Vladimir Putin and the
New World Order

Russian Federation state symbol,
adopted 30 November 1993, from the old Russia/Muscovy symbol.

Vladimir Putin and the New World Order

Looking East, Looking West?

J. L. Black

ROWMAN & LITTLEFIELD PUBLISHERS, INC.
Lanham • Boulder • New York • Toronto • Oxford

ROWMAN & LITTLEFIELD PUBLISHERS, INC.

Published in the United States of America
by Rowman & Littlefield Publishers, Inc.
A wholly owned subsidiary of The Rowman & Littlefield Publishing Group, Inc.
4501 Forbes Boulevard, Suite 200, Lanham, Maryland 20706
www.rowmanlittlefield.com

PO Box 317
Oxford
OX2 9RU, UK

British Library Cataloguing in Publication Information Available

Library of Congress Cataloging-in-Publication Data
Black, J. L. (Joseph Laurence), 1937-
    Vladimir Putin and the new world order : looking east, looking west? / J. L. Black.
    p. cm.
    Includes bibliographical references and index.
    ISBN 0-7425-2965-7 (cloth : alk. paper)—ISBN 0-7425-2966-5 (pbk. : alk. paper)
    1. Russia (Federation)—Foreign relations. 2. Putin, Vladimir Vladimirovich, 1952- I. T
DK510.764.B58 2004
327.47—dc22

                                                                    2003015.

Printed in the United States of America

∞ ™ The paper used in this publication meets the minimum requirements of American
National Standard for Information Sciences—Permanence of Paper for Printed Library
Materials, ANSI/NISO Z39.48-1992.

Contents

Abbreviations

ABM	Anti-Ballistic Missile Treaty (1972)
APEC	Asia-Pacific Economic Cooperation Council
ASEAN	Association of Southeast Asian Nations
ASEM	Asia-Europe Meeting
CFE	Conventional Armed Forces in Europe
CIS	Commonwealth of Independent States
CTBT	Comprehensive [Nuclear] Test-Ban Treaty
CFDP	Council for Foreign and Defense Policy
CMEA	Council for Mutual Economic Assistance (Comecon)
CPRF	Communist Party of the Russian Federation (Zyuganov)
EAPC	Euro-Atlantic Partnership Council
EBRD	European Bank for Reconstruction and Development
EEC	Eurasian Economic Community
EU	European Union
FSB	Federal Security Service
G-7 (G-8)	Group of leading industrialized countries: United States, Great Britain, Germany, France, Canada, Japan, Italy, and Russia
GRU	Main Intelligence Directorate, MoD
IMEMO	Institute of International Economy and International Affairs (Moscow)
IMF	International Monetary Fund
ISKRAN	Institute of USA and Canada, Russian Academy of Sciences
KFOR	Kosovo Force (NATO)
LDPR	Liberal Democratic Party of Russia (Zhirinovskii)
MID	Ministry of Foreign Affairs

MoD	Ministry of Defense
MVD	Ministry of Internal Affairs
NAC	North Atlantic Council
NMD	National Missile Defense System
OSCE	Organization for Security and Cooperation in Europe
PACE	Parliamentary Assembly of the Council of Europe
PfP	NATO's Partnership for Peace Program
PJC	Russia–NATO Permanent Joint Council
PRC	People's Republic of China
RRF	Rapid Reaction Force
ShCO	Shanghai Cooperation Organization
SNF	Strategic Nuclear Force
START	Strategic Arms Reduction Talks
State Duma	Russian Parliament, Lower House
TACIS	Technical Assistance to the CIS
UN	United Nations
UNPROFOR	United Nations Protection Force
UNSC	United Nations Security Council
UNSCR	United Nations Security Council Resolution
WMD	weapons of mass destruction
WTO	World Trade Organization

Website, Documentary and Press Source Acronyms

CDSP	Current Digest of the Post-Soviet Press (www.currentdigest.o
FBIS-SOV	Foreign Broadcast Information Service. World News Conn tion (wnc.fedworld.gov)
Interfax	Russian independent press service
ITAR-TASS	Russian Government Press Agency (www.Itar-Tass.com)
JRL	Johnson's Russia List, Website
MID Website	www.In.mid.ru/bul_ns_en.nsf
NVO	*Nezavisimoe voennoe obozrenie,* weekly military newspa owned by *Nezavisimaia gazeta*
REDA	*Russia and Eurasia Documents Annual* (Gulf Breeze, FL: A demic International Press), annual volumes since 1988

Preface

Built-in obsolescence is the cross borne by anyone who wishes to write about on-going international affairs. In the early winter of 2002, I decided to end my narrative of Vladimir Putin and the new world order at the moment of the Putin-Bush summit in Moscow, scheduled for May later in the year. The reason for the decision was simple and, it seemed at the time, logical. That event promised to be an important turning point in the shaping of Russia's post-Yeltsin foreign policy, one that marked a certain culmination of the process initiated by Putin immediately following the crisis in America of 11 September 2001. It is quite likely that by the time this book appears in print, events will have passed and the summit's significance will be either muted or starkly clear. Nevertheless, a stopping point had to be found, and this is it. Overtaken by events or not, this book will serve both as a historical survey of Putin's early activities in the international arena and help account for the Kremlin's preferences in matters concerning international integrative organizations and agencies, regional conflicts and associations, and both bi- and multilateral relationships.

Throughout, I have attempted to provide an understanding of the Russian perception of the various phenomena under discussion. For that reason, the sources cited here are almost entirely in the Russian language. As a former "Sovietologist," I find it somewhat eerie to discover myself returning to the old practice of citing and decoding feature items from the Russian press. The difference between then and now, of course, is that at that time we struggled to read between the lines—now we read and try to digest the lines themselves. In fact, the Russian press still provides a very good indication of prevailing moods within the political and military elite establishments of Moscow. It is also still evident that if we are to understand Russian foreign policymaking, we must attempt to view international situations through the prism of Russian analysts and officials. Only then can we draw conclusions based on both our and their perceptions of current events and visions for the future.

This book is divided into two parts. The first is a chronologically organized st
of Putin's efforts to find a niche for Russia in the world, carried from his sudden
pointment as acting president at the end of December 1999 through the end of N
2002. His nearly five months as prime minister in 1999 serve as an introductory :
ting. The bookends for this work are the publication of Putin's "manifesto" on
last day of 1999 and the communiqués released after his quick sequence of meeti
with U.S. President George W. Bush, NATO Heads, and EU Heads of State, in l
May 2002. On both occasions, the official and popular Russian attitude tow
NATO were decisive considerations for the Kremlin's powerbrokers.

The second part focuses on Russia's attention to specific regions of the world ɑ
types of international activity. These include individual countries, such as China ɑ
Ukraine; regions—Central Asia and the Caucasus; integrative agencies, including
CIS; concepts and practices, among them matters of security and military refo
and the ambivalent Russian associations with so-called rogue states.

For many reasons, Russia's relationship with the first former Warsaw Pact co
tries to join NATO, Poland, Hungary, and the Czech Republic, are not treated s
arately here; nor are the Baltic States.

The cycle of estrangement and accommodation in Moscow's relationship v
NATO and the United States is an underlying concern throughout the volume, ɑ
the question of further NATO expansion is treated as a constant motivating force
hind Russian bilateral and multilateral affiliations. Thus, although Part II highlig
Moscow's interests in its Southern Tier, Central Asia, and the Far East, the quest
of Russia and the West remains the overarching theme. This is fitting, given
Kremlin's preoccupation with the West—domain of most of the world's wealth ɑ
power. And since November 1994, when Foreign Intelligence Service Director Y
genii Primakov first warned of the implications for Russia of NATO expansion eɑ
ward, Moscow's eyes have been riveted on the Atlantic Alliance.

Almost all major Russian foreign policy decisions since 1999 were shaped in vary
degrees in anticipation of the "second wave" of new NATO members scheduled for l
vember 2002. For that reason, NATO appears throughout this book, whether the R
sian two-headed eagle happened to be looking to the West or to the East.

The book is purposely chronological, with great emphasis placed on the seque
of events. This approach helps illustrate important patterns; for example, Putin's t
dency to make dramatic overtures to the East as preparation for negotiations with
West, and the consistency of Moscow's Cassandra-like warnings about the threaɩ
international terrorism long before the events of 11 September 2001.

Because of the thematic orientation of Part II, there will appear to be some duﬁ
cation, which, it is hoped, the reader will find both helpful and slight. Through
the text, references such as "see chapter 3" indicate that further information on
chronologically noted events or regional phenomena will be found elsewhere in
book. Rather than take up footnote space, there are also references to press rele
sources (ITAR-TASS), placed directly in the text, with a date; and because the t
and origin of a media source often is as revealing as the content of the feature it
or program, I have used footnotes rather than endnotes.

Acknowledgments

I owe thanks to Yurii Matashev, graduate student at Carleton University, for making a last-minute check of the Russian transliteration and translation used here; to Joseph Black, professor of English at the University of Tennessee, Knoxville, for copyediting; and to the Donner Canadian Foundation for funds that allowed the CRCR to subscribe to relevant newspapers and magazines, and to keep in constant touch with researchers and analysts in Moscow.

Introduction:
Where We Were in
January 2000

On 16 February 2000, NATO Secretary General Lord George Robertson met in Moscow with Acting President Vladimir V. Putin, Foreign Minister Igor S. Ivanov, and Defense Minister Igor D. Sergeev. Whereas Ivanov and Sergeev had been in their respective positions when Russia froze all relations with NATO some ten months earlier, Putin and Robertson were still relatively new at their jobs. Indeed, this meeting represented their first major venture into the realm of high-level East-West diplomacy.

A joint communication issued during the exchange of views was cautious and general, although it emphasized that cooperation was now a shared goal. Given the extent of the spontaneous anger at and mistrust of NATO that had burst out in Russia over the previous year, both Putin and Robertson could claim this conclusion as a victory. Yet it was still a far cry from the "partnership" envisioned by proponents of the Founding Act signed between Russia and the Atlantic Alliance in May 1997.[1]

Where had matters gone so badly wrong since then, and how did Putin expect to rectify the situation? The first question was answered in my earlier book, *Russia Faces NATO Expansion. Bearing Gifts or Bearing Arms?*, which covered Moscow's changing perceptions of NATO throughout the 1990s and the implications those changes had for Russian security and foreign policy initiatives. The second question is central to the present investigation. *Russia Faces NATO Expansion* carried the story chronologically to the early spring, 1999, when Yevgenii Primakov was dismissed from his post

---

1. See "Joint Statement on the Occasion of the Visit of the Secretary General of NATO in Washington, 16 February 2000," NATO Website (16 February 2000), and a report prepared by Vyacheslav Bantin and Irina Chumakova for ITAR-TASS (16 February 2000). On the Founding Act, see J. L. Black, *Russia Faces NATO Expansion. Bearing Gifts or Bearing Arms?* (Lanham, Md.: Rowman & Littlefield, 2000), pp. 52–54.

as prime minister. That study dealt primarily with the vicissitudes of post-So'
Russia–NATO relationships, and as a subtext featured Primakov as foreign ¿
prime minister. In the current work, the story is picked up and turned into a broa
study of how a later prime minister, suddenly named president on the last day
1999, labored to introduce order into the chaos of Yeltsin-era Russian foreign pol

Much of the text has been shaped by a graduate course I have conducted for
Institute of European and Russian Studies, successor to the Institute of Soviet ¿
East European Studies at Carleton University, Ottawa, Canada. The course, tit
"Russia and the New World Order, 1992 to the Present," is based on a simple ≤
nario, and attempts to explain that scenario and its manifestations: in Decem
1991, the USSR disappeared into the dustbin of history, leaving Russia as the ≤
heir of the Soviet Union's "Great Power" status; a nuclear arsenal; permanent me
bership in the UN Security Council, with veto rights; and a territory that left it ≤
the largest country in the world. Those advantages notwithstanding, Russia also
herited an economy in shambles, most of the USSR's international debt and in
national commitments, a military in disarray, and a very unhappy citizenry. Mc
over, it was a democracy much more in name than in substance.

In the international arena, the new Russia had no alliances and was surrounded
equally new or reconstituted states. Many of these newly independent countries I
bored bitter grievances against the Soviet Union, which they believed to be syno
mous with Russia. The new Russia did not have the USSR's strategic advantages
the Baltic Sea, in Transcaucasia, or in Central Asia. Old Moscow-directed integra
agencies, such as the Warsaw Pact, the CMEA, and even the worldwide commu
movement, had all vanished in a blink of an eye. The purpose of the course is to
how—and if—Russia found a place for itself in the new world order. It is a hist
course in that students start with a "where we were" analysis, and a current aff
course in that they conclude with a "where we are" analysis. This book encompa⸱
a synopsis of the students' and my own findings for the first two-and-a-half year⸱
the Putin presidency.

I

Two-and-a-Half Years
of Foreign Policy Experimenting

1

✢

Yeltsin's Legacy, 1999

NATO'S "FIRST WAVE" AS FRONTAL ATTACK

There were a number of turning points in Russia's relationship with the West generally and with NATO particularly after the dissolution of the Warsaw Treaty Organization in 1989. These have been studied in considerable detail both in Russia and in the West, though far too few attempts have been made to place the key moments into a comprehensive analysis of their consequences for Russia.[1]

One particularly significant moment came with begrudging Russian acceptance of NATO expansion eastward in the form of the Founding Act between the Russian Federation and the North Atlantic Alliance, signed in May 1997, and the formal admission two years later of Poland, Hungary and the Czech Republic during ceremonies marking the fiftieth anniversary of the founding of NATO. The Founding Act provided that a Permanent Joint Council (PJC) meet regularly as a forum for Russia–NATO discourse, and carried with it an ambiguous—and by no means binding—commitment from NATO not to move nuclear weaponry into its newly acquired territories.[2] Membership in the G-7, making it a G-8 even though Russia was

---

1. Among the interesting Russian monographs in this regard are Vadim Makarenko, *Kto soiuzniki Rossii?* [Who Are the Allies of Russia?], (Moscow: Stradiz FIAMP, 2000); *Rossiia i zakavkaz'e: Realii nezavisimosti i novoe partnerstvo* [Russia in the Caucasus. The Reality of Independence and New Partnership], edited by R.M. Avakov and A.G. Lisov (Moscow: ZAO Finstatinform, 2000); *Rossiia v Sovete Evropy: chto znaiut ob etom grazhdane Rossii* [Russia and the Council of Europe: What the Citizens of Russia Know About It], (Moscow: Komissiia po svobode dostupa k informatsii, 2000). See also Igor Ivanov, *Novaia Rossiiskaia diplomatiia. Desiat' let vneshnei politiki strany* [The New Russian Diplomacy. Ten Years of the Country's Foreign Policy], (Moscow: OLMA-Press, 2002), for the foreign minister's own very general account.

2. The Founding Act ("Osnovopolagaiushchii Akt") was published in Russia in *Rossiiskaia gazeta* (28 May 1997), and *Krasnaia zvezda* (29 May). It is available in English on the NATO website, and in *Russia and Eurasia Documents Annual, 1997*. (Hereafter *REDA.*)

3

not to be a partner in the original group's economic deliberations for another ʃ
years, was one of the prizes Moscow won in return for its signature. Immediate me
bership in the Paris Club of lender nations and, sometime in the near future,
mission to the World Trade Organization (WTO), also were promised.

At the time of the Founding Act President Yeltsin proclaimed proudly that
PJC would provide the Russian Federation with real input into NATO decis
making, at best with a veto, at least with a vehicle for bringing Russia's concerns
rectly to NATO for its consideration. Some officials and analysts countered the cc
munist and nationalist outcry that Russia had "capitulated" to NATO by express
the hope that the PJC would provide their country with a voice in European affa
They were all doomed to disappointment. Even before the document was signed ʃ
mally, U.S. President Bill Clinton rejected whatever faint hopes Russian authori
might have had for a veto.[3] The hope that consideration of Russia's interests mi
sway NATO policy was erased nearly as quickly by the Alliance's actual policies,
pecially in connection with it's newly adopted strategic concept and the crisis
Kosovo.

Another point of departure was the final stage in the "first wave" itself, in May
1999. It came at a very bad time for all sides. Russia was in a state of political dis
ray and an economic spiral downward. NATO's first air strikes against Yugoslavia,
24 March 1999, had themselves come at a bizarre moment diplomatically: Pri
Minister Yevgenii Primakov was actually airborne, flying to Washington to negoti
terms of a loan from the IMF. On hearing of NATO's decision in Yugoslavia, he
dered the plane to turn around and head back to Moscow.

It was at that point that Russia called a halt in its dealings with NATO. Exc
for its ongoing participation in peacekeeping operations in Bosnia, all further me
ings and negotiations were "frozen." Most Western politicians and journal
seemed not to take Russia's action seriously until later in the spring, after Mosc
consistently rejected further discussion and vocal (if not large) sectors of the pul
in all NATO countries began to look critically at NATO policy in Yugoslaʻ
Widespread outrage against NATO shook the apparent complacency in Washi
ton and other NATO capital cities, although it had little impact on the actual c
duct of policy. In Russia, Yeltsin's collapsing popularity and the harsh anti-NAT
anti-Washington tone taken on by all parties and blocs competing for seats in I
cember's Duma election caused governments in many NATO member states to lc
more carefully towards Moscow. Existing tensions had been exacerbated on 24 Aʃ
when NATO gave formal approval to its new strategic concept, affirming its int
tion to act "out of zone" and, implicitly, on a unilateral basis. The Russian react
was furious and immediate. NATO was accused by officials and the media
Moscow of becoming a self-styled "world policeman" and Russians were warı
that the Mediterranean and GUUAM (an association linking Georgia, Ukrai

---

3. See J. L. Black, *Russia Faces NATO Expansion,* p. 50.

Uzbekistan, Azerbaijan and Moldova) states were falling within the Alliance's self-proclaimed sphere of influence.[4]

By that time, the frustration of Russians with their loss of place in the world was by no means restricted to the foreign policy elite and feature writers. A few days after NATO's strategic interests were headlined, surveys revealed that up to 51 percent of Russians now felt threatened by NATO expansion, and only 24 percent were optimistic about the Founding Act.[5]

International debate rang with rhetoric reminiscent of the Cold War. In Russia, the bombing of Yugoslavia was a catalyst for a marked change in Russian popular attitudes towards the West, and NATO's strategic concept continued to come under fire from Russian commentators well into the summer. Thus, opposition to Slobodan Milosevic within Yugoslavia was perceived in Russia as support for both separatism and a "pro-West" stance in Yugoslav politics.[6] Russians were angry that the West did not want to give them a zone of responsibility in Kosovo and overjoyed with the sudden and symbolic Russian takeover of the Pristina airport.[7] Nevertheless, military contacts were resumed on 31 August and Col. Gen. Viktor Zavarzin returned to NATO HQ in Brussels. But his participation was limited exclusively to interaction on the peacekeeping operations in Kosovo.

In the meantime, Russia delighted whenever divisions appeared within NATO, or between the United States, the United Nations and European countries.[8] On the other hand, Russia's own war in Chechnya had compounded the growing unease everywhere, as NATO members, the EU, and the IMF threatened economic retaliation against Moscow. In response, the Russian government, media and public charged the West with hypocrisy in light of NATO action in Yugoslavia and Iraq. Hardliners on both sides of the new East-West divide tended to treat the crisis in Chechnya as part of a renewed Cold War competition for control of the Caucasus.

In June, for example, a *New York Times* editorial noticed that "Anti-American sentiment [has] sharply increased" in Russia, as had a fear that NATO had become a

---

4. See, for example, Vadim Solov'ev, Vladimir Mukhin, "NATO zaiavliaet o svoei gotovnosti k deistviiam vo 'vsemirnykh masshtabakh'. Minoborony RF formiruet geopoliticheskii protivoves" [NATO Declares Its Readiness for Operations on a "Worldwide Scale": The RF Is Creating a Geopolitical Counterbalance], *Nezavisimoe voennoe obozrenie*, No. 16 (30 April–6 May 1999). [Hereafter, *NVO*]. The full text of NATO's strategic concept was printed in this issue as well.

5. Interfax (28 May 1999). This was almost exactly two years after the Founding Act was signed. Results of the survey were printed in *REDA* 1999, Vol. 1 ("Poll. Majority of Russians Afraid of NATO"), p. 230.

6. See, for example, Maksim Yusin, "Nastupaet zakat Slobodana Milosevicha" [Advancing the Decline of Slobodan Milosevic], *Izvestiia* (17 June 1999); Valentin Romanov, "NATO obkatyvaet novuiu strategiiu. Voina v Yugoslavii vyiavila ostrye protivorechiia s mezhdunarodnym pravom" [NATO Opens Up a New Strategy. The War in Yugoslavia Has Revealed Sharp Contradictions with International Law], *NVO*, No. 25 (3–8 July 1999).

7. See, for example, Maksim Yusin, "Posle blitzkriga" [After the Blitzkrieg], *Izvestiia* (15 June 1999), and "Zapad ne doveriaet Rossii" [The West Does Not Trust Russia], *ibid.* (11 June 1999).

8. See, for example, Maksim Yusin, "Raskol v riadakh NATO" [Divisions in the Ranks of NATO], *Izvestiia* (29 June 1999); Vladimir Mikheev, "Mest' nizvergnutogo genseka OON" [Revenge of the Overthrown UN GenSec], *Ibid.* (26 May 1999), on a book by Butros Gali criticizing American behavior towards the UN.

"threat to Russia itself." The editorial writer went on to portray President B(
Yeltsin and his newly appointed prime minister, Sergei Stepashin, as valiant warri
against the resurgence of Communist and nationalist forces in their country. The (
missal of Primakov on 12 May 1999 was made to look wise, and hopes were rai
that Yeltsin, President Clinton and Strobe Talbott, the White House's top adviser
Russia, would cooperate on a "joint peace plan."[9]

As events were soon to demonstrate, these words were wishful thinking. Talb(
for one, was looked upon with considerable suspicion in Russia because of his ur
lenting advocacy of NATO enlargement and the accession of the Baltic States to
Alliance.[10] Even after he was fired as prime minister, Primakov was regularly tou
as a likely replacement for Yeltsin when the presidential office was vacated in J(
2000. The New York Times editorial notwithstanding, Primakov was still respectec
the West. He was assumed to be pragmatic, even in the face of his open sponsors
of a uniquely "Russian way" in both domestic and international affairs and his c(
sistent opposition to NATO expansion.[11] Stepashin was less well-known abroad, ;
much was made of the fact that he had been minister of the interior. In fact, the r
appointment merely represented a tradition of prime ministers with security and
enforcement career profiles. Primakov had himself been the head of the Foreign
telligence Service. Stepashin's appointment was quickly approved by the State Du(
itself recently humiliated by a failed attempt to force Yeltsin out of office on 1
counts of impeachment.

A new cabinet included few fresh faces in the power positions. Igor Sergeev (1
fense), Igor Ivanov (Foreign Affairs), Sergei Shoigu (Emergencies), and P;
Krasheninnikov (Justice), all stayed on. Vladimir Rushailo replaced Stepashin as
terior minister. The new government had little opportunity to set its own course
foreign affairs. Stepashin's first major speeches to the Federation Council and
Duma, 17 and 19 May, emphasized the desperate need for change in the econo(
sphere, including its "decriminalization." With the exception of a remark to the
fect that NATO strikes against Yugoslavia were, in reality, "strikes against Russia
he stuck closely to economic themes. Even though their government participatec
the joint peace plan for Kosovo worked out in Helsinki, with former prime mini(
Viktor Chernomyrdin heading the Russian delegation, the ongoing bombing

9. See "The Kremlin Looks West," New York Times (6 June 1999). In announcing Primakov's dismi
Yeltsin praised him for his "courage" and for stabilizing the critical situation in Russia's economy and
cial sphere. But he called on Stepashin to take greater initiative in the economic sector and in combat
organized crime (ITAR-TASS, 12 May 1999).

10. See, for example, Vladimir Abarinov, "Russkii razmakh i amerikanskaia delovitost'. Administra
SShA utochniaet politiku v otnoshenii Rossii" [Russian Range and American Know-how. The U.S.
ministration Defines its Policy in Relation to Russia], Izvestiia (21 October 1999). See also an interv
with Talbott, "My smozhem ustranit' nashi raznoglasiia" [We Can Erase Our Differences], Izvestiia
July 1999).

11. See J. L. Black, Russia Faces NATO Expansion, passim.

12. "Acting Prime Minister Sergei Stepashin Speech in the State Duma," ITAR-TASS (19 May 19
summarized in Rossiiskaia gazeta (20 May 1999).

Yugoslavia persuaded even moderate Russians that the United States was bent on world domination.[13] It was commonly believed in Moscow that NATO was Washington's shield bearer in this endeavour, charged with replacing the UN as the main agent for conflict resolution in world affairs. They were concerned as well that Russia would be left out of a settlement altogether.[14] As early as June broad segments of the Western media for the first time began to echo points of view already heard in Russia for years. On 10 June, a few days before NATO proclaimed victory and stopped its bombing raids, for example, former USSR President Mikhail Gorbachev's allegation that NATO had become an offensive alliance driven by an agenda set in Washington at the expense of the United Nations was quoted widely. He warned American readers that NATO members were beginning to question the dominance of Washington in the Alliance.[15] For years, Gorbachev had been accusing NATO leaders of deceiving Russia about NATO's intentions when the two Germanies were reunited in 1990, and had revived these charges in a recent book.[16]

A G-8 summit in late June served as a forum for Yeltsin to get the Russian perspective off his chest. He insisted that the UN and its Security Council must be enhanced in the realm of international peace and security, and was less than subtle in his plea that no country should take on for itself "the role of global judge and policeman" (ITAR-TASS, 20 June). Yeltsin's call for a global monitoring system became for awhile the rallying cry of Russia's ministry of foreign affairs, usually accompanied by warnings that events in Yugoslavia were omens of what could go wrong if their admonitions were not heeded. The Yugoslavia question overwhelmed the media in Russia, leading to a flurry of internal contingency planning and public musing on foreign policy.[17] Special attention was paid to what was perceived as a completely new, general offensive strategy adopted by NATO, transforming it into a bloc with global ambitions.[18]

Aleksandr Lebed, perennial presidential candidate and governor of Krasnoyarsk, had grabbed headlines by taking up this refrain. He told an interviewer on 10 June that Russia should send peacekeeping troops to Kosovo only if they served under the UN flag. Under NATO, whose troops would have "no motivation for which they would be willing to die," the peacekeepers would be open to attack by the more

---

13. See, for example, Dmitrii Gornostaev, "NATO b'et po svoim" [NATO Beats Itself], *Nezavisimaia gazeta* (1 June 1999).

14. See, for example, Dmitrii Gornostaev, "NATO idet na priamoi kontakt s Belgradom" [NATO Undertakes Direct Contact with Belgrade], *Nezavisimaia gazeta* (5 June 1999).

15. Gorbachev, "No, no, NATO," *The Boston Globe* (16 July 1999), an excerpt from the former USSR president's (then) forthcoming book, *Gorbachev: On My Country and the World.*

16. See J. L. Black, *Russia Faces NATO Expansion,* pp. 22, 31.

17. See, J. L. Black, for example Aleksandr Lata, "Voina na Balkanakh stimuliruet oboronku Rossii" [War in the Balkans Stimulates Russian Defenders], *NVO,* No. 24 (25 June–1 July 1999); Igor Korotchenko, "Kompromiss mezhdu NATO i Rossiei naiden" [Compromise Found between NATO and Russia], *ibid.;* Vadim Solov'ev, "Minoborony RF analiziruet itogi voiny na Balkanakh i uchenii v Rossii" [RF Analyzes Results of War in the Balkans and Training in Russia], *NVO,* No. 25 (2–8 July 1999).

18. See Valentin Romanov, "NATO obkatyvaet novuiu strategiiu" [NATO Rolls Out a New Strategy], *NVO,* No. 25 (2–8 July 1999). Strobe Talbott was seen as the mastermind of NATO's new strategic concept.

highly motivated Serbs. Lebed went on to ridicule Chernomyrdin's role as Moscc
special envoy whose task it was to mediate between Belgrade and NATO.[19] Mon
later, Lebed went too far, accusing the Kremlin of complicity in terrorist acts blan
on Chechens for the purpose of shaping the State Duma elections. This type
charge cost the once popular military figure any real chance of resurrecting his pi
idential ambitions.[20]

Whereas Lebed's credibility quickly dissipated at home, he could still draw the
tention of the foreign press and appeal to some of Russia's radical nationali
Strange bedfellows though they may have been in June, Lebed and Gorbachev w
aware of an emerging resentment in NATO against the informal control of
decision-making process by the big five: the United States, Britain, France, Germa
and Italy, sometimes referred to in the North American media as NATO's "kitcl
cabinet." Ironically, these countries represented the remnant of the Contact Gro
a six-power committee in charge of Balkan peacemaking before one member, Rus
disassociated itself as a result of the air strikes on Yugoslavia. From Moscow's ɪ
spective, the new "kitchen cabinet" harked back to the Cold War era when, a
1955, the foreign ministers of the United States, Britain, France, and West Germ:
met privately before every high-level NATO meeting to set priorities for the Alliar
This widely held opinion about collusion contradicted the enthusiastic repc
Stepashin brought back to Russia after a late June sojourn in the United Sta
"Most of our differences can be resolved," he said, claiming that his meetings w
Clinton and Gore had been very productive.[21]

In fact, the notion that Western countries had badly miscalculated by ignor
Russia's interests in Yugoslavia and elsewhere became commonplace. When NA
military action in Kosovo produced a victory, of sorts, Western rethinking of
affront to Russia began in earnest.[22] But Stepashin was not to be a beneficiary
that rethinking process. On 9 August, Yeltsin again sacked a prime minister :
cabinet, replacing him with Putin, a KGB agent before he was appointed head
the Federal Security Service in July 1998. From March to August 1999, Putin I
combined his position as FSB director with work as secretary of the Secuɪ
Council.

[margin annotation: act of conspiring to deceive — a secret agreement]

19. *Komsomol'skaia pravda* (10 June 1999), FBIS-SOV, No. 616 (17 June 1999). See also Dɪ
Gornostaev, Igor Korotchenko, "Vashington umelo ispol'zoval Chernomyrdina" [Washington Took
vantage of Chernomyrdin], *Nezavisimaia gazeta* (8 June 1999).

20. See, for example, Tamara Shkel', "Lebed' v perevode s frantsuzskogo" [Lebed Translated from
French], *Rossiiskaia gazeta* (1 October 1999). Lebed had been interviewed in *Le Figaro*, Paris.

21. See, for example, Vladimir Abarinov, Svetlana Babaeva, "Moskva i Vashington pokhlopali ɪ
druga po plechy" [Moscow and Washington Pat Each Other on the Shoulder], *Izvestiia* (29 July 199

22. See, for North American revisionist opinions, for example, Anatoly Lieven, "What Role for]
sia?" *New York Times* (14 June 2000); Harry Sterling, "NATO's Russian Roulette," *The Ottawa Cit*
(15 June 1999); "The Russian Affront," *The Ottawa Citizen* (15 June 1999); George Friedman, "Gɪ
ing a Wounded Bear," *The Ottawa Citizen* (16 June 1999), from "It's The Russians, Stupid," an ana
by Friedman for Stratfor Inc.; Thomas L. Friedman, "NATO or BATO?" *New York Times* (15 June 19
"BATO" referring to a "Balkan-Atlantic Treaty Organization"; Aurel Braun, "The West Is Dangero
Misjudging Russia," Toronto *Globe and Mail* (12 July 1999).

Putin Named Prime Minister

In an unprecedented step, Yeltsin also named Putin as his probable successor as president.[23] At that time, Putin was thought to be a friend of both Moscow's Mayor, Luzhkov, and Primakov, so the appointment was seen as a boost in the fortunes of the Fatherland-All Russia Party, founded and supported by Luzhkov with Primakov recently chosen as leader. Putin was thus Russia's fourth prime minister in seventeen months, reflecting ongoing instability in the country's political arena. The power ministers again held on to their posts, and the FSB position went to Nikolai Patrushev, also a former KGB official and a longtime associate of the new prime minister.

In his initial speech to the Duma, on 16 August, Putin promised to grant priority to the economic course set by his predecessor and said that foreign policy would be unchanged. "Foreign policy is the president's prerogative and cannot be influenced by cabinet replacements," he said prophetically. The "revival and consolidation" of Russia's defense capacity would also be a priority, he added, with special reference to the defense industry and military prestige.[24] The new government's position on world affairs was expressed unequivocally in September, when Foreign Minister Igor Ivanov addressed the UN General Assembly. A multipolar world and reliance on the United Nations to "regulate international relations" were his key recommendations, implicitly rejecting the apparent ascendancy of the United States and NATO.

At that time, the Russian position on NATO and Yugoslavia seemed to be gaining further public, if not official, credibility in the West. As late as September, NATO found itself defending its "victory" against charges that the bombing campaign against Serbian forces had failed. General Wesley Clark, supreme allied commander of Europe, for example, went on a public relations offensive, claiming that the European and North American media had fallen for propaganda out of Belgrade. Speaking at a press conference in Brussels, he insisted that in more than 3,000 missions (and 23,000 bombs) NATO forces had inflicted severe damage on Yugoslavia's military capabilities.[25] Perhaps he should have waited a few weeks, so that he could reflect on the bill for $100 billion in damages claimed against NATO by Yugoslav foreign minister, Zivadin Jovanovic, at the United Nations. Russia supported the Yugoslav claim. Jovanovic was speaking about civilian damages: housing, bridges, and refugee-related costs. The claim went nowhere, but a political point was made.

A report to the U.S. Congress, in October, revealed NATO errors in timing and targets, and gave Russian commentators a chance to point out flaws inherent in Western assertions of military superiority, though they were well aware of the potential for disaster of their own as Russia's armed forces were drawn back into

---

23. On this, see for example, Aleksandr Privalov, "Yeltsin prozrel. On uvidel svoego preemnika" [Yeltsin's Eyes Opened. He Saw His Successor], *Izvestiia* (10 August 1999).

24. "Vladimir Putin govorit o glavnom" [Vladimir Putin Speaks about the Main Things], *Rossiiskaia gazeta* (17 August 1999).

25. See a report on this press conference, "NATO Insists Kosovo War Was a Success," *Ottawa Citizen* (17 September 1999).

Chechnya. The U.S. report was delivered to the Senate Armed Services Commit
by Defense Secretary William Cohen and General Henry H. Shelton. Cohen ;
Shelton played down the lapses, claiming decisive victory and praising the precis
of NATO's U.S.-led air raids. There was as well recognition of the fact that Serb
ethnic cleansing of Albanian civilians began in earnest after, not before, NATO
strikes got underway. The purpose here was not to excuse the action of Serbian
tionalist forces, rather it was to suggest that NATO policy had unexpected cor
quences. European military forces came in for criticism too, and Cohen repeated
earlier complaint that NATO had lost the propaganda war.[26] The Russian press ;
gleefully reported stories from Britain, on the eve of Jiang Zemin's visit to Lond
that NATO's bombing of the Chinese embassy in Belgrade had not been a mistak
Peering out from behind the Kremlin walls, it seemed to Russian analysts that NA'
was consumed by internal sniping: in November, for example, France's Ministry
Defense noted that a number of the bombing missions in Yugoslavia had been c
ducted by American forces outside the framework of NATO and its procedures.
some cases, indeed, the United States had conducted raids which French presid
Jacques Chirac would not have approved. Russian observers pounced on all sign:
dissension and misgiving in NATO, and relayed them to their reading public.[28]

Rising Tension between Moscow and Washington

At the diplomatic level tensions had increased between Moscow and Washing
over the summer of 1999. By the time that the seventy-eight-day bombing campa
ended, it was far too late for fences to be mended easily. Russian peacekeeping fo1
remained in Kosovo, but their line of command remained contentious. Whe1
Russia interpreted the Helsinki agreement to mean that its troops would be un
their own, autonomous command, the United States expected Russian troops to :
low the orders of a NATO commander in the field. NATO was startled, and m
cautious by Moscow's successful transfer of troops to the airport at Pristina in Ju
to which the United States retaliated by requesting that Hungary, Romania and E
garia refuse airspace access to Russia. Russia tested the waters shortly afterwards
conducting military exercises near Iceland.

A diplomatic tug-of-war ensued. On 3 July, an American assistant army attac
Lt. Col. Peter Hoffman, was declared persona non grata by the Kremlin, presuma
in response to an American decision to expel an official in the Russian mission to
United States and charge him with spying. It was in the first week of July as well t

---

26. For a summary of the Cohen-Shelton report, see Elizabeth Becker, "Military Leaders Tell Cong
of NATO Errors in Kosovo," *New York Times* (15 October 1999).

27. See, for example, Maksim Yusin, "NATO vnov' opravdyvaetsia" [NATO Again Justifies Its
Izvestiia (19 October 1999). Yusin referred to reports from the *Observer*.

28. See, for example, Vadim Solov'ev, "Pobeda s ogovorkami" [Victory with Reservations], *NVO*,
46 (26 November–3 December 1999).

NATO forces blocked air corridors necessary to transport Russian peacekeeping forces to Kosovo, delaying their arrival. This dispute was related to the Russian military's desire to command a sector of its own, in connection with which Moscow accused the United States of "provocation" (Interfax, 3 July 1999).

Elsewhere, the Russian high command had a special interest in the future of the Baltic region, especially after the three Baltic republics applied for admission to NATO and were accepted as legitimate candidates. Since late in 1997 the danger of the Baltic Sea becoming a NATO sea had been such that the Russian foreign and defense ministries spoke then of a "red line" across which the Alliance must not step.[29] On the map, that red line was drawn around the external borders of the former USSR. The willingness of the Baltic States to "prostitute" themselves, in the Russian mind's eye, by offering support to NATO in Yugoslavia was especially galling. In mid-1999 there was even talk of the ongoing navy reform resulting in a larger Russian presence on the Baltic.[30] Unrealistic as this ambition may have been in light of Russia's inability to finance the existing fleet, proponents of a larger Baltic fleet couched their arguments in terms of NATO activities there.

It was the renewed conflict in Chechnya that most exacerbated the rift in Russia–U.S. relations. In this connection, the Russian media was far less polite than Ivanov had been in New York in September. Furious over criticisms levelled at Yeltsin's leadership by Al Gore in October, and affronted by the widespread condemnation of Moscow's use of force in Chechnya, Russian writers accused the U.S. of attempting to "humiliate" their country. The roots of Western "Russophobia are deeper and more poisonous than the fear of a revival of Russian military strength," one author commented in the Kremlin's own newspaper.[31] "The United States is seeking to create a *pax americana* at Russia's expense," the author continued, "and therefore conveniently forgets all the negative aspects of NATO's military ventures in the Balkans." Needless to say, one of the consistent Russian worries was that NATO might offer support to the Chechen rebels, as they had to Albanians. When Chechen President Aslan Maskhadov actually asked for help from NATO in October, Russian columnists growled that "Russia is not Yugoslavia" and reacted angrily to complaints lodged by the European parliament against Russian actions in Chechnya.[32] Some consolation was offered by U.S. Ambassador James Collins, who was quoted to the effect that Washington strongly supported Russia's fight against terrorism. In answer to a direct question, Collins went on to say that Chechnya was clearly part of the

29. On this see J. L. Black, "Russia and NATO Expansion Eastward. Red-lining the Baltic States," *International Journal*, LIV: 2 (Spring 1999), 249–266.

30. See an interview with Vladimir G. Yegorov, commander of the Baltic Fleet, "Usilenie positsii na Baltike vozmozhno" [It Is Possible to Strengthen Position on the Baltic], *NVO*, No. 23 (18–24 June 1999).

31. Yevgenii Vasil'chuk, "Zamorskie notatsii polezny dlia rossiiskogo zdorovia" [Lectures from Overseas Are Beneficial for Russia's Health], *Rossiiskaia gazeta* (29 October 1999).

32. See, for example, Nikolai Paklin, "Chechnya ne Kosovo, NATO ne pomozhet" [Chechnya Is Not Kosovo. NATO Will Not Help], *Rossiiskaia gazeta* (13 October 2000).

Russian Federation and must be subject to Russian law. He hoped only that the]
man and civil rights of citizens of Chechnya be respected.[33]

After President Clinton failed, during an early November meeting in Oslo, to ʃ
suade Putin to soften Moscow's military tactics in Chechnya, the chances of a mut
strategic agenda dimmed noticeably. Putin even prepared an explanatory message
the *New York Times,* which was printed on 14 November under the heading "Why
Must Act." He understood Clinton's concerns and urged Washington in its turn to
derstand Russia's position. The Russian president asked what the American gove
ment's reaction would be if there were rebellions by militiamen in Montana or Ida
or bloody incursions like those that took place in Dagestan: what if "Suddenly, an
plosion. Dwellings in Watergate or in the center of Manhattan are turned into pile:
rubble. Hundreds are killed, thousands maimed, many are left crippled. Chaos ¿
panic engulfs the city, and then the entire country"? Terrorism has no borders, he c
tinued, and no state is safe from it. Americans must comprehend the realities of
conflict in southern Russia and recognize them as part of the widening ambition:
international terrorism and the influence of the "secret leader of the terrorists" Osa
bin Laden, who was funding terrorism in Chechnya, and whom the Americans ¿
loathe. Chechen rebels were called "criminals" and "mobsters." The Putin essay ¿
was published in Russia, with an admonition that it should be read by everyone.[34]]
same issue of the Russian-language paper carried a piece titled "Double Standard. :
Laden Prepares War Against the USA," and another describing how an Islamic jil
was proclaimed openly against Russia, in the center of London.[35] These Russian wa
ings were to have special resonance two years later, on 11 September 2001, but t
were ignored in 1999 as feeble attempts to justify Moscow's campaign in Chechny
In a simultaneous feature item highlighting the importance of Yeltsin's upcom
participation in the Organization for Security and Cooperation in Europe (OSCE
Istanbul, the growing divide between Russia and the United States was illustrated
the remark that "if Russia remains in the 'family of civilized nations,' as the Americ
understand it . . ., then there will be nothing good in store for us."[36] The most ʃ
found consequence of this mutual name-calling was an increase of anti-American
among the Russian public.[37]

---

33. "Posol SShA Dzheims Kollinz: Chechnia—chast' Rossii i dolzhna zhit' po zakonam Rossii" [l̩
Envoy James Collins: Chechnya Is Part of Russia and Must Live According to Russian Law], *Rossiis.
gazeta* (27 October 2000).

34. "Pochemu my dolzhny deistvovat'" [Why We Must Act], *Rossiiskaia gazeta* (16 November 19
Putin, "Why We Must Act," *New York Times* (14 November 1999). The English-language version
worded somewhat differently, but the message was the same.

35. "Dvoinoi standart. Ben Laden gotovit voinu SshA" [Double Standard. Bin Laden Prepares
against the USA], *Rossiiskaia gazeta* (16 November 1999); Yurii Yershov, "Rossii ob'iavili dzhikhad. V
glii" [Jihad against Russia Announced. In England], *Rossiiskaia gazeta* (16 November 1999).

36. Viktor Sokolov, Nikolai Ul'yanov, "Boris Yeltsin lichno vozglavit delegatsiiu Rossiiu na St
bul'skom sammite" [Boris Yeltsin Personally Heads the Russian Delegation to the Istanbul Sumr
Nezavisimaia gazeta (16 November 2000).

37. See, for example, Luc Chartrand, "Russie. Trahie par l'occident?" *L'Actualité* (1 Oct 1999), 62-
and *Rossiia i zapad: dialog ili stolknovenie kul'turnykh sviazei* [Russia and the West. Dialogue or Clas
Cultural Connections], (Moscow: Rossiiskii institut kul'turologii, 2000).

As the dates for the OSCE summit neared, Russian political groups pressured the government not to make concessions either in its opposition to NATO action in Yugoslavia or in its own behavior in Chechnya. Leading the way was the Anti-NATO Commission of the State Duma, which issued a formal statement calling for a "firm stand" against any interference in Russia's internal affairs by "NATO countries and their allies."[38] Russian analysts of all political stripes tended to treat the meeting as a test of Russia's influence, especially in the Balkans and Caucasus, and many writers expected the meetings in Istanbul to be openly anti-Russian.[39]

Others wanted to ensure that the OSCE's prerogatives were not coopted by NATO. Chief of the General Staff of the Russian Armed Forces General Anatolii Kvashnin told a conference at the foreign ministry's Diplomatic Academy that the structure of European security should be built on the OSCE. This had been a Russian position since the early 1990s when NATO began seriously to speak of expansion. Because NATO is a military bloc, its expansion eastward must be treated as a threat, Kvashnin said, even though there may be none (ITAR-TASS, 15 November 1999). His perspective was echoed on 17 November by Serge Karaganov, Chairman of the Council for Foreign and Defense Policy (CFDP), who recommended against the opening of a NATO mission in Moscow. NATO's air strikes against Yugoslavia, "in spite of and with lack of respect for Russia's interests," were such that even this prominent and normally moderate foreign affairs adviser recommended that there be no cooperation whatsoever with the Atlantic Alliance (ITAR-TASS, 17 November).

OSCE SUMMIT AT ISTANBUL, NOVEMBER 1999

As the summit opened in Istanbul on 18 November, Russian, American and European leaders recognized that their projected main goals, agreements on human rights and limitations on military deployments in Europe, were going to be difficult to achieve. One part of the revised OSCE treaty stipulated that violations of human rights in one member nation became a matter of concern for all members. Sergei Rogov, director of the Institute for the USA and Canada (ISKRAN), Russian Academy of Sciences, was quite objective about Russia's dilemma and not very optimistic about his country's chances of reaching a modus vivendi with the leading OSCE members. Pointing out that the "common European home" advocated in the 1980s by Gorbachev had been overtaken by NATO expansion, which marginalized the OSCE itself, he acknowledged that the situation in Chechnya (over which "the West has no juridical or moral right" to interfere) had greatly complicated European

---

38. (ITAR-TASS, 15 Nov 1999). For the Anti-NATO Commission, see *Russia Faces NATO Expansion,* 32, 43.

39. See, for example, Dmitrii Gornostaev, "Fon vstrechi—antirossiiskii" [Background of the Meeting is Anti-Russian], *Nezavisimaia gazeta* (17 November 1999).

relations for Russia. Unless some common ground could be reached, he said, a r
Cold War would ensue.[40]

Moreover, it was no secret that Russia had long since been violating the Conv
tional Armed Forces in Europe (CFE) agreement about levels of weaponry allov
in specific zones. Thus, as delegates arrived in Istanbul, Russia was in the unenvia
position of being in violation of two of the central articles for OSCE negotiatic
Moscow tried to defuse the situation by making important concessions. It agreec
adhere to the schedule for withdrawing from military bases in Georgia and, by 20
removing its 2500 troops from Moldova. In light of the fact that Russian forces
cently had crossed the Georgian border to attack alleged arms routes into Chechr
these concessions were greeted with relief, above all in Tbilisi.

The OSCE gathering generated much comment in Russia, including anti-Ameri
and anti-UN observations from an unusual source, Gorbachev. The former US
president told reporters that East-West relations were clearly deteriorating once ag
and cited criticism levelled against Russia at Istanbul by Clinton and other West
leaders. Gorbachev claimed that American leaders were taking advantage of the c
flict in Chechnya to "back Russia into a corner" and called the UN's Kofi Annan :
NATO's former General Secretary Javier Solana "puppets" of Washington (Inter
24 Nov). Though few mainstream analysts went as far as Gorbachev, most conclue
that Russia gained little from the OSCE session and that the meeting ensu
NATO's status as the sole collective security guarantee in Europe.[41] At Istanbul,
fact that France's Chirac was the leading critic of Russia on the Chechnya questi
and the recent selection of Solana, a "hawk" in the Russian vision of NATO exp
sion, to head up the European Union's (EU) foreign policy apparatus, were omin
developments for Moscow.[42] Putin had had his fill of Solana already, during a late C
tober EU summit in Helsinki. Expecting to discuss trade with his country's larg
collective trade partner, the Russian delegation found itself instead suffering conde
nation for its bombing attacks on Groznyy, the capital of Chechnya. Solana I
summed up the EU position, greatly angering Russian delegates.[43]

Obviously, Russia's relationships with all the major European integrative agenc
had soured badly. The post OSCE summit comments coincided with the publi
tion of the results of a survey suggesting that up to 80 percent of Russians now
lieved that the West was "unfriendly" to Russia (ITAR-TASS, 24 November). On

40. Rogov, "Zapad vozrozhdaet kholodnyiu voiny" [The West Resurrects the Cold War], *Nezavisin
gazeta* (17 September 1999). In his "A Geostrategy for Eurasia," Brzezinski urged the United States to
a greater role in Eurasia, providing it with "benign American hegemony." See *Foreign Affairs*, Vol. 76,
5 (September/October 1997), pp. 50–64.

41. See, for example, Aleksandr Sabov, "Evropa do i posle Stambula" [Europe before and after Is
bul], *Rossiiskaia gazeta* (23 November 1999); El'mar Guseinov, "Stambul Rossiia ne zabudet" [Russia
Not Forget Istanbul], *Izvestiia* (20 November 1999).

42. For a typical angry Russian reaction to Solana's EU appointment, see Nikolai Paklin, "I ty, Sola
[Et tu, Solana?], *Rossiiskaia gazeta* (17 November 1999).

43. See, for example, Maksim Yusin, "Nam ne v chem opravdyvat'sia pered Zapadom" [We Don't F
to Justify Ourself to the West], *Izvestiia* (23 October 1999).

other hand, Clinton's modifying comments to the effect that Russia had not only the right to defend itself against rebellion, "terrorism and unlawfulness," but an obligation to do so, was played up in the Russian media.[44]

Oddly, it was with NATO that Moscow was actually making the most progress. Solana had been replaced as general secretary on 14 October by the Rt. Hon. Lord George Robertson, Britain's Secretary of State for Defence. One of Robertson's first acts had been to call for renewed cooperation between NATO and Russia. In a long essay prepared specifically for a Russian audience, he said that a full strategic partnership from which both sides could benefit must be restored. Defending NATO's action in Yugoslavia, Robertson pointed out that Russia could help maintain the peace in Kosovo and that a mutual "new beginning" was essential for European security.[45] Other sides were heard from, to be sure. An almost simultaneous interview with Slobodan Milosevic's brother, Yugoslav ambassador to Moscow, presented a strikingly different picture of Robertson's ambitions for his country. Borislav Milosevic harshly attacked Bernard Kouchner, the UN's representative in Kosovo, for "illegal decisions" and charged NATO with supporting him and abetting Kosovo's move towards independence from Yugoslavia.[46]

Feelings still ran very high in Moscow and the ongoing crises in the Balkans tended to focus Russian attention on NATO and Washington. One military analyst accused NATO and Washington of purposely taking advantage of Russia's diminishing military budget to strengthen their own military position while demanding "Russia's essentially unilateral disarmament." Citing sources from the General Staff Main Intelligence Directorate (GRU), he claimed that Western arms manufacturing firms were helping to destroy the Russian industrial–military complex, and at the same time "squeezing" Russia out of its traditional areas of influence in Europe, the Near and Middle East, Transcaucasia and Central Asia.[47] An analogy with 1941 was drawn to urge Russians to prepare for all eventualities by strengthening their military.

Turning to the Nazi image to drum up support for their version of world affairs was an old Soviet propagandist trick, and an effective one. It had been revived in the mid-1990s as part of the Russian communist and nationalist rhetorical explanation of NATO expansion, often explained as a return of Germany's *Drang nach Osten* (Drive to the East). The image abounded again in the late 1990s as the second wave of NATO expansion eastward loomed larger. To make the image of the enemy more

44. See, for example, "Bill Klinton: Rossiia stolknulas' v Chechne s miatezhom i nasiliem" [Bill Clinton: Russia Is Faced in Chechnya with Rebellion and Violence], *Rossiiskaia gazeta* (19 November 1999).

45. Dzhordzh Robertson, "Novoe nachalo" [New Beginning], *Nezavisimoe voennoe obozrenie*, No. 43 (5–11 November 1999). This piece appeared as well in *Nezavisimaia gazeta*. An interview with Robertson, conducted by Vladimir Katin, was printed in the *NVO* cited above. See also Vladimir Skosyrev, "Smena karaula v NATO" [Change of the Guard at NATO], *Izvestiia* (3 August 1999), where Robertson's Scottish and labor background were stressed.

46. "Borislav Miloshevich: Voina protiv Yugoslavii prodolzhaetsia" [Borislav Milosevic: the War against Yugoslavia Is Continued], *Rossiiskaia gazeta* (3 November 1999). The interview was conducted by foreign affairs specialist Vladimir Lapskii.

47. Sergei Ptichkin, "GRU znaet vse. I otkuda iskhodiat ugrozy Rossii—tozhe" [The GRU Knows Everything. Including Where Threats to Russia Come From], *Rossiiskaia gazeta* (23 November 1999).

vivid, and threatening, it also had become common to equate Islamic-based terr
ism with Nazism.[48] Dominated as it was by the left in 1999, the State Duma and
Anti-NATO Commission tended to lead the way in formal diatribes against the W
generally and NATO particularly. In doing so, it served unwittingly as a mouthpi
for a government over which it had almost no influence, but which had to mute
own responses for reasons of diplomacy.

When, in spite of agreements reached at Istanbul, NATO's parliamentary asse
bly adopted a resolution that Russia immediately withdraw its forces from Mold
and Georgia, the Duma again issued an angry rebuke, accusing NATO of con
dicting its own claims to want a renewed relationship with Russia (Interfax, 25 I
vember). Such sentiments help explain the favorable publicity granted to a serie:
meetings between Russian defense personnel and their Yugoslav counterparts, <
minating with a high-powered delegation to Belgrade. Led by the minister of
fense, the delegation met with Slobodan Milosevic and negotiated the strengthen
of military ties between Russia and Yugoslavia. The new agreements were rela
mostly to military-technical assistance and were not intended to supersede exist
UN sanctions against Yugoslavia, but they included strongly worded warnings ab
any move towards a "greater Albania" in Kosovo. Speaking to reporters, Russia's
fense minister noted that Moscow would prefer that Russia and NATO cooperate
terms of the 1997 Founding Act, but that NATO's habit of overriding the autho
of the UN Security Council, and its disregard of Russia's concerns, made this i
possible.[49] Nor was Russia fully satisfied with agreements reached in Istanbul on
justments to the CFE Treaty.[50]

Col. Gen. Leonid Ivashov served as the defense ministry's mouthpiece for the r
hard line. It was left to him to announce that the defense minister would not atte
the NATO sessions set for 2–3 December in Brussels. He added that Chief of S
Kvashnin would not participate in a session of the PJC's chiefs of general staff, z
that Foreign Minister Ivanov would not be available for a later PJC foreign mini:
gathering (Interfax, 1 December). Ivashov took his ministry's message even to au
ences in NATO countries, such as Greece, with which the Russian Black Sea F
was actively developing contacts.[51] Speaking to a press conference in that cour
later in December, he blamed NATO for redividing Europe and said that the acc
sion of any CIS country to NATO would greatly "exacerbate" Russia's relations w

---

48. See, for example, Yakov Etinger, "Metastazy natsizma" [The Metastasis of Nazism], *NVO*, No
(3–9 December 1999). For reprints of the "Nazi" image used mostly by the communists in the 1990s
Russia Faces NATO Expansion, pp. 138ff.

49. See, for example, Igor Korotchenko, "Moskva i Belgrad ukrepliaiut voennoe sotrudniches
[Moscow and Belgrade Strengthen Military Cooperation], *Nezavisimaia gazeta* (28 December 1999)

50. On this, see Vladimir Mukhin, Viacheslav Proshkin, "Ustanovlen novyi rasklad sil v Evrope" [
Establishment of New Allocation of Strength in Europe], *NVO*, No. 48 (10–16 December 1999). '
long analysis of the CFE Treaty included charts of the new apportioning of conventional forces.

51. See, for example, Sergei Ukhanev, "Drug iz NATO. Chernomorskii flot RF razvivaet kontak
Gretsiei" [A Friend from NATO. The RF Black Sea Fleet Develops Contacts with Greece], *NVO*, No
(2–9 December 1999).

the Alliance. It would push Moscow towards closer cooperation with states outside NATO, Ivashov said, and raise international tensions still further (Interfax, 16 December). At that stage, Prime Minister Putin found nothing with which to disagree in the foreign and defense ministry conviction that relations with NATO must remain frozen.

Taking the High Road: the Draft National Security Concept

The RF Security Council had approved a draft National Security Concept on 5 October 1999, amending a predecessor adopted in 1997.[52] When the draft version was published a few weeks later, it attracted considerable attention both at home and abroad. The timing was right, for Russia was just beginning to take seriously Washington's proposal that the ABM Treaty of 1972 be amended so that the United States could construct its own national missile defense system (NMD). The possibility of amendments to the ABM had been raised officially as early as January 1999, when President Clinton sent a letter to Yeltsin in which American plans to develop and test an NMD were outlined. Moscow responded only after news of the proposal was leaked to the Russian media and an outcry arose that the United States was increasing its potential for nuclear defense at a time when Russia was retrenching. The fact that the American position was based on the premise that new threats existed from maverick countries such as North Korea was seen as a particularly flimsy rationale for interfering with the ABM. It was in October that the U.S. Congress refused to approve the Comprehensive Test Ban Treaty (CTBT) and signalled its support of Clinton's proposal to amend the ABM Treaty unilaterally. The Kremlin and Russia's mass media reacted strongly, suggesting that any subsequent NMD system would threaten Russia and lead to a renewed arms race.[53]

Little wonder then that the draft Security Concept raised nuclear deterrence to doctrinal level as the only means Russia had to guarantee its safety against major aggression, or that on 4 October Yeltsin ordered a full review of Russia's draft military doctrine then under study at the collegium of the ministry of defense (ITAR-TASS, 4 October). Russian officials and columnists scoffed at a common Western perception of the Concept as threatening, responding that the new edition was a direct consequence of NATO's eastward expansion, and the concomitant diminishing stature

52. "Kontseptsiia natsional'noi bezopasnosti Rossiiskoi Federatsii. Odobrena na soveshchanii chlenov Soveta bezopasnosti Rossiiskoi Federatsii 5 oktiabria 1999 goda" [The Russian Federation Concept of National Security. Approved at a Meeting of the RF Security Council, 5 October 1999], *NVO*, No. 46 (26 November–3 December 1999). For a translation, see *REDA* 1999, Vol. 1.

53. See, for example, Sergei Sokut, "SShA nachinaiut stroit' 'velikuiu amerikanskuiu stenu'" [The USA Begins to Construct a "Great American Wall"], *Nezavisimaia gazeta* (5 October 1999); Dmitrii Gornostaev, "SShA nachali publichnoe davlenie. Plany Vashingtona napriamuiu ugrozhaiut interesam bezopasnosti Rossii" [The USA Begins Public Pressure. Washington's Plans Directly Threaten Russia's Security Interests], *Ibid.* (19 October 1999); Sergei Sokut, "Real'no li vernut' mir k vremenam kholodnoi voiny?" [Will the World Really Return to the Cold War Time?], *Ibid.* (22 October 1999).

of existing mechanisms of international collective security such as the United 1 tions Security Council and the OSCE.[54] Western criticism was downplayed as 1 of the "rebirth of a great country, whose opinion on the world stage cannot be nored." Brzezinski, for instance, was bitterly criticized in the Russian press for tell the *New York Times* (24 November) that Moscow should give up its pretensions ; world power ("it is time for the Russian leaders to sober up"). The Russian me constantly accused Western leaders of applying "double standards" because tl seemed indifferent to the terrorist acts committed against Russian citizens Chechen rebels.[55] In mid-November 1999, the Duma turned the table on West critics, adopting an official statement blaming the crisis in Chechnya on "inter tional terrorist centers" and calling on all states and international organizations combine efforts against international terrorism.[56] But just as Putin's essay in the *N York Times* was met with indifference, little attention was paid in the West to statement issued by Russia's elected parliamentarians.

Politics of Change

During Putin's half year as prime minister, the Russian political arena was domina by bloc, party, and ever-changing coalitions positioning themselves for the electi to the Duma. By October, thirty-two blocs and movements had qualified for the I cember election, though by registration time the number was down to twenty- Relations between the legislative (Duma) and executive (president and cabir branches of government had been strained for some years, and by 1999 the mut hostility was the greatest since 1993, when Yeltsin had resolved political crisis by dering his troops to shell his own parliament building. Early in 1999 the Duma jected a proposal for political accord from Yeltsin and soon afterwards the t branches were pitted against each other in a long and bitter impeachment bat Caught up in the electioneering, Duma members had not been much interestec opposing Putin's nomination as prime minister, and they confirmed him on 16 z gust by a vote of 232 to 84.

Within a few weeks, however, the tone of the general election campaign was tensified by terrible bomb blasts in September, blamed on Chechen terrorists ; used by candidates as evidence that Russia was descending into chaos and anarc Four explosions in less than a month—two in Moscow, the others in Buinaksk ;

---

54. See, for example, "Novyi vzgliad na Kontseptsiiu natsional'noi bezopasnosti" [New Views (Concept of National Security], *Rossiiskaia gazeta* (6 October 1999); Vadim Solov'ev, "Osnovop gaiushchie dokumenty po natsional'noi bezopasnosti ne obrazuiut edinogo paketa" [Fundame Documents on National Security Are Not Formed in a Single Packet], *NVO*, No. 46 (26 Novemb(December 1999).

55. See, for example, Vladimir Kuznechevskii, "Chto eshche i komu nado ob'iasniat'?" [What Needs to be Explained and to Whom?], *Rossiiskaia gazeta* (2 November 1999).

56. "O situatsii v Chechenskoi Respublike" [About the Situation in the Chechen Republic], *Rossiis. gazeta* (19 November 1999).

Volgodonsk—causing some 400 deaths, and the discovery of huge caches of explosives in a Moscow suburb, contributed to great uncertainty and anger.

The reaction in Russia was not unlike the mood that was to spread across the United States two years later, though the Russian population had long before lost whatever sense of invincibility it might have once had. A sweeping anti-terrorist operation named *Vikhr* (Whirlwind) was launched across the country with support from a frightened population. Communist leader Zyuganov took advantage of the situation to argue that the entire government was paralyzed and helpless. But such comments were not new. A "For Victory!" bloc formed already in July, led by the communists, drew analogies between the victories of 1945, which "confirmed the vector of Russian history," and the sorry state of the current "Motherland in captivity." With an extraordinary, almost wartime, appeal to patriotism, they invoked the great military heroes of Russia's past and called for "nationwide unity to give battle against the destroyers who are killing our Motherland." Signing the original appeal were Zyuganov and a wide cross-section of military, literary, and public figures, many of the extreme left.[57] These ideas, in a less extreme format, were incorporated into the published Communist platform (People's Patriotic Union) in November.[58] For the first time in a decade, the communists were mainstream, at least on this issue. The Fatherland-All Russia group, Our Home is Russia, and Zhirinovskii's LDPR tried just as hard to co-opt nationalist sentiment and Russia's historical "legacy"; the first two parties called on all "patriotic and democratic forces" to rally against Russia's enemies, and the last named party claimed that it would "totally finish off the insolent bandits [in the Caucasus], no matter what the West may say." National unity was the most common theme, almost at any cost.[59] At any rate, Putin offered his support to a Unity Coalition (nicknamed *Medved* [Bear]), formed only in the autumn with the support of Yeltsin's behind-the-scene election strategists and led by Shoigu. By early December, polls were ranking Unity in second place, behind the Communists and just ahead of Fatherland-All Russia. At election time, the Luzhkov-Primakov coalition fell even further behind: the Communist Party took 24 percent of the votes, Unity 23, Fatherland-All Russia 13. Only three other parties (Union of Right-Wing Forces [8.5], Zhirinovskii Bloc [5.9], and Yabloko [5.9]) earned enough votes to win a share of the Party allocation in the Duma.[60]

The election results revealed some important trends. In the first place, the previously important Our Home is Russia, led by Chernomyrdin and second behind the

---

57. "Za pobedu" [For Victory], *Sovetskaia Rossiia* (29 July 2000).

58. "Politreklama: KPRF: Vstavai, strana ogromnaia! Za pobedu!" [Political Platform: CPRF: Arise, Great Country! For Victory!], *Rossiiskaia gazeta* (23 November 2000).

59. Zhirinovskii Bloc, "Politreklama. Vybiraite: Kto-za gosudarstvo?" [Political Platform. Choose: Who Is for the State?], *Rossiiskaia gazeta* (18 November 1999); "Vera-Sila-Svoboda. Iz programmy dvizheniia 'Nash dom—Rossiia'" [Truth-Strength-Freedom. From the "Our Home is Russia" Movement Program], *Rossiiskaia gazeta -Dom i otechestvo* [Supplement], (30 April 2000); Fatherland-All Russia, "Politreklama. Ver'te tol'ko delam!" [Political Platform. Believe Only Deeds!], *Rossiiskaia gazeta* (9 December 1999).

60. Full details are in "Obshchie itogo vyborov deputatov . . ." [General Results of the Election of Deputies . . .], *Rossiiskaia gazeta* (31 December 1999). See also *REDA* 1999, Vol. 1.

Communists in 1995, this time failed even to break the five percent ceiling and w
no bloc seats. On the other hand, Unity, formed only a few weeks before the el
tion, did surprisingly well. Its success, attributed by some to a well-financed (on
half of the government) publicity campaign that relied on mudslinging agai
Luzhkov and Fatherland-All Russia, was a victory for Prime Minister Putin. Pu
in turn, owed his great popularity at that time to his hard stance on Chechnya. /
other new coalition, the Union of Right-Wing Forces, or "young reformers," led
yet another former prime minister, Sergei Kiriyenko, also surprised observers w
the extent of its returns. The CPRF remained the single largest party in the Dui
winning slightly more of the Party/Bloc percentage than it had in 1995. But the l
wing coalition itself declined, as the Agrarian, Socialist, Stalinist, and splinter Cc
munist factions did very poorly. The new Duma had a more multipolar members
than its predecessor, which had been dominated by the left and divided into only t
large, competing perspectives. In short the 1999 Russian election resulted in the f
Duma from which the executive side of government could expect to draw subst
tial support on many major issues. Calmness in the domestic political arena seen
possible for the first time since the early 1990s.

International associations were still problematic. Among the steps taken by
Russian government in 1999 to reestablish its traditional partnerships was a tr
agreement with Cuba (Moscow, 14 May). This was followed by a joint statement
the foreign ministers of Russia and China announcing a common diplomatic fr
against NATO's activity in Yugoslavia and for the primacy of the UN in resolving
ternational conflict (Beijing, 2 June). A protocol on economic cooperation v
signed with India (New Delhi, 29 July), and a "good neighbors" discussion was h
with the Iranian foreign minister (Teheran, 28 November). In December, the RF
curity Council prioritized Russia's ties with CIS countries and Putin told repor
that Russia needed to build long-term relations with those countries "on the basi:
realism" (Interfax, 15 December). This priority was later to be entrenched in Russ
new foreign policy concept. Within the CIS, a key step towards further integrat
came with the signing, on 26 October, of a five-state (Russia, Belarus, Kazakhstan, K
gyzstan and Tajikistan) Customs Union. Five weeks later, the long-discussed Rus
Belarus Union Treaty finally was made official by Yeltsin and Belarus Presid
Aleksyandr Lukashenko.[61]

Looking westward, the situation was quite different. Generally, Yeltsin's last y
in office had seen the disintegration of whatever order there had been in Russian f
eign policy. The partnership with the United States envisioned by Yeltsin in the e;
1990s had long since dissipated. Talk of membership in the EU was no longer he;
vague promises of entry into the WTO had come to naught, and accession to the G
7 was by no means complete. A new East–West divide had taken shape since the m
1990s, to the extent that some Russians now spoke of a new "iron curtain" impo

---

61. See "Moskva, Kreml', 8 dekabria, 12 chas, 15 min" [Moscow. The Kremlin, 8 December, 12:
Rossiiskaia gazeta (9 December 1999) for speeches by the two presidents.

further east than the first one and designed by Western leaders to keep Russia out of Europe. Even Moscow's turn to Eurasia had not yet been firmed up, except in arms sales and paper accords on the world situation, and the Customs Union notwithstanding the CIS was poised on the brink of disintegration. In addition to the debilitating and consuming tensions between Russia on the one hand, NATO and the United States on the other, Moscow was faced with great difficulties in its bilateral relations with Ukraine, France and, because of a huge debt, even its most consistent Western friend, Germany.

In December 1999, the International Monetary Fund (IMF) again postponed a long-awaited third tranche of a multibillion-dollar loan, citing technical reasons, though most observers attributed the reluctance to pay to the Russian army's actions against rebels and civilians in Chechnya. The EU cautiously followed the IMF example, threatening on 10 December to tighten up trade restrictions against Russia unless changes were made in Moscow's policies towards the dissident republic.

On the last day of the month, Yeltsin suddenly delivered a short resignation speech to the Russian people on television, taking his own population and the international community by surprise. Russia needs "new people—clever, energetic and strong," and able to cope with a new "knot of problems," was his somewhat plaintive message.[62] Those problems were handed off to Prime Minister Putin, who was named Acting President.

---

62. "Obrashchenie Borisa Yel'tsina k zhiteliam Rossii" [Statement of Boris Yeltsin to the Citizens of Russia], *Rossiiskaia gazeta* (5 January 2000).

2

✝

Setting the Stage, 2000

A NEW YEAR'S EVE HANGOVER

Acting President Putin's first weeks in the presidential office were devoted to personnel changes, policy formulation, and the conflict in Chechnya. Teams of experts worked diligently to prepare final versions of the national security concept and a new military doctrine, the first of which was ready in January, the second by early February. In July, a new codified foreign policy vision was to complete a triad of blueprints for Russian policymakers to follow.

Putin's security and military documents, to be discussed in detail in chapter 7, and the foreign policy blueprint that is analyzed later in this chapter, were to a certain extent holdovers from the old Soviet habit of codifying approaches into systematic schema. In 1992–1993, as Russia under Yeltsin attempted to define a new place for itself in world affairs, new security, military and foreign policy doctrines abounded. As we come to their successors in this examination of Putin's first year as president, analogies with Russia's first post-Soviet year will be drawn, mostly to see which notions have survived and which ones have disappeared.

The new head of state ended 1999 with a ringing message to the Russian people in which, among other things, he spoke clearly and firmly about the "Russian Idea" and the enormous value of patriotism. Soon to be called Putin's "Manifesto," his televised speech was riddled with old stereotypical visions of a "genetic code" pushing Russians towards a highly centralized state system, and praised the "paternalistic roots" ingrained in Russian society. "The public," he proclaimed, "looks toward the restoration of the guiding and regulating role of the State." Claiming that he did not favor an "official ideology of any kind," the acting president added that "for the majority of Russians, the word [patriotism] still retains its original, positive meaning." Without it,

23

Russians would no longer be a people and their country no longer an important st;
Whereas Western observers tended to react to phrases such as these with some ala:
doubtless they mirrored the sentiments of the majority of Russians. Analysts in R
sia enthused over Putin's approach, and a few even heard in them echos of Peter
Great. None seems to have noticed (or bothered to mention) the striking simila
between Putin's claims about Russia and the infamous Article 6 of the Soviet Con
tution which read: "The leading and guiding force of Soviet society and the nucl
of its political system, of all state organizations and public organizations, is the Cc
munist Party of the Soviet Union."[1] Yeltsin's Constitution of 1993 transferred mi
of the old CPSU role directly to the presidency. This was not about to change.

As the presidential election drew closer, Putin regularly returned to the notion t
Russia had lost an empire but still had potential as a great power. On receiving
own registration card for the presidential campaign, he spoke also of restoring R
sia's moral fiber. Shortly thereafter, in an "Open Letter" to Russian voters publisl
on 25 February, the aspiring president wrote that "we need a strong Russia, nor
inspire fear, but to ensure that we are not ignored. Offending us will cost more tl
it is worth."[2] Campaign rhetoric of this type encouraged pundits from abroad to p
tray post-Yeltsin Russia as aggressive in international affairs. They offered Fore
Minister Ivanov's trips to Vietnam and North Korea (9–14 February), Russia's s
cessful testing of a Topol-M ballistic missile, continued work on a nuclear power :
tion in Iran, and the delivery of a guided-missile destroyer to China (the sale hav
been arranged during Yeltsin's tenure in office) as proof of this new pudding.
though the implications of these particular events for Russia's relations with the W
were tempered by qualifying statements, even concessions, from Putin, few of
traditional suspicions were allayed on either side. In late January 2000, for examj
the Russian press printed sections from President Clinton's State of the Union
dress which expressed Washington's hope to cooperate more fully with Russia ;
China,[3] but accompanying editorials tended to doubt his sincerity.

Russia's external affairs continued to be complicated by the brutal civil war
Chechnya. Talk that PACE (Parliamentary Assembly of the Council of Europe) '
likely to drop Russia as a member because of Chechnya pushed Putin into a bit (
corner, though it did not undermine his soaring popularity at home. Indeed, his i
age as proponent of a "Russia first" policy was strengthened by Putin's defense of
army's action in the dissident republic. PACE's British chair, Lord Russell-Johnst
visited Moscow for discussion in January and Putin agreed that he could t
Chechnya and judge the situation for himself. But when rebels seized the mom
and sought international recognition for their leadership, Moscow objected vi

---

1. Article 6 appeared for the first time in the Brezhnev Constitution (Fundamental Law), of 1977,
it reflected the reality of the USSR's political system since 1917–1918. For Putin's "Manifesto," see Pt
"Rossiia na rubezhe tysiacheletiia" [Russia on the Brink of the Millennium], *Rossiiskaia gazeta* (31
cember 1999).

2. See, for example, Putin, "Otkrytoe pis'mo Vladimira Putina k rossiiskim izbirateliam" [Open L(
to the Russian Voters], *Izvestiia* (25 February 2000).

3. "Shiroko shagaet Amerika" [America Takes a Long Step], *Rossiiskaia gazeta* (27 January 2000).

ously. To the Kremlin's horror, the "Foreign Minister of Ichkeria," Ilyas Akhmadov, was hosted by the U.S. State Department on 14 January, as a "private citizen." The foreign ministry accused the United States of supporting terrorists. In the long run only Afghanistan's Taliban government recognized Aslan Maskhadov as the head of an independent Chechen government. Only Washington's stance on Chechnya was left openly ambiguous. On the other hand, India, China, and Iran strongly supported Russia's policy on Chechnya. The strategic rhetoric and diplomatic maneuvering with Russia on one side and the "West" led by the United States on the other seemed to have come full circle.

A hectic round of delegations from other foreign ministries visited Moscow hoping to discover Putin's plans for Russia in the international arena; their presence kept the issue of Russia's cooperation with the Atlantic Alliance high on the list of subjects for discussion. Most of the visitors expressed some sympathy for Russia's position facing "terrorists" in Chechnya, calling however for a political solution to the crisis. Among the prominent tourists were German foreign minister, Joschka Fischer and Italian foreign minister, Lamberto Dini, who came to Moscow separately in early January. Cuban foreign minister, Felipe Perez Roque, spent 25–27 January in the Russian capital, and invited Putin to Cuba (see chapter 12). U.S. secretary of state, Madeleine Albright arrived on 30 January and left on 2 February; she was followed by French foreign minister, Hubert Vedrine, from 3 to 5 February. NATO's general secretary was scheduled to arrive in Moscow sometime in February. This last-named visit depended on an agenda that included specific terms for Russia's return to the PJC, so there was doubt that the meeting with Robertson would actually take place. Javier Solana was among other important visitors. One of their aims, of course, was to see just how far Putin intended to push his new version of Russian nationalism.

In the meantime, the NATO question kept Moscow's foreign and defense officialdom on the alert. The Russian media had been using NATO's actions in Yugoslavia as a rationale for Moscow's very forceful policy in Chechnya and, by the end of 1999, had taken advantage of growing rifts within NATO to demonstrate the propriety of their own government's policies. When a group of Western law professors (from Canada, Greece, Norway and Britain) charged sixty-seven NATO country leaders with war crimes before a United Nations tribunal in The Hague, the Russian media reacted with great enthusiasm, and kept the issue in front of the Russian public from December 1999 through January 2000.[4] Western press and TV paid far less attention to the matter.

---

4. See, for example, Kseniia Fokina, "NATO otvetit pered sudom" [Will NATO Answer before the Court?], *Nezavisimaia gazeta* (28 December 1999); "Yeshche tri toma dokumentov o zlodeianiiakh SShA i NATO v SRYu. Prestupnikov—k sudy!" [Three Volumes More of Documents on the Villainies of the USA and NATO in Yugoslavia. Criminals to Court!], *Sovetskaia Rossia* (15 Jan 2000). Dossiers in support of these charges were submitted to Carla del Ponte, chief prosector for the UN International Criminal Tribunal for the Former Yugoslavia, in November 1999. It became a matter for public discussion when the White House issued a statement criticizing the idea that NATO might be held to account for such actions. For an account of the charges, see Marcus Gee, "Are Western Leaders War Criminals?" Toronto *Globe and Mail* (29 January 2000).

Russian observers had watched with interest when NATO decided formally to examine its doctrinal option of "first strike" with nuclear weapons. Within a 1 weeks of the decision to follow-up on the review proposed by Canada's Lloyd ⌐ worthy at a foreign ministers' conference in Brussels (December 1999), irritated sponses from NATO's nuclear powers became common. Russian strategists begar look for weak links in NATO's chain, as their Soviet predecessors had done si France's disengagement from the Alliance in the 1960s.

Increasing violence in Kosovo gave Russia an opportunity to offer comprom The violence divided NATO, especially as peacekeeping troops themselves came der attack from, mostly, Albanian separatists. In January 2000, Col. Gen. Ivashov sisted that "there is no alternative to Russia–NATO cooperation and Moscow is rea to restore relations with the Alliance." Coming from one of the most outspoken ai NATO "hawks" in the upper echelons of the ministry, this was a clear concession, r tivated perhaps by the PACE dilemma and Putin's new emphasis on pragmatism. Ivashov set two unequivocal conditions: the UN Security Council Resolution (L SCR) 1244, which guarantees the territorial integrity of Yugoslavia, had to be ma tained; and NATO must show that it was serious about building good relations w Russia.[5] Indeed, UNSCR 1244 was certainly in danger of becoming redundant. February, interethnic violence in the divided city of Mitrovica placed some of 37,000 NATO-led troops in danger and caused important political groups in seve NATO countries, but above all in the United States, to urge their governments withhold funds and perhaps even withdraw troops from such peacekeeping tasks.

It was at this point that the EU rose collectively in protest against the selectior Jörg Haider, head of the Austrian Freedom Party, to a coalition government in t country. Oddly, Haider's alleged fascist inclinations upset the Russian public and ficialdom far less than it did their Western counterparts. Russian pundits ponde the apparent discrepancy between constant Western harping on the value of dem racy and the importance of free elections, and their willingness to pressure a fell EU member-state into overthrowing a "people's choice" when they happened no like him. One observer likened the Washington and EU approach to Austria a Western version of the Brezhnev Doctrine.[6] From Moscow's perspective, such consistencies in the American approach to European affairs provided good oppor nity for rhetorical point-making, but made long-term policymaking very difficul

ALBRIGHT IN TOWN AGAIN

Of the many visitors to Moscow, Madeleine Albright was perhaps the most cru for Putin, for he claimed on several occasions that the normalization of relations w

---

5. RFE/RL Newsline (31 January 2000).
6. Yevgenii Grigor'ev, "Zapad obkatyvaet svoiu 'doktrinu Brezhneva'," [The West Rolls Out Its C "Brezhnev Doctrine"], *Nezavisimaia gazeta* (3 February 2000). The sanctions were not lifted until 12 : tember 2000.

Washington was a top priority in foreign affairs. The sentiment appeared to be mutual. Russian ambassador to Washington, Yurii Ushakov, had said in January that "cooperation between our countries is a strategic imperative,"[7] and U.S. Deputy Secretary of State Strobe Talbott echoed that feeling on more than one occasion. Russian experts on Russian-American relations agreed, but continued to suspect Washington's motives—especially as Talbott was seen as the leading advocate of Baltic admission to NATO in the Clinton administration. ISKRAN Director Rogov emphasized that the "buddy Boris—buddy Bill" epoch was over and had been for quite some time. He blamed vacillating and incompetent Russian leadership, meaning Yeltsin, for much of the difficulty and congratulated Albright for her optimism. The crux of the problem between the two countries, however, was the Clinton administration's continued reluctance "to grant due consideration to Russia's legitimate interests." America would have to bend before true rapprochement could be reached, Rogov concluded.[8]

On 2 February, Albright delivered a speech to the Diplomatic Academy in Moscow, making the point that Russia and the United States had more interests in common than they had differences. She insisted, indeed, that the world was "multipolar" and not the American-driven "unipolar" one that some Russians claimed it to be. Logic compels Russia and the United States to work together, she proclaimed, in part because their nuclear arsenals "provide overwhelming deterrence against direct attack by any rational adversary."[9] Russian analysts took her remarks to mean that Washington intended to cooperate, but if she had hoped to earn support for the proposed amendments to the ABM Treaty—a central part of her address—she was doomed to disappointment. Yet the opening was still there. On 14 February, President Clinton told CNN that Russia had the right to fight terrorism on its own territory, causing the Russian media to exult that Washington was beginning to recognize that Russia must not be isolated.[10] The two presidents apparently had found common ground. A few days later in February, Putin sent a personal message to Clinton with the recently appointed head of Russia's Security Council, Sergei Ivanov, and said that Russia–U.S. relations were now his top foreign policy priority (Interfax, 16, 21 February).

As a former member of the Foreign Intelligence Service and deputy director of the Federal Security Service (FSB), Lt. Gen. Sergei Ivanov brought special experience to his new post. He met with Samuel Berger, presidential national security adviser and his

---

7. "Takaia slozhnaia materiia" [Such a Complicated Matter], *Rossiiskaia gazeta* (11 January 2000).

8. See esp. Sergei Rogov, "Strannyi period v otnosheniiakh Rossii i SShA" [A Strange Period in the Russia-USA Relationship], *Nezavisimaia gazeta* (8 February 2000). Rogov is one of Russia's most important scholars of the strategic relationship between Russia and the USA.

9. "Secretary of State Madeleine K. Albright Speech at the Diplomatic Academy" (2 February 2000), Information Resource Center, US Embassy, Ottawa. For a detailed Russian summary, see Madlen Olbrait, "SShA khotiat videt' v Rossii stranu mirnykh reshenii" [The USA Wants to See in Russia a Country of Peaceful Decisions], *Dipkur'er NG*, No. 3 (17 February 2000).

10. See, for example, Dmitrii Gornostaev, "Klinton pokhvalit Putina" [Clinton Will Praise Putin], *Nezavisimaia gazeta* (16 February 2000); and Interfax (16 February 200).

host in the United States, Albright, and the heads of both the FBI and the CIA. At t
time, settling the dispute over Washington's proposal to amend the ABM Treaty, a
in Russia, persuading the Duma to ratify START-II, were what Putin believed to be
keys to their mutual future. START-II was gaining support from the Russian milit
as well and, in spite of stiff opposition from the communists, the Duma also was le
ing towards ratification.[11] The ABM question was more difficult, yet even here sig
from the Kremlin suggested that compromise might be possible (see chapter 7).[12]

ROBERTSON NEXT IN LINE

Russia's uneasy relationship with NATO was still the major stumbling block whe
came to international security issues. In fact, within a few days of the Albright n
sion to Moscow all the old anti-NATO charges began showing up in the Russ
media either as commentary on specific issues or in connection with the Russ
presidential election campaign. The on-again, off-again planned visit to Moscow
Robertson provided grist for much of the discourse. For weeks, no specific dates w
set for the General Secretary's visit because they disagreed on the agenda.

The projected visit was preceded by aggressive position-taking in Moscow. Ivasl
led the attack, rejecting any kind of military "diktat" from Washington, synonym
with NATO, and accusing the Americans of both "hypocrisy" and "hegemony se
ing." There was no hint here of compromise on the ABM question. One of
Yeltsin-Primakov pointmen in Russian opposition to NATO expansion, Ivashov
viously now expected to perform this task for Putin. "The eastward NATO expans
is the Sword of Damocles overhanging the Western direction of bilateral relations,"
wrote on 11 February, accusing Strobe Talbott of offering direct support for Baltic
cession in his January statement. Ivashov's outbursts were a constant reminder of h
deeply rooted the distrust of Washington was in some Moscow circles.[13]

Other observers were more conciliatory. They watched carefully as Robert:
spoke to reporters in Bulgaria, Romania and Moldova (see chapter 8), and conclu
that NATO was sincerely trying to stabilize relations with Moscow.[14] Significan

---

11. V. Krylov, "Pochemu dolzhen byt' otklonen dogovor SNV-2" [Why START-II Must be Rejec
Sovetskaia Rossiia (5 February 2000). Zyuganov called START-II ratification "seriously dangerous to
country."

12. See, for example, V.N. Tsygichko, A.A. Piontowskii, in *Voennaia mysl'* No. 1 (Jan/Feb 2000
which "anti-missile defense" ("Star Wars") systems are defended if the ABM Treaty could be amende
the basis of a mutual agreement rather than unilaterally as Washington had threatened to do.

13. See Ivashov, "Rossiia ne priemlet silovogo diktata SShA. Iskrennost' Moskvy stolkivaetsia s l
meriem Vashingtona" [Russia Rejects Forceful Diktat from the USA. Moscow's Sincerity Clashes
Washington's Hypocrisy], *Nezavisimaia gazeta* (11 February 2000); and Vsevolod Ovchinnikov, "Skol
otkos k konfrontatsii" [Slippery Slope to Confrontatsii], *Rossiiskaia gazeta* (8 February 2000).

14. See, for example, "NATO Secretary General's Visit to Russia Confirmed," a long report filed 1
Brussels by A. Mineev for ITAR-TASS (14 February 2000), and Viktor Sokolov, "RF razmorozit otnoshe
s NATO?" [RF Defrosts Relations with NATO], *Nezavisimaia gazeta* (12 February 2000); "Gensek N/
pribyvaet v Moskvu" [NATO GenSec Arrives in Moscow], *Rossiiskaia gazeta* (16 February 2000).

even while congratulating Romania as "an important strategic partner" Robertson offered his hosts no guarantee of admission to NATO.[15] After he finally set down in Moscow on 15 February, the meetings appeared to go well for Russia, whose officials and media insisted that it was NATO that was most actively seeking accommodation while Russia held to its position that relations would "unfreeze" only after Russia was guaranteed real input into NATO via the Founding Act. The government press claimed victory, saying that its "firm convictions" had won the day. A joint "statement" announced that Russia and NATO would "intensify their dialogue in the Permanent Joint Council" and that both sides would "contribute towards building a stable and undivided Europe" (ITAR-TASS, 16 February).[16] Most analysts took care to remind readers that NATO was "continuing its expansion to the East"—referring usually to Robertson's prior visits to Ukraine, Moldova and Bulgaria and the Baltic States—in the face of Russian objections.[17]

Ivashov continued to carp. In Geneva delivering a report on Russia's military doctrine while Robertson was in Moscow, he presented a much less sanguine perspective. His main point was that "the United States is brainwashing the world . . . even the Russian people" into believing that it and its NATO allies have a right to interfere in domestic affairs "under the pretext of protecting human rights." This trend, he claimed, and NATO's new strategic concept "which views Russia as one of the most probable enemies, although in a concealed form"—is what had to be taken into account in the new Russian military doctrine. Ivashov agreed that Russia had no choice but to cooperate again with NATO, yet that cooperation must be on Russian terms. It was obvious that the Kremlin was going to be far more reserved under Putin than it had been with Yeltsin as president.[18]

As he was leaving Moscow, Robertson told reporters that NATO and Russia were, in fact, already "strategic partners on the world stage." It was not clear what he meant by that, but after the NATO leader left town, Ivashov set out what "strategic partner" meant to the Russians: equal participation in assessing crisis situations and their resolution (ITAR-TASS, 19 February). Both visions clearly awaited confirmation in practice. Coincidentally, presumably, on 17 February the monthly diplomatic insert to *Nezavisimaia gazeta* carried a long interview with Jack Matlock, former U.S. ambassador to the USSR and outspoken critic of NATO expansion eastward. Matlock

15. On this, see Viacheslav Samoshkin, "Rumyniia prositsia v NATO" [Romania Asking to be Admitted to NATO], *Nezavisimaia gazeta* (15 February 2000).

16. See, for example, Viktor Sokolov, Vladimir Mukhin, "NATO khochet pomirit'sia s Moskvoi" [NATO Wants to Reconcile with Moscow], *Nezavisimaia gazeta* (16 February 2000); Viktor Sokolov, Vadim Solov'ev, "Kreml' i NATO pomirilis'" [The Kremlin and NATO are Reconciled], *Nezavisimaia gazeta* (17 February 2000); Vladimir Kuznechevskii, "V Kreml'—za primireniem" [To the Kremlin, for Reconciliation], *Rossiiskaia gazeta* (18 February 2000).

17. See, for example, Anatolii Shapolov, "Vizit. Gensek—v Belokamennoi" [The Visit. General Secretary Is in Moscow], *Rossiiskaia gazeta* (17 February 2000); and Vladimir Mukhin, "NATO khochet pomirit'sia s Moskvoi," *op. cit.* (Fn. 16).

18. See the series of ITAR-TASS releases from Geneva, prepared by Konstantin Pribytkov, (16 February 2000), and "Russian General Accuses United States of 'Brainwashing the World,' Pushing toward 'New Cold War,'" FBIS-SOV, No. 216 (16 February 2000), Paris (North European Service).

was frank in his criticism of both Washington and Moscow in the Kosovo affai
the United States and NATO for relying on force too hastily, and Russia for its ʀ
sive, unhelpful attitude. But NATO expansion came in for his greatest reproach
diluted NATO itself, and excluded Russia from major security decisions in Euro
Both could be fatal decisions.[19]

While the Russian government held on to its tenuous position in Kosovo, thrʀ
ening to withdraw after every real or perceived affront, opposition political leaʀ
continued openly to support Yugoslavia and Milosevic. The head of the Russian
People's Union, Sergei N. Baburin, flew to Belgrade in mid-February as an obseʀ
to a Socialist Party of Serbia Congress. He praised a Milosevic address, claiming ʀ
the Serbian president wanted "social justice," and advocated the immediate uniоʀ
Russia, Belarus and Yugoslavia.[20] Shortly after Baburin's return to Moscow,
Duma approved a statement "On the Violation of UN Security Council Resolut
1244 (1999) on the Kosovo Settlement," accusing KFOR of abetting Albanian ʀ
aratism and "lawlessness by criminal groups" in the province of Kosovo and Mʀ
hija. The statement singled out Bernard Kouchner, the UN secretary general's ʀ
cial envoy, for charges of duplicity and called for a convocation of the UN Secu
Council to deal with the issue.[21] Putin and Robertson had discussed this matter
ready (Interfax, 21 Feb), so the Russian government ignored the Duma Statemeʀ

RETHINKING FOREIGN POLICY

These emotion-evoking foreign considerations were minor compared to the mu
ple obstacles faced by Putin as he tried to find a niche for Russia in world affairs. ʀ
wards the end of February, at its eighth assembly, the influential nongovernmeʀ
CFDP began discussing a detailed draft report on Russian foreign policy. The coʀ
cil had been established in 1992 to bring together and reconcile different pointʀ
view from Russia's intelligentsia about the direction Russian foreign policy shо
take. At that time it included such diverse figures as Foreign Minister Anʀ
Kozyrev, Sergei Stankevich, Yeltsin's main political adviser, Georgii Arbatov, tʀ

---

19. Matlock, "Zhestkii podkhod po Metloku" [Tough Approach According to Matlock], *Dipkur'er*.
No. 3 (17 February 2000). The same issue of *Dipkur'er NG* carried Madeleine Albright's speech undeʀ
rubric, "SShA khotiat videt' v Rossii stranu mirnykh reshenii" [The USA Wants to See in Russia a Cʀ
try of Peaceful Intentions].

20. Baburin's commentary was carried in a press release issued in Belgrade (Tanjug, 29 February)ʀ
also Yevgenii Popov, " 'Mirotvortsy' NATO razzhigaiut pozhar . . . Kosovska-Mitrovitsa—pylaiushʀ
ochag" ["NATO Peacekeepers Kindle a Fire . . . Kosovo-Metohija are the Burning Hearths], *Sovets.
Rossiia* (26 February 2000), and "Miloshevich neset poteri. No vsia bor'ba eshche vperedi" [Milosevic
fers Losses. But the Entire Struggle Moves Ahead], *Rossiiskaia gazeta* (10 February 2000), for a very ʀ
pathetic, and long, piece on Milosevic, the EU and Albanian separatism.

21. "Diskreditirovat' OON—nedopustimo.—O narushenii rezoliutsii Soveta Bezopasnosti O
1244 (1999) po kosovskomu uregulirovaniu" [To Discredit the UN Is Unacceptable. On the Violatiо
UN Security Council Resolution (1999) on the Settlement], *Rossiiskaia gazeta* (22 February 2000).

director of ISKRAN, and thirty-four others.[22] Karaganov, deputy director of the Institute of Europe, Russian Academy of Sciences, was the CFDP's founding director and remains in that post to this day.

The 2000 report, the fourth prepared by the CFDP, was summarized in March by Karaganov well before its final version was ready. He decried the "inaccurate idea of the world and [Russia's] place in it" and "incorrect priorities" held to by Yeltsin's political elite, most of whom were still in office. The CFDP quite realistically described Russia as only a "virtual-reality great power."[23] Russia's place in the world economy was declining, and about half of its population lived in poverty. Moreover, Russia lagged far behind in the information revolution. While "the country's 'greatness' and 'prestige'" is debated, the authors warned, Russia may miss out on the "post-industrial development" taking place everywhere else.

The report was more traditional on strategic matters: it was America's desire to impose its will that caused military force to be employed against Iraq and Yugoslavia, and NATO to move "out of zone," making the world unstable and unpredictable. The tendency in the United States to ignore Russia and Russia's own self-isolation, also were dangerous because they encouraged the xenophobic elements in Russian politics and society to grow more extreme. Karaganov pulled no punches.

To help choose the right policy, the CFDP set out the directions available to Putin's team: (1) increased militarization and reliance on anti-Western partners (Iran, Iraq, China), and the CIS; (2) acquiescence to Western leadership; or, (3) multipolarity, that is, the existing official policy. These options were put forward as the obvious options already mooted by Russian foreign policy shapers for some time. In their stead, the Council offered a fully new approach called "selective engagement," and placed economic recovery at the most urgent of government's priorities. There followed a very short list of "vitally important Russian interests," including an "unconditional" nuclear capacity. The "'great power' phantom" should be renounced, confrontations avoided as well, and foreign investments attracted. Tough rhetoric should be avoided, in part because "our threats are no longer feared." The candor of the Council's report was refreshing, even startling. It remained to be seen how persuasive it was.

In the meantime, ongoing U.S. criticism of Russian actions in Chechnya and Washington's presumed hand in influencing the IMF and the EU into putting economic pressure on Moscow, rankled the Russian leadership and media. Repeated incidents of American interference in what Russia regarded as its internal affairs did not help. For example, the Russian foreign ministry reacted furiously to remarks by a U.S. State Department official, James Rubin, who accused Russian troops of war crimes in Chechnya (Interfax, 21 February). A few weeks later, Foreign Minister

22. On the Council and its membership, see Suzanne Crow, "Competing Blueprints for Russian Foreign Policy," *RFE/RL Research Report*, 1: 50 (2000), 45–50.

23. Sergei Karaganov, "A New Foreign Policy. What Is Russia to Do? What Is to be Done with Russia?" *Moscow News*, No. 9 (8–14 March 2000); for the Russian version, see *Moskovskie novosti* (29 February–6 March 2000). 5, 11; and for earlier strategies offered by the Council for Foreign and Defense Policy, see *Russia Faces NATO Expansion*, pp. 12, 34, 98.

Ivanov denounced bitterly a U.S. House of Representatives bill allowing American
thorities to impose sanctions against Russian firms if they sold nuclear or rocket te
nology to Iran (Interfax, 3 March). Ivanov's statement came shortly after yet anot
"inspection" of a Russian tanker by a U.S. destroyer in the Persian Gulf (ITAR-TA
1 March). The irritants in Moscow–Washington relations were starting to fester.

In early March, the Russian foreign policy and military leadership repeated
mantra about Moscow's participation in the forthcoming NATO Council of Defe
Ministers' meeting. Attendance would not be ruled out, Ivanov told a corresponde
but a decision in this regard would depend entirely on NATO's "readiness for c
structive dialogue" (ITAR-TASS, 2 March). He and his colleagues were especi:
concerned about looming new crises in Kosovo and the attitude of NATO memb
("malicious slander") to Russia's military action in Chechnya.

At that time, Russia's media was growing more critical of the ABM amending {
mula, treating it as a threat to their own country's nuclear deterrence safety netwc
Lt. Gen. Nikolai Zlenko, for example, explained that, contrary to much of
hoopla around the Putin-Robertson communication, all Russian relations w
NATO were still frozen, with the exception of joint activities in Kosovo. The L
national missile defense system and consequent ABM amendment proposals are '
rected against the Russian Federation." Only the rhetoric had softened, he add
nothing else had changed .[24] Other analysts in Moscow asserted that Washington
pressuring the EU to give up any pretension of organizing its own peacekeep
forces independently of the Atlantic Alliance. To be sure, Russia had been gre:
concerned earlier when the EU began to debate collective security matters, imply
that new members, including former Soviet states, might be joining a security, rat
than strictly economic, bloc. Yet America's objections were deemed more omin
because they were seen as evidence that Washington hoped to maintain NATC
"the main forum for resolving security matters in Europe and beyond." Even the g
ernment press accused Washington of trying to impose its will on the EU.[25]

This type of perspective made the next big episode more startling than it mi
otherwise have been.

"Russia Wants to Join NATO"?

An international media frenzy was let loose on 5 March (the anniversary of Stal
death) when Acting President Putin answered BBC reporter David Frost's questi
"Is it possible that Russia will ever join NATO?" with "Why not? I do not rule

---

24. "Po ugroze i reaktsiia" [For Every Threat There Is a Reaction], *Rossiiskaia gazeta* (1 March 20
Zlenko was then first deputy chief of the RF Defense Ministry's Main Directorate for International I
itary Cooperation. He was responding to questions by American journalists.
25. Leonid Gladchenko, "Samostoiatel'nost'? Pozhaluista! No Tol'ko v ramkakh NATO" [Independe
Sure! But Only within NATO], *Rossiiskaia gazeta* (2 March 2000). See also N.I. Ryzhkov, former U
prime minister, on this, "Mir posle agressii NATO. Ostrov Svobody v tsentre Evropy" [The World :
NATO's Aggression. An Island of Freedom in the Center of Europe], *Sovetskaia Rossiia* (2 March 2000

such a possibility." As Russian officials rushed to clarify, headlines in the West screamed that Russia wanted to join NATO.[26] Keeping the upcoming presidential elections firmly in sight, the CPRF reacted with staged fury. Zyuganov accused Putin of failing to understand foreign policy and termed his remarks "naive and unpardonable." Repeating the accusation leveled often in the 1990s by Yeltsin and Primakov, that NATO expansion was the worst mistake since World War II, Zyuganov resurrected the *Drang nach Osten* image. "Our fathers and forefathers did not liberate Europe from fascists for the NATO military alliance to . . . pose a threat to Russia's national security," he thundered.[27] Even the leader of the purportedly liberal Yabloko, Grigorii Yavlinskii, called Putin's statement a tactical error, pointing out that by implication it granted legitimacy to pretensions in Ukraine and the Baltic States.

Putin backtracked almost immediately, telling reporters in Ivanovo that his response had been a hypothetical answer to a hypothetical question (Interfax, 7 March). Lord Robertson, who at first "welcomed" the notion as a sign that Moscow was willing to cooperate more fully with NATO, agreed that it was a "purely hypothetical" issue. On further thought, he added that Russian membership was "not on the agenda"—a position that many Russians, including Putin, took to mean that NATO did not want Russia's adherence to the Alliance.[28] It was this Robertson afterthought that was to be remembered in Moscow.

Deputy Duma Chairman Vladimir Lukin (ambassador to the United States, 1992–94, and one of the founders of Yabloko), agreed with Putin's approach, noting correctly that the acting president had gone on to tell Frost that Russian membership would be considered only "if Russia becomes a full-fledged partner." In the same breath Putin had reiterated that Moscow still objected to NATO expansion and that he was most concerned about the potential for Russia's isolation in the new world order.[29] With the exception of very critical commentary from the left-wing press in Russia, Putin's stance soon was treated as a logical response in the circumstance; the idea of Russian entry into NATO came to be regarded as something that could come about only if the Alliance reformed itself.[30]

---

26. See, for example, Giles Whittell, "Russia Wants to Join NATO," *Ottawa Citizen* (6 March 2000). For a detailed examination of the Western response, see Ira Straus (US Coordinator, Committee on Eastern Europe and Russia in NATO), "The Pitiful Western Response to Putin on NATO," Johnson's Russia List JRL, No. 4157, #11 (9 March 2000).

27. Interfax (5 March 2000). See also L. Nikolaev, "Putin—skoree poklonnik maiora Pronina, chem Dzheimsa Bonda, no ochen' khochet v NATO. Zlopoluchnyi zavtrak s Frostom" [Putin Admires Major Pronin More than James Bond, But He Very Much Wishes to Be in NATO. Ill-fated Lunch with Frost], *Sovetskaia Rossiia* (7 March 2000).

28. Putin made this point on 18 April, on ORT, speaking from Sevastopol, where he was meeting with Ukraine's Leonid Kuchma. See Ira Straus, "Putin Responds to NATO's Unresponsiveness," JRL No. 4258 (18 April 2000).

29. The full script of the interview was published by ITAR-TASS on 6 March. See also Interfax (5 March 2000), and "Rossiia v izoliatsii ne budet" [Russia Will Not Be Isolated], *Rossiiskaia gazeta* (7 March 2000), where the 'isolation' issue is given pride of place. For quick reactions from foreign pundits and statesmen see JRL, No. 4150, nos. 2, 3.

30. See, for example, Dmitrii Gornostaev, "Putin v NATO ne zovet" [Putin Is Not Invited into NATO], *Nezavisimaia gazeta* (7 March 2000).

At any rate, senior officials of the Russian defense and foreign policy departme
rushed to have it known that they still considered NATO expansion a "poten
threat" to Russia.[31] Sergei Ivanov gave the final answer to the Putin–NATO myst
on 16 March. Repeating his earlier explanation, "it was a hypothetic answer to a
pothetic question," the Security Council chairman went on to say,

> and why not, if NATO develops from a military–political organization and becomes ;
> political one, replacing the OSCE, which we think is on its last legs? On the condition
> of course, that Russia is admitted as an equal member, enabling it to influence decisions
> But, if our relations with NATO develop the way they did in Kosovo, the question wil
> automatically be struck off the agenda.[32]

Perhaps the best lines were those in an editorial prepared for the *Moscow Ti*
where a partially tongue-in-cheek writer said that all nations should join NAT
uniting the entire world under Washington's leadership in preparation for joint
fense against aliens from Mars. Willingness to join NATO has become the new
mus test for "international political correctness," the editorialist proclaimed, bu
reality it is a meaningless formality, one which Russia will, in fact, never take up

Public pronouncements by all political parties on this and other matters w
shaped to a greater or lesser extent by the presidential election campaign. The Cc
munist Party consistently emphasized the degree to which the Kremlin had fallen
der the sway of foreign influences, above all the American leadership. Zyugaı
blamed the Yeltsin regime and its reliance on the West for the growth of pornoɡ
phy and violence in Russia, and accused Putin of softening his early approach to
West. The CPRF leader adopted an aggressively patriotic theme, promising to bc
the combat readiness of the Armed Forces and prepare them to "rebuff any aggı
sor."[34] Putin's casual comment to the BBC about Russia joining NATO was used
the communist press for weeks to prop up charges that "NATO-lover" Putin was
verting to the pro-Western stance of a type that had cost Kozyrev his job in the n
1990s.[35]

Zhirinovskii and his LDPR cohorts also furiously bashed the West. All in vair
would seem: according to at least one poll taken in early March, the Russian pul
seemed not to follow the communist and nationalist line. To a question about wh
Russia's best interest lay in the international sphere, 28 percent approved cooperat
with NATO, and another 9 percent advocated membership in the Alliance. Gi

---

31. Russia "has not changed its negative attitude towards NATO expansion" eastward, Col. (
Ivashov reiterated at a news conference held on 9 March (ITAR-TASS, 9 March 2000).

32. Sergei Ivanov, "Rossiiu tesniat. No ne vytesniat" [Russia Is Pushed Back. But Will Not Be Expell
Rossiiskaia gazeta (16 March 2000).

33. "NATO Can Hold Back Aliens," *Moscow Times* (7 March 2000).

34. See "Obrashchenie k narodu Gennadiia Zyuganova, kandidata v Prezidenty Rossii" [Russian I
idential Candidate Gennadii Zyuganov's Appeal to the People], *Rossiiskaia gazeta* (14 March 2000).

35. See, for example, Viacheslav Tetekin, "Pristyp 'NATOliubiia'" [Attack of the "NATO-Lovers"
ease], *Sovetskaia Rossiia* (14 March 2000).

that only 17 percent favored the creation of a defensive alliance against NATO, the pro-Western trend seems to have made a bit of a comeback from the angry and dominant anti-West and anti-American sentiments generated by NATO's bombing of Yugoslavia and Iraq. More significantly, 66 percent had a "good, or mostly good" attitude towards the United States.[36]

THE PJC THAWS—SOMEWHAT

On 15 March 2000, the PJC met to discuss issues beyond military cooperation in Kosovo for the first time in a year.[37] Head of the Russian military mission to NATO, General Viktor Zavarzin, had resumed his chores in Brussels a week beforehand. Much was made in Russia of Putin's "initiative" vis-à-vis NATO, though the Council actually had been meeting since July 1999 on matters relating to peacekeeping operations in Kosovo. The situation in Yugoslavia, above all in Kosovo, was still high on the PJC agenda, but broader issues related to arms control and each other's new strategic concepts also were explored. Not surprisingly, in light of the upcoming elections, the Kremlin claimed success in that the PJC agreed to abide by the conditions set in UNSCR 1244, and participate in a broadly based mutual exchange of information (ITAR-TASS, 15 March).

Interestingly, the PJC meeting coincided with a blistering open lecture on Russia's national security concept delivered by Sergei Ivanov to the Moscow State Institution of International Relations in Moscow. Outlining growing threats "to Russia and the remainder of the international community from international terrorist organizations, which have chosen Russia as the bridgehead for their far-reaching plans," he found NATO culpable for Russia's weakened condition.[38] NATO, after all, acted in Yugoslavia as "prosecutor, judge, and executioner, ignoring the UN and the OSCE, not to mention Russia." Ivanov referred to NATO's strategic doctrine, which the PJC was discussing at that very moment, as a strategy for enhancing the Alliance's "own security and unquestionable leadership based on military superiority."

Much of this spleen was driven by the Kosovo question. A bizarre U.S. offer of a $5 million reward for Milosevic and other alleged Serbian war criminals was treated with disgust by the Russian media, which also foresaw an Albanian proclamation of independence for Kosovo with NATO either acquiescing to or even abetting their

---

36. Slightly less than 20 percent had no opinion about alignments, and 28 percent preferred that Russia join no military bloc. The poll was conducted by the All-Russia Public Opinion Research Center (VtsIOM), 28–31 January; results printed in *Trud* (7 March 2000).

37. "Otnosheniia s NATO vosstanavlivaiutsia" [Relations with NATO Are Re-Started], *NVO*, No. 9 (17–23 March 2000); D. Gornostaev, "Rossiia i NATO snova sovetuiutsia" [Russia and NATO Are Talking Again], *Nezavisimaia gazeta* (16 March 2000).

38. Ivanov, "Rossiiu tesniat. No ne vytesniat" ["Russia Is Being Pressed Back. But Is Not Expelled"], *Rossiiskaia gazeta* (16 March 2000).

claim. A separation movement in Montenegro was generally predicted as well.[39]
Moscow all talk of world affairs inevitably turned back to NATO and Yugoslavia

ANNIVERSARY OF NATO ATTACK ON YUGOSLAVIA

On 21 March 2000, a few days before the actual anniversary of the onset of NAT
seventy-eight-day bombardment of Yugoslavia, Lord Robertson issued a report pr.
ing the accomplishments of that campaign. In "Kosovo One Year On" the NA'
secretary general lauded peacekeeping and military and police forces for post-bor
ing developments, such as the resettling of 1.3 million former refugees, school op
ings, and a reduction in crime. He enthusiastically offered up numbers for land-m
clearing, the distribution of building supplies and firewood, and the number of m
ical treatments provided by NATO.[40]

Presumably the report satisfied the already converted, angered opponents
NATO behavior in Yugoslavia, and won few new converts. Assurances that the
liance "acted to uphold international law in Kosovo," and achieved its "humani
ian objectives against a ruthless, unprincipled cynical opponent," rang pretty holl
to Russian analysts. Robertson's address prompted another flurry of reassessment:
events in Kosovo, and even many Western journalists reached conclusions
amenable to the position taken by the secretary general. These were reported w
relish in the Russian media.[41] His acknowledgement that, "of course, some incide
occurred where there were unintended civilian casualties" was greeted with deris
even in some normally conservative circles.[42] Less than a week prior to Roberts<
celebratory presentation, in fact, Pentagon officials were warning that further war
tween Serbian and Albanian Kosovar troops was looming, and predicted a "
spring" into which NATO forces could be drawn. As events seemed either to c
tradict or weaken the impact of Robertson's claims, Russian monitors seized uj
such projections as proof of NATO's collective duplicity. Moscow's left recharged
the old analogies between NATO and Nazi Germany. The communist paper *So*

---

39. See, for example, Grigorii Danin, "Milliony za golovu Miloshevicha" [Millions for Milose
Head], *Rossiiskaia gazeta* (16 March 2000); Maksim Yusin, "NATO gotova zashchitit' chernogort
[NATO Is Ready to Defend the Montenegrins], *Izvestiia* (15 March 2000); "Ne NATO boiatsia alban
boeviki" [The Albanian Fighters Are Not Afraid of NATO], *Krasnaia zvezda* (14 March 2000).

40. "Remarks by Lord Robertson, NATO Secretary General, at the press conference to mark the
anniversary of the air campaign," NATO On-Line Library (21 March 2000).

41. See, for example, Kseniia Fokina, "Rasstrela v Rachake ne bylo" [The Executions in Racak Did
Happen], *Nezavisimaia gazeta* (25 March 2000), which discusses a report from Finland to the effect
alleged killings at Racak, in South Kosovo, which were used as a formal reason by NATO to initiate
tacks against Serb forces, did not happen. Taras Lariokhin, "Priznanie genseka. NATO ispol'zovala pr
Yugoslavii radioaktivnye snariady" [Acknowledgement by the General Secretary. NATO Used Radioac
Missiles Against Yugoslavia], *Izvestiia* (23 March 2000).

42. See, for example, Maksim Yusin, "Voina mifov" [War Myths], *Izvestiia* (24 March 2000), in wl
NATO leaders were accused of conducting a "mass propaganda campaign" about Serbian genocide aga
Albanian Kosovars to persuade their citizens that an air attack was only the last resort. Even Rober
did not claim, a year later, that the "genocide" had taken place before NATO attacked.

skaia Rossiia, for example, published a front page photo of picketers carrying placard messages such as: "Putin=Yeltsin, Yeltsin=Clinton, Clinton=Hitler!"[43]

In addition to picketers gathered in front of both the American and Polish embassies, a rally organized on Moscow's Slavianskaia Ploshchad was joined by members of the Union of Serb Communities, who accused NATO of intriguing with separatist Albanians. Various Orthodox churches, including the huge Savior Cathedral in central Moscow, held services commemorating the victims of NATO bombing (ITAR-TASS, 24 March). Solidarity with Serbia was in the air, as Slavic Brotherhood associations (who called Polish entry into NATO a "betrayal" of their ethnic heritage) organized evenings of Russian and Serbian music. Exhibitions of Serbian art and writing were featured in several locations in Russia; and poets and writers were invited to the House of the Writers Union for a meeting denouncing NATO "hegemonism." A conference held in Belgrade from 24 to 27 March, under the witness-leading title "Consequences of NATO Aggression against Yugoslavia," was widely reported in the Russian press. Russian reporting of the conference made much of the presence of delegates from Canada, Britain, India and Germany. The conference concluded, not surprisingly, that Washington was to blame for everything. In Russia even the most moderate papers sympathized with Serbs and angrily denounced both NATO's actions and Robertson's claims of success.[44] The benefit of the doubt granted Washington and NATO in earlier public opinion surveys was dissipating quickly.

The most direct and meaningful Russian criticism of Robertson's self-congratulatory remarks, however, came from the foreign minister. Writing in *Nezavisimaia gazeta* on 23 March under the title, "Kosovo Crisis, One Year On," Igor Ivanov rebutted almost every claim of achievement offered by NATO's secretary general.[45] Vladimir Lapskii, a seasoned observer of international affairs, covered the same ground for the government paper. Delineating the huge material and ecological destruction inflicted upon Yugoslavia, he called Kosovo a "colony of NATO" and asked rhetorically who gave NATO the right to "interfere unceremoniously in the affairs of other states."[46] This was very much the standard Russian public perspective.

---

43. *Sovetskaia Rossiia* (21 March 2000); see also, Yevgenii Popov, " 'Mirotvorchestvo' NATO mnozhit chislo zhertv v Kosove. Most . . . vdol' reki!" [NATO "Peacekeeping" Increases the Number of Dead in Kosovo. Bridge . . . Along the River!], *Sovetskaia Rossiia* (18 March 2000); see also Viacheslav Tetekin, "Svintsovoe mirotvorchestvo. Pozornaia dlia SshA i NATO godovshchina krovavoi agressii protiv SRYu" [Lead Peacekeeping. A Shameful Anniversary for the USA's and NATO's Bloody Aggression Against Yugoslavia], *Sovetskaia Rossiia* (23 March 2000).

44. See, for example, Aleksandr Sukhotin, "Kogda Miloshevich—za skobkami. Evropa nashla v Kosove svoiu Chechniu" [When Milosevic Is Out of Brackets. Europe Found Its Own Chechnya in Kosovo], *Obshchaia gazeta* , No. 12 (23–29 March 2000). The communist press still led the way in vitriolic analyses. See Viacheslav Tetekin, "Konferentsiia v Belgrade: obshchestvennost' 40 stran mira osuzhdaet agressiiu NATO. Okhota za skal'pom Yugoslavii" [Conference in Belgrade: The Public of 40 Countries of the World Condemn NATO Aggression. Hunting Yugoslavia's Scalp], *Sovetskaia Rossiia* (30 March 2000).

45. Igor Ivanov, "Kosovskii krizis: god spustia" [Kosovo Crisis, One Year Later], *Nezavisimaia gazeta* (23 March 2000).

46. Vladimir Lapskii, "Balkany: politiki so vzryvatelem" [The Balkans: Politicians with a Fuse], *Rossiiskaia gazeta* (23 March 2000).

Obviously, little seemed to have changed insofar as mutual regard was concern
On the twentieth, NATO forces and KFOR peacekeeping troops began a three-w
training exercise in Kosovo, named Dynamic Response 2000. Russian protests, c
cial and in the media, that the maneuvers were in violation of UNSCR 1244,
couraged Albanian separatism and were unnecessary anyway ("Against whom
NATO's response intended?"), fell on deaf ears outside Russia.[47] On the face of
there were incongruities about the exercise: Russian peacekeeping forces with KFC
were not invited to participate; it took place in Kosovo, part of Yugoslavia, with
any reference to Belgrade; and it followed closely after the Robertson visit to Mosc
where so many promises of Russia–NATO handholding had been made.

Leonid Ivashov chose this moment—nearing the anniversary of Moscow's offi
"freezing" of its relations with NATO—to say that any talk of opening a NA'
mission in Moscow was "premature" (Interfax, 22 March). Instead, a group
deputies led by Ryzhkov introduced a resolution in the State Duma "On the *i*
niversary of the Beginning of the North Atlantic Treaty Organization Aggress
against the Republic of Yugoslavia," in which they charged NATO with unt
death and destruction during the bombing, and more currently of "crudely vio
ing" the UNSCR 1244 "which maintains the sovereignty of Yugoslavia over Kos
and Metohija."[48]

There followed a flurry of ambiguous official comment: Igor Ivanov assured an
terviewer with RTR TV that Russia "does not now intend" to withdraw its pea
keepers from Kosovo—but it might if the situation worsens and if it begins to
pear that Kosovo could be separated from Yugoslavia (Interfax, 23 March). On
same day, Ivanov used his interview with *Nezavisimaia gazeta* to blame NATO
ethnic clashes and growing crime in Kosovo.[49] On the other hand, Ivashov, in w
could be called a reverse "good cop–bad cop" routine, told a press conference t
this was an appropriate time for further Russia–NATO cooperation, but that the l
was in NATO's court. It was up to NATO to make the hard decisions about obse
ing the letter and law of UNSCR 1244 (Interfax, 23 March). He announced as v
that Chief of the Russian General Staff Kvashnin would, after all, attend a counci
NATO chiefs of staff planned for 10 May.

All these assurances did not resonate well for NATO's image in Russia. At the (
of the month the Public Opinion Fund, a public organization founded in 1990 *i*
associated with the *Nezavisimaia gazeta,* asked 1,500 Russians if they thought
NATO as "an aggressive or a defensive military bloc." The Fund then compared
results with responses to a poll on the same question asked in 1997:

---

47. See, for example, Konstantin Chuganov, "Balkanskii uzel. Uchebnoe vtorzhenie" [Balkan K
Training Invasion], *Rossiiskaia gazeta* (21 March 2000); Anatolii Bystrov, "Mirotvortsy briats
oruzhiem" [Peacekeepers Rattle Sabers], *NVO,* No. 9 (17–23 March 2000).

48. "K godovshchine agressii protiv Yugoslavii. Chernaia letopis' NATO" [To the Anniversary of
Aggression against Yugoslavia. NATO's Black Chronicle], *Sovetskaia Rossiia* (18 March 2000).

49. *Nezavisimaia gazeta* (23 March 2000), *op. cit.,* fn. 46. For a summary of the RF foreign mini
statement, see Interfax (23 March 2000).

NATO	February 1997	March 2000
Aggressive bloc	38%	56%
Defensive bloc	24%	17%

In 2000, supporters of Zyuganov and Zhirinovskii tended to choose "aggressive" at a rate of 68 percent; and men (64) more than women (49). Surprisingly, people with higher education also saw NATO as an aggressive bloc. Responses to a question about Russia joining NATO, showed 30 percent were in favor and 43 percent opposed; on whether Russia might enter NATO some time in the future, the answer was more even, 39–32 percent, with the "no's" still ahead.[50] It would seem that mistrust of NATO had risen since January, accompanied however by an "if you can't beat them, join them" sense of resignation. Given that NATO and the United States were generally seen as synonymous in Russia, this poll would suggest as well that the opinion on America had reversed over the previous three weeks.

PUTIN'S FIRST-ROUND VICTORY, 26 MARCH

During March, of course, the attention of the Russian government and media was focused much more on their own presidential election than it was on NATO. Moscow's most cynical journalists hinted that the West knew this and was trying to get away with what it could while Russia was looking elsewhere. At any rate, within hours of his first-round election victory on 26 March, with 52 percent of the votes cast to his communist opponent's slightly less than 30 percent, Putin firmed up the foreign ministry. His very first cabinet decision was a one-year extension of term to Igor Ivanov. On the same day, he raised Aleksandr Losyukov to the rank of deputy foreign minister with a mandate to monitor Russia's relations with Asian-Pacific countries, specifically to prepare the way for presidential visits to China, India and Japan.[51] This was especially important, for it was assumed that Putin's first major venture overseas as president would be to the G-8 summit scheduled for Okinawa, 21–23 July.

WHAT NEXT?

Russian journalists and deputies were anxious to see what Putin's first moves in the foreign policy sphere would be and, as early as 29 March, flocked to a short-notice press conference with Aleksei Arbatov, deputy chair of the Duma Defense Committee and Yabloko member. The conference had been billed as "The Future of Russian Policy."

Conjecturing about Putin's plans, Arbatov pointed out that prior to the election the president's views had been moderate and compromising: at home the government must intervene in the economy, but also preserve the market economy; Russia

50. *Fond obshchestvennogo mnenia* (29 March 2000), *www.fom.ru.*
51. Interfax (27 March 2000). His predecessor, Grigorii Karasin, was sent to Britain as ambassador.

needs discipline—and democracy; the principles of federation must be retained, the RF needs streamlining and the powers of governors in republics should be stricted. In foreign policy, Russia must be a world power and at the same time operative. Now Putin had to make choices. He was elected with a mandate to br order back into the country, to resuscitate national pride and dignity, and strengtl the role of the state. Nationalist forces, clearly, were where his political stren resided. Arbatov referred to the "Why not?" response to the BBC's question ab joining NATO, calling it a positive signal to the West, but a mistake—Putin have to learn not to improvise. According to Arbatov, the new president's real po was best represented in a recently approved military doctrine (see chapter 7): re the unipolar world of Washington and NATO and, more importantly, place a "m stronger emphasis in the military field to resist" NATO's "Balkan model," by wh he meant the use of force to resolve regional disputes.[52]

It was obvious that there would be no major changes in foreign policy bef Putin's formal inauguration. Sergei Ivanov made that clear in an interview publisl in *Nezavisimaia gazeta* on 31 March. Repeating an opinion expressed in most m; pronouncements on Russian foreign policy during the late 1990s, he said that greatest threats to Russian security were still internal. But times had changed: in nal threats (interethnic conflict; organized crime; and terrorism) were now exa bated by well-defined external pressures. These included the increased use of forc solve international issues; growing differences in approaches to arms control and armament questions by Russia and the United States; the resilience in "certain" co tries of Cold War attitudes; and unprecedented international terrorism. In this he explained again and rendered more graphic the basic themes of Russia's equ new Concept of National Security (see chapter 7).[53]

Putin spread this message as well. In his first postelection trip outside Moscow, told nuclear weapons designers in Snezhensk (formerly the secret Chelyabinsk- that their work was vital to the country and growing even more important. In presence of foreign journalists, he promised to reduce the numbers of Russia's clear weapons and to win ratification of START-II—at the same time emphasiz the need to make nuclear weaponry research and maintenance more efficient dependable. This was no Cold War-style posturing, rather it was well in line with program of strengthening, securing and stabilizing the state.[54]

52. "The Future of Russian Policy. Press Conference with Alexei Arbatov," National Press Institute March 2000); JRL, 4216, No. 6. Similar opinions were expressed in Boris Sibirskii, "Poiavilis' laiushchie vstupit' v NATO" [There Are Those Who Wish to Enter NATO], *Nezavisimaia gazeta* March 2000). The new military doctrine finally was approved by presidential decree in April, but its tents had been widely known and discussed well before that.

53. Sergei Ivanov, " 'Glavnye ugrozy bezopasnosti Rossii—- vnutrennie'. Sekretar' Soveta bezopasr RF Sergei Ivanov otvechaet na voprosy NG" ["The Main Threats to Russia's Security Are Internal." retary of the Security Council Sergei Ivanov Answers Questions from NG], *Nezavisimaia gazeta* March 2000). The Concept of National Security was approved in mid-January 2000.

54. For reports on the speech, see Yekaterina Grigor'eva, "Pervyi vizit posle vyborov" [First Visit the Election], *Nezavisimaia gazeta* (1 April 2000), and Márcus Warren, "Putin Defends Nuclear Arsei *Ottawa Citizen* (1 April 2000).

It was at this juncture, 29–31 March, that Baltic governments released a plethora of public statements about the wisdom of their membership in both NATO and the EU (see chapter 9). A tour by Lord Robertson, who expressed unambiguous sympathy for Baltic memberships in NATO, triggered statements from the presidents in Riga, Tallinn and Vilnius about the merits of their candidacies, and sharp rebukes from Kremlin officials. As a result adamant adherents to Yevgenii Primakov's "red line" across which NATO must not expand—former USSR republics generally, the Baltic States specifically—raised their heads in Moscow's foreign ministry.[55] It didn't help that General Wesley Clark, NATO Supreme Commander Europe, informed an audience in Vilnius on 3 April that Russia's new military doctrine "represents a turning away from the previous policy of increased openness and cooperation with the West."[56]

Russian commentators could not see such words as anything other than mischievous, and further evidence that NATO was paying no attention whatsoever even to its most recent public endorsement of collaboration with Russia. In excerpts published on 1 April from *In the First Person. Conversations with Vladimir Putin,* Putin himself said that relations with NATO were strained because "we do not feel ourselves equal participants in the [decision-making] process" and referred to Yugoslavia as evidence of NATO's indifference to Russian interests.[57]

Tensions in Kosovo continued to provide Russian nationalists with counterpoints to Western complaints about the RF's actions in Chechnya and the often-expressed foreboding about a Putin-led KGB coopting the political and economic agenda in Moscow. In early April, the MID protested the arrest of Bosnian Serb leader Momcilo Krajisnik by French peacekeepers, as an act outside their mandate; and the communist press began to replay the previous year's bombing of Yugoslavia by NATO as a sign of things to come—even to highlighting an obscure report that traced the "origin of NATO-fascism" to the United States's "criminal" action in Korea a half-century earlier.[58] In its turn, the MoD circulated papers accusing NATO of aiding and abetting pan-Albanian schemes for dividing Yugoslavia still further.[59]

Events in Yugoslavia were important, but the newly elected Russian president's first and most obvious chore was to stabilize the economy: that is, attract foreign investment;

---

55. On the "red line", see J.L. Black, "Russia and NATO Expansion Eastward: Red-lining the Baltic States," *International Journal,* 44: 2 (Spring 1999), 249–266; and Aleksei Liashchenko, "Strany Baltii rvutsia v NATO" [Baltic Countries Strive for NATO], *Krasnaia zvezda* (26 April 2000).

56. For Clark's comments (reported by Reuters, 3 April 2000), see JRL, No. 4223. See also "Gensek NATO khvalit Moskvu" [NATO General Secretary Praises Moscow], *Izvestiia* (31 March 2000).

57. "Ot pervogo litsa. Ya schitaiu chto gosudarstvo dolzhno . . ." [In the First Person. I Believe the Government Must . . .], *Rossiiskaia gazeta* (1 April 2000).

58. See, for example, a rather strange report by Yevgenii Popov, "Prestupleniia SShA v Koree polveka nazad. Tak nachinalsia NATOfashizm!" [USA Crimes in Korea a Half-Century Ago. How NATO-fascism Began!], *Sovetskaia Rossiia* (4 April 2000). See also Viacheslav Tetekin,"Otchego v rossiiskom MIDe brataiutsia s Vukom Drashkovichem?" [Why is the MID Fraternizing with Vuk Drashkovic?], *Sovetskaia Rossiia* (8 April 2000). Maksim Yusin suggested, however, that Putin was too pragmatic to make a fuss over "a person like Krajisnik," see "Nochnoi arest" [Night Arrest], *Izvestiia* (4 April 2000).

59. See, for example, Yurii Pankov, "Na porokhovoi bochke" [On a Powder Keg], *Krasnaia zvezda* (6 April 2000); see also Yaroslav Yastrebov, "NATO razygryvaet chernogorskuiu kartu" [NATO Plays the Montenegro Card], *Krasnaia zvezda* (13 April 2000).

rebuild the tax system; restructure the financial system to suit IMF standards (
other IMF tranche was delayed in March); set agriculture on a more solid footi
so that Russia would not have to depend on foreign food aid; and repair the so
safety network, to halt the declining life expectancy and birth rate. Putin also hac
act on his promise to curb the economic power of the so-called "oligarchs."
achieve any of these herculean tasks, he would have to use levers other than his (
success story to that point, the revival of Russian national consciousness. Like on(
his predecessors in momentous times, M. S. Gorbachev, Putin knew that foreign
fairs could still play a significant role in getting the domestic situation under cont
In 1985–87, Gorbachev made himself Russia's most aggressive spokesman abro
travelling far more than any of his precursors among the Soviet leadership. By p
sonally turning skeptical Western leaders into believers in his desire for rad
change, against great odds, Gorbachev brought the Cold War to an end, officiall
least. Putin took the direct route as well, setting out in the spring.

After a quick postelection tour of Russia itself, Putin opened up a diplomatic
fensive, visiting Ukraine, Belarus and Britain in the final third of April, and meet
with newly appointed Japanese prime minister, Yoshiro Mori, in St. Petersburg.
agenda in Europe included foreign investment, arranging for debt forgiveness, h
in integrating with the EU and WTO, and getting back on schedule with the II
and the London and Paris Clubs of creditors. Putin especially hoped that the lc
of Russia's positions on NATO expansion, the Balkan crisis, and arms reduct
mechanisms would be recognized.

Mori's official visit to Moscow, his own first foreign venture since replacing
very ill predecessor, was the initial manifestation of what was to be Putin's much
celerated search in the Far East for friends. Mori promised more loans to Russia,
sisting that he was eager to conclude a peace treaty and complete the process beg
with the "Declaration on Constructive Partnership" signed by Yeltsin and th
Prime Minister Keizo Obuchi in November 1998. The Putin-Mori working meet
was part of the preparations for the July G-8 summit in Okinawa.

PACE STEPS ON MOSCOW

Earlier in April, the Russian president-elect stressed his country's desire for coope
tion, especially in the field of economics, and promised the ratification of STAI
II. But shortly before debate on START-II was to begin in the Duma, the natior
ists were to have their day. On 6 April, the Parliamentary Assembly of the Cour
of Europe voted 78 to 69 to strip Russia of its voting rights, and called on mini:
rial representatives to suspend its membership in the CE because of human rights
olations in Chechnya. The vote, in effect, rejected a long ten-point memorand
submitted to it by the Duma on 4 April in response to the initial PACE commit
recommendations, and in which Russia's parliamentarians insisted that the situat
in Chechnya was an internal matter that could be resolved only "on the basis of

Russian Federation Constitution and respect for the state's sovereignty and territorial integrity."[60] On learning of the rejection, the Russian delegation stormed out of the meeting in Strasbourg, angrily promising to carry on without, as Speaker of the Duma Gennadii Seleznev put it, "our European teachers."[61] *Izvestiia* claimed that PACE had "robbed the Russian delegation of the right to be heard."[62] This was the first time in its fifty years that the then-forty-two-nation Council had suspended a member.

While the presidential staff tried to downplay PACE's decision, Russian elected officials and many senior ministry personnel voiced outrage. An official statement from the foreign ministry said that PACE had shown a lack of respect for the Russian people and that the assembly had allowed itself to be highjacked by Cold Warriors (ITAR-TASS, 7 April). This line was repeated in the communist press, on the front page under a screaming headline "Driven Out of Europe."[63] Sergei Ivanov charged that the PACE decision would aid and abet international terrorism (Interfax, 7 April). This came shortly after he attended a meeting with Putin and Javier Solana, who was visiting Moscow as an envoy from the EU. *Rossiiskaia gazeta* called the vote "blatantly anti-Russian" and claimed that PACE was denying Russia its right to "territorial integrity." Dmitrii Rogozin, in Strasbourg as chair of the Duma's Committee of International Affairs, answered an interviewer's query as to who were the most active countries in "the anti-Russian campaign" by accusing "Georgia, Hungary, France and the Netherlands. Mainly East Europeans, of course."[64] *Krasnaia zvezda,* ministry of defense organ, blamed PACE for its "hypocrisy and double standards," and for defending "bandits." Journalist Vladimir Katin pointed out that Russia paid some $25 million annually to the Council of Europe, and all it got in return is a "slap in the face."[65] A writer for the independent *Obshchaia gazeta* complained that a "wall much stronger than the Berlin Wall has risen between the new Russia and the former satellites of the USSR."[66] The fact that, apparently, a representative

---

60. Russian State Duma, "O situatsii v Chechenskoi Respublike" [On the Situation in the Chechen Republic], *Rossiiskaia gazeta* (4 April 2000). The Council of Europe was founded in Strasbourg in 1949 and now includes 44 member countries. Russia joined in 1996. Its mandate is to coordinate European regulations in areas of human rights, culture and education, and constitutional reform.

61. ITAR-TASS (7, 8 April 2000). For a pre-vote warning and suggestion that a vote against Russia would not be significant, see Kseniia Fokina, "Kto boitsia mery Robinsona" [Who is Afraid of Robinson's Measures], *Nezavisimaia gazeta* (5 April 2000). Mary Robinson is UN High Commissioner for Human Rights.

62. Vladimir Dunaev, "Golovomoika. Evropeitsy ne zakhoteli slushat' golos Rossii" [A Scolding. Europeans Do Not Wish to Hear the Voice of Russia], *Izvestiia* (8 April 2000).

63. See "Goniat iz Evrop" [Driven Out of Europe], *Sovetskaia Rossiia* (8 April 2000).

64. Rogozin, "Sama sebia vysekla" [Did Itself a Disservice], *Rossiiskaia gazeta* (8 April 2000). The interview was conducted by telephone. See also Vladimir Lapskii, "LitseMERY [HypoCRITICAL Measure], *Rossiiskaia gazeta* (8 April 2000), for the "blatantly anti-Russian" comment; "MID Rossii nedoumevaet" [Russia's MID Is Puzzled], *Rossiiskaia gazeta* (8 April 2000).

65. Katin, "Rossiiu ne mogli nakazat', poetomu postaralis' oskorbit'" [Since Russia Was Not Punished, They Tried to Insult Her], *Nezavisimaia gazeta* (8 April 2000); Vadim Markushin, "PASE zashchishchaet banditov" [PACE Defends Bandits], *Krasnaia zvezda* (8 April 2000).

66. Boris Yunanov, "Oderzhali porazhenie" [They Earned a Defeat], *Obshchaia gazeta,* No. 15 (13–19 April 2000).

of Maskhadov's Chechen government attended the meeting and physically attac[
a member of the Russian delegation outside the hall further raised the hackle:
Russians—many of whom truly believed that they had been set up by a powe
anti-Russian cabal within PACE.[67]

On 11 April the Duma passed a resolution, 374 to 21, harshly condemn
PACE's decision, calling it "insulting." But there wasn't much else the Russians co
do, other than lobby visiting statesmen. In addition to the EU group, which
Moscow on that day after arranging to send a team to Chechnya, the head of
OSCE at that time, Benita Ferrero-Waldner (Austria's foreign minister), was
Moscow for a three-day visit. Putin's demeanor was one of relative moderati
claiming only that PACE was making a mistake by isolating Russia, and t
Moscow had many other European links. The Russian president tended to port
Russia as the protector of Europe from "extremism," and stressed the continued
evance of the "common European home" approach introduced by Gorbachev.

Russian officials and even the Duma got over their initial outrage and follov
Putin's lead. The Duma backtracked somewhat, adding to its resolution (383-3-1
provision that Russia's parliament continue "its constructive dialogue and coope
tion" with PACE if it could be based on "mutual respect."[68] Journalists and TV ta
ing heads soon calmed down as well, pointing out that PACE's resolution was mer
a recommendation to the Council of Europe Committee of Ministers, and that R
sia should wait and see what the CE's final decision would be. They expressed "
wilderment" about PACE and even two weeks later, in connection with the Dur
adoption of a position "On the Position of the Parliamentary Assembly of the Cor
cil of Europe on the Question of the Situation in the Chechen Republic," cc
plained that PACE's "efforts to isolate Russia plays into the hands of extremists
In the meantime, Russia had still to build bridges with Europe. Rogozin made r
plain to the Duma.[70]

In fact, the overall Russian tone in the PACE affair was notably more tempe
than it would have been just a year or so earlier. It remained to be seen if this wa
sign of new confidence, of subservience, or of a fatalistic expectation of such poli
from Europe. The potential financial cost to Russia of PACE's antagonism could
be taken lightly, however. By mid-April the European Commission, executive bo
of the EU, had slashed its funding of projects in Russia under the Techn

---

67. See, for example, Vladimir Dunaev, "Golovomoika" [Scolding], *Izvestiia* (10 April 2000); and E
Yunanov, "Chto PASEesh', to i pozhnesh'" [One Reaps What They Sow], *Obshchaia gazeta*, No. 14 (6
April 2000).

68. "On the Position of the Parliamentary Assembly of the Council of Europe on the Issue of the
uation in the Chechen Republic," Press Release, Russian Federation Embassy in Ottawa (12 April 20
See also Aleksandr Sadchikov, "Patriotizm naiznanku. Duma priznala PACE odumat'sia" [Patriotism
side Out. Duma Calls on PACE to Re-think], *Izvestiia* (13 April 2000).

69. "Politicheskomu uregulirovaniiu meshaiut boeviki" [Political Settlement is Hindered by Gunm
Rossiiskaia gazeta (18 April 2000). See also interview with Minister of the Interior Vladimir Usti
"Strasti po prokurature" [Passions over the Procuracy], *Rossiiskaia gazeta* (18 April 2000).

70. See, for example, Anna Kozyreva, "Dialog s Evropoi prodolzhaitsia" [Dialogue with Europe is C
tinuing], *Rossiiskaia gazeta* (13 April 2000).

Assistance to CIS Countries (TACIS) by more than two-thirds. The TACIS annual allocation of some 130 million euros to Russia was reduced by 90 million and earmarked for specific projects such as those related to human rights, assistance in democratic reforms, and nuclear safety. Officials in Brussels were frank about the reasons for taking this step, that is, to fulfill an earlier EU decision to reduce help for Russia under TACIS because of Chechnya.[71]

A few Russian commentators took advantage of the moment to criticize the Kremlin, admonishing Russia's leadership for doing little to persuade Europe that they belonged. *Izvestiia,* especially, mourned Russia's lost chances of integration with Europe: "Europe gave us the boot. Our isolation from the Old World and the West generally has never been more real in the modern history of Russia." In contrast to the usual angry protests, the *Izvestiia* writers added that "we would do better to blame ourselves." Communist writers also blamed Putin and his predecessors, yet remained adamant that Russia should go it alone. One headline spoke of Russia's "flogging" in Strasbourg.[72] For the most part, it was assumed that the divide between Russia and Europe had widened, to Europe's disadvantage.[73]

START-II ADOPTED ANYWAY

The settling down effect was most clearly felt when the START-II was ratified by Russia's Sate Duma on 14 April in spite of all the fuss over PACE's action. Even though the communists and the LDPR had been hotly opposing ratification, advocates in the Duma easily carried the vote. Only Communists and Agrarians opposed, casting 131 negative votes. Zyuganov called it "capitulation." Later his party called START-II a "pro-American treaty."[74] But Unity, Yabloko, Union of Right Wing Forces, Fatherland-Our Home is Russia, Russia's Regions and the newly formed People's Deputies Group all voted unanimously or nearly unanimously in favor of the resolution. Even Zhirinovskii's LDPR, after railing against START-II for months, unanimously approved. This vote alone demonstrated the degree to which the new Duma had shaken

71. Interfax (18 April 2000). The TACIS program cut funding specifically of projects related to transportation, energy, and personnel training, and said that the freed-up money would be channelled into humanitarian aid for the people of Chechnya.

72. See Vasilii Safronchuk, "Porka v Strasburge" [Flogging in Strasbourg], *Sovetskaia Rossiia* (11 April 2000); El'mar Guseinov, Semen Novoprudskii, "V okno iz Evropy" [In the Window from Europe], *Izvestiia* (7 April 2000). The *Izvestiia* authors added that Moscow had done nothing to inform Europe about how it was going to end the war in Chechnya.

73. Kseniia Fokina, " 'Poslednee' preduprezhdenie" [The "Last" Warning], *Nezavisimaia gazeta* (7 April 2000); Aleksandr Sabov, "Igraia chuzhim knutom" [Flogged by a Foreign Whip], *Rossiiskaia gazeta* (6 April 2000); Aleksandr Sabov, "Evropa na odnom kryle?" [Europe with One Wing?], *Rossiiskaia gazeta* (11 April 2000). See also *Rossiiskaia gazeta* (7, 8, 12 April 2000).

74. Zyuganov, "SNV-2: Ratifikatsiia = kapituliatsiia. Ne igrat' sud'boi strany" [START-II: Ratification = Capitulation. Don't Play with the Fate of the Country], *Sovetskaia Rossiia* (13 April 2000). Viacheslav Tetekin, "SNV-2: Putin gotov ustupit' nazhimu SShA? Proverka na progibaemost'" [START-II: Is Putin Ready to Give Up to the USA?], *Sovetskaia Rossiia* (8 April 2000). The full voting list was carried in *Sovetskaia Rossiia* (15 April 2000).

the left-wing monopoly by which its predecessor could be characterized, and the r
willingness to work closely with the government on most issues.

Representatives of the government, above all officials in defense and foreign
fairs, portrayed this victory as a vehicle for placing Russia on the moral high grou
when it came to future proposals for amending the ABM Treaty. Both before and
ter the vote, they assured Russian audiences that the Kremlin had set conditions
lated to the ABM before they agreed to go ahead with endorsement (see chapter 7
Ratification of the Comprehensive Nuclear Test Ban Treaty (CTBT) by the Du
on 21 April raised Russia's bargaining profile still further (see chapter 7). Pu
claimed that the ratification "makes it possible to guarantee our security in a pa
with the United States," and was a "good, positive signal to the world community

Putin On Tour

Putin was thus able to set out on 16 April for his first major international tour w
the START-II endorsement firmly in hand. The president's task was bolstered as v
by analyses offered at a seminar chaired by German Gref. Well-known foreign a
strategic policy specialists, among them Andrei Kokoshin, Aleksei Arbatov, and S.
Rogov, and military figures Col. Gen. Yurii Baluevskii and Admiral Vladimir Kur
dov, agreed that Russia's present situation—"no enemies, but also no allies"—was :
bilized. It remained for Putin to ensure that the country would not be isolated fr
the international concert of nations.[77]

Belarus and Ukraine were neighbors and CIS members, with long and spe
(though very different) relations with Russia. So it was in London that the Russ
president was truly testing foreign waters. He met with Prime Minister Tony Blair a
Queen Elizabeth. Joint communiqués explained that the political leaders talked ab
Russia's economic plans and security issues, including Moscow's position on Wa
ington's NMD—which, in effect, would necessitate amendments to the 1972 AI
treaty.[78] In standard diplomatic language, both sides called the meetings construe
and successful, and the Russian media reported Blair's remark that Russia should
be isolated in world affairs. Both sides spoke of the need for deeper economic t

---

75. See, for example, Yurii Yershov, "Dogovor dorozhe brani" [Treaty More Valuable than Abu
Rossiiskaia gazeta (12 April 2000); Anna Kozyreva, "V gosdume. Yadernyi balans" [In the State Du
Nuclear Balance], *Rossiiskaia gazeta* (14 April 2000); Dmitrii Gornostaev, "Moskva vyigraet, odobriv
govor SNV-2" [Moscow Will Gain by Approving START-II], *NVO*, No. 13 (14–20 April 2000); Dm
Litovkin, "Strategicheskaia stabil'nost': byt' ili ne byt'" [Strategic Stability: To Be or Not To Be], *Kras*
zvezda (14 April 2000).

76. Putin, "Zaiavlenie v sviazi s ratifikatsieu . . ." [Statement in Connection with the Ratification .
Krasnaia zvezda (18 April 2000). The statement was released on 14 April.

77. On this, see Aleksandr Manushkin, "Rossiia vybiraet prioritety razvitiia" [Russia Chooses Its
velopment Priorities], *Krasnaia zvezda* (13 April 2000).

78. On the NMD, see Celeste A. Wallander, "Russia's New Security Policy and the Ballistic Missile
fense Debate," *Current History* (October, 2000). This is a useful summary of her much longer study
the subject (see under "Further Reading").

They seem also to have reached some meeting of the minds on Chechnya, after Putin agreed that a nongovernmental Russian commission should monitor human rights in that dissident republic. Most Russian commentators were enthusiastic about the tour, remarking that Putin might be stealing a march on Bill Clinton.[79]

There was not much substance to press release from London, although they indicated that Putin eschewed bluster while holding the line on national interest issues. Indeed, this had been the main advice offered by Sergei Karaganov during a press conference held just two days before Putin left Moscow. Karaganov was announcing the CFDP's forthcoming report, "Strategy for Russia: 2000 Agenda for the President." There were no major surprises in the CFDP report because its themes had been made public in March. Karaganov's blunt criticism that, "regrettably the country has no foreign policy strategy today, and not even a wholesale doctrine," had been heard before. But this time his audience was larger.[80]

He agreed that, of the options open to Russian policymakers, the current official concept of multipolarity correlated best to the country's interests. Yet it was expensive and Russia hadn't the resources to act as a global power. Moreover, multipolarity guaranteed confrontation with the West. It weakened the "pole" for which Russia stood, and might even draw Russia into taking sides in a China–America dispute. Karaganov urged again that Russia's strategic priorities be limited to selective engagement. First, stake out Russia's most vital interests and hold firmly to them. Then give up aspirations to superpower status, avoid confrontation, look to the future, and seek economic success by supporting Russian business abroad and attracting foreign investments to Russia. Finally—avoid "tough rhetoric, Nobody believes our threats anymore."

Karaganov's propositions mirrored in many ways projections for the future of Russian–American relations put forward by ISKRAN's Rogov in a paper published on 6 April. Rogov also stressed the need for realism on all occasions, and compromise in all but issues that were absolutely vital to Russia.[81] In April and May, this seemed precisely the direction in which Putin's team was moving. These well-known experts were by no means alone in their exhortation that Putin fine-tune Russian foreign policy priorities. As the PACE story unfolded, several regular watchers of foreign af-

---

79. The communist press was the exception, complaining that Putin's concessions were "presents" for Britain in return for future considerations. See, for example, Vasilii Safronchuk, "Golovki i golovy" [Leadership and Heads], *Sovetskaia Rossiia* (18 April 2000); Viacheslav Tetekin, "Ne prevratitsia li Gosduma v rezinovuiu pechat'?" [Will the State Duma Be Turned Into a Rubber Stamp?], *Sovetskaia Rossiia* (20 April 2000).

For an enthusiastic account, see Yelena Dikun, "London prinial Putina na sebia" [London Takes Putin as He Is], *Obshchaia gazeta,* No. 16 (20–26 April 2000); and for the idea that Washington might be worried about Britain and Russia becoming too friendly, Viktoriia Sokolova, "Vashington bespokoitsia" [Washington Is Worried], *Izvestiia* (14 April 2000).

80. Karaganov, " Ne nado gnat'sia za statusom sverkhderzhavy" [Russia Should Not Pursue Superpower Status], *Izvestiia* (14 April 2000). See also Karaganov, "New Foreign Policy. What Is Russia to Do? What Is to Be Done with Russia?" *Moscow News,* No. 9 (8–14 March 2000).

81. Rogov, "Rossiia i SShA na poroge XXI veka: novaia povestka dnia" [Russia and the USA on the Threshold of the 21st Century. A New Agenda], *Dipkur'er NG,* No. 6 (6 April 2000).

fairs pointed out that the EU normally was much more amenable to Russia tl
PACE's decision implied. Others called on the president to use his first foreign t
to demonstrate the promised "healthy pragmatism" in foreign policy, especially in
gard to Western Europe.[82]

In addition to his achievements with Duma and Federation Council resoluti
on START II and the CTBT, Putin worked out, temporarily, a modus vivendi w
both communist and nationalist opposition in the Duma. He was once commu
himself, of course, and already had established a niche among Russian nationalist
dint of his hard line on Chechnya. Other, smaller, successes began to accumulat
the domestic political arena. He persuaded the Federation Council to agree to
dismissal of Procurator General Yurii Skuratov, a task Yeltsin had been trying to
complish for two years. In late April, the Unity Party proposed that the president
aside the constitutional provision separating the legislative and executive bodies a
become an active party leader himself. Though Putin told the Unity congress that
was not prepared to break an important tradition, the offer made explicit what '
already assumed. Unity, the Duma's second largest party, was the president's hook
the lower house. Internationally, the U.S. administration made the encouraging
cision to lift sanctions imposed in March 1999 against Russian companies who I
been suspected of cooperating with Iran in missile technology.[83]

BATTLING OVER ARMS REDUCTION—AGAIN

Rogov's essay of 6 April foreshadowed a statement for American readers prepared
Foreign Minister Ivanov as he set out for New York to consult on nonproliferati
Published in the *New York Times* on 24 April, Ivanov's conviction that the "bal
now in the court of the United States" could not have been made plainer.[84]
knowledging the long delay in ratifying START-II, for which the bombing of Irac
1998 and Yugoslavia in 1999 were blamed, he stressed the close connection betw
START-II and the ABM Treaty. Ivanov warned readers that the collapse of the la
treaty would have a "domino effect" on existing disarmament agreements. The R
sian position was that the alleged threat from so-called maverick states was "at le
exaggerated." At the same time, Ivanov offered alternate paths to what he called
"disruption of strategic stability." The heading given Ivanov's essay by the *New Y
Times,* "A Challenge from Russia," was remarked upon by Moscow journalists v

82. See, for example, Dmitrii Gornostaev, "Rossiia provodit reviziiu vneshnepoliticheskikh priorite
[Russia Conducts Revisions to Its Foreign Policy Priorities], *Nezavisimaia gazeta* (12 April 20
Vladimir Katin, Viktor Sokolov, "ES nostroen druzheliubnee, chem PASE" [The EU Feels Better t
PACE Does], *Nezavisimaia gazeta* (11 April 2000).

83. Sanctions were imposed by the U.S. Congress in 1998, and subsequently vetoed by Clinton.
in March 1999, 10 Russian companies were blacklisted by the United States. See *Russia Faces NATO
pansion,* p. 137.

84. Ivanov, "A Challenge From Russia," *New York Times* (24 April 2000).

wondered why "a hand extended" by·Ivanov (who had called the piece "An Extended Hand") should be treated as a challenge.[85]

Perhaps this ostensibly minor difference in perception represented the true temper of the times. At any rate, Ivanov's published statement contradicted a speech delivered at the UN on the same day by Secretary of State Madeleine Albright. Speaking at the opening of a four-week conference revisiting the Non-Proliferation Treaty signed by the Soviet Union, the United States, Britain and fifty-nine non-nuclear powers in July, 1968, Albright denied that the United States was about to sabotage the ABM treaty and strategic arms control. Rogov insisted that American plans to amend the ABM could not be justified on the basis of exaggerated threats from North Korea or Iran; but that a trade-off was certainly possible. The United States could construct a limited defense system directed specifically against potential threats from third world countries, in return for deep cuts in long-range nuclear missiles as part of START-III.[86] It may be that Rogov was testing the waters on behalf of the foreign ministry, for this was the line it was soon to take.

On 25 April, Ivanov told the large international gathering that Russia was itself prepared to make deep cuts in its nuclear warheads. Not, however, if Washington went ahead with plans that would undermine the ABM, full compliance with which was still regarded by Moscow as a "prerequisite" to further negotiations on nuclear disarmament.

By the end of April it was apparent that the ABM/NMD issue had the potential of setting Moscow and Washington irrevocably against each other once again. This was a compelling reason why a summit between Putin and Clinton was arranged for June.[87] Russia's hand was strengthened somewhat by the fact that most European leaders were reluctant to support the American proposals for a national missile defense system. Canadian foreign minister, Lloyd Axworthy, also opposed the NMD, calling it dangerous and potentially destabilizing. But Russia could not rely on America's allies to help them out of this dilemma, so Igor Ivanov proposed an accommodation after pre-summit talks with U.S. officials in Washington on 26–27 April.[88] He suggested, as Rogov had, that Moscow might accede to an amendment of the ABM Treaty if Washington agreed to a very limited national missile defense program. Albright responded at a news conference that Russia's offer was not sufficient for America's perceived needs.

Russia's relationship with NATO also remained in partial limbo. On 24 April, three days after Russia's new military doctrine was published, it was made official that the first visit to Brussels by a member of Russia's high military command in over

---

85. Sergei Merinov, "Protianutaia ruka kak broshennyi vyzov"[Hand Extended as a Challenge], *Rossiiskaia gazeta* (26 April 2000).

86. These arguments are outlined in the *New York Times* (25, 26 April 2000), essays by Michael R. Gordon from Moscow, and Barbara Crossette from the United Nations.

87. For a Russian perspective on the importance of this summit and Ivanov's "successes" in New York, see Sergei Merinov, "Etot kapital eshche prineset dividendy" [This Capital Will Bring Us Dividends in the Future], *Rossiiskaia gazeta* (27 April 2000).

88. The significance of the upcoming NMD debate for RF-U.S. relations and President Clinton's desire to leave a legacy when he left office was noted already but Vladimir Lapskii, "Bill Klinton: Amerika sebe ne prostit . . ." [Bill Clinton. America Will Not Forgive Itself . . .], *Rossiiskaia gazeta* (26 April 2000).

a year would soon follow. Chief of the general staff, Gen. Anatolii Kvashnin's wo
explain the doctrine to the Alliance. Hardliner Leonid Ivashov and first deputy ch
of the RF armed forces general staff, Col. Gen. Valerii Manilov, both separately m:
it clear that Kvashnin's participation in the PJC should not be taken as a sign t
Moscow was softening its position on NATO ("there will be no jump into
NATO embrace").

At about this time, Ivashov was a keynote speaker at the launching of the sec
volume of a Russian-language white book on NATO "crimes" in Yugoslavia, ;
three days later voiced yet again the official line that full restoration of relations w
NATO would occur only if Russia was treated as an "equal partner."[89] Ivashov ad
that his ministry would use the PJC as a forum for discussing the implementatior
UNSCR 1244 in Kosovo, and he accused the West of conducting a campaign agai
Slavic unity, mentioning specifically U.S. policy against Belarus and its "seducti
of Ukraine. There were Russian analysts who saw the moment as one in which
Russian presence in Kosovo should be revisited. Writing for the *Obshchaia gazeta,*
example, Tamara Zamyatina pointed out that Russian soldiers located in the ethr
Albanian areas of Kosovo were in danger and that there already had been casualt
She suggested that it was time for the Russian command to take some initiative ;
not be afraid of aggravating its already tenuous ties with NATO.[90] This approach
well with the new mood of exuberance in Moscow.

THE MOOD IN RUSSIA

Just a few days earlier, Ivashov—he popped up everywhere in the media—ad p
claimed that the "rogue" state rationale for American amendments to the AI
Treaty was a "bluff, designed to confuse the world community about Washingt
real plans . . . to ensure its strategic military supremacy over the rest of the wor
(RIA Novosti, 28 Apr). If the USA went ahead with its plans to develop an NN
he continued, Russia would have to "adjust" its own commitments. Here was v
traditional Russian (Soviet) posturing, flying in the face of Karaganov's recomm
dations against aggressive rhetoric.

Even so, normally moderate Russian foreign policy aficionados also now assun
that the American attitude was "full speed ahead and damn the critics." Moscow
alysts noted that when Lloyd Axworthy invited NATO to propose arms reduct

---

89. Ivashov (Interfax, 27 April 2000). His speech was delivered on 24 April 2000. See also *M
dunarodnye organizatsii i krizis na Balkanakh: Dokumenty,* [International Organizations and the Cris
the Balkans. Documents] 3 Vols (Moscow: Indrik, 2000), which covers the years 1991–1995 and is hi;
critical of NATO. Communist writers were at the same time drawing analogies between American ac
in Korea during the 1950s and Yugoslavia in 1999, revisiting the "NATO-Fascism" article referred to
viously (fn. 52). See Yevgenii Popov, "'NATOfashizm': ot Makartura do Robertsona" ["NATO-Fasci:
From MacArthur to Robertson], *Sovetskaia Rossiia* (25 April 2000).

90. Zamyatina, "V kontingente vse spokoino . . ." [All is Calm in the Contingent], *Obshchaia ga:*
No. 18/19 (4–17 May 2000).

initiatives of its own, Washington vetoed it out of hand even though it came from such a long-time ally and neighbor as Canada. Axworthy's plan had included unilateral reduction of nuclear bombs, transparency about remaining stocks of nuclear gravity bombs, and a more inclusive arrangement to control the proliferation of ballistic missile technology.[91] The almost casual dismissal of the idea by the new American administration was taken as a sign that a "unilateralist" U.S. mission in international affairs had begun to take shape.

THE PRESIDENTIAL MANDATE

When Russians saw and heard Putin at his televised gala inauguration ceremony swear to uphold Russian dignity and honor in world affairs, they had more reason to believe his sincerity than they had of the vacillating and inconsistent Boris Yeltsin. Putin could stand in front of the Russian people with a message for which they had actual evidence. He told them that his task was to "take care of Russia" and that his goal was to champion Russia's dignity. "We must know our history . . . draw lessons from it" and again make Russia a "great, powerful and mighty state."[92] His implicit message in foreign policy was: "I have ratified START-II and the Non-Proliferation Treaty. This is not a sign of weakness, I am insisting as well that the ABM Treaty not be amended by the Pentagon; I am testing weapons systems; I have signed our new military doctrine into law; and I have kept my promises about Chechnya." At that time, these claims rang true.

The ceremony was created almost exclusively for Russians. No foreign leaders, even from the CIS, were invited (though Presidents Kuchma and Lukashenko met with Putin the day before the inauguration), and foreign countries were represented only by their heads of mission. Yeltsin attended and delivered a congratulatory and encouraging short address; Gorbachev was there, along with a wide cross-section of other prominent Russians. The atmosphere was joyous, marred only by the astonishing news that the Russian national hockey team had for the first time ever been eliminated in the first round of the world championships.

That shocker aside, the new president was able to turn his inauguration into a celebration of the rebirth of patriotism in Russia, an accomplishment facilitated by the fact that it coincided with the annual Victory Day holidays, commemorating the defeat of Nazi Germany. Statements by Yeltsin and the Patriarch linked the present occasion with the glories of Russia's past. Putin spoke again at a concert in Moscow devoted to Victory Day, proclaiming that "we are returning to the very essence of patriotism" (Interfax, 7 May). The next day he travelled to Kursk, the site of history's greatest tank battle, met veterans and dedicated a new memorial for the

91. Notes for an Address by the Honourable Lloyd Axworthy, Minister of Foreign Affairs, to the North Atlantic Council Meeting (24 May 2000), *Statement,* DFAIT (Ottawa).
92. Putin's speech was published as "Klianus' verno sluzhit' narodu" [Vow to Faithfully Serve the Nation], *Rossiiskaia gazeta* (11 May 2000).

actual Victory Day, that is, 9 May. Putin again stressed the importance of pride country.

Putin's success to that date showed him to have a broader popular and legislat base by far than Yeltsin had enjoyed even in his heyday. Both houses of the Fed Assembly upheld him and, given that Russia's (Yeltsin's) constitution allocates alm unlimited powers to the president anyway, the newly formed government was of a very good start.[93]

Russia's new confidence was reflected in the tone, or at least its public version Kvashnin's participation in the PJC three days after the inauguration. Earlier c versations between General Secretary Robertson and Russia's permanent represer tive to NATO, Sergei Kislyak, had set the stage for Kvashnin's appearance mooted the possibility of a Russian ministerial presence at the PJC foreign minis meeting set for Florence on 25 May. Russian press releases portrayed the Kvash delegation as cooperative and constructive, yet holding firmly to their positions Kosovo. The official message was that Russia was ready to unfreeze its relations w NATO, where Moscow merely wanted its voice to be heard and respected. Mani and Ivanov still served as Cassandras, yet the number of media commentators w pointed out that Russia's boycott of NATO had run its course and was in dange becoming counterproductive increased almost daily.[94]

Watching Russia's participation in international forums became an exercise unlike the practice of analyzing who was standing where in old Soviet lineups. F eign Minister Ivanov was also in Florence and attended the PJC meeting, but he fused to take part in the simultaneous PfP ministerial-level session, sending deputy, Yevgenii Gusarev. Shortly thereafter, Ivanov took part in the Council of rope Committee of Ministers meetings and reported that Russia would remain a member. He joined in debate on Kosovo and Chechnya, and the question of the commendation for suspension by PACE was not even raised (ITAR-TASS, 11 M Indeed, while Ivanov was out of the country, Yugoslav Defense Minister Gen Dragoljub Ojdanic was in Moscow (9 May) for discussions with his counterp Sergeev, and Kvashnin. Ojdanic was greeted as a visiting dignitary in Moscow des international law that obligated the RF minister of justice to arrest him. With exceptions, these sessions were reported enthusiastically in the Russian media, the Yugoslav guest spoke of Russia as his country's "ally."

In the matter of Serbians designated by the tribunal in The Hague as war cri nals, Russia and NATO remained quite opposed to each other. As we have se when the U.S. State Department printed "Wanted" posters offering $5 million information leading to transfer to, or the conviction of, Slobodan Milosevic and c ers by the tribunal, copies were reproduced in the Russian press and treated w great derision.[95] Foreign Minister Ivanov claimed on 24 May that the invitation

93. See Articles 80–93, "Konstitutsiia Rossiiskoi Federatsii" [Constitution of the Russian Federati *Rossiiskaia gazeta* (25 December 1993), for descriptions of the presidential powers.

94. See Viktoriia Sokolova, "Nazad v NATO" [Back in NATO], *Izvestiia* (11 May 2000). For Mani remark, ITAR-TASS (11 May 2000).

Ojdanic had been a result of internal miscommunication, a mistake that would not be allowed to happen again (ITAR-TASS, 24 May). But he complained at the same time that The Hague tribunal was biased and that the trial of Serbs was a political, not juridical, exercise.

Shortly after this flurry of excitement, members of Yugoslavia's opposition, including Vuk Draskovic, also visited Moscow, consulting with lesser lights in the government. On 29 May, Draskovic conversed with Deputy Foreign Minister Aleksandr Avdeev and in a joint statement they condemned Milosevic's crackdown in Belgrade. Other statements from the Kremlin urged unity among competing political forces in Belgrade. Aware that Milosevic's regime would not survive much longer, the Russian government avoided commitment to either side in what appeared to be a society moving towards civil war.[96] The Kremlin still needed Serbia as a foil to NATO expansion in the Balkans, but also expected that major changes in Belgrade were forthcoming. On 13 June, for example, the Russian foreign minister voiced mild disapproval of Milosevic's refusal to talk with the opposition, and in the same breath charged Bernard Kouchner with further abuses of UNSCR 1244 in Kosovo.

The Russian communist press treated incidents like the "Wanted" posters as part of a growing American indifference to the sensibilities of all Europeans, and scorned America's official attitudes towards Cuba, Iran, Iraq and even India. While disagreeing with Putin on a number of major domestic issues, the communists credited him for granting priority to "Russian dignity" over "high handed" recommendations from the United States.[97] Zyuganov remained resolutely opposed to any unconditionally renewed relations with NATO, contending that neither Clinton nor Vice President Al Gore were interested in Russia, rather they were seeking support for Gore's own presidential election campaign.[98]

As Putin's new cabinet took shape, military analysts noted with discernible relief that few changes were made in the country's security apparatus. The Security Council remained important and indeed was to increase its sphere of influence. A projected reconfirmation of the relationship between regular military forces, the special services and various intelligence organizations, did not occur; and Igor Sergeev was reappointed minister of defense. Additionally, Sergeev appeared to have been given

---

95. For a reproduction of the "Wanted" poster, see Steven Lee Myers, "Wanted, but How Badly?" *New York Times* (18 May 2000). Not all Russian papers sympathized with war criminals charged by The Hague tribunal. See, for example, Fedor Riurikov, "Skelety v shkafu. Gaagskii tribunal po byvshei Yugoslavii deistvuet medlenno, no verno" [Skeletons in the Closets. The Hague Tribunal on Former Yugoslavia Works Slowly, but Surely], *Obshchaia gazeta*, No. 20 (18–24 May 2000). Riurikov said that the true criminals must be punished for their crimes, but that SFOR should not take the law into its own hands.

96. On this, see. for example Konstantin Chugunov, " 'Otpor' vstrechaet otpor" ['Rejection' Meets Rejection], *Rossiiskaia gazeta* (27 May 2000).

97. See, for example, Viacheslav Tetekin, "Knut i prianik v odnom konverte" [Knout and Cake in the Same Envelope], *Sovetskaia Rossiia* (18 May 2000), and L. Nikonov, " 'Vsemogushchestvo i nevezhestvo'. Ili pochemu i v Yevrope ne liubiat Ameriku" ["Omnipotence and Ignorance." Or Why America Is Disliked in Europe], *Sovetskaia Rossiia* (11 May 2000).

98. Zyuganov, "Fal'shivoe druzheliubie" [False Friendliness], *Sovetskaia Rossiia* (13 May 2000).

"carte blanche" to regenerate military restructuring projects that had ground t
standstill during the preelection period.[99]

REGROUPING WITH NATO

On 23 May, NATO's Robertson finally accepted Putin's "Why not?" as a reasona
alternative to the stand-off between Russia and the Alliance. In a public remark
this effect, which followed shortly after nine other former Soviet republics or W
saw Pact countries issued a joint call for their own admission to NATO, he assu
listeners that Russian entry was not a bad idea, although it was unlikely to hapן
in the near future. Robertson had delivered an opening address to a meeting of r
resentatives of the nine applicant countries, Albania, Bulgaria, Estonia, Lat
Lithuania, Macedonia, Romania, Slovakia, and Slovenia, gathered in Vilnius, cap
of Lithuania. This was a high-level meeting, for with the exception of deputy miı
ters from Macedonia and Albania, each was represented by a foreign minister. Tl
bid for admission in the year 2002, the year set for NATO's next summit meeting

Robertson's comment preceded by a day, and obviously was connected to, I
Ivanov's participation in a PJC meeting—a decision that had been confirmed o
six days beforehand. The Russian foreign minister's few days in Florence w
marked by almost hourly press releases from ITAR-TASS and Interfax. He had flo
there directly from Minsk flushed with the apparent success of a CIS summit wh
strengthened the unity of the five-nation (Russia, Belarus, Kazakhstan, Kyrgyzst
and Tajikistan—with Armenia as observer), CIS Collective Security Pact. The tɑ
seemed to go well for him in Florence, where, Ivanov said, the dialogue was "frɑ
and pithy" and both sides hoped for the full resumption of the Founding Act. Strɑ
gic stability in Europe, the Balkan question, and the future scheduling of such mɛ
ings were the main topics of discussion. In addition to the PJC, Ivanov had priv
meetings with U.S. Secretary of State Albright and the foreign ministers of Germɑ
(Joschka Fischer), and Italy (Lamberto Dini).

There was no full meeting of minds, however. Secretary General Robertson rejec
Russia's accusation that the International War Crimes Tribunal was biased and po
cized.[101] And, although an agreement finally was reached in principle that a NATO
formation bureau could be opened in Moscow, a NATO proposition that it be gi
diplomatic status was firmly rejected. Ivanov's encouraging words about Russia–NAՐ
cooperation were qualified as well by his insistence that the relationship would be fı
normalized only "provided that the UN Charter and the Russia–NATO Founding.

---

99. Sergei Sokut, "Siloviki ukrepliaiut svoi pozitsii' [The Power Ministries Strengthen their Positic
NVO, No. 18 (26 May –1 June 2000).

100. At the Washington Conference, it was decided that the next summit would be held "no later t
2002" and, except for an unusual circumstance, no earlier than 2002.

101. An interview with Robertson was published in Russia: "Dzhorzh Robertson: 'My govorili s Igo
Ivanovym po mobil'nomu'" [George Robertson: "We Talked with Igor Ivanov by Mobile Phor
Izvestiia (25 May 2000).

are adhered to" (Interfax, 24 May). He was referring, of course, to the larger issues of NATO's willingness to act out of zone without a clear UNSC mandate. A more immediate issue was the tendency towards the distancing of Kosovo from Yugoslavia control in spite of UNSC Resolution 1244. These matters were closely related to the reasons for the freeze in Russia–NATO relations in the first place, and none were diminished in significance by the optimistic rhetoric heard in Florence. Seeing little reason to trust NATO, CPRF analysts predicted that nothing constructive was likely to emerge later from the Clinton visit.[102] Moreover, a meeting between PACE chairman Lord Russell-Johnston and Chechen President Maskhadov was greeted with fury in the Russian press and provoked an official protest from the Kremlin. Military spokesmen accused PACE of going "behind Russia's back" to deal with international terrorists, and even normally less interest-driven analysts treated the meeting as a very unsavory event.[103]

The deep-rooted differences in opinion between Russia and NATO did not prevent general support in Russia for a regrouping with NATO from gaining ground. Deputy head of staff for the Duma's international affairs committee, Vladimir Kozin, wrote in late May that despite wide differences, a permanent state of confrontation, "or even suspicion," was too dangerous for the world to allow. He proposed a "hotline" between Moscow and Brussels and regular Russia–NATO summits separate from PJC meetings.[104] According to polls, slightly more than half of the Russian population agreed that cooperation was necessary. A new survey conducted by the All-Russian Center for the Study of Public Opinion showed that the Kremlin's policy of moving closer to the West was approved by the majority, noting however that the West still needed to be seen to be taking Russia seriously.[105]

PREPARING FOR THE SUMMIT

During the meeting between Igor Ivanov and Albright, purportedly also to discuss strategic stability, arms export and regional conflict in the Middle East and the

---

102. The optimism of the Florence meetings was echoed in Vadim Solov'ev, "Al'ians soglasoval pozitsii s Rossiei" [The Alliance Agreed with the Russian Position], *Nezavisimaia gazeta* (24 May 2000), where an editorial said that Putin was right to renew relations with NATO and that Russia and NATO must be "strategic partners in Europe." See also Konstantin Chugunov, "Bosniia—shkola dlia NATO" [Bosnia Is a School for NATO], *Rossiiskaia gazeta* (24 May 2000). *Izvestiia* (24 May 2000) carried a similar message. In all three pieces, NATO's bombing of Yugoslavia still came in for bitter criticism. The communist press continued its attack on NATO, charging it with a new "propaganda" attack on Yugoslavia, since it could not justify bombing it again. See, for example, Viacheslav Tetekin, "Telebombardirovshchik NATO" [Television Bombardment by NATO], *Sovetskaia Rossiia* (20 May 2000); for an even more distrusting piece, see Vasilii Safronchuk, "Kreml' otkryvaet vtoroi front. Chto nam zhdat' ot vizita Klintona v Moskvu?" [The Kremlin Opens a Second Front. What Can We Expect from Clinton's Visit to Moscow?], *Sovetskaia Rossiia* (30 May 2000).

103. See, for example, Boris Yunanov, "Predsedatel' PASE poluchil nagoniai" [Chairman of PACE Gets a Scolding], *Obshchaia gazeta,* No. 21 (25–31 May 2000); Yurii Pankov, "Rossiia-NATO: trudnyi dialog" [Russia–NATO: Difficult Dialogue], *Krasnaia zvezda* (26 May 2000).

104. Kozin, "Developing Good Neighborly Relations," *Moscow Times* (26 May 2000).

105. Vadim Markushin, "O pol'ze protivovesov" [On the Benefits of Counterweights], *Krasnaia zvezda* (25 May 2000).

Balkans, agendas were deliberated for four conferences between the Russian ¿
American presidents, the first one set for Moscow, 4–6 June. At the same time,
bright's deputy, Strobe Talbott, was in Moscow, setting the stage for President Cl
ton's arrival. On 26 May, Albright delivered a speech about Russia at the Lonc
School of Economics. Clearly a presummit offering, Albright's address was rife w
encouraging words for the new Russian leader, and she quoted Gorbachev's re
ences to his country's place in a "common European home." But her remarks w
riddled with "ifs." For example, "If its new leaders back their promises with ̩
formance, we will enthusiastically support" Russia's attempts to integrate with
world economy. The question, she said, really is "how fully Russia is prepared
work with us."[106] Albright's talk was reported by some Russian papers as merely
inventory of what the state department thought was wrong with Russia. [107]

Albright chose also to mention with regret the Ojdanic incident and Russia's c
tinued opposition to American positions on NATO enlargement, Iraq and
Balkans. Her penchant for offering unwanted advice was an irritant to Russians a
indeed, she told the audience that advice is what Clinton would be offering to Pɪ
ident Putin. Words to the wise were precisely what Putin did not to want to hear,
pecially as Russian commentators were pondering whether Putin would be able
persuade Clinton to the Russian point of view.[108]

Well before Clinton arrived in Moscow, Putin heard a similar sermon from an
delegation to Moscow. On 29 May, President of the European Commission Romɑ
Prodi was enthusiastic about the future of economic cooperation and praised Put
first initiatives related to taxes and budgeting. He stressed that Russia had a long ɯ
to go before it could attract much-needed foreign investment and linked ɪ
dilemma to alleged human rights violations in Chechnya. Putin maintained t
Russia's war in Chechnya was against international terrorism and that he was
going to be turned away from his current policy there by the EU or any other ɪ
eign adviser. All in all, however, Russians saw their "partnership" with the
strengthening.[109]

This opinion had been confirmed by Javier Solana during an exclusive interv
with *Izvestiia.* Speaking in anticipation of the fifth Russia–EU summit set to oɟ
on 29 May in St. Petersburg, he made it clear that a "strategic partnership" betwᴇ
them would be "strengthened and developed further."[110]

---

106. "Speech by Secretary of State Madeleine K. Albright," London School of Economics (26]
2000). USA Embassy in Ottawa.

107. See, for example, Vasilii Safronchuk, "Kreml' otkryvaet vtoroi front," *op. cit.*, and L. Niko
"Sammit s Klintonom—test dlia Putina" [The Summit with Clinton Is a Test for Putin], *Sovetskaia Ro*
(30 May 2000).

108. See, for example, Nikolai Paklin, "Ugovorit li Putin Klintona?" [Can Putin Persuade Clintᴄ
Rossiiskaia gazeta (13 May 2000).

109. Viktor Sokolov, "Partnerstvo RF i ES ukrepitsia" [Partnership between the RF and the EU ʾ
Be Strengthened], *Nezavisimaia gazeta* (30 May 2000).

110. Solana, "Postroenie strategicheskogo partnerstva ˈmezhdu Evropeiskim Soiuzom i Rossiei" [
Construction of a Strategic Partnership between the EU and Russia], *Izvestiia* (26 May 2000).

Russian observers were fully aware that the domestic American discourse would help shape Clinton's position-taking in Moscow. Republican presidential Candidate George W. Bush called for an expanded NMD and accused his opponent, Al Gore, and Clinton of catering to Russia and consequently undermining the United States's ability to defend itself against new threats. On the one hand, as cochair (with former RF premier, Viktor Chernomyrdin) of the Joint Commission on Relations between the United States and Russia, 1993–1998, Gore laid claim to important foreign affairs experience. On the other hand, Bush was supported by a team of big-name former republican foreign policy statesmen: Henry Kissinger, Donald Rumsfeld, George Shultz, and Brent Scowcroft; and the Armed Forces' Colin Powell. Against this influential American team, Russian analysts insisted that if the United States went ahead with the NMD, China, and then India and Pakistan would immediately accelerate their programs for building weapons of mass destruction. "Irreparable damage" would be done to the arms reduction and nonproliferation processes.[111]

Shortly before Clinton's arrival in Moscow, Gore acrimoniously criticized Bush's proposal to broaden the NMD system planned by Clinton, terming his opponent's plan "nuclear unilateralism." Almost simultaneously, U.S. intelligence officials warned that even Clinton's program might set off a Cold War-style nuclear arms race between China, India and Pakistan.[112] It was hardly surprising, then, that Andrei Nikolaev, chair of the Duma's defense committee, recommended on 22 May that Putin make no new concessions to Clinton on arms control questions until the Americans worked out their own positions. Hoping to arrive in Moscow with support for the NMD from his country's allies, Clinton began his foreign tour in Portugal, where he attended an EU meeting. But his most important stop was Berlin, where he hoped to persuade Chancellor Gerhard Schröder to side with him in this matter. As it happened, Russian observers emphasized that Schröder's position was more closely aligned to theirs than to the American option.[113]

Although arms control issues dominated the presummit discourse, the question of NATO expansion was still an important consideration for Russians. After leading a Duma delegation to Washington for a Library of Congress conference on "The Open World," Nikolaev reported to the Duma that "at least half" of the U.S. Congress was not in favor of further expansion. NATO's "failure" in Kosovo had persuaded many of them that they should not have gone "over the head of the UN

111. See, for example, Konstantin Kosachev, "Respublikantsy reshili, chto 'Yadernyi zontik' im nuzhen: TsRU uzhe znaet, chto budet, esli Dogovor po PRO slomaiut" [The Republicans Have Decided That They Need a "Nuclear Umbrella". The TsRU Already Knows What Will Happen if the ABM Treaty Is Broken], *Nezavisimaia gazeta* (30 May 2000). Communists quoted Kissinger at length in their warnings to Putin to watch out for American duplicity, see L. Nikolaev, "Sammit s Klinton—test dlia Putina," *op. cit.*

112. See Michael R. Gordon, Steven Lee Myers, "Risk of Arms Race Seen in U.S. Design of Missile Defense," *New York Times* (28 May 2000). Gore's statement was delivered as part of a graduation ceremony at the United States Military Academy, West Point, on 27 May.

113. On this, see Dmitrii Gornostaev, "Berlin fakticheski podderzhal Moskvu v ee spore s Vashingtonom" [Berlin Actually Supported Moscow in Its Argument with Washington], *Nezavisimaia gazeta* (3 June 2000).

Security Council."[114] On the other hand, "beware of Russia" features in the Am
can press by Zbigniew Brzezinski and Jan Nowak caused a stir in Russia. Highlig
ing Putin's KGB background and linking the new Russian president's family o
nously to Lenin and Stalin, Brzezinski congratulated Clinton for NA'
enlargement eastward and reminded readers of his pledge of a second wave, "incl
ing the Baltics." Brzezinski went on to take a position strikingly antithetical to
one sensed by Nikolaev. He urged Clinton to show restraint in Moscow and not
drawn into "hastily contrived" agreements on missile defense, or any commitmen
assisting Central Asian regimes against Islamic fundamentalist pressure fr
Afghanistan.[115] Brzezinskii's opinion may not have had much influence on Ameri
foreign policy-making in 2000, but Russian commentators still treated his musi
as representative of widely held top-level behind-the-scenes attitudes.[116]

It would appear that cold warriors on both sides were nervous about the summit
Moscow, the summit was preceded by a public hearing called "NATO Aggression: W
Is Justice Silent?", attended by a number of Duma members, mostly of the left. Part
pants were treated to a fare of old Soviet-style explanations about the Balkans and An
ican "hegemonism," ensuring that another Moscow tradition was still alive and well

Other presummit positioning saw an outburst of confidence-building statemer
The MoD carefully outlined its hopes for the meeting, and Russia agreed to prov
troops for a PfP exercise scheduled for Iceland during the second week of June.[117]
Brussels Robertson told the closing session of NATO's Parliamentary Council t
the Alliance and Russia should be partners in Europe, and that he "[does] not r
out" eventual Russian entry into NATO; Sergei Ivanov assured reporters that Ru
would oppose Baltic admission to NATO diplomatically and not by force. It '
perhaps symbolic that Putin finally signed the law ratifying the CTBT on 29 M
thereby gaining an arms reduction edge for his meetings with Clinton—whose o
country still had not ratified. More importantly, in an interview with Ameri
NBC, Putin put forward an alternative proposal to the American missile defe
proposition. He suggested that Russia, Europe and NATO create a joint anti-mis
defense system for Europe.[118] The ensuing "we'll think about it" response fr

---

114. Another member of the Duma defense committee delegation to the USA echoed this opinior
the communist press. See interview with V.N. Volkov, conducted by V. Tetekin, "Chem zhe esl
ublazhit' Ameriky?" [What Else Will Satisfy America?], *Sovetskaia Rossiia* (3 June 2000).

115. Brzezinski, "Indulging Russia Is Risky Business," *New York Times* (31 May 2000). For the Rus
translation of the Nowak piece, originally from the *Washington Times,* see Yan Novak [Nowak], "
obustroit NATO bez Rossii" [How to Improve NATO without Russia], *Rossiiskaia gazeta* (30 May 20
discussed in chapter 7, fn. 20.

116. See, for example, L. Nikolaev, "Zbigniev Bzhezinskii daet sovety. Ne riskuite dostoinstvom" [Z
niew Brzezinski Offers Advice. Do Not Risk Dignity], *Sovetskaia Rossiia* (3 June 2000). See also Vi
eslav Tetekin, "Zachem edet v Moskvu g-n Klintop?" [Why Does Mr. Clinton Come to Moscow?], *Sc
skaia Rossiia* (1 June 2000).

117. On this compromise, see Vladimir Kuzar', "Strategicheskaia stabil'nost' i ekonomika" [Strat
Stability and the Economy], *Krasnaia zvezda* (3 June 2000); (ITAR-TASS, 29 June).

118. See, for example, Vladimir Yermolin, "Uzy protivoraketnoi druzhby" [Anti-Missile Ties of Frie
ship], *Izvestiia* (3 June 2000).

American officials was not very enthusiastic, to say the least. At any rate, most Russian commentators agreed with Western ones in that even the optimistic expected few serious results from the summit, while the pessimistic argued that Clinton was looking for the unilateral disarmament of Russia.[119]

In preparing for the meetings, Putin consulted with his senior defense officials (something that Yeltsin almost never did), and was advised that Russia should make its last stand, "as at Stalingrad," on the ABM question. Russia still had alternative courses of action, they claimed. Although it could not afford another arms race, it could add warheads to existing delivery systems. Moscow might also expand cooperation with China in developing strategic missiles and ABM systems of their own. India, Iran and Libya were potential sources of support, the military advisers noted. Other consultants, such as Aleksei Arbatov, insisted that there was some room for "profitable concessions," for example, on a second U.S. ABM district in Alaska in exchange for guarantees on START-III.[120] Almost everyone in the Moscow foreign policy establishment predicted a new arms race if the United States went ahead with the NMD on its own.

---

119. See, for example, Viacheslav Tetekin, "Lomovoi natisk" [Cavalry Charge], *Sovetskaia Rossiia* (25 May 2000), and *Izvestiia* (30, 31 May 2000).

120. See, for example, Viktor Litovkin, "Boegolovnaia bol'. Generaly sovetuiut Kremliu stoiat', 'Kak pod Stalingradom'" [War Headache. Generals Advise the Kremlin to Stand "as at Stalingrad"], *Obshchaia gazeta*, No. 22 (1–7 June 2000); and Viktoriia Sokolova, "Vse PROdumano" [Everything Is Thought about the ABM], *Izvestiia* (1 June 2000). She cited unnamed MoD officials who insisted that Russia must leave the ABM itself if the U.S. went ahead with its NMD.

3

✝

Summitry and Beyond, 2000

PUTIN MEETS CLINTON, JUNE 2000

On 4 June, the two presidents issued an important joint statement "on principles of strategic stability." They agreed "that the international community faces a dangerous and growing threat of proliferation of weapons of mass destruction" and that this threat represented a "potentially significant change in the strategic situation and international security environment." They disagreed on how best to combat the trend. Clinton hoped to reach an agreement on amending the ABM Treaty, allowing the United States to deploy over time a limited NMD system. Putin argued that his government was "against a cure that is worse than the disease."

All in all, however, pragmatism was a characteristic of the joint statement. Confirming that the ABM Treaty was "a cornerstone of strategic stability" (Art. 5), they opened the door, slightly, to mutually agreed amendments, "taking into account any changes in the international security environment" (Art. 9).[1]

Article 9 notwithstanding, the Russian head of state held to the position taken by Russian officials from the moment changes in the ABM had first been proposed. This approach did not represent a hankering for great power status, for by mid-2000 few people in Russia believed that their country was still a superpower, or even potentially one as long as its economy remained in its current condition of debilitation. A new sense of reality had emerged alongside Putin's appeal for patriotism. He had granted pride of place to economic recovery in his electoral campaign. Acting Prime Minister Mikhail Kasyanov stuck almost exclusively to economic concerns in a

---

1. "Joint Statement by the Presidents of the United States of America and the Russian Federation on Principles of Strategic Stability," Office of the Press Secretary, the White House, Moscow (4 June 2000).

preconfirmation speech to the Duma on 17 May, and the president's address to
Unity Party Congress, 27 May, also gave priority to the country's "successful e
nomic development." Putin declared at that time that only after economic recov
could other tasks, such as reestablishing the authority of the central governmen
Russia, be fully achieved.[2]

During the course of his stay in Moscow, Clinton participated in a call-in progr
for the independent radio station Ekho Moskvy and was the first U.S. president
speak to the State Duma. During a subsequent press conference, Clinton critici
Russian actions in Chechnya and urged Putin to allow impartial investigations of
man rights violations in that republic. Putin did not respond publicly. In the radio
terview, Clinton answered questions about the degree of "friendliness" between R
sians and Americans by asserting that the great majority of Americans wanted go
relations with a "strong, prosperous, democratic Russia" and that polls revealing n
ative attitudes merely uncovered feelings about specific issues, such as Chechnya.[3]

The Duma address contained more of the same. Clinton made no attempt
smooth over the many differences of opinion between the two countries on spec
international situations, NATO, Chechnya, Kosovo, Iraq, and so on. He recogni
the tremendous challenges Russia now faced in terms of its economic and soci
needs, and congratulated the legislature for ratifying both START-II and the CTE
Most important were Clinton's frank musings on how Americans and Russi
should now define their relationship. Again, he insisted that the United States
not want a weak Russia, rather it preferred a Russia "strong enough to protect its
ritorial integrity while respecting that of its neighbors."

To a certain extent, remarks such as these had been foreseen and preempted b
cross-section of the Russian media. On 1 June, for example, the Russian governme
main newspaper carried a feature article in which Vuk Draskovic's visit to Moscow
said to be an event orchestrated by NATO, so as to draw Moscow into the civil
pute in Yugoslavia.[5] Reporters for the Russian government paper also cut off at
pass Clinton's expected appeal for greater American–Russian cooperation. Nik
Paklin, a long-time cynic about Washington's good intentions, was especially wary.
described Clinton as a "lame duck" president wanting only to improve his "tarnisl
image" before leaving office. The call for a limited NMD was political, not strate;
because the likelihood of an attack from any so-called rogue state was "zero." At a
rate, the new U.S. NMD could not protect Europe, leaving the door open for

---

2. "Putin Address at the Unity Congress," ITAR-TASS (27 May 2000), supplied by the Embassy of
Russian Federation in Ottawa. Acting Prime Minister Mikhail Kasyanov, "Text of Speech to the S
Duma, BBC Monitoring Service" (17 May 2000). See also the more critical Yurii Nikiforenko, "Gr
manstvo 9-go prem'era" [Gref-ism of the 9th Premier], *Sovetskaia Rossiia* (18 May 2000).

3. "Interview of the President in Live National Radio Program with Ekho Moskvy," Office of the P
Secretary, the White House, Moscow (4 June 2000).

4. "Remarks by the President to the Duma," Office of the Press Secretary, the White House, Mos
(5 June 2000).

5. Konstantin Chugunov, " 'Maik Rusiia' v Serbii naraskhvat" ['Majka Rosija' in Great Demand in
bia], *Rossiiskaia gazeta* (1 June 2000).

Russian proposal of an all-European system that Putin was soon to reveal in Italy.[6] The communist press termed the speech an American "maneuver" on the Eastern Front, and continued vigorously to condemn the ratification of START-II.

The communist press consistently warned of U.S. duplicity and highlighted the differences between the two presidents. But the radical left influence was waning quickly. A small political demonstration outside the American embassy was featured prominently only in the communist press, which also gave prominence to picketers brandishing such English-language slogans as: "NATO—Murders," "Yanki, go home!," "Clinton—Tribunal, Rope."[7]

Although the Putin–Clinton meeting produced no surprises, there was a trade-off of sorts. Clinton agreed that the ABM was the centerpiece of American–Russian arms control negotiations, and Putin acknowledged that there might be some danger lurking in the "rogue" states.[8]

POST-SUMMIT FOREIGN POLICYMAKING IN MOSCOW

But Putin was taking no chances: even before Clinton departed Moscow for Kiev, Putin was headed for Rome, Germany and Spain. The Russian president was well aware of European concerns that a unilateral American action on the ABM Treaty might destabilize Russia–U.S. Relations. Hoping both to attract investment and win support for an alternative security plan, he employed rhetoric reminiscent of Gorbachev's "common European home" campaign and asserted that Russia's plan would protect the entire continent from any missile threat without infringing upon the existing ABM Treaty. Few details of the actual plan were available, though a vague seven-step conspectus for "European, Non-strategic Defense" was offered by Sergeev at NATO meetings on 9 June.[9] Viktor Kremenyuk, deputy director of ISKRAN,

6. Paklin, "Vladimir Putin predlozhit sozdat' evropeiskuiu sistemu protivoraketnoi oborony" [Vladimir Putin Will Suggest that a European Antimissile Defense System be Created], *Rossiiskaia gazeta* (7 June 2000); Paklin, "Soedinennye Shtaty v Evrope" [The United States in Europe], *Rossiiskaia gazeta* (2 June 2000); see also Dzhul'etto K'eza, "Pochemu doroga vedet v Rim" [Why the Road Leads to Rome], *Obshchaia gazeta*, No. 22 (1–7 June 2000).

7. *Sovetskaia Rossiia* (6 June 2000), photos on front page. It is worth noting here that communists began to win regional representation, at governor level, regularly by mid-2001, though most of the successful candidates tended to support Putin for practical reasons. For more suspicious and spiteful communist commentary, see, for example, L. Nikolaev, "Manevry na 'Vostochnom fronte'" [Maneuvers on the 'Eastern Front'], *Sovetskaia Rossiia* (8 June 2000); Vladimir Krylov, "Po-medvezh'i shchit slomali" [They Crush the Shield Like Bears], *Sovetskaia Rossiia* (6 July 2000); Gen. Yu. P. Maksimov, "Sberech' potentsial yadernogo sderzhuvaniia" [Retain the Potential of Nuclear Deterrence], *Ibid.* (18 July 2000).

8. *Kommersant* (6 June 2000). For a presummit summary of this issue by a Russian rocket engineer, in which the danger from "so-called rogue states" was treated in detail, see Sergei Kreidin, "Protivoraketnaia ugroza preuvelichena" [Antimissile Threat Is Exaggerated], *NVO*, No. 18 (26 May–1 June 2000). For a later analysis of the summit by Dmitrii Rogozin, who saw nothing much accomplished by it, see Rogozin, "Sammit sostoialsia. Glavnaia problema ne reshena" [The Summit Is Completed. Main Problems Not Solved], *NVO*, No. 20 (9–15 June 2000).

9. See Oleg Falichev, "Rossiia-NATO: Trudnyi put' k dialogu" [Russia–NATO: Tough Way to Dialogue], *Krasnaia zvezda* (14 June 2000).

encapsulated an opinion common to reporting on both "sides" when he predic
that the Russian proposal would probably be ignored by the United States, whei
the European leaders might be motivated to think about alternatives to Ameri
plans. Convinced that the United States was not much concerned about Islamic
tremists or international terrorists in Europe, Kremenyuk complained that
United States was not much interested in international terrorism and that Russia '
even "less interesting and important for the USA."[10] Putin was earnest about ł
suading European leaders that there were viable alternatives to American defe
plans, and he was supported in this ambition by Russian officials in Europe ʋ
were more outspoken against any further NATO expansion that might include
Baltic States than they had been since 1997.[11]

Russia's renewed presence at NATO HQ had been the subject of much expert b
in Moscow, most of which approved renewed cooperation. But it was recognized t
the level of trust between them remained much lower than it had been before NAT
war against Yugoslavia.[12] Most authorities in Russia agreed with Sergeev's commen
the effect that the PJC had become a forum for exchanging information, and was
a vehicle for making collective decisions. One writer called the meeting the "dialoː
of the deaf,"[13] while others reiterated the long-standing adage that, whereas Russia
not want a veto over NATO, the Kremlin must continue to insist that its opinion
be ignored and its security interest not be jeopardized.[14]

One sign of continued distrust, at least at the public level, was the reaction
Russia to a sixty-five-page report released by Amnesty International charging t
NATO's bombing campaign against Yugoslavia violated international law. The reɛ
appeared shortly after the chief prosecutor for the International Criminal Tribuı

10. Kremenyuk, "Mnenie eksperta" [Opinion of an Expert], *Obshchaia gazeta,* no. 23 (8–14]
2000). On this, see also V. Lapskii, "Poslednii vizit—ne posledniaia vstrecha" [The Latest Visit Is Not
Last Meeting], *Rossiiskaia gazeta* (6 June 2000), and Anna Kozyreva, "Prezident SShA v Okhotnom riː
[The President of the USA in Okhotny Riad], *Ibid.*

11. Sergei Sokut, "Blizhe v Vashingtonu, dal'she ot Pekina?" [Nearer to Washington, Further from
jing?] and Marina Vodkova, Sergei Startsev, "Putin predlozhit sozdat' obshcheevropeiskuiu sistemu Pl
[Putin Proposes to Create an All-European NMD System], *Nezavisimaia gazeta* (7 June 2000); see
Trud (7 June 2000).

12. Vadim Solov'ev, "Pochemu by Rossii ne vstupit' v NATO" [Why Russia Will Not Enter NAT
NVO, No.19 (2–8 June 2000); and "NATO i Rossiia otkryvaiut novuiu stranitsu sotrudniche:
Odnako uroven' doveriia ostaetsia nizhe, chem do razryva otnoshenii iz-za voiny v Yugoslavii" [NA
and Russia Open a New Page of Cooperation. However, the Level of Trust Remains Lower than be
the Rupture of Relations Because of the War in Yugoslavia], *ibid.*; Leonid Gladchenko, "Allo, Briuː
NATO i Rossiia gotovy k dialogu" [Hello Brussels! NATO and Russia Ready for Dialogue], *Rossiis.*
gazeta (10 June 2000).

13. For Sergeev's complaint in Brussels that Russia was kept out of any collective peacekeeping p
ning for Kosovo, see Interfax (9 June 2000). On the PJC as a forum merely for information exchange,
for example, Viktorina Sokolova, "Dialog glukhikh. Sergeev kritikuet al'ians za Kosovo" [Dialogue ol
Deaf. Sergeev Criticizes the Alliance over Kosovo], *Izvestiia* (10 June 2000); Kseniia Fokina, "Kosoʋ
absurd prodolzhaetsia" [The Kosovo Absurdity Continues], *Nezavisimaia gazeta* (10 June 2000),
Kommersant (10 June 2000).

14. Interview with Defense Minister Sergeev, who recently had attended a Russia–NATO JPC sess
"Mir na Balkanakh nevozmozhen bez Rossii" [Peace in the Balkans Is Impossible without Russia], ł
naia gazeta (15 June 2000); see also *Krasnaia zvezda* (10 June 2000).

Carla del Ponte, absolved NATO of·such charges. The foreign affairs committee of Britain's parliament also questioned the legality of NATO's action, calling it "dubious," though the committee added that the military action was "justified on moral grounds." Whereas all questioning of NATO's behavior in the Balkans was rejected vigorously by the Alliance leadership, Russia's media and officialdom overwhelmingly treated the accusations as true.[15]

An exclamation mark was added to Putin's European expedition when, on 9 June, it was announced that he had accepted an invitation from Kim Jong-il to be the first Russian president to go to North Korea, the "rogue" state most often named in Washington as the likely source of an irrational use of a nuclear missile. This visit was taken by some as evidence of a pattern in Russia's "intimidating" foreign policy. Putin's new tactics reminded an *Izvestiia* writer of the Soviet "divide and conquer" approach. Moscow's proposal of a Russia–European–U.S. joint anti-missile defense system was one such move. Scheduling stops in China and North Korea prior to the G-8 summit in Okinawa was another.[16] In each case, the Kremlin would demonstrate alternatives open to Russia if its interests were not considered appropriately in Washington.

The more commonly held Russian opinion of the planned state visit to North Korea was expressed by Rogozin, who caught up with Putin's delegation to Germany and Spain. "The visit will serve as diplomatic evidence that Russia does not accept the notion of 'rogue' states," the chairman of the Duma's international affairs committee told a Russian TV audience on 13 June. Moreover, Putin would convey firsthand impressions to the G-8 at Okinawa, proving that the "threat" worrying the U.S. State Department had been "completely made up."[17] Analysts for major Russian newspapers concluded that Putin wanted to demonstrate that Moscow still looked both east and west, and that Russia was still a great power (though not a superpower) with global interests.[18]

A high-powered follow-up to the summit in Moscow, also on 13 June, brought Putin, his chief of administration, Sergei Prikhodko, and Sergeev together with U.S. Defense Secretary William Cohen and Ambassador to Moscow James Collins. They hoped to resolve the apparent impasse over the NMD, in vain. The Russians again proposed a "political umbrella" for Russia, the United States and "other" countries,

15. The Amnesty International report (EUR 70/18/00), "NATO–Federal Republic of Yugoslavia, 'Collateral Damage' or Unlawful Killings? Violations of the Laws of War by NATO during Operation Allied Force," can be found at *www.amnesty.org/ailib*. The results of Del Ponte's investigation, "Final Report to the Prosecutor by the Committee Established to Review the NATO Bombing Campaign against the Federal Republic of Yugoslavia," can be found at *www.un.org/icty*.
16. Svetlana Babaeva, Yevgenii Krutikov, "Diplomatiia bol'shikh predlozhenii" [Diplomacy of Big Offers], *Izvestiia* (10 June 2000). Putin did not go to Cuba, but he held a well-publicized conversation with Fidel Castro and his foreign minister in New York.
17. BBC Monitoring, Russian TV (13 June 2000).
18. See, for example, Svetlana Babaeva, Yevgenii Krutikov, "Diplomatiia bol'shikh predlozhenii" [Diplomacy of the Big Proposition], *Izvestiia* (10 June 2000); Yurii Alekseev, Dmitrii Kosyrev, "'Vostochnaia' diplomatiia Putina nachnetsia s sensatsii" [Putin's "Eastern" Diplomacy Will Begin with a Sensation], *Nezavisimaia gazeta* (10 June 2000).

hoping to render amendments to the ABM Treaty unnecessary. The American p
ticipants still saw the threat from "rogue" states as pressing, claiming that North I
rea could produce intercontinental missiles by the year 2005. Sergeev disagreed. T
differences in opinion seemed carved in stone, as Cohen rejected the Russian pro
sition for a nonstrategic antimissile system as something that would not sat
America's security needs (Interfax, 13 June).

The defense ministry's Ivashov used the example of a hypothetical "threat" fr
North Korea and the real bombing of Yugoslavia to fortify Putin's proposals of a n
strategic antiballistic missile system for Europe, exclaiming at a press conference t
NATO's desire to draw Russia back into the fold "is part of an attempt to exoner
the Alliance for its action in Yugoslavia." Only a week earlier Ivashov told *Izves*
that he saw grounds for a "thaw" between Russia and NATO, but also admitted t
he remained a "hawk" when Russia was threatened. Ivashov included the NN
among those threats, and pointed out that Russia had not signed on to a single l
event for the year 2000.[19] So the lines remained drawn.

THE TWO-HEADED EAGLE LOOKS WEST TO GERMANY

Moscow's initiatives in Asia, which included plans for presidential participation
meetings of the Shanghai Five (see chapter 11) in Dushanbe on 5 July, before p
ceeding to Okinawa via China and North Korea, never overshadowed the NATO qu
tion. On 15 June, for example, Russian TV carried a long interview with a senior R
sian military analyst who called for increased Russian participation in NATO. Gen
Aleksandr Vladimirov, vice president of the collegium of military specialists, told an
terviewer for the Spetsnaz program that only within NATO could Moscow usefully
vocate its policies. The program interlocutors themselves proclaimed that, with
Russia, NATO was and would remain a tool of American foreign policy. Vladimi
was convinced that integration was the only way to curb NATO and to prevent an
ident "anti-Russia" sentiment from becoming dominant again in Brussels.[20]

On the other hand, the ministry of defense continued its cat-and-mouse ga
with NATO. It agreed to participate in a large PfP exercise scheduled to take pl
in Kazakhstan 11–18 September,[21] but hedged on joining a ten-day PfP training r
neuver with a naval phase on the Black Sea and a land phase close to Odessa. Ru

19. "Leonid Ivashov: 'Ya stanovlius' yastrebom, kogda vizhu ugrozu Rossii'" [I Become a Hawk W
I See Threats to Russia], *Izvestiia* (6 July 2000). For summaries of Ivashov's press conference, see IT
TASS and Interfax (14 June 2000). See also " 'Novoe myshlenie' Pentagona" [The Pentagon's "I
Thinking"], *Rossiiskaia gazeta* (14 June 2000), where U.S. military strategists were quoted to the ei
that Russia was neither an "enemy nor adversary."

20. BBC Monitoring: "Russian Integration into NATO Advocated by Russian Military Expert"
June 2000). See also "Sergeev-Koen: odin na odin: [Sergeev-Cohn: One on One], *Rossiiskaia gazeta*
June 2000).

21. Interfax (21 June 2000). The fourth such training exercise since 1997, it was expected that se
4000 troops from eleven countries would take part: The USA, Britain, Russia, Turkey, Kazakhstan, I
gyzstan, Uzbekistan, Azerbaijan, Georgia, Ukraine and Mongolia.

agreed only to send observers to the land phase, Cooperative Partner-2000.[22] The Sea Breeze exercizes with Ukraine as an active participant, of which this was a continuation, had been the subject of controversy since their inception in 1997. The communists were especially adamant that NATO not be allowed to strengthen its foothold on the Black Sea and in this, at least, the Kremlin tended to agree with them.[23] Moscow continued, indeed, to make it obvious that its full cooperation with NATO, though desirable, depended entirely upon NATO itself. Obstacles remained to be overcome. The notion that Russia wanted some kind of veto over NATO decisions was consistently denied, countered again in June with the often repeated assertion that all Moscow wanted was "to decide the complicated problems of security and stability in Europe by mutual resolve."[24]

To a certain extent, Vladimirov's observations represented the growing conviction that Washington and NATO's influence would be curtailed if only Russia could offer viable alternatives to its European neighbors. Security options were still proposed regularly, but it was Putin's state visit to Germany on 15 June that caused the Russian media to speak of a "new impetus for the entire foreign policy of Russia," and to hint that the president was moving towards reestablishing his country's sphere of influence "on the outskirts of the former Soviet Empire"—that is, previous Russian-dominated "space."[25]

Putin himself named Germany Russia's most important link to Western Europe, Russia's largest trade partner and its main foreign policy "partner." At the time, in fact, Russia owed far more money to Germany than to any other single country.[26] In addition to sessions with Chancellor Gerhard Schröder, Putin, Primakov and Igor Ivanov met with former German President Kohl and a group of leading German industrialists. The Russian contingent wanted more trade and investment. Defense Minister Sergeev discussed antimissile systems, Russia's relationship with NATO,

22. ITAR-TASS (19 June 2000). Participants in the land phase of the 19 June–1 July training exercise were: Britain, Belgium, Greece, Italy, Spain, Turkey, Netherlands, Germany, the USA, France, Azerbaijan, Georgia, Bulgaria, Romania, Russia, Sweden and Ukraine. In the naval phase, in addition to several NATO countries, were Ukraine, Azerbaijan, Georgia, Bulgaria, Romania and Sweden.

23. See, for example, "Generaly iz Briusselia uzhe doveriaiut ukrainskim khloptsam nesti flagi NATO" [The Generals from Brussels Already Trust Ukrainian Boys to Bear the NATO Flag], *Sovetskaia Rossiia* (22 June 2000); the exercise included some 40 warships, from 10 NATO countries (Britain, Belgium, Germany, Greece, Spain, Italy, Netherlands, USA, Turkey and France) and 6 PfP countries (Azerbaijan, Bulgaria, Georgia, Romania, Sweden and Ukraine). See "Ucheniia na Chernom more" [Exercise on the Black Sea], *NVO*, No. 22 (23–29 June 2000).

24. See Igor Korotchenko, "Na puti sotrudnichestva Rossiia-NATO sokhraniaiutsia prepiatstviia" [Obstacles Remain in the Way of Russia-NATO Cooperation], *NVO*, No. 21 (16–22 June 2000).

25. Aleksandr Sabov, "Komu v Evrope 'zharko' i komu 'kholodno'?" [Who in Europe Feels "Hot" and Who Feels "Cold'?], *Rossiiskaia gazeta* (20 June 2000). See also Vladimir Lapskii, "Rossiia—FRG: tretii razbeg" [Russia–FRG: A Third Start], *Rossiiskaia gazeta* (17 June 2000); Dmitrii Gornostaev, "Peregovory po shirokoi programme" [Negotiations on a Broad Program], *Nezavisimaia gazeta* (17 June 2000).

26. As of 1 January 2000, Russia owed Germany $26.3 billion, followed by Italy ($6.4bn), Japan ($4.0bn), the USA ($3.8bn), and France ($3.7bn). See "Dolgi dostanutsia i vnukam" [Debts Will Be Left for Our Grandchildren], *Ekonomika i zhizni*, No. 17 (April 2000). On this debt, see Semen Novoprudskii, "Rossiiu nachinaiut shantazhirovat' vneshnim dolgom" [Russia Begins to be Blackmailed for Its Foreign Debt], *Izvestiia* (29 June 2000).

and other security-related matters with his counterpart, Rodolf Scharping. App
ently, Baltic security was on their agenda, as was the CFE and something referrec
as a "European defense identity." One day prior to these sessions, Putin ensured t
NATO would be the subtext by telling a gathering at the German Economy Ho
that Moscow still strongly opposed the Alliance's expansion and asked rhetorica
"If Russia can't join NATO, why is NATO moving towards our borders?" Accord
to Russian press reporting, he found a sympathetic audience in Germany.[27]

There was a circumstantial sign of a modus vivendi with Germany over furt
NATO expansion on 21 June, shortly after Putin's return to Moscow. At that ti
Walter Kolbow, state secretary of Germany's defense industry, told an audience
Tallinn that it was incumbent upon the Alliance to secure Moscow's agreement
fore any more states be added to the NATO roster. In his opinion Russia would h
no right to prevent enlargement in 2002, yet placating Moscow was crucial to Eu
pean security. Coming as it did so soon after Putin's meeting with Schröder ;
amidst a flurry of "glad to have you back" remarks from NATO leaders, obser\
from the Baltic States and East Central Europe took Kolbow's remarks to mean t
Russia had a de facto, if not de jure, veto on further NATO expansion.[28] If so, tl
a potential for a Moscow–Berlin axis already had significant ripple effects for R
sian foreign policy. Kolbow's encouraging commentary came on the same day t
the CIS heads of state, meeting in Moscow, released a communiqué linking wc
strategic stability with the inviolability of the ABM Treaty.

Even while it considered resolutions condemning perceived threats to press fi
doms in Russia, the Council of Europe appeared also to be catering to Russia. Its
cision on 26 June not to act upon PACE's recommendation that it suspend Russ
membership in the Council caused one Moscovite to exult that "European gove
ments, for the sake of preserving good relations with Russia, are prepared to confr
their own representatives . . . ."[29] The debate at Strasbourg, however, left a sour ta
in the mouths of Russian participants. Although the official procedures went tl
way, the delegation was subjected to considerable verbal abuse from the floor. E
the final document was believed by some to be roundly anti-Russian.[30]

27. See, for example, Dmitrii Gornostaev, "Udachnoe zavershenie visita Putina" [Putin's Successl
Completed Visit], *Nezavisimaia gazeta* (17 June 2000), and an interview with the German ambassadc
Russia, Ernst von Shtudnitz, *Izvestiia* (22 June 2000).

28. This analysis was offered by Paul Gobles in "Russia: Analysis from Washington—A de Facto Ve
CDI Russian Weekly, no. 107 (JRL, No. 5), 23 June 2000.

29. *Kommersant* (28 June 2000); see also Dmitrii Gornostaev, "V Strasburg pozvali Kiseleva i Doret
[Kiselev and Dorenko Are Called to Strasbourg], *Nezavisimaia gazeta* (28 June 2000), and Alan Ka:
"Plody boikota Rossiei PACE okazyvaiutsia gor'kimi" [The Fruits of PACE's Boycott of Russia Tui
Out to be Bitter], *Nezavisimaia gazeta* (30 June 2000).

30. See, for example, Maksim Sokolov, "Ne nerviruite bol'nykh" [No Nervous Pangs], *Izvestiia* (29]
2000), and El'mar Guseinov, "Otluchenie. Chast' vtoraia" [Excommunication. Part Two], *Izvestiia*
June 2000). Two Yabloko members of the delegation, Aleksandr Shishlov and Sergei Ivanenko, and Ui
of Right-Wing Forces deputy Sergei Kovalev, attended the meeting anyway. For an interview \
Kovalev, see Boris Yunanov, "Pravo golosa ili golos prava" [The Right to Vote, or a Voice for Rig
Obshchaia gazeta, No. 26 (29 June–5 July 2000).

The Council of Europe's decision coincided with the opening of hearings in the State Duma on Russia's relations with NATO. Conducted by the committee for international affairs and attended by representatives of the leading foreign policy ministries and agencies, the hearings heard a consistent theme. Resumption of close ties with NATO is important, but difficult to achieve. Even without the once powerful and pushy Anti-NATO Committee, which was not reconstituted in the new parliament, the atmosphere of distrust was strong. Deputy Foreign Minister Yevgenii Gusarov pinpointed the problem—the NATO bombing of Yugoslavia had destroyed whatever faith most participants had in NATO's claims of good intentions (ITAR-TASS, 27 June). In so many words, he restated Primakov's old line: Moscow will regard membership of any former Soviet republic as a decision aimed directly against Russia. The communist press held hard to the inviolable "red line" as well, and cautioned readers not to fall into the anti-Milosevic trap.[31]

To consolidate its deliberations, on 28 June the Duma adopted a decree "On Measures to Strengthen Relations between the Russian Federation and the Federal Republic of Yugoslavia." A harsh and explicit condemnation of NATO's behavior in Yugoslavia, the decree called on Russia's government to expand diplomatic and trade relations with the FRY, promote that country's association with the Russia–Belarus union, lobby to have sanctions against it lifted, and insist on the full implementation of UNSCR 1244.[32] A short time later, Ivashov—who once said in an interview that the PfP programs were merely "rehearsals for attacks on Russia"—illustrated what the lingering anti-NATO sentiment meant in practice. He condemned Russian participation in most of the PfP undertakings as a waste of time and money, while still calling for closer ties with NATO. His remarks to an *Izvestiia* interviewer reminded readers that the Kremlin's real sensibilities about NATO had changed very little since the bombing campaign began more than a year earlier.[33]

Ivashov's rancor was likely triggered by events in Washington. A day or so before he was interviewed, Jesse Helms and the U.S. Senate Committee for Foreign Affairs recommended restrictions on aid to Russia by the United States, the IMF, World Bank and the EBRD because of Chechnya. This action was described in Moscow as an "anti-Russian" provocation.[34] Clearly, the good feelings generated by the Putin/Clinton meeting were fleeting.

When, on 1 July, the president stamped final approval on Russia's new Russian foreign policy concept, Igor Ivanov remarked that the document was characterized

---

31. See, for example, a long interview with N.I. Ryzhkov, former USSR prime minister, "Kosovskii klin" [The Kosovo Wedge], *Sovetskaia Rossiia* (4 July 200). Perhaps it is no coincidence that, in an editorial on Russia's foreign policy, the paper *Yadernyy kontrol* [Nuclear Control] (4 August 2000), called Putin's approach to foreign policy "a continuation of the Primakov doctrine." See FBIS-SOV, No. 1014 (2000). On the Duma's Anti-NATO committee, see *Russia Faces NATO Expansion, passim.*

32. "O merakh po ukreplenniiu otnoshenii mezhdu Rossiiskoi Federatsii i Soiuznoi Respublikoi Yugoslaviei" [On Measures to Strengthen . . .], *Rossiiskaia gazeta* (6 July 2000).

33. Ivashov, "Ya stanovlius' yastrebom, kogda vizhu ugrozu Rossii" [I Become a Hawk When I See Threats to Russia], *Izvestiia* (6 July 2000)

34. See, for example, Andrei Litvinov, "Vashington ne khochet pomogat' Rossii" [Washington Does Not Want to Help Russia], *Nezavisimaia gazeta* (27 June 2000).

by its realism. "Mutually beneficial pragmatism," in which Russia recognizes its o
limitations, was the new policy's central theme according to the foreign mini:
(ITAR-TASS, 1 July). The minister of defense missed the point, blaming the Uni
States for "destroying the strategic stability" of Europe and the world by threaten
to amend the ABM Treaty. Speaking to the leading military weekly, Sergeev repea
at length all the arguments against amending the ABM, noting opposition tc
among America's own European allies.[35]

The interview was a mirror of the active lobbying Kremlin officials were carry
out all over Europe. Moscow's opinions were, in fact, shared in varying degrees
most G-8 leaders and on a number of points Russian concerns seemed vindicated
week prior to the Okinawa summit, for example, the failure of the third NMD
in the USA was greeted with great relish in Russia, many commentators suggest
that Clinton should welcome the failure "with relief," for he now had a reason
cancel the program.[36] On 1 September Clinton announced that he would not
thorize a go-ahead for the NMD precisely because he could not gain support fo
from his allies. The glee in Moscow was palpable.

The failed U.S. test itself had been preceded in Moscow by a meeting (5–6 July)
tween German and Russian officials on strategic stability. Klaus Erich-Schariot, direc
of the German foreign ministry's political department, and Georgii Mamedov, dep
foreign minister of Russia, discussed disarmament, the NMD, and nonproliferatior
preparation for the G-8 summit. It was obvious that there had been a meeting of mir
On 5 July as well, Putin and China's Jiang issued joint statements in Dushanbe, wh
the Shanghai Five was meeting, offering unconditional support for the ABM treaty
the "cornerstone of strategic stability and the basis of further reduction of strategic ;
offensive weapons" (Interfax, 5 July). Putin was still riding very high in domestic po
larity ratings. But he was not to have his way in everything: a survey released in Mosc
showed that the Russian population supported his every policy, foreign and domestic
with one striking exception: only 30 percent agreed that Russia should join NATC

NEW FOREIGN POLICY CONCEPT

The new Concept of Foreign Policy had a long gestation period. Approved by
Security Council as early as 24 March, it mirrored principles laid out in both the
curity concept and new military doctrine. According to Igor Ivanov, its innovat
was to bring Russian foreign policy "closer to life, and to the tasks which we are

35. Igor Sergeev, "SShA razrushaiut strategicheskuiu stabil'nost'" [The USA Is Destroying Strategic
bility], *NVO*, No. 22 (23–29 June 2000). The interview was conducted by Vitalii Tret'iakov, editor-in-c

36. See, for example, Yurii Vasilkov, "Prazdnichnye gulian'ia v Moskve po sluchaiu neudachnogo zapi
rakety-perekhvatchika" [Celebratory Gathering in Moscow on the Failed Launch of the Interceptor Miss
Rossiiskaia gazeta (11 July 2000); Boris Talov, "Tretii pusk v nikuda?"[Third Launch to Nowhere?], *R
iskaia gazeta* (7 July 2000); Vladimir Lapskii, "PROval. Dvoinoi promakh—v kosmose i na zemle"[N
System-Pros and Cons: Double Failure, in the Cosmos and on Land], *Rossiiskaia gazeta* (12 July 2000)

37. *Kommersant* (7 July 2000). In March only 23 percent had agreed with Putin on the NATO quest

complishing in this country," something its 1993 predecessor had not done. The protection of Russian citizens abroad and support of economic interests worldwide were high on the ministry's list of priorities, and the ministry itself was to play a greater role in coordinating Russia's foreign economic activity.[38]

After some further tinkering, the main propositions of the concept were finally made public, but not yet published, by Ivanov at the end of May. The occasion was fitting: at a lecture dedicated to A.M. Gorchakov, famous nineteenth-century Russian diplomat.[39] Ivanov claimed that the new foreign policy took new international circumstances into account, above all the apparent inability of the world to move from its former bipolar structure to international partnership in creating stability. Instead, the period of transition had been marked by the growth of international terrorism, new "focal points of tension" close to Russia's borders, and regional conflicts. American attempts to build a unipolar world structure, in which the most developed states led by the United States would predominate, were part of the reasoning that shaped Russia's new foreign policy. Other important "circumstances" listed by Ivanov were: unilateral action camouflaged as "humanitarian intervention," allowing some countries and NATO to override the UN Security Council; threats to the inviolability of the ABM treaty; and NATO-centrism in Europe. Insofar as international terrorism was concerned, the new concept mirrored a position taken by Moscow for some time, that is, that an international terrorist network stretching through "Kosovo, Chechnya, Kurdistan, Afghanistan, the Sinkiang-Uigur autonomous region of China, Malaysia to the South Philippines" was threatening world stability.[40]

In light of these considerations, Russia chose to work towards a "democratic multipolar system of international relations," Ivanov announced. This system should have the United Nations at its apex, abetted by regional organizations like the OSCE and a complex of bilateral agreements between states. The Concept called for a policy that was balanced geographically: collectively the CIS countries were the most important to Russia, followed by the European Union. NATO could play a key part in Russia's constructive foreign policy considerations, but only if Brussels committed itself fully to the conditions set out in the Founding Act. Improved relations with the United States were essential, and the importance of Asia among Russian foreign priorities was said to be "growing." China and India were singled out as countries with which existing partnerships should be intensified.[41] Russian foreign affairs experts were pleased with the document.[42]

---

38. See "Novyi vzgliad" [New View], *Rossiiskaia gazeta* (30 March 2000), and ITAR-TASS (24 March 2000).

39. On Ivanov's lecture, see Ol'ga Romanova, "Nasledie Gorchakova aktivno ispol'zuetsia MIDom" [The Gorchakov Heritage Is Actively Utilized at MID], *Nezavisimaia gazeta* (24 May 2000).

40. See Igor Yadykin, "Kak ukrotit' 'anakondu'" [How to Tame the "Anaconda"], *Krasnaia zvezda* (15 July 2000).

41. For a summary and analysis, see Anatolii Repin and Nikita Shevtsov, "This Is the Very Foundation of Our Policy. Foreign Minister Igor Ivanov on the Updated Concept of Russia's Foreign Policy," *Trud* (26 May 2000), translated in FBIS-SOV, No. 531 (1 June 2000).

42. See, for example, Viacheslav Nikonov, " 'Doktrina Putina' v tselom uzhe yasna" [On the Whole, "Putin Doctrine" Is Clear], *Dipkur'er NG,* No. 10 (1 June 2000).

When the Concept finally was released to the public in July, Ivanov announ
that the point of the exercise was "to make our policy more rational, more profita
in the political and economic sense."[43] In fact, Putin's state of the nation addres:
both houses of parliament on 8 July provided a foretaste of the Concept's m
points: economic realism and regional security.[44] In that fifty-minute televi
speech he spoke also of a Russia "strong and confident in its strength" and one
which "unity is bonded by patriotism."

The 1993 foreign policy position had never been published, but the new prea
ble gave an indication of the earlier document's tone: the "expectations" at that ti
of "equitable, mutually advantageous and partnership relations with the surround
world" had turned out to be false. New priorities on the international arena now I
to be set, and the United States, which implicitly had been of the first rank in 19
dropped well down the list. The Concept also clarified Russia's new attitude towa
NATO: cooperation with the Alliance is important "in the interests of security a
stability on the continent," but only insofar as the Founding Act prevents the
ployment of threatening forces ("conventional armed forces, nuclear weapons a
the means for their delivery") on the territory of new members. NATO's s
proclaimed right to act "out of zone . . . without the sanction of the UN Secu
Council" was condemned and the phrase "Russia maintains a negative attitude to
expansion of NATO" was included. NATO had not been an issue in 1993.

Asia was assigned a strong presence in the new Concept. India and China still
the way in importance, but special provision was provided for improving relatio
with Japan. Iran, too, was singled out as especially important to Moscow. A "mu
polar" system of international relations was again advocated. It was not clear h
Moscow hoped to achieve that goal, although a reform of the UN, raising the efl
tiveness of the Security Council while maintaining a right of veto for its perman
members, was among the document's many recommendations. The new doctr
was again greeted with enthusiasm by most of Russia's critics, though some conc
was voiced about the prominence given to Asia and the apparently diminished :
nificance of the United States in the Kremlin's list of foreign policy prioritie
Putin's own opinions on such matters were summarized during a press confere

---

43. See Aleksei Liashchenko, "Zashchita interesov lichnosti, obshchestva i gosudarstva—glav
zadacha rossiiskoi vneshnei politiki" [Defending the Interests of the People, Society and the State Are
Main Tasks of Russian Foreign Policy], *Krasnaia zvezda* (11 July 2000).

For the Concept: "Kontseptsiia vneshnei politiki Rossiiskoi Federatsii" [Foreign Policy Concept of
Russian Federation], *NVO*, No. 25 (14–20 July 2000). It appeared as well in *Rossiiskaia gazeta* and *N
visimaia gazeta* (11 July 2000). For a discussion by "experts," see Valerii Sychev, Avtandil Tsuladze, '
Have the Concept, But How Can It be Implemented?", *Segodnya* (11 July 2000), translated from
Novosti, JRL, No. 4397. Sergei Karaganov, V. Nikonov, and A. Pikaev were interviewed.

44. Putin, "Kak Rossiiu my stroim" [How We Are Building Russia], *Rossiiskaia gazeta* (9 July 200(

45. See, for example, Aleksandr Sukhotkin, "Novymi podkhodami—po vneshnei politike" [By M(
of New Approaches in Foreign Policy], *Obshchaia gazeta*, no. 28 (13–19 July 2000), and his "Aziat
smotriny . . ." in the same issue (see chapter 10). For an enthusiastic review: Vadim Solov'ev, "Vn
nepoliticheskaia kontseptsiia utochniaet voennuiu doktrinu" [Foreign Policy Concept Clarifies Mili
Doctrine], *NVO*, No. 25 (14–20 July 2000).

held for Russian and foreign journalists as he set out to attend the G-8 summit in Okinawa. "We want to be partners" with the West, he replied to one question, adding pointedly that he planned also to work out a new and improved relationship with Japan and North Korea.[46]

The left was not displeased with Putin's willingness to upgrade relationships with former Soviet allies, many of which were regarded with suspicion in the West. This tendency was not new, for Primakov had adopted it explicitly. But Primakov's policy-making had been mitigated by Yeltsin's consistent leaning towards the West. There were no such restrictions on President Putin, who agreed to visit Tripoli after an invitation from Qaddafi was handed him in Moscow by Libya's foreign minister. Western leaders watched with increasing alarm as Moscow's links to Cuba, North Korea, Iran and Iraq also were reactivated or strengthened in the summer of 2000.

The emphasis on economic interests was timely and supported enthusiastically by Russian leaders of all political stripes. Throughout the winter and increasingly in the summer, Russian economic planners had expressed alarm over trends that, if not halted, could prove disastrous by the year 2003. A looming "catastrophe of 2003" became a buzzword for Russia's media and officials. The key to this perceived pending calamity was the accumulation of payments on the foreign debt, predicted to increase by about 50 percent until, by 2003, they reached an astronomical annual sum of $17 billion. Negotiations with the London and Paris Clubs of creditors brought some relief and rescheduling, at least with the former group, but not much.

Selective investment, domestic and foreign, was another source of anxiety. Though investment grew steadily in 2000 in industry and consumer sectors, it declined in other areas, prompting forecasts of disaster in infrastructure deterioration: housing, roads, communication systems, schools, hospitals, and so on. The inability of Gazprom, for example, to invest in new pipelines was typical. Because Gazprom provided almost all of Russia with energy at less than world prices, it could not accumulate large amounts of investment capital of its own. Thus it needed foreign or government help to construct pipelines to carry gas abroad. Adding to Russia's gloomy picture was an assumption that the currently high world oil prices, the source of much of Russia's economic salvation, would drop sharply by 2005, or even earlier.

Other projections for 2003 included the exhaustion of Russia's fixed capital, and a demographic line that would show a dramatic increase in the number of pensioners and a drop in the number of young people moving into the work place. On 13 September, an ad hoc State Duma Commission made up of Duma deputies and representatives from both the government and the presidential administration was set up to work on the "2003" phenomenon.

In light of such prognostications, made more frightening by a series of disasters that struck Russia in the summer—fires, explosions, accidents, and the terrible tragedy of the *Kursk* (see page 77), Putin needed to act quickly on the economic priorities set in his own foreign policy file.

---

46. "My khotim partnerstva, a ne preferentsii" [We Want to Be Partners, and Not Special Status], *Krasnaia zvezda* (13 July 2000).

THE TWO-HEADED EAGLE LOOKS EAST TO OKINAWA

Before that, however, Putin established a presence for himself in the internatio
arena. By the time he arrived in Okinawa on 21 July for the G-8 summit, the pr
dent of Russia had behind him an extraordinarily eventful trip through the Russ
Far East and Asia, where he tapped a bountiful wellspring of approval for his fore
policies from the Shanghai Five, North Korea and China. Putin's government co
even boast of a small pre-Okinawa victory after a proposal from the U.S. and Eu
pean G-8 foreign ministers that their document include a criticism of recent pol
cal actions by Slobodan Milosevic was scrapped.[47] The success of Putin's Eastern t
was such that analysts in Moscow began speaking of the resurrection of Russia as
great Eurasian power.[48]

Even though Russia still was not represented at the pre-G-8 conference of (
members on the world economic scene, Putin was the focus of media attention at
summit itself. His picture graced the front pages of newspapers around the worl
eyeball-to-eyeball with Clinton, practicing Judo with Japanese experts—and all ot
leaders complimented his demeanor and contribution. An obvious improvem
over the erratic and sometimes unintelligible Yeltsin, Putin was taken seriously.

Contentious issues raised at the earlier Putin–Clinton summit faded rapidly i
the background at Okinawa. The Russian president arrived armed with internatio
backing for his vision of world affairs. His stance on the ABM and NMD had w
strong official approval at both the Shanghai Forum and in Beijing, where the R
sian opinion was carried almost verbatim in joint public communiqués; his effort:
ameliorate the image of North Korea as a "rogue" state were appreciated ;
prompted Clinton to say that he would "look into" Pyonyang's offer to give
building a nuclear arsenal in return for assistance in launching satellites "for pea
ful purposes." Putin also handed Clinton proposals for START-III talks. The t
presidents expressed their desire to cooperate in the field of strategic stability and
iterated their June support of the ABM Treaty (Interfax, 21 July). Moscow's cc
mentators were very optimistic about their country's progress in the internatio
arena, though they acknowledged that Russia was not the economic equal of any
the other seven leaders. Their country was still the IMF's largest borrower and l
not yet been admitted to the World Trade Organization (WTO) or the EU. But
them the important matter was that in the G-8 Putin was treated as an equal by
other seven leaders. They claimed to believe that his "bombshell" testimony ab

---

47. ITAR-TASS (12 July 2000). The meeting took place in Miyazaki, 12 July, to discuss the age
and final document of the G-8 summit. Ivanov and the U.S.'s Strobe Talbott held a private meetin
Miyazaki as well, where apparently they argued about the NMD and Chechnya.

48. See, for example, Vsevolod Ovchinnikov, "Golovy Rossiiskogo orla smotriat i na Zapad, i na '
tok" [Heads of the Russian Eagle Look Both to the West and to the East], *Rossiiskaia gazeta* (28 J
2000); see also Vadim Solov'ev, "Voenno-politicheskaia situatsiia v Azii" [The Military–Political Situa
in Asia], *NVO*, No. 24 (7–13 July 2000), a translation of a London Report with particular signific;
for Russian specialists; Svetlana Babaeva, "Progulki po Azii" [Stroll through Asia], *Izvestiia* (6 July 20
Vladimir Kuzar', "Ispytanie Vostokom" [Experiencing the East], *Krasnaia zvezda* (18 July 2000).

North Korea helped persuade at least three other countries (Germany, France and Canada) to oppose Clinton's ABM amendment proposals.[49]

Whereas the G-8 summit was hailed as a great success for Putin personally, few of Russia's international concerns were dispelled by it. While Putin was basking in the media limelight in Okinawa, the Norwegian foreign ministry announced that it would consider participating in the American system, prompting an angry retort from Moscow (Interfax, 21 July). The coinciding public controversy over the fate of Russia's elite rocket forces (see chapter 7) caused Russian experts to look more anxiously than previously at any potential change in the balance of power in the North. Strategic Missile Forces Academy specialist Vasilii Lata took this moment to caution that any talk of cooperation by Washington could be cover for a Pentagon plan to gain access to the Russian systems.[50] Robertson rejected the allegation and, in an unusually long conversation with Russian reporters, promised that NATO would take a careful look at Russia's proposal for a nonstrategic anti-missile system. He added that there were no real obstacles to full Russia–NATO cooperation and cited the planned opening of a NATO information office in Moscow as a vehicle for laying to rest "untrue" assumptions about NATO that abound in Russia.[51]

In light of these events on the international scene, discussion of Russian and NATO strategic doctrines at the ambassador level PJC on 24 July must have seemed a little redundant. The Russian military remained skeptical. Col. Gen. Manilov was invited to brief ambassadors on Russia's military doctrine (Interfax, 25 July). On returning to Moscow, Manilov explained to journalists that NATO's strategic concept was still unsettling. Alleging that NATO had granted itself the right to use force outside its "zone of responsibility" even without a mandate from the UNSC, he called the Alliance a source of instability in the world. From the MoD's perspective the ball was still in NATO's court.

But the military was in no position to challenge Putin's authority. Opinion polls conducted later in July showed that his approval rating had increased by some 10 percent, to 73 as compared to 61 percent in June. In terms of confidence he was far ahead of his closest competitor, Zyuganov (46 percent); Primakov followed with 10 percent. The successful visits to the Russian Far East, North Korea, China and Japan—all covered thoroughly by Russian TV—were assumed by analysts to be the main factors in the rise in the president's popularity.

49. See, for example, Aleksandr Sabov, "Vosem' uvazhaemykh gospod na fone globusa" [Eight Respected Gentlemen against the Global Background], *Rossiiskaia gazeta* (29 July 2000); Vladimir Kuzar', "Rossiia podtverdila status velikoi derzhavu" [Russia Confirmed Its Status of Great Power], *Kraznaia zvezda* (25 July 2000); Dmitrii Gornostaev, "Na okinava Rossiia sygrala na ravnykh" [At Okinawa Russia Played as an Equal], *Nezavisimaia gazeta* (25 July 2000).

50. Interfax (21 July 2000); Lata, former deputy chief of the main staff of Strategic Missile Forces (RVSN), was interviewed for *Vremya-MN* (21 July 2000).

51. Igor Korotchenko [interviewer], "NATO zhelaet znat' podrobnosti o nestrategicheskoi PRO" [NATO Wishes to Know the Details of the Non-strategic NMD], *NVO*, No. 27 (28 July–3 August 2000). The interview was conducted in Brussels.

There were a few cautionary voices out there, alerting listeners that too much
liance on "odious regimes" could undermine Moscow's credibility (see chapter 1
Receiving representatives from sanctioned governments (Serbia, Iraq, Libya), and l
bying for greatly accelerated economic and arms deals with China, Iran, and In
would have their consequences. But opinions such as these were rare and the gen
view was summarized in a strongly supportive commentary from Roy Medvedev, o
of the best-known dissident historians under the old Soviet regime. In a long c
pouring on priorities in foreign policy, Medvedev concluded that the president l
won the respect of government leaders in both East and West. Congratulating Pu
for not setting superpower ambitions for Russia, Medvedev rejected Karaganov's cl
that Moscow might become overextended. Russia needs to behave like a "great
clear power" to guarantee its national interests, Medvedev insisted.[52] Medved
newspaper essay echoed the biting criticism of NATO, especially for its actions in
Balkans, contained in his book on Russian policy and politics published in 1999.
had concluded that monograph with the opinion that "the conflict in the Balk
shows that the expansion of NATO to the East is a real danger for Russia, whicl
will have to take into consideration in its plans and policies."[53]

Medvedev's conclusion in August was prophetic. In point of fact, Putin's new v
came in for closer scrutiny in mid-summer, 2000, as observers began to look for c
crete results from his various proclamations about reform in Russia. The commur
press led the assault, counselling that the president's plans to integrate more fu
with the world economy and to "return to western civilization" harbored great pe
Spiced with references to Madeleine Albright and Zbigniew Brzezinski proclaim
America's right to direct the new world order, one long essay in the communist pi
declared Western civilization "aggressively egocentric," "despotic and totalitaria
The often quoted Jack Matlock statement that the West "deceived Russia" by pro
ising no further NATO expansion if Moscow agreed to a reunified Germany
used to substantiate the communist author's charge that the West also was "cyn
and immoral."[54] His point was that Putin had embarked on the wrong path. A
strident, but equally concerned writer for *Izvestiia* wondered if Putin actually kr
which way his "eagle" should be looking. Is he "a Westernizer or a Slavophile, an
vocate of forcing Russia into 'world civilization' (as the pax americana is often a
increasingly called), or a proponent of the 'special Russian way?'" Petr Akopov ask
Akopov's answer to his own query broke with the common opinion by claiming t
Putin did not know which way to go.[55]

---

52. Medvedev, "Vladimir Putin. Novye aktsenty vneshnei politiki" [Vladimir Putin. New Emphas
Foreign Policy], *Rossiiskaia gazeta* (8 August 2000).

53. Medvedev, *Politiki i politika Rossii. Vremia i bremia vybora* [Politics and Policy of Russia. Time
Burden of Choice], (Moscow: Prava cheloveka, 1999), pp. 214–15.

54. Vladimir Litvinenko, "Opasnye dogmy" [Dangerous Dogmas], *Sovetskaia Rossiia* (3 August 20
Later, the communist press referred to Brzezinski as a "harsh russophobe and enemy of our coun
Sovetskaia Rossiia (12 September 2000). On Matlock's statement, see Black, *Russia Faces NATO Ex*
sion, 22. Incidentally, Medvedev also had picked out Brzezinski for criticism.

55. Akopov, "Vy kuda, grazhdanin polkovnik?" [Which Way Do You Go, Citizen Colonel?], *Izve*
(15 August 2000).

This latter essay was especially timely, since it appeared shortly after two horrendous incidents reminded the Russian public and media of their country's deterioration and vulnerability. On 9 August an explosion rocked the metro tunnel in Moscow's Pushkin Square, killing 11 and injuring some 90 others. The public and media immediately blamed Chechen terrorists, and at least one Chechen was detained by the police. The Chechen government led by Maskhadov denied any involvement and Putin cautioned citizens against jumping to conclusions. But the realities of civil war in Russia were again brought directly to the minds of Moscow's population.

THE *KURSK* TRAGEDY AND THE EAGLE'S
SUSPICIOUS GLARE WESTWARD

A few days later, the pride of Russia's nuclear submarine fleet sank to the bottom of the Barents Sea carrying 118 sailors with it. No foreign or rebel villains could be found to blame for the *Kursk* tragedy of 12 August. To be sure, there were attempts to blame the West by some senior naval officers, and Defense Minister Sergeev continued to do so. But these charges were not taken seriously by the Russian media, which was well aware that long-standing underfunding of the Russian armed forces was one source of the problem (see chapter 7).

A public backlash emerged as the saga dragged out for well over a week.[56] Putin's aura of success began to fray, and both the high command and government officials came under attack for their slowness in requesting help from foreign countries. The Russian media and public swiped at Putin for remaining at the Black Sea resort of Sochi (where he was meeting with Central Asian leaders in preparation for a CIS summit), during the first week of the disaster. In the long run, as emotions cooled, Putin's approval rating did not drop very much. He took personal responsibility, refused proffered resignations from both Sergeev and naval chief of staff, Admiral V. I. Kuroedov, and promised substantial compensation to the families of the *Kursk* crew.[57] August 23rd was declared a mourning day for the *Kursk* victims.

In addition to myriad questions about the competence, funding and capability of Russia's navy raised in connection with the *Kursk* tragedy, broader political and foreign policy issues came to the fore. One of Russia's most respected military affairs writers, Vadim Solov'ev, for example, warned that "it is wrong to hold illusions about defense," implying that Russia could not afford to maintain a superpower type fleet in northern waters. Other analysts challenged the high command's "first reflex . . . to hide the truth." They accused the authorities of lying and demanded that someone

---

56. See, for example, "Tragediia 'Kurska': rovno nedelia" [The *Kursk* Tragedy: Exactly a Week], *Rossiiskaia gazeta* (19 August 2000). For more on the *Kursk,* see chapter 7.

57. On Putin's survival of this dramatic moment, see Yevgenii Krutikov, "Avariia podvodnoilodki 'Kursk' ne stala politicheskoi katastrofoi" [*Kursk* Submarine Accident Fails to Become Political Catastrophe], *Izvestiia* (24 August 2000).

be held accountable for what happened to the *Kursk.*[58] Vadim Solov'ev denoun
both the navy leadership and the ministry of defense for lying before and after
event, thus causing the tragedy and, by obfuscating, making it worse.[59] A writer
Izvestiia charged that the entire rescue attempt was conducted to "salvage Russia's p:
tige as a great power, and keep the military secrets safe." In fact, the *Kursk* affair m
the Russian military's claim that it represented a superpower ring pretty hollow.

Nationalists and communists took advantage of the crisis to call for the rejuve
tion of Russia, blaming the Yeltsin–Putin regime for the debilitation of their nati
One group, led by the CPRF's Zyuganov and including a religious leader, writ
academicians, editors of left-wing newspapers (*Zavtra, Sovetskaia Rossiia*), a gen
and an admiral—and two people who were instrumental in the attempted cc
against Gorbachev in 1991—published a petition against the "insane economic p
icy, which destroyed the Soviet Union and is now finishing off Russia." Four d
later, 26 August, Zyuganov called for the immediate creation of a National Salvat
Program to rescue Russia from the "monstrous, terrible and criminal" conditi
produced under the "slogans of 'democratization' and 'market reform'."[60]

All of a sudden, the press was on the offensive in what had been a somewhat des
tory and fatalistic fight against increasing government control over the media. C
commentator used the incident to criticize Putin's reliance on the power minist
and further centralization to govern the country; another pundit highlighted
preponderance of military-related spending set in the 2001 federal budget, over o
third of the total amount, coming at the expense of "human investments" and e
that "will not ensure the security of the people."[61] Calling the budget "highly n
tarized," Lyubov Kizilova echoed worries expressed already in late 1999. This cc
plaint did not stop Sergeev from defending the navy in a nationally televised in
view on 21 August by claiming that the Armed Forces had been "stripped a
robbed" of its financing over the previous decade. He reiterated the suspicion th
foreign submarine had been involved. Sergeev said this again four days later (In
fax, 25 Aug), prompting one writer to grumble that the minister's explanation ty

---

58. See, for example, Vladimir Yermolin, "Na dne. K-141 zadykhaetsia ot bespomoshchnosti ac
ralov" [At the Bottom. The K-141 Suffocates because of Helplessness from the Admirals], *Izvestiia*
August 2000); Georgi Bovt, "Otdaite chest'. Lzhivaia informatsiia o tragedii 'Kursk' topit reputatsiia vc
nykh" [Salute. False Information about the *Kursk* Tragedy Taints the Reputation of the Military], *Izve*
(18 August 2000).

59. Solov'ev, "Dolzhnostnaia nepravda, dovedshaia do tragedii" [Obligation of Falsehood, Which
to the Tragedy], *Nezavisimaia gazeta* (18 August 2000); Larisa Kalliona, "Moglo li byt' inache?" [Cou
Have Been Different?], *Izvestiia* (22 August 2000). The author assumed that the high command k
that the rescue campaign was fruitless, and that the sailors were long since dead.

60. Zyuganov, "Neobkhodimaia programma natsional'nogo spaseniia" [A Necessary Program of
tional Salvation Program], *Sovetskaia Rossiia* (26 August 2000); "V chas bedy" [In the Hour of Troul
Sovetskaia Rossiia (22 August 2000). The two members of the 18 signers of this latter appeal who pa
ipated in the anti-Gorbachev coup were General V. I. Varennikov and V. A. Starodubtsev.

61. Lyubov Kizilova, "Novaia metla po-tikhomu metet" [New Broom Sweeps Softly], *Izvestiia* (21
gust 2000); on criticism of the power ministries, Marina Kalashnikova, "Stavka na 'silovikov' mozhe
opravdat'sia"[Stake on the Power Ministries May Not Be Justified], *Nezavisimaia gazeta* (18 August 20
See also chapter 7.

fied a "wave of lies" that would make even full disclosure forever suspect. Elsewhere, Solov'ev sharply criticized Sergeev and military officialdom for treating the public "like fools" and for falling back on the "old set of past stereotypes"—foreign intrigue—to explain Russian mistakes.[62]

When LDPR leader Zhirinovskii charged that the *Kursk* was sunk by a Norwegian torpedo ordered by the United States (RIA Novosti, 18 August), few people paid any attention. Bizarre assertions were expected from him. Sergeev's stubborn accusations, however, angered members of the British and Norwegian rescue teams, who called the defense minister's charges domestic propaganda and a mirror of Soviet Cold War behavior. An unusual difference in popular and official attitudes emerged. Whereas the ministry of defense continued to attribute the accident to a collision, most likely with a foreign ship or submarine, the Russian public and media appeared to appreciate the sympathy and immediate offers of assistance coming from the West, and gave the collision claim short shrift.[63] As government investigative agencies struggled to find the cause of the *Kursk* tragedy the collision theory continued to leak from military circles.[64] At about the same time, the military affairs weekly *NVO* carried a full two-page report, with diagrams, in which the cause of the accident was attributed almost exclusively to a "foreign submarine." It was hinted as well in the same issue that Putin and Clinton may have agreed to cover this story up during their twenty-five-minute telephone conversation shortly after news of the tragedy was made public. The trade-off, the authors implied, was financial aid from the United States in return for Russian silence during Al Gore's election campaign. There was a strange irony to this piece, for it was introduced and supported by the very Vadim Solov'ev who some three weeks earlier had called the MoD hypocritical and dishonest for blaming the tragedy on foreign intervention.[65] The debate raged on.[66]

On the other hand, the Russian media soon grew irritated with doomsday analysis from western pundits who used the *Kursk* tragedy as evidence that everything was going wrong in Russia. One mainstream writer in Moscow called this pattern of

62. Solov'ev, "Tragediia, umnozhennaia lozh'iu" [Tragedy Compounded by Lies], *Nezavisimaia gazeta* (23 August 2000); Viktor Litovkin, "Lodku snova pytaiutsia utopit'. Komu nevygodna pravda o gibeli 'Kurska'" [Trying to Drown the Boat Again. For Whom Is the Truth about the Sinking of the *Kursk* Not Beneficial], *Obshchaia gazeta*, No. 34 (24–30 August 2000).

63. For a Radio Ekho Moskvy (19 August 2000) interview with Admiral Eduard Baltin, former commander of the Black Sea Fleet, who used a computer-simulated reconstruction to "prove" that a collision with a foreign ship was the most likely cause, see JRL, No. 4467.

64. For an interview with Popov, "Eto—voennye moriaki!" [This Is a Military Seaman!], *Rossiiskaia gazeta* (20 September 2000).

65. See Vadim Solov'ev, "Vladimir Putin i Bill Klinton sgovorilis'" [Did Vladimir Putin and Bill Clinton Collude?], and Valerii Aleksin, "Veroiatnee vsego, 'Kursk' protaranila inostrannaia submarina" [Most Probably the *Kursk* was Rammed by a Foreign Submarine], both in *NVO*, No. 34 (15–21 September 2000). Igor Milhal'tsev, one of the designers of Russia's deep sea rescue vessels, disagreed with the theory that the *Kursk* could have been hit by another submarine; see Yurii Rost, " 'Miry' otkroiuy taini tragedii" [The "Mirs" will Unlock the Mystery of the Tragedy], *Obshchaia gazeta*, No. 39 (28 September–4 October 2000).

66. In late October, Yurii Rost was strongly critical of the government for not informing the public about the sequence of events related to the *Kursk*, and also rejected the "collision with a foreign vessel" theory; but that image continued to appear. See Rost, "Pravda o 'Kurske' nepod'emna" [The Truth about *Kursk* Unconfirmed], *Obshchaia gazeta*, No. 43 (26 October–1 November 2000).

analysis part of "a rabid campaign of slander and attack on Russia, its people, ar and especially its president . . . ." Most decided, after a week, that the terrible ev could not be blamed on Putin, and several called the search for villains irresponsi and reflecting sometimes the "voices of hatred" waiting to be heard.[67] By the enc September 2000, opinion polls showed an upswing in Putin's approval rating.

There were other reasons for the Western horizon to appear murky to the t\ headed Russian eagle in August. A Russian representation to the UNSC on 18 Aug accused the United States and Britain of violating "international law" by bombing I (see chapter 12), and the PACE issue reappeared at more or less the same time. Dmi Rogozin announced that a delegation from the Duma committee on international fairs would go to New York on 1 September for a UN conference of parliament speakers. Though the conference's main topic was global international security, it came a forum for discussion of the PACE decision to restrict Russia's participatior its voting procedure. A group representing PACE was scheduled to visit Mosc shortly before the matter was opened to negotiation in Strasbourg on 25 Septembe A closely monitored election in Chechnya for an empty Duma deputy seat, on 20 , gust, was part of this new endeavor to erase the blots on Russia's reputation in the W But the election was accompanied by much violence and brought little comfort those who hoped to see the situation in the breakaway republic calmed.

August was not a good month for the eagle's Eastward glance either. When No Korea's Kim Jong-il told South Korean journalists that his earlier promise to put end to his country's missile program in exchange for booster rockets to launch sa lites was "a joke," made to Putin only in passing, the Russian president's foreign p icy initiative began to lose its luster. Although Foreign Minister Ivanov maintaii that North Korea could still be trusted to cooperate, damage had been done Moscow's Asia initiative. The North Korean leader's insistence that his cour needed to build missiles because their sale to Iran and Syria brought in necessary come compounded the problem.

THE UN MILLENNIUM SUMMIT

August 2000 was a terrible month for the Russian people as well. In addition to Pushkin Square explosion and the *Kursk* tragedy, a fire in the Ostankino televis

---

67. On the "voices of hatred," see Mikhail Chulaki, "Ne vrazhdui" [Not Hostility], *Obshchaia ga:* No. 35 (31 August–6 September 2000). See also Igor Maksimychev, "Politizatsiia Tragedii" [Tra_{g\} Politicized], *Nezavisimaia gazeta* (24 Aug 2000); Yurii Vasilkov, "A kto-to utonul v slovakh" [But S\< People Drown in Words], *Rossiiskaia gazeta* (23 August 2000); and "Strastnaia nedeliia" [Passio Week], *Izvestiia* (26 August 2000); Viktor Dvurechenskikh, "Preobrazhenie tragediei" [Transforma through Tragedy], *Nezavisimaia gazeta* (26 August 2000).

68. At least one Russian religious figure chastised his own compatriots for scorning PACE's empl on human rights as "double standards." See Father-Superior Veniami (Novik) of St. Petersburg, "Idec vyshli i politologi" [Ideology Is Higher than Political Ideas], *Obshchaia gazeta,* No. 34 (24–30 Au 2000); see also Alan Kachmazov, "Lord Zhadd Chechenskii" [Lord Judd of the Chechens], *Izvestiia* September 2000). The PACE committee was in Moscow 18–22 September.

tower on 27–28 August, and two further urban bomb blasts (in Ryazan and St. Petersburg), were devastating to Russians' peace of mind.

But September opened with Clinton's decision not to go ahead with the NMD. Putin's government was energized, and hailed the U.S. president's resolve as a "well-thought and responsible step" (Reuters, 2 September). Moscow's unwavering opposition to any amendment of the ABM was an undoubted factor in Clinton's decision not to authorize the NMD program, but by no means the only one. Other compelling reasons included the likelihood that the NMD would push China to escalate the arms race, the danger of alienating some of America's own NATO allies, the failure of the system itself in tests, and considerations related to the U.S. presidential election campaign. The Russian media grabbed credit for their country anyway.[69] Vadim Solov'ev crowed that Russia had won a "military–diplomatic victory in the second round of 'Star Wars'" and linked Putin's success directly to his initiatives vis-à-vis China and North Korea.[70] It was recognized, however, that the NMD was merely postponed and that the "breakthrough" on this issue was mostly a matter of breathing space until after the U.S. presidential election.[71] An interview with Condoleeza Rice, who said that the United States had been much too "soft" on Russia, helped confirm this suspicion. As the most likely adviser on Russia to George W. Bush if he won the election, her viewpoint (published in the United States and noted in Russia) was taken seriously in Moscow.[72]

The postponement of the NMD altered the agenda, somewhat, for Putin at the three-day UN Millennium Summit arranged to begin in New York on 5 September. Over 150 heads of government attended the largest diplomatic gathering in history. Secretary-General Kofi Annan opened it with a call for collective UN action to set straight most of the world's wrongs—an ambition seen by many commentators as unrealistic when the UN itself might not have a promising future. The Russian president was in an ideal position to "work the room" with the NMD decision in hand. He was scheduled to meet privately with Clinton and some 20 other heads of state.

Putin's calendar served as visible evidence of the Russian approach to world affairs and the "rogue states"—talk with them, rather than isolate them as the Americans were inclined to do. In addition to a meeting with his American counterpart and German Chancellor Gerhard Schröder, Putin talked with Israel's Ehud Barak, Cuba's

69. Yelena Shesterina,"SShA otkladyvaiut ocherednoe ispytanie NPRO" [The USA Suspends the Next NMD Test], *Nezavisimaia gazeta* (2 September 2000), said that "Washington has recognized clearly, though unofficially, the victory of Russian diplomacy." Vasilii Safronchuk, "Razymnoe reshenie Billa Klintona" [A Wise Decision by Bill Clinton], *Sovetskaia Rossiia* (5 September 2000).

70. Vadim Solov'ev, "Rossiia vyigrala i vtoroi raund 'zvesdnykh voin'" [Russia Won the Second Round of Star Wars as Well], *NVO*, No. 33 (8–14 September 2000).

71. On this see, for example, Viktor Litovkin, " 'Podarok' Kvashninu ot Klintona" [A "Gift" to Kvashnin from Clinton], *Obshchaia gazeta*, No 36 (7–13 September 2000), who predicted that even Al Gore, if elected, was likely to resurrect the NMD for select areas; and Safronchuk, *op cit.*, who noted that George W. Bush would adopt an unlimited NMD if he was elected.

72. See, for example, L. Nikolaev, "Larri dovolen, Shenderovich net" [Larry (King) Is Fair, Shenderovic Is Not], *Sovetskaia Rossiia* (12 September 2000); Nikolaev, "Umerit li Zapad 'pyl emotsii'?" [Has the West's "Emotional Ardor" Died?], *Sovetskaia Rossiia* (14 September 2000).

Fidel Castro, Iran's Mohammad Khatami, and China's Jiang. He appeared for a l(
interview, with translator, on *Larry King Live* (8 September) and joined Kofi Anı
for the opening of a Russian avant-garde exhibition at the Guggenheim Museu
His foreign minister met Madeleine Albright and together they issued a statem
agreeing to cooperate in reforming the United Nations.[73]

The Putin/Clinton session was preceded by a final meeting of the Russia–L
strategic stability group, chaired by Mamedov and Strobe Talbott. The group, wh
had met first in July, was relieved of its most formidable stumbling block when
NMD project was delayed. The delay made more meaningful a joint declaration
strategic stability signed by the two presidents (Interfax, 6 September), pledging
maintain existing disarmament agreements and to bring the nuclear test-ban tre
into force as soon as possible. The declaration was important to the Kremlin on t
counts: it included specific measures rather than the usual ambiguities and, it was
sumed by some, would compel Washington to ratify existing nonstrategic agı
ments. Together, the joint declaration and the agreement with Albright were tal
by several Russian analysts to mean that Putin finally had decided that Russia ′
ready to regain its rightful place among the leaders of the new world order.[74]
both counts, the optimism would be proven premature.

On 6 September, Putin told the UN gathering that the ABM was an effici
mechanism for disarmament and nonproliferation, and indirectly criticized
United States and NATO when he said that only the UNSC had the right to sa
tion "extreme measures" in crisis situations. He proposed an international confere
on preventing the militarization of space, under the UN umbrella and in Mosc
and again named "terrorism" as the most dangerous threat to international peac
Naturally, the NMD was perceived in Moscow as precisely the vehicle for the U
directed militarization of space.

The Russian media gave Putin high marks for his performance in New York, hi
lighting his efforts to rejuvenate the United Nations.[76] Foreign Minister Ivanov, w

---

73. "Joint Statement by the Minister of Foreign Affairs of the Russian Federation and the Secretar
State of the United States of America, 7 September 2000." U.S. State Department (11 September 20
On Putin and Larry King, "Larri King: Vy optimist?" Vladimir Putin: Nesomnenno" [Larry King: Are
an Optimist? Vladimir Putin: Undoubtedly], *Rossiiskaia gazeta* (12 September 2000).

74. See, for example, Aleksandr Ignatov, "Strategiia 'globalizatsionnogo liderstva' dlia Rossii" [
"Strategy" of Global Leadership for Russia], *Nezavisimaia gazeta* (7 September 2000). See, for exam
Marina Volkova, "Sovbez vzialsia za mirotvorchestvo" [Security Council Adopts Peacemaking], *Neza
maia gazeta* (8 September 2000), for the view that the United States would now have to ratify nonstı
gic agreements. This initiative was the most recent in a series of such joint declarations by the U.S.
RF presidents: the first was signed on 2 September 1998, in Moscow; the second on 20 June 199
Cologne; and the third at the G-8 in Okinawa, July 2000.

75. "President of the Russian Federation Vladimir V. Putin Address to the Millennium Summit
September 2000). Embassy of the Russian Federation in Ottawa. See also Dmitrii Kozyrev, "Yubilei
sudoroga OON" [Jubilee Convulsion of the UN], *Nezavisimaia gazeta* (7 September 2000).

76. See, for example, Dmitrii Kosyrev, "Dogovoru po PRO prodlili zhizn'" [Agreement on the N.
Has Been Extended], *Nezavisimaia gazeta* (5 September 2000); "Budushchee OON reshat glavy g
darstv: [The Future of the UN Lies with the Main States],′ *Nezavisimaia gazeta* (5 September 2000); V:
Safronchuk, "Debiut V. Putina v OON" [Putin's Debut at the UN], *Sovetskaia gazeta* (12 September 20

stayed on in New York for the fifty-fifth session of the UN General Assembly, put on a show of toughness, insisting that Russia would not go ahead with START-III until the ABM Treaty was guaranteed and calling again for the UN to lift its sanctions against Iraq. These points were raised by him as well in meetings held separately by foreign ministers from both the UNSC permanent membership and the G-8 countries (ITAR-TASS, 13, 18 September).

Ivanov himself addressed the Millennium Assembly on 18 September, expanding upon some very specific Russian interests. International terrorism and an "abhorrent manifestation of extremism" were his targets. He called on the UN to put an end to this "direct threat to security and stability" by adhering strictly to existing resolutions: no support, no safe havens. Ivanov also made an indirect appeal on behalf of the CIS's huge Russian diaspora, saying that the UN should not accept situations where some people "have no right to use their mother tongues [and] are deprived of citizenship and work on ethnic grounds." No doubt he meant Latvia and Estonia. Russia introduced a draft resolution of support for the ABM Treaty to the General Assembly, causing Russian analysts to claim that their country had taken the initiative and could not be excluded from among the leadership in the march towards international security.[77]

At about that same time the MoD printed a summary of threatening situations for Russia, placing "international terrorist organizations and groups" at the top of its list. The second category included hot spots of vulnerability in former Soviet republics, among them the Russian "enclaves" in the Baltic republics and Kaliningrad. NATO's new tendency to operate outside the mandate of the UNSC led the way in the third category; the proliferation of weapons of mass destruction, the American NMD, and religious-ethnic extremisms fell into the final three groups of threats.[78]

POST-MILLENNIUM REEXAMINATION OF FOREIGN POLICY

As Putin and Ivanov made their presence felt in New York, the general direction of Russian policy in the international arena was being scrutinized in Moscow by think-tank, academic, ministry and media analysts.

Communist researchers took Putin's remarks in New York as direct criticism of America and NATO for policies related to Yugoslavia and Iraq.[79] Yugoslavia already had special status in Moscow. In late August, the parliament in Belgrade had ratified a free trade accord with Russia, making it the first country outside the CIS to have

---

77. "Statement by Igor S. Ivanov, Minister of Foreign Affairs of the Russian Federation at the Millennium Assembly in New York" (18 September 2000). Embassy of the Russian Federation in Canada, News Release. On this, see Dmitrii Gornostaev, "Protivoraketnaia oborona—problema global'naia" [Anti-Missile Defense is a Global Problem], *Nezavisimaia gazeta* (19 December 2000).

78. Sergei Orlov, "Voennye ugrozy dlia Rossii" [Military Threats for Russia], *Kraznaia zvezda* (20 September 2000).

79. See, for example, Vasili Safronchuk, "Tri dnia v sentiabre" [Three Days in September], *Sovetskaia Rossiia* (12 September 2000).

such an agreement. Election campaigning in Yugoslavia during September was l
terly conducted and, even though the opposition was poised to win, they, and m
foreign observers, assumed that Milosevic would act illegally to retain his positior
power. His own campaign tactics included slogans calling votes for the opposit
votes for NATO, and labelling his opponents traitors. Russian communists natur:
treated this as a reasonable equation. The Russian foreign ministry, also seeing pl
emerging everywhere, fed Milosevic's paranoiac campaign, going so far as to acc
NATO of planning to deploy troops in Montenegro in violation of the Russ
NATO Founding Act.[80] These extreme statements notwithstanding, the Russ
government and media were not as supportive of Milosevic as one might have
pected given the earlier rhetoric in his favor. Russia opposed the idea of an elect
in Kosovo.[81] Several Russian observers predicted that a Milosevic victory would ca
Yugoslavia to disintegrate further, and recognized that full Serbian recovery was lik
only under new leadership.[82]

The future of Yugoslavia represented only one of the issues deemed unresol
and destabilizing by analysts in Russia. Putin's recently acquired image as a seri
and pragmatic leader was fine, they said, but too much remained undone. For
ample, reports that the restoration of full Russia–NATO cooperation was discus
informally on 14 September by Energy Minister Sergei Shoigu and Lord Robert:
in Garmisch, Germany, were treated as more of the same—as fruitless diplomac
Accounts of the meeting concluded that not a lot of progress had been made, e
though both sides had been saying for some time that accommodation between th
was essential.

On that same day an interview with the Swedish ambassador to Russia, who s
that Russia would never be a member of NATO or the EU, was published
Moscow. Sven Hirdman claimed not to be levelling criticism, rather he believed t
Russia was too large—straddling East and West—to fit the mandates of eit
NATO or the EU. A Russian squabble with China, for example, or a Central As
country, could draw NATO into a situation far beyond its means or interests. T
opinion was neither new nor particularly startling, though it was rare for a diplor
to express it.

More importantly, Hirdman offered up an alternative that fit neatly with pro
sitions the Kremlin had been putting forward since the late 1980s. His point ›

80. ITAR-TASS (15 September 2000). The ministry spokesman was referring to statements by U.S.
Force Commander Europe General Gregory Martin, who said that NATO might deploy troops if
grade uses force in Podgorica. See also Dmitrii Gornostaev, "RF i zapad sporiat o vyborakh v Kos(
[The RF and the West Argue about an Election in Kosovo], *Nezavisimaia gazeta* (16 September 20
and Gregorii Danin, "NATO gotovitsia k novomu vtorzheniiu v Yugoslaviiu" [NATO Prepares for a l
Invasion in Yugoslavia], *Nezavisimaia gazeta* (21 September 2000).
81. Georgii Stepanov, "Moskva protiv vyborov v Kosovo" [Moscow Is against Elections in Koso
Izvestiia (11 July 2000).
82. See, for example, Aleksandr Sukhotin, "Strasti po Slobodanu" [Passion over Slobodan], *Obshc
gazeta*, No. 38 (21–27 September 2000).
83. Shoigu and Robertson were participating in a seminar on international security, ITAR-TASS
September 2000).

that if a Eurocorps could serve as an alternative to NATO in Europe then the security interests of both Russia and Ukraine would be satisfied, at the same time making NATO less necessary.[84] The same could be said about the EU's rapid reaction force (RRF), to consist of 60,000 troops deployable by air and sea to enforce peace in European hot spots.

Hirdman's position was supported by the launching in September of a new Russian study titled *Russia and European Security Institutions Entering the 21st Century*. Presented by Moscow's Carnegie Fund, the book of eight separate essays portrayed the further expansion of both NATO and the EU as potential threats to Russia. In the case of NATO, the threat was not so much a matter of territory as it was the change in NATO's self-prescribed mission—which one author said constitutes a problem, not just for European, but also for global security.[85]

Other contributors saw certain advantages to EU expansion and encouraged close Russian association with it. They explained as well that Russia should raise its presence in OSCE missions and institutions, putting that agency forward again as an alternative to NATO for guaranteeing European security.[86] In summing up, the book's editor, Dmitrii Trenin, warned that Russians should not expect too much, but concluded that full rapprochement between Russia and the EU was essential for both sides.

Wider schema for Russia's future in the rapidly globalizing world were put forward by other scholars and analysts. Among these was a proposal that Russia adopt a strategy for "globalization leadership," put forward by Aleksandr Ignatov, director general of a branch of the Presidential Business Management Department. Published in *Nezavisimaia gazeta*, the proposal included a complex accounting for why Russia moved in "cycles of support for globalization and isolationism."[87] Ignatov complained that Russia was blocked from real participation in globalization by a "World Government" dominated by a "Hasidic/para-Masonic group" which treats Russia merely as a holding tank of natural resources for "The New World Order." In contrast to earlier proclamations by the radical right, Ignatov came up with a novel solution, that is, join them by becoming a world leader.

His strategy was complex and sweeping, including the adoption of two official religions—Christianity and Islam, and creating a ministry of ideology and propaganda. In foreign affairs, Ignatov advocated keeping out of any military blocs: instead, be a major player in blocs led by "Germany in Europe, Japan in the Pacific, and Iran

---

84. Hirdman, " 'Ya vliublen v Russkuiu kul'turu" ["I Am in Love with Russian Culture"], *Dipkur'er NG*, No. 13 (14 September 2000). See also an interview on Russia with the Swedish foreign minister in the same issue.

85. See summaries of each essay in *Rossiia i osnovnye instituty besopasnosti v Evrope* in the Carnegie Institution website, where it says that the book was published in June. The study is summarized as well in Sophie Lamroschini, "Russia: New Study Sees NATO, EU Threat," JRL, No. 4572, #4 (20 September 2000).

86. Russia's position on the OSCE was expressed fully by RF deputy foreign minister, Yevgenii Gusarov, in a long interview published in August; see Gusarov, "Sila i slabost' OBSE" [Strengths and Weaknesses of the OSCE], *Krasnaia zvezda* (1 August 2000).

87. Ignatov, "Strategiia 'globalizatsionnogo liderstva' dlia Rossii" [Strategy of "Globalization Leadership" for Russia], *Nezavisimaia gazeta* (7 September 2000).

in the Islamic world." The United States was only barely mentioned, and that as "
'America state' threat . . . transformed into an 'American super-corporate' threat" d
ing the next twenty-five to thirty years. One can only hope that Ignatov's propo
were not representative of advice listened to by President Putin.

PACE and the EU Looming Large

A series of meetings between senior Russian and European officials in Septem
brought both the question of Russia's role in PACE and the projected EU expans
back into the limelight. The PACE delegation to Moscow attended Duma sessi
on human rights in Chechnya and sent representatives again to that republic. Wh
in Strasbourg on 28 September, PACE resolved that Russia must end its abuse of
man rights in Chechnya (85-5-2), the decision actually represented a breakthrou
of sorts. It was reached with far less anti-Russian hyperbole than previously. Rogo
attended as an observer and reported this fact to the Duma, emphasizing that the
olution called on the rebels to stop similar abuses, especially hostage-taking, and p
pare to negotiate. PACE asked foreign countries not to provide aid to the rebels.

At about the same time, that is, the last week of September, Moscow was the
of separate visits by Germany's Schröder, Swedish Prime Minister Göran Perss
and French Foreign Minister Hubert Vedrine. The Armenian president was
Moscow on 26 September. The Russian media buzzed as these leading Europeans
tolled the importance of expanded trade with Russia, and called for the clarificat
of Russia's relationship with the EU. Vedrine, who was there in part to smooth
way for an EU-Russia summit planned for Paris in late October, echoed Russia's
sition on Iraq; and, in light of the current fuel crisis, Germany seemed anxiou
make deals for Russian oil and gas. Persson was important because Sweden
scheduled to take over the chairmanship of the EU in January 2001, so his insiste
that Russia be a key player in the EU's Northern Dimension initiative (see chap
9) and that its relations to the EU be defined more clearly was good news. It was
Schröder visit, however, that attracted the most attention in Russia's media, incl
ing visions of a Russia–Germany–United States balance of power.[89] Some Russ
commentators hoped that the EU could be persuaded to write off its debts.[90]
difference between the welcoming attitude towards the EU and the lingering disti

---

88. Interfax (28 September 2000). The resolution asked Russia to punish servicemen guilty of
crimes, end its block posts (and the alleged extortion at them), stop illegal arrests and physical abuse of
tainees, restore a judicial system to Chechnya and facilitate the return of refugees to their homes. See
Irina Dement'eva, "Chechenskii sled vedet v Dumu" [Chechen Tracks Left in the Duma], *Obshchaia ga*
No. 39 (28 September–4 October 2000), who noted that the PACE delegation heard a wide variet
opinion in the Duma; and "Prava RF v PASE mogut byt' vosstanovleny v nachale 2001 goda" [The
Rights in PACE May Be Resurrected at the Beginning of 2001], *Nezavisimaia gazeta* (28 September 20

89. See, for example, Leonid Slutskii, "XXI vek: Balans interesov v treugol'nike SShA-Ros
Germaniia" [The 21st Century: A Balance of Interests in the USA-Russia-Germany Triangle], *Neza
maia gazeta* (26 September 2000). On Schröder's visit, see *Izvestiia* (26 September 2000).

90. See, for example, Aleksandr Kuronov, Andrei Litvinov, "Finansisty v kol'tse srazheniia" [Finan
in the Battle Ring], *Nezavisimaia gazeta* (28 September 2000).

of NATO was made clear with the arrival in Moscow of Norwegian Jan Peterson, head of NATO's Parliamentary Assembly, for informal discussion with Russian deputies. This visit prompted attacks on the idea of further NATO territorial expansion from both Russia's left and right, especially as Norway was a vocal supporter of Baltic accession to NATO.[91]

Plans for regular Russian–EU consultations were mooted at the same time in Brussels by Deputy Prime Minister Viktor Khristenko, Javier Solana, the EU's representative for foreign and defense policy, Gunther Verheugen, in charge of EU expansion, and others (ITAR-TASS, 28 September). Khristenko, who told Solana that he would like European defense to be on the agenda for another Russia–EU summit set for April 2001, recognized that the EU would soon expand and hoped that Russia's interests would be considered when that time came. This position sounded familiar to everyone who had been following the Russia–NATO dialogue over the previous eight years. But circumstances had changed. By the year 2000, the EU was Russia's main trading partner, accounting for some 35 percent of the country's foreign trade. Russia was buoyed as well by what appeared to be a major shift in American defense policy. In a presentation to NATO defense ministers on 10 October, U.S. Defense Secretary Cohen said that NATO soon would have to share responsibilities for European security with the EU, as the latter organization's own defense capabilities grew. He referred specifically to the RRF. An EU defense ministers' communiqué in late November lent substance to the RRF by pledging troops (over 100,00), ships (100) and planes (400) to the force and making it capable of removing EU nationals from hot spots and providing armed combat troops for peacekeeping duties. A press release made it clear that the RRF was intended neither as a European army, nor as an alternative to NATO; rather, it would be an added security vehicle for Europe.

The Russian foreign and defense ministries were busy elsewhere. On 28 September, Kasyanov was in Norway, where closer interaction in military matters was discussed; a military delegation from India toured Russia during the same week, signing agreements to increase their expenditures on Russian planes. But the entire question of "whither Russia" remained unclear. In addition to the expansion of the EU and projections about NATO's "second wave," Russian onlookers began to predict a U.S.–Germany rivalry for leadership among individual industrialized countries. According to Leonid Slutskii, deputy chairman of the Duma's international affairs committee, the admission of Poland, the Czech Republic and Hungary to NATO was an enormous boon to German economic interests. It would be greatly to Russia's advantage, therefore, to play an "independent economic and political role" between the United States and Germany. The domination by either one of Russia, with its huge natural resource base and large size, would spell the economic downfall of the other. Moreover, the new "Germany party" (as opposed to an "America party") in Russia was led by Putin himself, raising the opportunity for a more balanced world in which Russia might again be a major player. Utilizing the "objective and inevitable U.S.–German contradictions" should be a mainstay of our new foreign

91. See, for example, A. Safarii, "Bez nas skuchaet 'starshii brat' iz NATO" [Without Us the "Elder Brother" from NATO is Getting Bored], *Sovetskaia Rossiia* (21 September 2000).

policy, Slutskii concluded, in tones reminiscent of Lenin's predictions about imperialist rivalries.[92]

PRESIDENTIAL ELECTIONS I: YUGOSLAVIA

The Russian government placated PACE and the EU by announcing that it favo neither side in the 24 September Yugoslav elections, and stating publicly that it not believe that NATO would interfere in Yugoslav affairs. The Kremlin complair only that the Western media and many Western leaders themselves took sides by cusing Milosevic of election fraud even before the elections took place. In this stance, the government in Moscow was not strongly supported by the Duma. Cc munists openly supported Milosevic as the "only leader in eastern Europe not succumb to the dictates of NATO"[93] and portrayed Vojislav Kostunica as a comp mise candidate, pushed to the forefront by the West.

After the Yugoslav election commission claimed that Kostunica barely failed win the necessary 50 percent majority, Putin offered to send his foreign ministeı Belgrade as mediator and invited the candidates separately to Moscow. From Kremlin's perspective, in fact, Kostunica was an ideal replacement for Milosevic. was a vocal proponent of rule by law and hoped to bring his country back into Council of Europe and the OSCE. More importantly for Russia, he seemed an likely servant of the West, for his often-expressed Serbian patriotism resembled Russian patriotism touted by Putin.[94] Opinions were not uniform, of cou whereas LDPR leader Zhirinovskii sent telegrams to Putin and other Russian g ernment leaders demanding support for Milosevic, and claiming that Kostur would bring Yugoslavia into NATO (Interfax, 29 September), Yabloko leader Yav skii publicly exhorted Milosevic to step down (ITAR-TASS, 2 October). A comr nist observer of the first round of voting called it a contest between those who wo go with "bowed heads to the West hoping for generosity from traditional enen and those who would continue the struggle to preserve independence."[95] The day

92. Leonid Slutskii, "XXI vek: balans interesov v treugol'nike SShA-Rossiia-Germaniia" [21st Cent A Balance of Interests in the U.S.–Russia–Germany Triangle], *Nezavisimaia gazeta* (26 September 20 Yelena Shesterina, "Rossiia mozhet polozhit'sia na Germaniiu" [Russia Can Rely on Germany], *Neza maia gazeta* , *ibid.*

93. See, for example, Viacheslav Tetekin, "Zapad: agitbomb ne zhalaet'!" [The West: Agitation Bo Are Not Wanted!], *Sovetskaia Rossiia* (16 September 2000).

94. On this, see Maksim Yusin, "Serbskaia oppozitsiia zhdet pomoshchi ot Rossii" [Serbian Opposi Awaits Help from Russia], *Izvestiia* (30 September 2000).

95. Viacheslav Tetekin, "Vybory pod bombami provokatsii i lzhi" [Elections under Bombs, Prov tions and Lies], *Sovetskaia Rossiia* (28 September 2000). See Kseniia Fokina, "Na vyborakh v Yugos pobedivshikh ne budet" [There Will Be No Winner in the Yugoslavian Election], *Nezavisimaia gazeta* September 2000); Georgii Stepanov, "Neuzheli Milosevich proigral?" [Has Milosevic Really Lost?] "Rezhim chrezvychainykh vyborov" [An Extraordinary Regime of Elections], *Izvestiia* (26, 28 Septeml Konstantin Chugunov, "Tol'ko by ne vybrali grazhdanskuiu voinu" [If Only They Won't Select (War], *Rossiiskaia gazeta* (28 September); Maksim Yusin, "Svoboda v obmen na vlast'" [Freedom in change for Power], *Izvestiia* (29 September 2000); Vasilii Safronchuk, "Bespretsedentnyi nazhim na goslaviiu" [Unprecedented Pressure on Yugoslavia], *Sovetskaia Rossiia* (26 September 2000).

ter the sudden and astonishing revolution unfolded in Belgrade on 5 October, Igor Ivanov flew to that city and met with Milosevic and Kostunica separately. He congratulated the latter on his "victory" and agreed with Milosevic that he should still play a role in the new Yugoslavia. In return, Milosevic, still head of Yugoslavia's largest party, conceded the election on public television. Simultaneously, Putin released an official statement: the current "direct violence" must be ended; peaceful solutions must be found; Russia will help (ITAR-TASS, 5 October).

Putin's recognition that Kostunica had won came only after much wavering, leaving Russia with potential headaches. Milosevic's brother Borislav was still in Moscow serving as ambassador for a government he could no longer logically represent; Milosevic's son Marko, widely believed to be a thug and a crook, fled to Russia, where he was not welcomed but was allowed to stay temporarily. Within a few days he was turned away even from China's borders.

Admonishing the government at first for its lack of resolve in the early postelection period, noncommunist Russian pundits soon began to praise Putin for cutting off any chance of a Milosevic return to power and urging him to take full advantage of his new relationship with Kostunica.[96]

Duma deputies were caught off guard. On 4 October they had passed a resolution recognizing the official results of the 24 September elections, thereby agreeing that a second round should go forward. Borislav Milosovic, who had been interviewed sympathetically on that same day, and many deputies claimed that Kostunica was little more than a puppet of NATO and Washington.[97] When Putin acknowledged Kostunica, Seleznev and the communists objected. The communists, in particular, remained very suspicious of what territories Yugoslavia would be expected to give up in return for aid from the West.[98] With all this contradiction, it was very difficult for Moscow to establish itself as a major player in the new Yugoslavia.

The mainstream papers now turned fully against Milosevic, accusing him of corruption and tyranny. Still, NATO was most culpable, blamed now for giving Milosevic the means to co-opt Serb nationalism and stay in power for as long as he did.[99] Officials in Moscow now began to exhort Kostunica to forestall any direct U.S.

---

96. See, for example, Maksim Yusin, "Milost' k padshemu" [Mercy to the Fallen] and "Poteriavshii stranu" [Those Who Lost the Country], *Izvestiia* (7 October 2000), where Ivanov and Putin are credited for cutting off Milosevic; and Dmitrii Gornostaev "Rossiia priznala Koshtuniysu prezidentom" [Russia Recognized President Kostunica], *Nezavisimaia gazeta* (7 October 2000). Earlier, the press was quite discouraged with Putin's "missed" opportunities, see Georgii Stepanov, "Serb i molot. Slobodan Miloshevich vybiraet grazhdanskuiu voinu" [Sickle and Hammer. Slobodan Milosevic Chooses Civil War], *Izvestiia* (6 October), and *Kommersant* (6 October), where it was said that "Russia's voice is timid."

97. See, for example, Vasilii Safronchuk, "Natovskii ockal" [NATO's Grin], *Sovetskaia Rossiia* (3 October 2000).

98. For the interview with Borislav Milosevic, see *Kommersant* (4 October 2000); see also Dmitrii Gornostaev, "Kreml' stanovitsia posrednikom v Yugoslavii?" [The Kremlin Becoming a Mediator in Yugoslavia], *Nezavisimaia gazeta* (4 October 2000). On 6 October, the Duma refused to congratulate Kostunica (ITAR-TASS, 6 October 2000). For the continuing communist suspicion of Kostunica and his connection with Western aid programs, see Vasilii Safronchuk, "Koshtunitsa prinosit prisiagu" [Kostunica Swears In], *Sovetskaia Rossiia* (10 October 2000).

99. See, for example, Konstantin Chugunov, "Yugoslaviia zabyla, kak zhit' bez sanktsii" [Yugoslavia Forgot How to Live without Sanctions], *Rossiiskaia gazeta* (11 October 2000), *Kommersant* (11 October 2000).

intervention on behalf of Montenegro or Kosovo.[100] Worry about the future
Kosovo, especially the possibility that it might slip into a state of independence
noticed while Yugoslavia rebuilt, was the subject of regular "pay attention" pie
Kouchner was portrayed as opportunistic, ready to take advantage of Serbia's crisi:
ignore UNSCR 1244.[101] Kostunica's quick visit to Moscow on 27 October ea
some of Russia's concerns.[102] The new Yugoslav president and Putin issued a jc
statement pledging economic and technological cooperation: Putin agreed
reschedule the huge Yugoslav gas debt (perhaps as much as $600 million), and prc
ised tangible aid to the war-damaged country—though it was not clear just h
much aid Russia was in a position to deliver. The trip was important for Russia
that it confirmed that the Kremlin was still relevant to Yugoslavia, or at least g
that impression. Moscow offered Kostunica unconditional support for UN
1244.[103] It seemed to some observers that the new Yugoslav leader was preparing
play a Tito-like role, that is, maintaining and benefitting from a middle path betwe
Russia and the West. In the long run that would not have been a bad solution
Moscow. The fate of Milosevic would serve as a test of this compromise.

PRESIDENTIAL ELECTIONS II: THE UNITED STATES

Whatever the chances of a timely resolution to the Yugoslav impasse, or of closer
sociation with the EU, Russian foreign policymakers were sensitive to the fact t
their destiny would be shaped to a certain extent by the results of the American p
idential election. This reality was brought home starkly in mid-September when
U.S. Congress released a 209-page report on United States–Russia relations. 1
commission responsible for the report was chaired by Republican Christopher C
Blaming the Clinton administration for failing to ensure that Russia became der
cratic, market oriented, and an ally of the United States, the commission recc
mended that less American money be spent on the Russian state and more on
people. It advocated land reform, an improved legal system, and a better investm
environment before further American assistance was made available to Russia. 1
many details were provided as to how this wish list could be accomplished, but
importance of the report is that it forewarned of the tough stance on Russia that
publicans were likely to carry with them into the White House. The long-te

---

100. See, for example, Kseniia Fokina, "Kosovo stanet respublikoi? [Will Kosovo Become a Republ
Nezavisimaia gazeta (17 October 2000).

101. See, for example, Sergei Rudchenko, "Kuda dreifuet krai Kosovo" [Where the Province of Ko:
is Drifting], *Rossiiskaia gazeta* (25 October 2000).

102. On this, see for example, Maksim Yusin, "Koshtunitsa opredelilsia" [Kostunica Decided], *Izve*
(24 October 2001).

103. "Joint Declaration by Presidents of Russia and Yugoslavia," ITAR-TASS (27 October 2000).
also Georgii Engel'hardt, "Koshtunitsa edet v Rossiiu za pôdderzhkoi" [Kostunica Goes to Russia for ?
port], *Nezavisimaia gazeta* (27 October 2000).

implications of the Cox report were pondered in Russia, with mixed results—though angry, puzzled, and nervous would describe most responses.[104]

Inasmuch as the Clinton Administration rejected the Republican dominated committee's various recommendations, and Albright angrily denied their implications, it was obvious to Russian observers that if Bush was elected, Washington's official approach towards Moscow would change dramatically.[105] Bush raised the question of Chernomyrdin's honesty in his dealings with Al Gore during one of the presidential TV debates; the Congress threatened to resurrect sanctions against Russian firms dealing with Iran; and State Department officials again met with Ilyas Akhmadov, separatist Chechnya's ("Ichkeria's") unofficial "envoy" in Washington. These campaigning incidents may have seemed insignificant in the West, but they generated media and official outbursts in Moscow and added to the atmosphere of deep suspicion of Republican motives.[106]

NEW CONSIDERATION: MIDDLE EAST—CENTRAL ASIA

The presidential competition in the United States did not distract officials from other important matters. Spillover from the long-standing civil war in Afghanistan continued to worry Russia and other CIS countries in Central Asia (see chapter 10). One consequence of continuing intrusions, or threatened ones, by Taliban forces on the territories of Tajikistan was a much strengthened CIS Collective Security Pact. Meeting in Bishkek on 11–12 October, the Pact members (Russia, Belarus, Kazakhstan, Kyrgyzstan, Tajikistan, Armenia) agreed to work closely together against "international

---

104. L. Nikolaev, " 'Russkaia politika' Vashingtona" [The "Russian Policy" of Washington], *Sovetskaia Rossiia* (26 September 2000); Maksim Zarezin, "Podderzhka reform s posleduiushchim razoblacheniem" [Support for Reforms Subsequently Unmasked], *Rossiiskaia gazeta* (6 October 2000); "Sled krestovogo pokhoda. Amerikanskaia zhurnalistka i russkaia tragediia" [Trace of the Christian Crusade. American Journalist and the Russian Tragedy], *Sovetskaia Rossiia* (17 October 2000); See, for example, Tamara Mikhailova, "Gilman vriad li goden k upotrebleniiu"[Gilman Unlikely to Be Fit for Human Consumption], *Rossiiskaia gazeta* (5 October 2000). The *Moscow Times* documented evidence of ballot-stuffing, vote-buying, bribery and rigging of vote counts to bring some 2.2 million votes to Putin, enabling him to win in the first round. Right or wrong, the Russian population was staggeringly indifferent to such charges.

When Thomas E. Graham was accused of encouraging a "forget Russia" attitude. His offending piece appeared in the *Christian Science Monitor* (26 October 2000). The "forget Russia" is not, in fact a Graham preference, rather he describes it as a prevailing mood in some parts of Washington. The Mikhailova reference is to Benjamin Gilman, chair of the U.S. International Relations Committee.

105. On this, see Dmitrii Gornostaev, "Olbrait vstupilas' za Putina" [Albright Stands Up for Putin], *Nezavisimaia gazeta* (29 September 2000); Leonid Nikolaev, "Madam Olbrait ob'iasniaetsia s kongressmenami. 'Russkaia politika' Vashingtona" [Madame Albright Explains Herself with Congressmen. The "Russian Policy" of Washington], *Sovetskaia Rossiia* (30 September 2000); and "Vedushchii amerikanskii ekspert konstatiruet" [Leading American Expert States], *Sovetskaia Rossiia* (28 October 2000).

106. See, for example, Vladimir Dunaev, "Aiatolly v ozhidanii bomby" [The Ayatollahs Wait for Bombs], *Izvestiia* (28 September 2000); "V SShA opublikovano sekretnoe pis'mo Chernomyrdina Goru" [A Secret Letter from Chernomyrdin to Gore Is Published in the USA], *Nezavisimaia gazeta* (18 October 2000); Aleksandr Sadchikov, "Za karman—k otvetu" [Out of the Pocket to Answer], *Izvestiia* (26 October 2000). See also *Sovetskaia Rossiia* (19 October 2000).

terrorism," "political and religious extremism," drug trafficking and, more specific:
"Islamic fanaticism."[107] Russian specialists advised that joint campaigns against '
ternational bandits" were a key component in strengthened ties between Rus
China and the states of Central Asia.[108]

The Akhmadov incident aside, there was also a lingering hope that the Uni
States might be drawn into an anti-terrorist coalition. A terrorist attack resulting
multiple deaths on the frigate USS Cole turned Washington's media tempora
away from electioneering and back to the question of terrorism. Putin had b
pointing to international terrorism as the greatest danger to global security for a l
time, and the RF foreign ministry repeatedly had asked that the problem be deba
in the UNSC. Events of the fall of 2000 lent credence to Moscow's assertion tha
was fighting international terrorism in Chechnya, if not yet for its specific activit
that republic. On 16 October, in fact, the U.S.–Russia working group on the ter
ist threat from Afghanistan met in Moscow. Representing Washington was Un
secretary of State for Political Affairs Thomas Pickering. Russian cochair was \
cheslav Trubnikov. The group, which first met in early August, discussed the l
Cole case along with its scheduled agenda related to Afghanistan and terrorism.

The concurrent outburst of violence between Israelis and Palestinians, disrupt
the slow-moving peace process in which President Clinton had been so closely
volved, found Moscow in an unusually conciliatory mood. Though the Du
blamed Israel in a draft resolution of 12 October, albeit in milder tones than pr
ously, the Kremlin made a point of casting no blame. The official Moscow line '
less harsh towards Israel than the UN Security Council resolution, which attribu
the violence mostly to decisions made in Tel Aviv. It would seem that Russian p
cymakers now viewed the Middle East in a much larger context than its Soviet pr
ecessors had done. In a feature on international terrorism, for example, the gove
ment newspaper attributed "50 percent" blame for events in Israel to each side.
the same editorial the author went on to say that it would take another "outrageo
anti-U.S. terrorist act, such as that committed against the USS Cole, to persu
Americans to rethink their position on Chechnya.[109] He was right, as an even m
dramatic incident, nearly a year later, was to prove.

---

107. On this, see chapter 10 on Central Asia, and Vladimir Berezovskii, "Sodruzhestvo sozdaet kol
tivnye sily bezopasnosti" [Commonwealth Creates Collective Security Pact], Rossiiskaia gazeta (12 O
ber 2000), and Yekaterina Tesemnikova, "Kiev i Tashkent prodolzhaiut sblizhenie" [Kiev and Tashl
Continue to Merge], Nezavisimaia gazeta (14 October).

108. See, for example, Stanislav Alekseev, "Formiruetsia banditskii internatsional. Protivostoiat'
stremizmu mozhno tol'ko sovmestnymi usiliiami Rossii, Kitaia i gosudarstv Tsentral'noi Azii" [A Ba
International Is Formed. To Counter Extremism Is Possible Only by Joint Efforts of Russia, China
the States of Central Asia], NVO, No. 37 (6–12 October 2000).

109. Vladimir Lapskii, "Chetvertaia voina Izraelia s arabami?" [The Fourth War of Israel with the Aral
Rossiiskaia gazeta (14 October 2000); see also Il'ya Maksakov, "Rossiiu prostiat za bor'bu s terrorizmo
[Will Russia Be Forgiven for Its Struggle against Terrorism?], Nezavisimaia gazeta (14 October 2000); M
anna Belen'kaia, Dmitrii Kozyrev, "Blizhnii vostok: chas provokatorov" [The Middle East: Hour of Prov
teurs], Nezavisimaia gazeta (14 October 2000), "Moskva stala mekkoi dlia izrail'tian" [Moscow Beco
Mecca for Israelites], Nezavisimaia gazeta (26 October 2000). On 11 October, both the Rossiiskaia gazeta
Nezavisimaia gazeta praised their government for its "balanced" approach to the "new" Middle East cris

Before October 2000 was out, the Israeli prime minister was in Moscow bearing the message that his country and Russia faced the same enemy, that is, extremism. In fact, both sides in the Middle East appeared to want the Russian Federation to be more involved in the peace process.[110] Igor Ivanov, who had only a few days earlier met with both Kostunica and Milosevic in Belgrade, now sat separately with Barak and Arafat, though in neither case was it clear how Russia could serve as mediator.[111] Reality set in when Putin was not invited to participate in the summit at Sharm el-Sheik, Egypt, where, in meetings facilitated by Clinton and Egypt's Mubarek, Barak and Arafat worked out a modus vivendi for stopping the violence. Moscow's position was that it would attend only if invited at the highest level, that is, if Putin himself were asked to take part. An invitation to Ivanov was not enough. It would seem, however, that Russia was best out of it. Putin could freely congratulate Clinton for his "courage" in chairing the meeting, escape being part of a decision that would, inevitably, satisfy neither side, and still be available for mediating work if called upon.

Comforting as this scenario might have been, several Russian analysts were beginning to wonder if their leader knew what he was doing. An entire series of disparate international events, the crises in Yugoslavia and the Middle East, Putin's visits to India and meetings with Kuchma and Lukashenko, upgraded integrative structures in the CIS after congresses in Astana and Bishkek, evoked words of warning. Well-known commentator and vice-president of the Reform Fund, Andranik Migranian, concluded that Putin, forced into making Solomon-like choices, had done the right thing by turning back to the CIS.[112] Greater attention to Russia's large Slavic neighbors and to Eurasia would lead to more satisfactory results in the country's search for a niche in the new world order. Towards the end of October, however, Migranian's prognostications were already dated.

RUSSIA–EU SUMMIT

On 27 October, Putin departed Moscow for the sixth EU–Russia summit in Paris, which opened a few days later with Chirac presiding (France held the rotating presidency at that time). Hoping to attract foreign investment, the Russian president briefed EU leaders on his efforts to speed up market reforms. There was discussion as well on European energy purchases from Russia and clarifications of the implication for Moscow of the EU's expansion to include former USSR republics and allies from East and East Central Europe. Following the EU meeting, Putin began an

---

110. See, for example, *Kommersant, Krasnaia zvezda* and *Nezavisimaia gazeta* (26 October 2000).

111. One Russian commentator said that Russia's offer to mediate in Yugoslavia was useless—see Liliana Bulatovich, "Rezhim zaleg na sokhranenie" [The Regime Is Taken to Bed], *Obshchaia gazeta*, No. 40 (5–11 October 2000)—for Yugoslavs already had made their choice.

112. Migranian, "Rasstavanie s illiuziiami. Moskva, predprinimaia vneshnepoliticheskie shagi, uchitsia trezvo smotret' na sobstvennye vozmozhnosti" [Parting with Illusions. Moscow, Adopting Foreign Policy Steps, Is Learning to Look Soberly at Its Own Possibilities], *Nezavisimaia gazeta* (27 October 2000). This was a full-page essay.

official state visit to France, with which Moscow's relationships had become qı
strained, especially over the conduct of war in Chechnya. This was the Russian pı
ident's first visit to France in any capacity.

To prepare himself, Putin had granted an interview to French journalists
Moscow) and held a nearly two-hour conversation with French specialist on Rus
Hélène Carrère d'Encausse.[113] During the interview, Putin answered questions ab
Russia's status as a great power, rejecting the idea that Moscow had any hegemo
ambitions. Responding to a query about Russia and the EU, he reiterated the be
that Russia is fully European and that its association with the EU should and wo
expand at all levels—though he agreed that Russia was not yet prepared to be a me
ber. EU expansion, even to the Baltics, was treated by Putin as something that co
be to Russia's advantage. He added, gratuitously, that NATO expansion was quit
different matter. Russia's opposition to NATO expansion was "logical, comprehei
ble and obvious," and would be consistently opposed by the Kremlin.[114]

The comment about NATO was not idly made. At a time when Russia was sch
uling major reductions in its armed forces personnel (see chapter 7) and planning
reduce its strategic nuclear weapons via START-II and -III, an outburst of Ameri
enthusiasm for the admission to NATO of the Baltic States was especially unv
come. The appropriation by the U.S. Senate on 24 October of some $20 millior
assist in preparing the Baltic States for integration with NATO reminded Russ
policymakers that the next wave of NATO expansion was scheduled for 2002 (
chapter 9). The possibility of former Soviet republics joining the Alliance streng
ened the hand of military conservatives, among them Sergeev, who opposed cut:
military personnel.

All in all, the EU summit marked another successful foray for Putin.[115] Its fifte
nation membership endorsed Putin's economic reform program, supported the ҏ
sibility of an early Russian association with the EU itself, and cautiously endor
Russia's hope to enter the WTO by the year 2002. Nonetheless, in addition to
pervasive but improving, economic problems, Russia, which had applied to enter
WTO in 1993, still was caught in a bind. WTO practices would require Russia
reduce tariffs against imports and solve the dilemma of its high subsidies to agric
ture. Neither of these conditions was very appealing to Moscow.

In the meantime, diplomatic negotiations with the French government led to
tle more than mutual acknowledgement that the atmosphere had improved.[116]
the business side, a deal valued up to $2 billion between Gazprom and Gaz de Fra

---

113. On the conversation with D'Encausse and Putin's visit to France, see the series of essays in ⅃
kur'er NG, No. 16 (26 October 2000).

114. "Russian President Reiterates Concern at NATO Expansion," Russian TV (Moscow, 29 Octι
2000), BBC Monitoring. JRL, No. 4608.

115. See, for example, Vadim Markushin, "Kholod kak stimul k sblizheniiu" [Cold as a Stimulu:
Closeness], *Krasnaia zvezda* (1 November 2000).

116. On this, see Yelena Dikun, "Putin podaril frantsuzam svoe serdtse. No dogovorom eto oform
be bylo" [Putin Presented His Heart to France. But No Treaties Are Drawn Up], *Obshchaia gazeta,*
44 (2–8 November 2000).

to construct a pipeline through Belarus, Poland and Slovakia was announced on 31 October. There were still many details to be worked out, including Poland's reluctance to cut off Ukraine (see chapter 9).[117]

Perhaps the most important consequence of the EU summit was the clarification of Russia's expectations in its developing relations with Western Europe. In addition to their explication in Putin's interview, these hopes were laid out by Deputy Foreign Minister Ivan Ivanov for *Le Figaro*. The message was simple: Moscow wanted to market oil and gas to Europe, and in return expected the European Investment Bank to invest substantially in Russia's energy industry; it wanted support for pipeline construction through Poland and for its claims against Ukraine's practice of siphoning off gas from existing transit lines. Ivan Ivanov raised the issue of NATO expansion and warned that Europe must take Russia's interests into account before NATO admitted the Baltic States. His essay ended with the common dual admonition: "Greater Europe must not exist without Russia . . . Russia is an inalienable part of Europe."[118]

Putin named the summit the "political zenith" of Moscow's relations with the EU (Interfax, 30 October), and the Russian media enthusiastically endorsed the energy deal, the EU's commitments to Russia, and the "new impulse" to Russian–French relations.[119] Their relief was apparent, for much had been at stake when Putin set out for Paris. In presummit musings about the importance of the session, most analysts had not been very optimistic. Negotiations with France were expected to be especially difficult, particularly because of the French public's distaste for Russia's actions in Chechnya.[120] In the end, however, Europe's energy requirements persuaded the EU of Russia's importance, and the opinions Russia and France shared on the ABM, NMD, and Iraq won the day. Interestingly, Putin hinted that Russia might consider accepting payments for its energy resources only in Euros, a move that some saw as a means of devaluing the U.S. dollar.[121] The agreement with the EU was treated by some Russian analysts as a major, and perhaps final, step away from the Cold War divide in Europe.[122] Such presentiments may have been premature. For Russians, the litmus test of the resilience of Cold War attitudes still depended largely on NATO's plans for the future.

---

117. The new accommodation with France was enthusiastically praised in Russia. See, for example, *Rossiiskaia gazeta, Izvestiia,* and *Nezavisimaia gazeta* (1, 2 November 2000).

118. *Le Figaro* (1 November 2000), summarized in Donald G. McNeil, Jr., "Putin in Paris, Where Talk Is Mainly of Business," *New York Times* (1 November 2000).

119. Nikolai Paklin, "Frantsuzskie dialogi Vladimira Putina" [The French Dialogues of Vladimir Putin], *Rossiiskaia gazeta* (1 November 2000). See also an interview with the head of France's lower house of parliament, who led a parliamentary delegation to Moscow on 12 October, *Izvestiia* (13 October 2000).

120. See Arkadii Vaksberg, "Parizh—eto ne prazdnik" [Paris Is No Holiday], *Obshchaia gazeta,* No. 47 (26 October–1 November 2000); and Nikolai Paklin, "Parizhskii dubl'" [Paris Double], *Rossiiskaia gazeta* (27 October 2000). On the other hand, *Nezavisimaia gazeta* (28 October 2000) had published an interview with Javier Solana, the EU's foreign policy chief, who said that the EU was prepared to help Russia.

121. On this, see Dmitrii Kosyrev, Vladislav Kuz'michev, "Putin podderzhal evro" [Putin Supports the Euro], *Nezavisimaia gazeta* (1 November 2000)

122. See, for example, "Myi otdaliaemsia ot razdela Evropy i 'Kholodnoi voiny'" [We Are Moving Away from the Division of Europe and the "Cold War"], *Rossiiskaia gazeta* (31 October 2000).

NATO AND THE U.S. PRESIDENTIAL ELECTION—AGAIN

The raised level of discussions with the EU inevitably brought the problem of NA'
and NATO expansion to the forefront of Russian policy deliberations. A few days
ter a reaffirmation of their opposition to NATO expansion by Putin and others d
ing their stay in France, Russian parliamentary delegates to a Russian–German c
ference titled "NATO and Russia: Strategic Partnership or Cooperation?" proclain
in Berlin that NATO enlargement was harmful to Russia's interests. They also
couraged dialogue, insisting that accommodation could and should be reached.[123]

The NATO issue was driven as well by the final days of the U.S. presidential el
tion campaign, when Russian planners had to prepare for changes in their relati
with the United States if the Republican candidate succeeded. Officialdom and
alysts assumed that divisions between the two countries would be less ambigu
than previously and that George W. Bush would take a tougher stance than Al G
on both the ABM and NMD. Observers in Moscow also believed that whatever p
erential treatment Russia might have enjoyed from the Clinton–Gore team wo
quickly disappear. Some felt that the change would be a good thing, making the
lationship more pragmatic, with less direct "meddling" by economic reform-obses
American officials. Several Russian observers even believed, rashly it was to turn c
that the isolationist tendency of Republican politicians might prevent Washing
from taking dramatic risks overseas.

When it became apparent that Bush might win without a majority of the Am
can people behind him, Russian onlookers became less sanguine. Rogov, for exa
ple, predicted that a final Bush victory could cause radical changes in the Russia–L
relationship, and newspaper commentators wrote ominously about the danger c
quick adoption of the NMD, a "slide into a new arms race," and aggressive Am
can interference with Russia's advanced standing with China, India and Iran.[124]
was believed in some circles that no matter who won, the end of the campaign wo
at least allow Russians to separate more easily the real from the theatrical in tl
dealings with America.

The weeks prior to the American election had seen a flurry of shoring-up fore
visits by the Russian prime minister, Mikhail Kasyanov. In Turkey on 23–25 Oc
ber, he negotiated a much-improved relationship on matters of trade and general

123. The Russian delegation was led by Andrei Fyodorov, of the CFDP. See also a long, strongly ʒ
NATO diatribe in the communist press, published at the end of October, but referring to a confere
held in Garmisch in September, Yurii Nikiforenko, "Poka igraem v krizis. Deputat Gosdumy—v
tovskom Tsentre Marshalla" [While We Play at Crisis. State Duma Deputies in NATO's Marshall C
ter], *Sovetskaia Rossiia* (24, 26 October 2000).
124. See, for example, the front-page feature, Dmitrii Gornostaev, "Amerika poka ne smogla izl
prezidenta. K sozhaleniiu, budushchee Rossii slishkom zavisit ot iskhoda vyborov v SshA" [America
Has Not Elected a President. Unfortunately, the Future of Russia Depends Closely on the Outcom
the Election in the USA], *Nezavisimaia gazeta* (9 November 2000). For the Rogov commentary see
terfax (8 November 2000). M. S. Gorbachev, however, insisted that there would be no major cha
(ITAR-TASS, 8 November 2000).

operation (see chapter 8); a few days later, Kasyanov was in Beijing, signing some 14 new agreements. There he offered a strong public statement in support of China's position on Taiwan, and confirmed their joint opposition to the NMD. Significantly, the concept of a Moscow–Beijing–New Delhi "axis" was revived (see chapter 11). The uncertainty of the immediate aftermath of the U.S. elections allowed for another kind of initiative: on 13 November, Putin released a statement saying that Russia was willing to work towards an even deeper cut in nuclear weapons than the ones envisioned by START-II and -III. These cuts would be tied to the "retention and strengthening of the ABM Treaty."[125] He again urged the U.S. Senate to complete the ratification of START-II and other anti-missile accords. Obviously, Putin wanted his position on the public record before a new administration grew comfortable in Washington. Russian officials interpreted this as "putting pressure" on the new U.S. president, no matter who it was to be, and they repeated warnings that if the new U.S. administration went ahead with the NMD the "entire system of nuclear security" created by the international community would be jeopardized.[126] It was also true, of course, that Russia could not afford an escalation of the arms race, or even the maintenance of its current stockpile.

Within days of his statement, Putin was off to Brunei for an Asia–Pacific Economic Cooperation (APEC) meeting, where globalization issues were to be discussed and bilateral meetings with world leaders, among them Bill Clinton, could be held (see chapter 10). While he was away, the Russian foreign ministry announced that it was "too early" for Moscow to consider rejoining the PfP, reminding journalists that the Partnership for Peace initiative in 1994 was mainly for countries that hoped eventually to join NATO (Interfax, 16 November).

November was, in fact, a month characterized in Moscow by foreign policy breakthroughs, most of them minor and for the most part predictable but with the accumulated effect of making Russia appear unusually busy in the international arena. On 3 November, Igor Ivanov notified the Clinton administration that Russia intended to restart arms sales to Iran, unilaterally withdrawing from a 1995 agreement between Viktor Chernomyrdin and Al Gore. The announcement came four days prior to the U.S. presidential election and prompted an immediate warning from Secretary of State Albright that there would be consequences, including the possibility of sanctions against Russian firms. President Clinton protested the action to Putin during their meeting in Brunei, but the Russian decision went into effect on 1 December anyway.

The sale of an AWACS-type system to China was confirmed by Beijing on 18 November. A few days later, Igor Ivanov completed a tour of the Middle East, and on the 24th Putin facilitated an agreement between Yasser Arafat and Ehud Barak to restore at least some security cooperation in the midst of the sudden post-Sharm el-Sheik

---

125. Text of "Putin Statement on Arms Reduction" (13 November 2000). Embassy of the Russian Federation in Canada.

126. See, for example, Aleksandr Babakin, quoting senior Russian military personnel, "Chem otvetit Amerika?" [How Will America Respond?], *Rossiiskaia gazeta* (16 November 2000).

outbreak of conflicts. Though the agreement was only a small step towards slow
down the spiral of violence—Arafat telephoned Barak from Moscow with Putin
tening—it signalled Russia's return to the peace process of which it had been a cosp
sor in the early 1990s. In terms of image, this was a diplomatic coup for Putin, as
Israeli and Palestinian governments agreed to reopen their joint liaison offices in
field. Although it was stretching reality somewhat to claim, as Russian officials did, t
Putin had worked a "miracle" in the Middle East arena, this new circumstance marl
a repudiation of the U.S.-brokered summit in Egypt and raised the Russian profil
the region. One expert's consideration that "Russia has awakened from a long dir
matic slumber" was perhaps more to the point.[127] By this time, in Russia only the cc
munists were consistently blaming Israel for the recurring crisis.[128]

Rumors contributed to Russia's image as a player in the "Great Game." It '
hinted at mid-month, for example, that the United States had asked Russia for h
in launching a joint military action against international terrorist Osama bin Lac
in Afghanistan (see chapter 10). The Kremlin's reaction to this suggestion was to v
for details. None were forthcoming. Moscow's approval of the EU's plans to buil
small military force of its own was much less equivocal. On 20 November, the
announced its members' pledges to provide troops, planes and ships for the rapid
action force envisioned for the year 2003. Amid denials in Western Europe that
RRF would in any way negate NATO's role in crisis management, Russia offered
cooperation. Putin discussed this matter with Tony Blair, in Moscow for his f
meeting with the Russian president. Britain proffered tentative approval for Rus:
involvement in joint security measures for Europe. In this case, Moscow's posit
signaled yet another change from the Yeltsin years. For most of the nineties,
MoD had vigorously opposed the idea of a European army, especially if Russia '
to be excluded from it.

The EU's decision sparked a bitter public row in London between Blair and 1
mer Conservative prime minister, Margaret Thatcher, and drew criticism fr
prominent Americans, such as former U.S. defense secretary, Caspar Weinber;
Generally, however, Washington sided with the RRF as a means of placing an o1
for conflict resolution in Europe more directly on the Europeans themselves. Fr
Russia's perspective, of course, a common European defense policy was a good th
if it would help diminish the continent's dependence on the United States.[129] On

---

127. Vladimir Dunaev, "Virtual'nyi sammit v Moskve" [Virtual Summit in Moscow], *Izvestiia* (25
vember 2000). For the "miracle" comment, see *Novye Izvestiia* (25 November 2000). See also Vlad
Lapskii, "Blizhnii vostok: Vremia meniat' posrednikov"[Near East: Time for Change in Intermediar
Rossiiskaia gazeta (21 November 2000), who pointed out that Clinton was no longer the logical me
tor, and that it was time for Russia to step in. *Kommersant* (25 November 2000) claimed that Russia
"saved" the Middle East from war. See also *Nezavisimaia gazeta* (30 November 2000) for an interview v
Vasilii Sredin, deputy foreign minister and presidential envoy to the Middle East.

128. See, for example, Vasilii Safronchuk, "I. Ivanov opiat' zanialsia Blizhnim Vostokom" [I. Iva
Again Is Devoted to the Near East], *Sovetskaia Rossiia* (14 November 2000)l Gennadii Zyuganov, "Ro
i Palestina" [Russia and Palestine], *ibid.*

129. For a full analysis of the Blair visit, see Maikl Bin'on [Michael Binyon], "Zachem Toni Bleru ru
aktsent" [Why Does Tony Blair Need a Russian Focus], *Obshchaia gazeta*, No. 47 (23–29 November 20

November, for example, Igor Ivanov urged the EU to play a stronger role in ensuring strategic stability in the world, and offered "constructive cooperation" in such matters. In his opinion, recent developments had set Russia–EU relations on a path towards "strategic partnership."[130] Projections such as these were matters for the relatively distant future and undoubtedly would be rethought no matter which new administration finally settled into the White House in Washington.

It appeared, in fact, that Ivanov had a few issues to work out himself. At the OSCE summit in Vienna, 27–28 November, the third and final stop in his seven-day trip through Europe with stops in Warsaw and Berlin, Ivanov obstinately rejected absolute timetables for the long-promised OSCE mission to Chechnya and Russian troop reductions in Georgia and Moldova. Because the OSCE requires consensus for any resolution to be adopted, there were no joint declarations on these matters. In light of assurances given by Moscow to the Istanbul OSCE meeting in 1999, the apparent change of heart flew in the face of the recent good turn in Russia–Europe relations. Moreover, they ran counter to the long-standing Russian advocacy of the OSCE as the core of a new, non-NATO-based security system for Europe.[131] Because of its demands related to Chechnya, the OSCE was now labelled interventionist by Moscow. To be sure, Ivanov said that the troop reductions would take place anyway, but he would not be dictated to by the OSCE—especially on Chechnya. The foreign minister was especially bitter about what he called Western "double standards" on the Chechen issue, a posture the Russian delegation tried to illustrate by asking, to no avail, that discussion of German neo-Nazis, and Basque and Irish "terrorists" be placed on the agenda.

In fact, Russia's behavior at the OSCE summit reflected its anxiety about intensified challenges to security in the North Caucasus and Central Asia. Just prior to the Vienna meeting Defense Minister Sergeev claimed that "religious extremism, separatism and international terrorism," with a well organized and heavily financed center in Afghanistan, now represented a powerful army—rather than individual terrorists—and must be taken more seriously. In response to these perceived threats, Moscow ordered the creation of rapid reaction forces of its own, one unit for the North Caucasus Military District, the other for the Volga–Urals Military District. Alleged NATO "plans" to increase its influence in Georgia and Azerbaijan were among the other official reasons given by the MoD for the creation of this force.[132] The connection between Russia's decisions at the OSCE conference, the new corps deployments, and allegations about NATO remained unstated, but not hard to discern. Indeed, one needed only to have examined the Foreign Policy Concept of July to see this coming.

130. As quoted in an AP report from Berlin, where Ivanov was still in the midst of his European tour. Ivanov repeated the offer to cooperate with the EU's RRF to Germany's Foreign Minister Fischer the next day.

131. See the *Novye izvestiia* (28 November 2000), for the opinion that the OSCE was now interfering in the domestic affairs of Russia, contributing to new divisions in Europe.

132. See Interfax (22 and 23 November 2000) for the actual comments from Sergeev and the announcements about the crisis management force. Drug trafficking was another task set for the new units, which were expected to include some 50,000 men by 2003. On Sergeev's posture, see "Chto takoe Amerika, eto chto . . . TsK?"[What Is America, . . . Is it the Central Committee?], *Rossiiskaia gazeta* (25 November 2000).

Putin's firmness in international affairs was abetted by the extraordinary m
made of the U.S. presidential election count in Florida, a political crisis that c
ried well into December, leaving the U.S. government rigidly focused on inter
matters. Analysts on both sides of the ocean believed that Russia was taking
vantage of this unusually long lame duck period to strengthen its hand for the
evitable next wave of negotiations with Washington. Renewed standing as a M
dle East peace cosponsor, and a prepared military player in the Caucasus a
Central Asia, an upgraded economic-energy association with the EU, and a "g
and oil" partnership with China and India, all were solidified in that period. 1
sentencing on 7 December of U.S. businessman Edmond Pope to twenty years
espionage both enraged American officials and gave the Russians yet another c
to play in the future.[133] His pardon a few days later was, presumably, played fc
future IOU.

THE NATO QUESTION NEVER FAR FROM THE SURFACE

The EU summit in Paris had marked a turning point, of sorts, in Russian anal'
of its relationship to Europe's integrating agencies, NATO and the EU. Increasin
debate among Russians about their future in a common European home feature
diminishing relevance of NATO and the growing significance of the EU in Eu
pean political, economic, and even security matters. NATO enlargement was s
characterized as a relic of Cold War attitudes sure to harden dividing lines in 1
rope. EU enlargement, on the other hand, if it coincided with the liberalizatior
trade and economic contacts with Russia, could lead to a mutually beneficial bre
through in Russia–West relations and elimination of Cold War hangovers
Though this opinion may well have been a classic "wishful thinking" phenomen
it nevertheless represented a sea change in the Kremlin's approach to Europe and
United States.

Moscow's opinion made little difference to NATO, whose Parliamentary Asse
bly adopted a "Resolution on NATO Enlargement" when it met in Berlin on 21 1
vember. The resolution emphasized the "positive impact" of NATO's last round
admissions and urged Assembly members "to continue keeping Russia, . . . activ
engaged in the creation of a stable Euro-Atlantic security network via, among ot
things, the NATO–Russia Founding Act." From the Russian perspective, this con
iatory note was contradicted by the resolution's conclusion, which called on the
sembly to issue invitations, no later than during NATO's 2002 summit, to any st

---

133. Pope had been detained for some months for purchasing designs, said by the Russians to be
cret, of a high-speed torpedo. His lawyers claimed that Pope was researching civilian commercial use:
the torpedo technology and that the purchase was made openly.

134. See, for example, Anatolii Adamishin, "Naskol'ko bezopasna nyneshniaia Evropa? Sl
radikal'nykh zhagov dlia Rossii i Zapada" [How Secure Is Europe Now? Six Radical Steps for Russia
the West], *Nezavisimaia gazeta* (2 November 2000). Adamishin is a former deputy foreign minister.

meeting the criteria for NATO membership as laid out in 1995.[135] During the second week of December Sergeev was in Brussels for conversations with NATO defense ministers. He arrived at the JPC meeting armed with a list of areas in which Russia and NATO could cooperate, met bilaterally with William Cohen, and offered some ameliorating conditions related to Russian arms sales to Iran. Some sources suggest that Sergeev's motive may have been a time-honored attempt to divide NATO by appealing mostly to its major European members while Washington's presidential campaign results remained in doubt.[136] Putin's summertime proposal of a European–NATO–Russia nonstrategic defense system for Europe remained open for discussion, and Cohen's public concern about the EU's RRF played into Moscow's hands. Sergeev held firm on some issues, driving home again Russia's opposition to NATO's promised "second wave" of members. The Baltic States and southeastern Europe were singled out. He repeated as well the refrain that if the USA withdrew from the ABM treaty, there would be a new arms race.[137]

Sergeev's posturing proved to be in vain. Soon after his foray into NATO's center the EU's long-anticipated "reform" summit in Nice made short shrift of any idea of an independent and strong European army. Even Russia's friends, Germany and Britain, made it plain that the RRF would rely mainly on NATO. The wide distribution in December of a U.S. defense department report, "Strengthening Transatlantic Security," also dampened Moscow's optimism about major changes of direction in Europe. The report emphasized that the United States had no intention of leaving Europe and urged the further enlargement of NATO. Washington's support of NATO and the PfP, whose role the report enhanced, as facilitators for the rebuilding of economic and security mechanisms in southeastern Europe (Balkans) was highlighted. The onus was left directly on Russia to make the right decisions in the complex Washington–NATO–Moscow relationship. Insofar as Baltic admission to NATO was concerned, the U.S. Defense Department had not backed off from its earlier position of support. Referring directly to Russian objections to Baltic inclusion, the report emphasized that: "no non-NATO country will have a veto over Alliance decisions."[138]

---

135. NATO Parliamentary Assembly, Committee Resolution 301, "Resolution on NATO Enlargement," Berlin (21 November 2000). NATO website. In an interview published in a Russian newspaper, NATO Deputy General Secretary Klaus-Peter Klaiber told Russians that expansion would help guarantee Russian security, but that membership for Russia itself was only a theoretical question: Yevgenii Grigor'ev, "Rossiia mozhet stat' chlenom NATO tol'ko teoreticheski i tol'ko cherez mnogie desiatiletiia" [Russia Can Be a Member of NATO Only Theoretically, and Only after Many Decades], *Dipkur'er NG*, NO. 18 (23 November 2000).

136. See, "Russia–NATO Relations Improving?" Jamestown Foundation Monitoring (7 December 2000); and Igor' Korotchenko, "Rossiia i NATO vozobnovliaiut polnomasshtabnoe partnerstvo" [Russia and NATO Resume Full-Scale Partnership], *Nezavisimaia gazeta* (7 December 2000).

137. See, for example, *Krasnaia zvezda* (7 December 2000); Dmitrii Satonov, "Marshal [Sergeev] rasseivaet tuman" [Marshal Sergeev Dissipates the Fog], *Izvestiia* (6 December 2000); Igor Korotchenko, "Rossiia i NATO vozobnovliaiut polnomasshtabnoe partnerstvo" [Russia and NATO Re-establish Full-Scale Partnership], *Nezavisimaia gazeta* (7 December 2000).

138. U.S. Department of Defense, *Strengthening Transatlantic Security. A U.S. Strategy for the 21st Century* (December 2000), 39.

President Putin's last two overseas visits for the year 2000 were to America's nei
bors, Cuba and Canada. In Cuba, Putin and Castro condemned the continuing L
quarantine of the island. Putin acknowledged that Russia should not have turned
back on Cuba in the early nineties, and promised greatly expanded trade. The NN
was harshly criticized and vague commitments were made to the effect that work
the nuclear energy plant started by the USSR in the early 1980s and closed in 1S
might begin again. In the end, however, the plant was abandoned by mutual c
sent. There was much media excitement in both countries about renewed links
tween Moscow and Havana, but not much substance followed. Putin wanted to <
cuss Cuba's debt to Russia, judged in Moscow to be about $20 billion; Castro
not want to acknowledge, at least publicly, that the debt existed.[139]

Putin flew directly to Ottawa from Havana, and Russian commentators emp
sized that Canada always had refused to participate in the American embargo of Cu
Promises of expanded Russian–Canadian trade were made in this case as well, w
about the same results as the Cuba visit.[140] More important for public relations p
poses was Prime Minister Jean Chrétien's endorsement of the ABM as a "cornerst<
of strategic stability" and a less direct rejection of the U.S. NMD project. Comin
the very moment that President George W. Bush expressed enthusiasm for the NN
and Secretary of State designate Gen. Colin Powell privately voiced doubts about
feasibility,[141] the Canadian position added to the impressive list Putin had compi
of countries "supporting" the Russian position in this matter.[142]

On the other hand, Chrétien balked at Putin's suggestion that his governm
serve as a mediator between Moscow and Washington on the ABM and NMD
sues. He reminded Putin that Canada was, after all, a long-time ally of the Uni
States, and he agreed to endorse Russia's WTO bid. Just as Putin was settling b
down in Moscow, the major EU countries, led by France, also spoke out against
NMD. The summit in Canada left the United States as the only G-8 country
which Putin had not paid a state visit since becoming president.[143] As it happen

---

139. Dmitrii Gornostaev, "Putin i Kastro sovmestno pokritikovali SshA" [Putin and Castro Joi
Criticized the USA], *Nezavisimaia gazeta* (16 December 2000); Gornostaev, "A pri chem zdes' Ssl
[What Is the USA Doing Here?], *Dipkur'er NG,* No. 19 (7 December 2000).

140. See, for example, Boris Yunanov, "Neutrachennye illiuzii" [Rediscovered Illusions], *Obshc<
gazeta,* No. 50 (13–20 December 2000).

141. Russian commentators regarded Powell as a "hardliner" in relation to Russia, see, for exam
Mikhail Khodarenok, "Simptomy smeny kursa" [Symptoms of a Change in Course], *NVO,* No.
(22–28 December 2000).

142. Canadian ambassador to Moscow, Rodney Irwin, wrote in the Russian press that Canada rega<
the Ottawa summit as a major event, praising the direction of Putin's reforms, while noting that m
still had to be done on Moscow's new government structure, military reforms, the state debt, and Ch<
nya. See Rodni Irvin [Irwin], "Kanada privetstvuet Putina. Nashi strany ob'ediniaet ne tol'ko liubo
khokkeiu" " [Canada Welcomes Putin. Our Countries have More in Common than Hockey], *Neza
maia gazeta* (16 December 2000).

143. For a Russian commentary, in which Canada's opposition to the NMD was highlighted n
strongly than was warranted, see "PRO, klen i 'Topol' "[Missile Defense, Maple Leaf and Topol'], *i
iiskaia gazeta* (20 December 2000). Topol' refers to a Russian missile and is the word for poplar tree.

among mainstream Russian analysts only communists claimed to be truly threatened by a Bush presidency.[144]

On 25 December, Putin summed up his own first year during a long interview with television and press journalists. His main point in the international affairs sphere was that Russia must find some middle way between the "imperial ambitions" of the Soviet era and the need to "understand clearly our own national interests, . . . to formulate them clearly and to fight for them."[145]

Russia's leading foreign policy experts agreed with their president. Early in December Sergei Rogov raised the issue of Russia's place in the world and urged Moscow to take advantage of its "unique role" as the geographic link between Europe and Asia. Blaming Yeltsin and Kozyrev for expending all Moscow's energies on military-political questions related to NATO expansion, ignoring regional economic problems, and isolating Russia from Europe, he exhorted the Kremlin to adopt a wiser Eurasian policy and to demand a Russian presence at all transcontinental negotiations.[146]

At a year's-end roundtable organized by the editorial board of *Mezhdunarodnaia zhizn,* journal of the ministry of foreign affairs, most participants argued that Russia still had not broken fully away from Soviet foreign-policy habits. They looked to the future and saw the dilemma of Russia's place in the world in economic terms: globalization and regional integration. They were much less worried about threats from the West, though NATO expansion was regarded as a real irritant, than they were about internal deterioration. If any external danger existed it would come from the South and the Far East. The "phantom of superpower" status was criticized, but seen as a natural consequence of Russia's transitional nature. For different reasons, the experts found Putin's overall approach competent and refreshing in comparison with the Yeltsin years.[147]

---

144. See, for example, Leonid Nikolaev, "Bush i Rossiia" [Bush and Russia], *Sovetskaia Rossiia* (19 December 2000); Svetlana Chervonnaia, "Vashington meniaet vneshnepoliticheskuiu doktrinu. Gossekretar' Busha Kolin Pauell i sovetnik po natsional'noi bezopasnosti Kondoliza Rais—simvoly 'respublikanskogo videniia mira'," [Washington Changes Foreign Policy Doctrine. Bush's State Secretary Colin Powell and National Security Adviser Condoleeza Rice are Symbols of the "Republican World View"], *Nezavisimaia gazeta* (19 December 2000).

145. "Vladimir Putin: pozitivnye tendentsiii est', no poka eto tol'ko tendentsii" [Vladimir Putin: There Are Positive Tendencies, But They Are Only Tendencies], *Nezavisimaia gazeta* (26 December 2000); also in *NVO,* No. 49 (29 December 2000–11 January 2001).

146. Rogov, "Rossiia mezhdu Evropoi i Aziei: poisk strategii" [Russia between Europe and Asia: The Search for a Strategy], *Dipkur'er NG,* No. 19 (7 December 2000). This essay covered two full pages in the bi-monthly newspaper insert.

147. See Dmitrii Gornostaev, "Paradoks preemstvennosti. Ob itogakh goda Putina vo vneshnei politike. 'Kazhetsia, za god osobykh oshibok vo vneshnei politike my ne nadelali' " [A Continuing Paradox. About the Results of Putin's First Year in Foreign Policy. "It Seems that It Was a Year in Which Serious Mistakes in Foreign Policy Were Not Made"], *Dipkur'er NG,* No. 20 (28 December 2000); and *Mezhdunarodnaia zhizn,* RIA Novosti translation, CDI Russia Weekly, No. 135 (4 January 2001). Participating in the round table were: Anatolii Adamishin, vice-president of System joint-stock corporation and former minister for the CIS; Yurii Kapralov, director of the foreign ministry's security and disarmament department; Valerii Nikolaenko, secretary general of the CIS Collective Security Council; Viacheslav Nikonov, president of Politika Foundation; Anatolii Torkunov, rector of the Institute of Internal Affairs of the ministry of foreign affairs.

Putin himself must have been especially satisfied with the way in which his ov
tures to Europe had produced results. Successful tours to Britain, Italy, Germa
France, Spain, Austria and Sweden all raised Russia's profile well beyond what Yel
had achieved. Buffeted by the problems of Chechnya and slow economic recov
Putin was nevertheless a key presence in European security considerations, and
forged new links with the EU. NATO enlargement remained, festering in the ba
ground, even as relations with the Alliance were provisionally restored. In this n
ter, above all, much would depend on the approach taken to Russia by the new B
administration—and the early signs were not encouraging.

4

‡

Negotiating from Strength, 2001

Although both the Russian and foreign media made much of Putin's accomplishments during his first year as head of the Russian state, no one suggested that international tensions had been greatly eased. In fact, international dividing lines still were drawn quite clearly in the sand. Russia and China were both anxious to keep or regain status as major powers in the international arena and to keep the United States out of their traditional spheres of influence. Russia was not doing very well in this regard, as its helplessness during the Yugoslav crisis and NATO expansion illustrated clearly enough. Putin's ambition for 2001 had to be a "Plan B," that is, find an alternative to absolute predominance of Americans—or join them. The hiatus in American politics caused by an awkward changeover in presidential administrations, and the cold warrior verbosity of Republicans on the campaign trail, left Putin with few choices as to where to direct his foreign affairs energy. With the limited exception of Russia's neighbors in Central Asia and the fruitless association with "rogue" states and China, the only practical direction to go was towards Europe and the EU.

Even Putin's critics acknowledged that Russia's standing in the world was now higher than it had been during Yeltsin's last few years in office. And the government continued to invest in patriotism, issuing a decree providing 178 million rubles' support for the "Patriotic Education of Citizens of the Russian Federation." In contrast to earlier programs, which called for school curriculum changes, the new bill allocated funds for museums, research, sports, conferences, and even for patriotic "propaganda" in the mass media.[1]

---

1. See Decree of the Russian Government, "Gosudarstvennaia programma, 'Patrioticheskoe vospitanie grazhdan Rossiiskoi Federatsii na 2001–2005 godu" [State Program, "Patriotic Education of Citizens of the Russian Federation for 2001–2005"], *Rossiiskaia gazeta* (12 March 2001).

The Russian economy had not improved much, but even that was enough the y 2000 was called Russia's best since the collapse of the USSR. This was a key part the new image, though skeptics cautioned that progress depended too heavily high world oil prices. Foreign investment was up, the political arena had stabiliz and the state system was more centralized than it had been for some time. Yet e Putin admitted in December that "a huge number of our citizens endure extre hardship and live in poverty."[2] Capital flight was still a serious problem, crime a corruption ran rampant, and the government's failure to invest in infrastruct (electrical power grid, roads, pipelines, bridges, railways, etc.) was recognized as d gerous by Russian planners. Nevertheless, the president was still popular and trust

In foreign policy, the new year began with an almost giddy crisscrossing of fore statesmen in Moscow. On 17 January, French defense minister, Alain Richard, c cluded meetings with Igor Sergeev with assurances that his country and Russia h views on international affairs that "largely coincide." They claimed to have agreed long-term military production cooperation and on questions of global strategic curity (ITAR-TASS, 17 Jan). Just after Richard was leaving, Japan's foreign minis Yohei Kono, arrived to discuss an agenda for a summit between the Russian a Japanese presidents, tentatively set for Irkutsk in February; Yugoslav foreign min ter, Goran Svilanovic came to Moscow that same day, shortly after Borislav Milc vic left town. A PACE delegation headed by British Labour M.P. Lord Judd pas through the Russian capital as well, on its way to checking out the human rights uation in Chechnya; and the Latvian foreign minister, Indulis Berzins, showed up a working visit in his capacity as chair of the Council of Europe's committee of m isters. They didn't all get to see the president, but the negotiation frenzy was clea part of Russia and Europe's attempt to get their relationships in order before the r U.S. administration was fully in place.

BRACING OR EMBRACING THE NEW U.S. ADMINISTRATIOI

Russia had normalized relations with the EU generally during 2000 and especi: with Germany and Britain, and also had built up close relations with China and dia. Russian–American relations were, on the other hand, left in limbo while R sians awaited clarification of a Bush policy towards Moscow. Washington a Moscow picked away at each other. Stories in the American media accused Russi: deploying nuclear missiles in Kaliningrad and the Russian foreign ministry char; Washington with START-II violations.[3] The question of Russian arms sales to I

---

2. "Vladimir Putin: Pozitivnye tendentsii est', no poka eto tol'ko tendentsii" [Vladimir Putin: There Positive Tendencies, but They Are No More than Tendencies," *Nezavisimaia gazeta* (26 December 200

3. For the immediate Russian reaction to the Kaliningrad tale, see Interfax (4 January 2001). For a tailed refutation and counter-accusation, see Viktor Litovkin, "Bliudo dlia povtornogo razogreva. ˊ ticheskoe yadernoe oruzhie kak 'vechnyi dvigatel'" spekuliatsii" [A Dish for Reheating. Tactical Nuc Arms as "Eternal Engine" of Trading], *Obshchaia gazeta*, No. 3 (18–24 January 2001).

angered U.S. congressmen, and Russian officials still rejected any amendment to the ABM or the notion of an NMD for the United States.

In the first few weeks of the year, it seemed that both Russians and Americans were staking out territory. In the United States, chairman of the Senate Committee on Foreign Relations and old Cold Warrior Jesse Helms kicked sand in the Russian face, telling the American Enterprise Institute on 11 January that Russia must not be allowed to have a "sphere of influence in what [it] ominously calls the 'near abroad.'" He came out firmly in support of further NATO expansion to the east, referring specifically to the Baltic States.[4] The Helms message flew in the face of an earlier report from the Carnegie Endowment for International Peace, which called for a "renewal" of U.S.–Russia relations on the basis of pragmatic, rather than emotional, considerations. Compromise on arms reductions and the NMD were the Endowment's main recommendation. Most importantly, from Moscow's perspective, the authors of "An Agenda for Renewal" strongly recommended "NATO should not consider expansion of membership to states on the territory of the former Soviet Union before 2005." Instead, NATO should "take Putin at his word" and strive to make the PfP and the PJC work effectively; moreover, the alliance should make it clear that eventually Russia itself would be welcomed into NATO.[5] The question of NATO's projected "second wave" was still haunting East–West relations.

A few days after the Helms diatribe, U.S. authorities arrested Pavel Borodin, one of Putin's former mentors and state secretary for the Russia–Belarus Union, on the basis of an international warrant from Switzerland. He was charged with money laundering. Neither the Russian press nor Russian politicians seemed much interested in the merits of the case. Choosing to regard it solely as a political matter, Foreign Minister Ivanov called in the U.S. ambassador and demanded Borodin's immediate release. Putin also openly defended him, as did the State Duma. They all pointed to Borodin's diplomatic status and treated the arrest as an "anti-Russian" act.[6] In the midst of all this fuss, an interview with Genrikh Trofimenko, long-time Soviet expert on American–Russian relations, revealed that the old notions lay very close to the surface in some Moscow circles. Referring mostly to the Clinton era, Trofimenko told his interlocutor that "America is now suffering from moral lawlessness and absolute permissiveness," and that Washington is trying to "subordinate all independent countries to U.S. diktat." In fact, he expected more "decency" from the

---

4. Jesse Helms, "Towards a Compassionate Conservative Foreign Policy," American Enterprise Institute (11 January 2001).

5. Carnegie Endowment for International Peace, Russia and Eurasia Program, *An Agenda for Renewal. U.S.–Russian Relations* (Washington, 2000), pp. 20–21. Contributors to this report were: Anders Aslund, Thomas Carothers, Thomas Graham, Stephen Holmes, Andrew Kuchins, Anatol Lieven, Michael Mc-Faul, Martha Brill Olcott, and Jon Wolfsthal.

6. See, for example, Natalya Kozlova, "Okhota na Borodina nachalas' v Amerike"[The Hunt for Borodin Began in the United States], *Rossiiskaia gazeta* (19 January 2001). For more, Lidiia Andrusenko, "Borodin ostaetsia v Amerikanskoi tiur'me" [Borodin Remains in an American Prison], *Nezavisimaia gazeta* (20 January 2001), and Nikolai Paklin, "Borodin gotov ekhat' v Shveitsariiu—no ne v naruchnikakh" [Borodin Is Ready to Go to Switzerland, but Not in Handcuffs], *Rossiiskaia gazeta* (23 January 2001).

new Republican administration and called for a pragmatic discussion of world aff
with Powell and others.[7] A similar stance was taken by Aleksei Podberezkin, heac
the *Dukhovnoe nasledie* (Spiritual Heritage) movement, who foresaw a return to "pı
matism and realism" on both sides, as opposed to the "imaginary principles," or '
manticism" with which he characterized Clinton's approach to Russia. Post facto R
sian analysis of the Clinton team's approach to the Kremlin tended to expose 1
distrust, especially of Albright and Talbott.[8] Vladimir Lapskii also saw pragmatism
placing romanticism in Russia–U.S. relations, but gave Clinton full marks for try
to help while the Yeltsin government squandered most of their best opportunities
     The communists were far less hopeful, as was their wont,[10] and even Seı
Karaganov warned that Putin's "patch-up" practices and a tendency to return to f
mer Soviet policies, such as increased (and "not very useful") friendships with I
and Cuba, could make it hard for the Bush administration to find room for cc
promise with Russia. Among other things, Karaganov repeated his earlier warni
against reliance on the "absurd" notion of a multipolar world. Former Soviet pr
dent Gorbachev made his presence felt on this issue too. Blaming both sides fc
"noticeable deterioration" in Russian–American relations, Gorbachev urged the r
U.S. administration to acknowledge that a secure new world order could not
achieved without Russia's participation, and recognize that the world is necessa
diverse and need not be a model of America to succeed.[11]

BACK TO EUROPE

Of all the diplomatic activities in which the Kremlin was involved in early 2001,
most productive was a series of negotiations with Germany. These talks were moː
about Russia's huge Soviet-era debt to that country, more than $20 billion of the $
billion total Soviet debt. Just before the end of the year, Prime Minister Kasyaı
had talked with Chancellor Schröder in Berlin, discussing with him and German
nanciers the possibility of turning payment of the Russian debt to Germany into
vestment in the Russian economy.[12] Russian minister for economic developme

---

     7. Trofimenko, "Dialog s uchetom realii" [Dialogue Heeding Current Realities], *Krasnaia zvezda*
January 2001).
     8. Podberezkin, "Vashington i Moskva meniaiut orientiry" [Washington and Moscow Change Cou
Nezavisimaia gazeta (11 January 2001), and Nikolai Paklin, "Sorok tretii" [Forty-Three], *Rossiiskaia ga*
(20 January 2001), who quoted both Thomas Graham of the Carnegie Institute and Stephen Cohe
support his thesis that the Republicans were likely to be better partners than Clinton's team had been.
     9. *Rossiiskaia gazeta* (20 January 2001), and *Izvestiia* (20 January 2001).
     10. See, for example, Nikolaev, "Tuman rasseivaetsia" [The Fog Is Lifting], *Sovetskaia Rossiia* (16 Jɑ
ary 2001).
     11. See Vasilii Safronchuk, "Putin nachinaet dialog s buzhem-mladshim" [Putin Begins Dialogue ᴠ
Bush-the-Younger], *Sovetskaia Rossiia* (30 January 2001); M. S. Gorbachev , "Kak ya predstavliaiu ﹖
rol' Ameriki" [What I Think about the Role of the Americans], *Nezavisimaia gazeta* (10 January 20
and Karaganov in *Sogodnya* (20 January 2001).
     12. "Vladimir Putin: Pozitivnye tendentsii est', no poka éto tol'ko tendentsii" [Vladimir Putin. There
Positive Tendencies, but They Are No More than Tendencies], *Nezavisimaia gazeta* (26 December 200(

German Gref, carried out even more detailed negotiations with his German counterpart, Werner Muller. Although the problem of the debt was not fully resolved, for no rescheduling was agreed upon, there was a consensus that more German investment would be forthcoming, especially in the energy and agricultural sectors.

A week later Schröder was Putin's first European visitor in 2001, and the debt again was a central point for consideration, along with the American NMD. By that time, Russia had announced that it would not be able to pay its $1.5 million installment to the Paris Club nations for the first quarter, evoking a quick negative response from Berlin. Putin attempted to ameliorate the situation by promising to reexamine the question of returning works of art looted in Germany by the USSR in 1945 back to Germany. The Russians promised Schröder that the debt would be paid, however, and the chancellor left Moscow satisfied, apparently.

Foreign Minister Ivanov carried the Russian campaign for accommodation to Rome, where he told his counterpart, Lamberto Dini, that Russia would accept "considerable new limits to strategic offensive weapons" if the USA would reconsider the NMD. He appeared to have Dini's support, as well as that of the EU's Solana, with whom Ivanov also met (Interfax, 15 Jan). Like other Russian spokesmen, Ivanov yet again made it clear that Russia could not accept further NATO expansion eastward or any unilateral amendment to the ABM Treaty (ITAR-TASS, 15 January). The still unscheduled EU enlargement was quite acceptable to Ivanov, as long as it did not adversely affect Russia's economic relations with new EU members.

It was obvious that Russia preferred integration with Western Europe to a deeper commitment to China and/or further concessions to the United States, both usually in return for nothing. Germany was its best bet for large amounts of direct foreign investment, which, of course, China could not offer. Germany needed Russia's energy resources; Russia needed Germany's support in the EU and in geopolitical considerations. Both countries needed a resolution of the debt question. To make the hoped-for partnership more palatable, the Kremlin wanted also to change its image in the Caucasus, both at home (Chechnya) and abroad in Azerbaijan and Georgia.

BACK TO THE CAUCASUS

The fact that Putin's own first visit abroad in 2001 was to Baku was taken in Russia as a sign that the promised new direction in Russia's international affairs finally was taking shape. Few of the problems in either the Caucausus or Central Asia had been settled in 2000. The question here was not so much radical change, but a clear adherence to a pragmatic approach to foreign policy. In this regard analysts, even communists, were encouraged.[13] The propitious visit to Azerbaijan (see chapter 8) signaled

---

13. See, for example Dmitrii Gornostaev, "Posle simvoliki. O novykh marshrutakh rossiiskoi diplomatii" [After the Symbolics. New Directions in Russian Diplomacy], *Dipkurier NG,* No. 1 (18 January 2000); Vasilii Safronchuk, "Kavkazskii gambit Putina" [Putin's Caucasus Gambit], *Sovetskaia Rossiia* (16 January 2001).

that Moscow hoped to establish a better-balanced position in the South Caucas
where for some time it had relied almost exclusively on Armenian friendship, ¿
was moving towards confrontation with Georgia.[14]

A changed image in the Caucasus meant a return to the PACE dilemma. ']
PACE delegation to Moscow and then to Chechnya continued to doubt Rus:
commitment to human rights in the rebellious region, and even conducted heari
on the freedom of press in Russia. The Kremlin made an effort to appease PACE
connection with Chechnya, hoping that its lost voting rights in that body would
restored (Interfax, 22 January). In this endeavor Russia was successful. On 25 Ja
ary, the forty-three-nation Council voted (88–20, with 11 abstentions) to reinst
Russia's voting rights. Though PACE had little real influence in the affairs of Eu
pean countries, its decision was symbolically important to Moscow.[15]

AND THEN THERE WAS NATO

In the January rush of speculation about Bush's new administrative team the qu
tion of NATO expansion eastward still predominated. Towards the end of the mo
Defense Minister Sergeev updated the Russian government's position on this m
ter.[16] He was frank in saying that Russia and NATO needed a dialogue and tha
would be counterproductive not to come to terms with the Alliance. His appro:
was of the backdoor variety. He insisted that NATO's European members were
coming more active in NATO and were at the same time more appreciative than
United States of the role Russia should have in guaranteeing world security. The o
barrier to cooperation was mutual distrust, for which he added plaintively, "Russi
not to blame." The problem lay with NATO's disinterest in Russia's concern ab
expansion eastward. Sergeev concluded with a familiar mantra: the ABM must
be amended; the United States must not proceed with the NMD; and NATO
pansion eastward is a "bad political mistake."

No one doubted that Sergeev was speaking for his president, who made many of
same points in a well-publicized speech to diplomats on 26 January. The deploym
of an NMD by the United States will wreak "irreparable damage" on the current
chitecture of international relations and NATO's further expansion eastward was
solutely "unacceptable" to Russia, Putin asserted. He added that Moscow's upgrac
ties with China and India, greater integration of regional structures in Eurasia, and

14. Alan Kasaev, "Rossiia formiruet novuiu zakavkazskuiu politiku" [Russia Forms New Caucasus I
cies], *Nezavisimaia gazeta* (11 January 2001).

15. Ironically, not all Russians were pleased by the PACE decision. Russian human rights advo
Sergei Kovalev, for example, told Echo Radio listeners (26 January 2001) that the Europeans had been
ceived by Russia and that atrocities were continuing, though not so openly.

16. *Parlamentskaia gazeta* (23 January 2001). The interview was conducted by Oleg Falichev; and /
tolii Shapovalov, "Kadry Busha—delo ottsovskoe" [Bush's Personnel, a Matter Carried Out by his Fatl
Rossiiskaia gazeta (5 January 2001). He believed that, as a military man, Colin Powell would be m
more cautious about "admitting Romania and Bulgaria, not to mention the Baltic countries."

newed links with North Korea and Iran, were all part of Russia's normal balancing of its Eastern and Western outreach. Reminding his audience that Russia had taken unilateral nuclear disarmament measures in 2000 by ratifying START-II and the CTBT, he called for "reciprocal steps" from the new administration in Washington.[17]

A "constructive" telephone conversation between Putin and Bush on 31 January was unable to prevent existing dividing lines between their two countries from being drawn even more sharply in early February. At that time Donald H. Rumsfeld, on his first overseas venture since taking up his duties as the new U.S. secretary of defense, informed Russia and his country's European allies (at a European security conference in Munich), that the United States would move forward with the NMD project. These were Colin Powell's words as well. Rumsfeld expressed some concern about the European RRF, suggesting that its development might destabilize NATO. In light of the fact that this was Rumsfeld's second stint as defense secretary, having served in that capacity under President Gerald Ford, 1975–1977, many Russian commentators worried that he might be retaining too much baggage from the Cold War era.[18] They, and some Western analysts, began to use the term "unilateralism" in their predictions about the approach that the Bush administration might take under Powell, Rice, and Rumsfeld. Even in the best-case scenario, "unilateralism" meant that Washington would do whatever it wanted in international affairs and assume that their allies would be drawn in its wake, even if reluctantly. In the worst case, the notion implied that American power was such that it need not be subject to the same rules of behavior it demanded of other nations. Wary of this possibility, by February 2001, Russian observers were more attentive to trends in Washington than they had been for some time. Among other things, they were faced with the reality that, in contrast to the pretence of the Clinton government, Bush's new team made no attempt to consider Russia its equal in world affairs.

Moscow's concerns were heightened somewhat when it was reported that Solana had taken a different approach to the Powell–Rumsfeld stance on the NMD than he had to Ivanov's earlier complaints about it. Solana now acknowledged that the United States had the right to deploy such a system and noted that the ABM was a matter between the United States and Russia, "not a Bible" for European states. A wellspring of distrust of Solana, built up in Russia while he served as secretary-general of NATO but diminished after he had become spokesman for the EU, resurfaced.[19]

---

17. APP summary (Moscow, 26 January 2001), JRL, No. 5042. See also Sergei Merinov, "Pezidentskaia Roll Call" [Presidential Exchange] *Rossiiskaia gazeta* (30 January 2001), on the differences between the Putin and Bush views on strategic arms reductions.

18. The Russian communist press accused Washington of being in a "frenzy" of Cold War thinking; see Leonid Nikolaev, "Vashington v Yarosti" [Washington in a Frenzy], *Sovetskaia Rossiia* (8 February 2001). See also Aleksandr Sabov, "Geopolitika. V Miunkhene vse ostalis' pri svoem" [Geopolitics: Everyone Sticks to Their Guns in Munich], *Rossiiskaia gazeta* (6 February 2001), where statements made at the Munich conference on world affairs by Rumsfeld, Sergei Ivanov, and others were analyzed. Rumsfeld's accession had already been looked upon with some concern; see Vladimir Malevannyi, "Pentagonovskii tiazheloves" [Pentagon Heavyweight], *NVO,* No. 2 (26 January–1 February 2001).

19. On this, see Aleksandr Karpukhin, "Chto na dushe u Khav'era Solany?" [What Is in Javier Solana's Soul?], *Nezavisimaia gazeta* (31 March 2001).

At the annual international economic conference in Davos, Switzerland, Russ
delegates were confronted with the looming question of NATO expansion. All th
Baltic presidents were present, openly lobbying for entry into both NATO and
EU, and gaining support from the Czech Republic, Hungary and Poland, with ot
northern countries (Denmark, Norway and Ireland) also acquiescing. Interestin
some Russian observers saw the new Bush administration in Washington, and po
bly Germany, as the Kremlin's only potential ally in keeping NATO from expand
further. Temporarily oblivious to their own long-standing opinion that NATO ·
the American spearhead in Europe, they now claimed that the United States did
want NATO watered down. It was asserted as well that Washington disliked
growing strength and autonomy of the EU.[20]

Whereas the NMD was then the most irksome issue between Moscow and Wa
ington,[21] the overarching Russian concern on the world stage continued to be
threat of international terrorism. An explosion in a Metro station in central Mosc
on 5 February was quickly blamed on terrorists by Moscow's Mayor Yurii Luzhk
even as the FSB and police said that it could also have been related to organi
crime. The Russian public immediately linked it to Chechen rebels, whom they
lieved to be supported by a wide-ranging international terrorist organization fun
by Osama bin Laden and associated with the Taliban in Afghanistan.[22] Paradoxic:
this latter belief also provided a good opportunity for Russian–American coop
tion, one that Moscow had been recommending for at least a year. In a detailed
sessment of global threats to the United States, CIA Director George Tenet told
U.S. Senate Intelligence Committee on 7 February that international terrori
above all Bin Laden and his "network," represented the "most immediate and seri·
threat." The Taliban was harshly criticized both for supporting Bin Laden and
participating in international drug trafficking, although there was little evidenc(
support the latter charge.

This approach did not mean that Putin's graphic warning to American reader:
the *New York Times* nearly a year-and-a-half earlier was now taken seriously. Inde
the moment was wasted, for Tenet went on to group Russia together with Bin La(
and China as global threats. A week later Rumsfeld compounded the insult by
cusing Russia of assisting "Iran, North Korea and India" with missile technolc
helping them threaten "the United States, Western Europe and countries in the M
dle East." Russian officials reacted furiously, accusing Rumsfeld of Cold War rh(
ric and of kowtowing to American defense contractors who would profit greatly fr

20. See, for example Dmitrii Gornostaev, "Opiat' problemy s NATO. Ekspansiia al'iansa plius sozd
sistem PRO?" [Problems with NATO Again. NATO Expansion Plus the ABM Systems?], *Dipkurier* .
No. 2 (1 February 2001).

21. On this, see for example, an interview with Andrei Kokoshin, former head of the RF Secu
Council, "My vstupili vo 'vtoroi yadernyi vek'" [We Have Entered a "Second Nuclear Age"], *Dipku
NG*, No. 2 (1 February 2001).

22. Reports said that 15 people were injured in the explosion on the Belorusskaia station platforr
of whom had to be hospitalized.

the NMD.[23] The tension was exacerbated on 16 February when American and British fighter planes conducted air strikes against five Iraqi radar stations outside the "no fly" zone, the first such raid since December 1998.

Nevertheless, there were flashes of optimism in Moscow. In several interviews conducted shortly after a visit to the United States, Sergei Rogov pointed out that the ascendancy of remnants from the elder George Bush's team was not necessarily a bad thing. The first Bush president had, in fact, spoken regularly of an international security system extending from Vancouver to Vladivostok, whereas it was Clinton who advocated NATO expansion eastward. Rogov was not particularly worried about Tenet's remarks either, noting that the CIA director had not called Russia an enemy. He was concerned, however, about what he called "very misleading" and negative western press reports about Russia and recommended that the Kremlin conduct a more skilled public relations campaign.[24] Few other specialists were as hopeful, especially in light of the raids on Iraq. Two columnists for a mainstream paper, for example, called the raid the natural "Bush reflex," that is, not knowing what to do "he will launch a rocket."[25]

PUTIN'S "ALTERNATIVE"

Shortly thereafter, Putin finally released details of the alternative security plans for Europe he had first vaguely offered in the spring of 2000. On 21 February, at the end of a three-day visit by Lord Robertson to Moscow, Russian officials revealed some particulars of its nonstrategic missile defense proposition on an all-Europe-based defense against short- and medium-range missiles. President Bush responded favorably, seeing this as a potential trade-off for his own NMD, whereas Moscow saw it as a counter to the U.S. initiative. A test of the two positions would come three days later when Foreign Minister Ivanov and Secretary of State Powell met in Cairo. This was the first direct contact between senior representatives of the two governments. In anticipation of this meeting, Dmitrii Gornostaev wrote that Russia must reaffirm its stand on the ABM so that the Bush administration would hold no illusions about Moscow's position. "Lately," he wrote, the American side "has become excessively harsh and arrogant," forcing Russia to respond firmly.[26] By that time, of

23. See Interfax (9 February 2001) for RF foreign ministry charges that Tenet was "hawkish" and "gloomy" and ITAR-TASS (15 February 2001) for comments that Rumsfeld was relying on Cold War rhetoric. See also Vasilii Safronchuk, "I. Ivanov raz'iasniaet pozitsiiu Rossii" [I. Ivanov Explains Russia's Position], *Sovetskaia Rossiia* (6 February 2001).

24. For these interviews, see Rogov, "Kuda poduet veter s Potomaka?" [Where Do the Winds from the Potomac Blow?], *Krasnaia zvezda* (14 February 2001) and *Segodnya* (17 February 2001).

25. Dmitrii Kosyrov, Marianna Belinkaia, "'Refleks Busha'" [The "Bush Reflex"], *Nezavisimaia gazeta* (20 February 2001). In a later commentary, Gennadii Gerasimov said that the NMD was unlikely to work and that it was doomed to go the way of Reagan's Star Wars at great cost both financially and diplomatically; see "Much To Do About Nothing," *New Times,* No. 10 (March 2001).

26. Gornostaev, "Opiat' Pro PRO. O lozhnoi interpretatsii—umyshlennoi i neumyshlennoi" [Again about the ABM: False Interpretations, Deliberate and Not]. *Dipkur'ier NG,* No. 4 (1 March 2001).

course, Moscow was well aware that Washington would go ahead with the NMD
matter what Moscow thought.[27] It remained to make the best of it.

On a broader front, Robertson's tour had generated a flood of official and perso
statements supporting further cooperation with NATO, simultaneously with f
opposition to NATO expansion eastward. To cite but a few examples: in Lond
Yobloko leader Yavlinskii circulated a memorandum to members of the Trilat∈
Commission denouncing NATO expansion (11 February); General Nikolaev, lea
of a Duma defense committee delegation to NATO HQ, accused NATO memt
of expanding so as to capture the Central European arms market (ITAR-TASS,
Feb); Putin told journalists in Vienna that Russia was strongly opposed to NATO
pansion (8 February); as did Sergeev in Belgrade and Bosnia-Herzegovina (Inter
7–8 February), Seleznev in Moscow (20 February), and so on.

Sergeev and his ministry's leading Cold Warrior, Ivashov, raised the pitch of a
NATO expansion rhetoric. Sergeev told members of a Norwegian parliamentary
egation that Russia would have to "adopt measures" if the Baltic States were adn
ted to NATO (Interfax, 8 and 19 February), and Ivashov accused the United Sta
of conducting an "information war" against Russia. In an ITAR-TASS (16 Februa
release, Ivashov declared that NATO's "further eastward enlargement was a threai
Russia's national security. 'Our stance is immutable on this and is clearly indica
in the Military Doctrine of Russia'." This was all very familiar, but confusing. 1
same individuals, and others also, fell over themselves demonstrating that Ru
wanted to cooperate with NATO, even to upgrade its participation in the PfP.

At the opening of NATO's first information office in Moscow, Robertson hin
that Russia might eventually join the Alliance. Russian analysts questioned his
cerity, in part because his remarks coincided with American and British bomb
raids on Iraq. The fact that the air attacks were not a NATO operation made li
difference.[28] In response to a direct question from a journalist in Moscow, Rob∈
son said that NATO did, indeed, plan to invite new members in 2002.[29] At any r
as the weeks passed officials in Moscow made it known that they were interestec
joining NATO if it became a strictly political body, and the Duma agreed to resu
relations with NATO's General Assembly.

The Cairo meeting on 25 February was anticlimactic: Ivanov and Powell agr
to be constructive on the Iraq question and that Saddam Hussein must not gain
cess to weapons of mass destruction. It was decided to speed up negotiations on a

---

27. See, for example, Eduard Lozanskii, "Novaia amerikanskaia mechta" [The New American Dre
Obshchaia gazeta No. 6 (8–14 February 2001).

28. Speaker of the Duma, Seleznev, a communist, openly doubted Robertson (Interfax, 20 Febru
2001). See also Vasilii Safronchuk, "NATO vse zhe budet rasshiriat'sia na Vostok" [NATO Will Exp
to the East Anyway], *Sovetskaia Rossiia* (27 February 2001). Unity house leader, Gryzlov, and Rog
both said that Russia should eventually join NATO (ITAR-TASS, 19, 20 February 2001).

29. "Ne konfrontatsiia, a dialog" [Dialogue, Not Confrontation], *Krasnaia zvezda* (20 February 20
See also an essay prepared by Robertson for the Russian press, "Chto khochet skazat' gensek NATO sv
vizitom v Rossiiu?" [What Does the NATO GenSec Wish to Say by Visiting Russia?], *Rossiiskaia ga*
(17 February 2001).

reduction.[30] These, to be sure, were "getting acquainted" talks and few specifics were expected from them. For a while, at least, much of the heat was taken out of the Russia–America relationship. Time would tell.

In Moscow, the NATO question was intricately connected with the problem of EU expansion. A delegation from the EU arrived in Moscow on 14 February and, among other things, discussed mutually beneficial projects in transportation, including the Trans-Siberian railway, gas pipelines from the Barents Sea through Murmansk and Karelia to Finland, Sweden and the EU, and the future of Kaliningrad. From the Russian perspective these discussions went very well and, indeed, provided hope that some understanding could be reached with the Baltic States and Poland by providing them access to Russia–EU undertakings. Putin already had been invited to Poland to discuss pipelines and further cooperative ventures (Interfax, 7 February). Igor Ivanov spoke to the EU about forming a "real partnership" and Anna Lindh, Sweden's foreign minister and head of the delegation, concurred, as did Javier Solana. By that time the EU's share of Russia's trade turnover approached 40 percent.

Putin's offer later in February to accept the NMD if it was widened to include the defense of Europe and Russia took Western leaders by surprise, though NATO's Robertson had provided some forewarning of Moscow's change of heart (see chapter 7). Russia itself worried about threats from the "south", a geopolitical term including even those countries to which it was selling weapons: Iran and Libya. For the Kremlin, Islamic "terrorism" was a consuming reality in the Caucasus and Central Asia. Putin agreed that Washington had reason to be concerned about "rogue" state behavior. The hint here was that in spite of everything said by Russia's general staff and ministry of defense officials NATO was not considered a threat by Putin's government; rather, it was Russia's only viable ally in the long run. In light of stern warnings against NATO expansion offered to German foreign minister Rudolph Scharping, who visited Moscow on 30 January, Sergeev's aggressive comments in Belgrade on 7 February, and continued railings from Manilov and Ivashov, it is obvious that there was a communications problem in Moscow.[31]

SERGEI IVANOV GOES TO WASHINGTON

It was hoped that some of the issues separating Moscow and Washington would be ameliorated when Sergei Ivanov traveled to the United States for meetings with Powell and Rice on 15 March. In Washington, Russian observers tended to put on a

---

30. The communist press was not impressed, seeing great risk in believing soothing words from Powell and Rice. See especially *Sovetskaia Rossiia* (1 March 2001).

31. Sergeev had said, "Russia will compare the consequences of NATO expansion with its own national interest." Interfax (30 January, 7 February 2001), and ITAR-TASS (2 February 2001). On 30 January, Sergei Ivanov told Scharping that Russia hailed the restoration of Russia–NATO relations, but said that further expansion was absolutely unacceptable; in February, Sergeev added that Russia planned to participate much more in the PfP in 2001, especially in projects close to the Russian border; and Manilov (2 February) insisted that any revision of the ABM would "emasculate" the treaty and cause Russia to retaliate.

brave face over the Republican takeover. They claimed to be looking forward to "chumminess" and a "healthy pragmatism" that would find Russia treated as par America's European interests, no longer subjected to a narrow "Russia policy" anc the mercy of "Russia advisers," such as Strobe Talbott.[32] Almost all the subjects ca ing tensions between them were raised in those brief meetings, but agreement reached on only two of them: the need to resist extremism jointly, and the need maintain dialogue. There was wide divergence on the matter of arms sales to Ira

The visit of the Iranian president to Moscow almost at the same time made conversation in Washington more sensitive than it might have been at another ti Putin and Foreign Minister Igor Ivanov had pronounced the sale of weapons and 1 ther cooperation with Iran an important phase in Russia's foreign policy. T openly resented America's objections, though they stopped short of adopting Iranian claim that the two countries were strategic partners (see chapter 12).[33] C specific result of the Washington meetings was that the Russian–American Cc mission headed previously by Premier Viktor Chernomyrdin and Vice President Gore, which had reached the secret and controversial agreement on Iran in 1990s, was abolished—to be replaced by an as-yet-unnamed intergovernment me anism for regular contact.

PUTIN'S POSITION OF STRENGTH

Putin's fearless stance in face of the apparent new American approach to world aff was in part a consequence of his successes at home. A communist-inspired vote nonconfidence in the Duma was turned back easily on 14 February, and opinion p showed that the president's popularity remained very high, with an approval ratin; well over 60 percent. On the other hand, other surveys showed that the United St; ranked number one among countries that the Russian population believed w threatening to Russia. The 34 percent of responders who named the United State Russia's chief potential enemy were a full 8 percent greater in number than in a si ilar poll taken in May 2000. China was a very distant second place at 5 percent. / other 34 percent said that Russia had no enemies.[34] These results represented a change in opinion over the previous year when, even in light of NATO's bombing tacks on Yugoslavia, the United States was regarded more favorably.

32. *Strana.ru* (15 March 2001); and *Kommersant* (14 March 2001), where Ivanov was urged to t carefully lest Russia "lose its last lever of influence on" the NMD and NATO. One writer was encoura seeing in the Bush administration a more pragmatic approach than Clinton's, Maksim Makarychev, " kakaia Moskva nuzhna Vashingtonu?" [So What Kind of Moscow Does Washington Need?], *Rossiis. gazeta* (15 March 2001). See also Andranik Migranyan, "Vneshniaia politika Rossii: ispytanie Iran [Russian Foreign Policy Tested by Iran], *Nezavisimaia gazeta* (15 March 2001), where the "coincidei of Ivanov's trip to Washington and the Iranian president's arrival in Moscow is pondered.

33. See, for example, Maksim Yusin, "Opasnaia sdelka" [Dangerous Transaction], *Izvestiia* (14 M. 2001), where Washington's objections were called "counter-productive."

34. On this poll, see Avtandil Tsuladze, "Odinokaia Rossiia. Vragov u nashei strany okazalos' bol'she, cl druzei" [Lonely Russia. It Seems That Russia Has More Enemies than Friends], *Segodnya* (15 March 20

"SPY MANIA"

A new espionage incident drove Russian public opinion about Americas down still further. The arrest in Washington of an FBI agent, Robert F. Hanssen, who was alleged and later convicted of spying for Russia and the USSR for fifteen years, raised the specter of a new Cold War in a different way. A few weeks later a young American, J. E. Tobbin, was detained in Russia on drug charges, though the press and officials made much of his apparent "intelligence" training and treated the affair as a "spy scandal."

A new period of "spy mania" quickly emerged.[35] Rumors that the United States had a surveillance tunnel under the RF embassy building in Washington were picked up by the Russian and American media and, though denied, had a surprisingly long life in 2001. A story broke in March (Moskovskii Komsomolets, 7 March) that a Russian intelligence officer had defected from the RF embassy in Ottawa, Canada, in December 2000. In late March, Powell ordered six Russian diplomats to leave the United States and declared four of them persona non grata for spying. Some forty others were asked to leave, the largest eviction since 1986. Moscow quickly retaliated in "tit-for-tat" expulsions of their own.[36] Name-calling quickly became the order of the day. A second round of Rumsfeld charges that Russia was a leading distributor of "weapons of mass destruction" (18 March) and the Kremlin's immediate response that he was still living in the Cold War era that the international community no longer accepted, was typical of the gutter diplomacy of the time. Scheduled meetings between American State Department officials and representatives of the Ichkerian (Chechen) "government"-in-exile on 26 March further soured the Russian–U.S. relationship. In the latter case, Russian spokesman Sergei Yastrzhembskii accused the U.S. State Department of "abetting terrorism," and head of the Duma's committee for international affairs, Dmitrii Rogozin, said that the United States should be added to the list of countries "who officially support terrorism."[37] The fact that these meetings coincided with a coordinated series of terrorist bombings in the North Caucasus, close to Chechnya's borders, in which twenty people were killed and over 100 injured, made the issue especially infuriating to Russians. Stories that Chechen

---

35. See, for example, Robert Shemak, "Administratsiia SShA predlagaet 'razmen' diplomatami [The U.S. Administration Suggests "Exchange" of Diplomats], *Rossiiskaia gazeta* (24 March 2001); and Vladimir Malevannyi, "Operatsii v dvoinom zazerkal'e" [Operations in a Double looking Glass], *NVO*, No. 8 (2–15 March 2001).

36. The process of expulsion and withdrawal was not completed until 1 July 2001 when the last of forty-five staff members at the U.S. embassy in Moscow left Russia for the United States. Among other things this was a very expensive exercise for both countries.

37. For the Rogozin remark, Interfax (27 March 2001). See also "Zachem zhe privechat' terroristov?" [Why Give Terrorists Red-Carpet Treatment?], *Rossiiskaia gazeta* (23 March 2001), where it was asked how could Americans meet with "people who blow up apartment blocks . . . kill hostages . . . and high-jack planes." Russian anger at this meeting was widespread—see for example, Aleksandr Shumili, "Mno-gokratnyi dostup" [Frequent Access]; "Drug vraga. Rossiia i Amerika perekhodiat na emotsii" [Friend of an Enemy: Russia and America Move towards Emotion], *Izvestiia;* and *Rossiiskaia gazeta* (22 March 2001)—and it did not recede quickly; see Markus Makarychev, "V Gollivude—gladiator, v gosdepe—ter-rorist" [Gladiator in Hollywood, Terrorist in the State Department], *Rossiiskaia gazeta* (28 March 2001). The meeting referred to was with Ilyas Akhmadov, foreign minister of Ichkeria.

fighters were crossing into the Balkans and making contact with NATO peaceke
ing troops made the rounds of Russian journalism as well.[38]

By the end of March the early relatively comfortable feeling about the new Am
ican administration had faded almost out of sight in Moscow. Even though Pu
played down the obvious rift with the United States, most Russian analysts ɛ
many public officials began to present a uniform picture of Washington as
source of a one-way Cold War campaign. One writer accused Washington of ado
ing the style of the former USSR, calling Rumsfeld and company "hypocritic
"strategically immature," and, if not "evil," then unable to understand how
world works.[39] As usual, ISKRAN's Sergei Rogov took the positive view, seeing
current crisis as a prelude to serious negotiations, after the dust settled around
Bush foreign affairs team. He did admit that American rhetoric had "toughen
and that Russia's niche in U.S. foreign affairs had been "purposely diminishe
They are trying to put "psychological pressure" on Moscow, he wrote, adding t
Russians must not panic. America's hard line was a way for Bush to claim legitimɛ
it was a "bluff" that eventually will be replaced by a more sensible dialogue. G
bachev weighed in, blaming pseudo "ultra-patriots" on both sides for the anta
nism.[40] At any rate the "spy mania" was declared over in a telephone conversat
between Igor Ivanov and Colin Powell on 28 March. An *Izvestiia* editorial said t
"Cold War-2 is over today."[41]

It was at about this time that Gorbachev reemerged as a celebrity in the Russ
political arena, a development that Putin casually promoted. The "mutual attracti
between them, as one writer noted, was their ambition to restructure and mode
ize Russia by weaving a centrist path between right and left. It was important ɛ
that Gorbachev still commanded considerably more attention in the West than
did in Russia, making him a valuable ally in Europe and North America and
threat at home.[42] It was also in mid-to-late March that analysts tended to reflect
Putin's first year as the elected President of Russia. Most report cards were laudat
pointing to his continued popularity and his more or less fulfillment of promises
lated to the economy, political stability and foreign affairs. There were warnings t
breakthroughs would have to come soon, especially in Chechnya, though there

38. See, for example, Timofei Borisov, "Zachem chechentsam NATO?" [Why Do Chechens N
NATO?], *Rossiiskaia gazeta* (30 March 2001).

39. See, for example, Gleb Pavlovskii, "SShA? USA? Amerika v sovetskom 'prostranstve ekspan;
[The USA or the USSR? America in the Soviet of "Space Expansion"], *Nezavisimaia gazeta* (27 M:
2001); Georgii Il'in, "Bitva za Kavkaz. Amerikanskaia viza protiv rossiiskoi" [Battle for the Caucasus
American Visa against Russians], *Izvestiia* (22 March 2001).

40. Gorbachev "Liubitelei poigrat' v ul'trapatriotizm khvataet i v SShA, i v Rossii" [People Who
to Play the Ultra-Patriotism Role in Russia and the USA], *Nezavisimaia gazeta* (27 March 2001); Ro
"Ne stoit vpadat' v isteriku. Vysylka diplomatov—preliudiia k peregovoram" [No Hysteria. Expel
Diplomats is a Prelude to Negotiations], *Nezavisimaia gazeta* (28 March 2001).

41 .Aleksandr Shumilin, "Gosdep upolnomochen predlozhit' " [State Department Authorizes Res
tion], *Izvestiia* (29 March 2001).

42. See, for example, Dmitrii Furman, "Putin vozvrashchaetsia ottuda, kuda ne doshel Gorbacl
[Putin Returns from Where Gorbachev Did Not Go], *Obshchaia gazeta*, No. 12 (22–28 March 200(

no suggestion anywhere that Putin's position could be placed in jeopardy anytime in the near future.[43]

THE EU PRIORITY

In keeping with the Kremlin's expressed priorities, which placed Europe well ahead of the United States in levels of importance, Sergei Ivanov began a working visit to France on 20 March. He was able to discuss regional security matters with Foreign Minister Vedrine and Defense Minister Richard, and was received by President Chirac. At the same time, Igor Ivanov completed a five-day tour of the Balkans, meeting officials in Belgrade, Kosovo and Macedonia. The Russian media took advantage of Ivanov's presence there to cast blame on a "confused" NATO generally, and the United States particularly, for a looming crisis between Kosovo Albanian rebels and the Macedonian government.[44] As the situation heated up, and American state department officials met with representatives of the Chechen separatists movement, some Russian analysts began to treat Albanian separatist intrusion on Macedonian territory as part of an "international terrorist campaign in the guise of Islamic Fundamentalism." Officials repeated this message as well. Defense Minister Sergeev, for example, openly accused NATO of promoting "the creation of [ethnic Albanian] illegal armed groups" to divide Yugoslavia. NATO and the United States "supports separatism," he charged on 26 March.[45]

The arrest of Slobodan Milosevic in Belgrade was another Balkan complication for Moscow. With the exception of the communist leadership, Russian authorities agreed that Milosevic should be tried for crimes against the Serbian people, but there was a consensus that he not be turned over to the tribunal in The Hague. That such a step would lend credence to NATO action against Yugoslavia and separatism,

43. See, for example, Anatolii Yurkov, "Protsess poshel. Khorosho, chto v obratnuiu storonu" [Process Started. It is a Good Thing That It Started in Reverse], *Rossiiskaia gazeta* (24 March 2001), who concluded, after noting both successes and failures, "The guy is doing his job."

44. See, for example, Yekaterina Glebova, "Vesennee obostrenie voiny" [The Spring Activization of War], *Obshchaia gazeta*, No. 11 (15–21 March 2001), who saw the Macedonia crisis as a "moment of truth" for those who bombed Yugoslavia and believed completely in the Albanian rebels. See also Anatolii Shapovalov, "Zachistka v bufernoi zone" [Cleansing in the Buffer Zone], *Rossiiskaia gazeta* (16 March 2001); Kseniia Fokina, "V Makedonii prodolzhaiutsia boi" [Fighting Continues in Macedonia], *Nezavisimaia gazeta* (16 March 2001), and Maksim Yusin, "Bol'shaia voina" [Large War], *Izvestiia* (16 March 2001). None were more delighted with NATO's potential embarrassment than the communists; see Vasilii Safronchuk, "Bessilie i bespomoshchnost' NATO i OON" [Weakness and Helplessness of NATO and the UN], *Sovetskaia Rossiia* (20 March 2001).

45. On Macedonia and "international terrorism," see Sergei Sergeev, "Voina v Makedonii mozhet stat' prologom Tret'ei mirovoi" [The War in Macedonia Could Be a Prologue to the Third World War], *Rossiiskaia gazeta* (27 March 2001); for Sergeev's remarks, Interfax (26 March 2001). *Krasnaia zvezda* (20 March 2001); he quoted the Macedonian prime minister, blaming the "West" for the crisis. See also Yekaterina Glebova, "Balkanskii zasov" [Balkan Bolts], *Obshchaia gazeta*, No. 13 (29 March–4 April 2001). Not surprisingly, the communists blamed the United States and NATO exclusively; see "Zashchitniki Makedonii" [Defenders of Macedonia], *Sovetskaia Rossiia* (24 March 2001).

benefiting only NATO and the American position in the Balkans, was the unifc
stance taken in Russia.[46] Russian communists, however, already having equated
defense of Milosevic with the "struggle against the American 'new world order,' "
sued a strong statement against his arrest.[47]

At the time, the foreign ministry was busy finalizing plans for Putin to have bi
eral discussions with EU leaders in Stockholm on 23 March. These sessions were v
important to Moscow because they were intended as sounding boards for Russ
readiness to join the WTO, make its vast energy sources available to Europe, ¿
open up negotiations on European security matters. Top EU leaders already had ·
ited Moscow twice since January, and regular EU–Russia summits were schedu
for May and October. Thus Putin had far greater direct access to European leac
than to the American president.[48] He was bolstered in this relationship by the R
sian public who, opinion polls demonstrated, were now much more favorably (
posed towards Europe than they were to the United States.[49] The simple fact that
enlargement would have a significant economic impact on Russia made it very i
portant to Moscow that NATO's plans be postponed until the effects of EU's grov
were seen.

HOUSECLEANING

Within a week of the Stockholm meeting, Putin's first major cabinet shuffle t(
place. The most striking changes came in the ministry of defense. Sergeev was (
missed and replaced by Sergei Ivanov. This move had been expected for some til

46. See, for example, Maksim Shevchenko, "NATO sozdala na Balkanakh rezhim etnicheskoi se
gatsii" [NATO Creates a Regime of Ethnic Segregation in the Balkans], *Nezavisimaia gazeta* (21 M:
2001), who charged NATO with discrimination against the Serbs; see also Konstantin Chuganov, "
grad na etot raz ne poluchit opleukh? [Will Belgrade Not Receive a Slap in the Face This Time?] *R
iskaia gazeta* (3 April 2001), where it was claimed again that Washington speaks the language of "
mata"; and *Izvestiia* (3 April 2001).

47. See Zyuganov's statement, "V Belgrade arestovan S. Milosevich. Zaiavlenie" [S. Milosevic Arre
in Belgrade. Statement], *Sovetskaia Rossiia* (3 April 2001), Vyacheslav Tetekin, "Obvineniia S. Milosevi
ne pred'iavleny. Pirrova pobeda" [Charges Are Not Presented to S. Milosevic. Pyrrhic Victory], *Sovets.
Rossiia* (5 April 2001), Tetekin, "Skhvachen Miloshevich, zatem—sem'ia . . . Chto dal'she?" [The Sei
of Milosevic, Then—His Family . . . What's Next?], *Sovetskaia Rossiia* (10 April 2001), and, eaı
Tetekin, "Pod zashchitoi naroda" [Behind the Shield of the People], *Sovetskaia Rossiia* (27 March 200

48. See, for example, Leonid Gladchenko, "16 person iz ob'edinennoi Evropy. Plius Vladimir Pu
[Sixteen People from United Europe. Plus Vladimir Putin], *Rossiiskaia gazeta* (22 March 2001); Aleks:
Pap, "Po stokgol'mskomu schetu" [According to the Stockholm Calculation], *Obshchaia gazeta,* No
(22–28 March 2001), a German political analyst who pointed out that, though Russia has chosen Euı
as opposed to the United States, Europe cannot make such a distinction; and Dmitrii Chernogor
"Putina zhdut v Stokgol'me" [Stockholm Awaits Putin], *Dipkur'er NG,* No. 5 (22 March 2001).

49. See Avtandil Tsuladze, "Bol'shaia ten' malen'kogo medvedia. Rossiia meniaet orientatsiiu" [
Large Shadow of a Small Bear. Russia Changes Orientation], *Segodnya* (23 March 2001); and *N
izvestiia* (24 March 2001). To the question, "What is more important, partnership with the United Sı
or with Europe?" the answer was 46% Europe; 28% equally; 10% with Unites States. To the quest
"To whom are you better disposed?" the answer was 51% Europe, 11% United States.

but its ripple effects were not so foreseen (for more detail see chapter 7). Much was made of the fact that Ivanov was the first civilian in Russian history to hold this post, though Igor Rodionov gave up his rank during his final year as minister, and Ivanov himself had been a Lieutenant General. One of his new deputy ministers, Lyubov Kudelina, was the first woman to reach that level in defense. Kudelina had been deputy minister of finance, and was now expected to oversee the military budget.[50] Minister of the Interior Vladimir Rushailo took Ivanov's chair on the Security Council, and his place was taken by Boris Gryzlov, head of the Duma's Unity Party. Yevgenii Adamov was dismissed as atomic energy minister and replaced by nuclear scientist Aleksandr Rumyantsev. On the face of it, these changes seemed not to be very extensive, yet they marked the passing of Yeltsin's baton off to a new team not in the slightest way beholden to Putin's predecessor. Political commentators tended to be very optimistic about the changes.[51] Sergei Ivanov already had been acting for Putin as if he were a vice president, a position not included in the Russian constitution, so his prominence was nothing new.

STATE OF THE NATION

A few days later Putin delivered his second annual address on the state of the nation, concentrating mostly on the economic and social policies of his government. Whereas he was able to boast that political disintegration had been curbed, he voiced concern over the economy and the threat of further violence emanating from Chechnya. Capital flight was still a serious problem, more taxation was forthcoming, and new foreign borrowing was to be limited. Foreign policy was barely mentioned, although NATO was singled out as an "organization that all too often ignores international opinion and the terms of international agreements when reaching its decisions." In connection with this last remark, Putin stated that it was the unequivocal Russian position that the UN Security Council is the only legitimate source for authorization of force in international relations. Integrative processes in the CIS were to be stepped up, and association with Europe were now top priorities.[52] Russian analysts again praised Putin for his pragmatism and commented upon the diminishing significance of the United States on Moscow's foreign policy horizon.[53] One well-known expert credited Putin with restraint, for not "shouting back" on what he saw

50. Sergei Ptichkin, "Armeiskii rubl' v zhenskikh rukakh" [Army Budget in Woman's Hands], *Rossiiskaia gazeta* (30 March 2001).

51. See, for example, Svetlana Babaeva, Viktoriia Sokolova, "Peresadka v organakh" [Transplant in the Agencies], *Izvestiia* (29 March 2001), who said that the new team would move from talk to action on reform; *Segodnya* (29 March 2001), agreed, saying that conditions were now right for reform.

52. Putin's Address to the Federal Assembly of the Russian Federation, the Kremlin (3 April 2001), issued by the Embassy of the Russian Federation in Ottawa.

53. See, for example, Aleksandr Shumilin, "Dva Ivanova i Solana" [Two Ivanovs and Solana], *Izvestiia* (5 April 2001). See also Yurii Pankov in *Krasnaia zvezda* (7 April 2001), and an interview with Sergei Karaganov in *Segodnya* (6 April 2001).

as America's new reliance on the "language of ultimata." He called Bush's foreign p
icy approach "primitive and conservative."[54]

Symbolically hammering this point home were the facts of the EU's Solana's v
to Moscow on 2–3 April to discuss European strategic concerns with the new Se
rity Council head, Rushailo, and the addresses by Putin and Gerhard Schröder to
St. Petersburg Dialogue, an annual summit of Russian and German officials. 1
topic of the latter meetings was "Russia and Germany on the Threshold of the 2
Century." The heads of state spoke at the opening session, but the remainder of
Dialogue was left to 100 middle-level officials (fifty from each country). Putin a
Schröder enjoyed a personal meeting and the respective foreign ministers also carr
on private discussions. European strategic interests, the Balkans, ABM/NMD,
expansion were all on the agenda and, even though Schröder made it clear to Pt
that NATO was the key player in European security, the new common ground
tween Russia and a Europe with Germany as its leader was evident.[55]

IMAGE PROBLEMS AND STILL UNCERTAIN
RELATIONS WITH WASHINGTON

Moscow had a few storms to weather before the new foreign ministry could be tal
more seriously than its predecessor. In the first instance, there was a new probl
with Russia's image abroad, always a difficult task for the ministry to mana
Gazprom's takeover of large parts of the former Vladimir Guzinskii media holdir
including the NTV, Russia's independent TV channel, was interpreted by some
home and many abroad as a state-driven attempt to regain control of the press. N'
journalists staged sit-ins and supported large street demonstrations against Gazpr
and the government. Western journalists and politicians thundered that press fi
doms were being threatened again in Russia. Gazprom responded with revelati
about the huge debt owed by Guzinskii's Media-Most empire. The fact that the R
sian state owned 38.4 percent of Gazprom, which in turn held 46 percent of
NTV shares, is what worried many commentators. Yet few suggested that
takeover was illegal. For the most, the Russian public supported the government
this matter, seeing it as an action against the hated oligarchs.[56]

---

54. Dmitrii Gornostaev, "Voprosy iz Moskvy: Dostatochno li u SShA mudrosti, chtoby vesti l
struktivnyi dialog s RF?" [Questions from Moscow: Is There Sufficient Wisdom in the USA to Carry
a Constructive Dialogue with the RF?], *Dipkurier NG.*, No.6 (2001). Gornostaev believed that, so
Bush's administration seemed incapable of dealing with big issues such as the ABM, NMD, NATO
pansion or Russia's debt to Western financial institutions.

55. On Solana's visit, see Aleksandr Shumilin, "Dva Ivanova i Solana" [Two Ivanovs and Sola
Izvestiia (5 April 2001), where the EU's "independence" from the U.S. was highlighted.

56. See, for example, Leonid Slutskii, "Slovo i otrazhenie" [Word and Reflection], *Nezavisimaia ga*
(13 Apr 2001), who warned that the huge cutbacks in Russia's foreign broadcasting apparatus allo
"foreign ideologists," mostly American, a free hand in broadcasting falsehoods to the Caucasus and C
tral Asia. On the Guzinskii case, see *REDA* 2000 and 2001.

And the traditional problems still awaited resolution. In addition to the ongoing issue of NATO expansion, on 18 April a visit by the Iraqi vice president, the highest ranked official to come to Moscow from Baghdad in fifteen years, spotlighted another source of tension between Moscow and Washington. The Yugoslavia vortex still lay between them as well. Oddly, a little moral high ground had been retaken on 11 April when a Russian peacekeeping soldier was shot and killed by an Albanian sharpshooter in Kosovo. NATO's Robertson and George W. Bush both called Igor Ivanov to offer condolences, and Russia's nationalists and communists who had been vigorously condemning NATO for its demands that Milosevic be tried in The Hague exploited the death as evidence of NATO disarray in the Balkans. Igor Ivanov and Powell met the next day in Paris and discussed a wide range of international issues central to both governments, after which Ivanov appeared more optimistic than previously about the future of Russian–American cooperation.[57]

He proposed strategic stability talks with the United States and acknowledged that cooperation between them was essential on a wide front of world security issues, the resolution of regional conflicts, and combating anti-terrorism, organized crime and drug trafficking. A document released at the Ivanov–Powell meeting reflected this mutual need, but the Russian foreign minister made certain that reporters knew that he blamed Washington for whatever impasse was still in place (ITAR-TASS, 14 April). The fact that his next stop was a two-day (17–18 April) working session in Minsk, Belarus—whose President Lukashenko was still anathema in Washington—served as an exclamation mark to Ivanov's comments in Paris.

The appointment of Alexander Vershbow as ambassador to Moscow, after a long delay on the part of the Bush administration, was appreciated by most Russian analysts. Vershbow's nomination worried some officials in the Russian military because of his long experience with NATO, but more of them took it as a sign that Washington thought Moscow important. Moreover, Vershbow was assumed to be Powell's candidate and Powell was thought to be much more constructive in his approach to Russia than Rumsfeld.[58]

THE NATO QUESTION REVISITED

Another outburst in April of Baltic officialdom taking their case for entry into NATO to representatives of both the European countries—for example Poland, Germany, Norway—and the United States, caught Russia without a useful reply. In

---

57. The Russian communists pledged formal support for Milosevic; see "Zaiavlenie predstavitleei rossiiskoi obshchestvennosti" [Statements of Representatives of the Russian Public], *Sovetskaia Rossiia* (21 April 2001).

58. See, for example, Dmitrii Gornostaev, "Gost' priiatnyi. No trudnyi" [A Troublesome but Pleasant Guest], *Dipkurier NG*, No. 7 (19 April 2001). In "Poslom SShA v Moskve budet Aleksandr" [Alexander Will Be U.S. Ambassador in Moscow], *Rossiiskaia gazeta* (19 April 2001), Maksim Makarychev agreed that even though Vershbow was a strong supporter of NATO expansion, he at least knew Russia.

Washington, Powell told a Latvian delegation that Russia would never have a v
over the admission of a Baltic state; and in Warsaw the Polish government ope
supported Lithuanian admission. The Russian press took up the question again,
ten using the ongoing perception of Albanian "aggression" in Macedonia as an
ample of the danger of NATO's selective use of force, and pointing out that the
liance's 1999 strategic concept made Russia a potential target. After further NA'
expansion, Russia would clearly be on NATO's "periphery" and "in and around
Euro-Atlantic area," both regions set out in the concept as open to military act
even for entirely internal crises. Territorial disputes, abuse of human rights, org
ized crime, and many related circumstances conceivably could be perceived and
fined by NATO as reason for intervention in Russian affairs. Farfetched as 1
sounded to many Western analysts and politicians, history and current realities m
them real to the Russian foreign policy elite.[59]

Paradoxically, there was still widespread optimism among Russia's foreign aff
elite that the Bush administration could be dealt with, whereas Clinton's team l
been too "slippery" to pin down to mutually beneficial policies. Vladimir Lu
deemed the Moscow–Washington relationship "unhealthy," but called the Repu
cans "pragmatic" and open to compromise; Andrei Fedorov proclaimed the "der
cratic romanticism" period over and looked for a more pragmatic approach from
Republicans.[60]

EURASIA ON THE HORIZON

One by-product of the tensions between Russia and the United States was a fir
ing up of the Russian nationalist claim on Eurasia as Russia's potential source
strength. On 21 April, Aleksandr Dugin, a philosopher of geopolitics and heac
the National Bolshevik Party, announced the creation of a new public and pol
cal movement called *Eurasia*. Its purpose, he said, was to spread the Eurasian i
as a national idea and to oppose "American-style globalization" (ITAR-TASS,
April). In a 1997 book titled *The Basics of Geopolitics: The Geopolitical Future
Russia,* Dugin had urged that the old Soviet empire be renewed to oppose "
lanticism, strategic control by the USA" and "liberal values," and spoke of the r

---

59. For a summary, see Norma Brown, "Counting the Cost of NATO Expansion," *Moscow Times*
April 2001). Brown is a retired U.S. diplomat formerly attached to the American OSCE missioı
Kosovo. The CPRF called the Duma dialogue with NATO parliamentarians "self-deluding." See Dɪ
Safarin, "Klyki miroliubiia. Illiuziia dialoga dumtsev s natovtsami" [Peaceloving Fangs. The Illusion of
alogue between Duma and NATO Members], *Sovetskaia Rossiia* (19 April 2001).

60. Maksim Makarychev, "Larri, ty ne prav. Nyneshniaia politika administratsii SShA mozhet priʲ
k izoliatsii strany, schitaet vitse-spiker Gosdumy RF byvshii posol v SShA Vladimir Lukin" [Larry, Yɾ
Wrong! The Current Policy of the USA Administration May Lead to the Isolation of the Country, Th
Former Ambassador to the USA and Deputy Duma Speaker Vladimir Lukin], *Rossiiskaia gazeta* (25 Ⱥ
2001); Andrei Fedorov, "Moskva-Vashington: est' vozmozhnost' poniat' drug druga"[Moscow, Wash
ton Have a Chance to Understand Each Other], *Nezavisimaia gazeta* (25 April 2001).

Eurasia as the wellspring of a civilization with values superior to the current Western one.[61]

To a certain extent, Dugin and others in Russia were turning Samuel Huntington's *The Clash of Civilizations and the Remaking of World Order* (1996) on its head, taking advantage of the isolation into which NATO expansion threatened to cast Russia to resurrect nineteenth-century Russian ideas of a great Eurasian civilization becoming dominant. *Eurasia's* first executive included former members of the radically anti-Semitic *Pamyat* (1980s) movement and the National Bolshevik Party (1990s), that is, Dugin himself, Mufti Talgat Tadzhuddin, of the Central Muslim Spiritual Administration, Orthodox Abbott Ioann Ekonomtsev, rabidly Zionist Israeli politician A. Eskin, and television personality Mikhail Leont'ev. All of these persons could be said to have strong fascistic tendencies; the *Eurasia* movement itself advocated the strongest possible support of President Putin.[62]

An even stranger version of history began to crop up in Russia, as a so-called New Chronology excited notice. A theory developed by mathematicians using astronomical and statistical data "proved" to their satisfaction that a vast Russian empire encompassing all of Eurasia and even the British Isles existed up to the early seventeenth century, gained popularity in 2001.[63] Fringe movements such as these caused more humor than disquiet, but they were nonetheless byproducts of a wider search for a "Russia Idea" championed by advocates of the multipolar ideal in world affairs—such as Yevgenii Primakov—and by Putin's own references to the importance of patriotism. In mid-2001, there was indeed some concern that Russia might revert to the nationalist back-to-the-wall approach that Karaganov, Rogov and others with broader outlooks so strongly rejected.

BUSH ANNOUNCES COMMITMENT TO NMD

On 1 May President Bush finally unveiled a sweeping new American defense strategy, presenting the basic outline of massive cuts to his country's nuclear arsenal and a concomitant reliance on a missile defense umbrella. His plan called for sea, land, air and even space-based anti-missile systems, though no details were offered about cost, or deployment schedule; nor were details provided on how many of America's 7,200 warheads might be cut. The Russian official reaction was surprisingly muted,

---

61. See, for explication, Charles Clover, "Will the Russian Bear Roar Again?" *Financial Times Weekend* (2–3 December 2000). X, and Vladimir Trenin, *Russia on the Border Between Geopolitics and Globalization* (Moscow: Carnegie, 2001), Chapter 3, "The End of Eurasia." A. G. Dugin, *Osnovy geopolitiki: geopoliticheskoe budushchee Rossii* (Moscow: Arktogeia, 1997), an English summary of which can be found on the Arktogeia website.

62. See Aleksandr Maksimov, Orkhan Karabaagi, "Evraziitsev prizvali na gosudarevu sluzhbu. Teper' chinovniki obuchaiutsia geopolitike po Duginu"[The Eurasianists Have Been Recruited to Serve the Sovereign. Now Officials Learn Dugin's Geopolitics], *Obshchaia gazeta,* No. 22 (31 May- 6 June 2001).

63. On this, see N. I. Khodakovskii, *Tretii Rim* [Third Rome] (Moscow: Aif-Print 2002).

probably because Bush had telephoned Putin beforehand to tell him of the plan a promised in-depth discussion about the project.

Nongovernmental reactions were mixed. Communist leader Zyuganov issue formal statement condemning Bush's announcement on behalf of the CPRF Du members.[64] Russian military experts claimed that the NMD system as propo would be easy to bypass (ITAR-TASS, 2 May); analysts from other sectors poin out that the United States was going to have their NMD no matter who objec and recommended that Moscow make the best of Bush's apparent willingness consult.[65] The widespread skepticism about the seriousness of consultation v allayed somewhat by Bush's acknowledgement of the need to improve relati with Russia and willingness to meet with Putin before the G-8 meeting in the su mer.[66] Rogov resurrected the specter of Washington acting unilaterally, even in face of contrary international agreements, and warned his own government to p ceed with great care.[67] Led by Dmitrii Rogozin, left-wing factions in the Du threatened to declare START-II null and void—but didn't. Representatives of CPRF called the American approach to disarmament a one-sided "Wild We position.[68]

Within a few days an eighteen-person American delegation, headed by L Deputy Secretary of State for Defense Paul D. Wolfowitz, set out for Moscow fc one-day (11 May) preliminary discussion on arms control. As it happened, neit Sergei nor Igor Ivanov was able to meet with the delegation. The foreign minis was in Finland, having just returned from India where he and the Indian prime m ister issued a joint statement (7 May) in support of the ABM Treaty. Several Russ participants in the discussion later noted their disappointment with the Ameri position, calling it "selfish" and driven by domestic political and financial conce rather than international security considerations (Interfax, 11 May).[69] Even Pr dent Putin told a large audience of veterans on Red Square that in this day and

---

64. Zyuganov, "Zaiavlenie" [Statement], *Sovetskaia Rossiia* (4 May 2001); Leonid Nikolaev, "Zagov Bushki—Rossiia molchit" [As the Bushes Begin to Speak, Russia Is Silent], *Sovetskaia Rossiia* (4 May 20 Viacheslav Tetekin, "Chto ustraivaet Busha v konsul'tatsiiakh s Putinym? Igra v PRO-poddavki" [W Bush Likes in Consultations with Putin? Play at NMD-Giveaway], *Sovetskaia Rossiia* (5 May 2001).

65. See, for example, Mikhail Kalmykov, "A New Phase in Russian–US Relations," an ITAR-TASS port filed in Moscow, in English (3 May 2001); *Izvestiia* (4 May 2001); Yurii Yershov, "Reshitel'nyi Bu skromnaia Evropa" [Decisive Bush and Modest Europe], *Rossiiskaia gazeta* (4 May 2001); Dmitrii Go staev, "Dzhordzh Bush smenil ton" [George Bush Changed Tone], *Nezavisimaia gazeta* (4 May 2001).

66. On this, see especially Aleksei Arbatov "The Americans Do Not Know Themselves What 1 Want from the ABM," *strana.ru* (3 May 2001).

67. See Rogov, "Americans Are Seeking Ways to Achieve Total Superiority in Military Sphere," *stran* (3 May 2001); Rogov, "Shchit i Bush. SShA namereny vyiti iz Dogovora po PRO. Chto eto znachit Rossii?" [The Shield and Bush. The USA Intends to Withdraw from the ABM Treaty. What Does ' Mean for Russia?], *Rossiiskaia gazeta* (5 May 2001).

68. For the communist position, see Vladimir Krylov. "Pentagon okrylen" [The Pentagon Is Che Up], *Sovetskaia Rossiia* (17 May 2001).

69. See Maksim Makarychev, "Bush poka idet naprolom" [For the Time Being Bush Pushes on gardless], *Rossiiskaia gazeta* (12 May 2001), on a *New York Times* assessment of Bush's first 100 days, w ing that Bush may alienate all of his allies, let alone Russia and China.

no country should attempt to construct exclusive security systems, "it is impossible to build a safe world for oneself alone."[70]

Russian and American positions on the ABM Treaty were antithetical, Bush implying that it was a relic of the Cold War and Putin insisting that it be maintained. Russian Foreign Service officials made this point at every available venue. The Kremlin's quandary was worsened when a PACE general assembly in Strasbourg raised the possibility of restrictions against Ukraine because of political turmoil there. Russia supported Ukraine and found itself caught in debates again about Chechnya and organized crime. Angry at charges that the "mafia" controlled Russian business, the leader of the Russian delegation accused PACE of applying "double standards" to Russia and Ukraine.[71] At almost the same time, Moscow came in for a rough ride from delegates to a meeting in Bratislava, Slovakia, where representatives from nine former Soviet and Warsaw Pact countries met to discuss admission to NATO. Needless to say, many Russian analysts interpreted the meeting as a NATO plot to further isolate and weaken Russia in Europe.[72] Letters of strong support from American Senators Jesse Helms and Trent Lott, a vigorous speech by Vaclav Havel, who could not "imagine Russia as a NATO member," and a report from an American Slovak organization accusing Russia of promoting criminal organization in East and East Central Europe, drew more angry outbursts from the Russian diplomatic community. Havel was a special target of Russian invective for insisting that any concessions to Russia on the matter of Baltic admission to NATO would be tantamount to resurrecting the old Molotov-Ribbentrop Pact.[73]

These difficult times were ameliorated somewhat by a two-day stay (15–16 May) in Moscow by Kofi Annan, who made it plain that he wanted Russia to become more involved in the Middle East peace process and to assist in strengthening the role of the UN in international conflict resolution.[74] The Russian ministry of foreign affairs seized the moment to deplore officially the failure of the United States to pay its dues at the UN. Generally, however, the ministry still attempted to avoid taking sides in the Middle East, and criticized extremism on both sides.[75]

---

70. Putin's speech commemorated Victory Day, 7 May. For an optimistic approach, see, for example, Prof. Viktor Kuvaldin, "Vashington–Moskva: novyi start" [Washington–Moscow: New Start], *Nezavisimaia gazeta* (12 May 2001). Kuvaldin, a historian, saw the Bush government as one much easier to deal with than the more opportunistic Clinton administration.

71. See Leonid Slutskii "Ne nado pugat' 'russkoi mafiei'" ["Russian Mafia" Must Not Be Used to Frighten People], *Rossiiskaia gazeta* (5 May 2001); see also an interview with Lord Russell-Johnston, PACE president, who told the same newspaper that Chechnya was a strong handicap to Russia in PACE.

72. See, for example, Fedor Luk'ianov, "V Bratislave vystroilas' ochered. V NATO" [A Queue Is Formed in Bratislava. For NATO], *Rossiiskaia gazeta* (15 May 2001).

73. See, for example, Aleksei Marinin, "Chego ne dogovorivaet Vatslav Gavel" [What Vaclav Havel Is Not Saying], *Rossiiskaia gazeta* (23 May 2001); Viacheslav Tetekin, "Userdnyi Gavel. NATO zatiagivaet poias . . . Vokrug Rossii" [Zealous Havel. NATO Tightens Its Belt . . . Around Russia], *Sovetskaia Rossiia* (31 May 2001); and reports from Paris AFP (North European Service) and ITAR-TASS (10–12 May 2001). Delegates came from Slovakia, Slovenia, Lithuania, Estonia, Latvia, Romania, Bulgaria, Albania and Macedonia. See also Christopher P. Winner, "Havel Warns Russians on NATO," *The Prague Post* (16–22 May 2001).

74. See, for example, "Kofi Annan mozhet rasschityvat' na Moskvu" [Kofi Annan Can Count on Moscow], *Rossiiskaia gazeta* (16 May 2001). This was an interview.

75. See, for example, Vladimir Lapskii, "Blizhnii Vostok na grani voiny" [Middle East Is on the Brink of War], *Rossiiskaia gazeta* (6 June 2001). Lapskii urged Moscow not to take sides.

RUSSIA–EU SUMMIT AND THE NATO QUESTION

The Bratislava meeting of NATO aspirants and a subsequent NATO Parliament
Assembly session held in Vilnius and boycotted by the Russian Duma highligh
the importance in Moscow of closer association with the EU.[76]

Links to the EU were a clear Russian foreign policy priority in late May, whe
Russia–EU summit was held in Moscow. One result of the meetings was the creat
of a semiautonomous thirty-person committee of leading figures from both side;
discuss further integration, and even the possibility of Russia joining the EU. 1
committee was headed in Russia by Vladimir Ryzhkov, a Duma deputy. A conco:
tant survey showed that slightly more than 60 percent of the Russian population s
ported integration with the EU. Another contemporary poll, this time of fore
policy experts in Russia, demonstrated how the turn to the EU coincided with gr(
ing concern that the Baltic States would soon be admitted by NATO. In list
the "threats to national security" the experts ranked international terrorism and
lamic fundamentalism first and second (61 percent), Russia being economic:
uncompetitive third (54.8 percent), and NATO's eastward expansion close behin(
52.9 percent.[77]

Few of the experts believed that Russia would or could recover superpower sta:
the majority thought Russia should balance its interests between West and East, ;
Yevgenii Primakov was credited with providing the basic premises of the country's c
rent policy in international affairs. The CFDP's Karaganov, one of the loudest R
sian voices in support of membership in the EU, exhorted a press conference in J(
to take Ryzhkov's committee work to heart. If not, then Russia was in danger of
coming isolated from emerging new giant blocs in Europe, North America, and A
lagging behind in technology and eventually missing out on modern developmen

The question, of course, was how committed Europe was to Russia, at least
yond the friendly diplomatic rhetoric commonly employed by Schröder, Bl
Vedrine and other European leaders and ministers. Russia already provided ab(
one-third of Europe's oil and gas, and one-half of Germany's. Oil companies fr
Germany, The Netherlands and Italy had made huge investments in Gazprom, ;
Europe's energy dependence on Russia was likely to rise. Moreover, Russia's turr
Europe for support of the ABM and opposition to the NMD was not a one-v
street. Russia had long been an easy foil for European countries to use against dc
inance by the United States, especially in the UNSC. France, for example, I
adopted a position like Russia's in matters of sanctions against Iraq, oil explorat
in Libya, and so on. Thus, they tended to feed on each other in international affa

---

76. In his attack of Havel, noted above, Aleksei Marinin emphasized the importance of Russian
ticipation in the affairs of the EU, an integrative agency much broader than NATO.

77. Georgii Bovt, "Rossiiskaia elita izbravliaetsia ot imperskikh ambitsii v pol'zu provintsializma" [
vey of Foreign Affairs Experts. Russia's Elite Sheds Imperialist Ambitions in Favor of Provinciali;
Izvestiia (25 May 2001).

78. "Press Conference with Sergei Karaganov, Chairman of Foreign and Defense Policy Council
June 2001), *www.fednews.ru/*, an *Argumenty i fakty* press conference.

and it is clear that Russia hoped to use its European connections to oppose the further expansion of NATO eastward. And by mid-2001 it was still the NATO question that was potentially the most divisive in Europe, and between Russia, Europe and the United States.

The publication of the survey results noted above preceded by a week the meeting of NATO parliamentarians in Vilnius, capital of Lithuania, whose parliament is an associate member of the Assembly. This was the first NATO meeting on former Soviet territory. Although the agenda for the meeting included further Alliance expansion, the American NMD project, and violence in the Balkans, all subjects vital to Russian interests, the Russian associate delegation withdrew rather than appear to acquiesce in the matter of Baltic membership in NATO. The Duma adopted a resolution (230-2-4) calling on Putin to upgrade Russia's resistance to NATO's eastward expansion, especially in the case of the Baltic republics (Interfax, 23 May). This was largely a Communist Party and Agrarian motion, for most members of the government-supporting parties failed to vote. NATO Assembly resolutions are nonbinding, but their gatherings serve as important forums in which delegates may have their opinions heard. In this case, the Baltic States and advocates of their adherence to NATO received disproportionate media attention, greatly worrying Russians that a fait accompli was in the works.[79] One week later Zyuganov issued a formal statement calling on Putin to act on the Duma resolution. His statement was carried in the communist press under the general rubric of "NATO's Guerillas Preparing to March to the East."[80]

Russia wavered slightly by sending one destroyer to take part in a PfP BALTOPS exercise on the Baltic Sea with fifty other NATO and Baltic country ships (Interfax, 23 May), and anxiety about all the subjects discussed in Vilnius was eased somewhat by promises of direct discussions with Washington on all of them except NATO. With the possible exception of the communists, who called such thinking a "mirage," most Russian mainstream political movements and their media agencies accepted the Ivanov and Powell consultation as lead-up to the Putin–Bush summit in Slovenia on 16 June with a surprising level of optimism.[81] They also tended to downplay stories appearing in *Der Spiegel* and another German magazine on 21 May that Schröder and Bush secretly had agreed to hold back financial aid to Russia as long as

79. See, for example, Viktor Litovkin, "Partnerstvo radi istiny" [Partnership for the Sake of Truth], *Obshchaia gazeta*, No. 20 (17–23 May 1001), a review of a recent book by Aleksei Arbatov where the question of NATO expansion is seen as a wellspring of ongoing friction between Russia and the U.S., and Viacheslav Tetekin, "Userdnyi Gavel . . . ." [Zealous Havel . . .], *op cit.*, for voting data on the Duma resolution "O merakh po protivodeistviiu rasshireniiu NATO" [On Measures Taken against NATO Expansion].

80. Zyuganov, "Zaiavlenie NPSR" [Statement of the National Patriotic Union of Russia], *Sovetskaia Rossiia* (2 June 2001).

81. See, for example, Ksenia Fokina, "Moskva i Vashington sblizila PRO?" [Does the ABM Bring Moscow and Washington Closer Together?], *Nezavisimaia gazeta* (22 May 2001). For the suspicious communist perspective, Vasilii Safronchuk, "Kreml', Belyi Dom i evropa" [The Kremlin, the White House and Europe], *Sovetskaia Rossiia* (22 May 2001), and Leonid Nikolaev, "Yiun'skii sammit Putina s Bushem. Liublianskii mirazh" [June Summit between Putin and Bush. Lyublyana Mirage], *Sovetskaia Rossiia* (24 May 2001).

capital flight continued and that Bush blamed Russia for arming Iran. Putin tern
the publication a "provocation," but there was little lasting rancor over the ir
dent.[82] The Russian president's sanguine approach notwithstanding, the fact t
Schröder's comments were excused in Germany rather than denied suggests t
Putin's "friendship" with the German leader had pretty shallow roots.

Noting that the previous months had been marked by Cold War language fr
many circles in America and some in Russia, and that a new wave of NATO exp
sion was looming, they called for a fully new "principled" stand in Moscow. Ima
making or -changing seemed to be the mainstay of their prospectus. The new
proach itself must begin with an accelerated program of reform in Russia, above
with "the active implementation of the postulates of an open civil society based
democratic principles and a market economy." Overcoming autarchy, integrat
Russia into the economic, financial, information and cultural institutes of the wo
and creating mechanisms for constructive dialogue, were the centerpieces of their
sion. Early warning systems to forecast troubling issues between the two countr
interparliamentary programs, and confirmation of rule of law and ownership rig
also were conditions they hoped to achieve. An unusual characteristic of the grou
advocacy is that the onus was placed on Russia to change, even though most of
blame for the current chill was attributed to American intransigence.[83] Much c
cern remained, however, as writer Dmitrii Kosyrev worried that Russia did not h
enough cards to bring to the bargaining table, that Washington was not likely to t
much heed even of its more traditional allies, such as Canada and Britain, and t
Putin would have a difficult time balancing Moscow's interests between East ε
West.[84]

PUTIN–BUSH SUMMIT, 16 JUNE

This and other approaches were debated vigorously in Russia as the Putin–Bε
summit neared. Academician Vitalii Tsygichko wrote in a long essay on the pot
tial for a Russia–United States partnership that Sergei Ivanov had too little foresig
Bush's proposals for a completely new relationship with Russia were very promis
and, if consummated, good for both sides. Russia would be able to integrate with
"civilized world" and America would have a partner with which to contain a rapi
rearming China. Russia should aspire to partnership with the United States ε

---

82. Interfax (21 May 2001); Fokina and Nikolaev (see above, fn. 8) held opposing views on the
Spiegel affair.

83. Sergei Oznobishchev, Igor Runov, "Chto delat' s Amerikoi? Neobkhodima novaia povestka dlia ι
iisko-amerikanskikh otnoshenii" [What to Do with America? A New Agenda for Russian–U.S. Relat
Is Necessary], *Dipkur'er NG*, No 8 (24 May 2001). The authors were both members of the Associatio

84. Dmitrii Kosyrev, "Ponravitsia li Bush Putinu. Rossiisko-amerikanskii dialog nachalsia. Vazl
chtoby on poluchilsia priiatnym" [Will Putin Like Bush? Russian–American Dialogue Began. It Is
portant That It Goes Pleasantly], *Dipkur'er NG*, No. 8 (24 May 2001); Kosyrev, "Uravnenie Put
[Putin's Equation], *Dipkur'er NG*, No. 9 (7 June 2001).

Japan for economic and strategic reasons, Tsygichko insisted, for the swelling population of China and its territorial needs "pose a potential threat to Russia."[85] There was a feeling as well that Russia was now willing to negotiate on the NMD, but that Moscow would argue from a position of some strength: Europe's growing dependence on Russian oil and gas, Russia's strategic and arms trade partnership with China and India, and its resumed arms sales to "rogue" states such as Libya, Iran, North Korea and Syria.[86]

In the meantime, the question of NATO expansion eastward was still the topic on which Moscow was less flexible than any other, including even the NMD/ABM issue. On 6 June, the head of the Security Council, Vladimir Rushailo, made Russia's still-rigid stand plain to the president of the NATO Parliamentary Assembly, Rafael Estrella, during talks in Moscow. We will have to take "commensurate measures" if NATO's infrastructure draws closer to Russia's borders, he warned (ITAR-TASS, 6 June). A few days later, Washington's Rumsfeld assured Baltic delegates to a meeting in Turku, Finland, that NATO membership would not be subordinated to negotiations with Russia over the NMD.

The itinerary of the two presidents as they wended their way towards the medieval Brdo Castle, Ljubljana, Slovenia, illustrated their separate agendas nicely. Bush went first to Spain, then to Brussels for a NATO summit, to Sweden to meet with EU leaders, then to Poland where he delivered his most important presummit speech. A brief Special Meeting of leaders of the nineteen NATO members on 13 June provided observers with a foretaste of the issues that separated Moscow and Washington, and also of divisions within NATO itself. New memberships and the NMD topped the list, but there was no immediate consensus on how long NATO troops should be expected to stay in the Balkans, NATO support for Europe's RRF, or relationships with the states assumed in the West to be mavericks. The Russia question was an overarching one, however. At a press conference held in NATO HQ, Bush said that the Alliance should "reach out to Russia's leaders . . . with a message that Russia does have a future with Europe." At the same time he denigrated the ABM as a relic of the Cold War, committed his own country to enlarging NATO, and called on other members to raise their level of spending on defense.[87]

---

85. Vitalii Tsygichko, "S Amerikoi—vmeste ili porozn'" [With America, Together or Separately], *Nezavisimaia gazeta* (9 June 2001); see also Igor Korotchenko, "Sergei Ivanov debiutiroval v NATO" [Sergei Ivanov Debuted at NATO], *ibid.*, where it was pointed out that Ivanov still argued against the United States withdrawing from the ABM.

86. On this, see Svetlana Babaeva, "Perevod s ritorichskogo" [A Switch from the Rhetorical], *Izvestiia* (8 June 2001); Yevgenii Grigor'ev, "Nakanune liubliany atmosfera otnoshenii RF-SShA tepleet na glazakh" [On the Eve of Ljubljana RF–USA Relations Can Easily Be Seen], *Dipkur'er NG*, No. 9 (7 June 2002); and Yevgenii Bai, "Takie pokhozhie prezidenty" [These Presidents Are So Alike], *Izvestiia* (8 June 2001, an interview with Rice.

87. Press Conference, NATO HQ, Brussels (13 June 2001), NATO website, *www.nato.int.* For a communist perspective on American plans, see an analysis of the opposing views on Russia held by Steven Cohen (in *The Nation*) and Jeffry Taylor (in May issue of the *Atlantic*) by Leonid Nikolaev, "V SShA zhdut ot Rossii 'chasa strashnogo suda'," [In the USA They Expect from Russia "The Ordeal of Terrible Justice"], *Sovetskaia Rossiia* (14 June 2001). Cohen was regarded as a friend of Russia, Tyler as an "open Russophobe."

There were no surprises here. Prior to leaving Washington, Bush met with co
spondents from major newspapers in the countries he planned to visit, and oth
Mikhail Kozhokin, editor-in-chief of *Izvestiia*, was there and reported that the Am
ican president again explained that NATO's move eastward was "logical" and that
planned to "firmly advocate NATO expansion." The U.S. president, with C
doleeza Rice beside him, also claimed to be looking forward to building a "c
structive relationship" with a fully democratic Russia based on rule-of-law, "libe
and democracy, free and fair elections."[88] With the Florida fiasco in mind, Russ
cynics wondered what it was that Bush meant by the last-named qualification.

In Warsaw, Bush called for NATO to open up places to all eligible countries "fr
the Baltic to the Black Seas," clearly including the Baltic States and excluding R
sia. Baltic officials were ecstatic, believing that their membership was now assur
Russian commentators did not miss the significance of the choice of Warsaw
Bush's major address, for until the Special Meeting Poland was the only Europ
country to have agreed unconditionally with America's NMD proposals.[89] After
meeting, Washington officials claimed that Britain, Spain, Italy and Hungary a
had come around to their point of view.

The Russian president's road to Slovenia was very different than that of his Am
ican counterpart. Putin flew to Slovenia after a meeting in Shanghai with the pr
dents of China and the four other Shanghai Five members. They attended a two-
gathering (see chapter 10), where that organization celebrated its fifth annivers:
admitted Uzbekistan to its ranks, and announced an agreement to counter join
"extremists, separatists and terrorists." The now six-member regional group (Rus
China, Kazakhstan, Kyrgyzstan, Tajikistan, Uzbekistan) changed its name to
Shanghai Cooperation Organization (ShCO), enabling Putin to arrive in Slove
with authentic credentials as a Eurasian leader and with a reconfirmed friend
China. He conveyed a verbal message from Jiang Zemin to Bush (Interfax, 15 Ju
In a joint communiqué, Jiang and Putin called for constructive relations with
United States, yet strongly condemned the NMD—as did the other four ShC
members. The symbolism of Putin's itinerary echoed his arrival at his first G-8 me
ing in Okinawa via China and North Korea almost a year earlier.[90] In light of the
vious advantage to Washington of a strategic partnership with Russia against a m
tant China, the expressions of comradeship between Putin and Jiang had spe
significance.[91] Continuing his meaningful journey, following the meeting with B

88. Aleksandr Shumilin, "Bush bol'she slushal" [Bush Listened More than He Talked], *Izvestiia*
June 2001); Svetlana Babaeva, Georgii Bovt, "Vladimir Putin i Zhordzh Bush: vstrecha kharakte
[Vladimir Putin and George Bush: Meeting of Characters], *Izvestiia* (16 June 2001).

89. See, for example, Aleksandr Sabov, "PRO prezidentov"[About the Presidents], *Rossiiskaia gazei*
June 2001). "PRO" also is the acronym for the NMD.

90. On this, see Aleksandr Sabov, "Novoe myshlenie ili khorosho zabytoe staroe?" [New Thinkin
Long-Forgotten Old Thinking], *Rossiiskaia gazeta* (16 June 2001).

91. For one perspective on this, see George Friedman, "NMD Initiative Obscures Larger U.S. Ot
tive," Stratfor Global Intelligence Report (29 May 2001); for a quite different and harshly anti-Putin v
see William Safire's, "Putin's China Card," *New York Times* (18 June 2001).

Putin went directly to Belgrade and Pristina (Kosovo), where the Russian and American positions had been consistently at odds. Adding emphasis to their differences, Putin promoted adherence to the UNSCR 1244, making it clear that Moscow would not accept the separation of Kosovo from Yugoslavia, and blamed NATO for the crisis in Macedonia.

Pundits on both sides of the Atlantic agreed that the first Putin–Bush meeting itself resulted in nothing remarkable.[92] Yet there was something of substance behind the enthusiastic backslapping and almost gushing compliments about each other's honesty, frankness, and willingness to behave constructively; that is, it was important that they made their positions on a number of central issues clear to each other.[93] They invited each other to visit their capital cities, and they redeclared that their countries were not enemies. On the other hand, the NATO divide was not set aside even during this rare moment of intimacy. In fact, the ambiguities of NATO membership was represented starkly when Putin introduced a 1954 note from the Soviet government to NATO suggesting that the USSR participate in the Alliance. At that time the idea had been rejected out of hand, just as it had been when Putin brought it up casually in the interview with David Frost in March 2000. "They don't want us" in that "military organization," he continued in Slovenia, and NATO is "moving towards our border. Why?"[94] Even if this document-waving incident was merely in response to Bush's Warsaw speech, it contradicted Putin's quick denial of the significance of his "theoretical response to a theoretical question" asked earlier by the BBC.

Immediate post-summit interviews with the major players in the United States, Bush, Powell and Rice, all put a very positive spin on the meeting. But reality set in quickly on Putin's return to Moscow. There the Russian president threatened a new arms race if the United States unilaterally abrogated or revised the ABM Treaty, promising that in such an event START-I and -II and all other arms control treaties would immediately be discarded. Skeptical analysts were told that defense funding would not be a problem, for multiple warheads could be mounted on existing missiles. Russia's obvious inability to cover the costs of a new arms race was less important here than the timing of Putin's remarks, which came during a three-hour interview with American journalists in the Kremlin library. These were the strongest words about the ABM from Putin in three months. At the same meeting the Russian president was asked

---

92. It had been predicted on both sides of the Atlantic Ocean that little would be accomplished at the meeting. In Russia Sergei M. Rogov, Director of ISKRAN, noted that American policy towards Russia had not yet been formulated and was very skeptical about various offers of aid in return for accommodation on the NMD. See Interfax (15 June 2001) and Aleksandr Sabov in *Rossiiskaia gazeta* (16 June 2001), op. cit.

93. Deputy Director of ISKRAN Viktor Kremenyuk was one Russian specialist to make this point; see Anatolii Shapolov, "Ne triumf, no besspornaia udacha" [Not a Triumph, but an Indisputable Success], *Rossiiskaia gazeta* (19 June 2001). See also Vitalii Dymarskii, "29 chasov na Balkanakh" [29 Hours in the Balkans], *Rossiiskaia gazeta* (19 June 2001).

94. "Press Conference by President Bush and Russian Federation President Putin" (Brdo pri Kranju, Slovenia, 16 June 2001), transcript released by the United States Embassy in Canada, Ottawa.

about the value of his KGB background, to which he was reported to have replied t
he owed to the KGB his "patriotism and love of motherland."[95]

It was obvious by the end of June 2001 that, while the level of direct talks betw
senior Russian and American officials had risen (Igor Ivanov and Powell were c
ducting weekly telephone conversations), public posturing at the presidential ¿
ministerial level had intensified—making it more difficult for either side to b₁
very much.

95. On this meeting with journalists, see report by two of them: Christian Caryl, "A Conversation ʋ
Putin. He Speaks 'Western.' But . . .," *Newsweek International* (2 July 2001); and Paul Quinn-Ju
"Master of the Moment," *Time* (2 July 2001). A transcript of the meeting is available on the websi₁
the Russian Federation Embassy in Ottawa.

5

✝

The Mandate Revisited, 2001

June appeared to be the month for surveys of Russian opinion on the government's foreign policy. Two consecutive polls demonstrated that public attitudes towards the West had not changed much since the radical downturn caused by NATO's bombing of Yugoslavia. More than a third (34 percent) of 1,600 respondents named the United States as the greatest threat to Russia. China was again a distant second at 5 percent. These were more or less the same results as the poll taken in March, and demonstrated that the Russia–U.S. Association had a lot of work to do if it still hoped to alter the image of the enemy in Russia. Another survey listing Russia's main allies saw over 40 percent choose Belarus first, with China second at 22 percent. The anomaly in relation to China was strictly regional in origin. A large percentage of the residents of Russia's Far East regard China as a menace, whereas in other regions most citizens do not.[1] More interesting was a demonstrable coincidence between public and elite (elected deputies, diplomatic staff, foreign affairs "experts") opinion on foreign affairs matters.[2]

Within a few weeks of the Putin–Bush summit, reflections on that event began to shift away from anticipation of great friendship. The *Rossiiskie Vesti* "club of experts" met shortly after the summit and debated its significance. Aleksandr Yusupovskii, adviser to the Federation Council, judged that Putin's handshaking and backslapping in Ljubljana may have signalled a propaganda victory for Russia, but achieved nothing for the state. His opinion was disputed by other panelists, most of whom felt that

---

1. For more details on these two polls, see Interfax (15 June 2001), and *strana.ru* (30 June 2001). Japan ranked third, at 3 percent; 9 percent named other states and 15 percent believed that the RF had no enemies. The 1,600 respondents were queried in 100 communities from all seven federal districts.

2. On this, see Mikhail Gorshkov, "Narod i 'partii' pochti ediny" [The People and the "Parties" Are Almost as One], *Izvestiia* (30 June 2001). Gorshkov is the head of the Russian Independent Institute of Social and Ethnic Studies, which conducted separate polls of the "elite" and "ordinary citizens."

Russia had gained by the summit. Michael Binyon, diplomatic editor for the L
don *Times,* cited evidence of a clear strategy on Putin's part, that is, a quiet dif
macy based on perceptions of strength and will. Not playing up his prior meet
with China in Shanghai, for example, could be taken as a sign of a subtlety unkno
in the Yeltsin era. There was a consensus that the China factor, the ShCO's collect
accommodation with Iran, and Moscow's friendship with New Delhi, made Ru
much stronger as a negotiator than was generally assumed.[3] The group also belie
that Russia's ties with Germany gave the anti-NMD campaign added substar
Later events suggest that this may have been a conclusion based on wishful thinki
Nonetheless, Aleksei Arbatov drew similar inferences quite separately from the *R
iiskie Vesti* club.[4] He pointed out that the United States had not yet ratified STAI
II, and must not be led to believe that Russia would disarm unilaterally.

Almost every expert agreed that NATO expansion eastward was a tougher quest
for Russia than the NMD.[5] A related sore spot was the still unfolding saga of
goslavia. The arrest in Belgrade of Slobodan Milosevic in April and the later decis
to hand him over to the war crimes tribunal in The Hague raised eyebrows in Ru
because even those who disliked the Serbian leader took exception to the unconsti
tional nature of the latter act.[6] Washington and Brussels were accused of buying
extradition of Milosevic by an angry opposition in Belgrade and also widely in R
sia, where the previous year's "Wanted" posters and large reward were remember
NATO's ambitions were blamed by Russian officials for the crisis in Macedonia
well.[7] The heads of both houses of parliament, Stroev and Seleznev, spoke bitt
against Kostunica's decision. Although the Russian government was fairly mute on
subject, its own mainstream press joined the CPRF in charging that the West bou
Milosevic from Kostunica.[8] The sound and fury did not mean that Milosevic w

---

3. On this, see, for example, Maikl Bin'on [Binyon], " 'Bol'shaia vos'merka' za zheleznym zanaves
[The "Big Eight" behind an Iron Curtain], *Obshchaia gazeta,* No. 29 (19–25 July 2001).

4. See Arbatov, "Golovnaia bol' ot golovnykh chastei" [A Headache from War Heads], *Obshc
gazeta,* No. 26 (28 June–4 July 2001); and "Vneshniaia politika khorosha dlia vnutrennego upc
bleniia" [Foreign Policy Is Good for Domestic Consumption], *Rossiiskie vesti* (27 June–3 July 2001).

5. The communists were the most critical; see Vasilii Safronchuk, "Kukushka i petukh" [Cuckoo
Rooster], *Sovetskaia Rossiia* (19 June 2001), and Leonid Nikolaev, "Vstrecha v Liubliane—klubok nej
imaniia" [Meeting in Ljubljana, a Bundle of Misunderstanding], *Sovetskaia Rossiia* (21 June 2001),
they certainly did not stand alone. See, for example, Yelena Dikun, "Prezidenty pogovorili po-muzh
[The Presidents Spoke as Men], *Obshchaia gazeta,* No. 25 (21–27 June 2001).

6. See, for example, Liliana Bulatovich, "Serby otkryvaiut iashchik Pandory" [Serbs Open a Pand
Box], *Obshchaia gazeta,* No. 14 (5–11 April 2001).

7. See, for example, Vasilii Safronchuk, "Yugoslaviia na grani raspada" [Yugoslavia on the Brink of
integration], *Sovetskaia Rossiia* (3 July 2001); and "Miloshevich otvergaet sudilishche" [Milosevic Rej
the Court], *Sovetskaia Rossiia* (5 July 2001), where a "Stop NATO" movement in Yugoslavia was h
lighted; see also a rant by University of Ottawa (Canada) Professor Michael Khossudovski, [Maikl K
sudovski], "Amerikanskaia voina v Makedonii" [The American War in Macedonia], *Sovetskaia Rossiia*
July 2001); Kseniia Fokina, "Albantsy otvergli plan NATO" [Albanians Reject NATO Plan], *Nezavisin
gazeta* (10 July 2001).

8. See, for example, Konstantin Chuganov, "150 millionov za golovu Miloshevicha" [150 Million
Milosevic's Head], *Rossiiskaia gazeta* (2 June 2001), and "Belgrad sdaet Miloshevicha za chetyre milli
dollarov" [Belgrade Gives Up Milosevic for 4 Billion Dollars], *ibid.* (27 June 2001); Boris Yunanov, "1
loboden" [Unfree], *Obshchaia gazeta,* No. 27 (5–11 July 2001); Vasilii Safronchuk, "A sud'bi k
[Judged by Whom?], *Sovetskaia Rossiia* (10 July 2001).

popular figure in official circles, for mainstream analysts accused him of "morally violating his own people" and called the public sentiment behind him in Russia a "collective fit of insanity."[9] The complaints were rooted more in a distrust of NATO and American motives than they were in protecting the Serbian leader.

Roundtables and consortia on foreign policy and strategic planning were the order of the day. Yet another discussion group made up of senior experts from ISKRAN and the ministry of defense debated the ABM during the first week of July, and reached a consensus that amendments to the ABM were conceivable as long as Russia's interests were protected. Most participants assumed that the American conviction of the need for an NMD had more to do with the domestic economy than it did with any fear of maverick states. Russia's best bet, they concluded, was to stay calm and let the Americans play the hand out by themselves.[10] A lengthy report prepared by Aleksei Arbatov, who was part of neither group mentioned above, also called for compromise on missile defense. Viktor Litovkin was especially cynical, calling Putin's threats "virtual warheads" frightening "no one."[11]

A common denominator in the wide-ranging discourse was the specter of nuclear-armed China. ISKRAN's Kremenyuk inferred that in the long run America was much more worried about China than it was about Russia, and this notion was heard again in Arbatov's report. The concept of a Russian, American and Chinese mutual arms agreement as the solution to the NMD/ABM debate was heard far more often from Russian "experts" in 2001 than calls for a Moscow–Beijing partnership against the U.S. position.

A statement by U.S. Deputy Defense Secretary Paul Wolfowitz that the ABM treaty could be amended unilaterally within months exacerbated the situation. Igor Ivanov subsequently complained that, in spite of promises of consultations made at Ljubljana and regular telephone conversations with Colin Powell, his ministry still had no clear idea about America's intentions. An internal twenty-four-page memorandum circulated to every U.S. embassy in July telling its diplomats that Washington would go ahead with the NMD in spite of the ABM Treaty caused special consternation in Moscow.[12] Donald Rumsfeld repeated the gist of this message on 13 July.

---

9. Boris Yunanov, "Nesloboden" [Unfree], *Obshchaia gazeta*, No. 27 (5–11 July 2001).

10. "Kruglyi stol. PRO et contra" [Roundtable. PRO (NMD) and Contra], *Rossiiskaia gazeta* (3 July 2001).

11. Viktor Litovkin, "Putin prigrozil virtual'nymi boegolovkami" [Putin Threatens with Virtual Warheads], *Obshchaia gazeta*, No 26 (28 June–4 July 2001). Arbatov, "Eshche raz o PRO. Dostizhima li formula stabil'nosti" [Once More on the NMD. Will We Achieve a Formula for Stability?], *Nezavisimaia gazeta* (4 July 2001); for the interview with Arbatov, "Golovnaia bol' ot golovnykh chastei. Chto stoit za nashim 'otvetom Bushu'" [A Headache from Warheads. What Is behind Our "Answer to Bush"], *Obshchaia gazeta, ibid.* See also Vadim Solov'ev, "Putin daet otvet na 100 let vpered" [Putin Gives an Answer for 100 Years in the Future]. *NVO*, No. 23 (29 June–5 July 2001), where Putin is criticized for reverting to traditional rhetoric.

12. On this, see Vadim Solov'ev, "Pentagon zapuskaet mekhanizm razvertyvaniia NPRO" [The Pentagon Launches a Mechanism for Developing the NMD], *NVO*, No. 24 (6–12 July 2001); and Solov'ev, "SShA forsiruiut vykhod iz dogovora po PRO" [The United States Accelerates Withdrawal from the ABM Treaty], *Nezavisimaia gazeta* (13 July 2001).

Russia was disappointed as well when the protocol on Russia's accession to WTO was postponed indefinitely after talks in Geneva in late June.[13] The blow ' softened a few weeks later when the EU opened an information office in Moscov and both the World Bank and the EBRD expressed renewed interest in investing Russia. These events and an early July sortie to Moscow by France's Chirac sugges that Europe's concern about Russian behavior in Chechnya and alleged threats freedom of the press were now relegated to the back burner. In fact, on 2 July Pt and Chirac signed a strategic agreement based on a mutual belief in the value of clear deterrence as a means of guaranteeing strategic stability in Europe.

Not everyone was impressed with these European initiatives. Moreover, the e nomic value of membership in the WTO was being questioned by critics who lieved that the struggling Russian manufacturing sector would suffer irrepara harm under the organization's regulations. There were larger issues opened up discussion as well. For example, the concept of "humanitarian intervention as par the new world order" was the subject of a very long and acerbic treatise by Vagif (seinov, director of the Institute of Strategic Investigation and Analysis, and mem of the CFDP. Concluding that such interventions were now inevitable, and e' sometimes necessary, he urged practitioners to conduct them only under the auspi of the UN and with the participation of all the regional organizations concern above all, the EU, CIS, and NATO. NATO's "aggression" in Yugoslavia was citec the way in which "humanitarian intervention" could too easily become "humanit ian war."[15] It was time for Russia again to look Eastward for comfort.

FRIENDSHIP TREATY WITH CHINA AND THE G-8 IN GENO

The NMD and ABM were discussed by Putin and Jiang Zemin in Moscow, wh Russia and China signed a new Good Neighborly Treaty of Friendship and Coof ation on 15 July, the first such treaty since 1950. Riddled with clichés about the n for a "multipolar world" led by the UN (and not Washington), and an emph upon the ABM Treaty as the "cornerstone" of world strategic stability, the treaty ' proclaimed by both signatories. It strengthened Putin's hand at the G-8 summit Genoa much as the visit to Beijing had given him legitimacy just prior to the G-{ Okinawa the previous year.[16] Putin also had met with Jiang shortly before his f

---

13. For an example of Russian anger, see Yevgeni Arsyukhin, "Shiroko zakrytaia dver' vstretila r iskuiu delegatsiiu na peregovorakh po VTO v Zheneve" [Doors Wide Shut Met Russian Delegatio WTO Talks in Geneva], *Rossiiskaia gazeta* (4 July 2001).

14. A roundtable of experts in Moscow all concluded that Russia one day would be a member of EU, but they recognized that their own economic problems had to be resolved first; see Georgii Ilyuc "Evrosoiuz nadeetsia kogda-nibud' priniat' Rossiiu v svoe lono" [European Union Hopes to Take Rt to Its Bosom One Day], *Izvestiia* (31 July 2001).

15. Guseinov in *Vestnik analitiki*, No. 3 (2001), summarized as "Sovremennaia 'filosofiia internats alizma'" [The Contemporary "Philosophy of Internationalism"], *Nezavisimaia gazeta* (7 July 2001).

16. On this see Sergei Luzianin, "Kitai i Rossiia podpishut novyi dogovor" [China and Russia Will : a New Treaty], *Nezavisimaia gazeta* (13 July 2001); and Aleksandr Lukin, "Rossiia-Kitai: druz'i soperniki?" [Russia and China: Friends or Rivals?], *Nezavisimaia gazeta* (3 August 2001).

summit with George Bush in June 2001. This time, however, President Bush could come to the G-8 with an NMD success story, a test finally having succeeded on 14 July. The completed trial brought a quick end to Russia's chortling over earlier failures and prompted an outburst of new accusations that the United States was threatening to undermine the entire architecture of nuclear disarmament and nonproliferation treaties. Putin and Jiang immediately reiterated their support for a multipolar world and the ABM Treaty.

Most Russian analysts were genuinely impressed with Putin's performance at the G-8, insisting that he was accepted as a full member even though Russia still was not asked to attend the major economic session. A potential for self-delusion in this regard was remarked upon in some higher circles. Yevgenii Primakov, for example, advised Russians against falling for appearances. This was a very dangerous moment, he implied, noting that the NMD could make the United States invulnerable, able to "blackmail" Russia and China, and behave as it wished in world affairs.[17] A sign of things to come was Condoleezza Rice's post-G-8 trip to Moscow in late July. Hyped at first by Russians who saw the need for agreement before the ABM (and conceivably START-II) was subverted, the meeting netted nothing for Moscow. In fact, the Kremlin was compelled to deny rumors that it had offered gratuitous concessions on the ABM.[18]

NATO MEMBERSHIP RE-REVISITED

A few weeks before the G-8 summit in Genoa the notion of Russia joining NATO resurfaced. George Bush hinted at such a possibility shortly after the meeting in Slovenia, where Putin had waved the 1950s Soviet document, and Rice confirmed that it was not out of the question. During a three-day visit to Moscow in mid-July, Canadian Prime Minister Jean Chrétien was quite open in saying that Russian membership should be considered seriously by the Alliance, and Italy's new prime minister, Silvio Berlusconi, voiced a similar opinion. Putin stepped into the discussion, telling an Italian journalist on 16 July and a Russian press conference two days later that NATO should either disband or admit Russia.[19] Towards the end of the month Chancellor Schröder told an interviewer for *Stern* that he would welcome Moscow's accession to NATO—sometime in the future.

All of a sudden, analysts and commentators were again mooting the subject, with a wide range of conclusions. Ironically, just prior to the Genoa meeting Putin uttered

17. "Yevgenii Primakov: Nam nuzhno uchityvat' geopoliticheskie ugrozy"[Primakov: We Need to Take Geopolitical Threats into Account], *Izvestiia* (1 August 2001); see also Sergei Merinov, Nikolai Paklin, "Fotografiia na pamiat' o 'bolshoi vos'merke'" [G-8 Souvenir Photograph], *Rossiiskaia gazeta* (24 July 2001).

18. On this, see Yurii Yershov, "Zontik dlia Kondolizy Rais. Yadernyi . . ." [Umbrella for Condoleezza Rice. A Nuclear One . . .], *Rossiiskaia gazeta* (26 July 2001), and an interview with Stefan Sestanovich, an American diplomat under Clinton, in *Obshchaia gazeta*, No. 30 (26 July–1 August 2001).

19. ITAR-TASS (16 July 2001. The journalist was in Moscow, reporting a pre-G-8 story for *Corriere della Sera*.

his toughest words yet against NATO expansion. Speaking at a press conference
some 500 Russian and foreign journalists on 18 July, the Russian president scor[...]
the idea that NATO had become a political organization. If it was, he said, "why
[it] bomb Yugoslavia?" He repeated the old Primakov message that NATO expans[...]
merely opened up new dividing lines in Europe, "pushing the wall directly to Rus[...]
borders." His alternatives to NATO's expansion were, one, to dissolve NATO and
place it with a unified European security space; two, allow Russia to join NATO;
three, create a completely new type of inclusive organization, based on the OS[...]
Obviously, he did not expect any of these routes to be taken by NATO.[20]

By that time, of course, Russia's official stance towards NATO had changed s[...]
stantially since the year in which relations had been frozen. In July 2001, the mini[...]
of defense renewed its peacekeeping activities in Kosovo and offered to participate i
NATO/UN peacekeeping undertaking in Macedonia if such became necessary. In f[...]
Russia urged the UN to take action in that tense region. A director for the NATO
formation Office in Moscow was finally appointed—German diplomat Rolf Welber
nearly six months after the office was declared open; a new Sea Breeze exercise was c[...]
pleted on the Black Sea, with Russian observers present; and Russian officers again w
contributing to joint operations-planning at NATO Supreme Headquarters.

This did not mean that the sometimes gaping differences between the Atlantic
liance and Russia had dissolved. Unresolved problems, from relatively minor iss[...]
such as the setting up of a NATO Military Liaison Office in Moscow, to overar[...]
ing concepts of how European security should be guaranteed, remained. Russia [...]
determined to oppose any NATO "out-of-zone" action without a UNSC mand
and any more NATO expansion eastward. The latter principle was restated in 11 J
by a foreign ministry representative to a conference on European and global secu
held in Athens.[21] From Moscow's perspective, the future of NATO and Russia's pl
in the new world order were intricately connected. A larger NATO would render
OSCE irrelevant in security matters and further undermine the importance of R
sia's veto powers in the UNSC. American unilateralism would be greatly facilitat
Clearly, much hinged on the results of the proposed discussion between the Pu
and Bush administrations on global security and strategic stability. A number of R
sian analysts saw the solution in Russian accession to NATO. That was, first, so[...]
thing that Europeans, especially Germany, might advocate so as to avoid havin[...]
"mindlessly follow" the American lead in everything and, second, as a way to an
European security system.[22]

---

20. "Vladimir Putin's Press Conference with Russian and Foreign Journalists," *strana.ru.* Full m[...]
script in translation, BBC Monitoring (Russian TV, Moscow, 18 July 2001).

21. Interfax (11 July 2001). The statement was made by Deputy Foreign Minister Yevgenii Gus[...]
who said that NATO expansion made no "military or diplomatic sense" other than as a means of is[...]
ing Russia and making it into a buffer state between West and East. For a discussion of Russian p[...]
opinion and NATO, see William Zimmerman, "Survey Research and Russian Perspectives on NATO
pansion," *Post-Soviet Affairs,* 17: 3 (July/September 2001), pp. 235–261.

22. See Yurii Pankov, "Zachem Rossiiu priglashaiut v NATO" [Why Is Russia Invited to NAT[...]
Krasnaia gazeta (11 August 2001). See also Dmitrii Gornostaev, "Cautious Invitations Should Be Tre[...]
Cautiously. Continued Debate on Prospects for Russia Joining NATO," *strana.ru* (9 August 2001).

Ambassador Vershbow did tell a radio interviewer on 15 August that there were no obstacles to considering Russia's membership to NATO; yet there was little real bending on America's part. He hedged when asked more precise questions, and made it clear that Russia could prevent neither NATO enlargement, nor American deployment of its NMD system.[23] In short, on the truly major issues Washington would do what it wished.

America's announced plans to withdraw from the ABM treaty drew more charges of American unilateralism from Russian analysts and almost always generated critical comment from senior Russian officials about NATO expansion eastward, above all about Baltic membership. The Russians were trying to make the best out of a bad situation, sometimes playing the China or "rogue state" cards, sometimes shrugging the ABM question off as out of their hands. But on the NATO expansion question they were consistent.[24]

Defense Minister Ivanov went on the offensive on the home front. On 26 July he told a Russian press conference that NATO expansion accomplished nothing other than to move its infrastructure closer to Russia's borders. He resurrected all the old rhetorical queries: "Why was it all necessary? Does Russia threaten anyone?" and then a few days later downplayed the problems facing the ABM, admitting that it was the United States's right to opt out of the agreement. President Putin repeated this latter message in early September. In both cases the Russian leaders went on to speak strongly against further NATO expansion, especially in the Baltics.[25]

"ATTACK ON THE USA" AND RUSSIAN–AMERICAN RELATIONS

All bets were off after the horrendous terrorist attacks on New York and Washington on 11 September. Putin was the first leader of a foreign country to contact Bush directly, and offered strong support. Within a day of the event all nineteen NATO member states invoked Article 5 of the Alliance's founding charter, which declares that an attack on any one member is considered an attack on all members. On the

---

23. The long interview of Vershbow was conducted by Ekho Moskvy on 14 August 2001 (Interfax, 15 August 2001).

24. On this, see especially, Aleksandr Sabov, "Pochemu malye shazki luchshe bol'shikh skachkov" [Why Small Steps Are Better than Large Steps], *Rossiiskaia gazeta* (14 August 2001). The communists remained very distrustful of Donald Rumsfeld, who visited Moscow in mid-August; see Vasilii Safronchuk, "Ramsfeld serditsia na Rossiiu" [Rumsfeld Is Angry at Russia], *Sovetskaia Rossiia* (21 August 2001), and called NATO expansion a "provocation and absurd." See S. Anchukov in *Sovetskaia Rossiia* (28 August 2001).

25. Interfax (30 August 2001); *strana.ru* (2 September 2001) Ivanov, "Glavnye kriterii—bezopasnost' Rossii" [Russia's Security Is the Main Criterion], *Krasnaia zvezda* (26 July 2001); Viktor Ozerov, "Russia Firmly against NATO's Eastward Expansion," *Parlamentskaia gazeta* (5 September 2001), translated for JRL, (CDI Russia Weekly, No., 170); and "Putin Softens Tone on Baltic Quest for NATO," *Jamestown Foundation Monitor* (6 September 2001). In the latter piece it is suggested that because Putin said that Russia did not plan any "campaign of hysteria," the tone had softened. Putin's strong opposition against Baltic admission was acknowledged.

13th an unprecedented Russia–NATO Permanent Joint Council declaration cal
on "the entire international community to unite in the struggle against terrorism
The two sides agreed to "intensify their cooperation under the Founding Act to
feat this scourge." Interestingly, less than three weeks prior to 11 September Pu
had moved to strengthen Russia's own Anti-Terrorist Commission by adding
deputy directors of the Federal Security Service, the Russian Foreign Intelligence S
vice, and the Russian Federal Protection Service, and the first deputy finance mii
ter to its ranks. Four sitting members were removed to make room for the r
blood.[27] On 21 August, a new cabinet post was created: deputy foreign ministei
charge of international cooperation on the fight against terrorist. The post went
former first deputy director of the FSB, Anatolii Safonov. Almost simultaneousl
new military commander was put in place in Chechnya.[28]

Sympathizing sincerely with Americans, Russian analysts, officials, and the pi
immediately began also to reflect on the significance of the event to their own cor
try: some used it as evidence that the NMD was pointless. A few offered various v
sions of "I told you so" and drew analogies with Russia's strife in Chechnya.[29]
early as 13 September, for example, head of the RF Security Council Vladii
Rushailo warned that Russians must "learn from the American mistakes" a
pointed out that the Russian government had regularly called for global solidarity
the "fight against this evil."[30] The communist press claimed that "the American p
ple are paying for the policies of their government" and remarked on the irony t
the United States was now planning to fight Osama bin Laden though they had or
inally funded him, as they had Saddam Hussein.

It was clear that for the moment, at least, Russia's long-standing clarion call agai
international terrorism as the main threat to world security would have resonance
the United States. Consultations on joint operations, especially in Afghanistan,
gan almost immediately. Even China was brought into the act, as prime ministers
the Shanghai Cooperation Organization met in Almaty, Kazakhstan, on 14 Septe
ber and vowed to fight the "global danger" of terrorism (Interfax, 14 Septemb
There was some concern that Russia not be dragged into a conflagration that to
on a "West" versus Islam character, and Putin made it clear that his cooperation

---

26. NATO press release, "Statement." Extraordinary Session of the NATO–Russia Permanent J
Council at Ambassadorial Level (13 September 2001).

27. "Obnovlen sostav Federal'noi antiterroristicheskoi komissii" [Changes in Federal Anti-Terr
Commission Membership], *Rossiiskaia gazeta* (25 August 2001).

28. Timofei Borisov, "Generala Moltenskogo predstavliat' ne nado" [General Moltenskoi Needs No
troduction], *Rossiiskaia gazeta* (11 October 2001). Lt. Gen. Vladimir Moltenskoi took over from Va
Baranov.

29. See, for example, "Terakt v SshA" [Terrorist Act in the USA], *Izvestiia* (12 September 2001); *K
mersant* (12 September 2001); *Komsomol'skaia pravda* (12 September 2001). The communist press,
Zyuganov, expressed deep sympathy and called for an immediate destruction to international terror
See, for example, "Khirosima v n'iu-iorke" [Hiroshima in New York], *Sovetskaia Rossiia* (13, 15 Sept
ber 2001).

30. "Rossiia dolzhna uchest' oshibki Ameriki" [Russia Must Learn from American Mistakes], *Ne.
isimaia gazeta* (13 September 2002). Similar quotes were drawn from a dozen other political leaders
scholars in Russia.

not include participation in any bombing attacks.[31] Russian military experts employed the terms "global danger," and "global threat" often, repeating their earlier characterization of the civil conflict in Chechnya.[32] The general sense was that Russia should help the United States in any program directed against international terrorism, but not condone indiscriminate attacks against alleged "rogue" states.[33]

Moscow found itself in a difficult position. On the positive side for policymakers was the rush of Western countries to join an anti-terrorist crusade which Russia had been urging them to do for years. On the negative side was the potential either for chaos in Central Asia, or for a major American military presence on the ground in the region—or both.[34] Assistance more extensive than intelligence exchange could place Russia's newly developed relationships with Iran, Iraq and the Arab community at large in jeopardy. Analysts and officials soon began to wonder what Russia might get in return for its contribution. Even Karaganov warned that unequivocal siding with the United States on this matter could make Russia vulnerable. As early as 17 September, he prodded the government to join the anti-terrorist coalition with NATO—along with China and India—and to request concessions on the NMD and NATO expansion (Interfax, 17 September). Russia had the most to lose, he said, and so should not balk at asking for quid pro quos. The Russian president demanded nothing, at least publicly.

By 24 September, Putin's initial wariness had been overcome. His decision nearly two weeks earlier to join with the United States had been taken almost alone; by the 24th he had rallied his cabinet around him and almost single-handedly, turned the Russian foreign policy agenda into a clearly pro-Western one.[35] In a speech televised that evening, he said that Russia would, in fact, participate in "search and rescue missions" if there was an American attack on Afghanistan and would open up its air space for "humanitarian" U.S.-led missions. He agreed as well to help persuade Uzbekistan and Tajikistan to open up air bases to a coalition force, after first having

31. See, for example, Andrei Fedorov, "Rossiia stoit pered vyborom" [Russia Facing a Difficult Choice], *Nezavisimaia* (14 September 2001).

32. See, for example, Yevgenii Moskvin, "Epokha miatezhni voiny nastupila vnezapno" [An Epoch of Guerilla Soldiers Arrives Unexpectedly], *NVO*, No. 34 (14–20 September 2001).

33. See, for example, Sergei Ptichkin, "Prikryt li kreml' ot ataki s vozdukha?" [Is the Kremlin Protected from Attack from the Sky?] *Rossiiskaia gazeta* (14 September 2001), and "Rossiia mozhet sygrat' svoiu partiiu" [Russia Can Play Its Own Game], *Nezavisimaia gazeta* (15 September 2001). See also *Izvestiia* (15 September 2001).

34. See, for example, Vladimir Mukhin, "SShA ishchut voennye bazy v SNG" [The USA Seeks Military Bases in the CIS], *Nezavisimaia gazeta* (15 September 20021); Yekaterina Tesemnikova, "Baku i Tbilisi khotiat ispol'zovat' gnev Ameriki sebe na pol'szu" [Baku and Tbilisi Want to Take Advantage of American Anger], *Nezavisimaia gazeta* (19 September 2001); Marina Volkova, Dmitrii Gornostaev, "Putin protiv uchastiia Rossii i SNG v novoi Amerikanskom voine" [Putin against the Participation of Russia and the CIS in the New American War], *Nezavisimaia gazeta* (22 September 2001); Vladimir Mukhin, "Pentagon v Tashkente" [The Pentagon Is in Tashkent], *Nezavisimaia gazeta* (28 September 2001).

35. On this, see Marina Volkova, "Vtoroi front prezidenta" [The President's Second Front], *Nezavisimaia gazeta* (26 September 2001); Natal'ia Melikova, "Tsarskii podarok" [Tsarist Gift], *Nezavisimaia gazeta* (27 September 2001). See also Vladimir Mukhin, "Pentagon v Tashkente" [The Pentagon Is in Tashkent], *Nezavisimaia gazeta* (28 September 2001).

pressured them not to do so. In this way Moscow forestalled the possibility of
Central Asian neighbors working closely with the United States while Russia was
standing on the sidelines.[36]

Public reaction to the announcement was mixed. All sectors of society were
termined that their country never again be bogged down in a war in Afghanist
The left interpreted the entire battle plan as an American plot to gain control of C
tral Asia. So the government's message was not an easy one to sell at home. Putin
pected Western complaints about Russian action to Chechnya to become less s
dent, and in this regard at least the Kremlin had some short-term success. Sho
after Russian General Procurator Vladimir Ustinov told the press that "we have c
right proof of a direct connection between the Chechen terrorists and sponsors
Afghan territory, . . . Bin Laden," the American State Department issued a public
mand that Chechen rebels cease any links they might have had with Osama
Laden.[37]

Within 24 hours of Putin's startling turnaround, he was in Berlin consulting w
the German leadership and business community. He spoke to the Bundestag in
ent German and expressed his pleasure with the apparent reversal of Berlin's posit
on Russia's campaign against separatists in Chechnya.[38] He candidly questioned
contradiction between NATO now asking for unwavering loyalty from Russia, wl
offering no mechanism through which Russia could take part in "drafting and m
ing decisions related to European security situations." Almost simultaneously,
German ambassador in Moscow hinted that his country would not oppose Russ
membership in NATO; Russia's foreign minister addressed the UN General Asse
bly and urged that the coalition against terrorism be conducted by the UN; a
Moscow and Teheran agreed to joint action against terrorism.[39] German and An
ican leaders both expressed sympathy for Russia's difficulties in Chechnya.

RUSSIA IN NATO—YET AGAIN?

Putin spent three days in Brussels as well, on an official visit to the Belgian gove
ment and to discuss strategy with both the EU and NATO leaderships. Although
spent several hours with NATO's Robertson on 2 October, he pointedly did not v
NATO Headquarters. That being said, the Russian president called for closer Russ

---

36. The communist press saw an American plot to win influence in Central Asia emerging. See Va
Safronchuk, "SShA podbiraiutsia k srednei asii" [The USA Slowly Approaches Central Asia], *Sovets*.
Rossiia (25 September 2001); see also Vladimir Mukhin, "Pentagon v Tashkente" [The Pentagon I
Tashkent], *Nezavisimaia* (28 September 2001).

37. See Dmitrii Severnyi, "Chechnya uchitsia zhit' po zakonam" [Chechnya Learns to Live by the L
Rossiiskaia gazeta (21 September 2001).

38. "Remarks by President Vladimir Putin of Russia in the Bundestag . . ." (25 September 2001), t
script in English on the Embassy of the Russian Federation in Canada website; see also Mal
Makarychev, "Tak pobedim!" [We Will Win!], *Rossiiskaia gazeta* (26 September 2001).

39. See Aleksei Bolotnikov, "Iran uzhe opredelilsia" [Iran Has Already Decided], *Nezavisimaia* (20 !
tember 2001).

NATO ties and announced that his country was prepared to support major changes in Europe's security structures. Among other things, he said that there was a need for new "agencies" to handle the current crisis. Coupled with a statement from Colin Powell in Washington on 3 October to the effect that the events of 11 September caused a "seismic sea change of historic proportions" in the U.S.–Russian relationship, and an accompanying flurry of talk about the potential of Russia as a NATO member, it seemed that the wheels of fortune were spinning quickly in Moscow's favor.[40] Powell ended his commentary by saying "nothing is beyond consideration these days," pointedly referring to a possible future Russian membership in NATO. How times had changed, or so it appeared.[41]

General Secretary Robertson's plan to set up a special Russia–NATO "think tank" to discuss what Putin called "qualitative change" in Russia's relationship with NATO was characteristic of the sudden change in atmosphere. The Russian president would not acquiesce to expansion without a major transformation of NATO itself, however, and made it plain that Russia was more interested in an alliance with NATO than he was in actual membership.[42]

Nevertheless, chatter about Russian membership in NATO continued in October: British Defense Minister Geoffrey Hoon, Ambassador Vershbow, and Polish President Kwasniewski all offered qualified support to the idea.[43] Only Sergei Karaganov among Russia's prominent foreign affairs experts took such statements at face value. "The advantages of NATO membership for Russia would outweigh the disadvantages," was his not very compelling endorsement.[44]

Russia quickly became a facilitator for American involvement in Central Asia, asking only that Washington inform Moscow before any major agreement was made with a country in the former Russian sphere of influence. Although an arms deal was signed with Iran (see chapter 12) on 3 October with no complaints from the United States, the new arrangement was a mixed blessing for Russia: an American presence in Uzbekistan (Rumsfeld was in Tashkent on 3 October) and Tajikistan could in the long run reduce Moscow's influence in the region; or, if the United States conducted

---

40. For commentary on the new interest in Russia becoming part of NATO, see Ira Straus, "How Russia Can Get into NATO," *Moscow Times* (3 October 2001).

41. On this, see Viktor Kremenyuk, "Ne nado davit' na Briussel'"[We Must Not Pressure Brussels], *Rossiiskaia gazeta* (4 October 2001).

42. On this, see Maksim Makarychev, "NASHestvie v NATO" [Our Move towards NATO], *Rossiiskaia gazeta* (4 October 2001); and Andrei Avdoshin, "Rossiia vozvrashchaet status velikoi derzhavy" [Russia Gets Back Its Status as a Great State], *Ibid.*

43. See an interview with Vershbow, Megan Twohey, "An Old Hand at the Helm," *Moscow Times* (12 October 2001).

44. For the relevant interview with Karaganov, see *Trud* (20 October 2001), translated in JRL (CDI Russia Weekly, No. 177). He too called it only a "theoretical possibility" and noted that Russian entry would turn NATO into a much larger military-political body with a quite different philosophy. For the opposite view, in which it was said that, in spite of the "pointed friendliness," nothing really had changed between Russia and NATO, see Yevgenii Grigor'ev, "Golubushka, kak khorosho!; Tak govoriat na zapade o politike Rossii, no neizmenno gnut liniiu na rashirenie NATO" [My Dear Fellow, Don't Worry! That Is What They Say about Russian Policy in the West, but the Hard Line on NATO Expansion Is Unchanged], *Nezavisimaia gazeta* (24 October 2001).

raids from those countries and then left without providing guarantees of protect
from Wahhabite retaliation, then Russia could find itself with a badly destabili
frontier. Moreover, there was concern that international terrorism might upgrade
activities in the Caucasus to ease the pressure against Afghanistan's Taliban.[45]

Public opinion surveys showed the Russian people to be very sympathetic w
Americans and eager to be part of an anti-terrorist coalition. They were overwhel
ingly opposed, however, to retaliation without a named and proven target.[46] De
sions by the CIS heads of state seemed to mirror these opinions. On separate d
they (in Moscow) and their security ministers (in Dushanbe) adopted stateme
on combining efforts against terrorism, noting that the UNSC resolution 13
adopted unanimously on 28 September, should be the guiding mandate for any jc
operation. And Russia decided to sell $30 to 45 million worth of arms to the Nor
ern Alliance, the only credible opposition to the Taliban in Afghanistan. Where n
essary, Iran agreed to act as middleman in these deliveries.[47] Shortly thereafter, Wa
ington accepted the Northern Alliance as its main ally on the ground ins
Afghanistan, indirectly making Iran an ally as well.[48]

There was another complication for Russia. Osama bin Laden had been reviled
Russia for a long time as the kingpin of international terrorism, but specialists on
Islamic world warned that the attack on "terrorist number one" must not be allowed
drive a wedge between Islam and the West—within which the Kremlin now obviou
included itself.[49] Putin exhorted the CIS leaders gathered in Moscow on 28 Septem
not to allow the struggle against terrorism to become a war between civilizations

The "we are in this together" with America mood was sustained, however. Co
doleeza Rice helped by telling an interviewer from a Russian paper that the threa
international terror would bring the Russian and American governments "closer
gether." Their relationship was on the agenda for a Putin–Bush meeting at
Shanghai G-8, and President Bush began to speak of his "friend Vladimir."[51]

---

45. On this, see Konstantin Totskii, "A Security Alert," *Obshchaia gazeta,* No. 39 (27 September–2
tober 2001), FBIS-SOV, No. 1001 (5 October 2001). Totskii named Chechnya, Dagestan, Georgia
Azerbaijan as possible targets; and Maksim Yusin, "Khoroshikh terroristov ne buvaet" [There Are
Good Terrorists], *Izvestiia* (4 October 20901).

46. For a cross-section of political opinion in Russia, see Maksim Glikin, "Party Bosses Show Way
of Crisis: They Lead in Different Directions," *Obshchaia gazeta,* No. 39 (27 September 2001);, Fl
SOV, No. 1001 (2 October 2001); Il'ia Medovoi, "Slabost', kotoruiu ne pobedit' siloi" [Weakness, Wl
Cannot Be Defeated by Force], *Obshchaia gazeta,* No. 38 (20–26 September 2001).

47. On this, see Igor Korotchenko, "Lend-liz ot Sergeia Ivanova" [Lend-Lease from Sergei Ivan
Nezavisimaia gazeta (4 October 2001).

48. On this irony, see Maksim Yusin, "Dzhorzh Bush nashel glavnogo soiuznika" [George Bush Fo
the Main Ally], *Izvestiia* (19 October 2001).

49. See, for example, Adam Dol'nik, "Terrorist nomer odin" [Terrorist Number One], *NVO,* No
(21–27 September 2001).

50. See, for example, "Islamskii mir Rossii" [The Islamic World of Russia], *Izvestiia* (17 October 20
Viktor Timoshenko, " 'Ne dopustit' voiny tsivilizatsii' " ["Don't Allow a War of Civilization"], *Neza
maia* (29 September 2001).

51. For the interview with Condoleeza Rice, *Izvestiia* (15 October 2001). See also Aleksandr Shum
"Osobennosti 'tekushchego momenta', Dzhordzh Bush otsenil 'drug Vladimir' " [A Special "Momen
Time," George Bush Valued "Friend Vladimir"], *Izvestiia* (13 October 2001).

Indeed, Putin had to make some very tough choices. Full support for the American effort was looked upon askance in many Russian political and economic circles. Russian business has many contacts and contracts with the Islamic world; other groups, including some within the military, were reluctant to offer their old ideological enemies unconditional aid, especially after taking so much abuse from the West themselves over their military's behavior in Chechnya and elsewhere.[52]

Widespread unease in Russia that Washington would utilize the anti-Taliban campaign to weaken Russia in Central Asia, did not fade away. The danger of America coming to dominate oil routes between the Caspian and Asia was all too real.[53] The problem for Putin remained the simple fact that Russian public opinion did not want to go as far as he did in promising help to the coalition: the bombing attacks, both their potential for effectiveness and the killing of civilians, had very mixed reviews in Russia. Communists called them "barbaric" and warned that there would be a major backlash among the world's huge Islamic population.[54] This was the reaction expected from the left, yet even Igor Ivanov insisted that the strikes should be directed only against the guilty, and the centrist State Duma issued a statement criticizing them.

In his capacity as deputy chair of the Duma defense committee, Aleksei Arbatov rejected the spreading opinion that America was coming "to stay" in Central Asia, on CIS borders. Instead, he worried that they might bomb terrorist locations and leave Russia "face to face" with a volatile Central Asia and an ongoing civil war in Afghanistan.[55] Shortly thereafter, a signed agreement between the United States and Uzbekistan guaranteeing Tashkent some protection in return for bases in that country confounded Arbatov's assertions somewhat.[56]

As American and British forces began bombing presumed terrorist-held targets in Afghanistan, the Russian foreign ministry issued a statement that both supported the action and demonstrated its somewhat different perspective. Charging that Afghanistan under the Taliban was a "world center" for international terrorism and

---

52. See, for example, Leonid Ivashov, "Global'naia provokatsiia" [Global Provocation], *Nezavisimaia gazeta* (10 October 2001); Michael McFaul, Nikolai Zlobin, "Pogruzhenie v 'tepluiu voinu'" [Immersion in "Warm War"], *Obshchaia gazeta,* No. 41 (11–17 October 2001); this last piece was published in the United States as "Moment of Truth for the Kremlin."

53. See, for example, statements by Olga Romanova, Russian TV commentator, on Ren TV (Moscow, 11 October 2001), translated by BBC Monitoring Service; and Sergei Sokut, "Rossiiskii otvet Amerike. Vashington usilivaet svoe vliianie v tsentral'noi azii, a Moskva delaet shag k persidskomu zalivu" [Russia Answers America. Washington Strengthens Its Influence in Central Asia, but Moscow Takes Steps in the Persian Gulf], *NVO,* No. 37 (5–11 October 2001); see also Oleg Cherkovets, "Obkladyvaiut . . ." [They Cover Up . . .], *Sovetskaia Rossiia* (13 October 2001), where the new "merging" with NATO was called a myth.

54. See, for example, "Net terrorizmu! Ostanovit' voinu!" [No to Terrorism! Stop the War!], and Yu.P. Savel'ev, "V Afganistane bombiat Rossiiu" [They Bomb Russia in Afghanistan], *Sovetskaia Rossiia* (11 October 2000); Vasilii Safronchuk, "Islamskii bumerang" [Islamic Boomerang], *Sovetskaia Rossiia* (16 October 2001).

55. Arbatov, "Amerikantsy prishli ne navsegda. No Moskva ne dolzhna pozvolit' im otbombit'sia i uiti" [Americans Have Not Come to Stay Forever. But Moscow Should Not Allow Them to Merely Bomb Sites and Leave], *Nezavisimaia gazeta* (11 October 2001).

56. On this, see Vladimir Berezovskii, "Tashkent i Vashington udarili no rukam" [Tashkent and Washington Strike a Bargain], *Rossiiskaia gazeta* (16 October 2001).

extremism, and of the production and illicit trafficking of drugs, Moscow fully proved the raids. The statement concluded with an admonition that "terrori wherever they are—in Afghanistan, Chechnya, the Middle East or the Balkan: must know that justice will come upon them."[57] The link between Russia's stand what they were fighting in Chechnya and the nature of Albanian military activi in the Balkans was implicit.

At roughly the same time, some of the hoped-for quid pro quos began to fade fr sight. American Secretary of State for Commerce Donald Evans was in Moscow 15 October and, apparently, made it clear that few concessions would be offered facilitate any fast-tracking of Russian membership in the WTO. From the Russ point of view, this attitude marked a change of heart and led to even more un tainties about Russia's integration into the world economy. It was significant, howe that President Bush called off three planned NMD tests, presumably to keep ABM out of the discussion when the two presidents met at Crawford, Texas.[58]

MEETINGS IN SHANGHAI AND DUSHANBE

It is worth pointing out that Putin and Bush added a separate statement of their o to an APEC anti-terrorist announcement from Shanghai. The APEC group rele made no reference to Afghanistan or Osama bin Laden; the RF–U.S. statement c and also included calls for joint action against nuclear proliferation, and the use chemical and biological weapons research. At a news conference, Putin and Bush vealed the extent of their intention to work together on terrorism, and their cont ued differences on the ABM and NMD.[59]

There were differences of opinion on other matters too, revealed as the Russi began dealing with the Northern Alliance directly. On his return from the AP meeting, Putin stopped in Dushanbe to meet with Tajik President Rakhmonov ɛ the president-in-exile of the Islamic Government of Afghanistan, Borhanoddin R bani, titular leader of the Northern Alliance.[60] Rabbani had been deposed in 1ɕ by the Taliban but was still recognized by the United Nations and most other stɛ as the legitimate head of Afghanistan's government. They were joined there by h

---

57. "Statement by Russia's Ministry of Foreign Affairs Regarding the Start of the USA's and G Britain's Counterterrorist Operation on the Territory of Afghanistan" (8 October 2001). Issued by the Embassy in Ottawa, Canada.

58. For one Russian reaction to this, see Valerii Volkov, who said that whereas the United States see now more flexible about the ABM, the depth of change would only be apparent after the meetin Crawford, "Do noiabria ne letaet" [It Will Not Fly Until November] *Izvestiia* (27 October 2001).

59. "Remarks by Bush and Putin at News Conference" (21 October 2001), transcribed by *eMe MillWorks, Inc.* For Russian analyses, see Vitalii Dymarskii, "'Neskuchnyi sad' v Shangkhae" [An "Ir esting Garden" in Shanghai], *Rossiiskaia gazeta* (20 October 2001), and Vsevolod Ovchinnikov, "P snova v Shankhae" [Putin Again in Shanghai], *Rossiiskaia gazeta* (18 October 2001).

60. Rabbani was not always regarded as a friend in Moscow. In early 1996, he was accused of sponso rebels in Tajikistan. In December of that year, however, he (along with representatives from the UN, and Russia) helped facilitate an accord between the warring factions in Tajikistan. See *REDA* 1996, Vol

of the Russian Security Service, Nikolai Patrushev, and Defense Minister Ivanov, so the meeting was not quite so "unscheduled" as the Russian official media later claimed it to be. In addition to the large supply of arms promised to the Northern Alliance, the Russian government already had delivered humanitarian aid for refugees, some 23,000 tons of tents, blankets and food to Kulob on the Tajik border with Afghanistan, by train, with much more promised (ITAR-TASS, 14 Oct). At the meeting in Dushanbe, Putin spoke firmly against the idea put forward by Pakistan and tentatively accepted in Washington, that some "moderate" members of the Taliban be included in any new Afghan government. Pakistan had been one of the few countries to recognize the Taliban as the legitimate government of Afghanistan. Moscow's role as chief sponsor of the Northern Alliance and in deciding the makeup of a future government seemed to be shaping up.

Taking no chances, the Kremlin continued its diplomatic offensive. Igor Ivanov spoke with Iran's foreign minister by telephone on 24 October and confirmed their joint support of the Northern Alliance. At about the same time, Italy's prime minister, Berlusconi, was in Moscow for a two-day visit, and just as he arrived on the 24th France's prime minister, Lionel Jospin, was leaving the city. So was the Israeli deputy prime minister, Natan Sharansky, who had come to Moscow for discussions with Igor Ivanov. A few days later the Chinese vice president, Hu Jintao, arrived in Moscow, followed a week or so later by the Indian prime minister. It was made clear at all these meetings that Russia did not wish to join NATO; rather, it hoped to establish a deeper association with Europe and participate in decision-making whenever security questions for Europe and Central Asia were raised. Russian analysts continued to stress the importance of Moscow playing a meaningful role in forming a post-Taliban government.[61]

PREPARING FOR A PUTIN–BUSH SUMMIT

It remained to be seen if the "seismic sea change" with America would have any substance, as cautionary views began to emerge on both sides. In the meantime, Putin ordered the closing of its surveillance base at Lourdes, Cuba, and large naval base at Cam Ranh, Vietnam, doubtless expecting, but still not demanding, an important reciprocal concession from the United States (see chapter 7).[62] Nevertheless, Russian analysts still worried that their country and the United States might become competitors—not partners—for influence in post-Taliban Afghanistan.[63] A timely appeal

61. See, for example, Yelena Melkumyan, "Mify i real'nost' antiterroristicheskoi kampanii" [Myths and Realities of the Anti-Terrorist Campaign], *Izvestiia* (27 October 2001), and "Spetsnazovtsy idut v Afganistan" [Specialists Go to Afghanistan], *Nezavisimaia gazeta* (27 October 2001).

62. On this, see Svetlana Babaeva, et al, "Bazovaia tsennost'" [The Value of Bases], *Izvestiia* (18 October 2001).

63. See, for example, Vadim Solov'ev, "Rossiia—SShA: partnersy ili soperniki?" [Russia–USA: Partners or Rivals?], *NVO*, No. 40 (26 October–1 November 2001).

to Russians by Lord Robertson appeared in the form of a long essay on the r
Russia–NATO relationship. Granting that Russia had a "special role" to play in
Caucasus, Central Asia and the Far East, the General Secretary claimed that, as p;
ners in an anti-terrorist coalition, NATO and Russia could be a powerful force in
world.[64]

The Russian foreign policy elite also prepared for the Crawford meeting, offer
Putin's team advice on what line to emphasize. The CFDP, for example, released a d
ument titled "Russia and the Globalization Processes. What Is to Be Done." In ke
ing with its earlier theses the Council urged Putin to drop the "multipolar" visior
the world and avoid confrontation with the United States. CFDP Director Karagai
proposed that the question of Russian membership in NATO be put directly to Pr
dent Bush. Aleksei Arbatov and Yevgenii Primakov were among the signatories of
document, which explains the subtext, that is, that NATO should postpone further
pansion eastward until a decision about Russian entry was reached.[65]

As the Washington/ Texas summit neared, Russian negotiators might have b
pleased by polls showing the Russian population adopting a more positive attitude
wards improved relations with the United States. Over 70 percent favored converge
between Russia and the United States according to a poll conducted in late Octol
many respondents referring to the mutual need to combat terrorism as the reason
this trend (Interfax, 1 November). Interestingly, though the Russian public had co
around to support their president's new association with America, there was little
pectation of any real reciprocity from the United States.[66] At least one prominent {
eign affairs analyst reminded readers of the failed great expectations generated by /
drei Kozyrev, who had been harshly blamed for putting all his policy eggs into the (
American basket. Even Sergei Rogov, who saw the moment as a great opportunity
Russia, was not convinced that Washington's need for Russian help would trans
into much flexibility on the major differences between the two countries.[67]

Russian observers waited for the results of the Washington–Crawford talks m
more anxiously than Americans did, for they marked the first real test of Put

64. Robertson, "Posle 11 sentiabria. Chego sleduet ozhidat' NATO i Rossii" [After 11 September. W
Comes Next for NATO and Russia], *NVO,* No. 40 (26 October–1 November 2001); this was printe
well in *NG* (23 October 2001).

65. For a summary of the CFDP report, see Yevgenii Verlin, "'Experts' Mandate to the President,"
mya MN (2 November 2001), translated for FBIS-SOV, No. 1102 (5 November 2001).

66. In addition to the railings of the communist press, see Sergei Stroka in *Kommersant-Vlast,* No
(6 November 2001), who said that Russia was being "taken in again." CPRF leader Zyuganov acci
Washington of following a path set by Hitler; see Zyuganov, "SShA idut ne po puti ruzvel'ta, a dorogc
urera" [The USA Does Not Follow the Path of Roosevelt, but Hitler's Road], *Sovetskaia Rossiia* (1
vember 2001).

67. S.M. Rogov, "De-fakto soiuzniki. Vstrecha Vladimira Putina i Dzhordzha Busha mozhet
istoricheskie rezul'taty" [De Facto Allies. A Meeting of Putin and Bush May Have Historical Resu
Nezavisimaia (13 November 2001); Sergei Kortunov reminded readers of Kozyrev's failures, and ·
tioned that Russia was giving up too much with little guarantee of any significant reciprocity from W
ington; Kortunov, "Litsom k litsu s Amerikoi" [Face to Face with America], *Rossiiskaia gazeta* (10
vember 2001), and Sergei Oznobishchev, Igor Runóv, "Tovarishchi po oruzhiiu ili brat'ia
razumu?"[Comrades in Arms or Brothers in Reason?], *Rossiiskaia gazeta* (10 November).

decision in September. The situation was further complicated by a Northern Alliance push right into the city of Kabul while Putin was in Washington. Within days of that event a Russian support team was in the Afghan capital, meeting with Rabbani (who was back in the city for the first time in five years), and hoping to ensure a strong Russian association with whatever new government emerged from the conflict.

PUTIN IN WASHINGTON AND CRAWFORD

There was one early surprise on 13 November, the first day of the Putin–Bush talks, and that came from the American president who proposed reducing the U.S. stockpile of over 7,000 nuclear warheads by two-thirds. Putin's response was somewhat stuttering even though he had made similar recommendations himself on more than one occasion. His general concurrence came with the rider that the reductions should follow from a written accord signed by both governments. Russia's own nuclear arsenal included about 5,800 warheads. In the subsequent press conference, Bush remarked that he was willing to make such cuts on the basis of a handshake— prompting pundits in Moscow later to wonder how the U.S. Congress and the Duma could ratify a handshake. Russia's communists were enraged, accusing Putin of capitulating to Bush and helping to violate the ABM Treaty.[68]

Shortly after his first meeting with Bush, Putin spoke to a select audience of American public and official figures at the Russian Embassy in Washington, welcoming them to "Russian territory." He set the stage for the next few days by stressing the solidarity between their two countries after 11 September, pointing out that Russian citizens had been killed by the terrorist acts in New York, and emphasizing the international character of modern terrorism. He called for a "full-fledged and permanent working alliance" to deal with such threats. Putin urged the anti-terrorist coalition to comply with UN resolutions and to utilize that institution as a medium for international unity against terrorism. It was then that he declared Russia ready for "deep" cuts in strategic arms, underscoring that he would need a written protocol— not just a handshake—before the reductions would be made possible. International relations cannot yet be built solely on trust, he remarked: Moscow and Washington still needed to rely "on the existing foundation of treaties and agreements in the sphere of disarmament and arms control."[69]

Coinciding with a flurry of public appearances by Putin in the United States were statements issued by officials in Moscow designed to sustain public awareness of

---

68. The CPRF bitterly criticized Putin for a "strategic capitulation . . . before the West," G.A. Zyuganov, "Strategicheskaia kapituliatsiia. Zaiavlenie" [Strategic Capitulation. Statement], *Sovetskaia Rossiia* (17 November 2001); see also Zyuganov, "Otstupat' dal'she nekuda!" [There Is No More Room for Retreat!], *Sovetskaia Rossiia* (10 November 2001); and Artem Vernidyan, "Putin i Bush narushat dogovor po PRO vmeste" [Putin and Bush Agree to Violate the ABM Treaty Jointly], *Sovetskaia Rossiia* (6 November 2001).

69. Russian Federation Ministry of Foreign Affairs, "Speech by President Putin of Russia before the Representatives of the American Public and US Political Figures, 13 November 2001, Russian Embassy in Washington." RF Embassy in Canada website. See also Maksim Makarychev, "Putina vstretil pustynnyi Vashington" [Putin Was Greeted by a Deserted Washington], *Rossiiskaia gazeta* (14 November 2001).

Russian positions on major international phenomena. Continued opposition
NATO expansion eastward was still de rigueur. Valentin Kuznetsov, a senior offi
with the ministry of defense, urged that the anti-terrorist campaign not be usec
an excuse to enlarge NATO; Rushailo issued a similar statement (Interfax, 14 ?
vember). Remarks such as these came in response to assertions from NATO car
date countries, especially the Baltic States, that international terrorism confirmed
need for a larger NATO. On 14 November, Foreign Minister Ivanov again rejec
the idea that the ABM was obsolete, and the assumption that the UN was the k
agency for managing post-bombing government-creation was mentioned sev
times. Putin met with the UN's Kofi Annan on his last day in the United States.

Towards the end of Putin's visit with the American president several joint cc
muniqués were circulated. These confirmed presidential determination to cut
clear weapon stockpiles, and continue wide-ranging consultations on their r
strategic relationship. They spoke also of joining hands in the fight against terrori:
the proliferation of weapons of mass destruction and both biological and chem
weapons, aggressive nationalism, religious intolerance, and so on. No details w
committed to writing, so it appeared in Moscow that Putin had not accomplisl
very much in terms of specifics. There had been much gushing, but little agreem
on the big questions of the ABM and NMD, or on NATO expansion. It was sig
icant that it was left to Tony Blair to take up the task of proposing a mechanism
Russian–NATO negotiations about upgrading their relations. Blair contacted Pu
in Moscow and advanced the idea of a new NATO/Russia body to focus on cooi
nating anti-terrorist activities and arms control. The suggestion was immediately
dorsed by Igor Ivanov. Canada had proposed a similar new approach. It was not cl
how the new mechanism would coexist with Lord Robertson's "think tank," or e
with the JPC. It appeared that the question of Russia actually joining NATO 1
had another fifteen minutes of fame.

Within a week of Putin's return to Moscow, Russian officials met with Checl
separatist representative Akhmed Zakaev at the Sheremetovo airport in Moscow. 1
tle was expected of the meeting—which was held under very tight security—
even less than that was achieved. The mood in Russian government circles had ha
ened by 20 November, when U.S. Under Secretary for Arms Control John Bolt
told a United Nations gathering that Iraq represented the most serious threat
launch a biological war campaign against his country. Some Russian analysts saw
remark as preparing the way for an attack on Iraq, an event that would greatly cc
plicate Putin's policies. By that time, it was understandable why Moscow was v
quick to get a delegation of their officials into Kabul to help negotiate a new g
ernment with the Northern Alliance.

On 26 November, in fact, more than 200 Russian troops from the Emerge
Measures Ministry entered Kabul and set up what they called a "humanitarian" c
ter in mid-city. Transport helicopters, construction crews and a mobile hospital
lowed. Although the move seemed to take everyone by surprise, Russian officials s
that it was done in conjunction with the U.S.-sponsored program to aid Afghans

fore winter set in. Putin announced that "President Rabbani and the Islamic State of Afghanistan" had requested the move, which had the effect of giving the Russians a step up in gaining the ear of the Northern Alliance dimension of the new Afghan government.

"NATO AT 20"

In the meantime, Lord Robertson visited Moscow and made much of the proposed new relationship between Russia and NATO. He and Putin saw the ongoing fight against international terrorism and the dangers posed by biological, chemical and nuclear weapons of mass destruction as the chief rationale for a new arrangement, but few details were forthcoming after the Moscow talks on 21 November. Blair's proposition, which must have come with the approval of Washington, projected some kind of Russia–NATO council with a mandate to discuss details of the current war against international terrorism, arms reductions, selected peacekeeping matters, and other "soft" security concerns. This scope suited Putin, who was blunt in saying that, although Russia would not "stand in queue" to join NATO, it was open to developing relations as far as the Atlantic Alliance itself was willing to go. Important foreign policy advisers in Russia, even those who advocated Russian membership in NATO, were encouraged that a Russia–NATO alliance might be worked out. Many Russian commentators assumed, rashly as it turned out, that a new Russia–NATO Council would compel NATO itself to transform itself.[70]

The government's position that the "20" format would "put Russia and NATO on an equal footing"[71] was not taken literally by analysts in Moscow. A warning from one writer that Russia would lose its "freedom to maneuver The notion of an association along lines of the "Group of 20" advocated by Britain and Canada was welcomed as a good compromise.[72] Robertson's two-day visit to Moscow, 22–23 November, also saw the "Group of 20" idea pushed forward.[73] There was muttering

---

70. See, for example, Sergei Sokut, "Moskva trebuet peremen v NATO" [Moscow Demands Changes in NATO], *NVO*, No. 43 (23–29 November 2001). For the interview with Karaganov, " 'Tret'ego puti' ne dano" [There Is No "Third Way"], *Obshchaia gazeta,* No. 47 (22–28 November 2001); in another interview with Mayak Radio (23 November) Karaganov said that "Russia will not be allowed to join NATO, . . . Russia's opinion will be taken into account only because it won't have the right to veto or enter NATO." FBIS-SOV, No. 1123 (27 November 2001).

71. Igor Ivanov to reporters in Moscow prior to a PJC ministerial meeting scheduled in Brussels on 7 December (Interfax, 5 December 2001).

72. Aleksei Pushkov, "Pochemu nam ne nado vstupat' v NATO" [Why Russia Should Not Join NATO], *Nezavisimaia gazeta* (27 November 2001); Aleksandr Sukhotin, "London zadumal reformu NATO" [London Thinks about NATO Reform], *Obshchaia gazeta,* No. 47 (22–28 November 2001).

73. See "Robertson: Nuzhno li vyryvat' rastenie, chtoby razgliadet' korni?" [Robertson: Does a Plant Have To Be Ripped Out to Examine Its Roots?], *Rossiiskaia gazeta* (24 November 2001); and an interview with Robertson, Aleksandr Sukhotin, "Genseku NATO nravitsia protsess" [NATO GenSec Is Pleased at the Process], *Obshchaia gazeta,* No. 48 (20 November–5 December 2001); Svetlana Babaeva, et al, "Al'ians. Rossiia i NATO nachinaiut stroit' novyi mir" [Alliance. Russia and NATO Start to Construct a New World], *Izvestiia* (23 November 2001).

among NATO member states as well, in Poland and France for example, where it ᵛ
assumed by some that a Russian veto over certain NATO decisions might be impl
from the new arrangement. The only common ground, it seemed, was a general
lief both in NATO and in Russia that Putin had given up on the idea that Ru
actually join NATO. Obviously, much work had to be done before the new plan ᵛ
to get off the ground.

Colin Powell was in Moscow over 9–10 December, smoothing the way for a
ture visit by George W. Bush.[74] The nature of NATO's new "partnership" with R
sia was discussed as well, after NATO foreign ministers met in Brussels on 6–7 I
cember and created what by then was being referred to as a "NATO at 20" jc
forum. By that time the U.S. State Department's enthusiasm for closer NATO
operation with Russia had cooled noticeably and it was made plain that Mosc
would have no veto over any NATO agenda item. On some matters, Moscow ᵛ
just as unbending and, according to at least one survey, the Russian population ᵛ
still not very welcoming to NATO. A public opinion poll conducted in Novem
found that only 14 percent of Russians would approve their country joining NAT
about the same number who would approve a defensive alliance with former So'
bloc countries and Soviet republics as a counterbalance to NATO (Interfax, 8 I
cember). In both cases these numbers marked only slight changes in attitudes h
by Russians in 1996.

Distrust of Washington and Brussels was the norm among both officials and
general public of Russia. Most Russian observers warned readers not to hold tl
breath if they assumed that NATO's foreign ministers in Brussels would take
long-held Russian positions into account during their deliberations.[75] The value
the series of Russian "concessions" made by the Kremlin to the United States ᵛ
widely questioned, and a majority of foreign affairs analysts believed that the new
liance' with the West would go the way of the Grand Alliance of the Second Wc
War once one of the sides no longer needed the other.[76] The communist pɛ
ridiculed Putin's advances to NATO, saying that the "Yankees decide what place R
sia will have in NATO," that is, at its feet.[77]

It is safe to say, then, that if there were any certainties in Moscow about the fut
of Russian, American, and NATO relationships, it was that uncertainty reigned.

---

74. See "Prezident SShA s radost'iu zhdet poezdki v Rossiiu" [U.S. President Looking Forward to
iting Russia], *Nezavisimaia* (1 December 2001). This was a front-page interview with Powell.

75. The communists insisted that Russia would end up with nothing, and NATO would have its
everywhere; see "NATO–Rossiia: novaia formula sotrudnichestva. Bublik s dyrkoi" [NATO–Russi;
New Formula for Cooperation. A Bun with Holes], *Sovetskaia Rossiia* (8 December 2001).

76. See, for example, Dmitrii Furman, "Druzhba protiv. Postignet li antiterroristicheskuiu koali
uchast' antigitlerovskoi?" [A Friendship Against. Will the Antiterrorist Coalition be Like the Anti-H
Coalition?], *Obshchaia gazeta*, No. 49 (6–12 December 2001); Valerii Yaremenko, "Lurdes brosɑ
Bor'ba vokrug Dogovoram po PRO teriaet vsiakii smysl" [We Are Throwing Lourdes Away. The Stru
over the ABM Treaty Loses Any Sense], *NVO*, No. 45 (7–14 December 2001); Marina Kalashnikova
NATO bez revoliutsii" [NATO Avoiding Revolutions], *Nezavisimaia* (8 December 2001); see also a
from Sergei Rogov for a strengthened Russia–U.S. Relationship, in *Krasnaia zvezda*, No. 229.

77. "Yanki ukazhut, gde mesto Rossii v NATO," *Sovetskaia Rossiia* (20 December 2001).

THE UNITED STATES WITHDRAWS FROM THE ABM

Putin's grand gesture of September and the "good ol' boy" atmosphere of Crawford, Texas, went all for naught, when on 13 December President Bush announced officially that the United States would withdraw from the ABM Treaty in six months.[78] In an official response to the American decision, Putin called it a "mistake" but said that the Russian government would remain calm. There would be no "anti-American hysteria," he told an interviewer for Britain's *Financial Times*.[79] Nevertheless, he immediately telephoned heads of government in China and India, agreeing with Jiang Zemin that they would act jointly if further response was deemed necessary.

Moscow had been told of the impending move two weeks beforehand by Colin Powell. Powell also had attempted to ease the blow on 10 December, when, during his first trip to Russia as secretary of state he opened negotiations on the arms cuts to which both governments had committed themselves. In a response to journalists he accepted the premise that there were international terrorists fighting in Chechnya, and a few days later (in Kazakhstan), he recognized that Russian membership in NATO would calm everyone's fears.[80] When it came to arms reduction, Putin insisted that the arms ceiling be given legal seal, in writing—and the U.S. administration agreed that that would be the central deal signed when he and Bush met in the spring of 2002. Rumors that senior American officials assumed, and said, that even a signed agreement would not be binding on them if they wished to rebuild their stockpile, placed Russian policymakers in an extraordinarily awkward position. As part of this discourse, Sergei Ivanov announced that the RF would not enforce START-II before the United States ratified it.

Russia's chattering and official classes were not so sanguine about the projected demise of the ABM: Aleksei Arbatov, Andrei A. Kokoshin, and Karaganov agreed that the United States withdrawal would strengthen the distrust of America in Russia and force Moscow to upgrade its own missile defenses.[81] The only saving grace left to the Russian government was the notion that coalition with the United States and NATO was more important than the ABM, but even that possibility was not

---

78. Russia was informed of this officially by U.S. Ambassador Alexander Vershbow on 13 December (Interfax, 13 December 2001).

79. The interview was published in Russia as "Bush menia nikogda ne obmanyval" [Bush Has Never Deceived Me], *Rossiiskaia gazeta* (18 December 2001).

80. See, for example, Vladimir Bogdanov, "Kolin Pauell ochertit nam krug" [Colin Powell Will Outline the Circle for Us], *Rossiiskaia gazeta* (11 December 2001); see also Sergei Kozlov, "Vstuplenie Rossii v NATO uspokoit vsekh" [The Admission of Russia into NATO Would Calm Everyone], *Nezavisimaia gazeta* (14 December 2001).

81. See Karaganov in *Nezavisimaia* (15 December 2001). For the interview with Kokoshin, "Nachalas' li era PROtivostoianiia" [Is It the Beginning of an Era of (NMD)-opposition?] *Rossiiskaia gazeta* (18 December 2001), and with Arbatov, "Eto ne prestuplenie, eto oshibka" [This Is Not a Crime, but It Is a Mistake], *Nezavisimaia* (14 December 2001); see also Marina Kalashnikova, "Vykhod SShA iz Dogovora po PRO byl by otkatom nazad" [USA Withdrawal from the ABM Treaty Would Be a Step Backwards], *Nezavisimaia* (15 December 2001).

promising by mid-December.[82] Across the political spectrum the press urged Ser
Ivanov to tell the JPC meeting in Brussels on 19 December that Russia would
think START-III and be less cooperative on arms reductions negotiations.[83] 1
Duma opened a formal discussion of a draft response to the American decision o
on 26 December, after chair of the international affairs committee, Dmitrii Rogo;
introduced a strongly worded resolution denouncing the unilateral withdrawal fr
the ABM.

The timing of Bush's announcement was especially galling to Moscow, for it ca
shortly after the first major victories over the Taliban and al-Qaeda in Afghanist
Wondering what happened to all the promised consultations and hinted-at de
Russian analysts saw this new development as further evidence that Washing
would exploit Russian offers of help in Afghanistan and renege on all promises o
they got what they wanted. That the withdrawal "first and foremost, put Russia
its place," and placed any notion of a multipolar world in abeyance was the opin
of one well-known foreign policy analyst.[84] Others took it to mean that the ne·
established rapprochement with the United States was flimsy and depended
much on American good will; that is, an intangible sentiment that had little cha
to prevail over the supercharged unilateralism seen then to prevail in Washingtor

There were other problems facing Putin's foreign ministry: first, the selection
Hamid Karzai (who has five brothers with successful careers living in the Uni
States), to serve as Afghanistan's interim prime minister by an American-bacl
gathering of Afghan factions in Bonn; second, the exclusion of Rabbani from ;
place among Karzai's proposed deputies undermined the potential of Russian int
ence in Kabul; and, third, the growing media anticipation of an American str
against Saddam Hussein. These trends caused Putin's to that date unassailable fore
policy initiatives to begin to look less rosy at home.

Russian diplomats worked overtime trying to shift the anti-terrorist campaigr
the aegis of the UNSC, to which it presented a report on 27 December. Inde
Deputy Foreign Minister Sergei Ordzhonikidze felt compelled to qualify Russ
support of UNSC Resolution 1373 setting up an international security force

82. See, for example, "Russia–U.S.: Generals Dissatisfied by the 'Close Friendship' ", *Argumenty i f*
No. 52 (December 2001), translated by Andrei Ryabochkin for WPS Monitoring Age
www.wps.ru/e_index.html. See also Mikhail Khodarenko, "Chuvstvitel'noe porazhenie Rossii" [Russia
fers a Strong Defeat], *Nezavisimaia gazeta* (18 December 2001), an interview with Col.-Gen. Vc
Kraskovskii.

83. See, for example, Igor Korotchenko, "Kremlevskie golubi v Evrope" [The Kremlin's Pigeons in
rope], *Nezavisimaia* (18 December 2001); Yevgenii Grigor'ev, "SShA sozdaet vakuum bezopasno;
Evrope" [The USA Creates a Security Vacuum in Europe], *Nezavisimaia* (18 December 2001).

84. Pavel Felgengauer, in "Washington Is Putting Russia in Its Place," *Moscow News* (18 Decen
2001). A similar view was expressed by Nikolai Zlobin, "Vykhod i PROshlogo" [Exit from the AI
Past], *Obshchaia gazeta,* No. 51 (20–26 December 2001).

85. See, for example, Aleksei Pushkov, "Rossiia i SShA: predely sblizheniia,"[Russia and the Un
States. Limits of Rapprochement], *Nezavisimaia* (27 December 2001); Andrei Artemev, Mikhail k
darenok, "Zapad demonstriruet Rossii novyi format sotrudnichestva" [The West Demonstrates a I
Format for Cooperation], *Nezavisimaia* (20 December 2001), an interview with Karaganov and Ivasl

Afghanistan. Although Moscow voted in favor of the resolution, which passed unanimously, Ordzhonikidze's emphasis that provisions for the UN to provide the legal framework for the force's activities and that the peacekeeper mandate "be exercised in coordination with the provisional Afghan administration" must be sustained (Interfax, 21 December), was a reflection of Moscow's disillusion with the fate of UNSC Resolution 1244 in Yugoslavia. The RF ambassador to Afghanistan, Vladimir Suprun, had taken up his post on 18 December, consolidating Russia's formal presence in Kabul.

YEAR'S END: WHERE DID MOSCOW STAND WITH WASHINGTON?

U.S. withdrawal from the ABM Treaty, a lull in the enthusiastic Russia–U.S. collaboration in Afghanistan, and fading hopes for a true partnership with NATO, left Moscow floundering in comparison to the great expectations that so characterized the early fall of 2001. Still, a group of Russian academics concluded in late December that a Moscow–Washington alliance was possible.[86]

To make that happen, some movement forward was necessary. Relatively minor points, such as the Jackson-Vanik amendment, and major issues related to unfulfilled promises of arms reductions, had yet to be dealt with. In late December, the Russian defense ministry issued statements vigorously blaming the U.S. defense industry for that country's withdrawal from the ABM Treaty. The Jackson–Vanik amendment was very important symbolically to the Putin government. It had been adopted by the U.S. Congress in 1975, after more than two years of debate on the Trade Reform Act to which it was attached. The amendment tied American trade with the USSR to the degree to which Moscow allowed its citizens to emigrate freely. It continues to function even though it has been waived on an annual basis since 1989. The Russian government has been trying to have it removed since 1993.[87]

Foreign ministries in Beijing and Moscow agreed publicly that the purpose of abrogating the ABM was to neutralize the nuclear deterrence potential of both Russia and China. In this connection a Russian–Chinese consultative group on strategic stability was created in Moscow on 19 December, at the end of a three-day series of meetings on security. Thus, both the perception and rhetoric of the Cold War era lingered on.

On the other hand, Russia's place in Europe, though still undefined in relation to NATO and the EU,[88] had been raised a notch during the previous year. Russia's new

---

86. Nikolai Dmitrievskii, " 'Ostorozhnye optimisty' staviat na sblizhenie s Zapadom" ["Cautious Optimists" Bet on Merging with the West], *Obshchaia gazeta*, No. 51 (20–26 December 2001).

87. On the Jackson-Vanik amendment and Russia, see William Korey, "Jackson-Vanik: Its Origin and Impact as Russia Nears 'Graduation' ", *The Harriman Review* (November 2002), pp. 1–15.

88. There was still some anger at the EU for "unfair" economic practices in relation to Russia, see for example, Aleksei Chichkin, "I sevriuzhku otkushat', i vodochkoi zapit' . . ."[Have a Cake and Eat It. EU Still Demands That Russia Open Its Customs Doors Widely, but Promises Nothing in Return], *Rossiiskaia gazeta* (11 December 2001).

status in Europe was given credence by the Italian foreign minister, who inforn
reporters in Moscow on 19 December that the RF position on a "new framework
strategic stability" was well received in Europe. Igor Ivanov's simultaneous statem
to the accredited foreign diplomats in Moscow that Russia hoped to achieve a "r
quality of international relations," though suitably diplomatically vague, had re
nance with his audience. Polish Prime Minister Leszek Miller was in town the n
day, and repeated the Italian minister's message in a somewhat different form. 1
official opening of a NATO military mission in Moscow, a presence the Kremlin I
long opposed, on 19 December (as part of the Belgian embassy), represented anot
stage in the new relationship to Europe. Putin's working visit to Britain on 21–
December helped confirm this new status. Small matters seemed to be adding up
a growing Russian profile in Europe, just as its new "partnership" with the Uni
States seemed to be fading.

We have seen that Europe had been granted pride of place over the United Sta
in the Foreign Policy Concept of the Russian Federation published in July, 2000.
a trade partner and as a potential source of credibility for Russia's vision of itself a
major player in international security issues, Europe was still of the utmost imp
tance to Moscow a year-and-a-half later. As the year 2002 dawned, however, th
was a danger that Europe was losing its relevancy as a collective force for inter
tional peace and security. Galvanized by the events of 11 September 2001,
United States was fully in charge of the international anti-terrorist campaign, prep
ing to send troops to Georgia and Yemen, and was threatening to attack Iraq, a
perhaps even Iran. The notion that "if you are not for us, you are against us"
peared to dominate thinking in Washington, prompting President Putin and
power ministers to ponder whether they had conceded too much.

6

✣

From "Axis of Evil" to "Vladimir and George," 2002

MOVING TOWARD PARTNERSHIP OR IRRELEVANCE?

January 2002 promised to be a busy month for Putin and his foreign policy team. The president was scheduled to visit Paris and Warsaw over three days beginning on 15 January. Before that, a ceremonial closing of the Lourdes base was planned for Cuba on 3 January and on the 7th foreign ministers from the Shanghai Cooperation Organization were set to meet in Beijing.[1] Each of these events had the potential for long-term significance and for controversy at home; they also promised closure of long-standing indecision.

The main concern in the MID, however, was the uncomfortable feeling that its exciting new relationship with Washington might be going the way of the Cheshire Cat. The first big post-ABM event in this regard came on 10 January when U.S. Assistant Secretary of State J. D. Crouch told a Pentagon briefing that some 4,000 nuclear warheads were going to be mothballed—not destroyed. From the perspective of Moscow this decision was in direct contradiction of what the much-praised arms reduction debate was all about. The euphoria initiated by the Putin–Bush announcements in Crawford, Texas, now appeared meaningless, and even the value of START-II was placed in doubt (Interfax, 12 January). The MID demanded that reductions in nuclear arms be "irreversible," to make any sense at all. In Moscow, Washington's evident reluctance to sign a meaningful treaty to replace the ABM made all the earlier warmth and apparent agreement on what needed to be done

---

1. The full dismantling of Russian facilities at Lourdes was said to be complete on 27 January (Interfax, 27 January 2002).

look like mere posturing.[2] Predictions of a new arms race suddenly reappeared
the Russian media.[3] These views were made official when they were incorpora
into the State Duma resolution on the ABM withdrawal, finally adopted (326
on 16 January. The deputies believed that the American decision "destroys the
isting international treaty system which ensures strategic stability . . . And pose
real threat of a new . . . arms race."[4]

Coupled with renewed American criticism of Russia in Chechnya, the change
heart on arms reduction negotiation struck many Russian analysts as a sign that
anti-terrorist coalition honeymoon was nearing its end. When, towards the end
the month, an official from the U.S. State Department again met with the Ichker
(Chechen) foreign minister, Ilyas Akhmadov, in Washington, the MID had li
choice but to condemn the meeting as "an unfriendly step with regard to Russia.

The growing assumption was that once the Taliban was defeated, and Russian h
no longer deemed necessary, then American attitudes had quickly reverted to pre
September form.[6] There were diplomatic troubles with Europe as well. In mid-Janu
Putin discussed European security with French President Chirac in Paris, and ca
away thinking they had agreed that any attacks on countries other than Afghanis
must come with a UN mandate, and after serious consultation within the anti-terro
coalition.[7] This accommodating moment seemed to have passed by the end of
month, when the French ambassador to Moscow participated in a meeting in P
conducted by French officials with Zakaev, incurring a strong rebuke from the Russ
ministry of foreign affairs. Well-known historian Yurii Afanas'ev advised that Put
hopes for a partnership with the United States "proved illusory."[8] Afanas'ev was am
the first prominent mainstream and moderate Russian writers to question Ameri

---

2. See, for example, Yevgenii Bai, "Yurii Baluevskii: Yadernye rakety budem pilit'" [Yurii Baluev
"We Will Saw Our Nuclear Missiles Apart"], *Izvestiia* (18 January 2002), which included commentar
Nikolai Zlobin, who remarked that because the United States sees itself as the victor in the Cold W
can pretty well do what it wishes, ignoring the concerns of Russia; Artur Blinov, "Incautious Dismantl
The Pentagon Does Not Want to Destroy Its Nuclear Warheads," *Vremya MN* (10 January 2002), tr
lated by WPS Monitoring Service, *www.wps.ru/e_index.html.*

3. See Aleksei Ivanov, Igor Ignatov, "Multiple Headaches: The Year's Results," *Tribuna* (9 Jan
2002), translated for FBIS-SOV, No. 0109 (14 January 2002).

4. Duma Resolution, "On Priority Measures in Connection with the US Decision Unilaterally to W
draw from the Anti-Ballistic Missile Treaty . . .," ITAR-TASS (16 January 2002). See also Mak
Makarychev, "God Busha" [Year of Bush], *Rossiiskaia gazeta* (19 January 2002).

5. Interfax (24 January). See also Vladimir Georgiev, "Yanki—v Chechniu!" [Yankee, to Chechn
Nezavisimaia gazeta (25 January 2002), where it was suggested that the Americans were much more
cient at defeating the Taliban than the Russians were in their long war against "terrorists" in Chechn

6. For general and not optimistic commentary, see Sergei Kortunov, Pavel Zolotarev, Boris Makarei
"Stakan napolovinu polon ili napolovinu pust. Chto stoit za sblizheniem Rossii s Zapadom" [The C
Is Half Full or Half Empty. What Stands behind the Rapprochement between Russia and the West], *i
iiskaia gazeta* (9 January 2002).

7. See, for example, Nikolai Paklin, "Shirak—Putin: otkrytaia povestka" [Chirac and Putin: An O
Agenda], *Rossiiskaia gazeta* (15 January 2002); Aleksandr Sabov, "Pochemu Amerika BYSHuet" [\
America Is Getting Angry], *Rossiiskaia gazeta* (16 January 2002); and Maksim Yusin, "Amerika narus
moratorii na kritiku chechenskoi kampanii" [America Breaks the Moratorium on Criticism of
Chechen Campaign], *ibid.*

8. Afanas'ev, "'Sootvetstvuiushchii poriadok' kak prolog griadushchei bedy" [The "Corresponding
der" as Prologue to Coming Troubles], *Obshchaia gazeta,* No. 52/1 (27 December 2001–9 January 20

commitments to universal human rights, and caustically criticize its manipulation of the media and other sources of information when it came to demonstrating the rightness of U.S. policy.[9] The "timid acceptance" of such U.S. manipulation by NATO and UNSC members "is extremely dangerous for humankind and above all for Russia," he concluded. If Afanas'ev's opinions represented a strong current of thought in Moscow's intelligentsia, then one could say that Putin's dramatic turn to the West was increasingly and more publicly seen as a failure. In fact, views like these began to show up in print with increasing frequency. "The prime target of U.S. strategic nuclear force is Russia," one analyst charged, adding that Washington was likely to attack Iraq next and work hard to keep Russia at arms length from NATO.[10]

Even such moderates as the prominent Americanologist Rogov worried loudly about "unilateralism" which, he said, seriously handicapped the development of trust in the Russia–U.S. relationship. Yabloko's Yavlinskii questioned the sincerity of the West and above all the United States when they claimed to want a strategic alliance with Russia. Yavlinskii was especially alarmed over what he saw as the growing influence in Washington of people with "ideologized, dogmatic foreign policy views."[11] Rogov and Yavlinskii both seemed genuinely puzzled by the lack of evident gratitude in America for Putin's initiative.

The NATO question was accentuated in mid-January when Moscow announced that Vice Admiral Valentin Kuznetsov was scheduled to replace Zavarzin at NATO HQ. The announcement triggered speculation about the value of the mission itself. Russia's recognition that enthusiasm for creating a new mechanism of cooperation between Russia and NATO was fading in Washington was featured with regret in an essay prepared by Igor Ivanov for publication in the *New York Times*. In that piece, which appeared on 27 January 2002, Ivanov also emphasized that, in light of the new types of threats faced by modern countries, any new system of international security would best be "conducted under the auspices of the United Nations and on the basis of strengthening international law."[12] The Russian foreign minister's message was mixed in that it was also an obvious effort to slow the deterioration in U.S.–Russian relations by extolling the advantages of the close association that had grown after 11 September. Several serious Russian reexaminations of Moscow's chances of becoming a partner with NATO were decidedly pessimistic; some assessments, in fact, hinted that Washington's NATO allies might become so alarmed at American unilateralism that the projected European army (RRF) was more likely to become reality, and that here was a route for Russia to follow.[13]

9. On human rights, see also Aleksandr Sabov, who discussed and criticized racial profiling in the United States, "Arabskii sindrom?" [Arab Syndrome?], *Rossiiskaia gazeta* (10 January 2002).

10. Aleksandr Kuranov, "Utrom kredity, vecherom sekrety" [In the Morning Credits, in the Evening Secrets], *Nezavisimaia gazeta* (19 January 2002).

11. Yavlinskii, "Druzhba na vremia ili soiuz navsegda? Rossiia i Zapad posle 11 sentiabria" [Friends for a Time or Allies Forever? Russia and the West after September 11], *Obshchaia gazeta*, No. 4 (24–30 January 2002); Rogov, "Rossiia i SShA pered vyborom" [Russia and the United States Are Faced with a Choice], *NVO*, No. 1 (18–24 January 2002).

12. Igor S. Ivanov, "Organizing the World to Fight Terror," *New York Times* (27 January 2002).

13. See, for example, Yuri Pankov, "U al'iansa krizis vozrasta. Voenno-politicheskoe obozrenie" [The Alliance (NATO) Is Having a Mid-Life Crisis. Military-Political Overview], *Krasnaia zvezda* (10 January 2002).

The foreign minister professed that his country was not interested in join
NATO; rather it hoped again to work jointly with the Alliance "in areas of sha
interest." By the time of Ivanov's writing, however, even noncommunist Russian
alysts had begun to nurture the old Soviet fear of encirclement, pointing to new
much enlarged American and British military bases or surveillance posts surrou
ing the Russian Federation—in Japan, South Korea, Central Asia and Kazakhst
Turkey, Cyprus, the Arab Peninsula, Northern Europe, and elsewhere. A comm
rhetorical query was whether the Caucasus was next.[14]

An unsatisfactory tour by Foreign Minister Ivanov through Central Asia, wh
it was clear that the new American and NATO presence gave heads of state so
real bargaining chips with Moscow, did not help the mood in MID. According
some reports Ivanov's reception in Turkmenistan and Uzbekistan had been noti
ably cool,[15] and even when U.S. Under-Secretary State Richard Armitage actua
referred to Central Asia as Russia's "sphere of influence," Moscow's pundits
mained skeptical.[16]

The Russian government was, in fact, working hard to maintain an edge, es
cially in the Southeast. Turkmenistan's President Niyazov travelled to Moscow
21–22 January to discuss, among other things, issues related to the Caspian S
and agreed with Putin that terrorism was the greatest threat to international sta
ity.[17] President Aliev of Azerbaijan arrived a few days later. He and Putin issu
joint statements about coordinating actions against international terrorism and "
treme separatism," implicitly referring to each other's main problems in Nagor
Karabakh and Chechnya. They also promised resolutions to disputes over
Caspian Sea, and signed agreements on further economic cooperation.[18] Iraq's Ta
Aziz showed up the very next day, joining Igor Ivanov in similar statements a
agreements.

Given the fact that these visits followed shortly after the arrival of a large dele
tion from the EU led by Richard Wright, who soothed Russian sensibilities ab
closer relations with Europe, the public impression of success was relatively s
tained.[19] Putin's trips to Paris and Warsaw were treated as triumphs in Moscow
spite of the glitch mentioned earlier. To a certain extent, the Kremlin benefitted fr
European reluctance to fall in line with increasingly bellicose Washington.

---

14. See, for example, Sergei Ptichkin, Aleksei Chichkin, "Otkuda Rossiia vidna kak na ladoni" [F
Where Russia Is Clearly Visible], *Rossiiskaia gazeta* (22 January 2002); and Vasilii Strel'tsov, "Gruziiu
toruiu my poteriali. Pentagon ne stremitsia v Zakavkaz'e, on tam uzhe" [The Georgia We Have Lost.
Pentagon Is Not Rushing into the Transcaucasus, It Is There Already], *Nezavisimaia gazeta* (20 Febr
2002).

15. See, for example, *Kommersant* (11 January 2002).

16. See, for example, Aleksandr Shumilin, "Gospred priznal Sredniuiu Aziiu 'zonoi vliianiia Rossii'" [I
State Department Recognizes Central Asia Is Russia's Sphere of Influence], *Izvestiia*, (24 January 2002)

17. See, for example, *Rossiiskaia gazeta* (22 January 2002).

18. See, for example, Vladimir Bogdanov, "Sblizhaemsia[Moving Closer Together], *Rossiiskaia ga*
(26 January 2002).

19. On the EU visit, see "Richart rait: Rossiia dlia Evrosoiuza—partner prioritetnyi" [Richard Wri
Russia Is the EU's Priority Partner], *Rossiiskaia gazeta* (23 January 2002).

THE "AXIS OF EVIL" BOMBSHELL

When President Bush referred to Iran, Iraq and North Korea in his State of the Union address, 29 January 2002, as a collective "axis of evil," his words landed with the impact of a diplomatic bombshell in the Kremlin.[20] Of the three, the question of Iraq was especially troubling because Russian foreign ministry officials had for a long time been lobbying both Baghdad and the UN for compromises on the stiff military and economic sanctions imposed by the latter body. Iraq's Deputy Prime Minister Aziz was in Moscow twice within a week towards the end of January—the second time the day after Bush termed his country "evil" and in danger of preemptive attack from the United States.[21] Aziz did not even wait to meet with Russian officials before he rushed home. During the Iraqi minister's first visit, on 25 January, Igor Ivanov had issued a firmly worded statement that the anti-terrorist campaign must not be aimed at Iraq. Kremlin officials at first remained mute about Bush's remarks, but there is little doubt that they caused great consternation. The rhetoric from Washington rendered Moscow's diplomacy in connection with Iraq and Iran impotent. Some Russian experts in military affairs began to take an American war against Iraq for granted and urge their own government to prepare a political—and principled—stand against that event; others urged that the Lourdes and the Cam Ranh Bay bases be reopened.[22]

Russia was not having much luck with its WTO application either. A World Trade Organization meeting in Geneva during the last week in January had been fruitless insofar as Russian delegates were concerned. Their complaints about over 100 "discriminatory measures" against Russian goods fell on deaf ears. One participant from Moscow reported back that "hypocrisy" and "double standards" dominated the sessions.[23] At about the same time, some relief was thrown Kasyanov's way during the World Economic Forum held in Washington in the same week. On 31 January, he was informed by the U.S. secretary of trade that the Jackson–Vanik amendment would no longer apply to Russia—soon; and that Russia was now considered to have a market economy.[24] But such assurances were not given much credence in Moscow, for good reason: although the latter promise finally was met in early June, the for-

---

20. See, for example, Vasilii Safronchuk, "SShA vbivaiut 'os' zla'," [The USA Hammers the "Axis of Evil"], *Sovetskaia Rossiia* (5 February 2002).

21. Bush had said, "I will not wait on events while dangers gather. . . . The United States of America will not permit the world's most dangerous regimes to threaten us with the world's most destructive weapons." State of the Union Address, 29 January 2002.

22. See, for example, Vadim Solov'ev, "Rossiia vozvrashchaet kubinskuiu bazu v Lurdese" [Russia May Retain Its Cuba Base at Lourdes], *Nezavisimaia* (6 February 2002). Vladimir Georgiev, "Voina v Irake nachnetsia v Sentiabre" [The War against Iraq Will Begin in September], *Nezavisimaia* (6 February 2002).

23. Fedor Lukianov, "VTO ne toropitsia otkryvat' ob'iatiia Rossii" [WTO in No Hurry to Embrace Russia], *Rossiiskaia gazeta* (31 January 2002).

24. See Yekaterina Vasil'chenko, Vladimir Gurvich, "Ekonomika 'lichnykh sviazei' v deistvii" [Economy of "Personal Ties" in Action], *Rossiiskaia gazeta* (31 January 2002); Vasil'chenko, "Kas'ianov otkryvaet Ameriku" [Kasyanov Discovers America], *Rossiiskaia gazeta* (5 February 2002). The Forum is usually held in Davos, Switzerland.

mer promise was rejected by the U.S. Congress shortly before the Bush visit
Moscow in May.

Putin's first public grumble about President Bush's "axis of evil" speech did
come until 1 February. While receiving the credentials of five new ambassador:
Russia, he remarked that international relations based on the "domination of (
center of force" was hopeless (AFP, 1 February).[25] The Russian position was offe
more aggressively two days later at the Munich Conference on Security Policy. An
ican Deputy Defense Secretary Paul D. Wolfowitz triggered a Russian rebuke wh
on the first day of the meetings, he and Republican Senator John McCain called
an assault against Baghdad. Wolfowitz told the startled gathering of 400 invi
guests from forty-three countries that the United States would go it alone if need
In addition to renewed conjecture on whether this rhetoric might even spell the (
of NATO itself, Sergei Ivanov accused Wolfowitz of applying double standards
failing to include Saudi Arabia among terrorist-supporting countries and said blur
that there was no evidence that Iraq had links with international terrorist organi
tions. Robertson weighed in as well, calling for both a radical upgrading of defe
expenditures by NATO members and voluntary restraints on American unilate
ism.[26] Sergei Ivanov took the opportunity also to condemn Western countries
meetings with representatives of the former Ichkerian (Chechen) government. "]
imagine," he said, if " a Basque separatist would be received in London or in Par
All such meetings represent "double standards" and should be curtailed, he advi
a press conference on 3 February. "Terrorists cannot be good or bad, moderate
not," he continued, referring to the discarded notion that there had been "mode1
Talibans"—wondering aloud how Russia's allies in the anti-terrorist campaign co
now behave in such a way towards Moscow.[27] The gloves were off. The very next (
Foreign Minister Ivanov was in Rome for a NATO–Russia conference on combat
terrorism, and listened to Robertson call for a vastly upgraded level of cooperat
between the two sides.[28]

Shortly thereafter Igor Ivanov was in New Delhi resurrecting Yevgenii Primak
idea of an axis of Russia's own making, that is, a Moscow–New Delhi–Beijing a

---

25. The official government paper covered the speech very cautiously at first, summarizing what w;
it with almost no analysis. See, for example, Maksim Makarychev, "Bush otchitalsia pered natsiei" [F
Reported to the Nation], *Rossiiskaia gazeta* (30 January 2002); Anatolii Shapovalov, "Bush isprosil—i
bilsia soglasiia" [Bush Asked For, and Got Consent], *Rossiiskaia gazeta* (31 January 2002).

26. This series of statements caused a buzz in the West as well; see, for example, Elizabeth Bum:
"Axis of Debate: Hawkish Words," *New York Times* (3 February 2002); Paul Koring, "America's Axi
Grind," *Globe and Mail* (31 January 2002). In Russia, even former foreign minister Andrei Kozyrev, ·
lost his job for being too pro-American, called Washington's position on Iraq "very awkward, very ;
plistic and inflexible . . ."

27. The communists charged that Yeltsin and now Putin had made Russia a "vassal" of the Un
States, that NATO was taking over all of Europe and excluding Russia, and so on. See, for example,
talii Rogal'skii, "Pis'mo iz N'iu-Iorka: Drug na rol' vassala" [A Letter from New York: A Friend for
Role of Vassal], *Sovetskaia Rossiia* (9 February 2002).

28. Lord George, "NATO–Russia Cooperation in Combating Terrorism: A Good Idea Whose 1
Has Come," Key Note Address at the NATO–Russia Conference on the Military Role in Combating 1
rorism (4 February 2002). Rome, NATO Defence College. NATO Website.

Ivanov sensed that the timing was now right to bring it up again, under the rubric of "trilateral cooperation." Yet this was not the only approach put forward in the winter of 2002. It was clear to several experts that the best way for Russia to compete in a world order now dominated by America was to develop their country's economic sphere: build up technology and utilize state resources, while avoiding military–political responses to imagined challenges. Mikhail Delyagin warned that the U.S. "crusade" against a new "evil empire" was primarily a vehicle for mobilizing American society and its economy, so would not be easily mellowed.[29] Vadim Solov'ev and Sergei Rogov, two of the best-known and highly placed analysts of Russia's relations with the United States, agreed that the conduct of all three members of the alleged "axis of evil" in the international arena was questionable, but challenged the notion of such an axis in the first place.[30]

Russian foreign affairs specialists made much of the fact that European countries and Canada were reluctant to follow Washington's lead in a crusade against the alleged axis of evil. Japan and South Korea were not supportive of the idea either, and they expressed this reservation to President Bush during his mid-February visit to those two countries. In fact, on 18 February Moscow welcomed the Iranian foreign minister for a two-day working visit just as Bush was landing in Tokyo; and the Iraqi ambassador to Moscow was widely quoted for congratulating Russia on its "rational" perspective on the "axis" concept. The Canadian prime minister, in Moscow for three days in February accompanied by a team of some 200 business people and officials, was persuaded to speak openly against any unilateral assault on Iraq.[31] Russia's parliamentarians put in their two cents worth as well when the Duma opened deliberations on a Statement submitted by its international affairs committee attacking the entire notion of "axis of evil" states. The Duma especially denounced the idea of using force without a UNSC mandate.[32]

Igor Ivanov was then completing a working visit to Paris and spoke of France as "a strategic partner of Russia." Ivanov professed that he and Hubert Vedrine held common positions on a wide-ranging set of issues, including the conviction that the fight against terrorism must be conducted within the limits set by international law. French officials and media echoed the Russian position that any military action against Iraq must fall within mandates provided and overseen by the UN. The specter of al-Qaeda and Taliban fighters gathering in Georgia's Pankisi Gorge region was discussed as well, and both sides emphasized the need for international cooperation in rooting them out. Widening the band of negotiations, heads of the Russian,

---

29. Mikhail Delyagin, "Oni sebe vse mogut pozvolit'" [They Allow Themselves Everything], *Rossiiskaia gazeta* (6 February 2002). For the economic position, see Sergei Shishkarev, "Nash otvet kersonu, ili Kak Rossii sleduet reagirovat' na vykhod SShA iz Dogovora po PRO"[Our Response to Curzon or How Russia Should Respond to U.S. Withdrawal from the Treaty], *Rossiiskaia gazeta* (30 January 2002).

30. Rogov at a news conference in Moscow (Interfax, 1 February 2002) and Solov'ev in *Nezavisimaia* (2 February 2002).

31. See ITAR-TASS (13 February 2002); Interfax (14, 15 February 2002).

32. See Interfax (18 February 2002), on the Duma Statement, and ITAR-TASS (11, 18 February 2002), for comments by Putin and the Federation Council's General Valerii Manilov.

Ukrainian, Belarusian and Polish security councils gathered in mid-February to ⟨ cuss regional security. This was the first time that a NATO country participatec discourse among the large Slavic states.[33]

OTHER MATTERS

Ivanov's remarks about the Pankisi Gorge were not coincidental. A few days earl the U.S. chargé d'affairs in Tbilisi told a Georgian newspaper that the United St; would like to create an anti-terrorist force within the Georgian defense minis Needless to say, this proposition had a ripple effect in Moscow, where officials l been pressuring Georgia for months to assist in fighting Chechen and other ten ists hiding on Georgian territory. The prospects of an American military (even ac sory) presence in the region was not welcomed by the Kremlin, to say the least. though Putin held true to form by shrugging off the significance of the potentia U.S. forces in Georgia, most analysts in Moscow saw the issue of the Pankisi Go as a real test of the Russian–American relationship.[34]

Moreover, the anticipated new association with NATO seemed to be go nowhere, as neither side was pushing it very hard and NATO maneuvers in the Ba and Barents Sea went ahead without any Russian input. On 22 February, Alexan Vershbow was partly responsible for resurrecting the issue at a conference on NA' held at St. Petersburg University. Insisting that Russian–U.S. relations were cl(than they had been at any other time in history, the ambassador called the projec NATO–Russia Council of Twenty a new forum in which Russia could work w NATO's nineteen members as an equal partner "on issues where our shared inter(make it sensible to do so."[35] The timing was fortuitous, for Russian politicians, f eign affairs analysts, and journalists already were asking what they had gained fr joining the U.S.-led anti-terrorist coalition. The media—even the governm press—was especially dubious, assuming that their government was retreating in face of inexorably expanding American hegemony. Even such minor promises as abolition for Russia of the Jackson-Vanik amendment had not been fulfilled, alone the larger accommodations expected on NATO and on arms reductions. T May summit between Putin and Bush was widely expected already to be yet anot "last chance" for Russia.

International developments being what they were, the once very hot topic of ⟨ bodan Milosevic and The Hague Tribunal had faded from the front pages

---

33. On this breakthrough see, for example, Yekaterina Grigor'eva, "Iz Moskvy v Kiev cherez NA' [From Moscow to Kiev, via NATO], *Izvestiia* (20 February 2002).

34. See, for example, Georgii Maitakov, "Amerikantsy prishli. Ne na tantsy" [The Americans F Come. But Not to Dance], *Nezavisimaia gazeta* (4 March 2002); see also Tamara Shkel' in *Rossiis; gazeta* (7 March 2002).

35. Vershbow, "NATO and Russia: Redefining Relations for the 21st Century" (22 February 20 Released by the U.S. Department of State. Also published in Russia: Vershbow, "NATO i Rossiia: N podkhod k vzaimootnosheniiam v XXI vekem," *Nezavisimaia gazeta* (4 March 2002).

Moscow. The opening of the actual—as opposed to media—trial of Milosevic on 12 February generated surprisingly little uproar in Russia, though the communists kept up their strident demand that he be freed, and continued to charge that NATO was the true war criminal in the Yugoslav affair.[36] Of course, much more distracting things were going on. In addition to a possible American military presence in Georgia, and actual presence in Indonesia and Yemen, the open threat to Iraq was especially worrisome. Kremlin officials watched Vice President Cheney's eleven-country tour of the Middle East with both dismay and relief. They worried above all that he was much more anxious to raise support for an attack on Iraq than he was in resolving the spiraling violence between Israel and the Palestinian Authority. With an eye on the future, they were relieved that so little support for an invasion of Iraq was forthcoming.

Russia's unhappiness about its image in world affairs was intensified by its dismal performance at the Winter Olympics in Salt Lake City. In addition to the generally poor showing, the loss of medals due to doping disqualification (cross-country skiers) and charges of bloc voting (skating) were especially humiliating. Moreover, Russian bureaucratic responses and orchestrated public outrage sounded so like the old Soviet approach—charging the West with conspiracies and threatening to withdraw from the Olympics altogether—that even a few commentators in Russia were embarrassed by it. The nineteenth-century words of Baron Pierre de Cubertin, "O sports, you are peace," reappeared everywhere as "O sports, you are war," or "O sports, you are dollars!"[37]

A concomitant trade "war" prompted by Washington's decision to raise a prohibitive tariff (30 percent) against steel imports from everywhere outside of North America, caused another stir in Moscow. Russia shared in Europe's dismay, the minister of finance calculating that the new tax could mean up to $1.5 billion loss to the Russian economy over the next several years. Russia retaliated by banning further poultry imports from the United States.[38] Health officials demonstrated that some of the poultry was infected by salmonella, and objected to the practice of injecting them with antibiotics, but the scale of the reaction was clearly political. The potential blow against the U.S. poultry export industry was large, for the sales amounted to some $600 million annually—considerably more than the annual loss to Russia in steel exports. In fact, fully one-half of American poultry exports go to Russia. The

---

36. See, for example, "Trebuem osvobozhdeniia Slobodana! Zaiavlenie KPRF, NPSR i SKP-KPSS" [We Demand That Slobodan Be Freed! Statement of the CPRF, NPSR and the SKP-KPSS], *Sovetskaia Rossiia* (12 February 2002).

37. See for example, Viktor Kozhemiako, "O, sport! Ty—dollar!" [O Sport, You Are Dollars!], *Sovetskaia Rossiia* (2 March 2002). This was a take-off on a well-known Russian song, "O, sport! ty—mir! [O sport, You Are Peace]; see also *Izvestiia* (26 February 2002); Yurii Rost, "Sport-Artur. Nanaiskaia bor'ba rossiiskikh chinovnikov na Olimpiiskikh igrakh" [Sport-Arthur. Nanaiskii Struggle by Russian Officials at the Olympic Games], *Obshchaia gazeta*, No. 9 (28 February–6 March 2002); Viktor Shenderovich, "Reportazh s lyzhni" [Reporting from the Ice], *ibid.*; Dmitrii Filipchenko, "Zimnie dopingovye Igry" [Winter Doping Games], *ibid.*

38. "Stal'nym serpom po nozhkam Busha" [Steel Sickle against Bush's Legs], *Izvestiia* (7 March 2002); Yevgenii Arsyukhin, "Kurinaia slepota" [Chicken Blindness], *Rossiiskaia gazeta* (12 March 2002).

ban went into effect on 10 March and was lifted on 23 April after the United St:
agreed to guarantee a better inspection process, but serious damage had been d₁
to the image of America in Russia. On the steel issue, even normally pro-America
ficials and analysts recommended that Moscow work with the EU to condemn
USA's new protectionism.[39]

Even though a compromise was reached in the matter of American poultry exp₁
to Russia and bilateral talks on steel calmed Russian concerns, the burst of ange₁
Russia was a long time simmering down.[40] A victory in the steel sector when in N
the United States agreed to compensate Russia for its losses, did not ease the gloo
feeling that Russia's economic and other interests were completely irrelevant
America.[41]

RUSSIA A POTENTIAL U.S. TARGET?

The event that depressed Russian analysts the most, and confirmed for them t
the much-hailed "partnership" with the United States had crumbled, was a gove
ment report delivered by the Pentagon to the U.S. Congress in January and "leak
to the *Los Angeles Times,* which then printed it on 9 March. The annual report, *I
clear Posture Review,* added four new potential nuclear weapon "targets" to the
ready much-publicized list of "rogue states": Russia was now among them. Russ
media and official reaction were marked by more anger and astonishment, mos₁
it sincere. Igor Ivanov called the *Review* a "Cold War" document, and Sergei Ivar
who was in the United States for a four-day official visit, protested Russia's tr₁

---

39. See, for example Aleksandr Livshits, "Rozhki Busha" [Bush's Horns], *Obshchaia gazeta,* No
(14–20 March 2002). The communists made much of what they called an American plot to foist dise₁
chicken legs off on unsuspecting Russians, for example, "Luchshe prevratit' marteny v inkubatory cl
pitat'sia amerikanskimi otbrosami" [Better to Turn Steel into Incubators than to Eat American Disca₁
Sovetskaia Rossiia (12 March 2002).

40. Kirill Pal'shin, "Rossiia vykhodit iz stal'noi voiny" [Russia Gets Out of the Steel War], *Izvestiia*
March 2002). See also Alla Startseva, "Despite Lifting of Ban U.S. Birds Still Frozen," *Moscow Times*
May 2002). The poultry issue actually was not resolved until the summer and the first regular shipm
of chicken back to Russia began only in September; See also George Bovt, "Kul'tura konsensusa daet
trudom" [Culture of Consensus is Hard to Master], *Izvestiia* (14 March 2002), who pointed out that
Russian ban on importing U.S. poultry would run out two weeks before the May summit; see also A
sei Chichkin, "Stal'naia druzhba protiv Ameriki" [Steel Friendship against America], *Rossiiskaia gazeta*
March 2002).

41. Because the sudden increase in tariffs against European steel coincided with a huge American
iff wall (29 percent) set against Canadian softwood lumber, potentially impoverishing the Canadian l
ber industry and putting thousands out of work, the feeling that America's long-standing rhetoric i₁
vor of free trade was sincere only when American industries (lobbies) were doing well, became a univ₁
worry. In the geopolitical arena, the Russian, European, and Canadian publics began to question the v
of partnerships with the United States. On this, see Aleksei Baliev, "Pervym delom—stal' i samole
[Steel and Aircraft First?], *Rossiiskaia gazeta* (26 March 2002). Several week later, Russia claimed vi₁
on the steel issue, announcing that the United States would compensate Russian steel producers for t
losses due to the prohibitive tariffs. See Vladimir Gurvich,̆ "Gref zanial stal'nuiu oboronu. I vyigral" [₁
Mounted a Steel Defense. And Won], *Rossiiskaia gazeta* (18 April 2002).

ment by the Pentagon.[42] Long lists of recent U.S. failures to fulfill commitments, broken promises, and threats—both alleged and real—were tracked by foreign affairs essayists who declared that Washington was "blackmailing" and isolating Russia. Several journalists accused Washington of wielding a big stick over Moscow to soften it up for the May summit between the two presidents—and not even speaking softly.[43] Others protested bitterly that Russia would soon be completely surrounded by American military bases, from the North Atlantic to the Pacific, just as it had been in the bad old days of the Cold War.[44]

Perhaps it should have come as no surprise, then, that in surveys conducted in February, Russian respondents demonstrated that the level of antipathy towards the United States had remained constant over the previous year; that is, about 60 percent were either indifferent towards or actively disliked the United States.[45] Feature articles on America's warlike stance on almost all major international issues and caricatures of members of the Bush administration in Rambo-style poses were not uncommon even in the main government print media.[46]

Nevertheless, Putin's public demeanor in the face of the presence of American troops in Georgia and the buildup of American and NATO bases in Kyrgyzstan was still nonchalant. Even a large NATO exercise in Norway and Poland in late February and early March seemed not to ruffle the Russian president, although deputy chief of general staff, Col.-Gen. Yurii Baluevskii, wondered, to journalists, why NATO was still enlarging in Russia's direction and conducting offensive training maneuvers with far more soldiers (40,000) than had been committed to fighting international terrorism (ITAR-TASS, 1 March). But the calm approach taken by the Kremlin could also have been a calculated strategic move to promote European and American support for a Russian alliance with NATO. Certainly, Sergei

---

42. See, for example, Marina Kalashnikova, "I Rossiiu vkliuchili v 'os' zla' " [And Russia Is Included in the "Axis of Evil"], *Nezavisimaia gazeta* (11 March 2002); Svetlana Babaeva, Dmitrii Safonov, "Obraz druga" [Friendly Image], *Izvestiia* (12 March 2002); "My popali v samuiu 'semerku' " [We Are among the "Seven"] *Rossiiskaia gazeta* (12 March 2002); "Rais i Pauell utochniaiut" [Rice and Powell Clarify], *Rossiiskaia gazeta* (12 March 2002); "I. Ivanov: Yadernaia doktrina SShA napisana v dukhe 'kholodnoi voiny' " [Igor Ivanov: USA's Nuclear Doctrine Was Written in the "Cold War" Spirit], *Sovetskaia Rossiia* (14 March 2002); Viktor Litovkin, "Ministr oborony snova ushel v razvedku" [Minister of Defense Again Went to Reconnoiter], *Obshchaia gazeta*, No. 11 (14–20 March 2002).

43. See, for example, Marina Kalashnikova in *Nezavisimaia* (11 March 2002), and Semen Novoprudskii, "Imperiia Dobra" [Empire of Goodness], *Izvestiia* (6 March 2002).

44. See, for example, Sergei Kortunov, "Yadernogo pariteta skoro ne budet. I ne nado" [Soon There Will be No Nuclear Parity. And No Need for It], *Rossiiskaia gazeta* (13 March 2002); Vladimir Urban, "Cam Ranh Base Will Become Green," *Novye Izvestiia* (4 April 2002), JRL, No. 200 (4 April 2002), on the likelihood of the U.S. leasing the Cam Ranh base in Vietnam when Russia finally moved out by 1 July; Mikhail Khodarenok, "Ozherel'e iz amerikanskikh baz" [A Necklace of U.S. Military Bases], *NVO*, No. 10 (29 March–4 April 2002).

45. Georgi Ilyichev, "Rossiiane stabil'no ne liubiat Ameriku" [Russians Are True to Their Dislike of America], *Izvestiia* (5 March 2002).

46. See, for example, Aleksandr Volkov, "Neizvestnaia Voina-2" [The Unknown War-2], *Rossiiskaia gazeta* (12 March 2002), with front-page drawings of Bush, Rice, Powell, Rumsfeld, and Cheney in Rambo, Batman, and other heroic character outfits.

Karaganov claimed that the CFDP's advice to avoid bluster finally had b[e]
heeded.[47]

George Robertson took a hand in mollifying Moscow by preparing a long es[say]
for *Izvestiia* in which he urged both sides to set aside "mutual suspicions" and ster[eo]
types so as to facilitate cooperation between Russia and NATO. The general sec[re]
tary repeated much of what Vershbow had said six weeks beforehand, claiming t[hat]
it was time to implement the much-ballyhooed new joint council. This encoura[ge]
ment coincided with other feature pieces from analysts in Moscow who advised [of]
ficials to be realistic: recognize that the United States used alliances and cooperat[ion]
only in its own interest. Bearing this reality in mind, Russia should empha[size]
"morality and ethics" in world affairs, all the time working hard to reach both [an]
arms reduction agreement with Washington and a consolidated "NATO at [20]
arrangement.[48] The formation of a "NATO–Russia Council" appeared to be the g[oal]
of a committee formed in Brussels, with that name, in late March. ISKRAN Di[rec]
tor Rogov led the Russian team, which collectively expressed some optimism ab[out]
a resuscitated partnership with NATO.[49]

The anti-terrorist coalition limped along as well. The results of a working visi[t to]
Moscow by Afghanistan's interim leader, over 12–13 March, was a sign of the r[ecent]
times. President Karzai acknowledged that Russian military and economic help [was]
important to his country, while making it clear that relations with America were [the]
number one priority (Interfax, 13 March). Indeed, a week later it was announ[ced]
that the Pentagon would "train" the new Afghan army.

Optimists in Moscow found a ray of hope in the fact that, as of 1 April, Ru[ssia]
took over the chairmanship of the UN Security Council. It was in that capacity, [the]
Permanent Representative at the UN Sergei Lavrov said, that Russia could lead [dis]
cussions on settling the Afghan question, the problem of Iraq, the Middle East, [and]
so on.[50] Pessimists, on the other hand, cautioned that Lavrov's excitement would c[ome]
as the UN Security Council itself slid inexorably toward irrelevancy.

GEARING UP FOR THE SUMMIT

In preparing for George W. Bush's visit in late May, the Kremlin had to face surp[ris]
ing recalcitrance on the part of a general public that now exuded a much more n[eg]
ative attitude towards American and NATO motives than their president and [gov]

---

47. See Karaganov in *Izvestiia* (26 February 2002). He was being interviewed on the 10th anniver[sary]
of the CFDP.

48. See, for example, George Robertson, "Rossiia i NATO: Vremia realizovat' sovmestnyi zam[ysel]
[Russia and NATO: Time to Implement a Joint Plan], *Izvestiia* (2 April 2002), and Maj.-Gen. R[omald]
Zolotarev (rtd) in *Nezavisimaia* (2 April 2002).

49. On this see Vadim Solov'ev, "Al'ians vnutri al'iansa" [Alliance within the Alliance], *NVO*, N[o.]
(15–21 March 2002); and an interview with Nicholas Burns, "Prioritety severoatlanticheskogo soiuz[a]
2002 god" [NATO Priorities for 2002], *ibid.*

50. "Russkii mestatz v OON" [Russian Representative in the UN], *Izvestiia* (3 April 2002).

cabinet did. It may be that Putin's personal popularity, and the constitutional power held by the presidency, rendered popular opinion on specific issues harmless to the government. Nevertheless, a survey of opinion conducted in March suggested that public trust in the United States as a partner had fallen to a level consistent with that of the summer of 1999—slightly lower even than February's survey had shown—when anger over the bombing of Yugoslavia caused a spontaneous anti-America/NATO outburst. The growth of anti-American sentiment was attributed to a sequence of specific events, such as the Olympic scandals and the "trade war," and a general feeling that Washington was forcing its policies on the rest of the world.[51]

Whatever the reason for the cooling of sympathies for the United States in the Russian Federation, the bitterness was reflected so strongly in the Russian media that Vershbow undertook a speaking campaign in mid-March to sooth Russia's feelings.[52] When Putin delivered his annual address to the Federal Assembly in April, the question of relationships with America was barely mentioned. In fact, reference to the United States came only within a single paragraph devoted mostly to the EU and NATO. Moscow's "main foreign policy priority" was still the CIS, the president told his parliamentary audience.[53]

Presummit Hot Spots

In addition to squabbles with the United States on such matters as the conduct of war against terrorism and looming crisis over Iraq, there were two other international "hot spots" over which Moscow and Washington were far apart.

The Middle East

Renewed violence in the Middle East in late March and early April had placed Moscow in a somewhat ambiguous position. On 4 April President Bush took a firm stand against the irrational elements on both sides. Demanding that Israel withdraw its troops from Palestinian cities and calling Palestinian suicide-bombers "not martyrs, but murderers," he changed his earlier hands-off stance. Colin Powell was sent to the region to act as mediator, ending scenarios still vaguely played out in Moscow that featured Russia coming to the rescue.

---

51. On this, see also Georgii Ilychev, "Obstruktsiia sleva po kursu. Rossiiane snova proiavliaiut anti-amerikanizm" [Obstruction on the Left. Anti-Americanism on the Rise Again in Russia], *Izvestiia* (9 April 2002); Mikhail Bernshtam, "Problemy Rossii nyneshnim SShA neinteresny" [At Present, the USA is Uninterested in Russia's Problems], *Izvestiia* (9 April 2002).

52. See, for example, Salavat Suleimanov, "Amerika uspokaivaet Rossiiu" [America Calms Russia], *Nezavisimaia* (14 March 2002); Lidiia Andrusenko, "Chem otvetit Putin na shantazh Vashingtona?" [What Will Putin Say to Washington's Blackmail?], *Nezavisimaia* (11 March 2002).

53. Putin, "Rossii nado byt' sil'noi i konkurentosposobnoi" [Russia Must Be Strong and Competitive], *Rossiiskaia gazeta* (19 April 2002). A translation of Putin's Address to the Russian Federal Assembly was available from the Russian Embassy in Ottawa, Canada.

Putin's position was an awkward one anyway. He had hosted Israeli senior offici
and his government arms industry officials had made important sales to that co
try. Moscow had been making a point for over a year of being balanced in its
proach to both sides in the conflict, which is more than could have been said
Washington. But Russia's friends, or at least main customers, included Iran and Ir
Important political people in Moscow, among them Primakov and Zhirinovskii, w
oppose each other on most other things, have much closer ties to the Arab wc
than to Israel; and the Russian public is far from free of the decades of Cold War
culcation which portrayed the Arabs as victim and Israel as America's agent for
ploiting them.[54] By April, their mutual position on the Middle East was added to
list of things analysts expected Putin and Bush to discuss.

Chechnya

Russian behavior in Chechnya was an old point of difference between the Kren
and the West, and had not disappeared even after Washington's post–11 Septem
recognition that terrorists were operating in the dissident republic. Tension surfa
after meetings between U.S. State Department officials and representatives of
rebel "Ichkerian" government resumed, and American officials began again to critic
Russian military activity in the region. Meetings between Carla del Ponte, prosecu
for the war crimes tribunal, and Maskhadov's envoys, and calls in PACE that ways a
means be found to prosecute people responsible for violating human rights in Che
nya, were thought in Moscow to be encouraged from Washington. The situation v
worsened when, in the first week of April, American-sponsored Radio Free Euro
Radio Liberty began to broadcast into the North Caucasus (from Turkey) in the lc
languages. Russian officials named this action interference in Russia's internal aff
and "incompatible" with the "common fight against terrorism."[55]

THE MERRY MONTH OF MAY, 2002

The month of May promised to be an extraordinarily important one for Russian f
eign policy. Indeed, in its final week the value of Putin's turn to the West would
put to its greatest test. After meeting with George W. Bush in Moscow and St.
tersburg from the 23rd to the 26th, Putin would travel to Rome where NATO he
of state would make the final decision on NATO's proposed new Council. The v
next day, 29 May, a Russia–EU summit was to open in Moscow. While they were
Moscow, Bush and Putin were expected to sign off on important arms reducti
agreements: a Declaration on Strategic Stability and an Agreement on the Reduct

---

54. See, for example, "Pered vsem mirom Izrail' demonstriruet gosudarstvennyi terror" [Israel Den
strates State Terror in Front of the Entire World], *Sovetskaia Rossiia* (2 April 2002).
55. On this see Anna Bladkhen, "Kremlin Angry as Radio Liberty Airs," *San Francisco Chronic*
April 2002), JRL, No. 200 (4 April 2002).

of Strategic Offensive Weapons. As a symbol of the convergence of important meetings, the official opening of a permanent NATO office in Moscow was lined up for 27 May, with Lord Robertson in attendance.

Important CIS meetings were planned for May as well. One of these, the Inter-State Council of the Eurasian Economic Community (Russia, Belarus, Kazakhstan, Kyrgyzstan, Tajikistan, with Moldova as an observer), was also to meet in Moscow; as was the CIS Collective Security Treaty group (Russia, Belarus, Armenia, Kazakhstan, Kyrgyzstan, and Tajikistan).

Draft agreements on both the NATO question and arms reductions had been made public before Bush set out for Moscow. Thus, preparation and prognoses for the summits in Moscow and Rome were granted equal time both by Russian punditry and in official statements.

THE NATO ISSUE AS LAST STRAW OR BREAKTHROUGH?

The fourth round of Russia–NATO consultations had opened in Moscow on 8 April at meetings chaired by RF Deputy Foreign Minister Yevgenii Gusarov and Assistant to the NATO GenSec for political affairs, Günther Altenberg. They expected to have a proposal ready for NATO foreign ministers meetings scheduled for Reykjavik, 14 May, where a final draft would be prepared to bring to the NATO leaders in Rome. The Russians, of course, hoped for a "functional" new council in which they would have a say equal to that of the nineteen members of NATO, at least on certain issues. This was not the approach taken by the most prominent NATO states. So the "sides" had a lot of work to accomplish in a relatively short time.

The unheralded "experts working group" on the question of Russia–NATO relations, called for by Robertson many months earlier, was also still doing its job. From 11 to12 April, the third and busiest session to that date, gathered in Brussels. Among the American representatives were former ambassador to NATO, Robert Hunter, and former ambassador to Moscow, James Collins. The Kremlin's interests were represented by Sergei Rogov and several other highly regarded experts. This group's long report to Robertson called for a formalized structure, that is, a Russia–NATO Council to ensure joint deliberations on matters of security. The "most important" question to be resolved between them was that of admitting the Baltic States to NATO. Although alternatives were proposed, no solution was reached other than a vague agreement that if Latvia, Estonia and Lithuania became NATO members, efforts should be made to integrate Russia more closely with Europe. Obvious differences between the Russian and American approaches to Iran and Iraq were noted, and wide-ranging observations were rendered on virtually all the complications inherent to the new, presumably upgraded relationship. This was rather a remarkable and frank report. Its publication in full in Russia gave rise to much discussion.[56]

---

56. "Doklad rabochei gruppy po otnosheniiam Rossiia-NATO" [Report of the Working Group on Russia–NATO Relations], *NVO*, No. 13 (19–25 April 2002).

Interestingly, shortly before the group's third meeting Rogov had defined
Russian readers what he called the "Bush Doctrine" and its role in determining
future of Russian–American relations. His purpose, it would appear, was to sust
optimism but also to caution against expecting too much. In short, Rogov ₚ
sented a pragmatic, realistic stand that Putin could not have made publicly, l
likely accepted privately. Rogov warned that Russia must not be forced into isc
tion or resume a confrontational posture towards America. Both trends wo
throw obstacles in the way of his country's economic and political recovery. T
new "Bush Doctrine," he claimed, was a formula for preserving American statu:
the only superpower in the world, meaning that Washington would attempt
contain any country (including Russia, but mainly China) deemed to be emerg
as a strong rival. Moreover, proponents of the Bush Doctrine would not rely on
ternational consensus, rather they would fall back on "unilateral action" quic
whenever necessary.

Even in light of the common front in the fight against international terrori:
Rogov saw some real danger in Moscow's new relationship with Washington,
cause it was fraught with "dangerous uncertainty." With this stance, Rogov, unv
tingly perhaps, encapsulated the significance of the forthcoming end-of-May su
mitry. He and others believed that anti-Russian forces were still at large
Washington, which explained why none of the concessions expected from that aɪ
terrorism alliance had been forthcoming. Rogov urged that the long-promised f
mation of a Russia–NATO Council be created right away, that an arms conƚ
regime be resuscitated, and that the United States recognize Russia's interests in f;
not just in name. Only then could a stable, mutually beneficial relationship t
shape.[57] His musings had no official standing, but doubtless they mirrored the "t
in the hall" at the Kremlin.

In early April, Russia's chances of significant gains at the summit had seen
slight. Leading Russian analysts worried that a deeper commitment to NA՝
would enable the Alliance to completely usurp the powers of the United Natic
the final resting place of Russian prestige as a victor in World War II, and pɪ
their country into a "backwater." Others urged the foreign ministry to resuscit
its own foreign affairs doctrine and focus on relations with the CIS.[58] Indeed,
April the approaching NATO summit in Rome was the hottest foreign affairs ɪ
dia subject, greater even than Bush's impending arrival in Moscow. It generatec
much discussion in Russia as had the events of May 1997, when Moscow sigɪ
the Founding Act with the Atlantic Alliance. NATO officials were interviewed ɑ
all the known Russian "experts" rushed into print their perspectives on the sɩ

---

57. Rogov, "Doktrina Busha i perspektivy Rossiisko-Amerikanskikh otnoshenii" [The Bush Doct
and the Future of Russia–U.S. Relations], *NVO*, No. 11 (5–11 April 2002).

58. See, for example, Dr. Artem Ulunyan, " 'Terroristicheskii polumesiats' ne svetit" [The "Terror
Moon" Does Not Shine], *Rossiiskie vesti*, No. 15 (April 2002). "Aleksandr Vershboi: Nash soiuz—
tizhimaia tsel'" [Alexander Vershbow: Our Alliance Is an Attainable Goal], *Rossiiskaia gazeta* (25 ₳
2002); see also Marina Kalashnikova in *Nezavisimaia gazeta* (25 April 2002).

ject.[59] On the political spectrum, the Left loudly opposed trusting NATO, equating the level of "threat" with that of Napoleon and Hitler.[60] Yet even the center and Right demonstrated mixed feelings. On 9 May, when the United States Permanent Representative to NATO, Nicholas Burns, reported that the Transcaucasus and Central Asia were now regarded officially as areas of interest to NATO, Russian analysts tended towards a doomsday approach.[61]

Russia seemed not to be asking a great deal as the negotiations over the "NATO at 20" wound down just prior to the Reykjavik meeting. With the exception of a few scattered, but still stern, comments about the pointlessness of further NATO expansion, the Kremlin plainly had accepted the inevitable. The Kremlin wanted—indeed needed—a carefully and openly constructed format defining the new Council's function and operation, with the questions to be debated precisely delineated. Russian officials hoped that the Council's decisions would be by consensus and that all member-states would be regarded as equals on it. In the meantime, military analysts continued to alert readers to the "NATOization" of former Soviet republics.[62]

It was also important to Moscow that the old PJC system be maintained so as to provide broader forums through which Russia could make its presence felt in NATO. Interestingly, on 23 April it was announced in Brussels that a Permanent NATO Mission in Moscow would open officially on 27 May, one day after the Bush–Putin Moscow summit was scheduled to close.

WARHEAD REDUCTION

The countdown towards the summit-laden end of the month began on 14 May when George W. Bush announced in Washington that a treaty cutting American and

59. See, for example, Dmitrii Rogozin, "Rossiia-NATO: sleduet li speshit' s 'dvadtsatkoi'?" [Russia-NATO: Is It Necessary to Hurry Up with the "Twenty"?], *NVO*, No. 12 (12–18 April 2002); Vadim Solov'ev, Salavat Suleimanov, "Proekty dlia dialoga s Rossiei" [Drafts for Dialogue with Russia], *NVO*, No. 12 (12–18 April 2002), a front-page interview with Rolf Welberts, director of the NATO information bureau; Artem Ulunyan, "Rossiia khochet v NATO no po-svoemu" [Russia Wants to Work with NATO but in Its Own Way], *Rossiiskie vesti*, No. 14, (17–23 April 2002); Svetlana Babaeva, "Novoe rimskoe pravo. 28 Maia Putin soedinit Rossiiu s NATO" [A New Roman Law. On 28 May Putin Unites Russia with NATO], *Izvestiia* (17 April 2002); Yurii Yershov, " '19+1' prevrashchaetsia v 'dvadtsatku' " ["19+1" is Transformed into "Twenty"], *Rossiiskaia gazeta* (24 April 2002).

60. Ivashov, "Udushlivye ob'iatiia NATO" [The Suffocating Embrace of NATO], *Sovetskaia Rossiia* (16 May 2002); see also Viacheslav Tetekin, "Briussel'skii lokhotron" [The Brussels Washing Machine], *Sovetskaia Rossiia* (18 April 2002). Ivashov was back in the red press a few weeks later, blaming the terrorist attack on the World Trade Center "not on Osama bin Laden, but on two powerful groups," the Bush administration and the people around it, and "transnational oligarchies." See Ivashov, "Mezhdunarodnaia situatsiia i mirovoi kriminal" [The International Situation and World Criminals], *Sovetskaia Rossiia* (1 June 2002).

61. See, for example, Aleksei Lyashchenko, "Rossiia–NATO: novyi format" [Russia–NATO: New Format], *Krasnaia zvezda* (15 May 2002), and "Pozitsiia amerikanskikh kongressmenov" [The Attitude of American Congressmen], *ibid.*

62. See, for example, Vitalii Dymarskii, Aleksandr Sabov, "Nulevoi variant. Rossiia i NATO khotiat stroit' svoi otnosheniia s chistogo lista" [Zero Option. Russia and NATO Want to Build Their Relations from Scratch], *Rossiiskaia gazeta* (16 May 2002); see also *Izvestiia* (16 May 2002), and *Krasnaia zvezda* (16 May 2002).

Russian nuclear arsenals would finally be signed on 24 May, in Moscow. B
claimed that this event would mark the final demise of the Cold War, the passing
which had been reported regularly since 1990. Putin expressed his satisfaction w
the agreement too, for the promised treaty marked a victory of sorts for the Kre
lin. Putin had insisted on a binding treaty when, at their American summit in I
vember 2001, Bush had quixotically suggested that a handshake was all that ·
needed to make the reductions happen. The new agreement also granted Ru
some face-saving status as a partner in arms control negotiations.

That being said, Russian acquiescence in the face of Washington's insiste
that America be allowed to store, not destroy, superfluous long-range missiles, a
withdraw from the treaty at short notice (three months), was treated as a ma
diplomatic failure in unofficial Moscow. The standard complaint was that
United States won its treaty while giving up nothing. Russian analysts harked b.
to earlier Russian concessions, such as removing military bases from Cuba a
Vietnam, for which their country also had gained nothing in return.[63] The d
agreement required both sides to cut their deployed strategic nuclear warhead:
between 1,700 and 2,200 by the year 2012. Russian, and some American, cri
argued that the treaty had more to do with enabling the United States to upgr:
its own nuclear warhead apparatus, and even to develop new ones, than it l
with traditional arms control. In light of reports submitted in May by the U
Joint Atomic Energy Intelligence Committee to the effect that the Russians w
preparing nuclear tests themselves on the arctic island Novaia Zemlia—char
resolutely denied by Moscow—suspicions were raised that America was look
for an excuse to conduct tests of its own.[64] One mainstream commentator, for
ample, thought Russia had blinked in these negotiations.[65] On the other ha
Vyacheslav Nikonov, president of the Politika Foundation, insisted that no ma
its several weaknesses and American bias, the proposed treaty was better than
treaty at all.[66]

In case no quid pro quo was forthcoming from the West, the Kremlin shored
its Eurasian connections prior to the summit. On 14–15 May the CIS Collective
curity Treaty group met in Moscow and transformed itself into an international r
itary-political bloc with a formal charter and legal foundation. Presidents of
member countries of the Collective Security Treaty Organization (CSTO), Rus
Armenia, Belarus, Kazakhstan, Kyrgyzstan, and Tajikistan, were open—if unrea
tic—in claiming the new body could serve as a regional counterweight to NAT

---

63. See, for example, Dmitrii Chirkin, "America Got Treaty, and Russia Nothing," *pravda.ru* (14]
2002).

64. On this, see for example, Thom Shanker, "Administration Says Russia Is Preparing Nuclear Te
New York Times (12 May 2002).

65. Georgii Bovt, "Bush prislushalsia k Putinu lish' v odnom" [Bush Heeds Putin's Idea—on Just (
Point], *Izvestiia* (15 May 2002).

66. Vyacheslav Nikonov, "Will Russia Benefit from New Russian–American Accords?" *Trud* (18]
2002), translated by RIA Novosti for JRL.

The CSTO immediately announced plans for joint officer training and scheduled rapid-reaction forces exercises.[67]

It was no coincidence that the defense ministers of the Shanghai Cooperation Organization were meeting in Moscow on the same day that the CSTO was proclaimed. They too issued a joint communiqué announcing a sharp upgrade in joint management of regional security and defense matters. Heads of military in Russia, Kazakhstan, China, Kyrgyzstan and Tajikistan agreed to create a standing mechanism and several working bodies to facilitate cooperation against "terrorism, separatism, and extremism." These events passed almost unnoticed in the West.

NATO AT REYKJAVIK

Within hours of the arms reduction pronouncement, NATO's foreign ministers in their turn proclaimed the last rites of the Cold War. At Reykjavik, formal approval was given to the establishment of the new joint body made up of the nineteen NATO members and Russia. Issues to come before the Council were set out clearly: counterterrorism, controlling the spread of weapons of mass destruction (nuclear, chemical, biological), missile defense, certain regional crises, civil emergencies, and other security-related matters. Russia would not become a member of NATO; nor would it have veto power over core NATO decisions, participate in NATO war-planning, or, clearly, have any influence over NATO's plans to enlarge its membership. The agreement was booked to be formally ratified by NATO and Russia at the Rome summit. Russian experts commenting on the Reykjavik decision were not impressed.

The tone was set by Karaganov, who insisted that the new Council solved almost none of Russia's security problems and remarked that Russia had made its major mistake in 1997 when it signed the Founding Act legitimizing NATO expansion. Another prominent writer about NATO and Russian foreign policy, Marina Kalashnikova, predicted that Russia would be expected to contribute heavily to the anti-terrorist coalition by not opposing U.S. presence in Central Asia or the Transcaucasus, granting flyover rights, providing intelligence, and so on, and still obtain very little in return.[68]

In the meantime, Moscow carried on with its alternative foreign policy-making: on 16 May, Egyptian Foreign Minister Ahmed Maher arrived to sign agreements on strengthening economic ties. He took the opportunity, likely at the urging of Russia,

---

67. On this, see Yekaterina Grigor'eva, "Vostochnyi al'ians" [Eastern Alliance], *Izvestiia* (15 May 2002); Vladislav Vorob'ev, "Drug s drugom bez opasnosti. Cherez 10 let posle sviego sozdaniia Dogovor stal Organiizatsiei" [Together without Danger. Treaty Became an Organization 10 Years after Its Creation], *Rossiiskaia gazeta* (15 May 2002); Interfax (14, 15 May 2002). The formal creation of the new CSTO was scheduled for 1 November 2002, after documents had been prepared and discussed.

68. Sergei Karaganov, "Prokommentirovat' . . . Karaganova" [Karaganov Comments on the Russian–NATO Meeting in Reykjavik], *Nezavisimaia* (16 May 2002); Marina Kalashnikova, "Pax Americana vskladchinu" [Pax Americana Pooled], *Nezavisimaia* (16 May 2002).

to state openly that his country opposed an attack on Iraq. A few days later the
gerian Chief of General Staff and defense minister flew into Moscow to negoti
military hardware upgrades and purchases. On the same day, the North Korean 1
eign minister began an official three-day visit. At a meeting in St. Petersburg, also
20 May, the transport ministers of Russia, Iran and India signed the long-discus
charter creating a North-South international transportation corridor.

Coincidentally, the results of yet another survey of public opinion about NA'
appeared in the Russian press on 15 May, demonstrating that over 50 percent of
1,500 respondents still saw the Atlantic Alliance as an "aggressive military blc
About 52 percent went so far as to call NATO a potential threat to the Russian F
eration.[69] A second poll showed an improvement in Russian attitudes towards
United States, that is, close to 59 percent felt "very good, or good" about the Uni
States, a clear rise above the 48 percent of a month earlier (Interfax, 18 May). S
picion of NATO was alive and well in Russia, whose public and media still diver;
in this one matter from their overwhelming confidence in almost all other poli(
adopted by President Putin. The "experts," however, still pushed for a Russia–U.
NATO dialogue.[70]

On 23 May Russia announced that it would formally withdraw from the STA]
II on 14 June when the ABM Treaty was scheduled to be officially dissolved. STA]
II was dead already anyway because the United States had never ratified it, so (
can only presume that this was a way of portraying Russia's consistent good int
tions in the face of American reluctance to make any concessions.[71]

After the Offensive Arms Reduction Treaty was signed on 24 May cynicism ;
reigned supreme in Moscow. Rogov bent a little, calling it a new window of oppoi
nity while reminding readers that the first such "window" —the summit of Novem
2001—had been in danger of closing because of the United States's subsequent uni
eral withdrawal from the ABM Treaty. Marina Kalashnikova now admitted that a t
American–Russian "friendship" was possible, yet pointed out how easily the "bala
of forces" could be upset by puzzling over the U.S. Congress's almost concomitant
fusal, on 23 May, to waive the Jackson–Vanik amendment for Russia.[72]

The cautious optimism and outright skepticism offered up by most of the Russ
"experts" in foreign affairs was quite in contrast to the mushy bliss represented
statements made by Bush, and to a lesser extent by Putin. Even before the sumi

---

69. *Izvestiia* (15 May 2002). The 1500 respondents were surveyed in 100 locations across the RF.

70. On this see, for example, Nikolai Dmitriev, " 'Okno vozmozhnostei' vse eshche otkryto" [
"Window of Opportunity" Is Still Open], *Obshchaia gazeta*, No. 21 (23–29 May 202). See also Svet
Babaeva, "Moskve i NATO podgotovili soglashenie o 'dvadtsatke' " [They Prepared a Treaty on
"Twenty" for Moscow and NATO], *Izvestiia* (15 May 2002).

71. See *Gazeta* (23 May 2003), *www.wps.ru/e_index.html.*

72. Kalashnikova, *Nezavisimaia gazeta* (28 May 2002); Rogov, "Kapituliatsiia ili perekhod k part
stvu? Rossiia dolzhna ispol'zovat' 'okno vozmozhnostei' " [Is It Surrender or Transition to Partners
Russia Must Utilize the "Window of Opportunity"], *NVO*, No. (24–30 May 2002); Vladimir Geor;
"Rossiia i NATO nachinaiut virtual'nuiu druzhbu" [Russia and NATO Begin a Virtual Friendship], *N
visimaia* (28 May 2002).

took place, an interview granted to ITAR-TASS by President Bush and Mrs. Bush in Washington on 22 May bemused many readers in Russia. Seeking a way to demonstrate that the two presidents shared a lot of interests, President Bush came up with, "we love our wives, and we love our daughters. We love our countries, we love the outdoors," comments that were derided by cynics on both sides of the Atlantic.[73]

SUMMIT COUNTDOWN

Everyone had advice for Putin and Bush as the Moscow summit loomed closer. Grigorii Yavlinskii, fading star of the fading Yabloko party, for example, wrote that the abrupt turnaround in Russian foreign policy after 11 September 2001 also marked a dramatic change in the Russian leadership's "value system." He urged Russian and Western readers to give Moscow time for that change to settle in, so as to facilitate Russia's assimilation into Western civilization.[74] Although most analysts did not agree with Yavlinskii's final point, almost all of them switched positions as the summit dawned, putting on their optimistic caps for the moment.[75]

   The summit itself took place with the expected fanfare: the arms reduction treaty was signed and the Cold War was declared over—again. Putin and Bush issued a Joint Declaration on 24 May in which a "new strategic relationship" was announced. Political cooperation was promised on a wide cross-section of international hot spots, most of them close to Russia's borders in Central Asia, the South Caucasus and Afghanistan. The soon-to-be-signed "NATO at 20" was portrayed as the centerpiece of the new association. Economic cooperation also was stressed, and yet another promise that Russia eventually would be excused from the Jackson-Vanik amendment was made. Collaboration against the spread of weapons of mass destruction and international terrorism, and for nonproliferation, were also part of the wide-ranging set of mutual interests. Missile defense teamwork was another. Separate joint statements were issued on energy policy, counterterrorism, the Middle East, economic relations, and people-to-people contacts.[76]

---

73. ITAR-TASS (22 May 2002); the interview was printed under the caption "Bush: the USA and Russia Are No Longer Enemies" in *Rossiiskaia gazeta* (23 May 2002). It is worth mentioning here that later in the summer a biography of Putin's wife appeared in Russia and presented a rather harsh picture of Putin's attitude towards her.

74. Yavlinskii, "Dver' v Evropy nakhoditsia v Vashingtone. Vizit Busha: o chem nuzhno dogovorit'sia" [The Door to Europe Is in Washington. The Upcoming Visit of Bush: What Should Be Negotiated], *Obshchaia gazeta*, No. 20 (16–22 May 2002); see also Viktor Litovkin, "Stolknovenie yadernykh boegolovok" [Collision of Nuclear Warheads], *ibid.*, for a less than optimistic view of the planned arms reduction agreement to be signed by Bush and Putin.

75. On this see, for example, Yuliia Kuz'mina, "Okno novykh vozmozhnostei" [Window on New Opportunities], *Rossiiskaia gazeta* (23 May 2002), for a summary of projections by various "authoritative Russian international experts," among them S.M. Rogov.

76. The arms reduction treaty appeared in Russia as "Dogovor mezhdu RF i SshA o sokrashenii strategicheskikh nastupatel'nykh potentsialov," *Rossiiskaia gazeta* (25 May 2002). The series of joint declarations, "Sovmestnaia deklaratsiia," appeared in the same issue of the *RG*. See also Nikolai Paklin, "Rossiia vkhodit v NATO. No ne vstupaet" [Russia Is in NATO. But Has Not Joined It], *Rossiiskaia gazeta* (28 May 2002).

The two sides did not agree on everything, for Putin made it clear that he did accept Washington's positions on Iran and Iraq. Indeed, he pointed out that h American-, European-, and Japanese-based companies had been working in th countries directly or indirectly with impunity. Appeals such as these were, of cou made to the broad public audience, for Putin knew very well that they would fall deaf ears in Washington.

RUSSIA–NATO COUNCIL

The two presidents then rushed off to join eighteen heads of NATO states in Roi where, on 28 May, a "Declaration by Heads of State and Government of NA' Member States and the Russian Federation" created the Russia–NATO Coun This Council replaced the PJC and will operate on a vague principle of consens Chaired by the NATO Secretary General, it will meet at the level of defense mii ter twice a year and at the ambassadorial level on a monthly basis. Heads of state ε government will meet only "as appropriate."

As Russia had hoped, specific areas for discussion were laid out for the Counci deliberate: the struggle against terrorism, crisis management, nonproliferation, aι control, theater missile defense, search and rescue at sea, military-to-military co eration and defense reform, civil emergencies, and a category called "new threats ε challenges." This quite inclusive menu notwithstanding, Russian expert analysis ν still very mixed. Even the deputy director of ISKRAN complained that the agι ment would not benefit Russia very much. Viktor Kremenyuk called it a loser's commodation but concluded that Russia had no choice but to go along with i Others pondered the "consensus" principle, noting that as NATO grew larger Council might eventually be constrained to vote on a pressing issue, something t the original body had not done.

The communists, of course, hated everything about the week of Bush's appε ance in Moscow and Russia's new association with NATO. Demonstrations were ganized outside the American embassy in Moscow, with participants shouting sults and waving placards carrying such slogans as "Bush is worse than Hitler!" ε accusing Putin of "capitulation."[78] More specifically, the CPRF Central Commit met on 25 May and adopted a resolution outlining in detail what the party belie' were the gravest threats to Russian security. Above all others, the resolution said, foreign policy of "Putin and the oligarchs . . . threaten the very existence of country." The CPRF also condemned the just-signed arms reduction treaty as a

---

77. See , for example, Kremenyuk, "Ne nado shapkami" [No Need for Braggadocio], *Rossiiskaia ga* (29 May 2002); see also Svetlana Babaeva, " 'Troika', 'Vos'merka', 'Dvadtsatka' " [The Troika, the Eight, the Twenty], *Izvestiia* (28 May 2002), who said that the new Council probably benefits everyone, but tioned that Russia would be treated no more as an "equal" than it had been in the G-8. See also *Izve* (29 May 2002), where it was suggested that NATO needed Russia more than Russia needed NATO.

78. See, for example, front-page photos of demonstrators and their placards, *Sovetskaia Rossiia* (25] 2002).

hicle weakening Russia's security. The resolution was printed on the front page of the party's main newspaper and trumpeted in speeches by Zyuganov and others. None of its content was surprising, although the shrillness of its tone was a bit of a throwback.[79]

WINDING DOWN

As the excitement over the new arrangement with NATO and the Putin–Bush summit faded, the EU convention took over Moscow's front pages. Already in April, Russia had made it plain that it supported EU expansion, with the one caveat that the interests of Kaliningrad should be protected. The EU demanded that Russian citizens acquire visas to travel through Lithuania or Poland to reach and return from Kaliningrad. Prime Minister Kasyanov had taken this matter directly to EU leaders during a meeting in Brussels on 24 April,[80] pointing out that there were nearly a million crossings annually by train alone and that Russians should not have to buy visas to go from one part of their own country to another.[81] At the EU summit in Moscow a month later, Putin made a strong statement against visas for Kaliningrad and implied that the EU's treatment of this issue was a measure of its willingness to cooperate with Moscow. Even this direct appeal was turned down at that time.[82] Russian public reaction was mostly of the "I told you so" variety.[83]

The EU and Russian leaders issued a joint statement on Kaliningrad and supplementary joint positions on crisis settlement, security, energy, the Middle East and India–Pakistan (ITAR-TASS, 30 May), but they lacked substance insofar as Russian observers were concerned.[84]

By the spring of 2002, as our period for study came to an end, the two-headed Russian eagle was again looking nervously to both east and west. Moscow's reach to

79. "CPRF CC Zaiavlenie, 'Ob ugroze natsional'noi bezopasnosti Rossii'" [CPRF CC Statement on the Threat to the National Security of Russia], *Sovetskaia Rossiia* (28 May 2002); see also Viacheslav Tetekin, "Ob'iatiia i obrazy Rimskoi aviabazy" [The Embrace and Images of the Roman Airbases], *Sovetskaia Rossiia* (30 May 2002).
80. See Yekaterina Vasil'chenko, "Glotok ekonomicheskoi svobody" [A Drop of Economic Freedom], *Rossiiskaia gazeta* (25 April 2002).
81. The official Russian figures have 960,000 by train, 620,000 by car annually.
82. In September, a proposal of a special "Kaliningrad Pass" for travel through Lithuania, good until 2005, was put on the table for discussion at the EU.
83. See Yurii Yershov, "Kaliningradskii oreshek" [Kaliningrad Tough Guy], *Rossiiskaia gazeta* (30 May 2002), and Vladimir Bogdanov, "S popravkoi na Ameriku" [Amended to Suit America], *Rossiiskaia gazeta* (30 May 2002), a statement prepared for the newspaper by Sergei Oznobishchev, Director of the Institute of Strategic Assessments in Moscow. On earlier pessimism about the likelihood of Russia's quick entry into the WTO, see Aleksei Chichkin, "Kak iz Evrazii popast' v WTO?" [How Can One Get into the WTO from Eurasia?], *Rossiiskaia gazeta* (14 May 2002).
84. Maksim Medvedkov, "Rossiia ne postupitsia pravami Kaliningradtsev" [Russia Will Not Yield the Rights of the People of Kaliningrad], *Rossiiskaia gazeta* (31 May 2002). Medvedkov is a Duma deputy and one of the leaders of the Russian delegation to the Russia–EU summit. See also Yekaterina Grigor'eva, Olga Bubenko, Yelena Myazina, "Status. Bystro" [Status. Quickly], *Izvestiia* (31 May 2002).

the east and south will be examined in more detail in Part II of this study. In
West, the main if not sole focal point of Part I, much had been accomplished:
NATO question had again reached some sort of a resolution; a modus vivendi I
been arranged with Washington; a new arms reduction agreement with the Uni
States was in the bank; the EU had become Russia's main trading partner; payme
on the foreign debt were being made regularly; and Russia had become a player
be reckoned with in the G-8. But Russia was at odds with the EU on certain pol
cal issues, it was still far from being admitted to the WTO, and both NATO and
United States were, as one Russian put it, "oozing" into several of Moscow's tra
tional spheres of influence. A reading of any cross-section of the mainstream me
and official statements in May 2002 revealed that there was a strong sense of dis
lief in Russia in the durability of any of these developments. Their permanence
still to be tested.

Our chronological overview, in fact, has revealed just how shallow Moscow's m
"unshakeable" positions, such as those on the ABM, the NMD, and NATO exp
sion, had been. If the new relationships in the West with NATO, the United Sta
and the EU prove to be unworkable, and the recently upgraded integrative mec
nisms in the East are unfruitful, then Putin's to-date much-praised pragmatism n
eventually be interpreted as mere backing-down.

II

The Two-Headed Eagle
Faces East and West

7

✝

Debating Security and Defense

YEAR ONE

Thrust into the presidential chair by Boris Yeltsin on the last day of 1999, after only three months as premier, Putin was compelled to find a source of legitimacy for himself quickly. In part because of the ongoing conflict in Chechnya and in part because of the upcoming presidential elections, he took the most appealing route by placing military and security matters very high on his list of priorities. The purpose of this chapter is to track the shaping of a distinctive "Russian Way" in military–strategic affairs during Putin's first two-and-a-half years in office.[1] To maintain the integrity of this account of security and defense thinking, there will be some repetition of materials covered in Part I, but it will be kept to a minimum.

Within hours of the appearance of his "Manifesto" on the last day of 1999 (see Chapter 1), Putin was visiting troops on the ground in Chechnya. In the course of bestowing honors on some of them, he promised to rehabilitate Russia's military–industrial complex and augment government expenditures on the military by over 50 percent. The acting president's impulse for revitalizing the military had been illustrated already on 31 December 1999, when he ordered the reintroduction of "elementary military training" in Russia's general school.[2] The edict called for courses on military preparation and lessons in patriotism for youngsters at age of fifteen, effectively restoring a program offered for years in the USSR but cancelled in 1991. As

---

1. The "Russian Way" was an approach to defining Russia's role in international affairs, and indeed to the government's action on domestic matters, espoused by Yevgenii Primakov. See *Russia Faces NATO Expansion, passim.*

2. "Polozhenie o podgotovke grazhdan Rossiiskoi Federatsii k voennoi sluzhbe" [Resolution on the Preparation of Citizens of the Russian Federation for Military Service], *Rossiiskaia gazeta* (13 January 2000).

we have seen, the simultaneously printed "Manifesto" singled out patriotism as a l
saver for the Russian people and state, and resuscitated the notion of a "Russ
Idea" as part of a new direction for the country.[3] These documents marked the ·
set of a conscious effort to raise the prestige of the armed forces, to the extent t
some observers worried about the remilitarization of Russian society.[4]

NEW SECURITY CONCEPT

Early in January 2000, Putin signed into law the first of three major blueprints
defining Russia's place in the world, the Russian National Security Concept. 1
other two documents were a new Military Doctrine (see below), and the new F
eign Policy Concept (see Chapter 3). A new draft of the Security Concept, amei
ing the 1997 version, had been adopted by the Security Council in October 19
As premier, Putin had ordered it reworked so as to more clearly define "terrorisi
the meaning of a "multipolar world," and the methods by which Russia could gu
antee national security. The amended Concept allowed the ministry of defense to
ploy nuclear weapons against any truly dangerous attack, nuclear or conventiona
The Concept replaced the notion of "partnership" when referring to the West w
"cooperation," a more standoffish stance than the one taken in the mid-19S
Whereas security suppositions from the late 1980s had seen western countries as
nign in their relations with the USSR and Russia, the new edition revived a visior
the West generally and the United States particularly as potential threats. Moscc
real worry, however, was revealed in the opening lines of the document wheri
claimed that Russia would promote a multipolar world in the face of "attempts
create a structure of international relations based on the domination of the inter
tional community by developed western countries under U.S. leadership."
Some foreign observers claimed to be surprised by this Soviet-style vision of wc
affairs. They should not have been. It echoed Defense Minister Sergeev's written
marks in December 1999 to the effect that NATO expansion eastward was "clea
the most significant threat to Russian security," along with the danger of the wc
being subject to American "military-force diktats."[6] This time, however, the vis

---

3. Putin, "Rossiia na rubezhe tysiacheletiia" [Russia on the Eve of the Millennium], *Rossiiskaia ga*
(31 December 1999). As we have seen in the introductory chapter, this long statement came to be ca
Putin's "Manifesto."
4. On the school program, see Alan Kachmazov, Andrei Stepanov, "Bol'shaia peremena" [Long Rec
Izvestiia (5 February 2000). The "problem" of militarization was discussed in connection with the def
industries, and discounted, by Aleksei Shlunov, "Krizis VPK: podmena poniatii" [Crisis of the Mili
Industrial Complex: Secretly Changing Concepts], *NVO*, No. 9 (17–23 March 2000).
5. "Kontseptsiia natsional'noi bezopasnosti Rossiiskoi Federatsii" [National Security Concept of
Russian Federation], *Rossiiskaia gazeta* (18 January 2000); *NVO*, No. 1 (14–20 January 2000). P
signed the Concept into law on 10 January.
6. Marshal Igor Sergeev, "Osnovy voenno-tekhnicheskoi politiki Rossii v nachale XXI veka" [Basis of
Military-technical Policy of Russia at the Beginning of the 21st Century], *Krasnaia zvezda* (9 Decen
1999). Sergeev was making an appeal for further funding for military-technical infrastructure and equipm

was shaped more by the Kremlin's understanding of NATO's action against Yugoslavia in 1999 than by lingering Marxist–Leninist ideology.

The potential for internal crises, which had dominated the Concept's 1997 predecessor, was by no means ignored; the new version highlighted conflicts occasioned by "international terrorism." In this regard, both the plan and the public discourse that preceded its adoption featured the preservation of public unity and Russian national self-consciousness to a much greater degree than had the 1997 document.[7]

START-II AND THE CTBT

This new attitude was witnessed first in arms reduction talks. When Al Gore's national security adviser, Leon Fuerth, met with then Security Council Chairman Sergei Ivanov in Moscow on 14 February, the question of START-II and the ABM Treaty featured prominently in their deliberations. Ivanov made it plain, in public statements at least, that further cuts in Russian armaments were possible only if the ABM Treaty remained untouched. In a long address to the Moscow State Institute of International Affairs, he declared that any unilateral changes to the ABM Treaty would lead both to "the destruction of global strategic stability" and to the "militarization" of space. NATO was characterized in the speech as Washington's front line in its quest for world dominance.[8]

Battle lines over policy began to form as ratification of START-II finally was scheduled for debate in the Duma. An orchestrated campaign against ratification quickly shaped up in the oppositionist press, with the communist *Sovetskaia Rossiia* leading the charge as it had been doing since 1995. First out of the blocks was none other than Igor Rodionov, Yeltsin's strongly anti-NATO defense minister whose sacking in 1997 was called "appeasement" of NATO by the Union of Russian Officers.[9] The government apparatus was led by Putin, Sergeev and Foreign Minister Ivanov. They urged parliament to approve START-II as a means of redressing, somewhat, the growing lack of parity in Russian–American missile holdings. As official debate drew nearer, the decision by PACE to suspend Russia's voting rights triggered a new outburst of anti-START-II rhetoric. Opponents of START-II quickly spotted a plot, ranting that PACE was participating in an "anti-Russian" campaign engineered in Europe or Washington; advocates saw ratification as a way to cut spending on missiles and as a card with which to gain leverage in the debate over amending the ABM Treaty.[10]

---

7. See, for example, Ramazan Abdulatipov, "Doktrina natsional'noi bezopasnosti Rossii. Poka gospodstvo 'edinstva' bez ucheta 'mnogoobraziia'" [The Russian Doctrine of National Security. "Unity" Still Prevails without Taking "Diversity" into Account], *Nezavisimaia gazeta* (29 January 2000).

8. Sergei Ivanov, "Rossiiu tesniat. No ne vytesniat" [Russia Is Being Pushed Back. But Will Not Be Pushed Out], *Rossiiskaia gazeta* (16 March 2000). Foreign Minister Igor Ivanov made similar remarks; see Interfax (14 February 2000).

9. See *Russia Faces NATO Expansion*, p. 57. *Sovetskaia Rossiia* 's first attack on START-II had been printed on 8 April 1995.

10. See, for example, Yurii Yershov, "Dogovor dorozhe brani" [Ratification Is Better than a Quarrel], *Rossiiskaia gazeta* (12 April 2000).

In an essay printed on 30 March, Rodionov, now a Duma deputy, called ratifi
tion of START-II an "unconditional capitulation of Russia to the USA and NAT(
He contended that acquiescence would render Russia vulnerable to attack and h
dire consequences for "all mankind."[11] In the long run, however, voting opposit
to START-II was limited to deputies from the Communist Party, which called r
fication an act of treason, and their Agrarian allies. Most media commentators s
ported the government position, though both sides blamed the long delay in rat
cation on NATO expansion.[12]

When the Duma finally ratified on 13 April,[13] Putin commented that it was n
up to the United States to act ("the ball is in their court") and warned that if
ABM were altered unilaterally all arms reduction agreements were off. STAR1
called on both sides to cut their nuclear arsenals by about one-half before 200;
leaving Russia with 3000 warheads, and the United States with 3500—and pa
the way for further cuts provided for in START-III. START-III proposed to le
both sides with 1500 warheads. The Duma complemented its approval of STAR1
the next day by adopting a resolution ensuring that Russia's Strategic Nuclear Fc
(SNF) remained the "key instrument of the national defense." The resolution
manded that the SNF must be funded and combat-ready and must not be weakei
in any way because of START-II or -III.

Ratification a week later of the CTBT, which the U.S. Senate had rejected on
October 1999, gave Putin another step up on the arms reduction high ground ;
paved the way for a strong Russian presence at the UN Non-Proliferation Tre
Conference scheduled to meet in New York from 24 April through to 19 May.[14] 1
dorsement of the CTBT may have been more symbolic than consequential, for o
Britain, France, and now Russia of the nuclear powers had ratified, but symbolisr
important in diplomacy generally, and in the United Nations particularly. And R
sia was not averse to showing strength when and where it could. On 18 Ap
Moscow announced that it planned to test its fleet of cruise missiles in South R
sia, explaining that it needed to do so because of U.S. army deployment of cru
missiles in Yugoslavia. A government press analyst said that the Russian military l
drawn conclusions from the "shameful NATO action in the Balkans" where
United States "showered their monstrous strike power down on sovereign

---

11. Rodionov, "Slom shchita. SNV-2—bezogovorochnaia kapituliatsiia Rossii pered SShA i NA⁻
[Destruction of the Shield. START-2 is Russia's Unconditional Capitulation to the USA and NAT
Sovetskaia Rossiia (30 March 2000).

12. See, for example, Vladimir Belous, "Bezal'ternativnyi variant. Esli Rossiia ne ratifitsiruet SNV-2
tem samym podygraet amerikanskim planam razvertyvaniia PRO" [Variant without Alternative. If Ru
Does Not Ratify START-II, That Will Play into the American Plans to Deploy the ABM], *NVO*, No
(7–13 April 2000).

13. START-II was approved in the Duma 288–131, and by the Federation Council on 19 A
186–18-6. See Valentin Kuznetsov, "K miru bez yadernoi ugrozy" [Towards a World without Nuc
Threat], *Krasnaia zvezda* (13 May 2000).

14. See Vladimir Lapskii, "Vtoroi Dogovor v tret'ei Dume" [Second Treaty in Third Duma], *Rossiis,
gazeta* (15 April 2000). The USA, India, Pakistan and China had not yet signed the agreement.
CTBT was ratified by the Russian Duma 298–74-3.

goslavia."[15] Thus, NATO remained the specter shaping Russian military policy, as it had been since the mid-1990s.

The negotiating advantage that the ratified CTBT gave the Kremlin was deemed very important by noncommunist commentators, some of whom insinuated that the United States's failure to respond might well be part of a plan to modernize its nuclear arsenal and develop an NMD.[16] Communists, however, continued to rail against the Kremlin's "capitulation" to American pressure on arms control, highlighting what they called anti-Russia, hegemonic commentary from the U.S. press. The piece by Jan Nowak (see Chapter 2), former national security adviser and longtime employee of Radio Free Europe, drew special ire.[17] Nowak's reference to enlarged NATO membership as an "important tool of constructive American influence in this [the Balkans] crucial region" was proof of the pudding for Russian pundits. His call for a new wave of admissions to NATO, including Romania, Bulgaria and the Baltic States, precisely to combat what Nowak called an "expansionist mentality among Russia's ruling elite" struck them as nothing less than bizarre.

Anxiety about perceived Western indifference to the Kremlin's initiatives was alleviated somewhat when the federal law on ratification of START-II was finally published on 6 May. Article 2 of the law gave Russia the right to withdraw from the treaty "in exercise of its sovereignty" and listed the "extraordinary circumstances" that would make such withdrawal necessary. These included American unilateral withdrawal from the ABM Treaty of 1972 and the deployment by the United States or NATO of "nuclear weapons on the territory of states that have joined the North Atlantic Treaty Organization after the date of signing of the START-II Treaty," that is, since 1993.[18] The federal law on ratification therefore gave Russia a legislated guarantee of diplomatic action in the case of unexpected buildups, even non-nuclear, in the new NATO member countries. This is precisely what had been missing from the 1997 Founding Act between Russia and NATO, a point for which Yeltsin had been castigated from all sides in Russia.[19]

---

15. Boris Talov, "Superstrely XXI veka" [21st-Century Super Arrows], *Rossiiskaia gazeta* (21 April 2000).

16. See, for example, Anna Kozyreva, "Yadernye ispytaniia pod zapretom?" [Are Nuclear Tests Banned?], *Rossiiskaia gazeta* (22 April 2000).

17. On Nowak's "What NATO Can Do for Russia," *Washington Times* (19 April 2000), see "Otkryli yashchik Pandory" [They Opened Up Pandora's Box], *Sovetskaia Rossiia* (25 April 2000). On Nowak's praise for Hungary's help to NATO's "peace mission" in Yugoslavia, the Russian editorial writer added punctuation marks "(?!!)." See also Yan Novak [Nowak], "Kak obustroit' NATO bez Rossii" [How to Improve NATO without Russia], *Rossiiskaia gazeta* (30 May 2000), accompanied by scathing commentary from Vladimir Lapskii.

18. See Article 2, sections 2, 4, "O ratifikatsii Dogovora mezhdu Rossiiskoi Federatsiei i Soedinennymi Shtatami Ameriki o dal'neishem sokrashchenii i ogranichenii strategicheskikh nastupatel'nykh vooruzhenii" [Russian Federal Law, on the Ratification of the Treaty between the Russian Federation and the United States of America on the Further Reduction and Limitation of Strategic Offensive Arms], *Rossiiskaia gazeta* (6 May 2000). The law was signed by Putin on 4 May.

19. V. Shport, "SNV-2: bezopasnost' na paritetnykh nachalakh" [START-II: Security on a Parity Basis], *Krasnaia zvezda* (16 May 2000). The interview was conducted by Col. Anatolii Antipov.

NEW MILITARY DOCTRINE

The second major schematic for defense, a draft of new military doctrine, ⁊ brought before the Russian Security Council on 4 February 2000. It too exci knee-jerk reactions in the West, even though its content had been known for m; months.[20] The fact that neither set of guidelines was any more "aggressive" in t(than defense strategies approved in all other nuclear powers, or in NATO, did prevent Western commentators from finding something foreboding in them.

The military doctrine was seen differently in Moscow. As Aleksei Arbatov pu(the new doctrine served as a warning to the United States that Russia would reac pressured too strongly. Otherwise, the only thing innovative in the doctrine was somewhat more strident tone.[21] Several mainstream Russian analysts linked changes closely to the "growth of new threats to Russia, including the expansior the North Atlantic Alliance."[22] One of the doctrine's chief architects, Col. G Manilov, first deputy chief of the Armed Forces General Staff, later noted that new doctrine emphasized the prevention of conflict, partnership with all states t do not contravene the UN Charter, and deterrence. The Pentagon's complaints w ludicrously hypocritical, he and others argued, for the United States still had a fi strike policy of its own. Indeed, some writers worried that, with its technological periority, NATO could have ultimate control over Russia's defense-related surv lance and electronic communications systems.[23]

Military commentators tended also to emphasize the transitional nature of new military doctrine and insist that it would be revised again when Russia's milit situation was stabilized. Several political authorities saw the doctrine as a comp mise between strongly held differences of opinion between defense officials and g ernment bureaucrats, and suggested that Moscow's version was in part a respons(NATO's one-year-old new strategic doctrine.[24] In fact, most strategic analysts Russia agreed that the doctrine simply brought Russia's strategic principles into l with those of the United States, Britain, and France.[25]

---

20. See, for example, Vladimir Yermolin, "Novaia voennaia doktrina Rossii" [The New Russian N tary Doctrine], *Izvestiia* (13 October 1999).

21. Arbatov, "Everything is for the Elections! With this Tactic, Putin Approaches the Military [trine," *Obshchaia gazeta* (10 February 2000), translated for FBIS-SOV, No. 0211.

22. See Aleksandr Shaburkin, "Rossiia meniaet voennuiu doktrinu" [Russia Changes Its Military [trine], *Nezavisimaia gazeta* (5 February 2000).

23. Sergei Shikin, "Rossiiskii oboronnyi zakaz— pod kontrolem NATO? [Russian Defense Ord(Under the Control of NATO?], *Rossiiskie gazeta* (8 February 2000); Manilov, "Doktrina est'— voin; ne bylo" [There Is a Doctrine, if Only There Won't Be War], *Rossiiskaia gazeta* (23 February 2000).

24. Vadim Solov'ev, "Zerkalo novoi voennoi doktriny. V nem otrazhaetsia strategicheskaia kontsep NATO. No poka lish' v obshchem" [Mirror of the New Military Doctrine. NATO's Strategic Conce] Reflected in It. But Only for Now], *NVO*, No. 11 (31 March–6 April 2000); the same essay appeare *Nezavisimaia gazeta* (30 March 2000). See also a long essay by Col. Gen. Valerii Manilov, "Glavnyi terii— natsional'nye interesy Rossii" [The Main Criteria Are the National Interests of Russia], *Kras; zvezda* (21 March 2000).

25. See for example, Vladimir Dvorkin, "Doktrina Sergeeva ne zhestche predydushchei" ["Sergeev's [trine" No Tougher than Its Predecessor], *Nezavisimaia gazeta* (19 February 2000). Dvorkin is alleged t(the author of the section in the doctrine on the use of nuclear weapons. Karaganov, "New Military [trine Guarantees Russian Security," RIA Novosti—Moscow Diary (21 February 2000), JRL No. 4127

Doubtless, the timing of the release of the draft rendition had domestic political implications. Russia's presidential elections were scheduled for March and Putin had little time to campaign. In an "Open Letter to Russian Voters" (25 February), the aspiring president spoke of both the military doctrine and Security Concept as means by which Russia could regain respect in international affairs. He lauded the army for "recovering from a long crisis with honor,"[26] and explained that Russia and Russians could no longer be ignored as they had been when the UN and NATO made decisions concerning Iraq and Yugoslavia. It is not hard to understand Putin's popularity with the armed forces, who voted for him at a noticeably higher rate than the civilian population.

The new military doctrine was finally approved by Putin on 21 April, after a lengthy Security Council discussion, which he chaired. Government press releases called the document a "doctrine of deterrence" in which nuclear armaments would be used only "in case of an exclusive threat to the country's existence." General Manilov labelled it a "Russian military–political manifesto."[27] It is worth mentioning that both real and perceived NATO behavior was cited as explanation throughout the revision. Among the defining factors of military–political "situations," for example, were the "spread of nuclear weapons," current "attempts to weaken existing mechanisms for safeguarding international security" (the UN and OSCE), and the "use of coercive military actions as a means of 'humanitarian intervention' without the sanction of the UN Security Council."

In its final rendering, the often mentioned endorsement of nuclear first-strike reads as follows:

> The Russian Federation reserves the right to use nuclear weapons in response to the use of nuclear and other types of weapons of mass destruction against it (or) its allies, as well as in response to large-scale aggression using conventional weapons in situations critical to the national security of the Russian Federation.

This cannot be said to differ substantially from military doctrines adopted by the United States, or by NATO.

TESTING THE CONCEPT

The Kremlin's long-standing grievance that the West was deaf to Russia's international concerns had resurfaced in Moscow on 20 March when NATO and KFOR troops mobilized for a three-week training exercise in Kosovo. The exercises, to

---

26. "Otkrytoe pis'mo Vladimira Putina k rossiiskim izbirateliam" [Open Letter of Vladimir Putin to Russian Voters], *Izvestiia* (25 February 2000).

27. For a long essay on the doctrine by Manilov, see "Voenno-politicheskii manifest Rossii" [A Russian Military-Political Manifesto], *Rossiiskaia gazeta* (26 April 2000). See *Vremya novosti* (28 April 2000) and *Izvestiia* (22 April 2000) for similar praise. For the final version of the military doctrine, "Voennaia doktrina Rossiiskoi Federatsii" [The Military Doctrine of the Russian Federation], *NVO*, No. 15 (28 April–11 May 2000). It was printed as well in *Nezavisimaia gazeta* (21 April) and *Rossiiskaia gazeta* (25 April).

which Russian peacekeeping forces were not invited, were intended as a signal to S
bian and perhaps Albanian extremists that NATO would act if civil war erup
again. There was little pretence that "Dynamic Response 2000" was a peacekeep
operation; rather, it was a show of force by some 1,500 soldiers, 1,100 of whom w
American. Russian commentators joined the Serbian chorus by calling it an act
aggression, and repeatedly charged that the maneuver violated UNSCR 1244.[28]

Whatever the case might have been, Russia's response to what its leaders belie
to be a destabilizing trend in the Balkans and elsewhere included military train
exercises of its own. A three-day Russian–Armenian command-post training sess
was initiated under Russian command on 28 March. On the same day the CIS a
vated a planned "Southern Shield-2000," involving troops from Russia, Kazakhst
Kyrgyzstan, Tajikistan and Uzbekistan, with observers from Belarus and Armei
More significantly, on 27 March the Russian navy successfully test-launched a t
listic missile from an underwater nuclear-powered submarine in the Barents S
finding a target on the Kura range in Kamchatka. This was the Northern Fleet's s
ond such successful attempt, offering evidence that Russia still owned daunting
taliatory power.

THE ABM TREATY AND THE NMD

Widening debate between Moscow and Washington over the ABM Treaty was
focus of attention in May as Russia prepared to host President Clinton. Aleksei
batov spoke of this divide in an invited presentation to the Carnegie Non-Prolif
tion Project in Washington. The primary reason for START-II's confirmation in R
sia was not because Duma members thought the United States wanted Russia a
partner for cooperation and security; rather, it was because they and the Russian p
lic "think that the nuclear threat is great." Moreover, they believe that the Uni
States demands superiority.[29]

Russia needed START-II to maintain some semblance of parity, he argued,
wittingly (perhaps) reactivating the discourse of the 1960s. In addition to a "fea
American nuclear superiority and the fear of the United States," which Arbatov
sisted was real, START-II was assumed to be a further guarantee of the "viability a
validity" of the ABM Treaty, a fact confirmed by Article 2 of Russia's START-II i
plementation law. Russia had done its part. If the Americans would only follow s
then a real breakthrough in arms control could be achieved and the two count
could more easily accommodate each other "on European affairs, on Iran, on Ch
and many other issues of international security." If not, they would both be fa
with serious threats to their national security.

28. United Nations Security Council Resolution (UNSCR) 1244 guarantees the territorial integrit
Yugoslavia.
29. "Arbatov on U.S.–Russia Relations," Carnegie Endowment for International Peace, *Prolifera
Brief,* Vol. 3, No. 16 (18 May 2000).

The MoD held its collective breath and then was greatly relieved on 4 June when Putin held his ground and Clinton was persuaded to share in a declaration calling the ABM "a cornerstone of strategic stability."[30]

Almost simultaneously with Clinton's departure from Moscow the next day the Russian president and his defense and foreign ministry officials fanned out across Western Europe to relay the Kremlin's still vaguely defined security "alternative" to the NMD. As we have seen, Putin visited Rome and Berlin; Sergeev went to Brussels for discussions with NATO. At the same time, military analysts and technicians assured Russians that their country was well able to deal with a unilateral U.S. withdrawal from the ABM agreement. Director general of the Russian Agency for Control Systems, Vladimir Simonov, for example, told readers of *Izvestiia* that Russia was fully prepared for any eventuality and that its response to the United States doubtless would be "adequate."[31] In this regard it is noteworthy that in his preconfirmation speech to the Duma, Acting Prime Minister Kasyanov acknowledged that Russia would have to specialize in its defense spending. "It is vital," he said, "to concentrate efforts on equipping [the army] with new state-of-the-art hardware," and he called for selective but large spending increases on defense.[32]

Russian military protestations seemed a little overwrought, for high-level negotiations were taking place. START-III and ABM were subjects of meetings held in Geneva, 28–30 June, and Russia–U.S. consultations on strategic stability were scheduled for Oslo on 19 July. Nevertheless, the minister of defense accused Washington of "destroying strategic stability" and the commander of Russia's Strategic Rocket Force (RSVN), Col. Gen. Vladimir Yakovlev, outlined measures available to Moscow if the USA deployed an NMD system. These included increasing the number of warheads on existing IBMs, withdrawing from agreements on the liquidation of intermediate- and shorter-range missiles, and even threatening continental Europe. Here was heady stuff, providing visions of a "next stage" previously kept out of the press. One Russian writer went so far as to introduce Yakovlev's revelation as a "step towards a nuclear missile war"; hardliner Ivashov tended to agree.[33]

---

30. "Joint Statement by the Presidents of the United States of America and the Russian Federation on Principles of Strategic Stability," Office of the Press Secretary, the [Russian] White House, Moscow (4 June 2000), Article 5. In Article 9 the door was left open to "mutually-agreed" amendments to the ABM if the international situation changed.

31. Simonov, "Nash otvet SShA budet adekvatnym" [Our Response to the USA Will Be Adequate], *Izvestiia* (9 June 2000).

32. "Vystuplenie Mikhaila Kas'yanova v Gosudarstvennoi Dume 17 maia" [Statement of Mikhail Kasyanov to the State Duma on 17 May], *Rossiiskaia gazeta* (18 May 2000).

33. Oleg Odnokolenko, "Wait for an Answer. Asymmetrical Answer," *Segodnya* (22 June 2000). This report on the Yakovlev speech to graduates of the Peter the Great Missile Academy is a translation from RIA Novosti, carried in the CDI Russia Weekly, #107. See also a summary in Interfax (21 June 2000); and Yakovlev, "Bezopasnost' Rossii nadezhno obespechena" [Russian Security Is Reliably Guaranteed], *Krasnaia zvezda* (5 July 2000); Sergeev, "SShA razrushaiut strategicheskuiu stabil'nost'" [The USA Destroys Strategic Stability], *NVO*, No. 22 (23–29 June 2000). See also Gen. Leonid Ivashov, "Protivoraketnaia oborona: ukreplenie strategicheskoi stabil'nosti ili novyi vitok gonki vooruzhenii?" [Anti-Missile Defense: Strengthening Strategic Stability or a New Stage in the Arms Race?], *Krasnaia zvezda* (29 June 2000).

No wonder that the failure on 8 July of America's third test of the NMD syst
caused great celebration in Russia.

MILITARY REFORM DRAWS HEADLINES

An unexpected public outburst in July lent credence to stories of a sharp divide
tween the army's general staff and the ministry of defense. On 12 July, after a clo
meeting of generals, Chief of Staff Anatolii Kvashnin called for the elimination of
strategic nuclear rocket forces as a separate branch of the military, suggesting t
they be folded into the air force. He wanted more funds spent on ground forces
cause they would bear the brunt of any real conflict. Sergeev rejected Kvashnin's id
out of hand, calling them "madness" and a "crime against Russia." Although
chief of staff cited mostly economic reasons for his proposals, the media treated
affair as a serious and dangerous rift in the ranks, some calling the recommendat
an attempted "coup in Russia's military."[34] Senior officers of the strategic nucl
forces urged Kvashnin to reconsider, and leaked their letter to him to the press. 1
dispute suggested that the "free hand" in administrative changes allegedly gi
Sergeev by Putin some months earlier was open to question.

Putin ordered Sergeev and Kvashnin to settle the matter privately. They met w
the president, carried on discussions in Sochi with Putin's security adviser, Sei
Ivanov, and finally offered up a reconciliation of sorts on public television. No
tails were given, but final decisions on the military reform were left to the preside
The public part of the brief outburst threw into stark contrast the two oppos
forces within the military: Sergeev representing the traditional nationalist cro
current, to whom the separate missile force remained a symbol of Russia's status a
great power; Kvashnin representing the new pragmatism, aiming to maintain Ru
as a regional power by channelling more resources into modernizing the conv
tional forces.

Kvashnin was the clear loser in the public mind, where emotion and fear do
nated. He was raked over by nationalists and liberals alike, who accused him of
dermining Russia's status as a great power, weakening his country's position in a
reduction negotiations with the United States, and diminishing the significance
nuclear deterrence.

Even the normally conciliatory Rogov sided openly with Sergeev, terming
"Kvashnin Plan" a "strategic capitulation" to the United States. Vasilii Lata, forr
deputy chief of the Strategic Rocket Forces (RSVN), upbraided the General Staff
endangering Russia's "reliable shield" against American aggression. Several pro
nent foreign affairs analysts warned that the "Kvashnin Principle" was but a "tip

---

34. In "Rakety ostaiutsia v stroiu" [Rockets Remain Ready to Launch], *Izvestiia* (13 July 20
Vladimir Yermolin called it "one of the fiercest battles ever fought within the walls of the Russian Def
Ministry." For communist outrage, see "Ataka Genshtaba na RVSN" [Attack of the General Staff on
Rocket Forces], *Sovetskaia Rossiia* (15 July 2000).

the iceberg," and said that such matters must be solved soon or Russia's credibility in world affairs would be affected.[35] The communist press exhorted the ministry of defense to follow the guidelines set in Russia's new military doctrine, and retain a capacity for "nuclear deterrence."[36]

The defense ministry outburst was surprising only because it was so noisily public. Military reform had, in fact, long been a topic of interest. Its failure to materialize even after the new military doctrine was adopted had been the subject of a detailed analysis by General Nikolaev as recently as early July.[37] His alarmist description of the state of Russia's preparedness for war, which included a scenario in which Poland might draw Russia into a nuclear conflict with NATO, may have played a role in the Kvashnin–Sergeev debate. NATO expansion eastward and its air strikes against Yugoslavia were capitalized on by Nikolaev as examples of how unprotected Russia was—they reminded him of the events of 1939 to 1941.

Former secretary of the Security Council Kokoshin echoed Nikolaev's concerns, but from quite a different perspective. Blaming NATO's actions in Yugoslavia for the further development of nuclear potential in both India and China, he predicted that within a decade both countries would have greatly increased their nuclear capacity. "The planned American NMD will only make this situation worse," he said. "War tensions (India–Pakistan; China–Taiwan; Iran–Afghanistan) will grow, and only Russia will be in a position to serve as mediator."[38]

At any rate, Putin left the final decision about Kvashnin's recommendation up to the Security Council, scheduled to meet on 11 August. But he took no chances.

---

35. For the "Kvashnin Doctrine", see Sergei Sokut, "Igra bez Kozyrei' [Play without Trumps], *Nezavisimaia gazeta* (15 July 2000); Rogov, "Strategicheskaia kapituliatsiia. 'Plan Kvashnina' i yadernaia politika Rossii" [Strategic Capitulation. The "Kvashnin Plan" and Russia's Nuclear Policy], *Nezavisimaia gazeta* (26 July 2000). See also Vadim Solov'ev, "Podkovernaia bor'ba generaliteta vyryvaetsia naruzhu" [Under-the-Rug Struggle of the Generals Comes to Light], *NVO*, No. 26 (21–27 July 2000). Solov'ev agreed with Rogov. Lata, now a specialist with the RVSN Academy, was interviewed for *Vremya-MN* (21 July 2000), summarized in Interfax (21 July 2000). See *Nezavisimaia gazeta* (18 July 2000) for the point that the dispute would be simmering away from the public eye until it was resolved, and that there would be a political loser in the game, probably Sergeev.

36. Army General Yu.P. Maksimov, "Sberech' potentsial yadernogo sderzhivaniia" [Retain the Potential for Nuclear Deterrence], *Sovetskaia Rossiia* (18 July 2000). Maksimov was chief of the RVSN, 1985–1992; see also Col. Gen. N.E. Solovtsov, "Raketnyi krizis" [Rocket Crisis], *ibid.* (22 July 2000). Solovtsov is head of the RSVN Academy. See also Ye.B. Volkov, "Do kakogo urovnia mogut byt' sokrashcheny RVSN?" [To What Level Can We Cut the RVSN?], *Sovetskaia Rossiia* (27 July 2000); Yu. P. Savel'ev, "Shchit i mech zvezdnykh voin. 'Klimat doveriia' sozdaet nadezhnaia sila" [Shield and Sword of Star Wars. A "Climate of Trust" Is Created by a Reliable Force], *ibid.*

37. Nikolaev, "Voennaia reforma buksuet" [Military Reform Is on the Skids], *NVO*, No. 23 (30 June–6 July 2000). Nikolaev had been writing regularly on military reform. See his "Abstraktnaia doktrina abstraktnogo gosudarstva" [Abstract Doctrine of an Abstract State], *ibid.*, No. 46 (26 November–3 December 1999), "Voiska idut v gory" [Troops Go Uphill], *ibid.*, No. 5 (11–17 February 2000).

38. Kokoshin, "Kakie konflikty i soiuzy zhdut Rossiiu vo vtorom yadernom veke" [What Conflicts and Alliances Await Russia in the Second Nuclear Century], *Izvestiia* (27 July 2000). These points were repeated for an English-speaking audience by Igor Ivanov in an essay published in the September/October issue of *Foreign Affairs*, which appeared shortly after President Clinton postponed a decision on authorizing the NMD; Ivanov, "The Missile-Defense Mistake: Undermining Strategic Stability and the ABM Treaty," *Foreign Affairs* (September/October 2000).

Shortly before that meeting, he weakened Sergeev's position by dismissing and re signing six senior generals from their posts, among them Col. Gen. Anatolii Sitr chief of procurement and armament, and Col. Gen. Boris Dukhov, chief of an missile defense.[39] These generals had all been appointed by Sergeev.

Putin's direct hand in military reform was made apparent when his opening dress to the Security Council, 11 August, was printed.[40] Their task, he said, was prepare a military planning strategy for the period up to 2015. This was a "natio wide issue" because of the tremendous resources needed for the country's defense a security requirements. Putin sharply rebuked the military establishment for its inn nal polemics, and ordered it stopped. The missile corps was later offered a reprie and a decision on its fate was postponed until 2006.

THE *KURSK* FACTOR

There was a terrible irony in the timing of this meeting, for the military was st gered while the Council sat. It was then that the pride of the Russian navy, the n clear submarine *Kursk,* sank to the bottom of the Barents Sea with its crew of 1 men.[41]

The navy had been in the news for much of the spring as a beacon of light in otherwise troubled military apparatus. In April, naval command scheduled a thi month Battle Group tour of duty in the Mediterranean. A Black Sea Fleet rec naissance ship, the *Kilden,* already had been sent through the Straits (16 Februa 27 April) on a mission to monitor the Persian Gulf and provide a presence, in li of American seizures of Russian oil tankers. The new project sparked some exc ment, for it was the first such undertaking in four years. The Group would inclu an aircraft carrier and a heavy guided-missile cruiser, about which the governm press waxed enthusiastic. Analysts pointed out that the new military doctrine cal for the protection of Russia's commercial activities on the world's oceans, and so claimed that this expedition showed that the military's "financial problems are be

---

39. On this see *Moscow Times* (1 August 2000). The other "reassigned" generals were: Maj. Gen. / tolii Shatalov, chief of the defense ministry press service; Gen. Nikolai Karaulov, chief of rocket and tillery directorate; Lt. Gen. Aleksandr Zobnin, chief of the military's foreign economic relations; and (Gen. Stanislav Petrov, chief of biological, chemical and radiation defense.

40. Putin, "Strategiia voennogo stroitel'stva—obshchenatsional'naia problema" [Military Plann Strategy a National Problem], *Krasnaia zvezda* (16 August 2000). See also Vadim Solov'ev, Vladimir lasov, "Prezident rezko meniaet kurs voennogo reformirovaniia" [The President Sharply Alters the Co of Military Reforms], *NVO,* No. 28 (4–10 August 2000), and Alan Kachmazov, "Okopnaia pravda. Vo Ministerstva oborony s general'nym shtabom prodolzhaetsia" [Trench Truth. War of the Ministry of fense with the General Staff Continues], *Izvestiia* (2 August 2000), who called it a "cockfight" that no would win and that the people of Russia would be the losers.

41. It was also at that time that the navy was orchestrating a press campaign stressing the importa to Russia of its dominance on the Black Sea and the need to keep NATO forces out; see, for exam Sergei Usov, "Na puti 'iz variag v greki' " [On the Way "from the Varangians to the Greeks"], *Kras zvezda* (11 August 2000).

solved."[42] Most importantly, Russia was now "showing its face" in areas where its presence had been fading.[43]

The feeling of confidence dissipated quickly as a horrified Russian public watched the *Kursk* saga for more than a week. The media began to question military financing with an increasingly sharp eye. The largest part of the naval budget had been allocated to the nuclear-powered ballistic-missile submarine fleet, which by 2000 numbered only about eighteen (from sixty-two in 1990). Speaking at a Navy Day celebration at Baltiisk in July, Putin had pledged that, "if we want Russia to flourish and be a strong, successful and influential country in the world, we are obligated to provide for the fleet. And that is what we will do."[44] But it was left to Chief of Naval Staff, Admiral V. I. Kuroedov, who had written glowingly of a new naval strategy for Russia in May, to clean up the *Kursk* shambles.[45]

In his own Navy Day contribution, Kuroedov had outlined the means whereby Russia's navy could "maintain the fatherland's flag throughout the world's oceans." He called for a systematic delineation of Russia's national interests at sea, a determination of whence threats to those interests might come (the USA and NATO mentioned specifically), and a list of priorities in financing and developing a "unified naval strategy." Another senior naval officer, director of operations Vice Admiral Nikolai A. Konorev, told interviewers that the fate of the navy would be determined by economic decisions, and highlighted his concerns by pointing out that "one must not forget that the USA and NATO countries continue intensively to strengthen and complete their naval forces."[46] It was clear already that the navy's vision of the international strategic dynamic was locked in a time warp to a greater extent, even, than the army's.

When the *Kursk* sinking was first announced, suspicion of the West surfaced almost immediately, and blame-casting took on an old Soviet-style format. Admiral Vladimir Chernavin hinted to interviewers that the accident might have been the result of a collision with an American submarine, secretly monitoring Russia's North Sea exercise. A NATO presence was insinuated even in the noncommunist, government press.[47] Sergeev voiced and held to his mantra that "irrefutable evidence"

---

42. Aleksandr Babkin, "Voennyi flot pospeshit na pomoshch' torgovomu?" [Will the Navy Hurry to Help the Merchant Marine?], *Rossiiskaia gazeta* (27 April 2000). The Mediterranean tour was postponed, and rescheduled in March 2001.

43. See, for example Valerii Aleksin, "Voennye moriaki idut v sredizemnomor'e" [The Naval Fleet Goes into the Mediterranean], *NVO*, No. 14 (21–27 April 2000). An interview with Vice Admiral Nikolai Mikheev.

44. See Mikhail Timofeev, "Glavnyi parad v Baltiiske" [Great Parade in Baltiisk], *NVO*, No. 28 (4–10 August 2000).

45. Kuroedov, "Interesy Rossii v Mirovom okeane" [Russia's Interest in the World's Oceans], *Krasnaia zvezda* (24 May 2000).

46. Valerii Aleksin, "Ustoichivost' flotu pridaet ekonomika" [Stability of the Fleet Depends on the Economy], *NVO*, No. 27 (28 July–3 August 2000), an interview with Konorev. Vladimir Kuroedov, "Rozhdaetsia novaia morskaia strategiia Rossii" [The Birth of a New Naval Strategy for Russia], *ibid.*

47. See, for example, Nikolai Cherkashin, Sergei Ptichkin, "Podvodnyi kreiser terpit bedstvie" [Submarine Cruiser Suffers Disaster], *Rossiiskaia gazeta* (15 August 2000); Nikolai Cherkashin, "Bitva za 'Kursk'" [Battle for the *Kursk*], *Rossiiskaia gazeta* (16 August 2000).

proved an "external influence or a collision."[48] As late as 22 August the governm
newspaper, *Rossiiskaia gazeta,* carried a very long treatise made up of interviews w
naval intelligence experts who insisted that the collision theory was the correct on
and the United States was the most likely culprit.[49] The sense that only a collis
could explain the accident did not go away; but neither did rumors that the *Ku*
might have been sunk by "friendly fire," that is, a torpedo from a Russia cruiser
participating in the exercise.[50]

Though it was not surprising that the Russian navy did not immediately turr
NATO for help when the *Kursk* went down, the media and public soon began to
cuse the navy command of failing to act quickly enough to save Russian lives. Pu
finally stepped in five days after the accident and ordered Kuroedov to seek fore
assistance. Cold War attitudes were criticized by the Russian public and the h
command was censured for its inability to tell the truth. The media also blamed '
tally inadequate operational funding" and called for immediate resolution of the
litical and financial impasse in the military.[51] All of Russia's security ills were brou
starkly into focus by this one calamity.

Sergeev's appeal, in December 1999, for infrastructure, training and technol
funding was granted macabre credence by the events of August. The accident
spired a wave of demands that the entire military structure be overhauled, mode
ized and made efficient.[52] Indeed, the announced draft budget for 2001, appro
by the government on 21 August and sent to the Duma, already had included a s
stantial increase for the armed forces and other power ministries to slightly over o
third of the total. The defense allocation itself was scheduled to rise to 206,324
lion from its current 140,852 billion rubles. In light of the accident, individ

---

48. ITAR-TASS (17 August 2000), Interfax (22 August 2000).

49. Captain First Rank Nikolai Cherkashin, "Kto taranil atomokhod 'Kursk'?" [Who Rammed the
clear Submarine *Kursk*?], *Rossiiskaia gazeta* (22 August 2000). The long essay was comprised mostly c
interview with Rear Admiral Anatolii T. Shtyrov, of naval intelligence, who aggressively discredited
USA and NATO's "internal explosion" theory and insisted that the accident must have been caused
collision.

50. See, for example, Vadim Solov'ev, "Vladimir Putin i Bill Klinton sgovorilis'?" [Did Vladimir Putin
Bill Clinton Collude?], and Valerii Aleksin, "Veroiatnee vsego, 'Kursk' protaranila inostrannaia submai
[It Is Most Likely That the *Kursk* Was Rammed by a Foreign Submarine], *Nezavisimaia gazeta* (12, 13
tember 2000). The author of these two essays said also that the collision was probably with a U.S. sub
rine, and that Putin may have agreed to keep the story secret, after a phone conversation with Clinto
return for financial aid. Admiral Vyacheslav Popov, commander of the Northern Fleet, continued to ac
the American and/or British navies of causing the accident; see *Rossiiskaia gazeta* (20 September 2000).
possibility of a "friendly fire" accident, that is, a torpedo from the cruiser *Peter the Great*, was raised
member of the Duma investigating committee, and vehemently denied by the ministry of defense.

51. See, for example, Valerii Aleksin, "Podlodku 'Kursk' spasaet ves' flot" [The Submarine *Kursk* Is
ing Saved by the Entire Fleet], *Nezavisimaia gazeta* (15 August 2000), and "V redaktsii razdaiutsia
doumennye zvonki chitatelei—neuzheli nel'zia spasti podvodnikov?" [Editorial Office Receiving C
fused Phone Calls from Readers Asking "Are We Really Not Able to Save the Submarine Crev
Rossiiskaia gazeta (16 August 2000). See also *Segodnya* (17 July 2000).
A chronological chart of the accident was printed in *NVO*, No. 31 (23–31 August 2000), along
the names of the 118 sailors.

52. See, for example, Vadim Solov'ev, "Bolezni armii i flota zagoniaiut vovnutr'" [Ailments of the A
and Navy Are Driven Inside], *NVO*, No. 30 (18–24 August 2000).

Duma members began clamoring for more defense spending even before debate on the budget opened.

MILITARY REFORM AND THE FEDERAL BUDGET FOR 2001

New budget considerations compelled the government finally to timetable much discussed reductions in armed forces personnel. On 7 September the press reported forthcoming cuts of some 350,000 servicemen from the 1.2 million army, navy and air force by the year 2003. The armed forces would then number about 850,000 members. Troops of the ministry of the interior, railway and border guard services also were to be reduced. The RVSN question was answered as well: the strategic missile force divisions would be reduced in number by 2006 and gradually amalgamated with the air force.

The forces reduction plan itself and the eventual integration of the Strategic Missile Troops into the air force sparked further controversy: some analysts called the plan "insane" and insisted that it would cost, rather than save, the armed forces.[53] Others said the decrease in personnel could in no way make up for the increased budget expenditures, because the increase actually represented a reduction in the percentage of GDP that was supposed to go the military. There seemed to be near consensus outside the government that the "too little, too late" approach would be a disaster.[54] Apparently, the Duma Defense Committee also believed that the draft 2001 budget failed to provide enough funding for the military and adopted a resolution offering to raise national defense spending by 52 billion rubles, by projecting a 3.5-percent share of the GDP, as opposed to the 2.6 percent allocated in the draft budget.[55]

Much of the posturing on the military budget was political, and effective only in that the senior officer corps was made to appear to stand in the way of serious reform. In late September, Putin back-pedaled on the proposed release of huge numbers of armed forces personnel, saying that the process would have to be more carefully thought out. Public debate on how to deal with what many saw as a bloated military, over-officered yet stuck with tens of thousands of ill-nourished, ill-equipped, and ill-disciplined soldiers, brought apparently endemic problems out in the open, just as it had in the 1980s. The inability of the military to fill its quota of

---

53. See, for example, Viktor Litovkin, "Reformatorskii zigzag" [Reformative Zigzag], *Obshchaia gazeta*, No. 37 (14–20 September 2000).

54. See, for example, an interview with General Andrei Nikolaev, "Predlagaemyi oboronnyi biudzhet na 2001 god dlia armii nepriemlem" [Proposed Defense 2001 Budget for the Army Is Not Acceptable], *Nezavisimaia gazeta* (15 September 2000), who said that the increased spending on the military was actually a decrease in the military's share of the GDP; see also *Nezavisimaia gazeta* (16 September 2000) where the absorption of the RSVN is criticized.

55. See, for example, General Andrei Nikolaev, "Planiruemye voennye assignovaniia nedostatochny. Komitet gosdumy po oborone nameren sformirovat' biudzhet vosstanovleniia vooruzhennykh sil" [Proposed Military Allocations Are Insufficient. The Duma Defense Committee Intends to Create a Budget to Resurrect the Armed Forces], *NVO*, No. 35 (22–28 September 2000).

recruits, due mostly to draft-dodging, was another dilemma. Some specialists argued that the cuts were absolutely necessary, but that they should fall heaviest on the more than a million civilian workers in the military sector.[56] Most analysts were well aware that little would be done while the future of the ABM and NMD remained uncertain.

STEPS FORWARD, STEPS BACKWARD

A step towards order was taken early in November when the defense ministry announced a more specific plan to reduce military personnel (by 365,000) between years 2001 and 2003.[58] The cuts included 240,000 officer positions, about 380 which were at the level of general. The downsizing was designed to provide the ministry more money to spend per soldier. A step backward came a week before the State Commission inquiry into the *Kursk* tragedy was scheduled to meet. Kuroedov announced that a collision with a NATO submarine, British or American, was navy's "position," not a mere possibility; and the government newspaper carried a series of articles in which the collision theory was given much credence.[59] Still, Commission drew no definitive conclusions about the cause of the accident. In many minds the collision theory was pushed by officialdom to defuse the horror of learning that sailors had survived the explosion only to die while awaiting rescue.

The collision theory had been lent credibility a few weeks earlier by an astonishing volte-face on the part of respected military analyst Vadim Solov'ev. In the early days the *Kursk* affair, Solov'ev angrily had accused the ministry of defense of hypocrisy and deception in its blame-casting. In September, however, he published a full front-page feature charging Putin and Clinton with collusion: Russia agreed to ignore collision evidence in return for financial aid. One might think that the "rammed" track was being overplayed here, but it is noteworthy because few Russians believed even Solov'ev. The military-image die was cast. During the preinquiry hype, public suspicion of the armed forces' tendency towards disinformation as its main defense was scored, and opinion polls suggested that the collision theory was not taken very seriously.[60]

---

56. See, for example, Boris Yamshanov, "Voennaia mashina ne dolzhna buksovat'" [The Military chine Must Not Go into a Skid], *Rossiiskaia gazeta* (29 September 2000).

57. See, for example, Liubov Kudelina, "Uvelichivat' oboronnye raskhody—ne v pol'zu armii" [To crease Defense Spending Will Not Benefit the Military], *Izvestiia* (27 September 2000), an interview Deputy Finance Minister Kudelina; and Boris Yamshanov, "Ne chislom, a umeniem" [Not Numbers Ability], *Rossiiskaia gazeta* (28 September 2000).

58. Interfax (31 October 2000).

59. Serge Ptichkin, " 'Kursk' raskryvaet tainy" [*Kursk* Unveils Secrets], *Rossiiskaia gazeta* (27 October 2000), " 'Nikto iz nas ne mozhet podniat'sia naverkh'" ["None of Us Can Get Up"], *ibid.* (28 October Sergei Bazarov, "Odin . . . Ili dvoe? Versiia gibeli K-141" [One . . . Or Two? Versions of the Sinking of 141], *ibid.* (4 November 2000).

60. See Viktor Litovkin, "Fakty bez dokazatel'stv" [Facts without Evidence], *Obshchaia gazeta,* No (9–15 November 2000). For the Solov'ev piece, "Vladimir Putin i Bill Klinton sgovorilis'?" [Did Vlad Putin and Bill Clinton Collude?], *NVO,* No. 34 (15–21 September 2001). This article had appeared a days earlier in *Nezavisimaia gazeta,* but with less fanfare (see footnote 50). The new feature item was companied by a large front-page caricature of Putin and Clinton lowering the *Kursk* into a grave.

At about the same time rumors began to fly of a looming reshuffle in Putin's government directly related to security matters. It was assumed by many observers that Sergei Ivanov, chair of the Security Council, was being groomed to take over the ministry of defense, or even the prime minister's office. The fact that Ivanov was relieved of military duties as a Lt. General in the Federal Security Service (FSB), a rank too low for easy transition to the defense post, was treated as one signal in this regard. It was reported as well that Ivanov was behind the disbanding of state arms-sales agencies *Rosvooruzhenie* and *Promeksport* in November. According to the official explanation the two agencies were competing against each other and thus keeping prices for Russian weapons down, a problem addressed by creating a new, single body called *Rosoboroneksport* (Russian Defense Export Agency), now chaired by Andrei Belianinov, an Ivanov associate.[61]

In the arms reduction sphere, an important initiative was taken by Putin when he told reporters on 13 November that Russia would consider cutting its nuclear arsenal even more than START-III envisioned. To be sure, he had a quid pro quo in mind. Putin added that further reductions would depend on the United States withdrawing plans to introduce an NMD. Putin hoped that current discussions of a new code of conduct for nonproliferation, and the creation of a Global Missile and Missile Technology Control System (GCS), would greatly diminish the need for NMD's, or any amendments to the ABM.[62] A few days after his statement on warhead reductions, Putin spoke strongly on the importance of sustaining the Conventional Armed Forces in Europe Treaty. The occasion of his remarks on 19 November was the tenth anniversary of the Treaty, which he used to criticize "poorly thought-out bloc [NATO] policy, and the use of force bypassing the UN Security Council." The American response to such admonitions was muted, necessarily, because of the ongoing U.S. presidential election debacle and the simple fact that Madeleine Albright, Strobe Talbott and others in the foreign policy sector were preparing to leave office.[63]

---

61. Rosvooruzhenie had been chaired by Aleksei Ogarev; Promeksport by Sergei Chemezov. Belianinov had been Ogarev's deputy. For a detailed analysis of the nature, and politics, of these two agencies, see Viktor Litovkin, "Iskusstvo Rodinu prodavat'. Kto zarabotaet na oruzhii" [The Art of Selling the Motherland. Who Will Earn Money on Weapons], *Obshchaia gazeta*, No. 21 (25–30 May 2000); Litovkin, "Putin uvolil 'ten' Sem'i'" [Putin Is Freed from the "Shadow of the Family"], *Obshchaia gazeta*, No. 45 (9–15 November 2000); and Vadim Solov'ev, "Gosposrednik vnov' poluchaet monopol'nye prava" [State Broker Again Receives Monopoly Rights], *NVO*, No 42 (10–16 November 2000). The last-named article included full models of the new arms export structure.

62. Text of "Putin's Statement on Arms Reduction" (13 November 2000), Embassy of the Russian Federation in Canada. S. M. Rogov, director of ISKRAN and specialist on arms control, discussed the issue of arms control and Russian–American relations in detail in "Nuclear Arms Reduction and Defense Reform in Russia," Carnegie Endowment for International Peace, *Russia and Eurasian Program*, 2: 12 (November 2000).

63. For Putin's statement on 19 November, "Nuzhna armiia, sposobnaia dostoino obespechit' bezopasnost' Rossii" [An Army Is Needed, Especially Trained to Guarantee the Security of Russia], *Krasnaia zvezda* (24 November 2000). According to at least one prominent Russian analyst, another "scandal" was looming because the U.S. military was "violating" the 1987 treaty on liquidating short- and intermediate-range missiles by testing the Hera ballistic missile; and America needed some leadership before this could be stopped. See Sergei Sokut, "Vashington reanimiruet 'Pershingi'" [Washington Reanimates Pershings], *Nezavisimaia gazeta* (17 November 2000).

Moscow had problems of its own. Endless conflict in Chechnya and rising t
sions in Central Asia were both costly and threatening. Putin's popularity had res
at first on his commitment to resolving the Chechen crisis, which by year's end '
declared part of an expanded international anti-Russian terrorist campaign. Russ
officials began to meet openly with leaders of the anti-Taliban forces in Afghanis
and, in November, the defense ministry announced its rapid reaction force (RRF)
both the Caucasus and Central Asia. Simultaneously, Putin reconfirmed the prc
ised deep cuts in military personnel, triggering consternation among the ser
ranks.[64]

Moreover, he shifted blame for the failure in Chechnya directly on to the milit;
lecturing the annual assembly of Russia's military commanders on the poor state
their leadership and training. Citing the military's sorry performance in Chechr
the president claimed that he would push harder for military reform and raise
standards for officer training. Early in 2001, in fact, conduct of operations in Che
nya was taken out of the hands of the military and turned over to the FSB. No n
ter the spin put on this change, it was a humiliating event for the ministry of
fense.[65] The tightening-up continued in November 2000 as Putin signed into la·
decree creating a commission for military cooperation between Russia and fore
countries. Naming himself chair of the commission, he effectively linked foreign ¿
military policy under his direct supervision.[66]

The entire issue of military reform and Russian security was discussed candidly
Secretary Sergei Ivanov in an interview conducted on 29 November. Ivanov mad
plain that the elaboration of security strategies in Russia now rested with the Se
rity Council, whose role in military reform and military policy had greatly increa
since its creation in 1992.[67] An immediate consequence of Ivanov's remarks wa:
extend the military reform question beyond the internal tactical discourse, and m
it a point of contention between the Russian executive and legislative branches.

The political debate was more complex than one over the merits of small, w
trained and equipped forces as opposed to a much larger, but poorly funded milit;

---

64. On the RRF, see Yurii Pankov, "'Razvesti' ES i NATO" [The EU and NATO "Separate"] *Kras;
zvezda* (22 November 2000). On confirming the military cuts, Boris Yamshanov, "Kazhdyi piat'yi, :
iz stroia!" [Every Fifth Step Out of Formation], *Rossiiskaia gazeta* (11 November 2000).

65. "O merakh po bor'be s terrorizmom na territorii Severo-kavkazskogo regiona Rossiiskoi Federa
[On Measures to Combat Terrorism on the Territory of the Russian Federation's North Caucasus Regi
Rossiiskaia gazeta (23 January 2001. The edict was signed by Putin on 22 January. Nikolai Patrushev, I
of the FSB, was put in charge and given until 15 May to come up with a key to defeating the separa
in Chechnya.

66. The commission included the prime minister as vice chair, senior people of the presidential
ministration, plus the ministers of defense and foreign policy, and the heads of both the Foreign Int
gence Service and the FSB, ITAR-TASS (18 November 2000).

67. Sergei Ivanov, "Strategiia bezopasnosti Rossii" [The Security Strategy of Russia], *NVO*, No. 45 (
December 2000); also in *Nezavisimaia gazeta* (29 November). See also Sergei Ptichkin, "Sovetskaia Ar;
ukhodit v proshloe, nachinaetsia stroitel'stvo Armii Rossiiskoi" [Soviet Army Is a Thing of the Past,
Organization of a Russian Army Begins], *Rossiiskaia gazeta* (23 November 2000), and "Kakoi flot nuz
Rossii" [What Kind of Fleet Russia Needs], *Krasnaia zvezda* (23 November 2000), for interviews '
Gen. Yurii Baluevskii of the Army General Staff Main Operations Directorate.

The Duma's defense committee took umbrage at Sergei Ivanov's presumption, complaining that elected deputies were being ignored by the closed forum of the Security Council. General Andrei Nikolaev remarked that in Russia the military had a broader function than defense of the country; that is, it also has a "morale-moral" purpose. He called for a more open deliberation on military reform for the reason that, whatever changes were adopted, all Russian society would be influenced by them. There should be a moratorium on "pseudo-reforms and large scale experiments," Nikolaev concluded, naming specifically the nuclear deterrent forces as something that should be left untouched.[68] This was very much the "old-guard" approach.

A communist review of the world's military situation was more pessimistic about Russia's ability to defend itself. For example, Yurii Kachanovskii, a professor in Khabarovsk, prepared a detailed prospectus on military reform beginning with a scenario in which the United States went ahead with the NMD while Russia's nuclear forces were weakened. The result, he said, could lead to the "real danger of a major war against Russia or the simple liquidation of it as a state with the loss of its territory and natural resources." Kachanovskii concluded that the currently proposed reform would leave the armed forces without "sufficient numbers of well-financed and highly trained" troops to defend itself, and called on the president to guarantee—by economic policies—resources for the military.[69] Sergeev disagreed, at least publicly, telling an interviewer that his ministry had to cut personnel because it could not afford to keep them—and grumbled that the Russian armed forces still would have the same tasks to perform.[70]

The president rejoined the military reform controversy towards the end of the year, demonstrating what side he would likely come down on in the crunch. On 25 December, Putin told a gathering of TV, radio and print journalists that Russia "must not have a large, loose army, rather it needs a small and mobile, highly professional and well-trained, and certainly technically well-equipped army." His approach sounded much more like Kvashnin's than Sergeev's.[71]

In the military and security spheres, Putin accomplished a great deal during his first year in office. He updated and signed off on long-debated military, security and

68. Interview with Army General Andrei Nikolaev, conducted by Viktor Litovkin, "Voenachal'niki v odinochku ne spraviatsia. Reforma armii— shag k grazhdanskomu obshchestvu" [Military Commanders Alone are Not Equal to the Task. Reform of the Army is a Step Towards Civil Society], *Obshchaia gazeta,* No. 48 (30 November–6 December 2000).

69. Kachanovskii, "Kto zashchitit Rossiiu v XXI veke?" [Who Will Defend Russia in the 21st Century?], *Sovetskaia Rossiia* (7 December 2000). Kachanovskii suggested eight ways in which the government could raise money for the armed forces. Yabloko's Aleksei Arbatov took a similar approach, pondering at .great length the dilemma facing Russia's armed forces: military needs vs available resources. Arbatov, "Dilemmy voennoi politiki Rossii" [Dilemmas of Russia's Military Policy], *NVO,* No. 43 (17–23 November 2000).

70. See interview with Sergeev, "Novyi biudzhet vnushaet optimizm" [New Budget Inspires Optimism] *Krasnaia zvezda* (16 December 2000).

71. Putin, "Armiia dolzhna byt' professional'noi" [The Army Must Be Professional], *NVO,* No. 49 (29 December 2000–11 January 2001); see also *Nezavisimaia gazeta* (26 December 2000). Though Putin called for a professional army, he noted that it was a "noble" if idealistic goal and certainly not something for the near future.

foreign policy conceptual guidelines. A new naval doctrine was under review and portedly nearly complete by the end of the year.[72] Though these long-winded bl prints have little to do with day-to-day policy-making, they provide a sense of wh Russia believes it should be in the international scheme of things and furnish pi ciples for practitioners to follow. On the other hand, military reform remained et real, though much talked about.

Driven largely by the *Kursk* crisis, defense budget allocations for 2001 were s stantially increased.[73] Even at that, early concerns that Russia was on the verge of militarizing were proven groundless, and perhaps even impossible. In spite of Put efforts, in fact, the prestige of the armed forces had not been elevated and, by the (of the year, there were misgivings afoot about its ability to defend the country.[74]

Issues related to the ABM, NMD, START-II and -III, CTBT and other inter tional arms control mechanisms and security arrangements all were still problem: as the year 2000 opened. Because these were all matters subject almost entirely Russian and American deliberation, their resolution had to wait until the new U administration was fully in place. Russia's military elite knew that NATO was lik to take in new members in 2002 and that the new wave could include former So' republics among them. References to contingency plans were often made, yet few alysts believed they had much substance. The main difference between January 2(and January 2001, however, is that during the intervening year Russia's positions international issues of defense and security had been given long-needed substa and form, and a "Russian Way" was more clearly discernable.

YEARS TWO AND THREE

Formulating Strategies as the Bush Team Moves In

As Putin's second year in the presidential office opened, the Russian media ' swamped with retrospective and prospective musings on Russia's security futt Even Grigorii Yavlinskii weighed in on the security question. Usually much m concerned with economic and domestic political questions, and the conflict Chechnya, he pointed out in a long sum-up of Russia's situation at the turn of new year that only the country's western borders were secure. In the south and sou east, Russia's frontiers were unstable and vulnerable. He sharply criticized Russ conduct of the Chechnya war, recommending again that a political solution

---

72. Leaks from the ministry suggested that a major rebuilding program was planned for the navy and previously postponed ventures into the Mediterranean had been rescheduled. Such news provided relic mariners who had foreseen Russia becoming a second-class naval state. See, for example, Mikhail k darenko, "Dal'nii pokhod otlozhen" [Long Campaign Postponed], *NVO*, No. 39 (20–26 October 200(

73. For a breakdown of budget allocations for defense in 2001, some 207 billion rubles altogether *Rossiiskaia gazeta* (10 January 2001). This amount was still a minute fraction of what is spent on the itary in the United States, where the new administration also was calling for defense allocation incre:

74. In addition to Arbatov's musings (see fn. 69), see Vadim Solov'ev, "Rossiia ne mozhet vesti bol'sl voinu" [Russia Is Unable to Conduct a Big War], *NVO*, No. 43 (17–23 November 2000).

sought. The ABM/NMD question was an unsettling one, Yavlinskii acknowledged, proposing that the United States and Russia agree on a dual strategic security system, "one for America and one for Europe and Russia."[75] Terrorism was the greatest threat to Russia anyway, he concluded in a section on security.

Putin's own comments to members of the diplomatic corps in which he stressed the need to create a positive image of Russia abroad were given greater meaning by a series of "spy" scandals and accounts of outrageous behavior on the part of Russian diplomats abroad. One Russian observer noted that what Putin really needed was deeds, not words: that is, to pay foreign debts, end the corruption, and behave "normally" abroad.[76]

Sergei Rogov hinted that it was too late for parity and that a dual system of sorts was already in place, one that was "simultaneously multipolar and unipolar."[77] Continuing that "only the United States was powerful enough to stand alone, produces almost half of the world's arms, accounts for fully three-quarters of global military research expenditures, and spends more on upgrading its own arms than "all other countries combined," Rogov left an impression of Russian weakness in the face of American power that was staggering in its implications.

It is true that Russia had no enemies, Rogov continued, but it also had no "dependable allies or partners." Furthermore, the UN and the OSCE were weakening as instruments of international security. In fact, he claimed, both institutions were being used to apply pressure on Russia while their security functions were being absorbed by NATO. Thus, Russia was in far greater danger than its government was willing to admit. It could not, and must not, get bogged down in an expensive arms race. Instead, it was imperative that economic reform go ahead, enabling military reform to proceed (not stall) on the basis of a wise use of resources. Only then would Russia be in a position to "preserve its status as a great military power."[78]

Rogov's treatise was replete with economic data and ended on an upbeat note. Strategic assessment specialists Aleksandr Konovalov and Sergei Oznobishchev were not so sanguine. Both worried about the new American administration and insisted

---

75. Yavlinskii, "Strana na pereput'e" [The Country at a Crossroad], *Obshchaia gazeta*, No.52/1 (28 December 2000–10 January 2001). Most of this long feature was, in fact, on the Russian economy, but the security issue was given far greater attention by him than usual.

76. See, for example, Andrei Kolesnikov, "Shutit' po-russki" [A Russian Joke], *Izvestiia* (30 January 2001). The Russian press continued to defend Borodin, who was arrested on 18 January in the John F. Kennedy International Airport on his way to attend the Bush inauguration, and claimed in an interview that his arrest was politically motivated: see, for example, *Izvestiia* (7 March 2001). Some were more balanced, for example, Aleksandr Sabov in *Rossiiskaia gazeta* (27 January 2001), and "Budet sidet'!" [He Will Do Time!], *Izvestiia* (26 January 2001). On the tragedy in Ottawa, Viktoriia Averbukh, "Dipgonshchik" [Diplomatic Driver], *Izvestiia* (30 January 2001).

77. Rogov, "Vektory bezopasnosti 2001 goda" [Security Vectors 2001], *NVO*, No. 1 (12–18 January 2001).

78. This position was taken as well by contributors to an important military historical journal. In "Voennaia reforma. Kakaia armiia nuzhna Rossii?" [Military Reform. What Kind of Army Does Russia Need?], *Voenno-istoricheskii zhurnal*, No. 2 (February 2002), 2–5, V .F. Fedorov and A.V. Tereshchenko used history to demonstrate that the Russian military always was able to adapt to new conditions, and that it would soon do so in 2002.

that, as a counterpoint, Russia's foreign policy should focus on becoming more ir grated with Western Europe.[79] Scheduled military reforms, specifically person cuts and a restructuring program, were assumed to be delayed until it was clear w policies George W. Bush's new administration would embark upon—though no ficial pronouncement was made to that effect.[80] One writer pointed out that, e before he took over the job as president, Bush had called for $6 billion to be set as to help Boeing upgrade research on the NMD.[81] There was a feeling in certain r itary circles, however, that pragmatic negotiations would push forward and if United States broke faith with the ABM, Russia was quite capable of expanding nuclear potential to render an NMD pointless—at least militarily.[82]

BUSH AND THE NMD

Other analysts in Moscow took President Bush's apparent plans to proceed with NMD unilaterally as an unprovoked slap in the face to President Putin, who had ready spoken positively about the potential for an arms reduction dialogue with United States. Their views on strategic arms are "very different," one such observer p nounced, exploiting Bush's own words to claim that the United States wants to "l the world toward greater security" on Washington's terms only. Another insisted t the NMD had little to do with "rogue" states, rather its purpose was to "reduce [R sian] retaliatory strike" capacity.[83] Sergei Karaganov had predicted this dichotomy a tle earlier, casting blame mostly on the Russian elite. He told an interviewer on 20 J uary that the Russian clamor for a "multipolar world" was absurd and cited upgra relations with Iraq and Cuba as examples of poorly thought-out policy.[84]

Security became a greater issue on 3 February when new U.S. Defense Secret Donald H. Rumsfeld told a European security conference in Munich that his g

---

79. Konovalov is president of the Moscow State Institute of International Relations and presiden the Institute of Strategic Assessments; Oznobishchev is director of the Institute. Their participation press conference with a moderator, on 15 January 2001, was printed by the Press Development Instit Federal News Service.

80. See Dmitrii Safonov, "Bitva pri ambitsiiakh" [Battle of Ambitions], *Izvestiia* (23 January 2001) the view that the struggle for reform was going on behind the scenes, with Kvashnin leading in a pc dispute with Sergeev.

81. See, for example, Viktor Litovkin, "Bush podkorrektiroval Kvashnina" [Bush Corrected W Kvashnin Said], *Obshchaia gazeta*, No. 2 (11–17 January 2001); Mikhail Khodarenok, "Voennaia refo poshla" [Military Reform Is On], *Nezavisimaia gazeta* (19 January 2001); and "Kremlin Stepping I from Defense Reform Plans?" *Jamestown Foundation Monitor* (19 January 2001). See also Yevgenii "PRO Busha" [Bush's NMD (or "About Bush")], *Izvestiia* (30 January 2001), on Bush wanting tc ahead with NMD.

82. See, for example, an interview with Maj. Gen. Vladimir Dvorkin, Chief of the Defense Mini Central Research Institute, *Izvestiia* (22 January 2001).

83. Konstantin Cherevkov, "Stabil'nost' na novoi osnove" [Security on a New Basis], *NVO,* No. 4 (February 2001); Sergei Merinov, "Prezidentskaia pereklichka" [Presidential Exchange] *Rossiiskaia ga* (30 January 2001).

84. Karaganov, "Na Moskvu budut davit' korrektno, no zhestko" [They Will Pressure Moscow C rectly, but Firmly], *Segodnya* (20 January 2001).

ernment would proceed with the NMD. Russian and Chinese officials reacted angrily. Igor Sergeev blustered that "powerful" Russian technology developed in the 1980s could be restarted; and the Chinese foreign minister repeated his warning that further NMD tests scheduled for May would have "a far-reaching and extensive negative impact on global and regional strategic balance and stability" (Interfax, 6 February).[85]

Later, during a television interview in America, Rumsfeld mused that Russia "knew" that the NMD posed no threat to them because it was limited in scale; Moscow was using the NMD discourse to protect the ABM treaty. When asked about similar concerns among America's European allies, he shrugged them off, explaining that as "rational" states and loyal allies the Europeans would come around to the U.S. position. Russia didn't seem to matter. It was part of the problem anyway, as a "proliferator itself" for selling missile technology to Iran, North Korea and other "rogue" states. Although he attributed Cold War thinking to his foreign and domestic opponents in this matter, Rumsfeld's own responses resonated with old notions and clearly reflected the unilateralism mentioned above.[86] From the Russian perspective, Rumsfeld himself had quickly become part of the problem.

Some order was brought into the NMD argument in late February when the Bush administration had its first direct meetings with European and Russian leaders. Britain's Tony Blair was in the United States for a "get-acquainted" session at Camp David and agreed with Bush to support a European defense force as long as it enhanced, rather than detracted from, NATO's military missions. Blair shared some of America's concern about missiles launched from maverick states, but to Moscow's relief refrained from endorsing the NMD. At a simultaneous meeting of foreign ministers in Cairo, Ivanov and Powell declared that they would approach their differences on missile defense constructively, and deal quickly with cutbacks in nuclear arsenals. A conference in Munich also saw the U.S. and Russian positions laid out, by Sergei Ivanov and Donald Rumsfeld, with no sign of any movement from either side.

The din of outrage emanating from the MoD in connection with the ABM was blunted in March when NATO's Lord Robertson reported in Washington that Russia's president actually accepted the notion that some form of NMD was necessary and that the "rogue" states were, indeed, a threat to peace. Robertson claimed that Putin had even used the "rogue" word in connection with Iran and North Korea during his visit to Moscow in mid-February. A concurrent ministry position paper, "Phases of European Missile Defense," represented a striking change from Moscow's prior intransigence and suggested that the Kremlin recognized that the United States

85. Well-known Russian foreign affairs analyst Andrei Piontkovskii commented on this confrontation a month later, and warned that Rumsfeld and Ivanov were both on a slippery slope dragging Russia towards a new Cold War, see "Khotiat li Russkie 'Kholodnoi voiny'?" [Do Russians Want a "Cold War"?], *Obshchaia gazeta*, No. 10 (8–14 March 2001). "Khotiat li Russkie voiny" [Do Russians Want War] was a well-known song during the Brezhnev era.

86. Interview on *The News Hour with Jim Lehrer* (14 February 2001). For a Russian communist perspective, Viacheslav Tetekin, "Pervaia zhertva 'Zvezdnykh voin'" [First Victim of "Star Wars"], *Sovetskaia Rossiia* (20 February 2001).

would go ahead with its program no matter what Russia or European countries sa In that case, Russia needed to avoid being marginalized in the debate about Eu pean security.[87]

MILITARY REFORM REVISITED

In addition to the alleged delay in reform, the military high command had suffe humiliation when, on 22 January 2001, the FSB was ordered to take over respoi bility for defeating separatists in Chechnya (see Chapter 4). Uniformed soldiers w to be cut from about 80,000 to 22,000 and secret service agents under the comma of Nikolai Patrushev, head of the FSB, were moved in. This changeover began on February and took about four months to be set fully in place.[88]

There was some good news for the navy, however. In late January, leaks about long-awaited new navy doctrine began to show up in the press. Rumors that Ru was again going to deploy globally as a maritime power were substantiated wl navy ships were sent simultaneously into the Pacific and Indian Oceans, for the f time in nine years.[89] There was an important, if grudging, navy concession latei the spring, when a government commission concluded that the *Kursk* had, inde been the victim of one of its own training torpedoes. Reporting this finding at a pi conference, Admiral Kuroedov added that there still might have been a collision w another submarine. It was also announced that the submarine would be raised on September and only then should final conclusions be drawn.[90] Nine months a that, in June 2002, a final judgement brought at least official closure to the *Kursk* fair: an internal explosion caused the accident.

There had been some renewed military association with NATO as well. In Feb ary 2001, Sergeev gave notice that Russian forces would participate in the I

---

87. For more detail see Michael R. Gordon, "Moscow Signaling a Change in Tone on Missile Defei *New York Times* (22 February 2001).

88. See Mikhail Khodarenok, "Rukovodit' operatsiei porucheno chekistam" [Chekists Are Ordere Head the Operations], NVO, No. 3 (26 January–1 February 2001).

89. See, for example, Nikolai Cherkasin, "Flot vykhodit v okean" [Fleet Begins Ocean Voyage], *iiskaia gazeta* (25 January 2001); Oleg Vladykin, "Grimasa velichiia. Rossiiskii Voenno-morskoi floi tuchil okeanskii pokhod" [Grimace of Greatness. The Russian Navy Wrings Out an Ocean Voyage], *shchaia gazeta*, No. 3 (18–24 January 2001). Not everyone was happy: the same issue of *OG* carri piece by Marina Tokareva, "Pochemu pogib 'Kursk' znaiut vse. Krome grazhdan Rossii" [Everyone Kr Why the *Kursk* Died. Except Russian Citizens].

90. Vladislav Kulikov, " 'Kursk' potopila torpeda. Takoe sensatsionnoe zaiavlenie sdelal vchera glav VMF admiral Kuroedov" [A Torpedo Sank the *Kursk*. Such a Sensational Statement Made This Eve by Admiral of the Fleet Kuroedov], *Rossiiskaia gazeta* (26 May 2001); see also "Istinnye prichiny g submariny zamalchivaiutsia" [The True Cause of the Sinking of the Submarine is Hushed-Up], NVO, 16 (11–17 May 2001), in which Oleg Erofeev takes the ministry to task for deceiving itself about its invincibility.

91. "Rossiia budet 'sderzhannoi' "[Russia Will be "Restrained"], *Rossiiskaia gazeta* (8 February 20 Aleksandr Sabov, "Geopolitika. V Miunkhene vse ostalis' pri svoem" [Geopolitics: Everyone Stuck to Guns], *Rossiiskaia gazeta* (6 February 2001). See also Vadim Solov'ev, "Ocherednyi zigzagi v voennykl nosheniiakh" [Customary Zig-zagging in Military Relations], *NVO*, No. 7 (23–29 February 2001).

though in a limited fashion only and in exercises close to Russia's borders.[91] The fate of the missile forces remained unresolved and almost always part of the NMD/ABM discourse in Russia. Indeed, several analysts urged Russia to forget about America's NMD, in part because Sergeev and others in the top military echelons seemed incapable of moving beyond a Cold War assumption that its primary purpose was to curtail Russia's retaliatory capacity against a preemptive strike.[92] China was frequently cited as a greater potential threat than the United States. In March as the new U.S. administration appeared to think of Russia as irrelevant, analysts were divided over whether the NMD was truly threatening or something that was unlikely ever to be in place anyway. Mostly the Russians advocated alternative security measures and hoped that these would be given a fair hearing in Washington.[93]

Rogov was back in March with a long study on the military policies of the Bush administration, in which he insisted that "it is not necessary to panic or be swayed by hysteria." Bush's "harsh rhetoric" notwithstanding, there was still opportunity for Russia and the United States to reach a compromise. He called Bush's administration a "new old team," noting the links key individuals (Cheney, Rice, Rumsfeld) had with the earlier George Bush presidency, and suggesting that they would have to adjust to new circumstances. Rogov exhorted his audience to adopt a "wait and see" approach.[94]

SERGEEV DISMISSED

Movement on the military reform front was made more likely when Marshal Igor Sergeev was dismissed on 28 March. As had been expected,[95] Security Council head, Sergei Ivanov, filled the position, touted as the first civilian in Russian history to head the defense ministry. Sergeev was shuffled off to an advisory capacity on security matters, including the NMD. The ministry was changed further when Deputy Finance

92. On this, see, for example, Andrei Piontkovskii, "Khotiat li russkie 'kholodnoi voiny'?" [Does Russia Want a "Cold War"?], *Obshchaia gazeta,* No. 10 (8–14 March 2001); Viktor Litovkin, "Razvedchiki raketchikov ne ponimaiut" [Intelligence Officers Do Not Understand Missilemen], *Obshchaia gazeta,* No. 4 (25–31 January 2001); Sergei Ptichkin, "Rabota nad oshibkami: Vpered, kosmicheskie sily!" [Working on Mistakes: Forward, Space Forces!], *Rossiiskaia gazeta* (27 January 2001).

93. See, for example, an interview with Aleksandr Yaklovenko, head of the foreign ministry's Department of Information, Dmitrii Chernogorskii, "Moskva ne vidit ugroz, opravdyvaiushchikh sozdanie NPRO" [Moscow Sees No Need for the U.S. National Missile System], *Nezavisimaia gazeta* (21 March 2001); and Boris Talov, " 'Zvezdnye voiny' sebe dorozhe" [The "Star Wars" Will Cost More than It Is Worth], *Rossiiskaia gazeta* (16 March 2001), who pointed out that the increase in America's military budget for 2002 is alone more than Russia's entire state budget.

94. Rogov, "Slova—groznye. A kakovy budut dela? O voennoi politike administratsii Busha" [The Words Are Terrible. But What Will Be Done? On the Military Policies of the Bush Administration], *NVO,* No. 9 (16–22 March 2001).

95. See, for example, Yevgenii Moskvin, "Kto vozglavit minoborony?" [Who Will Head the Defense Ministry?], *NVO,* No. 8 (2–15 March 2001).

96. The Kudelina appointment generated lots of comment, mostly favorable. See, for example, Sergei Ptichkin, "Armeiskii rubl' v zhenskikh rukakh" [Army Budget in Woman's Hands], *Rossiiskaia gazeta* (30 March 2001).

Minister Lyubov Kudelina was appointed deputy minister of defense, the first won
to hold such a high position in that ministry.[96] She was joined by two other r
deputy defense ministers, Gen. Igor Puzanov, former commander of the Moscow r
itary district, and Aleksandr Moskovskii, who also kept his post as deputy secretary
the Security Council. Former minister of the interior, Vladimir Rushailo, took c
Ivanov's chair of the Security Council and he, in turn, was replaced as minister
Boris Gryzlov, head of the Unity Party, usually seen as Putin's party in the Duma.

Putin explained that the changes would advance military reform and "demil
rize" Russian society, finally curbing fears raised during the first months of his p
idency when it appeared that he might have a fixation with resurrecting the pres
of the military. Little was said in Russia about the extent to which KGB/FSB p
sonnel were permeating the power ministries and the presidential apparatus. At a
rate, military reform stumbled forward. Within a few days of the announcemen
Sergeev's dismissal, general staff deputy chief, Col. Gen. Vladislav Putilov,
nounced that the army would be cut by 365,000 by 2004. He acknowledged t
this would cause tension within the armed forces, but it was clear that the Krem
was prepared for a showdown with the military elite.

Ivanov had an inside track to the budget and was reasonably well-respected wit
the ministry.[97] He had been doing part of the work of the ministry already. As head
the Security Council Ivanov had signed off on the military and security doctrines a
as recently as 19–24 March he had conducted talks in France and Poland on questi
of international security, the OSCE, Chechnya, the "struggle against terrorism," a
most importantly, the creation of a European nonstrategic missile defense systen
The military recently had gained a lobby in the Duma somewhat reminiscent of G
eral Lev Rokhlin's movement in support of the armed forces, when a new interfactio
group of deputies was formed. Calling itself Honor, Duty, Fatherland—Career O
cers, the new faction included thirty-four deputies from a cross-section of affiliatic
who agreed to support military reform. It was headed by Vice Admiral Valerii Doro
and included such luminaries as former defense minister Rodionov (Communi
Nikolai Kovalev (Fatherland-All Russia) and Aleksandr Gurov (Unity).[99]

Analysts predicted a new epoch and rapid movement towards military reform
and at first they seemed to be right, as more of Sergeev's key people were moved
of the top layers of the ministry: Vladimir Yakovlev was replaced as commandei
Russia's Strategic Rocket Forces by Col. Gen. Nikolai Solovtsov, and Ground Foi

97. See, for example, Boris Yamshanov, "Komu ustupil svoe mesto marshal Sergeev" [For Whom
Sergeev Step Aside], *Rossiiskaia gazeta* (30 March 2001); Vadim Solov'ev, "Prezident rokiruet silovil
[The President Rotates Military Staff], *NVO*, No. 11 (30 March–5 April 2001); *Izvestiia* (29 M
2001).

98. See, for example, Igor Korotchenko, "Moskva stroit evroPRO. S etoi tsel'iu Sergei Ivanov po
Frantsiiu i Pol'shu" [Moscow Builds a EuroNMD. For This Purpose Sergei Ivanov Visited France
Poland], *NVO*, No. 8 (30 March–5 April 2001).

99. ITAR-TASS (14 March 2001). On the Rokhlin movement, see *Russia Faces NATO Expansion*,
165–174.

100. See, for example, Mikhail Khodarenok, "Armiia ozhidaet korennykh peremen" [Army Exp
Radical Changes], NVO, No. 13 (13–19 April 2001).

Chief Col. Gen. Nikolai Kormiltsev was appointed deputy defense minister. One consequence of the latter appointment is that Kormiltsev could bypass his military boss, Kvashnin, and take matters directly to the minister. Kvashnin's earlier controversial recommendation that the rocket forces be amalgamated with other units clearly had won the day, but it was not so clear that Kvashnin himself would advance because of it.[101] Analysts noted that subsequent changes in personnel came slowly and cautiously, one of them pointing out that the most "implacable" critic of NATO and the United States, Ivashov, was not likely to be removed because the "anti-Americanist position is still in fashion in the Kremlin."[102]

RETHINKING DOCTRINE

George Bush's announcement on 1 May that the United States would start work on the NMD immediately had widespread political repercussions in Russia (see Chapter 4). In addition to the usual rush to find the proclamation's real meaning for Russia, there was a related spate of monographic writing about Russia's new military and strategic doctrines and how they were now to be applied. One of these, by Aleksei Arbatov, was a full-length book titled *The Transformation of Russian Doctrine: The Lessons of Kosovo and Chechnya.* A longtime commentator on Russia's role in world affairs, deputy chair of the Duma Committee on Defense and director of the Center of Geopolitical and Military Prognoses in IMEMO, Arbatov's opinions are taken seriously. The book, in fact, was sponsored by the George K. Marshal European Center, funded from American and German sources. The source of his support did not stop Arbatov from vigorously criticizing both the West's policies towards Russia and Russia's own policy-making, especially that of the MoD. That being said, the main problem as Arbatov saw it was the tendency of the United States and NATO to do what they wished in world affairs no matter the view held in Moscow.[103]

This was a widely held opinion, and one that prompted renewed exhortations from the foreign affairs elite in Moscow that the UNSC's role in conflict resolution be strengthened

As the Putin–Bush summit of 16 June loomed nearer, Russian officials regularly pronounced the inviolability of the ABM while speaking the language of compromise and consultation. More independent military and foreign affairs analysts played up the seriousness of any unilateral amendments by Washington and insisted that the

---

101. See "Peresudy" [Gossip], *Izvestiia* (29 April 2001), where in a debate on military reform it was said by both parties that the change was a victory for Kvashnin's policies; and in Mikhail Khodarenok, "V minoborony razgorelas' kadrovaia revoliutsiia" [A Cadre Revolution Has Broken Out in the Ministry of Defense], *Nezavisimaia gazeta* (29 April 2001), "far-reaching consequences" were expected.

102. Viktor Litovkin, "Kadrovaia spetsoperatsiia. Rukovodstvo armii meniaiut tikho" [The Special Operation. Army Leadership Changes Quietly], *Obshchaia gazeta,* No. 20 (17–23 May 2001).

103. For a description and review of Arbatov's book, *Transformatsiia rossiiskoi voennoi doktriny—uroki Kosovo i Chechni,* see Viktor Litovkin, "Partnerstvo radi istiny" [Partnership for the Sake of Truth], *Obshchaia gazeta* , No. 20 (17–23 May 2001).

NMD would not work.[104] The dispute intensified after the summit and headli
grabbing comments by Putin that, 1) Russia was ready to discuss amendments to
ABM Treaty, and 2) if the amendments were unilateral and Russia was not satisf
with them, a new arms race was inevitable.

Noting the sea-change in the Kremlin's official attitude on the inviolability of
ABM, Vadim Solov'ev explained that Putin was trying to make the best of a bad sit
tion. Yeltsin had done the same thing when it was clear that NATO expansion was
evitable, no matter how forcefully Moscow objected. He agreed that, if need be, Ru
could maintain its nuclear deterrence capacity by placing MIRVS on single-warh
missiles at relatively little cost. But he worried that Putin had not made it clear how
he was willing to compromise, leaving the atmosphere more muddied than pr
ously.[105] The notion that the so-called rogue states might, or even could, attack
United States with missiles was called unrealistic again by Russian officials. Former 1
fense Minister Sergeev, for example, took this message directly to Joseph Biden, ch
of the U.S. Senate International Affairs Commission, and claimed to have had so
success.[106]

It was at this time, in fact, that another of Sergeev's supporters in the MoD 1
his position. On 30 June, Putin signed a decree discharging First Deputy Chief
Staff Manilov, because of his "age"—sixty-two. It was true that this was the age
which senior officers were expected to retire, but there was a general feeling that
had been let go because he was seen as part of the Sergeev camp.[107] With Mani
out of office, the only remaining high-profile public anti-NATO ministry of defe
spokesman was Ivashov, and he reconfirmed his credentials as a hardliner in this
gard during a long interview with journalists from *Krasnaia zvezda* in early July
He and others in the MoD and MID pointed out that if the United States unila
ally withdrew from or violated the ABM Treaty then Russia might protect itself
arming the so-called rogue states.[109]

---

104. Oleg Grinevskii, "Dogovor po PRO soglasovyvali v tundre" [The ABM Treaty Was Agreed U
in the Tundra], *Dipkur'er NG*, No. 8 (24 May 2001); "Moguchaia fantaziia Pentagona" [A Powerful
tasy of the Pentagon], *Rossiiskaia gazeta* (16 May 2001); Sergei Ptichkin, "Amerikanskoi mechte mesh
rossiiskie S-300" [American Dream Is Blocked by the Russian S-300], *Rossiiskaia gazeta* (30 May 20

105. See, for example, Solov'ev, " 'Satana' dlia Vashingtona" ["Satan's for Washington"], *Nezavisir
gazeta* (21 June 2001). See also a long interview with A.D. Rotfeld, director of SIPRI, who was in Mos
earlier in June. The interview was conducted by Solov'ev: "Mir vstupaet v polosu narashchiv;
vooruzhenii" [The World Is Moving into the Realm of Increasing Arms], *NVO*, No. 20 (8–14 June 2

106. "Igor Sergeev: 'Izgoi nikogda ne smogut napast' na Ameriku' " [Igor Sergeev: "Rogue States
Never Be Able to Attack the USA"], *Izvestiia* (21 June 2001). Sergeev was attending a conference on
clear non-proliferation in Washington, 20 June.

107. See, for example, Serge Ptichkin, "Genshtab neset poteri" [General Staff Suffers Losses], *K
iskaia gazeta* (3 July 2001); see also Irina Petrova, "Komu komandovat' informatsionnym frontom?" [\
Will Command on the Information Front?], *Rossiiskie vesti* (4 July 2001), who saw Manilov as the la
the old Soviet-style propagandists, whose early career had been with the *Krasnaia zvezda*.

108. See Vladimir Mokhov, "Prioritety bezopasnosti v svete nyneshnei vneshnepoliticheskoi situa
[Security Priorities in Light of the Current Foreign Political Situation], *Krasnaia zvezda* (4 July 2001

109. Interview conducted by Mike Tricky for the *Ottawa Citizen* (18 July 2001). See also Va
Solov'ev, "SShA brosaiut novyi vyzov" [The USA Throws Out a New Challenge], *NVO*, No. 25 (13
July 2001); see also his "SShA forsiriut vykhod iz dogovora po PRO" [The USA Accelerates Withdr
from the ABM Treaty], *Nezavisimaia gazeta* (13 July 2001).

Russia had been providing weapons to some of these states for some time already, but for money and diplomatic points. The diehards were not taken very seriously. In fact, none of the aggressive responses impressed the more pragmatic Russian analysts. Aleksei Arbatov, for example, agreed with the tenor of Putin's remarks, but not with his timing. If they had been made much earlier, they may have drawn more precise declarations from Washington and perhaps even have "deterred America from tough unilateral steps." Viktor Litovkin, on the other hand, accused Putin of threatening the United States with "virtual warheads" and therefore "frightening no one."[110] And the "rogues" are much closer to Russia than they are to the United States,[111] so a change in the ABM status was not as important as whatever replaced it. The general sense among analysts was that whatever opportunity there had been for a constructive Russian initiative on the ABM and NMD, it was rapidly fading away.[112] The success of the first NMD test conducted by the Bush administration, though generally thought to be have been contrived, had a dampening effect on one dimension of Russia's argument against the proposed defense system, that is, that it wouldn't work.[113]

A sequence of post-Genoa "consultations" between American and Russian security hierarchies resulted in little more than promises to consult further. Rice visited Moscow in late July, followed by Rumsfeld in August; Col. Gen. Yurii Baluevskii travelled to the Pentagon on 7 August, and Sergei Ivanov came after him later in the month. After all this scurrying about, the only tangible offer, apparently, came from Rice, who was alleged to have proposed closer security arrangements in return for a Moscow promise not to arm North Korea and Iran.[114] The suggestion was rejected in Moscow, and Russian analysts began commenting upon the "futility" of such consultations.[115] They now believed the NMD program was directed against China, and the "rogue" state explanation was mere camouflage for what American strategic planners could not say publicly. A month after it was alleged that Rice made a tentative offer, a stalemate seemed to have been reached. The Rumsfeld tour prompted one Russian analyst to complain that Russia and the United States talked to each

---

110. Litovkin, "Putin prigrozil virtual'nymi boegolovkami. Ego zaiavlenie nikogo ne napugaet" [Putin Threatened with Virtual Warheads. His Statement Frightens No One], *Obshchaia gazeta*, No. 26 (28 June–4 July 2001); Arbatov, "Golovnaia bol' ot golovnykh chastei. Chto stoit za nashim 'otvetom Bushu'?" [Headache from Warheads: What Is Behind Our "Answer to Bush"?], *ibid.*

111. This would not have been so, of course, if Cuba was included among the "rogues." But Cuba had become irrelevant to everyone but Washington. It no longer could afford to buy arms from Russia, and Moscow would never allow itself to be drawn back into a situation like that of 1962.

112. See, for example, Litovkin, "Amerika preodolevaet Dogovor po PRO" [America Abrogates the ABM], *Obshchaia gazeta*, No. 29 (19–25 July 2001); Vadim Solov'ev, "Rossiia smenila gnev na milost'" [Russia Switches from Anger to Mercy], *NVO*, No. 27 (27 July–2 August 2001).

113. On this, see Yurii Yershov, " 'Potemkinskie predstavlenie' opasno dlia mira" ["Window Dressing" Dangerous to the World], *Rossiiskaia gazeta* (17 July 2001).

114. On the Rice visit see, for example, Ol'ga Tropkina, Ivan Rodin, "Chego zhdat' ot Kondolizy Rais?" [What to Expect from Condoleeza Rice?] *Nezavisimaia gazeta* (27 July 2001).

115. "Aleksei Arbatov: Konsul'tatsii s SShA ni k chemu ne privedut" [Aleksei Arbatov: "Consultations with the USA will be Futile"], *Nezavisimaia gazeta* (14 August 2001).

other like the blind to the deaf.[116] On his return to Washington, Rumsfeld told L television viewers that Russia was still driven by Cold War attitudes, implying t reasons for the impasse could be found in Moscow, not Washington (Interfax, August). Russian officials took the position that this was the kettle calling the black.

In the midst of all this consultation, futile or otherwise, Russia's long-awai naval doctrine was signed by the Russian president and published. The tim and location of its official announcement were chosen carefully: Putin selec Sevastopol, where he and Ukrainian President Kuchma were for the first time joir celebrating the Russian Navy Day, away from Moscow where the anniversary of *Kursk* disaster was being mourned. Analysts saw the announcement as part of overall military reform and the start of a process leading to the reestablishmen Russia as a naval power by the year 2020.[117]

The ABM debate petered out somewhat in August when the Russian governm signalled that it was willing to make "certain amendments" to the ABM Treaty to k it in place, only to hear from President Bush two days later, 23 August, that the Uni States would withdraw from the ABM "at a time convenient to America." Bush's gotiator John Bolton was in Moscow at the time and agreed with his Russian coun parts that the two sides should keep on talking anyway. Nevertheless, Russia was dangling, with few options. Defense Minister Ivanov adopted a notably less hawk tone than usual in a reply to a query about the apparently final American decisior opt out of the 1972 treaty. This was their "sovereign right," he said, adding that R sia would react calmly and encourage further consultation sessions.[118] Ivanov impl that NATO expansion eastward was now, again, the most pressing issue.

As we have seen in an earlier chapter, the terrorist attack on New York and Wa ington in September changed many things. Russian analysts began to reassess tl own defense against terrorism, even though their country had already been the t get of such acts for several years. They made it clear also that they believed that event had demonstrated weaknesses in American intelligence agencies and offe gratuitous advice on how to resolve that problem.[119] In fact, the day before the tack on America, the Duma reopened after the summer break with an increase Russia's defense budget as their first item for debate. By 19 October the bud

---

116. See Viktor Litovkin, "Pro i kontra. Rossiia i SShA razgovarivaiut, kak slepoi s glukhim" [Pro Con: Russia and the United States Talk Like the Deaf to the Blind], *Obshchaia gazeta*, No. 33 (16 August 2001). See also Vladimir Bogdanov, "Nashi liudi v Pentagone" [Our People in the Pentag *Rossiiskaia gazeta* (10 Aug 2001), who was encouraged that there was at least the appearance of fur consultations.

117. "Morskaia doktrina Rossiiskoi Federatsii na period do 2020 goda" [Russian Federation N Doctrine for the Period Up to 2002], *NVO*, No. 28 (3–9 August 2001); Sergei Ptichkin, "Morskaia c trina Rossii" [Russia's Naval Doctrine], *Rossiiskaia gazeta* (31 July 2001).

118. Interfax (30 August 2001). See also Andrei Piontovskii, "Moment dlia istinu" [Moment of Tru *Nezavisimaia gazeta* (4 September 2001).

119. See, for example, Igor Korotchenko, "Vashington ishchet vinovnykh" [Washington Searche: the Guilty Ones], *NVO*, No. 34 (14–20 September 20001); Vladimir Mukhin, "Rossiiskoe povtor N'iu-iurkskoi tragedii vozmozhno" [A Russian Repetition of the New York Tragedy Is Possible], *ibid*

already had passed its second reading with a national defense increase of roughly the equivalent of $10 billion. The announcements that Russia would be closing its surveillance base in Cuba (Lourdes) and would withdraw the military contingent from the Cam Ranh base in Vietnam were justified by the defense ministry as necessary economic measures. Putin had met senior officials at the ministry on 17 October to discuss military reform, with emphasis on the modernization of equipment, weapons, and training. Noting that the defense budget had been substantially raised for 2002, he insisted that more resources had to be found. Qualitative rather than quantitative growth was necessary, and duplicate structures and ineffective spending had to be eliminated. A program of armaments ordering had to be initiated immediately.[120] All this, it would seem, ensured the final victory of the Kvashnin approach to military reform.

The 11 September tragedy had also given new purpose to Russia's military presence in Central Asia. In fact, two days before the terrorist planes hit the buildings in New York, the president of Tajikistan celebrated his country's independence with praise for Russia's help in their fight against "extremism."[121] All this followed a period when the CIS Collective Security Group conducted a military briefing course on the concept of a "one-and-a-half war", that is, coordinating an NMD of its own against both NATO and the Taliban.[122]

Not surprisingly, the Russian press was filled with warnings against both their own country and the United States becoming involved in a land war in Afghanistan. One military expert insisted that access to the Central Asian airfields would not be of great advantage to American forces: existing bases were small, in terrible condition, and looted of much of their assets. Moreover, the relative isolation of the airfields meant that problems of logistics (weapons supply, fuels), and insufficient infrastructure (barracks), might create more problems than they could solve.[123] It may have been the daunting condition of Russia's own infrastructure that persuaded such analysts, wrongly, that America would not simply rebuild the bases they hoped to use.

It has already been pointed out that Russia's strategic decision to support the United States in all but actual fighting was a huge one: providing an air corridor, providing intelligence, acting as liaison with the Central Asian states, committing itself to search and rescue operations, and, significantly, providing the Northern Alliance with between $30–45 million in arms.[124] These were substantial commitments for

---

120. "Remarks by President Putin at a Meeting at the Defense Ministry of the Russian Federation, Moscow, 17 October 2001," Ministry of Foreign Affairs of the Russian Federation (18 October 2001), RF Embassy in Canada website.

121. See Nikolai Plotnikov, "Tverdyi otpor ekstremizmu" [Firm Rejection of Extremism], *NVO*, No. 33 (7–13 September 2001); Vadim Solov'ev, "Pravitel'stvo predlagaet uvelichit' voennyi biudzhet na tret'" [The Government Recommends an Increase in the Military Budget by a Third], *ibid.*

122. Peter Polkovnikov, "SNG vzialo na vooruzhenie kontseptsiiu 'polytora voin'" [The CIS Takes On the Concept of "One-and-a-Half War"], *NVO*, No. 32 (31 August–6 September 2001).

123. Mikhail Khodarenok, "Na ruinakh abustroit'sia trudno" [It's Hard to Base Yourself in Ruins], *Nezavisimaia gazeta* (26 September 2001).

124. On this, see Mikhail Khodarenok, "Rossiia delaet strategicheskii vybor" [Russia Makes a Strategic Choice], *NVO*, No. 35 (21–27 September 2001).

Russia's strained military and intelligence services, but a manageable commitm
nonetheless. And they had political manifestations. As details of Russia's role in
anti-terrorist coalition were worked out, Putin invested in the rejuvenated relati
ship with America by toning down Russian opposition to both the further expans
of NATO and the United States's NMD. The Russian and American presidents ag
hinted at compromises on the ABM, tied mostly to the potential for a much lar
than expected nuclear arms reduction, bringing the number of missiles retained
both sides down well below the 2,000 floor.

November's summitry in Washington, Texas, and New York led to promises
substantial mutual reduction in nuclear warheads. But the Russian military elite
adamant that the agreement be in a treaty format. As it happened, the conduct of
new war against terrorism, both in Chechnya and Afghanistan, worked to the
vantage of the military senior command in Russia at the expense of the bureaucr;
ministry of defense. Kvashnin, only recently embroiled in a bitter public disp
with former Minister of Defense Sergeev, now seemed to have greater promine
than Sergeev's successor, Sergei Ivanov.

Whereas Ivanov and Putin offered conciliatory commentary on the ABM iss
the military remained unyielding about the treaty's inviolability, and continued to
sist that their own missiles could penetrate the proposed American defense system
Retired senior officers lodged protests, some of them very bitter, about Putin's c
to the military, and his plans to phase out conscription. In fact, the defense mini:
announced a serious shortfall of new recruits available for the fall call-up beca
about 88 percent of the young men on the military register had gained exempt
one way or another. A spokesman for the defense ministry warned on 17 Novem
that the existing conscription system soon would not be able to guarantee to fill
army's personnel needs.[126]

Rumors that Putin was now an object of military political intrigue were lent
dence on 10 November when a group of retired generals and admirals publishe
scathing open letter to the president, Duma deputies, government members, ;
governors of the Russian Federation. They rejected Putin's new alliance with Am
ica, complained about the projected closure of bases in Vietnam and Cuba, and
jected to the arrival of American troops in Uzbekistan and Tajikistan. Military
form must be rethought, they demanded, before Russia is so greatly weakened a:
give up its leadership role even in the CIS.[127] They were supported to a certain
tent by Andrei Nikolaev, Chairman of the Duma Defense Committee, who argi

---

125. See, for example, Col. Gen. Nikolai Chervov (ret'd), "Vozvratnaia bomba" [Reversible Bomb:
Missile Defense System Will Save Them from Our Satan], *Rossiiskaia gazeta* (28 November 2001).

126. Dmitrii Ivanov, "Soldat nynche v defitsite" [A Deficit in Soldiers This Year], *Rossiiskaia gazeta*
November 2001).

127. "Sluzhit' Rodine!" [Serving the Motherland!], *Sovetskaia Rossiia* (10 November 2001). Va
Solov'ev, "Generaly ukhodiat v oppozitsiiu Kremliu. Ministr oborony Sergei Ivanov teriaet kontrol'
Vooruzhennymi silami, vsia nadezhda na prezidenta" [Generals Go into Opposition to the Kremlin.
fense Minister Ivanov Is Losing Control of the Armed Forces, All Hope Is Pinned on the President], *N
visimaia gazeta* (13 November 2001).

that the notion of a professional army was only weakly thought-out, that the infra-structure and wages were not nearly enough to attract good people into the armed forces, and that the plan was contradicted by scheduled reductions in the numbers of officer corps, contract soldiers, and NCO's. In short, many more details should be worked out before such plans were announced.[128]

All the myriad military-related issues were opened up for discussion at a military conference chaired by Prime Minister Kasyanov in early December. A keynote report from Kvashnin was a central subject of debate, in a session that was purposely wide-ranging. Although no firm conclusions were reached, it seems that most of the con-troversial issues were aired.[129]

U.S. WITHDRAWAL FROM THE ABM TREATY

When President Bush finally announced, on 13 December 2001, that the United States would withdraw from the ABM Treaty within six months, the Russian mili-tary reacted with a barrage of statements to the effect that no NMD could withstand a Russian attack. This approach was not new, but recently they had been endorsing active participation with NATO in setting the norms for international security. The general feeling was that, because of the campaign against international terrorism, the United States needed Russia as much as Russia needed to be integrated into the world security complex.[130] The Russian military was made more nervous as Ameri-can forces massed on Iraq's borders and the interim Afghan government formed in Bonn did not include Rabbani or other leaders closely associated with Russia.

Leonid Ivashov, discharged from his position in September before he reached retire-ment age, weighed into the battle, accusing Putin of getting rid of "independent thinkers" in the ministry of defense—meaning himself. His main complaint was that Russia's lack of a "geopolitical doctrine" had allowed the United States to challenge Russia's primacy in Central Asia.[131] Opinions such as these still percolated in the higher ranks of the armed forces, to the extent that analysts conjectured that statements

---

128. Valerii Batuev, "Disintegration of the Army as a Consequence of the Military Reforms?" *Vremya MN* (23 November 2001). Translated for the WPS Monitoring Agency, *www.wps.ru/e_index.html*.

129. See, for example, Boris Yamshanov, "Soldat net. Sluzhba idet" [There Are No Soldiers. Service Continues], *Rossiiskaia gazeta* (8 December 2001). See also Igor Korotchenko, "Armeiskaia verkhushka pod nadzorom FSB" [Army Hierarchy Monitored by the FSB], *NVO*, No. 45 (7–14 December 2001).

130. For three quite different approaches, see, for example, Sergei Rogov, "Bez paniki i s dostoinstvom" [Without Panic, but with Dignity], *Nezavisimaia* (18 December 2001); Yevgenii Grigor'ev, "SShA soz-daiut vakuum bezopasnosti" [The USA Creates a Security Vacuum], *ibid.*; and an interview with Lt. Gen. Vol'ter Kraskovsdkii, "Chuvstvitel'noe porazhenie Rossii" [Overwhelming Defeat in Russia], *ibid.*; see also Yevgenii Lisanov, "Ravnopravnoe partnerstvo SshA i Rossii— zalog stabil'nosti v mire" [Equal Russian-USA Partnerships a Guarantee for Global Security], *Krasnaia zvezda*, (4 December 2001]; Sergei Rogov, "Proryv sleduet zakrepit'" [Breakthrough Must Be Reenforced], *Krasnaia zvezda* (16 December 2001).

131. For the interview with Ivashov, "Leonid Ivashov: 'Likvidatsiia baz za rubezhom— strategicheskaia oshibka'" [Ivashov, "The Liquidation of Overseas Bases Is a Strategic Mistake"], *Nezavisimaia* (18 De-cember 2001). Ivashov was appointed vice president of the Academy of Geopolitical Problems in Moscow.

from Sergei Ivanov seeming to contradict Igor Ivanov, especially on Central Asia ¿
Afghanistan, were in some way an appeasement of hardliners still lurking within
senior officer corps.[132]

Concern about Central Asia threw the question of military reform into stark
lief, with some senior officers demanding that it be speeded up and others calling
a slowdown. There also were further public criticisms of the 2002 defense bud;
some specialists calling the large increases in certain budget items paltry whei
came actually to conducting serious reform.[133]

There were some compensatory moments. As a result of the visit to Moscov
Azerbaijanian President Aliev, Russia signed a ten-year lease on the Soviet-built (
bala missile-tracking station. In return Moscow recognized the station, over wh
there had been tensions since the collapse of the USSR, as part of Azerbaijan. ↑
station gives Russia a lookout over a huge southeast Asia region, which includes
dia, Pakistan and the Persian Gulf.

Hope persisted in Russia as well that the CFE would help neutralize the strate
consequences of the Baltic States joining NATO. On 11 January, Russia claimec
have achieved all the adaptations agreed upon at the OSCE meetings in 1999 at
tanbul, and now urged the NATO countries and especially the United States to 1
ify them. Five months later they were still waiting. And military reform contini
to confound the senior officer corps. A change in conscription rules caused mi
comment, as did an announcement outlining a new Russian arms program to 20
Most military observers found the new conscription rules contradictory and too
nient on the "no-shows," whereas the weapons procurement projection was seer
illusory because of the "trillions" it would cost.[134]

The apparent lack of movement in arms reduction talks after the American wi
drawal from the ABM was especially annoying to the MoD. Colin Powell told
U.S. Congress in February that Russia and America had agreed to disagree on
ABM, and would keep on negotiating arms reductions,[135] leaving Russian offic
objecting bitterly to the Pentagon's wish not to destroy nuclear warheads and tl
carrier vehicles, and instead to stockpile them. This was but one of the sore poi
regularly mentioned by Russia's ministry of defense. The Comprehensive Test I

---

132. On this, see Igor Korotchenko, "Mezhdy Kremlem i Genshtabami" [Between the Kremlin anc
General Staff], *Nezavisimaia* (21 December 2001); and Aleksei Arbatov, "Dogovor po PRO i terror:
[The ABM Treaty and Terrorism], *Nezavisimaia* (26 December 2001).

133. See, for example, Vladimir Georgiev, "Oboronnyi biudzhet-2002; virtual'noe povyshenie" [2
Defense Budget: Imaginary Increase], *Nezavisimaia* (17 January 2002). Georgiev also claimed that
troops "had come to stay" in Uzbekistan and Kyrgyzstan; Major-General (ret'd), Professor Vladimir [
nik, "Voennoi reforme nyzhna glubokaia operatsiia. Inache ee snova 'zagovoriat' generaly" [Military
form Needs a Profound Operation. Or Else the Generals Will Again "Discuss It"], *NVO*, No.3 (17
January 2002).

134. See, for example, Viktor Litovkin, "Prezident vypisal strane novoe oruzhie" [President Orders 1
Weapons for the Country], *Obshchaia gazeta*, No. 5 (31 January–6 February 2002); Oleg Vladykin,
poiman—ne voin" [Not Caught—Not a Soldier], *ibid.*; see also *Rossiiskaia gazeta* (6 February 20
where it was hoped that Russia would not get involved in another costly arms race.

135. See, for example, Maksim Makarychev in *Rossiiskaia gazeta* (6 February 2002).

Treaty (CTBT) remained unratified in the United States, and rumors began to circulate in January that the United States might even withdraw from the moratorium on nuclear tests.[136] Even Gorbachev was back in the news, alleging—in the United States—that Washington was too quick to turn to war as a solution to international problems.[137] Thus, the atmosphere in Moscow before scheduled 19 February arms reductions talks in that city was one of cynicism, at least if public statements from military officialdom reflected reality. Not many details were made public after that meeting, though representatives of each side mouthed the usual diplomatic assurances that all was going well, and their differences were minor. But differences there obviously were.

TENSIONS WITHIN THE MoD?

The planned change of leadership among Russia's NATO delegation was made official in February when Vice Admiral Valentin Kuznetsov was appointed military representative in Brussels. At about the same time the Russian media again acknowledged that the *Kursk* was sunk by one of its own torpedoes, and questioned the Russian navy's commitment to safety and the government's commitment to proper funding for the naval branch of the armed forces. One commentator remarked that the *Kursk* mystery would never truly be solved, but that it was likely a consequence of Russian "habitual slipshodness" and would remain a secret.[138]

That being said, the Baltic Fleet commander, Admiral Vladimir Valuev, offered few objections to the NATO strategic exercise Strong Resolve 2002 which took place on the territories of Poland and Norway in early March. The mild official reaction failed to preclude a related dispute within Russian military circles. It was assumed by nongovernmental analysts in Moscow to have been a test by the United States of Russian security capabilities. MoD officials were therefore obliged to speak out. Kvashnin, for example, strongly if belatedly criticized Sergei Ivanov's failure to take a stand against NATO's maneuvers in Poland and Norway, and even warned the armed forces to be prepared to repel an external attack.[139] On the other hand, Kvashnin himself was assailed by extremist Duma members for "capitulation" to NATO

136. On this, see interview with Andrei Kokoshin, "Rossii ostaetsia luchshe rabotat' golovoi" [The Best Choice for Russia Is to Improve Work with Brains], *Nezavisimaia* (30 January 2002).

137. See, for example, Mikhail Gorbachev, "Nas priuchaiut k voine" [They Train Us for War], *Rossiiskaia gazeta* (19 February 2002). On general Russian uncertainties related to the new western connection, see Alexei Arbatov, "Russian Security and the Western Connection," and Ivan Safranchuk, "An Array of Threats to Russia," in John Newhouse, ed. *Assessing the Threats. Instabilities, Proliferation, Terrorism, Unilateralism* (Washington: Center for Defense Information, 2002), pp. 59–84, 85–102.

138. See, for example, Marina Tokareva, "Koshelek gosudarstva ili zhisn' podvodnikov" [The Purse of the State or the Lives of the Submariners], *Obshchaia gazeta*, No. 6 (7–13 February 2002); see also Boris Yamshanov, "Tam, za gorizontom ostanetsia ekho: 'Kursk'" [An Echo Will Sound behind the Horizon: *Kursk*], *Rossiiskaia gazeta* (22 February 2002), and Interfax (11 February 2002).

139. On this, see, for example, Igor Korotchenko, "Armeiskoe dvoevlastie" [Dual Power in the Military], *Nezavisimaia gazeta* (6 March 2002).

and the United States. Some deputies labeled him a "traitor" for insisting that R
sia should fulfill its agreement to withdraw troops from Georgia.[140] Charges such
these represented the dogged resistance of nationalists to any decision that appea
to infringe upon their country's traditional military sphere of influence. Clearly
was difficult for many senior military officials to shake long-held belief syste
which held that American military policy was designed to ensure "absolute strate
dominance of the world."[141]

On the other hand, rumors abounded that Kvashnin was being groomed to
place Sergei Ivanov as minister of defense—sooner rather than later—though ot
names were heard as well.[142] A serious split between military command and the m
istry had been regularly rumored, and some analysts thought that Kvashnin had b
in charge all along anyway. Ivanov, the pundits insisted, had never been able to bu
a team at the ministry.[143] And Putin's much-ballyhooed promises of pay raises to
military were greeted with cynicism by armed forces personnel themselves, some
them going so far as to ridicule the presidential offer as a "protocol of intent," t
they would believe only when the money was in their hands.[144]

The military was rattled again when, in March 2002, the *Los Angeles Times* p
lished the leaked pentagon list of seven countries, among them Russia, against wh
the United States "targeted" nuclear weapons (see chapter 6). No one expected Wa
ington to actually launch strikes and no actual "targetting" existed (both sides w
on alert with "zero sights"), but the affair was very humiliating and put the Russi
on the defensive.[145] Military analyst Vadim Solov'ev harshly condemned b
Ivanovs for not being prepared for the consequent scandal when the Pentagon
was leaked to the press. Solov'ev spoke for many MoD insiders when he urged t
Russia's nuclear defense apparatus be upgraded.[146]

Calm settled in by the end of March 2002 as the military prepared for Putin's ar
reduction talks with Bush and the forging of a new relationship with NATO—b

---

140. On this, see Oleg Vladykin, "Kvashnin ob'iavlen predatelem" [Kvashnin Declared a Traitor],
shchaia gazeta, No. 10 (7–13 March 2002). This author charged the name-caller, Duma member C
nadii Gudkov, with foolishness and "hysteria."

141. On this, see for example, Vladimir Georgiev, "Amerikanskie protivorakety mogut imet' yade
boegolovki" [The American NMD Can Have Nuclear Warheads], *Nezavisimaia gazeta* (5 March 20C

142. See, for example, Igor Korotchenko, "Novyi pretendent na post ministra oborony" [New Ca
date for the Post of Minister of Defense], *NVO,* No. 9 (22–28 March 2002).

143. See, for example, Dmitrii Safonov, "Mezhdu Pauellom i Kvashninym" [Between Powell
Kvashnin], *Izvestiia* (28 March 2002). Safonov said that Kvashnin's strength was limited to the diplom
side; he could deal well with Colin Powell.

144. See, for example, Viktor Litovkin, "Generaly dorastut do chinovnikov" [Generals Will Grov
the Level of Civil Servants], *Obshchaia gazeta,* No.10 (7–13 March 2002).

145. See, for example, Viktor Litovkin, "Ministr oborony snova ushel v razvedku" [Defense Min
on Recon Mission Again], *Obshchaia gazeta,* No. 11 (14–20 March 2002); "I. Ivanov: Yadernaia dokt
SShA napisana v dukhe 'kholodnoi voiny'," [Ivanov: The USA's Nuclear Doctrine Was Written in
"Cold War" Spirit], *Sovetskaia Rossiia* (14 March 2002); and another Ivanov interview in *Rossiiskaia ga
(13 March 2002).

146. Solov'ev, "Yadernaia doktrina SshA" [The American Nuclear Doctrine], *NVO,* No. 9 (22
March 2002).

subjects dealt with at length elsewhere in this volume. It has been demonstrated already that military pundits had mixed opinions about the arms deal announced by Bush and Putin on 14 May and then signed off at the Moscow summit at the end of the month. There was even more polemic over the merits of Sergei Ivanov's proclamation in April that the promised higher wage scale for Russian servicemen would come into force as of 1 July. According to media reports, the level of disbelief in the armed forces had not diminished.[147] In fact, Putin signed a law regulating salaries and benefits in Russia's armed forces on 8 May, on the assumption that the changes would come into effect on schedule (ITAR-TASS, 8 May).[148]

Whether more money would soothe the potentially dangerous unrest amongst the armed forces remained to be seen. But this was but one of the military and security questions still unanswered by the end of Putin's first two-and-a-half years.

---

147. See, for example, Viktor Litovkin, "Sergei Ivanov obgoniaet Dumu" [Sergei Ivanov Gets Ahead of the Duma], *Obshchaia gazeta*, No. 14 (4–10 April 2002), and Salavat Suleimanov, "Armiia bez vospitatelei" [Army without Teachers], *NVO*, No. 14 (26 April–16 May 2002), on the dearth of NCO and officer instructors because of budget cuts.

148. Aleksandr Babakin, "Pogonnyi rubl'. Gosudarstvo budet platit' voennym bol'she, chem grazhdanskim chinovnikam" [Uniform Ruble. State Will Start Paying Servicemen More than Public Servants], *Rossiiskaia gazeta* (24 May 2002), and Dmitrii Safonov, "Voennye budut poluchat' bol'she chinovnikov" [Military Will Receive More than Officials], *Izvestiia* (21 May 2002); See also Savat Suleimanov, "Sovbez vnov' korrektiruet plan voennoi reformy" [Security Council Again Amends Plans for Military Reform], *Nezavisimaia* (4 June 2002).

8

✢

The Caucasus Vortex

THE NORTH AND SOUTH CAUCASUS IN 2000[1]

General

Shortly after Putin's election as president, his foreign policy advisers urged him to reestablish Moscow's primacy in the North Caucasus and reconfirm its role as a central player on the Caspian and Black Seas.[2] Russia's strategic considerations in the Caucasus were skewed badly in 1999 after civil war resumed in Chechnya. Continued bombardment, huge losses of military personnel and materiel, the slow but inexorable destruction of Chechnya's capital city, Groznyy, and the ever-growing number of civilian casualties and refugees—who spread out over the rest of the Caucasus—shaped Russian decision making at home and tarnished Russia's image abroad.[3]

In October 1999, Prime Minister Putin issued a statement on the results of his discussions about Chechnya with a group of prominent Russians. Acknowledging that he had heard mixed opinions, he nonetheless claimed there was a consensus believed that steady "strength of will" would resolve the crisis. The problem was "strictly internal," he announced, and the issue was the right of Russia's citizens to

---

1. A useful Russian starting point is R. M. Abakov, A. G. Lisov, eds. *Rossiia i zavkavkaz'e: realii nezavisimosti i novoe partnerstvo* (Moscow: ZAO Finstatinform, 2000).

2. See, for example, Vladimir Katin, "Sredizemnoe more—zona interesov NATO" [The Mediterranean Sea Is a Zone of NATO Interest], *Nezavisimaia gazeta* (29 March 2000); Aleksandr Dzasokhov, "Kavkaz dolzhen stat' stabil'nym" [The Caucasus Must Be Stabilized], *Nezavisimaia gazeta* (7 April 2000).

3. For a long and mournful essay on this see Ramazan Abdulatipov, "Zhertvennye tantsy na krugu" [Sacrificial Dances in a Circle], *Rossiiskaia gazeta* (11 September 1999). Abdulatipov was minister of federation and nationalities policy in Viktor Chernomyrdin's government.

"security and peace."[4] A few weeks later, a joint Russia–EU statement released a Putin's meeting with EU leaders in Helsinki demonstrated that the European coi tries were monitoring events in Chechnya closely and pressuring Moscow to av human rights violations in that republic (Interfax, 22 Oct). Russian commentat displayed a uniform resentment of what Foreign Minister Ivanov called "w orchestrated" economic coercion from the West. Accusing the IMF of blindly : lowing Washington's lead, Russian officials profiled Chechen rebels as agents of ' lamic terrorism" funded by strongly anti-American sources such as Osama Laden, and therefore just as dangerous to the West as they were to Russia.[5]

The civil war undermined the Russian government's negotiations with the Uni States on the ABM Treaty, with OSCE on human rights and the CFE treaty on tro deployment in Europe, and with the Russia's own State Duma on ratification START-II. By November 1999, Russian officials were accusing the USA of suppc ing rebels in Chechnya. For example, Sergeev charged that America's national in ests required that "the military conflict in the North Caucasus, fanned from the c side, keeps constantly smoldering." Suspicions such as these were fueled by wor that the United States was infringing upon Russia's traditional sphere of influenc the South Caucasus, above all by supporting oil pipeline construction to bypass R sia and Iran. The air was cleared—temporarily—between Russia and Western cri of its Chechnya policy at the OSCE Istanbul summit in November and Russia ' allowed to keep more weaponry in the Caucasus than previously permitted under CFE. But Moscow's program of highlighting the grave danger posed to the West terrorists like Bin Laden continued apace. Putin's November 1999 article in the *N York Times* was the best example of this approach, though it had long been a co mon position taken by the Russian media.[6] As we have seen, these warnings were r with indifference in the West.

The Chechnya problem overshadowed and shaped much of the Kremlin's dom tic and foreign policy. In denial about the plight of refugees and rejecting outri

---

4. "Zaiavlenie Predsedatelia Pravitel'stva Rossiiskoi Federatsii V.V. Putina dlia pressy po itogam k sul'tativnogo Soveshchaniia s gruppoi vidnykh rossiiskikh politikov po probleme chechenskogo u ulirovaniia" [Statement by . . . Putin for the Press on the Results of the Consultative Conference wi Group of Prominent Russian Politicians on the Problem of a Chechen Settlement], *Rossiiskaia gazet* October 1999).

5. See, for example, Gennadii Charodeev, "Boeviki zaprosili pomoshch' u terrorista ben Lad [Rebels Requested Help from Terrorist Bin Laden"], *Izvestiia* (18 September 1999); Vladimir Abari "Ben Laden finansiruet i gotovit chechenskikh boevikov" [Bin Laden Finances and Trains Chechen Fi ers], *Izvestiia* (29 October 2000); Vladimir Kuznechevskii, "Chto eshche i komu nado ob'iasniat'?" [W Else Needs to be Explained and to Whom?], *Rossiiskaia gazeta* (2 November 1999); Gennadii Charoc "Za vzryvami v Rossii viden sled ben Ladena" [Signs Lead to Bin laden for the Explosions in Rus *Izvestiia* (30 November 1999); Petr Fadeev, Svetlana Babaeva, "ZAPADnia" [Western Trap], *I* Vladimir Dunaev, "Ben Laden ishchet novoe ubezhishche" [Bin Laden Searching for a New Hic Place], *Izvestiia* (3 November 1999).

6. See, for example, Vladimir Dunaev, "Ben Laden dlia talibov dorozhe zlata" [Bin Laden Is W More than Gold to the Taliban], *Izvestiia* (16 November 1999); "Ben Laden gotovit voinu protiv SS [Bin Laden Prepares for War against the USA], *Rossiiskaia gazeta* (16 November 1999); Putin, "Poch my dolzhny deistvovat'" [Why We Must Act], *Rossiiskaia gazeta* (16 November 1999), that is, the I sian version of "Why We Must Act," *New York Times* (14 November 1999).

accusations that their troops were committing atrocities, the mainstream Russian media validated all Russian military activity by drawing comparisons with NATO behavior in Yugoslavia. As Western officials complained about Russia's application of brute force, Russian authorities raised the level of their accusations of hypocrisy: why, they queried, do NATO's spin doctors refer to civilian casualties in Kosovo as "collateral damage" and in the same breath designate civilian casualties in Chechnya victims of human rights abuses?

Official and private commentators in Moscow unanimously expressed both their right and their obligation to combat terrorism within their own borders. In fact, few foreign governments objected to Russia's right in this regard; rather, they tried to ameliorate the intensity of Russia's response to rebellion. Moscow explained away Western disapproval by constantly alluding to the involvement of "foreign" agencies in support of the rebels. Prominent military–political spokesmen, like Col. Gen. Ivashov, implied on more than one occasion that American objections to Russian policy in Chechnya had more to do with Washington's own ambitions for the Caucasus than with human rights.[7]

Among the foreign critics, however, it was the Council of Europe's position-taking on Chechnya that most angered Moscow. The American stance was expected. The intensity of European hostility took Russia by surprise and, as we have seen, it culminated in the PACE recommendation that Russia be suspended from the organization's list of members. This issue was still a sensitive one in June 1999, when the Russian parliamentary delegation refused to take part in a Council of Europe meeting where the PACE proposition was being debated. In the end, the Council declined to suspend Russia's voting privileges, a decision which Russian officialdom called a right step towards reconciliation. Yet the Council went on to express its disapproval of an apparent clampdown in Russia on the freedom of the press, to which Moscow replied by accusing Washington of rumor-mongering and telling the Council to mind its own business.

Later that same month, Russia was cited for "disproportionate and indiscriminate use of military force" against civilians in Chechnya by the UN Human Rights Commission. Russian observers treated this as further evidence of "double standards" employed in the West when judging Russian actions, and Manilov termed it "anti-Russian" (Interfax, 25 April).

Perhaps because they were then still MoD officials, Ivashov and Manilov were not so explicit in their rantings against the United States and the CIA for meddling in Moscow's sphere of influence as their Soviet mentors had been. Georgia, however, was indicted more openly, several times, of providing Chechen rebels with cover and weapons—either directly or by turning a blind eye to clandestine operations of

---

7. Ivashov, "Rossiia ne priemlet silovogo diktata SShA" [Russia Rejects Washington's Military Diktat], *Nezavisimaia gazeta* (11 February 2000). For Russia's attempts to consolidate some Islamic help against extremists in the Caucasus, see Dmitrii Koptev, "V edinstve nasha sila" [Our Strength Lies in Unity], *Izvestiia* (21 June 2000); see also Vladimir Mokhov, "'Otryvai i vlastvui'" [Divide and Conquer], *Krasnaia zvezda* (25 May 2000).

which they were well aware. President Shevardnadze and his officials repeatedly
nied such allegations, and at the same time stepped up their own chatter ab
Georgia as a future NATO member. Russian observers accused the Georgian pr
dent of drawing lines between "evil" Moscow and the "good" West.[8]

The South Caucasus, dominated entirely by the USSR before 1991, had bee
seriously troubling region for Moscow throughout the nineties. Russian national
and strategists bemoaned the loss of Russian influence in the region, blaming
United States, NATO, and international oil interests for seducing Azerbaijan a
Georgia into their camp with promises of great riches. Even when the bloody wa
Chechnya was attributed to international terrorism, there were the added hints t
Western and Arab financial syndicates contributed to the carnage for the purpos
gaining control of Azerbaijani oil.[9] In response, even the Russian-language pres
Azerbaijan periodically spoke of an alliance among Armenian, Iranian and Russ
nationalists to make Armenia strong at Baku's expense.[10] One cause of Russian (
trust was the Baku–Tbilisi–Ceyhan export pipeline agreement signed by Geor;
Azerbaijan and Turkey in Istanbul on 17 November 1999. Many details still hac
be worked out, but the scope of the project was such that Kazakhstan, Turkmenis
and Uzbekistan were expected to participate as well, while Russia, Armenia and I
were excluded. Needless to say, Russian officials and media protested vehemen
certain that American aspirations for control of the Caspian were behind the pr
ect.[11] Moscow's longtime worry about the South Caucasus was carried over into
sions of concentrated U.S. inroads into the North Caucasus, that is, onto the te
tory of the Russian Federation. For example, on 24 April 2000 Ivashov charged tl

> The United States is doing everything possible to "keep the system of local internal con
> flicts working and is using them skillfully" to weaken individual regions, . . . What hap
> pened to Kosovo "is being projected" onto the North Caucasus today. (Interfax, 24 April

Such remarks must have reflected a dominant sentiment among Moscow's fore
and defense elites.

A small first step in the restoration of Russian prestige in the South Caucasus `
taken during a pivotal CIS Heads-of-State summit held in Moscow towards the enc
June, 2000. The Russian foreign minister chaired a meeting between the leaders
Azerbaijan, Armenia and Georgia for an exchange of opinions on problems facing tl
region. But Putin's absence due to the *Kursk* crisis reduced the potential of the me
ing, as did continued rumors that Chechen rebels were basing on both Azerbaijan

---

8. See, for example, Alan Kasaev, "Eduard Shevardnadze reshil vstupit' v NATO do 2005 goda ne
raia na otritsatel'noe mnenie Rossii" [Eduard Shevardnadze Decided to Enter NATO in 2005 in Spit
the Negative Opinion of Russia], *Nezavisimaia gazeta* (26 October1999).

9. See, for example, Vladimir Kuznechevskii, Aleksei Chichkin, "Tochka pritsela: bol'shaia ne
bol'shoi terror" [Firing Line: Big Oil and Big Terror], *Rossiiskaia gazeta* (1 October 1999).

10. See, for example, *Zerkalo* (12 June 1999), FBIS-SOV, No. 617 (18 June 1999).

11. See, for example, Aleksei Baliev, Vladimir Fedorov, "Turetskii marsh kaspiiskoi nefti,. . . ." [
Turkish March to Caspian Oil], *Rossiiskaia gazeta* (29 November 1999).

and Georgian territory. Armenia was a beneficiary of the tension between Russia on the one hand, Georgia and Azerbaijan on the other. There was even talk in June of a Russian–Armenian–Greek military accord on the occasion of a visit to Moscow by the Greek president and defense minister. At that time, Greece and Cyprus represented a growing market for Russian military technology, a fact not lost on Turkey.[12]

Russia's direct association with countries of the South Caucasus is both bilateral and, through the aegis of various CIS agencies, multilateral. That is why a trend towards tightening up in the GUUAM (Georgia, Ukraine, Uzbekistan, Azerbaijan, and Moldova) began agitating Russian strategic planners in 1999–2000. GUUAM began in 1997 as an informal association of countries to form a transport corridor from Eurasia to Europe; Uzbekistan joined formally in 1999. Since that time there had been a movement for closer coordination of their economic interests, especially as talk of a free trade zone within the CIS faded. An allocation by the U.S. Congress of $45.5 million to GUUAM, and to Armenia, for military assistance in mid-September 2000 was jarring to Moscow. In light of other large expenditures by the United States on military aid, especially to Georgia and Uzbekistan, Russians foresaw a decline in the region's dependence on Russia, and an increase in those countries' reliance on NATO.[13]

But in 1999–2000 it was pipeline politics that most confounded Russia in the South Caucasus and the adjoining Black and Caspian Seas. Coinciding as it did with Russia's participation in upgrading the CIS Collective Security Pact and the creation of the Eurasian Economic Community (see Chapter 10), a tour of Central Asia by Turkey's President Amhet Necdet Sezer brought Moscow and Istanbul into direct competition. In Tashkent, Sezer made agreements to combine forces against terrorism and crime; in Ashgabat, he signed an energy deal that included contracts for long-term gas supplies to Turkey (ITAR-TASS, 11 October). Combined with the Baku–Ceyhan oil pipeline project, Turkmenistan's formal adherence to proposals for a Transcaspian pipeline to carry Turkmen gas to Turkey and another project to supply Turkmen electricity to Turkey, were a challenge to Moscow's diplomacy. Russian officials called these developments part of a NATO–American bid to gain control of CIS energy resources— mainly at the expense of Russia.[14] The Baku to Ceyhan oil pipeline achieved final agreement from Azerbaijan in October. But the Transcaspian gas pipeline was even more problematic for the Kremlin, which suspected that it might draw Turkmenistan closer to NATO, through Turkey's influence. Russia turned to Iran in the hope that jointly they could deny seabed construction rights to the pipeline consortium.

Pragmatically, Moscow also courted Turkey. In fact, relations with Ankara improved almost simultaneously with Sezer's trip to Central Asia, mainly as a consequence of a

---

12. On this, see, for example, Petr Akopov, Yevgenii Krutikov, "Kogda RAK na gore svistnet" [When the Greek Bird Whistles], *Izvestiia* (28 June 2000).

13. On this, see *Kommersant* (23 September 2000).

14. See, for example, Sergei Pravosudov, "SShA boriutsia za energoresursy stran SNG" [The USA Is Fighting for the Energy Resources of CIS Countries], *Nezavisimaia gazeta* (19 October 2000); see also Yaroslav Kliuchnikov, ". . . I more odno na piaterykh" [. . . One Sea for Five], *Krasnaia zvezda* (5 October 2000).

three-day Kasyanov visit to Ankara (23–25 October). It was as an energy provider t
Russia drew closer to Turkey, just as it had done with the EU. Russia had already b
supplying some 10 billion cubic meters of gas to Turkey annually, and agreed to p
vide more via the Blue Stream gas pipeline scheduled to go into service in 2001. E
trical power sourcing was negotiated as well, and both sides confirmed an interes
much-expanded trade relations. A common approach to terrorism was another imp
tant breakthrough and, according to one Russian commentator, opened the door t
new "Eurasia" with compatible Russia and Turkey as major players in it. Further mo
ings were arranged, including one by Armed Forces General Staff Chief Kvashnin,
discussions of Russian–Turkish military cooperation. During a short conversation w
the Turkish president, an invitation for Putin to visit Turkey was handed to Kasyano
This was a very encouraging meeting for Russian policymakers, and eased their an
eties about an aggressive Turkey angling for influence in the Caucasus, and Central A
as an agent for NATO and the U.S.A.[16]

Azerbaijan

Former USSR Politburo member and president of Azerbaijan, Heydar Aliev, on s
eral occasions condemned terrorism in Chechnya and, after meeting with Igor Iva
in September 1999, called for stronger ties between Baku and Moscow (ITAR-TA
2 September 1999). Yet he was widely distrusted in the Russian capital, where m
officials believed that Azeris were assisting the Chechen rebels.[17] Aliev lent crede
to Russian suspicions when he followed the example of Uzbekistan and refused to
new his country's participation in the CIS Collective Security Pact. In their turn, .
eris believed that the Russian delegation to the Minsk OSCE Group negotiating
fate of Nagorno-Karabakh was biased in favor of Armenia. Foreign policy advise
Aliev, Vafa Guluzade, who in the winter of 1999 recommended that Azerbaijan p
vide NATO with air bases for their raids on Yugoslavia, claimed in December t
Russia was only pretending to help resolve the conflict.[18] Needless to say, remarks s
as these fed Russian doubts about Azerbaijan still further.

Writers in Russia constantly took Azerbaijan to task for its turn towards NAT
claiming that promises of fortunes to be made in oil had drawn Baku into cat

15. See "Turki nam ne konkurenty. Oni nam partnery" [Turks Are Not Our Rivals. They Are Our I
ners], *Rossiiskaia gazeta* (25 October 2000); Aleksandr Sabov, "Vizit k blizhaishemu sosedu" [Visit
Near Neighbor], *Rossiiskaia gazeta* (26 October 2000).

16. See, for example, Arngolt Bekker, "K iugu—'Golubym potokom'" [Blue Stream to the Sou
Rossiiskaia gazeta (3 November 2000). Bekker, who was interviewed for this piece, is presiden
Stroitransgaz, and in charge of the Samsun-Ankara section of the Blue Stream gas pipeline. See also "
banov Says 'Blue Stream' Project Marks Important Cooperation," *Anatolia* (in English), (22 Noven
2000), FBIS-SOV, No. 1203 (22 Nov 2000).

17. See, for example, Gennadii Charodeev, "Boeviki zaprosili pomoshch' u terrorista ben La
Prichastny li Azerbaidzhan i Gruziia k sobytiiam v Dagestane" [Rebels Asked Help from Terrorist
Laden. Did Azerbaijan and Georgia Participate in the Events in Afghanistan], *Izvestiia* (18 Septen
2000).

18. *Turan* (10 December 1999), FBIS-SOV, No. 1216 (17 December 1999).

controlled by international oil barons, mostly in Washington, and connected perhaps even to events in Chechnya.[19] In February 2000, Azerbaijan's foreign minister, Vilaet Guliev, who had invited NATO to open an information office in Baku in 1999, repeated Guluzade's earlier offer and hinted that his country might eventually join NATO (Interfax, 10 February). He was aware that Azerbaijan would have to upgrade its armed forces greatly before it could reach NATO's standards, but cooperation with NATO and the PfP would increase. In April, when the PfP initiated courses on managing civil emergencies in Baku, hosting sixty-one delegates, Moscow commentators treated the event as one more step away from the CIS, and accused Washington of catering to both Baku and Tbilisi for the purpose of replacing Moscow as the main foreign power in the region.[20] Russian leaders were left with little choice but to concentrate on holding their own on the Caspian Sea, looking for closer ties with Iran and Kazakhstan, and raising the level of its influence in Armenia.

By the spring of 2000, the importance of the Caspian Sea region to Russia's economic and strategic interests had reached a point where the RF Security Council was compelled to set up a special committee to monitor events there. Warning that if the Kremlin did nothing, Turkey, Britain and the United States would soon take control of Caspian Sea resources (Interfax, 21 April), a Security Council spokesman said that the new committee would include heads and their deputies of Russia's power ministries, plus representatives of the fuel, energy and transport industries. An aggressive campaign for a Russian economic presence in the Caspian region was thus under way.

From the point of view of Russian nationalists, and oil barons, this measure came not a moment too soon. On 28 April, for example, the head of NATO's Military Committee, Guido Venturoni, arrived in Baku for discussions with Azeri Minister of Defense Safar Abaev. After the meeting, Abaev told reporters that Azerbaijan's participation in the PfP would increase and that the country's armed forces would be raised up to NATO standards (Interfax, 28 April). The NATO bogey notwithstanding, in June President Aliev welcomed RF Security Council Secretary Sergei Ivanov to Baku (ITAR TASS, 14 June). Subsequent statements by both men featured the need for stronger ties between their countries. Aliev invited Putin (through Ivanov) to his capital city and agreed himself to participate in the upcoming CIS Heads-of-State summit in Moscow on 21 June. The two security councils signed protocols of cooperation in matters of information exchange on security issues, and coordination of efforts to counter drug trafficking, crime and terrorism. Azerbaijan also agreed to join with Russia and other PfP troops in a Tsentrazbat exercise scheduled for Kazakhstan in September. This was the closest Moscow and Baku had been for several years.[21]

19. See, for example, Ivan Aibazovskii, "Azerbaidzhan khochet v NATO. Baku uvazhaet chechentsev" [Azerbaijan Wishes to Be in NATO. Baku Respects the Chechens], *Nezavisimaia gazeta* (19 February 2000).

20. See, for example, Asia Gadzhizade, "Baku i Tblisi dogovorilis' pod patronazhem vashingtona" [Baku and Tbilisi Reached an Agreement under Washington's Patronage], *Nezavisimaia gazeta* (25 March 2000).

21. On this, see Dmitrii Sergeev, "Azerbaidzhan: Novye nadezhdy" [Azerbaijan: New Hopes], *Izvestiia* (22 July 2000).

In fact, at that time Baku had very few attractive alternatives. Attempting to al with the West while maintaining good relations with neighbors Russia and Iran not an easy task. Aliev was still handicapped by sanctions imposed on his country the U.S. Congress in 1992. The sanctions, a consequence of the Azeri–Armenian over Nagorno-Karabakh and perhaps driven by the large Armenia lobby in the Uni States, prevented the American government from providing direct aid to Azerbaij Moreover, Azerbaijan's "great expectations" related to its oil and natural-gas resei had not been fulfilled. Proclamations in July 2000 of huge oil finds in parts of Caspian Sea controlled by Kazakhstan tended to diminish the significance of Baku the great energy game. For instance, when the final agreements on construction c tracts for the pipeline from Baku to Ceyhan were signed in October 2000, Russ analysts made much of the potential "unprofitability" of the relevant Azeri oil field

The new "closeness" with Russia predicted by Aliev and others was shaken in summer of 2000 when rumors began circulating that large groups of Chechen rel were hiding in northern Azerbaijan. On 18 August stories broke that rebel lea Maskhadov had relocated to Azerbaijan. The government in Baku rejected such mors as mischievous falsehoods, but could not prevent the still tenuous new Russ Azerbaijan relationship from being compromised.[23] Contentious issues were lurk close to the surface anyway. Azerbaijan, for example, was especially concerned wl Russia relocated military equipment from bases in Georgia to its military base Gyumri in Armenia. Defense Minister Abiev accused Russia of upsetting the bala of power in the region.[24] It remained for the communists of Azerbaijan and Ru to pick up the pieces and maintain a connection between the two countries that beginning to unravel.[25]

Armenia

The association between Russia and Armenia was already driven in large part Yerevan's complicated relationships with Azerbaijan and Turkey. As the plans for oil pipeline from Baku through Georgia to Turkey were finalized, Russian offic regularly proclaimed that its main purpose was to avoid using the territory of eit Russia or Iran. Few Russians were concerned that Armenia also was to be exclud

22. See, for example, Vladimir Mishin, " 'Zapadnyi marshrut' poluchil udar s severa" [The "Wes Route" Receives a Blow from the North], *Vremia* (19 October 2000).

23. On this, see El'mira Akhundova, "K Basaevu s pomoshch'iu FSB" [To Basaev with Help from FSB], *Obshchaia gazeta*, No. 30 (27 July–2 August 2000), and Bakhtiar Akhmedkhanov, et al., "Vc nye igry" [War Games], *ibid.* Armenian reports about this were refuted by at least one Russian invest tive reporter; see Vadim Rechkalov, "Chechenskie prizraki na granitse s Armeniei. Prizraki est', boev net" [Chechen Specters on the Border with Armenia. Specters, Yes; Militants, No], *Obshchaia gazeta*, 48 (30 November–6 December 2000).

24. Safar Abiev, "Bronia razdora" [Armor of Discord], *Obshchaia gazeta*, No. 43 (26 October–1 vember 2000).

25. See, for example, "Frank Elkaponi: 'Rossiia i Azerbaidzhan zhdut novye grani sotrudnichest [Frank Elkaponi: "Russia and Azerbaijan Wait for the New Side of Cooperation"], *Nezavisimaia ga* (17 December 2000).

In fact, Yerevan's own sense of isolation in the Caucasus had been an important catalyst in that country's turn to Moscow. In February 2000, an Armenian interparliamentary group was formed in Yerevan to lobby for their country's integration with the Russia–Belarus Union. Led by Agasi Arshakyan, who emphasized economic reasons for the union, the group held parliamentary hearings on the subject on 9 March (Interfax, 10 March). But not much was accomplished by it other than to stir the political pot and draw media attention.

Yet Armenia's isolation tended to be limited to its neighborhood. It still had a large diaspora and therefore a stronger lobby in North America and Europe than the other peoples of the South Caucasus. The one-sidedness of this lobby's influence was diminished considerably when the Azerbaijan and Georgian profiles were raised by NATO's needs in the Balkans in 1999 and, much later, by the anti-Taliban's coalition's needs in both the Caucasus and Central Asia. Armenia's ethnic lobby in the United States helped ensure that Yerevan continued to receive some $100 million in aid annually from the government of the United States. So Armenia could and can look both eastward, to Russia, and westward for support. Thus, the diaspora is extremely important to Armenia. It has little else to offer—and Azerbaijan has oil.

Although Armenia's strategic interests plainly lie with Russia, on 15 August 2000 the government in Yerevan announced that it planned to expand cooperation with NATO. Klaus-Peter Klaiber, the Atlantic Alliance's deputy secretary for political affairs, visited the Armenian capital and was presented with a plan for Armenia participation in seventy-five PfP programs for the year 2000–2001, greatly increasing its activity over previous years. In announcing the plan, the foreign ministry made it clear that increased participation in the PfP in no way diminished Armenia's commitment to the CIS Collective Security Treaty.

In September 2000, Armenia was allocated funds for military technical development by the U.S. Congress at the same time that monies were awarded to the GUUAM (see Chapter 10). This development did not worry Moscow, for it balanced at least symbolically the allocations to Azerbaijan and Georgia. Making certain that there would be no misunderstanding in this regard, Armenian President Robert Kocharyan travelled to Moscow, where he and Putin issued a joint declaration announcing an expanded "strategic interaction" between their two countries. Visa-free travel was confirmed and several economic accords were reached. There was no discussion of the still-mooted invitation to join the Russia–Belarus Union, as both sides proclaimed satisfaction with the status quo. Putin named Armenia a "traditional ally" of Russia, and there was a consensus among analysts that the two countries had a solid political relationship.[26]

---

26. See Ashot Melikyan, "Moskva zakliuchila s Erevanom soiuz. No ne takoi, kak s Belorussiei" [Moscow Concluded a Union with Yerevan, But Not Like That with Belarus], *Obshchaia gazeta,* No. 39 (28 September–4 October 2000); Armen Khanbabian, "Moskva i Yerevan udovletvoreny urovnem politicheskikh otnoshenii" [Moscow and Yerevan Are Satisfied with the Level of Their Political Relationship], *Nezavisimaia gazeta* (27 September 2000); Kocharyan,"My s Putinym myslim skhozhimi kategoriiami" [Our Thoughts Are in the Same Categories as Putin's], *Izvestiia* (27 September 2000).

Georgia

Georgia was Russia's Achilles heel in the South Caucasus. In October 1999, Ge
gian President Eduard Shevardnadze's public commitment to a bid for admiss
into NATO by 2005 set off the long-smoldering tensions between Moscow and T
lisi. Commentators in Moscow insisted that Shevardnadze was purposely alienat
his country from Russia, and this presumption remained constant throughout m
of the next two years.[27] Some observers argued that Georgia was being nudged in t
direction by Washington.[28]

Neither side missed an opportunity to snipe at the other. In response to every
mand that Russia withdraw its military forces from Georgian territory on schedt
Moscow reminded Tbilisi of the scheduled new visa regime, and charged Sheva
nadze with abetting Chechen rebels. The Georgian president protested on b
counts, threatening to withdraw from the CIS and to open still wider collaborat
with NATO.[29] Georgia's participation in the projected Baku–Ceyhan pipeline v
also a sore point, as was Tbilisi's debt to Russia for gas supplies. Indeed, on 2 I
cember 2000, Russia cutoff natural-gas supplies to that city, where it is used to t
power generators. The cutoff lasted four days, but a clear message had been sent. S
vardnadze replied that Georgia had the "right to select partners from those states t
respect its sovereignty, not by word but by deed," adding however that he thou
Tbilisi and Moscow should and could have a much better relationship.[30]

Hard feelings in Moscow towards Tbilisi were lightened somewhat during the C
heads-of-state summit held in Minsk over 29–30 November. During a reporte
strained meeting, Putin and Shevardnadze decided that their respective foreign m
isters would be given two months to draft a new Russia–Georgia treaty, though
Russian State Duma had not yet ratified an earlier one, signed in 1994 (Interfax,
November). The Russian president agreed that the newly instituted visa-regi
should not last long, claiming that it was strictly part of his country's anti-terro
campaign. That regime, which began officially on 5 December 2000, had bee
matter of contention for many months and by that time Georgia was the only C
country with such a relationship with Russia. On this issue, at least, fellow GUU/
members Ukraine and Azerbaijan, and Armenia, took up Georgia's cause.

Shevardnadze complained bitterly about the visa requirements, especially after it v
learned that similar regulations would not be set for Russia's borders with Abkhazia a

---

27. See, for example, Alan Kasaev, "Lis gotovitsia k pryzhku" [The Fox Is Prepared to Jump], *N
visimaia gazeta* (26 October 1999); Yevgenii Krutikov, "Gorez. Eduard Shevardnadze meniaet Rossii
NATO" [Mountaineer. Eduard Shevardnadze Exchanges Russia for NATO], *Izvestiia* (27 October 19
Nodar Broladze, "Shevardnadze rabotaet na perspektivu" [Shevardnadze Has a Future Plan in Mir
Nezavisimaia gazeta (15 February 2000).

28. See, for example, Aleksandr Tikhonov, "Tbilisi utochniaet prioritety" [Tbilisi Defines Its Priorit
Krasnaia zvezda (24 June 2000).

29. On this, see for example, Petr Akopov, "Gruziia ne khochet ni rossiiskikh voisk, ni viz" [Geo
Wishes Neither Russian Troops, Nor the Visas], *Izvestiia* (27 July 2000), and Dmitrii Koptev, "Gru
aktiviziruet kontakty s NATO" [Georgia Activates Contacts with NATO], *Izvestiia* (4 August 2000).

30. Shevardnadze, "U Gruzii s Rossiei mogut i dolzhny byt' ideal'nye otnosheniia" [Georgia and I
sia Can and Need to Have Ideal Relations], *Izvestiia* (14 November 2000).

South Ossetia, both technically part of Georgia. He also suggested that the CIS would be weakened and GUUAM strengthened if Russia continued to discriminate against Georgia.[31] The fact that some 500,000 Georgians then worked in Russia, sending home millions of dollars from their wages, made the new regime a very serious matter.

In their turn, Russian officials placed the blame squarely on Shevardnadze's shoulders, accusing him of ignoring Chechen bases on his territory and claiming that the purpose of a visa regime was to make it difficult for "bandit gunmen" to exploit Georgian laxness for easy access to Russia. Several Russian generals warned that Georgia might initiate "provocations" against their country.[32] In the meantime, the final withdrawal of Russian ordinance and personnel from Gudauta, its leased military base in Abkhazia, was started with the expectation that it would be completed by the end of the year (ITAR-TASS, 8 December).

After energy supplies used by power generators for Tbilisi were cut off again for a few days, for lack of payment, Russian Deputy Prime Minister Ilya Klebanov flew to Georgia. He spent two days in the Georgian capital, 23–24 December, and appeared to work out an accommodation with Shevardnadze, who told a Georgian radio audience that cooperation with Russia was now a top priority.[33] Economic accords were signed, though the debt issue was far from resolved and, although withdrawals from military bases in Georgia proceeded on schedule, it was also made clear that Russia preferred extensions of up to fifteen years. This desire was directly related to the Abkhazia issue, which at that time was probably more central to Russia–Georgian relations than Chechnya.[34]

THE NORTH AND SOUTH CAUCAUSUS IN 2001

General

There was a profound shift in Moscow's management of conflict in the North Caucasus in early 2001. During his year-end interview with Russian TV and press journalists, Putin said that the campaign in Chechnya must be finished by professionals, meaning special forces, and that the political side was now in the hands of the appointed president, Akhmad Kadyrov. He sounded optimistic that normalization would follow, if slowly.

Consequently, the PACE delegation led to Moscow by Lord Judd on 14–17 January, and then to Chechnya, was treated in a considerably more accommodating

---

31. See El'mira Akhundova, "Vizovyi rezhim dlia starogo druga" [A Visa Regime for an Old Friend], *Obshchaia gazeta*, No. 49 (7–13 December 2000).

32. See, for example, Marina Bondarenko, "Vizovyi rezhim v deistvii" [Visa Regime Underway], *Nezavisimaia gazeta* (7 December 2000), and Anatolii Kurganov, "Gruziia sama sebe obrekla na vizu" [Georgia Condemns Itself to Visas], *Rossiiskaia gazeta* (6 December 2000).

33. Shevardnadze weekly radio broadcast, FBIS-SOV, No. 1225 (25 December 2000).

34. See, for example, "Komu voina, komu . . . mat' rodnaia . . ." [He Who Is Concerned about War, His Motherland Is More Important], *Rossiiskaia gazeta* (22 December 2000).

manner than its predecessors had been. The visit was marked by an announcem
from the Kremlin, perhaps (but not likely) coincidentally, that seven Russian servi
men had been found guilty of crimes against Chechen civilians (Interfax, 16 Janua
Data released at the same time claimed that hundreds of cases against members of
armed forces had been launched since the second stage of the war had started (agai
sixteen officers, 153 conscriptees, and fifty contract soldiers and NCOs), and that t
process was going to continue apace. In addition to the hoped-for influence
PACE's reports, information of this type lent credence to the often ignored and li
ited protest from Russians concerned about their own army's behavior.[35]

Putin's need to end the conflict in Chechnya, his first explicit promise to the R
sian electorate a full year earlier, was cause for the radical shift in the conduct of
war. On 22 January 2001, he decreed that the Federal Security Service (FSB) wo
take over responsibility for defeating the separatists. To manage the new tactic,
"Operational Headquarters for the Command and Control of Counter-terrorist C
erations on the Territory of the Russian Federation's North Caucasus Region" was
up, headed by the FSB director and responsible to a board made up of represer
tives from the Kremlin's power ministries. The FSB was given until 15 May 2001
find the key to a successful operation.[36] In the meantime, the number of Russ
troops in Chechnya were to be reduced from 80,000 to about 20,000, and FSB p
sonnel were moved in. The changeover started already on 28 January.

In the political domain, the Russian government and media took a more sangu
than usual view of NATO's Lord Robertson's tour to Yerevan, Baku and Ashgal
where he urged greater association with NATO and promised further NATO
pansion eastward. He also claimed, disingenuously one must say, that NATO l
not been opposed to Russia joining its ranks during the furor of March 2000 a
that there were no obstacles against Russia doing so sometime in the future (In
fax, 16 January).

More important, however, was Russia's concomitant new approach to Azerbai
and its deteriorating relationship with Georgia (see below), and the active role in w
seemed to some to be a new direction in Russian foreign policy played by Azerbaij
President Aliev and Chairman of the Russian Security Council Sergei Ivanov.[37] Ot
ously, oil diplomacy was one of the motors driving the new Baku–Moscow relati
ship. Russia's LUKoil and Transneft had been pushing for the modernization of
Makhachkala (Dagestan) to Novorossiisk oil pipeline, assuming that the propo
Baku–Ceyhan pipeline had a dim future. If, as Russia hoped, an agreement betw

---

35. The charges, though, were mostly for fraud and theft, not atrocities; illegal arms dealing; the
arms and ammunition; loss of military property, and so on. In one case, however, a Col. Yurii Budanov
indicted for murdering and raping a Chechen girl. The case was still under review in the summer of 2(

36. "O merakh po bor'be s terrorizmom na territorii Severo-kavkazskogo regionu Rossiiskoi Federa
[On Measures to Combat Terrorism on the Territory of the Russian federation's North Caucasus Regi
Rossiiskaia gazeta (23 January 2001); Mikhail Khodarenok, "Rukovodit' operatsiei porucheno chekist
[Chekists Are Ordered to Head the Operations], *NVO*, No. 3 (26 January–1 February 2001).

37. On this see esp. Alan Kasaev, "Rossiia formiruet novuiu zakavkazskuiu politiku" [Russia Creat
New Transcaucasus Policy], *Nezavisimaia gazeta* (11 January 2001).

Azerbaijan and Armenia on Nagorno-Karabakh could be brokered by Moscow, then an entirely new situation would exist in the South Caucausus.

By the time that Sergei Ivanov was appointed minister of defense in March, the situation had changed again. The presidents of Armenia and Azerbaijan had met separately with the new American president, who made it plain that his administration planned to increase its involvement in the Caucasus and Caspian regions. Russian analysts suspected that American information agencies were intensifying their efforts to sway political and international thinking in the area and the government in Washington was preparing to challenge the predominance of Russian, British and French oil and gas interests there.[38]

Still, all three South Caucasus states attended the CIS summit in Minsk, 31 May–1 June, and some progress was proclaimed at least for public consumption. The Russian president met separately with each South Caucasus president and chaired meetings between them. Links between the GUUAM and the Eurasian Economic Community were reestablished.[39] Indeed, a few weeks later Uzbekistan, the newest member of GUUAM, was admitted also to the Shanghai Five. Tentatively, therefore, Putin began to draw the South Caucasus back into a mutually beneficial relationship with Moscow.

The Caucasus dilemma took on a different hue in the wake of the 11 September terrorist attacks on New York and Washington. America's sudden shift to a strongly anti-terrorist mood provided Russia with considerable more leeway in dealing with rebels in Chechnya and granted more credibility to its long-standing claims that its enemies in Chechnya were part of a global terrorist conspiracy. When the General Procurator in Moscow, Vladimir Ustinov, claimed that he had definite proof of links between Osama bin Laden and the Chechen rebels, he was immediately believed in Washington, and when he went further to accuse Afghanistan, Saudi Arabia, Turkey, Azerbaijan, Georgia, and even Latvia, of harboring Chechen fighters, he was taken much more seriously than he would have been a year earlier.[40] Because the events of 11 September brought Russia closer to the United States—and Iran—as part of a newly vitalized anti-terrorist coalition, they had different consequences for each of the South Caucasus states, as comments noted below will attest.

At any rate, Russia gained its first benefit from the 11 September crisis when the U.S. State Department demanded that Maskhadov cease all further contact with terrorists in Afghanistan. On 10 October a new Russian commander for Chechnya was appointed. Lt. Gen. Vladimir Moltenskoi replaced Valerii Baranov, with a mandate to tighten up operations there.[41] This decision came in the midst of rapidly rising

---

38. See, for example, Leonid Slutskii, "Slovo i otrazhenie" [Word and Reflection], *Nezavisimaia gazeta* (13 April 2001); "Mr. Bush's Caspian Diplomacy," *New York Times* Editorial (16 April 2001).

39. On this, see for example, Vasilii Safronchuk, "28-ia vstrecha v verkhakh" [28th Summit], *Sovetskaia Rossiia* (5 June 2001).

40. See Ustinov, "Chechnya uchitsia zhit' po zakonam" [Chechnya Learns to Live by the Law], *Rossiiskaia gazeta* (21 September 2001).

41. See Timofei Borisov, "Generala Moltenskogo predstavliat' ne nado" [There Is No Need to Introduce General Moltenskoi], *Rossiiskaia gazeta* (11 October 2001).

tension between Russia and Georgia over Chechen and Georgian militant atta
against Abkhazia (see below). In November the first meeting in two years betw
Russian and Chechen officials took place when a representative from Maskhad
government, Akhmed Zakaev, held a two-hour discussion with Viktor Kazantse\
presidential plenipotentiary for the Southern Federal District—at the Sheremet
airport in Moscow. Although some enthusiasm was generated for this meeting in
Western press, where it was called a breakthrough of sorts, Kazantsev himself l;
called it useless and unproductive.[42]

Armenia stood to gain the most from the changed international circumstances.
dependence on Russia and, to a lesser extent on Iran, for support against Azerbaij
and its relatively good relations with Washington, set the country up as one of
tential strategic significance. As its neighbors worried that Russia's influence mi
increase in the South Caucasus, the feeling in Yerevan was likely one of relief.

In addition to dashing Russian hopes for major concessions from the Uni
States, the quick victory of the anti-terrorist coalition over the Taliban promp
some analysts in Moscow to recommend that the American "method" be used
Chechnya, querying at the same time why Russian forces had taken so long to
feat a similar enemy within its borders.[43] The shine was quickly taken off this brig
if somewhat facetious, idea when the U.S. State Department again began meet
with Ichkerian emissaries, including Zakaev.[44]

Azerbaijan

Much of the tension between Moscow and Baku already had been eased, at least p
licly, as a result of Putin's state visit to Azerbaijan on 9–10 January 2001. The ev
was clearly a public relations success for both sides. Among other things, the Russ
president was awarded an honorary degree by the Slavic University in Baku. He ;
Aliev agreed on joint efforts on the Caspian Sea, more trade in energy, visa-l
arrangements at the borders, and the need for a rapid resolution of the Nagor
Karabakh conflict. Putin made it clear that a new level of relations with Azerbai
would in no way interfere with Moscow's association with Armenia.[45] Both si
condemned the spread in the Caucasus of "terrorism, extremism and aggressive s
aratism." Even the communist press saw renewed cooperation with Azerbaijan as

---

42. See Kazantsev, "'Ya uzhe zabyl o Zakaeve" ["I Have Already Forgotten about Zakaev"], *Rossiis,
gazeta* (22 November 2001); and Dmitrii Furman, "Absurdistskaia p'esa na chechenskii siuzhet" [An
surd Play on the Chechen Plot], *Obshchaia gazeta*, No. 47 (22–28 November 2001).

43. See, for example, Vladimir Georgiev, "Yanki—v Chechniu! Rossii pokazali, kak eto delaetsia" ['
kee, Go to Chechnya! Russia Has Been Shown How to Do It], *Nezavisimaia gazeta* (25 January 200

44. On this, see for example, "U Maskhadova est' tri predlozheniia. Ikh oglasil Akhmed Zak
[Maskhadov Has Three Proposals. Akhmed Zakaev Reads Them Out], *Obshchaia gazeta*, No. 5
January–6 February 2002).

45. On the perceived great success of the visit, see Asia Gadzhizade, Dmitrii Kozyrev, "Putin nachal
s Baku" [Putin Opens the Year in Baku], *Nezavisimaia gazeta* (10 January 2001); "Moskvu-Baku: N;
obshchii iazyk" [Moscow-Baku: We Have Reached Consensus], *Rossiiskaia gazeta* (11 January 2001).

important step forward, especially as it might dim that country's enthusiasm for NATO. Agreements with Baku must not interfere with Russia's traditional friendship with Armenia, communists argued. They warned also that an isolated Georgia might rush even more quickly into the arms of NATO.[46]

Stories of terrorist groups trained in Iran and located in Azerbaijan continued to appear in the Russian press, however, keeping alive the suspicion that the government in Baku was not a reliable associate.[47] The Baku–Ceyhan pipeline remained a point of contention between Azerbaijan and Russia, as did Aliev's continued insistence on closer ties to NATO. Rumors that he might invite Turkey to establish military bases on Azeri soil struck a discordant note as well, though these notions were denied in March. Moscow was quietly encouraged as the Baku–Ceyhan project seemed to have reached an impasse and Azerbaijan repeatedly failed to gain Western support for its case in Nagorno-Karabakh.

The question of Azerbaijan's relations with NATO was raised again in Moscow as Aliev set out for a visit to the United States on 3 April 2001. The Azeri president downplayed the matter himself, telling reporters that his country had no chance of admission to NATO, though he hoped that their association would grow. The matter was a special topic of concern in the Azerbaijan Russian-language press where, on 4 April, the pros and cons of an application were laid out. On the pro side, the potential benefits for Azerbaijan from NATO membership were obvious: no further domination from either Russia or Iran; NATO support in the Nagorno-Karabakh affair; and financial returns from bases leased to NATO, especially if the country became a strategic base for NATO operations in the Balkans, the Caucasus and even Central Asia. On the con side, the closer Baku moved towards NATO, the stronger Russia's ties with Armenia could become, and the likelihood of NATO being able to protect Azerbaijan from Russia and Iran on the Caspian was slim. All in all, the best path was the status quo—at least according to some Baku circles.[48]

Azeri nationalists took heart when the American budget for 2002 was announced in April and revealed an allocation to Baku of $50 million and, for the first time, none to Nagorno-Karabakh. Washington also still planned to assist Armenia, but the absence of funds for the Armenian-controlled region within Azerbaijan's borders was taken as a sign that the new U.S. administration would be more "balanced" in its approach to the Caucasus.[49]

All bets were off as ripple effects from the terrorist attacks on New York and Washington were felt in the South Caucasus. Azerbaijan faced greater insecurity because

. 46. See, for example, Vasilii Safronchuk, "Kavkazskii gambit Putina" [Putin's Caucasus Gambit], *Sovetskaia Rossiia* (16 January 2001).

47. See, for example, El'mira Akhundova, "Akademika 'zakazali' iranskie spetssluzhby?" [Academican "Killed" by Order of the Iranian Special Services?], *Obshchaia gazeta*, No. 10 (1–14 March 2001).

48. See E. Abulfatov, "NATO in Azerbaijan," *Baku zerkalo* (4 April 2001), translated for FBIS-SOV, No. 0405 (2001); and Armen Khanbabyan, "Aliev okonchatel'no opredelilsia?" [Has Aliev Finally Decided?], *Nezavisimaia gazeta* (29 March 2001).

49. See, for example, E. Abulfatov, "USA Plans to Allocate $50 Million for Azerbaijan," *Baku zerkalo* (12 April 2001), translated for FBIS-SOV, No. 0411 (15 April 2001).

Russia and Iran were brought closer together in their anti-terrorist policies, and b
joined the American-led anti-terrorist coalition. Airfields in the Central Asian co
tries became more important to the United States and NATO than Azerbaijan
sites, and tales of Baku officials providing tacit support for terrorists in Chech
were revived. As Washington increasingly ameliorated its stance against Russia's
tivities in Chechnya, Baku's star appeared to fade in the vision of the United St
and NATO. Or at least that was a concern. Moreover, security and stability in
region became more important to the major Western powers than oil and
pipeline routes.

After the events of 11 September, Azerbaijan again offered its territory to NA
for basing operations, and there was talk among pundits in Moscow that the ev
would widen the gulf between GUUAM, of which Azerbaijan is one, and the ot
members of the CIS. Moreover, Washington already had come under attack fr
Russian analysts for using allegedly the antiterrorism campaign as cover for its a
bitions to gain a foothold in the South Caucasus.[50] But this particular source of t
sion had been defused by Russia's immediate support for the anti-terrorist coaliti
The ongoing focus on Afghanistan took RF Minister of the Interior Gryzlov to B
on 23 October 2001 for discussion of anti-terrorist cooperation. A meeting of mi
was ensured, on this issue at least.

As a consequence of Moscow's energetic campaign to win back support in A
baijan during the winter of 2002, the relationship did in fact improve considera
Tentative agreements were reached on the Caspian Sea, pipeline transit, debt a
trade during a series of meetings in February and March. Even though the first su
mit of the "Caspian Five" leaders, meeting in Ashgabat on April, was a failure in
far as an accord on the division of access to oil deposits on the seabed was c
cerned,[51] the Moscow–Baku relationship brightened. A large role in the r
accommodation was played by the Azerbaijani president's son, Il'kham Aliev
prominent businessman who had grown up in Moscow.[52] Shortly thereafter, A
baijan and Russia reached its first real agreement on the Caspian Sea after ne
twelve years of dispute. They agreed on a border in the central sector of the Sea a
in light of a Russian–Kazakhstan accord a few days earlier, and Turkmenistan's d
sion not to protest, the possibility of an end to conflict over rights to oil deposits
foreseen.[53] Iran remained a stumbling block to full unanimity on the Caspian (
chapter 12), but great progress nonetheless had been achieved for the Russian ca

50. See, for example, Asia Gadzhizade, "Baku pomozhet Vashingtonu v bor'be s Talibami" [Baku
Help Washington in the Struggle against the Taliban], *Nezavisimaia* (14 November 2001).

51. On this failure, see a series of articles in *Rossiiskaia gazeta* (25 April 2002).

52. On this, see articles and interviews by Aliev himself, for example, Il'kham Aliev, "V nashikh
nosheniiakh nachinaetsia novaia epokha. I ne nado etogo boiat'sia" [A New Epoch Is Beginning in
Relationship. And There Is No Need to Be Afraid of This], *Izvestiia* (28 March 2002); Il'kham Aliev
nas vse poluchitsia" [Everything Will Work Out for Us", *Izvestiia* (25 April 2002).

53. On this, see Aleksandr Chichkin, "Kaspii dostali do dna" [Caspian Bottom Reached in a C
Rossiiskaia gazeta (24 May 2002). Russia and Azerbaijan signed a formal accord on a demarcation of
Caspian on 23 September 2002, greatly angering Iran.

Georgia

The respite engineered in the long Moscow–Tbilisi stare-down by Klebanov's visit to Tbilisi in December 2000 was short-lived. Inertgazstroi, the Russian company supplying gas for Georgia's main power generators, cut supplies yet again on 1 January 2001. It was claimed that an American-owned supplier (AES Corp.) was selling its gas to Georgia at too low a price. A compromise was reached, although Georgia was left vulnerable to the political uses of energy. The relationship was strained further when the Russian foreign ministry warned its citizens not to travel in Georgia because of the danger of kidnapping by Chechen rebel supporters, whom both the Russian media and government still suspected were acting in collusion with the government in Tbilisi.[54]

Other events exacerbated the situation. A call from Stalin's grandson, Col. Yevgenii Dzhugashvili, to build a "reformed" Communist Party in Georgia, dedicated to reunification with Russia, may not have been taken seriously in Russia but was treated as threatening in Georgia. And negotiations for Russian troop withdrawal from bases in Georgia reached a stalemate by February, as the Kremlin hedged on the established timetable. A step towards cooperation was taken in mid-February, however, when defense ministers Sergeev and David Tevzadze met in Tbilisi and agreed to resume military cooperation for the first time since 1998. This event did not prevent Shevardnadze from insisting that Georgia still hoped to join NATO. By that time, however, it was also obvious that there was not much enthusiasm for Georgia within NATO itself.

Russia's ability to pressure Georgia through the visa regime and energy supply cutbacks remained strong, and Russian analysts continued to chide Tbilisi for "wanting it both ways," that is, to join NATO by 2005 and still enjoy the advantages of free movement in, and energy from, Russia. Former Russian ambassador to Georgia, Feliks Stanevskii, for example, pointed out that the notion of a visa regime was first introduced by the Georgians themselves in the mid-1990s.[55]

It was left to the two presidents to resolve the issues between them. Shevardnadze and Putin met briefly and, according to both of them, constructively, at the 28th CIS summit held in Minsk between 31 May and 1 June. Putin lodged no objections later in June when Georgian forces took part in a large land-and-sea NATO exercise. Cooperative Partners 2001 began on Georgian territory and included some 4,000 servicemen, thirty-four warships and two submarines from ten states. Official statements from Tbilisi denied that there was anything anti-Russian about the Georgian role in the PfP undertaking, but Russian military analysts made their suspicion of Shevardnadze's long-term motive known.

---

54. See, for example, Boris Talov, "Viza dlia Tiflisa" [Visa for Tiflis], *Rossiiskaia gazeta* (5 January 2001); Aleksandr Baliev, "Rossiia snova spasaet Gruziiu?" [Will Russia Save Georgia Again?], *Rossiiskaia gazeta* (11 January 2001).

55. See, for example, Feliks Stanevskii, " Vizy na sovesti Gruzii" [The Visas Are on Georgia's Conscience] *Obshchaia gazeta*, No. 13 (29 March–4 April 2001). Stanevskii was ambassador from 1996 to 2000. This was a "polemic" with Yurii Rost whose "Liubov' i malen'kaia neumnaia politika" [Love and a Little Stupid Policy], *Obshchaia gazeta*, No. 8. (22–28 February 2001), was more favorably disposed towards the Georgians.

While Putin remained pragmatically aloof, the military hierarchy was so su:
cious of this operation, in which American, Ukrainian and Turkish military pers
nel also participated, that the Russian commander in the Abkhazian peacekeep
zone placed his forces on alert; and an analyst for *Izvestiia* asked rhetorically, "w
exactly are NATO preparing to separate and reconcile on the Black Sea coast wi
out Russia's participation." [56] The hint that Russia was a target of the training fo
was immediately denied in Tbilisi, but Russians remained unbelieving. At least (
Moscow-based writer reminded readers that the exercise would end on 22 June
day of tragic significance for our people." He was referring, of course, to the
niversary of the German invasion of the USSR in 1941.

The timing of the PfP operation was likely what generated such a bitter respo
in the Russian ministry of defense. On 20 June, Russia had actually set in mot
the final withdrawal of troops from its military base in Vaziani, in compliance w
promises it had made to the OSCE in 1999. Moscow had a vague agreement w
Tbilisi that the base would not then be occupied by a third power, but few exp(
assumed that this commitment would hold up for very long. For obvious reasc
Russia was reluctant to remove personnel from a base in Gudauta, on the Black
coast of Abkhazia. Still, Tbilisi's protests to the OSCE prompted Russia to proc
there too—but slowly. In his turn, Shevardnadze took a moderate stance on
weekly radio interview of 25 June, explaining first that the PfP exercise was a g]
success and no threat to Russia, and secondly that the Gudauta problem would
resolved mutually. Georgia's ambition to join NATO in 2005 was still on the dr:
ing board, he told his audience.[57]

In the long run, however, there seemed to be little chance of an understanding
tween Tbilisi and Moscow on Abkhazia generally or on the Gudauta base specificall
Georgia itself was on the brink of destabilization. Widespread corruption and the J
murder in Tbilisi of a popular Georgian television personality, Giorgi Sanaia, c
tributed to the discontent and undermined Shevardnadze's popularity. Doubt was (
on Georgia's suitability as a route for Caspian Sea oil, and there was a tendency to at
bute the murder to a Russian plot—lessening the likelihood of accommodation. Sh
ardnadze failed to attend a CIS summit of presidents held in Sochi over 1–3 Augus

Like Azerbaijan, Georgia was rendered more vulnerable by the consequences of
11 September events in the United States. Russia's realignment towards a larger ai
terrorist campaign in combination with the United States and other NATO countr
made Russia's bases in Georgia more important than previously. It also made it cert
that the Shevardnadze government would be pressed to act against Chechen rebels

---

56. See, for example, Maksim Zorin, "NATO—na Chernom more" [NATO on the Black Sea], *Izve*
(14 June 2001).

57. Shevardnadze Weekly Radio Interview (25 June), FBIS-SOV, No. 625 (26 June 2001).

58. See, for example, Boris Talov, "'My u vas pod zashchitoi, vy u nas v plenu',"['We Are under `
Protection, You Are Our Prisoners"], *Rossiiskaia gazeta* (6 July 2001); Viktor Litovkin, "Na meste sha;
marsh! Rossiia repetiruet nevozmozhnost' vyvoda svoikh voennykh baz iz Gruzii" [Standing in P]
Quick March! Russia Rehearses the Impossibility of a Withdrawal of Its Military Bases from Geor]
Obshchaia gazeta, No. 28 (12–18 July 2001).

Georgian territory. In fact, it appeared that a militant Georgian and Rebel Chechen joint attack on Abkhazia was stalled by Abkhazian forces shortly after the crisis of international terrorism was brought home so starkly to North America. Shevardnadze happened to be in Washington at the time, meeting with Bush, Cheney and Powell, speaking at Johns Hopkins University, and lobbying for aid and revitalization funding for GUUAM. His remarks at Johns Hopkins were taken in Moscow as very anti-Russian.[59] Simultaneous rumors of Georgian involvement in the shooting down of a UN observer helicopter, killing all aboard, made his task more difficult—but Russians were still concerned about the possibility of Georgia becoming a platform for further U.S. involvement in the Caucasus.[60] This particular worry was to prove prophetic.

On 11 October, Georgian troops were sent to the Abkhaz border. The next day, Shevardnadze gave Russian peacekeepers three months to get out of Abkhazia, in the face of protest from the Abkhazian leadership. Reports that Georgia would soon withdraw from the CIS resurfaced and Russia began "strengthening" its own borders with Georgia, including the Abkhaz section. Russian officials blamed Georgia for the escalation, and the Moscow media again equated Shevardnadze's position with abetting rebels in Chechnya. More than one Russian account insisted that Ruslan Gelaev, the Chechen leader involved in the attack on Abkhazia, was doing the Georgian government a favor in return for permission to resettle in Ajaria.

Others complained that Shevardnadze planned to draw NATO troops into the region to serve as peacekeepers, and accused him of actually arranging Gelaev's attack on Abkhazia.[61] The Duma adopted a formal statement strongly criticizing Georgia, and the official press consistently labelled the rebel group attacking Abkhazia "Georgian–Chechen bandit formations," laying the blame for the crisis directly on Tbilisi's power ministries.[62] Shevardnadze's threats to leave the CIS were greeted with scorn in Moscow, where media analysts rejected what they called "blackmail," and forecast war in Abkhazia and South Ossetia if Russian forces were compelled to withdraw in favor of "terrorists."[63]

---

59. On this and Shevardnadze's subsequent explanation see an interview with him, "Voiny ne budet, a mira uzhe net" [There Will Be No War, but No Peace Either], *Obshchaia gazeta*, No. 42 (18–24 October 2001).
60. See Bakhtiar Akhmedkhanov, "Abkhaziia gotova zashchishchat'sia. I ot gruzin, i ot chechentsev" [Abkhazia Prepares to Defend Itself. From Both Georgians and Chechens], *Obshchaia gazeta*, No. 38 (20–26 September 2001).
61. Alan Kasaev, "Abkhazskii front, Afganskoi voiny" [Abkhazian Front of the Afghan War], *Nezavisimaia gazeta* (10 October 2001); Timofei Borisov, "Pochemu gelaev poshel v Abkhaziiu?" [Why Did Gelaev Go to Abkhazia?], *Rossiiskaia gazeta* (11 October 2001); Borisov, "'Lis' blagoslovil 'Volka': Prezhde chem napast' na Abkhaziiu, Gelaev vstretilsia s Shevardnadze" ["Fox" Blesses "Wolf": Before Attacking Abkhazia, Gelaev Met with Shevardnadze], *Rossiiskaia gazeta* (12 October 2001); Andrei Sharov, "Beoviki blokirovany v Kodorskom ushchel'e" [Gunmen Blocked in the Kodori Gorge], *Rossiiskaia gazeta* (11 October 2001). See also "Molodoe vino voiny udarilo v golovu" [Young Wine of War Has Gone to the Head], *Rossiiskaia gazeta* (13 October 2001).
62. Oleg Galitskii, "Abkhazkaia pruzhina szhimaetsia" [Abkhazian Spring Tightens], *Rossiiskaia gazeta* (20 October 2001).
63. See, for example, Anatolii Chekhoev (a Duma deputy interviewed by Tamara Shkel), "Nuzhno li khlopat' dver'iu, vykhodia iz obshchego doma?" [Does One Have to Slam the Door When Leaving the Common Home?], *Rossiiskaia gazeta* (23 October 2001).

Georgia, in fact, seemed about to become unravelled. Protests demanding Sh
ardnadze's resignation over questions of corruption and poverty, a security raid on
independent TV station (Rustavi 2), and uncertainties over Abkhazia, all contribu
to a very volatile situation. On 1 November 2001, Shevardnadze dismissed his en
cabinet. Zurab Zhvania, his leading political opponent and speaker of parliame
turned in his resignation as well. All of this made destabilization in the region
even greater Russian worry. Moscow's distrust of Shevardnadze and his officials
highlighted in a long interview given by Putin to Moscow bureau chiefs of the le
ing U.S. media on 12 November just prior to his departure for Washington
Crawford.

In response to a question about Georgia's complicity in facilitating the transp
of terrorists from Chechnya to Turkey (whence they would then move on
Afghanistan), Putin said "certain quarters in Georgia are at the very least pander
to the operation of international terrorists on their territory." He avoided blam
Shevardnadze directly, but the message was clear.[64] Shortly thereafter, a bomb b
in a North Ossetian market was blamed by Russians (and Ossetians) on milita
based in Georgia. The situation seemed to be spiralling out of control.[65]

On 21 November, the Russian government took the initiative and demanded t
Georgia capture Gelaev and turn him over to Moscow (ITAR-TASS, 21 Novemb
Although nothing concrete came of this directive, within a month Moscow and T
lisi seemed to have reached a mutual change of heart. Negotiations were reopened
a friendship, security and cooperation treaty in Tbilisi on 21 December. Cochair:
the negotiating commission, Boris Pastukhov, head of the Duma's committee on
lations with the CIS, and Georgian foreign minister, Irakli Menagharishvili, both
fered optimistic words to the media, though neither claimed that the road to
commodation would be easy. A few days later Shevardnadze told reporters that 2(
would be a year in which Georgia's relations with Russia would be normalized (
terfax, 26 December).

In spite of regular comments from Shevardnadze in the New Year to the effect t
his country's relationships with Russia were important and needed normalizati
Georgia watchers in Moscow grew increasingly pessimistic as Tbilisi moved close
the West. As American acknowledgement of the international terrorist componen
the Chechen rebel movement faded, hopes from pressure on Georgia to close its g:
to Chechen militant operations diminished with it. Russian observers again be;
forecasting U.S. dominance of the Caucasus generally, and of Georgia particularl

---

64. "Vladimir Putin Talks with American Journalists," *Kommersant*, No. 206 (12 November 20
translation from RIA Novosti; JRL, No. 5541.

65. Russian communists were especially vigorous in their criticism of Shevardnadze, accusing hir
staying on as president against the will of the Georgian people. See Maria Tsvetkova, Andrei Matiash, "
taetsia, chtoby dokonat' gruziiu" [He Remains to Ruin Georgia], *Sovetskaia Rossiia* (3 November 20(

66. Vasilii Strel'tsov, "Gruziia, kotoruiu my poteriali. Pentagon ne stremitsia v Zakavkaz'e, on tam
prisutstvuet" [Georgia, Which We Have Lost. The Pentagon Is Not Rushing into the Transcaucasus,
Already There], *Nezavisimaia* (20 February 2002).

New rumors of Shevardnadze pulling his country out of the CIS flourished, although the Georgian ambassador to Moscow tried to lay them to rest as he prepared for an informal CIS meeting in Almaty, Kazakhstan (ITAR-TASS, 28 February 2002).[67]

The feeling that Georgia was "going West" was intensified in February/March when Russians suddenly learned of an American military presence in Georgia from Washington, not from Tbilisi.[68] Analysts were not impressed with an interview with Brzezinski, who said that Russians should be grateful for American participation.[69] As usual, Putin's reaction to the potential of American help in sealing the Pankisi Gorge was subdued. Officials in the ministries of defense and foreign affairs were not so dispassionate: they predicted U.S. interference in the Abkhazia question and a slow diminution of Russian influence in the region.[70] Abkhaz Prime Minister Arni Dzhergeniia proclaimed that his "country" was prepared to apply for associate relations with Russia if the U.S. military meddled in the regional dispute (Interfax, 28 February). The newly established U.S. presence in the Transcaucasus was the beginning of the end, according to one well-known writer who thought that even Armenia would eventually fall into the American camp, seduced by U.S. dollars and promises.[71] The Kremlin also worried that the Pentagon might take a hand in the Abkhazian affair crisis and regularly termed this new crisis a "test" of Russian–U.S. post–11 September relations.[72] The notion of some bigger plan being hatched in Washington was lent credence in the opinion of some Russian observers when the U.S. Congress pledged $1.5 million to Georgia in March for military-technical training.[73] Putin and Shevardnadze presented their quite different perspectives on the situation at the CIS heads-of-state

---

67. "Zurab Abashidze: Shevardnadze nikogda ne stavil vopros o vykhode iz SNG" [Zurab Abashidze: Shevardnadze Has Never Raised the Question of Leaving the CIS], *Izvestiia* (27 February 2002). Abashidze is Georgian ambassador to Russia. He was very defensive about Chechnya, the United States and NATO in this interview. Earlier he had insisted that Russian troops were not needed in the Gorge, "Zurab Abashidze: v Pankiskoe ushchel'e rossiiskim voennym nikak nel'zia" [Zurab Abashidze: Russian Troops Are Not Needed in the Pankisi Gorge], *Rossiiskaia gazeta* (31 January 2002).

68. See, for example, Aleksandr Chuikin, "Amerikanskii desant v Pankisskoe ushchel'e" [American Landing in Pankisi Gorge], *Izvestiia* (21 February 2002); Maksim Yusin, "Vtoroi Chechenskii front" [The Second Chechen Front], *Izvestiia* (28 February 2002); Georgi Bovt, "Pankisskii lev prygnul" [The Pankisi Lion Leapt], *ibid.* (1 March 2002).

69. Brzezinski, "Rossiia dolzhna aplodirovat' amerikantsam" [Russia Should Applaud the Americans], *Nezavisimaia gazeta* (7 March 2002).

70. See, for example, Mikhail Khodarenok, "Uchast' pobezhdennykh" [The Fate of the Defeated], *Nezavisimaia gazeta* (14 March 2002), and Mikhail Dzhimdzhikhashvili, "Ushchel'e obliubovali terroristy" [Terrorists Have Chosen the Kodori Gorge], *Obshchaia gazeta,* No. 8 (21–27 February 2002).

71. See, for example, Armen Khanbabyan, "Gruziia—eto tol'ko nachalo"[Georgia Is Only the Beginning], *Nezavisimaia gazeta* (14 March 2002), and Semen Novoprudskii, "Imperiia Dobra" [Empire of Goodness], *Izvestiia* (6 March 2002).

72. See, for example Vladimir Bogdanov, "Luchshe bez rezkikh dvizhenii" [Better without Sharp Movements], *Rossiiskaia gazeta* (2 March 2002); Oleg Galitskikh, "V Abkhazii vstrevozheny dazhe mimozy" [Even the Mimosas Are Anxious in Abkhazia], *ibid.*

73. Nodor Broladze, "Gruzinskie 'gornye strelki' zagovoriat po-drugomu"[Georgian "Mountain Riflemen" Will Speak Differently], *Izvestiia* (15 March 2002). In an interview published in Russia, Zbigniew Brzezinski said that Russians should welcome a U.S. presence in Georgia because Moscow had been complaining for so long about terrorists in the Pankisi Gorge: "Rossiia dolzhna soglasit'sia" [Russia Must Agree], *NVO,* No. 8 (15–21 March 2002).

meeting in Almaty. According to reports from that meeting, both were frank ab
their positions, and neither left much room for compromise.[74]

The Russian government press service released opinions from Georgia's par
mentary speaker, Nino Burdzhanadze, and Dzhergeniia in March, in which b
tried to appear accommodating.[75] In fact, however, the Gelaev case and Abkh;
were still very contentious subjects. In early April, Georgian troops who were s
posed to have been withdrawn from the Kodori Gorge (near Sukhomi) by 2 Ap
were accused of firing on Russian peacekeepers.[76] Promised observers from the U
and the CIS still had not been sent to the region and tensions between Moscow a
Tbilisi remained very high.[77] Russian analysts were concerned that the presence
American soldiers would make the government in Tbilisi overconfident, thereby
flaming the situation in Abkhazia, Ajaria, and South Ossetia. Indeed, the South (
setian speaker of parliament foresaw a new conflict looming between his repul
and Georgia.[78] Although CIS official observers arrived on the scene on 14 April, tl
left shortly afterwards, remarking only that their task had been accomplished. In
meantime, one Russian delegation led by a general appeared in Ajaria without h
ing consulted with the Georgia government, Abkhazia had threatened to mobiliz
Duma delegation had gone to Tbilisi to speak directly with Shevardnadze, and
level of tension caused some to warn even of a new war in the region.[79]

Georgian officials themselves were divided on the question of Russian, Ameri
and their own interests in the Pankisi Gorge. Nino Burdzhanadze granted an in
view to a Russian journalist in which she questioned Shevardnadze's wisdom in f
keeping quiet about militants gathering in the Kodori Gorge, and then calling
Washington for help without informing Russia. She made it clear, however, t
Georgia had little choice but to involve the Americans because Moscow could
have resolved the problem by itself.[80] A compromise was finally achieved when (
peacekeepers started a patrol of the Kodori Gorge in mid-May, accompanied

---

74. Vladislav Vorob'ev, "Razgovor bez sekretov" [Conversation without Secrets], *Rossiiskaia gazet*
March 2002); on the other hand see an interview with Shevardnadze, "Personally, I Have Faith in P
. . .," *Moscow News*, No. 9 (6–12 March 2002).

75. See "Gruzinskaia kosa i abkhazkii kamen'" [Georgian Scythe and Abkhazian Stone], *Rossiis.
gazeta* (23 March 2002).

76. See Madina Shavlokhova, "Georgia Breaks Protocol on Troop Pullout," *Moscow News*, No
(17–23 April 2002).

77. See, for example, Anatolii Shapolov, "Kodory razdora" [Kodori Discord], *Rossiiskaia gazeta*
April 2002).

78. Stanislav Kochiev, "V Gruzii nakhodiatsia uzhe 1000 amerikanskikh soldat" [1,000 U.S. Solc
Already in Georgia], *Izvestiia* (3 April 2002). Kochiev is the speaker of the South Ossetian parliamen

79. See, for example, Anatolii Shapovalov, "Abkhazia: Soldat ne mozhet byt' politseiskim" [Abkh;
A Soldier Cannot be a Policeman], *Rossiiskaia gazeta* (11 April 2002); Yevgenii Chubarov, Aleks;
Chuykov, "Kodorskii razdor" [Kodori Discord], *Izvestiia* (16 April 2002); Anatolii Shapovalov, "U m
zhenskoe litso" [A Mission with a Feminine Face], *Rossiiskaia gazeta* (16 April 2002).

80. Burdzhanadze, "Ne lgat' trudno, no mozhno" [Not to Lie Is Difficult, but Possible], *Obshc
gazeta*, No. 16 (18–24 April 2002). Burdzhanadze is the first woman to be speaker of Georgia's pa
ment. See also Igor Korotchenko, "Moskva ustupila silovomu nazhimu Tbilisi" [Moscow Yields to Sti
Pressure from Tbilisi], *NVO*, No. 13 (19–25 April 2002); and Anatolii Shapovalov, "Likha beda nach
[First Step Is Always the Hardest], *Rossiiskaia gazeta* (25 April 2002).

UN observers.[81] It would seem that in this case, Putin's—and perhaps also Shevardnadze's—patience won the day.

The relationship between Moscow and Tbilisi was not altogether smoothed over, for the NATO question continued to cause friction. In early June, Russia refused to serve even as an observer for a PfP training session in Georgia; and sent only the military attaché from the Russian embassy in Tbilisi to attend a ceremony officially handing over the Russian military base at Vaziani, from which Russia troops had withdrawn. That ceremony, presided over by the Georgian minister of defense, was attended as well by the chief of NATO forces in Europe and officers and NCO's from the U.S. force in Georgia. The Russian left and nationalists treated the event as a NATO infringement upon Moscow's traditional sphere of influence.[82]

CONCLUSION

Obviously, little had been resolved on the Caucasus front by the late spring 2002. Contentious points between Moscow and Tbilisi were far from settled by the end of May 2002. Moscow understood, however, that conflicts with Georgia had always moved away from the brink. A resurgence in Russian–American cooperation within the new Russia–NATO Council and in the still undefined coalition against international terrorism, in which NATO had been shunted to the sidelines, will mean that Georgia cannot look to Washington for any substantial help. For all that, the Russia–Georgia treaty promised by both presidents in 2000 and mentioned sporadically since that time is less imminent now than it was then.

Moscow's renewed and upgraded association with Azerbaijan, which includes strategic cooperation on the Caspian, and the continued status of Armenia as a Russian partner in the region, suggest that there is light for the Kremlin at the end of the long and dark South Caucasus tunnel. Even the Nagorno-Karabakh conflict with which Russia's Caucasus specialists had been grappling since the 1980s, no longer drove Moscow's dealings with Baku and Yerevan. The general accommodation was due in part to Putin's new and less combative relationship with the American president and that, in turn, was a byproduct of Putin's "turn to the West" in September 2001.

The normalization was very recent, however, and by the spring of 2002 nothing had occurred to test it seriously.

.

---

81. See Thomas de Waal, "Into the Georgian Quagmire," *Moscow News* (24 May 2002), on the general problem.

82. See, for example, "Natovskoe novosel'e na rossiiskoi baze" [NATO's Housewarming on a Russian Base], *Sovetskaia Rossiia* (6 June 2002).

9

✟

Ukraine and Belarus

UKRAINE, 2000[1]

Since 1992, Ukraine has been the largest territorial entity between Russia and Europe, and between Russia and NATO since the spring of 1999. Ukraine's westward neighbors are Poland, Slovakia, Hungary, Romania and Moldova; and to the east—Russia and Belarus. The Black Sea remains an extraordinarily important strategic region shared by Russia and Ukraine, and is increasingly vital to NATO. Ukraine was a founding member of the CIS in December 1991, but has consistently refused to join that organization's Collective Security Pact. It was also a founding member of the regional association GUUAM (see chapter 10), whose member states were distinguished within the CIS both by their rejection of the Collective Security Pact and the level of their participation in NATO projects. They have been the leading recipients in the CIS of funding per capita from the United States.

Kiev's relations with Moscow were an important part of the discourse particularly during the presidential election campaign in Ukraine during 1999. Nationalists saw a "Russian hand" lurking behind most things they did not like about current foreign affairs, while others worried that links with Russia were being precipitously cut off. Russian observers pondered the significance of this trend and often treated that election as a vote of confidence on the Ukraine–Russian relationship.[2] About 20 percent of the population of Ukraine is ethnic Russian.

---

1. For a useful preliminary overview, see Jennifer D. P. Moroney, "NATO's Strategic Engagement with Ukraine and Central Europe on the East–West Frontier," in James Clem, Nancy Popson, eds. *Ukraine and Its Western Neighbors* (Washington: Woodrow Wilson Center and Harvard Ukrainian Research Institute, 2000), 93–106; and on Russia–Ukraine relations during the 1990s, see *Russia Faces NATO Expansion,* Chapter 4.

2. See, for example, Ivanna Gorina, "V Kieve ishchut 'ruku Moskvy'" [The "Hand of Moscow" Is Being Sought in Kiev], *Rossiiskaia gazeta* (27 October 1999).

The NATO question was the first international point of contention between R
sia and Ukraine, and the longest-lasting one. It was introduced to the election ca
paign by left-wing groups and individuals in both countries. The Russian commu
press accused President Leonid Kuchma of turning Ukraine into a semi-colony of
United States and NATO, and other analysts in Moscow judged the widening li
between Ukraine and NATO as a direct threat to Russia.[3] Kuchma won the f
round of the thirteen-candidate election with 36 percent of the vote. He was v
ahead of communist Pyotr Symonenko (22 percent), who, with socialist leader Ol
sandr Moroz and the radical left's Nataliya Vitrenko, with 13 and 12 percent resp
tively, were collectively responsible for bringing outright opposition to NATO i
the forefront of Ukrainian politics. Kuchma's second-round victory on 14 Novem
was decisive (56–38 percent). His success, however, had little to do with his posit
on foreign policy, nor was it a result of any great popularity; rather he was seen as
best bet among a crop of not very compelling candidates. In light of the fact t
Kuchma's campaign on a populist platform of long-overdue market reforms, more
tegration with the West, and an end to corruption generated so little enthusiasm
him personally, the need for a change in direction was obvious. The first signal to i
affect came in his 30 November inaugural address when Kuchma made it clear t
Ukraine's most important strategic partner was Russia, from which it bought ene
and in second place was the United States, whence came credit and technical aid. T
question of strengthening relations with NATO was mentioned only in passi
Within a week of the inauguration, in fact, Kuchma (who called himself a "new" p
ident), was in Moscow negotiating with Putin and Russia's oil–gas tycoons for ene
supplies. The Russian media greeted Kuchma's success with cautious anticipation.

The elections actually confirmed trends that had become more and more p
nounced as Russia floundered and Western European countries appeared to beco
more acquiescent in what some called the new American hegemony. Ukraine's
had already turned to the national interest as a substitute for lingering allegiance
either class or old Soviet groupings. Even the Kaniv (Tkachenko, Moroz, March
Oliynyk) group was more patriotic than socialist in its diatribes against the West a
the IMF.[5] The Communist Party of Ukraine had won 113 seats, of 450, in
March 1998 parliamentary elections, followed distantly by the People's Movem
(Rukh) with forty-six and a combined Socialist and Peasants' Party with forty-fo

3. See, for example, Igor Yur'ev, "Soiuznik ili geopoliticheskii sopernik?" [Ally or Geopolitical Partn
NVO, No 42 (29 October–4 November 1999); L.M. Okov, "Pis'mo iz Kieva. Komu Kuchma v rad
[Letter from Kiev. Who Is Pleased with Kuchma?], *Sovetskaia Rossiia* (25 October 1999).

4. On the inaugural address and Kuchma's encouraging attitude to Russia, see Ivanna Gorina, "Leo
Kuchma, beregites' zhenshchin i opponentov" [Leonid Kuchma, Watch Out for Women and Oppone
Rossiiskaia gazeta (2 December 1999). See also *Izvestiia, Kommersant* and Viktor Timoshenko, "Za
privlekatel'nee vostoka" [The West Is More Appealing than the East], *Nezavisimaia gazeta* (16 Noven
2000); the latter piece is an interview with Ukrainian political scientist Dmitrii Vydrin, who said
Kuchma was now strong enough to dismiss "odious figures" in his government.

5. For the "Kaniv" group, see fn. 9, below; see also Taras Kuzio, "Nation-building in Ukraine. A Gr
ing Elite Consensus," Kennan Institute. *Meeting Report,* 18: 5 (2000).

Over twenty other parties and groups were represented, making it a very mixed body, with no faction able to dominate absolutely.[6]

Whereas Symonenko's presidential election platform stated unequivocally, "Ukraine will not be a member of NATO" and called for a "dynamic development of relations with Russia and Belarus,"—in the national interest—Kuchma's campaign statement on international affairs was ambiguous. He included "nonalignment" and "strategic partnership with Russia and other states" as part of his foreign policy projection, yet also insisted upon an "effective system of European security."[7] The foreign minister, Borys Tarasyuk, had risen to that office in April 1998 already well-known as a supporter of closer Ukrainian ties with NATO and he continued to represent a strongly pro-NATO position. Tarasyuk also lobbied hard to gain Ukrainian admission to the EU[8] and was opposed consistently and loudly on both counts by Oleksandr Tkachenko, the parliamentary speaker.[9]

The crisis in Kosovo had muddied the political scene in Ukraine, interrupting the slide towards the West. Even Tarasyuk took care to point out to NATO delegates to the Ukraine–NATO Commission in April that the people of his country were opposed to the bombing of Yugoslavia. Much later he was to denounce Washington's attempt to amend the ABM as well. In April the Ukrainian government had been concerned enough about NATO's bombing attacks against Yugoslavia to join the CIS Interparliamentary Assembly, of which it had been an observer only, and signed on to its statement that NATO's action was a "threat to peace and stability throughout the world" (Interfax, 3 April). Tkachenko led the Ukrainian delegation to St. Petersburg where the Assembly was meeting. On 23 April 1999, the Ukrainian Supreme Council adopted a resolution on relations with NATO, calling the Alliance an "aggressive military bloc whose leadership has usurped the right to punish any sovereign state, while disregarding the UN Charter and the norms of international

---

6. On this, see Paul D'Anieri, "Reforming the Rada: Getting the Funk out of Parliament," *Analysis of Current Events,* 12: 1–2 (January–February 2000).

7. Kuchma's election platform was published in *Ukrayina Moloda* (8 September 1999), and translated for FBIS-SOV, No. 913 (14 September 1999). See also "Leonid Kuchma Speech to the 'Our Choice—Leonid Kuchma' Electoral Bloc," *Uryadovyy Kuryer* (2 September 1999), translated for FBIS-SOV, No. 909 (10 September 1999). For Symonenko's platform, "Narodu ukrayini—gidne zhittia!" [A Good Life for the People of Ukraine!], *Holos Ukrayiny* (31 August 1999).

8. See, for example, "Tarasyuk, 'Zovnishnia popitika mae buti vivazhena i peredbachuvana, a diplomatiia—profesiyna'" [Tarasyuk, "Foreign Policy Should Be Balanced and Predictable, and Diplomacy Should Be Professional], *Holos Ukrayiny* (3 February 1999); and an interview with Tarasyuk, "Brussels Is the Gate to Unified Europe, but It Is Not Easy to Go through It," *Uryadovyy Kuryer* (25 May 1999), translated in FBIS-SOV, No. 428 (1 June 1999).

9. See, especially, Tkachenko, "Tezisy peredvibornoy programi kandidata u prezidenti ukrayni" [Theses from a Presidential Candidate's Pre-election Program], *Holos Ukrayiny* (18 August 1999); and "Zverennia kandidativ u Prezidenti Ukrayni Yevgena Marchuka, Oleksandra Moroza, Volodomira Oliynika, Oleksandra Tkachenka do narodu Ukrayni" [Address to the Ukrainian People by Candidates for President Yevhen Marchuk, Oleksandr Moroz, Volodymyr Oliynyk, and Oleksandr Tkachenko], *Holos Ukrayiny* (26 August 1999).

10. "Shchodo vidnosin Ukrayni i Organizatsiy Pivnichnoatlantichnogo dogovoru (NATO)" [Resolution on the Relations between Ukraine and the Organization of North Atlantic Treaty (NATO)], *Holos Ukrayiny* (27 April 1999).

law and human morality."[10] The Council recommended that the government ma
tain its nonaligned stance, revisit its informal relationships with NATO, submit
agreement with NATO to the Council for approval or rejection, and oppose ¿
NATO action in Yugoslavia outside the mandate provided by the UN. The gove
ment, which like its Russian counterpart is presidential in terms of actual author
ignored this resolution. So Ukraine's position remained frozen somewhere betw
Russia and the West, that is, in the so-called gray zone about which Kuchma and
foreign affairs advisers had expressed great concern throughout 1998–early 1999

The tide actually began to change after the Ukrainian presidential election. E
as the Ukrainian population and the opposition parties raged against NATO's act
in Yugoslavia and generally supported Russia's battle against "international terrori
in Chechnya, Kiev signed a plan for extensive cooperation with NATO to the y
2001 (ITAR-TASS, 15 December 1999). Simultaneously, Tarasyuk attended a re
lar meeting of the Ukraine–NATO Commission in Brussels and arranged coope
tion in military affairs—disarmament, conversion to peaceful uses, emergency sit
tion, and peacekeeping. The Commission had been created in May 1997, wl
Ukraine signed a "Distinctive Partnership" with NATO.

The left had not taken decisive advantage of the Yugoslavia windfall and, thou
it remained a major player in Ukrainian politics, could not prevent Ukrainian in
gration with NATO agencies from expanding beyond a point of no return. Ukra
ian troops had taken part in 469 Partnership for Peace events between 1994–
even though it had not formally joined the PfP until May 1996. This participat
included major exercises, such as the Sea-Breeze maneuvers on the Black Sea, wh
greatly angered Russia, and made it possible for NATO forces to use the Yavoriv r
itary testing grounds in the L'vov region, another decision that infuriated Russ
veteran and nationalist groups.[11] Altogether, Ukraine agreed to some 200 joint
tivities with NATO for the year 2000 alone.

Each Ukrainian step closer to NATO invoked anger in the Russia media.[12]
1–2 March 2000, the North Atlantic Council (NAC), NATO's nineteen-mem
ambassador-level decision-making body, gathered in Kiev. This was the first N
meeting on the territory of a non-NATO member. Robertson and Tarasyuk m:
a point of saying publicly that Ukrainian membership in NATO was not on
agenda, and that it would not be so in the near future. But these remarks did
tle to ease the Kremlin's concern. Russian ambassador to Ukraine, Ivan Aboim
commented that Russia was watching the situation closely and referred to all ty
of NATO expansion as "anti-Russia" behavior. There was little doubt in Mosc
that NATO's decision to meet in Kiev challenged Putin's new assertiveness in f
eign affairs. Putin's famous comment a few days later that Russia itself might ev
tually join NATO may well have been driven by a perception that the NA

---

11. See *Russia Faces NATO Expansion*, pp. 178–84, 186ff.
12. See, for example, Viktor Timoshenko, "Novye kontakty Ukrainy i NATO" [New Ukrainian C
tacts with NATO], *Nezavisimaia gazeta* (9 February 2000), and Andrei Dneprov, "Kiev prinimaet s
NATO" [Kiev Joins the NATO Council], *Nezavisimaia gazeta* (18 February 2000).

meeting in Ukraine was calculated to influence the upcoming Russian presidential election.[13]

The level of distrust of Ukraine among Russia's officials mounted steadily during the winter of 2000. A Russian Public Policy Center poll of officials and bureaucrats in February saw nearly 88 percent provide negative responses to questions about Ukraine's policy towards Russia. Highest among the reasons given for a clearly negative opinion of Ukraine was "the further deepening of Ukraine's cooperation with NATO" (84 percent). Other problems included the status of the Black Sea Fleet and Sevastopol, problematic border control between the two countries, and the standing of native Russian-speaking citizens in Ukraine.[14] The last-named source of animosity was to grow in significance.

Meanwhile, on 1 March 2000 NATO and Ukraine signed an agreement on the Status of Foreign Armies (SOFA) on Ukrainian territory, providing legal protection for foreign troops. The next day, the Ukrainian parliament ratified a new PfP agreement, plus an extra protocol which purported to upgrade the quality of joint military exercises, fund the retraining of officers, formalize access to Yavoriv, and channel NATO funds into the training of members of Ukraine's armed forces. This event was a clear victory for Tarasyuk. The Russian government press handled the redefined Ukraine–NATO relationship with greater aplomb than previously, noting that President Kuchma took care not to alienate Russia while his country was nurturing links to NATO.[15] In fact, Kuchma was "out of town" on vacation during the NATO meetings, delegating Tarasyuk to read his speech of welcome. The Ukrainian president was quoted in the Russian press saying that he wished to keep on good terms with both NATO and Russia, but his failure to reiterate Ukraine's long-standing promise (and constitutional requirement) to avoid bloc alignments was noted as well.[16] The Ukraine–NATO Commission post-meeting statement had at least one note of which Moscow would approve. It included a reaffirmation of their commitment to UNSCR 1244 as the basis for a "democratic and multiethnic Kosovo within the FRY."[17]

All such statements aside, the NAC meeting in Kiev marked a watershed in Russia–Ukraine relations, and gave nationalists in both Ukraine and Russia a target to rail at. The new agreements with NATO called for still more joint maneuvers, including participation in the Cooperative Partner-2000 exercise planned for the Black

13. A spokesman for Ukraine's foreign ministry took the opportunity to say that Russia, of course, has the right to act in its own interests, and that Ukraine, too, might apply for membership in NATO "when the time comes and circumstances are favorable." Kiev Internews (8 March 2000).

14. See Valeriy Chaly, Mykhail Pashkov, "Ukraine's International Image: The View from Russia," *National Security & Defence* [Kiev], No. 3 (2000), 60–67.

15. See, for example, Viktor Timoshenko, "NATO sobralas' v Kieve" [NATO Met in Kiev], *Nezavisimaia gazeta* (1 March 2000).

16. See, for example, Ivanna Gorina, "Ukraina v seroi zone. Nash partner po SNG pytaetsia dogovorit'sia s NATO. No i ne rassorit'sia s Rossiei" [Ukraine in the Gray Zone: Our CIS Partner Tries to Reach Agreement with NATO and Not Split with Russia]. *Rossiiskaia gazeta* (3 March 2000); Yanina Sokolovskaia, "Ukrainskii bufer" [Ukrainian Buffer], *Izvestiia* (2 March 2000).

17. "NATO–Ukraine Commission Statement" (1 March 2000), NATO Website (1 March 2000).

Sea on 19–30 June.[18] Viktor Timoshenko, a *Nezavisimaia gazeta* writer known
his dislike of Ukraine's westward leanings, claimed that NATO now had a new "p
form" in Kiev for intervention in the CIS.[19]

Moscow took notice as well of a groundswell of antagonism towards things R
sian sponsored by a cross-section of Ukrainian nationalist groups while celebrat
the 186th anniversary of the birth of Taras Shevchenko. "Anti-Russian" incidents l
been growing in Ukraine since 1999 and this had been remarked upon by the l
man rights commissioner in Moscow, Oleg Mironov, who complained to inter
tional human rights agencies in February that forced restriction of Russian
Ukraine was "a gross and explicit violation of the norms of civilized relations amo
people."[20] Other Moscow analysts treated the language crisis as an attempt by
tionalists in Ukraine to steal the political agenda from centrists by using Russian:
a scapegoat.[21] Moscow's ministry of foreign affairs also lodged official protests. l
the intensity of the dispute was highlighted in the Russian media when, on 9 Mar
a small group of eleven young Ukrainian nationalists, members of Samosti
Ukraine, occupied the Communist Party building in Kiev for a day, calling it a he
quarters of Russian communist imperialism in Ukraine. In L'vov, Western Ukrai
demonstrators picketed the mayor's office demanding that all Russian language p
lications be banned from schools and public libraries.

A few days later, Rukh Party leader Hennadiy Udovenko called on the mayor
Odessa to hand over office space used by the communists to the Rukh regional pa
saying that "we cannot forget crimes committed by the communists" against Ukra
ans (Internews, 13 March 2000). The language crisis was still attracting the attent
of Russia's communist press in April, when *Sovetskaia Rossiia* published an essay
the subject already submitted to, and rejected by, several Ukrainian newspapers.
author was Yurii Solomatin, a Russophile deputy in the Ukrainian parliament.[22]

Moscow was not about to give up on Ukraine, where, not surprisingly, many
the opinions on world affairs held by Russians were shared. Polls conducted by

18. A "show-down" was predicted by the author(s) of "Finally, NATO Tests a Resurgent Russia-
Kiev," Stratfor.Com Global Intelligence Update (2 March 2000).

19. Viktor Timoshenko, "NATO poluchila poligon v SNG" [NATO Received a Platform into
CIS], *Nezavisimaia gazeta* (3 March 2000).

20. Mironov also said that the "scale of language discrimination [in Ukraine] is mass and unpr
dented," ITAR-TASS (10 February 2000). See also Aleksandr Sokov, "Derusifikatsiia v deistvii—MID
protestuet protiv deistvii ofitsial'nogo Kieva" [Derussification at Work—Ministry of Foreign Af
Protests the Action of Kiev Officials], *Nezavisimaia gazeta* (4 February 2000); and Fedor Olegov,
grani 'lingvisticheskoi voiny.'" [On the Brink of "Linguistic War"], *Nezavisimaia gazeta* (16 Febr
2000). For an earlier piece on this issue, see Yuliia Kantor, "Russkii yazyk v Kieve—kraeugol'nyi kar
pretknoveniia" [Russian Language in Kiev, a Fundamental Stumbling Block], *Izvestiia* (4 August 199

21. See, for example, Ivanna Gorina, "Kak eto budet po-russki" [What This Would Be in Russi
Rossiiskaia gazeta (12 February 2000).

22. See Solomatin, "Dva pis'ma iz Kieva. 'Vimknit' tretii mikrokhvon', ili Zagonim russkii yaz
kurilki i tualety Verkhovnoi Rady Ukrainy" [Two letters from Kiev. Let's Leave Russian for Smoking
eas and Washrooms of Rada], *Sovetskaia Rossiia* (1 April 2000). Solomatin also is the head of a Kiev o
Society for Russian Culture, *Kievskaia Rus'*. The second letter was from Mikhail Koreichuk, of the "/
lytical center, *Russkaia obshchina*, in Kiev.

Ukraine Centre for Economic and Political Studies (UCEPS), a nonprofit public organization in Kiev, showed that in the winter some 46 percent of citizens surveyed had seen NATO as an aggressive military bloc.[23] Organizers of the survey attributed this response, up nearly 30 percent over a similar poll conducted in 1997, equally to the specific act of bombing Yugoslavia and to the more general consideration of NATO's interference in the affairs of a sovereign nation. Half of the respondents said that Ukraine should never join NATO, and slightly less than a quarter said that it should join within the next five to ten years. Nearly half had an unfavorable opinion of NATO enlargement.

As he was to do elsewhere, Putin took a direct hand in easing tensions. His first trip abroad after his election victory was to Kiev, where he and Kuchma agreed that they must settle their bilateral problems. These included Ukraine's huge debt for Russian gas, an obligation that Moscow was quite willing to hold over Kiev's head. In March, for example, Kuchma had complained that Russian pressure was such that it was driving Ukraine to look for alternate energy supplies, perhaps directly from Azerbaijan, one of its partners in the GUUAM.[24] Russia claimed that Ukraine owed about $3 billion, whereas Ukraine admitted to "only" about $1 billion. In either case, it was a lot of money. On 18 April, the two presidents agreed on continuous personal contact and told reporters that they had reached consensus on most issues, among them the gas problem, free trade, broad security issues, and human rights questions. Consultations on military–technical cooperation were scheduled and Russia agreed to consider supplying nuclear fuel to Ukraine.[25]

Like Putin, Kuchma came to these talks in a stronger position at home than he had been previously. On 16 April, he had been victorious by wide margins in a four-question referendum strengthening the presidency against a potentially militant parliament. In a 79-percent voter turnout (29 million), 85 percent agreed that the president should have the right to disband parliament if it did not approve the budget within three months; 89 percent said that deputies should not enjoy immunity; 90 percent called for the reduction of seats from 450 to 300; and 87 percent approved the idea of a bicameral parliament. Bilateral relations could therefore be worked out by two strongly entrenched presidents. Yet even their concerted efforts would not make certain disputes fade away.

The NATO question had not gone unnoticed during the visit. In Sevastopol, Putin told officers of the Black Sea Fleet, on the 18th, that Russia still objected strongly to further NATO expansion towards Russia's borders. He was hosted by Fleet Com-

23. Andriy Bychenko, Leonid Polyakov, "How Much of NATO Do Ukrainians Want?" *National Security & Defence,* No. 8 (August 2000), 13–14. The poll was conducted by UCEPS, 25 January–5 February 2000; 2,010 citizens were surveyed.

24. See Asia Gadzhizade, "Kuchma rezko kritikuet Rossiiu" [Kuchma Sharply Criticizes Russia], *Nezavisimaia gazeta* (18 March 2000). On the GUUAM (Georgia, Ukraine, Uzbekistan, Azerbaijan, and Moldova), see Chapter 10.

25. See ITAR-TASS, Interfax-Ukraine, and RF Embassy in Ottawa press releases (17–18 April 2000); Ivanna Gorina, "Tri vizita—tsel' odna" [Three Visits—One Goal. Vladimir Putin Actively Upholding Russia's National Interests. "Hello, Kiev!"], *Rossiiskaia gazeta* (18 April 2000).

mander Vladimir Komoedov, who had just prepared a long essay on Ukraine's fin
cial debt to the fleet and called for a revision of the 1997 treaty that divided the fl
The fact that the essay appeared in the Russian government newspaper just a few d
before Putin's arrival implies that its timely appearance was no coincidence.[26]

There were other sources of friction that could not be ignored. Asked by Russ
journalists about Chechen information centers in Ukraine, Kuchma answered t
there were none, though he acknowledged that a radical right-wing group had b
trying to give Chechens some assistance. According to the Ukrainian president,
ministry of justice had the situation well in hand. Russian reporters tended to t
this response with scorn, asking how Kuchma could possibly not know of what t
believed were extensive anti-Russian, pro-Chechen organizations operating ope
under the rubric "Free Caucasus." Putin's conciliatory approach did little to dispel
trust of Kiev among Moscow's fifth estate.[27] Radical nationalist Viktor Anpilov, for
ample, blamed all anti-Russian activities in Ukraine on the machinations of NA'
and the United States.[28] A long interview with President Kuchma in the Russian p
didn't help much. While repeating his position that Moscow and Kiev must be str
gic partners in all sectors, Kuchma irritated readers by attributing failures within
CIS to Russian imperial ambitions, or at least the specter of them.[29] His ambigu
stance was seen by many as a main obstacle in the way of improved relations.

Continued sporadic anti-Russian demonstrations in Ukraine kept the Russ
media busy accounting for what they called a virulent anti-Russian mood in t
country. To cite but one case, at the end of May thousands of demonstrators in L'
chanted "Down with Russians" and demanded that all Russians be expelled from
country. This particular group was protesting the death of a Ukrainian folk cc
poser, Ihor Bilozir, who was killed in a brawl, apparently with Russian-speaking
itors. Within the next few weeks, the L'vov city and oblast councils separately enac
resolutions limiting the use of the Russian language within their jurisdictic
Moscow's State Duma Committee for Nationalities Affairs retaliated by accus
Ukrainian nationalists of whipping up "anti-Russian hysteria."[30]

Ukrainian linguistic nationalists had their Russian counterparts, of course. In S
tember and October, demonstrators in several Ukrainian cities lobbied for Russ

---

26. Komoedov, "Dlia nas igraet Sevastopol'skii val's" [Sevastopol Waltz Is Playing for Us], *Rossiis.
gazeta* (14 April 2000). See also an earlier interview with Komoedov conducted by Natal'ia Aipapet
"Chernomorskii flot gotov vypolnit' liubuiu zadachu" [The Black Sea Fleet Is Prepared to Fulfill
Task], *Nezavisimaia gazeta* (8 March 2000).
27. See, for example, Ivanna Gorina, "Chego ne znaet prezident Ukrainy" [What the Ukrainian P
dent Does Not Know], *Rossiiskaia gazeta* (20 April 2000). The centers, apparently, were linked
Ukrainian nationalist group, the Ukrainian People's Self-Defense (UNSO) and its associate organizat
the Ukrainian National Assembly (UNA).
28. Anpilov, "Gogol' po ukrainski . . ." [Gogol in Ukrainian], *Sodruzhestvo NG*, No. 4 (26 April 20
29. For a description, see Aleksandr Maksimov, "Kto khochet postavit' Ukrainu na koleni?" [\
Wants Ukraine to Force Ukraine to Its Knees?], *Sodruzhestvo NG*, No.5 (31 May 2000).
30. See also Aleksei Popov, "Russkii yazyk pod zashchitoi evropeiskoi khartii. Mnogim v Kieve et
nravitsia" [The Russian Language Is Defended by the European Charter. Many in Kiev Are Not Ple
by This], *Sodruzhestvo NG*, No. 6 (28 June 2000).

to be given official status in certain areas: Kharkov, Luhansk, Donetsk, and Zaporizhzhya. The Nationalists in Russia were angered as well by Ukrainian participation in the Cooperative Partner-2000 naval exercises on the Black Sea, 19 June to 1 July, just as the earlier Sea Breeze projects had infuriated Russians, especially ethnic Russians living in Crimea. To demonstrate its disapproval, MoD authorities turned down an invitation to take part in the version of Sea Breeze scheduled for 2000, though they sent observers to the land phase of the operation. In its turn, Ukraine signed none of the military-defense protocols agreed to by most of the heads of state at the Moscow CIS summit in June, although Kiev did agree to various protocols on free trade.

A land-based component of the PfP exercise, Peace Shield-2000, wound down on 19 July, on the same day that Ukrainian Prime Minister Yushchenko completed a one-day working visit to Moscow. According to official reports, his four-hour meeting with Kasyanov went well, though no accord was reached on the Ukrainian gas debt. Within a few days, the Kremlin protested to a Kiev–Warsaw agreement that Moscow would not be allowed to construct a gas pipeline across Polish territory to Slovakia, bypassing Ukraine.

The same week had witnessed angry public accusations by officials from both countries. Ambassador Aboimov had taken the unusual step of accusing bureaucrats in Kiev of encouraging anti-Russian sentiment. The Ukrainian foreign ministry denied the allegation and retaliated by charging its Moscow counterpart with conducting anti-Ukrainian propaganda.[31] One consequence of this bickering was the formation of an interfaction group of deputies in Ukraine's parliament calling themselves "For the Union of Ukraine, Belarus and Russia" (ZUBR). Pavlo Baulin, a deputy from Zaporizhzhya, told journalists that his country had become a "socioeconomic disaster zone" because of its pro-West policy. He and his eighteen colleagues in ZUBR urged fellow deputies to link their "destiny with orthodox-Slav statehood" (ITAR-TASS, 22 July). In this, they echoed diatribes from Russian nationalist spokesmen such as R.V. Manekin, who blamed Ukrainian extremists and "Anglo-Saxon" duplicity for the wrong-headedness of any Ukrainian preference for NATO and the West over Russia.[32]

These events brought the question of Ukraine's association with NATO, which had been relatively dormant in Russia for a while, back into the media. Dmitrii Danilov, director of the European security division of the Russian Academy of Sciences' Institute of Europe, wrote that Kiev's indecisiveness on NATO expansion greatly complicated Moscow's decision making on security matters.[33] The issue was made more complex in August, when Washington threatened to stop financing

---

31. For a long essay by a Russian who travelled to L'viv to test the degree of anti-Russia feeling there, see Vadim Rechkalov, "Puteshestvie katsapa" [Trip of a Katsap (a Russian)], *Obshchaia gazeta*, No. 32 (10–16 August 2000). He found lots of it, he said.

32. Manekin, "Ukraina i Rossia. Chto delat'" [Ukraine and Russia. What to Be Done], *Russkaia mysl*, No. 6 (2000).

33. Dmitrii Danilov, "Kiev na rasput'e" [Kiev at a Crossroad], *NVO*, No. 26 (21–27 July 2000). See also Danilov's, "Ukraine's Co-Operation with NATO: Are There Any Grounds for Concern? A View from Moscow," *National Security & Defence* (Kiev), No. 8 (2000), 58–63.

nuclear disarmament in Ukraine if that country continued to send nuclear capa
bombers to Russia to help pay off its huge debt. Ukraine had been doing this for t
years, trading eleven bombers and approximately 700 cruise missiles in 1999
some $285 million in debt forgiveness. But an offer of ten more bombers in J
2000, caused the American government to withdraw some $7 million from the (
operative Threat Reduction Program it had with Ukraine.[34] Ukraine was in an av
ward position here. As the third-largest recipient of American financial assista
(behind Israel and Egypt), it could not afford to alienate Washington. Still, Ukra
continued its sensitive trade-offs with Russia.

Ukraine's growing links with Poland, a NATO country, also was reason for c
cern in Moscow, albeit a mostly watchful and resigned concern before 4 Septem
2000. On that date, Ukraine and Lithuania concluded an agreement on a coope
tive military structure, an act prompting Russian conspiracy theorists to see a Pol
hand in the background.[35] The actual agreement, signed in Vilnius, was rela
strictly to structural matters, and included consultation in the area of democr:
control over the armed forces, peacekeeping practices, and the establishment of a
sis for financing and planning. These circumstances did not allay MoD suspicior

Warsaw was more obviously central to the question of a gas pipeline to Eur
transitting Poland and bypassing Ukraine. A meeting in Paris on 29 August betw
Gazprom officials and Europe's four largest natural-gas distributors had reopened
matter. At that time, close to 90 percent of Gazprom's supplies to Europe cros
Ukrainian territory, so the loss to Russia of gas siphoned off in Ukraine had im
cations for Europe's supplies. The cost of a new pipeline via Belarus and Pol:
would have to be borne by the European companies, for Gazprom had insuffici
investment capital of its own.[36] As we have seen, energy resources from Russia w
increasingly in demand in Europe. So Moscow could afford to wait this one out.

A poorly thought-out, politically at least, NATO–Ukraine training exercise,
gravated the situation between Moscow and Kiev in September. Called Coss
Steppe-2000 and conducted in eastern Crimea, it was based on a scenario of an "e
nic rebellion in an eastern republic." A Ukrainian ministry of defense description i
plied that its forces were being trained to defend Ukrainian independence from R
sians. The MoD called it provocative.[38] Just as the Cossack Steppe military exer
concluded, another, called Transcarpathia-2000, got under way. Emphasizing en

---

34. The "threat" was proffered by Steven Pifer, U.S. Ambassador to Ukraine, on 7 August. On this
Stratfor.Alert Global Intelligence Update (11 August 2000). The bombers in question included Tu-
Blackjack heavy bombers.

35. See for example, "Protiv kogo druzhit' budem?" [Against Whom Will We Be Friends?], *NVO*,
33 (8–14 September 2000).

36. Gazprom supplies all of Russia with natural gas at much lower than world prices and cannot a
mulate large amounts of money for infrastructure investment, or so it claims.

37. For a discussion of this matter, see "Europe Hands Ukraine to Russia." *Stratfor.Alert* Global Ir
ligence Update (30 August 2000).

38. See, for example, Viktor Timoshenko, "Provodiatsia voennye manevry s provokatsionn
tseliami" [Military Maneuvers Conducted with Provocative Goals], *NVO*, No. 34 (15–21 Septen
2000). The Ukrainian paper referred to was *Flot Ukrainy*.

gency measures, for example, in times of serious flooding, this Ukraine-based program included twelve countries, almost all of them former Soviet republics or Warsaw Pact members, but excluded Russia.[39] Training sessions such as these fueled charges and countercharges pushing the two largest Slavic states along a collision course driven by small but vocal minorities on both sides.[40]

A bit of a break came Russia's way in late September, when Ukrainian Foreign Minister Borys Tarasyuk was dismissed by a Kuchma decree. Almost any replacement for Tarasyuk would have been received well in Moscow, but the appointment a few days later of Anatoliy Zlenko, former foreign minister and ambassador to both the UN and France, was especially welcomed. The sudden turn towards Moscow, if that is what it was, moved Moscow-based analysts to predict a much-improved relationship with Kiev.[41] Certainly, the "one less Westerner" approach taken by an editorial commentator illustrated the mood of observers in Ukraine who looked more to the East than to the West.[42]

Putin and Kuchma moved quickly to smooth the way for closer relations. A meeting of the two presidents in Sochi, set up primarily to discuss the Ukrainian gas debt, resulted in some guidelines being set for payments and for Russia's participation in Ukraine's gas transit network. In addition to Russia's natural-gas imports to Europe that pass through Ukraine, much of Turkmenistan's exports cross Ukrainian and Russian territory, making a coordinated transit policy important to the development of an economic partnership between the two largest Slavic nations. There were no quick solutions, however. Kuchma took exception to the almost simultaneous establishment of the Eurasian Economic Community (see chapter 10), complaining that it could spell the end of the CIS, especially as Russia still dragged its feet on a CIS free-trade zone.[43] On the other hand, some Russian columnists, many of whom prematurely claimed Russian "victory" in the "gas war," foresaw Ukraine becoming an associate of the Eurasian Economic Community because up to 40 percent of Ukraine's foreign trade is with Russia, Belarus, Kazakhstan and Tajikistan, four of its members.[44] Certainly, Kuchma made it plain that he wanted to improve Ukraine's

---

39. Hungary, Georgia, Belarus, Moldova, Slovakia, Poland, Romania, Slovenia, Sweden, Switzerland, Croatia and Ukraine.

40. "Ukraina i Rossiia: porozn' ili vmeste?" [Ukraine and Russia: Separately or Together?], *Nezavisimaia gazeta* (16 September 2000); see also statements by Stepan Gavrish, deputy speaker of the Ukraine Supreme Council, who stressed the commonalities between Russians and Ukrainians, *Nezavisimaia gazeta* (13 September 2000).

41. On this, see feature by Iryna Kutsyma in *Fakti i kommentari* [Kiev] (29 September 2000), translated by BBC Monitoring Service (2 October 2000). See also Gleb Parfenov, "Ukraina povorachivaetsia k Rossii" [Ukraine Makes a Turn towards Russia], *Ekspert,* No. 39 (16 October 2000). For Tarasyuk's opinions on Ukraine–NATO relations, see an interview with him in *Nezavisimaia gazeta* (16 May 2000).

42. Svetlana Stepanenko, "Odnim zapadnik ot men'she. Prezident Ukrainy uvoli 'druga' NATO" [One Westerner Less. President Kuchma releases a "Friend" of NATO], *Vremia novostei* (2 October 2000).

43. See, for example, Aleksei Popov, "Vsemirnyi bank i NATO 'idut v narod'" [The World Bank and NATO "Go to the People"], *Nezavisimaia gazeta* (12 October 2000); *Kommersant* (12 October 2000).

44. Aleksei Chichkin, "Vzamen pretenzii—kompromissy" [Compromise in Place of Complaints], *Rossiiskaia gazeta* (18 October 2000); Yekaterina Tesemnikov, "Kiev i Tashkent prodolzhaiut sblizhenie" [Kiev and Tashkent Continue to Merge], *Nezavisimaia gazeta* (14 October 2000), where it was said that Kiev was strongly opposed to the EEC.

relations with Russia, especially in the economic sector.[45] There was even so
muted discussion by political observers that the question of Ukraine joining
Russia–Belarus Union might be revisited.[46]

Poland's decision to negotiate pipeline transit with Gazprom and West Europ·
gas distributors (see chapter 3) put more pressure on Ukraine. Warsaw offered sol
by suggesting that Ukraine be involved in the project in some way, perhaps in a jc
venture, and insisting that the new pipeline not carry gas normally transit
Ukraine. The EU's decision in October to more than double its purchases of
from Russia and the need for a secure route through Poland had persuaded t
country to reconsider its earlier boast that it would protect Ukraine's interests at
costs. Ukraine attempted to resolve its own energy problems. A delegation was s
to Iraq, where an embassy was opened and negotiations under the UN-approved '
in exchange for food" program were started. Kiev also hoped for gas from Tu
menistan. Russian commentators were convinced, however, that Gazprom still h
the winning hand in this contest, noting that Turkmenistan would not prov
Ukraine with natural gas if it was not paid for, and that in the long run Poland ·
likely to be swayed by European energy concerns.[47] Direct negotiations betw·
Russian, Polish and European gas companies were set to open on 4 November 20

Shortly after the Putin–Kuchma meeting at Sochi, Foreign Ministers Ivanov ;
Zlenko hosted a press conference in which they outlined their areas of agreement ;
disagreement. Zlenko was in Moscow, where he was received by President Putin,
the purpose of fleshing out agreements related to border control, the legal statu;
the Sea of Azov and the Kerch Strait, and the Black Sea Fleet. A new concorda
was signed on cooperation in the field of television and radio broadcasting. Wl
congratulating themselves on this latter development, both foreign ministers
dressed somewhat testily the as-yet-unresolved issues of the cultural security of R
sians living in Ukraine, and Ukrainians living in Russia. Zlenko, for example, cc
plained about the "large amount of negative coverage" of Ukraine in the Russ
media. "Rude rhetoric," he called it, saying nothing about the realities of regulati·
restricting the use of Russian-language radio programming and newspaper circu
tion, raising the ire in Russia even of the normally temperate *Obshchaia gazeta*.
ferring to high taxes levied against newspapers published in Russia and sold

---

45. See, for example, Aleksei Popov, "Zigzagi ukrainskoi diplomatii" [Zigzags of Ukrainian Di
macy], *Nezavisimaia gazeta* (10 October 2000), and Viktor Timoshenko, Natal'ia Peroverta, " 'N
men'she ezdit v evropu'. Leonid Kuchma prizval chinovnikov po utran dumat' o Rossii," ["The Less
Travel to Europe the Better." Leonid Kuchma Calls on Officials to Think of Russia in the Mornir
Nezavisimaia gazeta (1 November 2000).

46. See, for example, Viktor Timoshenko, Liudmila Romanova, " 'Vsia pogoda delaetsia v Kremle' "
Weather Is Made in the Kremlin], *Nezavisimaia gazeta* (17 October 2000) and Alla Yaz'kov, "Ukrai
Rossiia: porozn' ili vmeste?" [Ukraine and Russia: Separately or Together?], *Nezavisimaia gazeta* (14
tober 2000).

47. See, for example, Sergei Pravosudov, Denis Prokopenko, " 'Gazprom' nadeetsia oboiti Ukra
[Gazprom Hopes to Go Around Ukraine], *Nezavisimaia gazeta* (20 October 2000); Aleksei Po
"Zigzagi ukrainskoi diplomatii" [Zigzags in Ukrainian Diplomacy], *ibid.*; E. I. Urinovskii, "Kuda t·
'golubye' reki" [Where Do the "Blue" Rivers Flow], *Sovetskaia Rossiia* (19 October 2000).

Ukraine, the Russian government press accused Kiev of declaring a "holy war" against the Russian language.[48] Prime Minister Yushchenko denied that there was discrimination against Russian-language speakers in Ukraine, listing to the media in Kiev the large number of schools, universities, theaters, periodical literature, and even newspapers that still functioned in Russian.[49] The issue continued to cause rage on both sides, even as some Ukrainian parliamentary deputies such as Boris Oliynyk, member of the European Parliament's committee on culture, tried to find a middle road. In an essay published in both Russian and Ukrainian, he categorically rejected the "dangerous slogan 'Ukraine only for Ukrainians' as racist," but insisted as well that Ukraine must be sovereign and that its language was central to achieving that end.[50]

The language issue aside, at the government level Russian–Ukrainian relations were much improved. Yushchenko flew to Moscow in mid-November to meet with Kasyanov. Both prime ministers insisted that they wanted to stop the decline in trade between their countries, and Yushchenko reiterated the Kuchma position that Russia was Ukraine's top priority as "partner."[51] Foreign Minister Ivanov replied in kind, with a long paper titled "Russia and Ukraine: On the Way to a Strategic Partnership."[52] The energy question was the one most in need of a quick fix, Yushchenko said, making it clear both that he was open to compromise and that access to energy resources was vital to Ukraine's survival as an independent country. A turning point was reached a week later when, after further Kuchma–Putin conversations in Minsk, Russia deferred the Ukrainian gas debt for ten years.[53]

Not to be outdone by Ivanov, Zlenko prepared a statement of his own on Ukrainian–Russian relations. Published in both Russian and Ukrainian newspapers, Zlenko's treatise echoed his Russian counterpart's article, but from the vantage point of Kiev. He saw the recent meetings between their respective presidents and prime ministers

---

48. Ivanna Gorina, "Kiev ob'iavil voinu rossiiskoi presse" [Kiev Has Declared War on the Russian Press], *Rossiiskaia gazeta* (27 October 2000). See, also Elena Glagoleva, "Ukrainskaia vendetta. Kiev izgoniaet rossiiskuiu pressu" [Ukrainians Vendetta. Kiev Exiles Russian Press], *Obshchaia gazeta,* No. 43 (26 October–1 November 2000), and "Press Conference with Minister of Foreign Affairs of the Russian Federation Igor Ivanov and Minister of Foreign Affairs of Ukraine Anatoliy Zlenko," Embassy of the Russian Federation in Canada, *News Release* (23 October 2000).

See also Taras Kuzio, "Giving Substance to the Ukrainian–Russian 'Strategic Partnership,'" *RFE/RL Newsline,* 4: 26, Pt. II (7 November 2000).

49. See "Yushchenko Denies Discrimination Against Russian Speakers," *RFE/RL Poland, Belarus and Ukraine Report,* 2: 40 (31 October 2000).

50. See Oliynyk, "Kto nami pravit?" [Who Rules Us?], *Sovetskaia Rossiia* (23 December 2000). See also Igor Guzhva, Dmitrii Kornilov, "Kogo Rossiia zashchishchaet na Ukraine? [Whom Does Russia Defend in Ukraine?], *Sodruzhestvo NG,* No. 10 (29 November 200).

51. See an interview with Yevgenii Marchuk, Secretary of Ukraine's Council of National Defense and Security, conducted by Viktor Timoshenko, "Moskva i Kiev ostaiutsia strategicheskimi partnerami" [Moscow and Kiev Remain Strategic Partners], *Nezavisimaia gazeta* (14 November 2000).

52. Ivanov, "Rossiia i Ukraina. Na puti k strategicheskomu partnerstvu" [Russia and Ukraine: On the Way to a Strategic Partnership], *Rossiiskaia gazeta* (25 November 2000).

53. See, for example, Viktor Timoshenko, "Yushchenko vydvinul ul'timatum i ostavil zaveshchanie" [Yushchenko Sent an Ultimatum and Left a Testament], *Nezavisimaia gazeta* (28 November 2000); and Aleksei Chichkin, "Ukraina soglasilas' platit' i den'gami, i imushchestvom" [Ukraine Agrees to Pay in Both Money and Property], *Rossiiskaia gazeta* (7 December 2000). The meeting took place on 1 December.

as singularly constructive, and pointed out that in foreign affairs, positions taker
Moscow and Kiev were generally much closer than usually is assumed—even
Black Sea Fleet question posed fewer problems than previously thought. "Destr
tive rhetoric" was blamed for the difficulties related to each other's diaspora, but i
appeared to be the only stumbling block in the way of a lasting "strategic partr
ship" based on pragmatism.[54]

Kuchma fairly gushed on 21–22 December as he and Putin met in St. Petersb
and signed the final memorandum on the gas question, claiming that Russi̇
Ukrainian relations had improved in all sectors. Long-term defense cooperation '
agreed upon as well, but Kuchma's credibility was badly scarred when he was accu
of arranging to have a journalist, Georgii Gongadze, kidnapped. Demonstrati·
against Kuchma took place throughout the country, and Ukrainian nationalists t·
advantage of the moment to accuse the president of catering to the Russians.[55]

Although all mutual difficulties had not been solved, Russia's improved relati·
with Ukraine was one of the high points of Putin's first year as president. This '
in keeping with priorities set out in Russia's new Foreign Policy Concept, in wh
the CIS had been placed on top of the list.

There was a blip on the screen early in 2001. Kuchma's momentary disgrace n
have made it easier for the Ukrainian ministry of communications to go out o
limb and order all television and radio channels to broadcast only in Ukrainian. 1
Russian response was quick and angry, even though it was obvious that many l·
broadcasters would ignore the order anyway.

The sudden outburst of ill will did not prevent meetings in Kiev between defe
ministers Igor Sergeev and Oleksandr Kuz'muk. Unprecedented joint agreements
over fifty land, air and sea operations were signed, and they agreed to disagree
NATO expansion.[56] Scattered but loud protest against any defense association w
Russia from Ukrainian nationalist groups (for example, Shchyt batkivshch·
[Shield of the Motherland]), failed to slow the process.[57] The outburst of bad p
licity also overshadowed a Kuchma order that his prime minister intensify
Ukraine–Russia relationship in light of the 22 December agreements (Interfax,
January), especially in matters of trade and industrial cooperation.

Cooperation between the two governments expanded on all fronts. Putin ȧ
Kuchma sat down together in Dnipropetrovsk on 11–12 February, and reache
consensus in the areas of aerospace and defense. More immediately, they agreed
setting a framework for parallel electrical grids.[58] A few days later, Zlenko and l

---

54. Zlenko, "Kazhdoe vremia umno po-svoemu" [There Is a Right Time for Everything], *Rossiis.
gazeta* (16 December 2000); *Zerkalo nedeli* (16 December 2000).

55. For Russian accounts, see, for example, Sergei Vlasov, "Nastupit li moment istiny" [Will the ·
ment of Truth Come?], *Sovetskaia Rossiia* (16 December 2000).

56. On this, see Igor Korotchenko, "Vo imia natsional'nykh interesov" [In the Name of National
terests], *NVO*, No. 3 (26 January–1 February 2001).

57. See, for example, Serhiy Chornous, "Commentary on Igor Sergeev's Visit to Ukraine," *Ukra̱
Moloda* (20 January 2001), translated for FBIS-SOV, No. 0131 (1 February 2001).

58. On this, see Chichkin, "Rossiia–Ukraina: Soshlis' na edinoi elektrotsepi" [Russia–Ukraine. Part
on the Same Electric Grid], *Rossiiskaia gazeta* (14 February 2001).

Ivanov met in Kharkov to discuss border cooperation with leaders of the Russian and Ukrainian border states. A consensus was reached on trade and joint enterprises. Zlenko spoke enthusiastically about Russia, Poland and the United States as Ukraine's strategic partners.

Further agreements were reached in April when Yushchenko flew to Moscow to discuss threats of anti-dumping legislation against the export of Ukrainian pipes to Russia. A deal was worked out, though Ukrainian analysts accused Moscow of using "dirty tricks" and ultimata.[59] Further reconciliation with Ukraine was foreseen in Russia, although everyone was aware that the political crisis in which Kuchma still found himself could compromise the relationship. The Ukrainian president's popularity sank precipitously and the split among Ukrainians over their government's inclination towards East or West intensified. Conspiracy theories abounded. Kuchma lashed out and accused anti-Russian nationalists in his country of engineering the crisis in which he was embroiled, and the Russian government newspaper charged "U.S. financial circles," naming George Soros, with manipulating the entire affair to gain control of Ukraine's resources.[60] Hysteria seemed to have won the day. On 26 April, however, wealthy industrialists and communists in Ukraine forged an unlikely alliance to force the dismissal two days later of the country's most popular politician, Yushchenko. A no-confidence vote was passed 263–69, demonstrating a clear inclination to the left and a real chill in the Ukraine–U.S. relationship. The IMF already had frozen promised financial assistance, and both the World Bank and the EBRD announced that they would hold off on loans needed for the completion of two Soviet-designed nuclear reactors. It was widely believed that Kuchma had undermined the prime minister privately even as he supported him publicly. Pro-reform forces were, in fact, purged from the government in Kiev and the government.

Ukraine's international standing deteriorated further when the PACE monitoring committee recommended that its membership be suspended. Kuchma again blamed people who "disapprove of our rapprochement with Russia" for the chaos in his country.[61] Russia supported Ukraine when the matter came to a PACE meeting in Strasbourg in early May, making a case against sanctions generally and suggesting openly that an "anti-Ukrainian" movement was encouraged by American anti-Kuchma forces.[62] Yushchenko's dismissal had compounded the political chaos in

---

59. See, for example, *Holos Ukrayiny* (13 April 2001).

60. See, for example, Andrei Grozin, "U amerikantsev svoe pristrastie k ukrainskim galushkam" [Americans Have their own Liking for Ukrainian Dumplings], *Rossiiskaia gazeta* (20 April 2001); Vladimir Bogdanov, "Yugoslavskii variant dlia Ukrainy" [Yugoslavia Scenario for Ukraine], *Rossiiskaia gazeta* (28 April 2001). See also an interview with the Ukrainian president, "Leonid Kuchma: Seichas ne do gitary" [Leonid Kuchma. No Time for Guitars], *Rossiiskaia gazeta* (18 April 2001).

61. "Leonid Kuchma: Seichas ne do gitary" [Leonid Kuchma: No Time for Guitars], *Rossiiskaia gazeta* (18 April 2001).

62. See, for example, Leonid Slutskii, "Bez 'osobykh mnenii'. Moskva podderzhala Kiev"[Without "Special Opinions." Moscow Supports Kiev], *Rossiiskaia gazeta* (4 May 2001). Slutskii, head of the Russian delegation, noted that even human rights activist Sergei Kovalev and Yabloko delegates supported Ukraine on this matter. See also Serhiy Kichihin, editor-in-chief of the Ukrainian Russian-language paper *2000*, whose editorial (11 May 2001) blamed the United States for using human rights issues against Kuchma because they were afraid that he was moving closer to Russia.

Kiev, a situation that Putin took advantage of by posting Viktor Chernomyrdin th
as ambassador on 10 May. The appointment was a sign of Ukraine's importance
Russia and it was widely believed that one of the new envoy's tasks would be to
gotiate a common Russia–Ukraine economic front to raise investment from, a
markets in, the European Union.[63]

Almost at the same time, Kuchma appointed Anatoliy Kinakh, generally seer
"pro-Russian," to the prime minister's post.[64] Chernomyrdin took his post seriou
carrying out long and apparently fruitful discussions with Kinakh, and celebrat
Russia Day (12 June) in Kiev with a much grander gala reception than any of
predecessors had sponsored.[65] The next day, Kinakh addressed an economic for
in St. Petersburg, promising closer economic cooperation between Ukraine, Ru
and the CIS, and expanding the horizon of what already had become the clo;
Moscow–Kiev relationship since the collapse of the USSR.

On the other hand, Ukrainian military personnel were no less active in the I
joining Georgian, Turkish, American and forces from six other countries in the (
operative Partners-2001 exercise on Georgian territory starting on 11 June; and
annual Sea Breeze training sessions opened in July. The fragile Russian–Ukrain
popular rapprochement was jolted anew when a dispute broke out over the pa
visit to Ukraine in June. The Russian Orthodox Church protested that Ortho
Christianity was being betrayed in Ukraine and charged the Vatican with prosely
ing. The dispute was not taken seriously by either government but the media a
public, especially the religious among them, tended to look upon the issue as anot
Ukraine—or at least Western Ukraine—versus Russia affair.[66] Allegations of rest
tions on the Russian language in the Ukrainian media continued to irritate the re
tionship at the public level.[67]

Outbursts of public upset did not set back the new state-to-state arrangemei
however. Recognition that it was in Russia's best interest to have all this cleared
was evident in the big buildup given a meeting between the presidents of Rus

---

63. See, for example, Tamara Shkel', "Naznachenie. Chrezvychainyi i polnomochnyi Chernomyr
[Appointment. Extraordinary and Plenipotentiary Chernomyrdin], *Rossiiskaia gazeta* (11 May 2001);
Sophie Lambroschini, Askord Krushelnycky, "Why Is Moscow Sending Chernomyrdin to Kiev?" *RFI
Weekday Digest* (11 May 2001).

64. Yuliia Timoshenko, "Novyi ukrainskii prem'er budet po-rossiiskim" [Yuliia Timoshenko. The I
Ukrainian Premier Will Be Pro-Russian], *Rossiiskaia gazeta* (12 May 2001). The Ukrainian politician I
oshenko was interviewed by Ivanna Gorina.

65. On the Chernomyrdin-Kinakh meeting, see an interview with Kinakh, "S priezdom V. C
nomyrdina reshatsia mnogie voprosy" [With the Arrival of V. Chernomyrdin Many Questions Wil
Decided], *Rossiiskaia gazeta* (2 June 2001).

66. See, for example, Mykola Biloblotskyy, "Prinimat' Papu—eto prestizhno" [It Is Prestigious to
ceive the Pope], *Rossiiskaia gazeta* (23 June 2001). Biloblotskyy was then Ukrainian ambassador to I
sia. See also Nikolai Paklin, "Chto stoit za vizitom glavy Vatikana na Ukrainu?" [What Lies Behind
Head of the Vatican's Visit to Ukraine?], *ibid.*, (20 June 2001).

67. See, for example, Andrei Kapustin, " 'Yesli nam poveriat, podderzhka budet obespechena' " [If I
Trust Us, Then Support Will Be Forthcoming], *Nezavisimaia gazeta* (4 July 2001); Ol'ga Solov'ianei
"Ukraina obeshchaet vorovat' Rossiiskii gaz i vpred'" [Ukraine Promises to Keep Stealing Russia's Ga
the Future], *Nezavisimaia gazeta* (12 July 2001).

Ukraine and Belarus, scheduled for 25 July in Vitebsk. The nominal purpose of the meeting was for the three presidents to preside over the opening of a Slavic Bazaar arts festival, but there was no doubt in anyone's mind that the questions of EU expansion and a pending presidential election in Belarus were to be the focus of private talks between them. As early as three weeks before the meeting analysts stressed the economic and strategic importance of Belarus to Russia, but demonstrated some concern about Lukashenko's erratic behavior. Ukraine's Kuchma was viewed as a much more reliable partner of Russia, and the dismissal of the "anti-Russian" Yushchenko was treated as proof of that in both countries.[68]

Kuchma and Putin celebrated Russia's Navy Day together in Sevastopol on 31 July and held private talks prior to the CIS summit of presidents set for Sochi on 1–3 August. Topics on their agenda included energy questions, naval cooperation on the Black Sea, and cultural exchanges. This, their seventh meeting in just two years, was marked by a clear recognition by Putin that Crimea was part of Ukraine. Thus, longstanding tensions between Russia and Ukraine dissipated further, notwithstanding carping from nationalists on both sides.

The two presidents met again in Kiev, where the Polish president joined them, in late August. A deal on gas was worked out and Poland agreed on a plan to export Russian gas to Europe through its territory; talks were held as well on Kaliningrad. The occasion was propitious, for Putin helped Kuchma celebrate Ukrainian Independence Day, marking, according to *Izvestiia,* a real "turnaround in Russian political consciousness" in regards to Ukraine. Prime Minister Kinakh informed reporters that expanded economic relations with Russia was the ideal vehicle through which Ukraine could, in fact, maintain its independence.[69]

The change in attitudes and perhaps more importantly the Russian media, was illustrated concretely in the form of reactions to a tragedy in early October; that is, when a Russian charter plane (Sibir Airlines) flying to Novorossiisk from Tel Aviv was blown up over the Black Sea, killing all seventy-seven people on board. Because of events related to the 11 September terrorist attack on the United States, it was immediately assumed to have been a terrorist deed—especially since most of the passengers were citizens of Israel. It soon appeared more likely, however, that it was an accidental hit by a land-to-air missile fired during a Ukrainian training exercise. The Ukrainian ministry of defense immediately issued a denial and even the Russia government was very careful not to accuse Ukraine of anything sinister. All in all, the reaction on both sides was far less hostile than it would have been a year earlier. In fact, Kasyanov was in Kiev as the news came out, and went ahead with the planned restructuring of Ukraine's gas debt. And by 13 October, when the Ukrainian president acknowledged that it was probably a Ukrainian missile that destroyed the Russian plane, Moscow was satisfied with profound apologies. The only concern, it seemed,

---

68. For a typical Russian perspective, see, Vladimir Kuznechevskii, "A Meeting of the Presidents of Belarus, Russia and Ukraine Is Planned for 25 July in Vitebsk," *Rossiiskaia gazeta* (3 July 2001), translated for FBIS-SOV, No. 0709 (12 July 2001).

69. Interview with Kinakh in *Rossiiskaia gazeta* (24 August 2001).

was who was going to pay compensation to both the airlines and the bereaved fa
ilies.[70] A few weeks later Kiev formally admitted responsibility and the defense m
ister resigned. How times had changed.

On 1 November 2001, a celebration invoked by Putin and called "Ukraine's Y
in Russia," that is, 2002, was kick-started by a series of cultural events across
country. Major negotiations on free trade opened at about the same time, with b
sides looking for compromise on a wider range of issues. For the first time in sev
years these talks were initiated in an atmosphere of optimism about their resc
tion.[71] It would appear, in fact, that the mutual attempts to upgrade their relati
ship in 2001 had met with some success. In November the Russian ministry of
nance announced that Ukraine was now Russia's top trading partner within the C
with a turnover volume worth $6.9 billion—up 12 percent from the first n
months of the previous year. Belarus ranked second at $6.8 billion, up about 14 p
cent over the same period.

Shortly thereafter, Moscow and Kiev finally resolved their gas problems, signin
package of documents in Moscow. Among other things the way was set for an ev
tual merging of their energy grids. On the cultural level an All-Russian Congress
Ukrainian Expatriates gathered in Moscow during the first week of December, a
showpiece event for Putin's "Ukraine's Year in Russia." The Russian president
dressed the large group and called for a "qualitative breakthrough" in Russia–Ukra
relations (Interfax, 10 December). Russian reporting on the event was glowi
Thus, even the cultural wars were winding down, if never far from the surface.

In February 2002, Kuchma even took advantage of Putin's initiative to visit T
men, Siberia, where a large Ukrainian diaspora lives and works. In interviews w
the Russian media, the Ukrainian president was very optimistic about his natic
new relationship with Russia. He noted that he and Putin had held nine perso
meetings in 2001 alone and that a strategic partnership was clearly in the interes
both countries.[72] A long statement by Igor Ivanov commemorating the tenth
niversary of the first protocol establishing diplomatic relations between Russia a
Ukraine corroborated the importance of the increasingly closer ties.[73] Moreover,
new relationship had spillover consequences for Moldova as opportunities for thi
way economic cooperation grew. A joint statement issued after a meeting betwi

---

70. On this, see Ivanna Gorina, "Kto streliat tot i strelochnik" [Whoever Fired Will Get the Blai
Rossiiskaia gazeta (13 October 2001). For notice of the new trade relations, see Yevgenii Arsiuk
"Ukraina–Rossiia: Torgovlia bez iskliuchenii" [Ukraine–Russia: Trade without Exceptions], *Rossiis.*
gazeta (18 October 2002).

71. See, for example, an interview with Volodymyr Honcharuk, a senior official in the European i
gration division of Ukraine's ministry of finance, "Cherez kompromissy—kak tsivilizovannye li
[Through Compromise, as Civilized People], *Rossiiskaia gazeta* (1 November 2001); Irina Savchei
"Segodnia poskupilsia—zavtra nedoschitalsia" [Grudged Today, Lost Tomorrow], *Rossiiskaia gazeta* (3
vember 2001).

72. "Leonid Kuchma: 'My otdelili zerno ot plevel'" [Kuchma: "We Have Separated the Wheat f
the Chaff"], *Rossiiskaia gazeta* (12 February 2002).

73. Ivanov, "Porozn', no vmeste" [Separate, but Together], *Rossiiskaia gazeta* (14 February 2002).

the heads of the Russian, Ukrainian and Moldovan governments in March 2002 confirmed this trend.[74]

Parliamentary elections in Ukraine on the last day of March revealed lingering ambiguities in the new partnership.[75] The party backed by Kuchma, For a United Ukraine, received only 13 percent of the vote; the Communists, who also supported association with Russia but disliked Putin, won 20 percent. Our Ukraine, headed by strongly pro-Western Yushchenko, was the largest single winner with 22 percent. Nearly thirty other parties split the remainder of the votes. Such divisions were potentially destabilizing and, in several regions, sparked vigorous anti-Russian campaigning. For example, a decision by the city council in Ivano-Frankivsk to recognize veterans of the Ukrainian "Galichina" SS Divisions as veterans in the war of freedom for Ukraine prompted an angry outburst from the Russian foreign ministry.

Generally, however, Russian observers were encouraged by the elections, claiming that it had gone in favor of the reformers and proponents of rapprochement with Russia.[76] Most analysts assumed that the pragmatism now dominating the executive branch of governing bodies in Moscow and Kiev would ensure a stable relationship between them. Some took a measure of pleasure from the fact that several members of the U.S. Congress were so concerned about the elections that they recommended that sanctions be imposed on Ukraine as an incentive for the government to sponsor further reform.[77]

The momentum for broadened economic cooperation continued apace. Preparing for an early April meeting in Moscow with Kasyanov, Ukrainian Prime Minister Kinakh again expressed Kiev's optimism and its desire to cooperate in any way that was beneficial to both countries.[78] There would have been no reason to doubt this message to reporters; indeed, less than a month later, Ukraine requested that it be allowed to sit as an observer on the Eurasian Economic Community. Putin, who at the time was meeting with Kuchma in Sochi on 17 May, saw no reason why Ukraine should not become a full member.

At that meeting, the two presidents signed an address to a joint session of the Russian and Ukrainian Academies of Science, and called for closer scientific cooperation.

---

74. *Nezavisimaia gazeta* (19 March 2002); "Sovmestnoe zaiavlenie prezidentov Rossiiskoi Federatsii, Respubliki Moldova i Ukrainy" [Joint Statement by Presidents of the Russian Federation, the Republic of Moldova, and Ukraine], *Rossiiskaia gazeta* (23 March 2002).

75. For a preelection assumption that the "Russian factor" would be a major issue in the results, see Vladimir Bogdanov, "Rossiiskii faktor ukrainskikh vyborov" [The Russian Factor in the Ukrainian Elections], *Rossiiskaia gazeta* (26 March 2002).

76. On this see Yekaterina Mikhailova, "Na Ukraine pobedili reformatory" [The Reformers Won in Ukraine], *Obshchaia gazeta*, No. 14 (4–10 April 2002); see also Vladimir Litvin, "Rossiiskii faktor ukrainskikh vyborov"[The Russian Factor in the Ukrainian Election], *Rossiiskaia gazeta* (26 March 2002), and Vladimir Bogdanov, "Zapad est' Zapad, Vostok est' Vostok" [West Is West, East Is East], *Rossiiskaia gazeta* (2 April 2002).

77. See, for example, Ivanna Gorina, "Amerikanskaia tragediia" [American Tragedy], *Rossiiskaia gazeta* (3 April 2002); Aleksandr Sabov, "Ukraina i Rossiia budut druzhit' domami" [Ukraine and Russia Will Be Friends from House to House], *Rossiiskaia gazeta* (6 April 2002).

78. "Anatolii Kinakh: 'Ya ne derzhus' za kreslo prem'era'" [Anatoliy Kinakh. "I Do Not Clutch the Prime Minister's Chair"], *Izvestiia* (9 April 2002).

They also expanded cooperation in the gas industry, recently the source of so mı tension between the two countries, and charted further economic interaction.

During Putin's short period as president a large body of bilateral agreements l been signed into law, fully normalizing the Russia–Ukraine relationship. This wa huge advance over the diplomatic rubble left by Yeltsin. The rhetoric of friends took a new twist in late May 2002, after the Russia–NATO Council was given o cial form. The Ukrainian government immediately announced that it was soon ing to set in motion a formal application for NATO membership. Moscow said t such a move did not at all bother the Kremlin.

Of course, it did.

Belarus

In the 1990s, the Republic of Belarus had taken positions on NATO expansion a relations with Russia that were diametrically opposed to those of Ukraine. The g ernment headed by Alyaksandr Lukashenko consistently and aggressively revi NATO's move eastward and portrayed itself as the front line in a redivided Euro To a certain extent, Lukashenko was right, in that Poland is his country's neight and the Russian and Belarusian military forces were closely integrated well before Charter of Union between the two countries finally was ratified in December 19 Lukashenko went so far as to talk big about rearming the nuclear missile sites on territory if similar weapons were sited in Poland.[79]

In practice the Union was primarily a military one. Military planners in Minsk cepted principles espoused in the draft Security Concept approved by the RF Se rity Council on 5 October. This Russian document treated military blocs (NAT as a real threat, and the later military doctrine both repeated this principle and s gled out "joint defense policy with the Republic of Belarus" as a specific means protection against such threats.[80]

On 7 October, a joint Russian–Belarusian meeting of military leaders discus mutual strategies in Moscow. Russian Minister of Defense Sergeev told the delegɛ that the year 2000 would be decisive in realizing full integration of their arn forces, at least in terms of planning and strategies. Indeed, the Duma had ratified September, a treaty on joint utilization of military infrastructure; and the two pr dents had agreed even earlier on the concept of joint defense. Decisions on a bud division had been reached, as had tentative accords on mutual deployment of r

79. On this see *Russia Faces NATO Expansion,* pp. 117–118, and S. J. Main, *Belarus–Russian Mili Relations (1991–1998)* (Surrey: Conflict Studies Research Centre, 1998); see also Ivan Rodin, "Sto m Aleksandra Lukashenko" [100 Minutes of Aleksandr Lukashenko], *Nezavisimaia gazeta* (28 Octɾ 1999).

80. "Voennaia doktrina Rossiiskoi Federatsii" [Military Doctrine of the Russian Federation], *Neza maia gazeta* (22 April 2000), Article 7. See also Peter Szszlo, "Russian-Belarusian Military Integratiɾ MA Thesis, Carleton University, 2001.

road troops. The submissive Belarusian press, especially Russian-language papers, was enthusiastic about this development.[81] Lukashenko played his part, taking the initiative by strongly defending Russian actions in Chechnya and urging the Duma in Moscow to ignore Western criticisms of the Union. During a rousing address to the Russian parliament on 27 October, the Belarusian president chastised Moscow for drawing back from the Middle Eastern arms market, only to have Western arms manufacturers move in. We need a common foreign policy so as to regain the primacy enjoyed by the USSR in that important region, he exhorted the Russian deputies.[82]

On the ordnance side, rumors that Belarus signed a contract to purchase MiG-29 fighter aircraft from Russia circulated in September 1999, after Aleksei Ogarev, then the head of *Rosvooruzhenie,* the Russian state-run arms dealership, said as much during an international exhibition. The MiG-29 is an all-purpose plane that can carry out air combat, interception, ground-attack and observation tasks—and is expensive. The Belarusian ministry of defense consistently denied, or made no comment on, the deal, saying that the funds could be spent much more wisely on upgrading existing equipment. Whether the deal was real or not, the potential for confusion in the new Russia–Belarus military link-up was apparent even to Belarusian writers.[83] This did not deter the joint collegiums of defense ministries from signing nine documents on military cooperation in October. According to Sergeev the accords were designed to promote further integration, including a single regional anti-aircraft defense system, a joint armaments program, and an operational and strategic infrastructure to implement their development. We have no enemy, a communiqué reminded journalists, but "if one appears, this group will be ready to face him" (ITAR-TASS, 6 October 1999).

A full version of the Union Treaty had been signed by Yeltsin and Lukashenko on 5 November but not celebrated in a public event until 8 December.[84] The importance of the military component of the Union was such that one day before the gala final celebration, it was announced that a joint military doctrine would be signed in the new year. The Treaty provided that the two nations unite but remain independent of each other, forming a political confederation by 2005, with a common tax system, customs laws, and currency. For practical reasons the economies of the two countries were expected to become the core of the Union. The structure was to be

81. See, for example, Yurii Strigel'skii, "Sluzhu Soiuzy! [I Serve the Union!], *Belorusskaia delovaia gazeta* (8 October 1999); and "Oboronnaia doktrina Soiuza" [The Union's Defense Doctrine], *Sovetskaia Belorussiia* (28 October 1999). See also "CIS Air Defense Forces Exercises Reviewed" *Belorusskaia delovaia gazeta* (1 September 1999), FBIS-SOV, No. 980 (1 September 1999).

82. See also Semen Novoprudskii, "Prezident Gosdumy. Aleksandr Lukashenko ocharovyvaet parlament" [President to the State Duma. Lukashenko Charms the Parliament], *Izvestiia* (28 October 1999).

83. See, for example, Yuryy Stryhelski, "MiG-29. Ghosts or Military Secret?" *Belorusskaia delovaia gazeta* (13 September 1999), translated for FBIS-SOV, No. 921 (24 September 1999).

84. On this, see "Moskva, Kreml, 8 dekabriia, 12 chas. 15 min" [Moscow. The Kremlin, 8 December, 12:15], *Rossiiskaia gazeta* (9 December 1999). Not all Russian analysts were overjoyed at the Union; see, for example, Yevgenii Krutikov, "Neravnyi brak" [Unequal Marriage], *Izvestiia* (9 December 1999).

overseen by a council of leaders—the two presidents, prime ministers and speak
of parliaments.[85]

According to the Union Treaty, "a regional armed forces group and the shaping
a joint defense contact will be completed" at that time, that is, by 2005.[86] Milita
defense integration was tightened already on 10–11 February 2000, when Russ
Deputy Prime Minister Ilya Klebanov led a delegation to Minsk to negotiate
agreement setting up a Russia–Belarus financial group to be called Defense Syste
Its purpose was to "design, manufacture, and market joint air-defense technolog
It is worth noting that the Russian delegation included Anatolii Kornukov, H
Commander of the Russian Air Force. Russian observers attributed the rapidity
Russia-Belarus military integration directly to "events in Kosovo and Chechnya, a
by NATO statements that the Baltic States might soon become members of the
liance."[87] Lukashenko's pronouncement on 10 February that, in accordance with
new military doctrine, Russia could use nuclear arms to protect Belarus, indica
the importance of this particular meeting.

Belying their haranguing of NATO for expanding eastward, Belarusian authori
claimed that they, like Russia, preferred to work closely with the Atlantic Alliance. D
ing a working visit by Igor Ivanov to Minsk, for example, both he and Ural Latyp
told reporters that they would be interested in working out some form of formal
cord with NATO, the latter foreign minister agreeing even that, if invited, Bela
would cooperate with the new (and previously reviled) German–Danish–Po
NATO corps headquartered in Poland. Unfortunately, these remarks coincided w
attacks by radical groups on a Russian diplomatic mission in Poznan, Poland, for wh
Russia blamed the Polish government. Ivanov cancelled a scheduled visit to Wars
and was supported by the Belarus media that spoke darkly of Poland's ambitions.[88]

Officials in Minsk were among the most vociferous lobbyists for Yugoslavia's
mission to the Russia–Belarus Union, introducing it as a motion in the fall of 19
and consistently supporting the idea through the winter of 2000. In addition to th
common Slavic ethnicity and animosity towards NATO, Minsk and Belgrade sha
political habits. Almost simultaneously in March, for example, Milosevic mo
against the independent media in his country and Lukashenko announced a ban
marches by opposition groups. Lukashenko's action followed a protest parade on

---

85. For an overview of the Union's prospects, from the Russian perspective, see an ITAR-TASS rep
"Tema dnia. Kliuchevye slova minskikh dialogov—rubl', gaz, viza" [Theme of the Day. Key Words of
Minsk Dialogues Are Ruble, Gas, and Visa], *Rossiiskaia gazeta* (4 December 2000). The forum here
a CIS meeting in Minsk. Yurii Godin, "Na puti k soiuznomu gosudarstvu" [On the Way to a Ur
State], *Sodruzhestvo NG*, No. 1 (26 January 2000).

86. Interfax (7 December 1999). The two states also were committee to producing a joint armam
program for the period 2001–2005. For documentation, see *REDA* 1999, Vol. 2., "Belarus."

87. See, for example, Col. Vladimir Mukhin, "Rossiia i Belarus ob'edin̄iaiut sily vozdushnoi i oboro
[Russia and Belarus Unite Air Defense], *Nezavisimaia gazeta* (2 February 2000). See also Yurii Godin,
puti k soiuznomu gosudarstvu" [On the Way to a United State], *Sodruzhestvo NG*, No. 1 (26 Janu
2000), and "Konvergentsiia Rossii i Belorussii" [The Convergence of Russia and Belorussia], *ibid.*, N
(29 March 2000).

88. See, for example, Nina Romanova, "Vizit v Pol'shu otmenen" [Visit to Poland Cancelled], *Sc
skaia Belorussiia* (26 February 2000).

March of some 20,000, demanding free elections and opposing union with Russia. In Belgrade, six nongovernmental radio and TV stations were closed, marking the most severe crackdown since the late 1980s. There were Russians who supported Yugoslavia's admission to the Union as well, among them Gennadii Seleznev, chairman of the State Duma. Nonetheless, a parliamentary commission created to study the question found little support among the political elite in Russia.

Belarusian support in Russia's quest to maintain the status quo in connection with the ABM Treaty was appreciated by Sergei Ivanov, who said as much in his 16 March speech on foreign policy to the Institute of International relations in Moscow.[89] Likewise, Lord Robertson's commemoration of the anniversary of NATO's bombing attacks on Yugoslavia was greeted in Belarus much as it was in Russia. Following Russia's lead, Belarus had suspended relations with NATO and the PfP after the Alliance launched its air campaign, and it lifted that suspension shortly after Russia did. But Minsk remained aggressive in its commentary on NATO expansion. In April, after the newly elected Putin visited the Belarusian capital, Lukashenko announced that an agreement to create a joint military organization with Russia had been struck, and was scheduled for signing in June. The consequent joint force of some 300,000 soldiers, would be deployed on the Belarus–Polish border. Moscow tended to distance itself from the enthusiasm shown by Lukashenko when he spoke of this arrangement, and Russian commentators calculated that the effectiveness of such a force would be slight if faced with an aggressively expanding NATO. Missiles, they said, would remain the crucial deterrent. One writer referred to a Kremlin press leak, that Lukashenko was told to be quiet because Europe would not be intimidated by a 300,000-man military group.[90] Within a month, however, the Russian and Belarusian defense stratagem was cinched up still further. A joint regional air defense complex was created, with tracking and intercept systems coordinated to monitor intrusions from the west. A combined training exercise was scheduled for August.

The close link between Moscow and Minsk in military planning was confirmed in Russia's new military doctrine, signed into law by Putin on 21 April 2000. It has been pointed out already that the Doctrine claimed that the RF was responsible for implementing a "joint defense policy together with the Republic of Belarus" and to maintain the defense capability of the Union State of Russia and Belarus. Significantly, the Doctrine authenticated Lukashenko's earlier statement that Russia's nuclear deterrence applies equally to its ally, Belarus.

Following the Russian example, the parliament in Minsk ratified the Comprehensive Test Ban Treaty on 27 April, one day after the first meeting of the Union State congress adopted a statement on Yugoslavia accusing NATO of "aggression" causing death and destruction in that country. Peacekeeping in Kosovo had "failed," the statement concluded. A trade delegation to Libya, led by Deputy Prime Minister and

---

89. Ivanov, *Rossiiskaia gazeta* (16 March 2000), *op. cit.*

90. Yelena Dikun, "London prinial Putina na sebia" [London Takes Putin for Itself], *Obshchaia gazeta,* No. 16 (20–16 April 2000). See also Viktor Litovkin, "Bodal'sia bat'ka s NATO" [Father Butted Heads with NATO], *ibid.*

Foreign Minister Latypow, in May, maintained the image of Belarus in lockstep w
Russia in its dealings with "rogue" states around the world.

Belarus's standing as a buffer state between Russia and NATO was continu:
harped upon by foreign policy commentators in Minsk. A tour through all th
Baltic capital cities by Gerhard Schröder in June prompted many questions ab·
Baltic State admission to NATO, and a feeling—perhaps wishful thinking on
Baltic part and paranoia on the Russian–Belarus part—that Schröder suppor
their entry.[91] Strobe Talbott, who was in Tallinn a few days later, added credibilit)
the rumors, however.[92] The notion of Belarus as a buffer state between Russia and
expanding NATO was regularly voiced in Minsk. In September, for example,
head of the Russia–Belarus Union's commission on security, defense and the fi
against crime described Belarus as the linchpin in Russia's strategic move to sepaı
the Baltic States from GUUAM, and the sole geographical region linking Russiɛ
Europe. (ITAR-TASS. 14 September).[93]

The question of Baltic admission to NATO was raised again in late October a
the U.S. Senate appropriated funds to help those three republics prepare for er
(see chapter 3). Putin almost immediately reiterated Moscow's opposition to such
pansion, and the already growing military relationship between Russia and Bela
was stepped up. In a probably unrelated incident, Lukashenko personally tende
an invitation to Yugoslavia to join the Union between Russia and Belarus—but
newly installed Vojislav Kostunica, who visited Moscow on 27 October, rejected
idea. Suspicions that the West was now buying Kostunica's support, already pre
lent in government circles in Belarus, were confirmed in Lukashenko's (and Russ
nationalist/communists') mind when it was reported that NATO spokesman Jaı
Shea told the Cambridge Club that NATO provided financial aid to Kostunica
help overthrow Milosevic, and would do so in Belarus against Lukashenko. The R
sian Duma's international affairs committee demanded that the ministry of fore
affairs attempt to verify these reports (Interfax, 22 November). Shea denied the a
gation, calling it completely fabricated, but the idea fell on fertile suspicious soi
both Moscow and Minsk.[94]

The problem with statements on behalf of the Union, however, was that the jc
organization still had little substance even ten months after ratification. The Un
structure (a Supreme Council, Parliament, Council of Ministers, Court, anɛ
Comptroller's office, plus a number of committees and an official newspaper)

91. See, for example, Viktoriia Sokolova, "Shreder pomozhet Baltii vstypit' v NATO" [Schröder '
Help Baltics to Enter NATO], *Izvestiia* (6 June 2000).

92. Maksim Yusin, "Amerika vstupilas' za pribaltov" [America Assumed Protection of the Baltic
gion], *Izvestiia* (9 June 2000).

93. Boris Bikkinin spoke of a Black Sea–Baltic cordon sanitaire made up of the Baltic States and (
UAM serving as a buffer zone between Russia and Europe—with only Belarus splitting it. See also E
Bikkinin, "Rossiia–belarus': geostrategicheskii soiuz" [Russia–Belarus: A Geostrategic Union], *Krasi
zvezda* (19 September 2000).

94. Shea's denial was taken at face value by the Russian government paper on the grounds that if it ʋ
true, Shea would never have mentioned it publicly. See *Rossiiskaia gazeta* (25 November 2000).

mained hollow, and there was only a vague public recognition that it existed—especially in Russia.[95] On 30 November, however, Lukashenko and Putin signed an agreement scheduling the introduction of a common currency, funded mostly by Russia.

Hollow shell or not, the Russian–Belarus institutional marriage had grown considerably during Putin's first year as president, especially in military matters. In late December Russia and Belarus agreed to produce a joint military doctrine and the Russian budget allocated some 800 million rubles for the preparation of the small joint armed force of about 300,000. Economic and other types of union had not advanced nearly so far, though these and other manifestations about Russia–Belarus integration proposals were confirmed by the new foreign minister of Belarus, Mikhail Khvastow, when he paid his first working visit to Moscow on 7–8 January 2001.

The December 2000 agreements had concrete results when, on 31 January 2001, customs controls on the Russia–Belarus border were abolished and a single customs regime was finally made official. Media commentary on both sides treated this event as a major step towards giving the Union some substance.[96]

It was about time. The year 2001 marked the fifth anniversary of the Union agreement, so much was made in both countries of the progress to date. Yet it remained primarily in the military and foreign policy spheres that they seemed most synchronized; indeed, the Belarus minister of defense was dismissed at almost the same time Sergeev was let go. Although Putin offered no obvious support for Lukashenko's domestic political policies, he regularly pointed to Belarus as Russia's partner in international affairs and its second most important trade partner. The Russian media tended to pick up on this and treated Minsk with greater sympathy than it had during the 1990s.[97]

On 5 April it was announced that Russia and Belarus would soon have a fully amalgamated air defense system with its control center located in Minsk, designed "so that that fairly important region, which borders NATO, has its own control body" (Interfax, 5 April). While making this announcement, Russian air force commander Anatolii Kornukov claimed that NATO and U.S. spy planes had been making twelve to fifteen intelligence-gathering flights weekly over the Russia–Belarus defenses. A few weeks later a new joint army group was formed to include the Belarus armed forces, the Moscow military district and units stationed in Kaliningrad. Sergei Ivanov, Russia's new defense minister, claimed that a command system for it was being planned (Interfax, 17 April). Although few military analysts saw the formation as truly important, Russian experts still stressed the necessity of a common military district, no matter its initial frailties. One proponent of this particular form of inte-

---

95. On this, see Maksim Glikin, "Vadim Borodin stroit novoe gosudarstvo" [Vadim Borodin Builds a New State], *Obshchaia gazeta,* No. 38 (21–27 September 2000).

96. See, for example, Chichkin, "Soiuz poluchit edinuiu tamozhniu" [The Union Will Gain a Single Customs House], *Rossiiskaia gazeta* (30 January 2001), and ITAR-TASS (31 January 2001).

97. See, for example, Aleksei Chichkin, "'Esli belorusy ne budut sebia chuvstvovat' inostrantsami v Rossii, a russkie—v Minske . . .'" [If Belarusians Do Not Feel Like Foreigners in Russia, or Russians in Minsk . . .], *Rossiiskaia gazeta* (28 March 2001).

gration stated that it was driven by the fact that NATO tanks had reached
Union's borders, "with their wide smiles," and also by religious extremism menac
from the south.[98]

A new Belarusian defense minister was appointed in May, that is, Leonid Malt:
who was considered an even stronger supporter of Belarus–Russian military inte{
tion than his predecessor. Clearly the Union was working in the military sphere
2002, if not well anywhere else; and Russian observers continued to look askanc{
Lukashenko's practices in domestic politics. In fact, when Liudmila Griaznov;
leader of the opposition in Belarus, and some 100 other antigovernment dem·
strators were arrested in Minsk in late March, and dozens more were detained
April, the Russian media roundly criticized the Lukashenko government. Parad{
cally, public opinion surveys revealed that an increasing majority of Russians wan
full union between the two countries.

CONCLUSION

By May 2002, Russia's relationships with Ukraine and Belarus both had chan{
substantially since Putin first took office. For the most part these changes were
Russia's advantage. Moscow and Kiev were decidedly closer than they had been
late 1999, especially in the economic sphere. Raging issues over energy, the Black
Fleet, Crimea, language, and even their respective relationship with NATO had b·
resolved, muted or, at worst, postponed. A significant part of that accommodat
depended, however, on the increasingly unpopular (both at home and in the W·
Kuchma's ability to stay in office.

The fact that Ukraine's economy continued to spiral down also ensured greater
liance on Russia. More to the point, was Putin's policy towards the governmeni
Kiev. He consistently impressed upon his power ministers the need for econoı
contacts with Ukraine and eschewed aggressive rhetoric on debt and language issu
A turning point had been achieved in June 2001, when long-term agreements w
reached on the gas debt, joint industrial development, and other forms of collabc
tion in the economic sector. The appointment of Chernomyrdin as ambassadoı
Ukraine was a major diplomatic success, and the decision to declare 2002 "Ukraiı
Year in Russia" was a stroke of political genius.

There had not been much consolidation in the Russia–Belarus Union, aside fr
growing military integration. Nor had the continued semi-isolation of Belarus fr
the concert of nations handicapped Russian policy to any extent. In this case as v
the entrenchment of President Lukashenko in office, and the extent of his unsav
reputation outside the country, were bound to ensure the status quo.

---

98. See, for example, Boris Yamshanov, "Vse my vyshli iz odnoi shineli" [Everyone Will Wear the S
Greatcoat], *Rossiiskaia gazeta* (26 April 2001). This was part of a four-page supplement to the *RG*, "Sc
Belarus'-Rossiia" [Union. Belarus–Russia].

Although certain nationalists in Russia, Ukraine and Belarus would deny it, the three countries remained closely related by their ethnicity, history and cultures. This reality has been a source of as much friction as it has of cooperation, and it by no means guarantees close cooperation in international affairs. Russia and Ukraine, for example, both want closer relationships with the EU—Ukraine eventually as a member, Russia as a trading partner. Disappointed in its economic association with Europe, Kiev has turned to NATO and the PfP as its main access to European governing and economic circles. In May 2002, the Ukrainian government announced that its long-term ambition was accession to NATO. Russia hopes only that the new NATO–Russia Council will work far better than the Permanent Joint Council established in 1997. If it does, then Ukraine's upgraded links with NATO might well be to the Kremlin's benefit.

The place of Belarus in Russia's foreign policy vision was still in limbo by May 2002, primarily because of the nature of the government in Minsk. Outwardly, Moscow has kept the relationship at arms length. Nevertheless, Russia is the only country Belarus can call an ally. The Union agreement between the two countries, and their close ties to both the CIS Collective Security Treaty Organization and the Eurasian Economic Community, make them each other's closest partners in the international arena. Belarusian dealings with India, China and the "rogue" states also follow the Russia model.

With the anomalous exception of Kaliningrad, it is Belarus and Ukraine that separate Russia territorially from NATO and from most of the candidates for membership in the EU. To date, Russian official doctrine has consistently stressed that the country's western borders are secure and unthreatened. It is in this connection that the Baltic States represent the only red flag in this picture. When they are admitted to NATO as members, the Atlantic Alliance will have reached the borders of Russia proper (not just Kaliningrad), and the Baltic Sea will have become a NATO Sea. Kaliningrad will then be cut off from Russia by a military bloc rather than merely by two foreign countries. Moreover, any threat from Russia over perceived violations of the human or civil rights of ethnic Russians in Latvia or Estonia could be deemed a direct challenge to NATO. Any major crisis in the Baltic could severely test Russian diplomatic friendship with Slavic Belarus and Ukraine.

10

✦

The CIS and Central Asia

THE CIS IN 2000

Eighty-five percent of the Russian Federation can be said to lie in the East, and 85 percent of its population lives in the West. It has been generally assumed in Moscow that partnerships in the East make Russia less dependent on the West and, as one essayist put it, the two-headed Russian eagle is at its strongest when looking in both directions. In 1999, the East–West divide became food for thought in all twelve members of the Commonwealth of Independent States. According to Russian analysts, NATO's air strikes against Yugoslavia had driven many CIS countries to commence upgrading their defense capacities, either looking to Russia for succor or seizing an opportunity to "go West." Even Ukraine agreed to join with Russia, Belarus and Armenia in condemning the bombing. In short, NATO's action had a distilling effect on the CIS, reminding all states that they could eventually be forced to choose between the Atlantic Alliance on the one hand, and Russia on the other.[1]

As preparations got under way in January 2000 for a late spring CIS summit in Moscow, observers in both Russia and the West treated it as somewhat of a last gasp. The CIS had existed for eight years, with an on-again, off-again membership of twelve countries, an extensive infrastructure of councils and committees, and a record of some 1,300 cooperative and integrative acts. Few of those acts encompassed the entire membership and they tended not to be very binding. The CIS had

---

1. See, for example, Vladimir Mukhin, "Otvet na agressiiu NATO imeetsia" [What Is the Response to NATO's Aggression (in the CIS)], *Nezavisimaia gazeta* (28 April 1999). For the two-headed eagle musing, see Vsevolod Ovchinnikov, "Golovy Rossiiskogo orla smotriat i na Zapad, i na Vostok" [The Heads of the Russian Eagle Look Both to the West and to the East], *Rossiiskaia gazeta* (28 June 2000).

divided into inter-regional groups defined, for the most part, by their bilateral r‹ tions with Russia. Only a few of the CIS countries could be counted as allies Moscow—Belarus, Kazakhstan, Armenia, and Tajikistan.[2] Kyrgyzstan leaned tow Russia as well, whereas Ukraine, Georgia, Azerbaijan, Turkmenistan, and Uzbekis were inclined more towards NATO and Western Europe—at least when it sui them. Moldova wavered somewhere in between, casting a wary eye on Romai Ukraine, and Russia, whose troops were scheduled to leave the Transdniester reg by the summer of 2000.[3]

As Putin's presidency first began to take on substance, Russia, Belarus, Kaza stan, Kyrgyzstan and, more recently, Tajikistan, had formed a vaguely defined C toms Union, called then the Central-Asian Economic Community. Only Tu menistan excluded itself. A second integrating movement, the GUAM (Geor; Ukraine, Azerbaijan, and Moldova—later joined by Uzbekistan to become G UAM), had as one of its purposes the export of Caspian Sea oil and other go‹ without involvement from Russia or Iran. A third was the Shanghai Five: Rus China, Kazakhstan, Kyrgyzstan, and Tajikistan. These organizations divided the (into competing regional associations, pushing the centralizing agencies of the cc monwealth into the background.

Yet the CIS muddled through. When its heads of state finally came togethei Moscow in June 2000, Putin's efforts to strengthen Moscow's position within the ı ritory once controlled by the USSR were already showing some results. Even bef the meeting the "struggle against fundamentalism and international terrorism" l become buzzwords for Moscow's drive to consolidate its position in the CIS ger ally, and in Central Asia particularly.[4] Although Ukraine and Georgia failed to s various protocols on military cooperation and defense-related accords, they part pated fully in economic agreements. In international affairs the Kremlin was s‹ ported by a joint CIS ministries of defense statement on behalf of the "inviolabi and integrity" of the ABM Treaty. The ministers warned that amendments to treaty could "undermine global strategic stability," and referred to events Afghanistan as a signal that international anarchy needed to be contained.[5] Head: all CIS states except Turkmenistan signed a resolution appointing Boris Mylnik former deputy chief of the Russian FSB's anti-terrorist department, chief of a r CIS anti-terrorist center.

---

2. Sergei Ivanov, head of the Russian Security Council, made this point in a speech to the Moscow S Institute of International Relations on 16 March 2000; see *Rossiiskaia gazeta* (16 March 2000).

3. For pessimistic Russian comment, see Aleksandr Sabov, "My uzhe ne druz'ia. No partner Konkurenty?" [We Are No Longer Friends. But Are We Partners? Competitors?], *Rossiiskaia gazeta* January 2000).

4. See, for example, Vladimir Yermolin, "Bezopasnost' na shesterykh" [Security for the Six], *Izve* (26 May 2000); Armen Khanbabyan, "Obshchaia ugroza kak faktor sotrudnichestva" [General Thre: a Factor for Cooperation], *Sodruzhestvo NG*, No. 5 (31 May 2000).

5. "Statement of the CIS Heads of State on Strategic Stability" (21 June 2000). Release by the Emb of the Russian Federation in Ottawa; see also Igor Sergeev, "Strategiia kollektivnoi bezopasnosti" [S egy of Collective Security], *Krasnaia zvezda* (21 June 2000).

As we have seen in an earlier chapter, the summit included special sessions between the South Caucausus heads of state, and voiced its strong approval of the establishment of a special commission chaired by Yevgenii Primakov to resolve the dilemma of Transdniester separation in Moldova. Moreover, a joint Russia–Moldova military exercise was planned, and executed from 7 to 12 August. These events were viewed inside and outside of Russia as part of Putin's attempt to reestablish Russia as the most influential power in the former Soviet territory. With the exception of the communist opposition, who worried that the CIS tail was now wagging the Russian dog—especially after Putin abolished the post of minister for CIS affairs in his own government in May—Russia's media looked very kindly on these trends.[6]

The importance of the CIS to Russia's new stance in international affairs was made especially clear in the Foreign Policy Concept. Under "regional priorities," the CIS was ranked first. Economic cooperation, "reciprocal openness," and strategic partnerships with all CIS members were urged, though qualified by an insistence that the CIS should "duly consider the interests of the Russian Federation, including the safeguarding of the rights of Russian compatriots."[7] And Russia made certain its needs were met. In August 2000, Moscow threatened to withdraw its support for the visa-free movement among member-states by November. Granted, this decision had been expected for some time; it was the timing that had added significance. Moscow claimed that it was a temporary maneuver, designed to make it less easy for terrorists and drug traffickers to move freely about the region, and more evidently to allow Moscow to deport noncitizens who had moved into Russia's cities by the thousands since the collapse of the USSR. Some pundits again predicted the end of the CIS.[8]

The visa-free travel agreement had its origin in 1992, when nine countries—Armenia, Belarus, Kazakhstan, Kyrgyzstan, Moldova, Russia, Tajikistan, Turkmenistan and Uzbekistan—signed what came to be known as the Bishkek Accord. Georgia joined in 1995. Since then various states had broken away and/or signed bilateral agreements of their own on visas with neighbors. Russia's notice of withdrawal, with ninety days' warning, was provided for in the Accord. Shortly after the announcement in 2000, however, Moscow's immediate purpose was exposed. It began to negotiate bilateral visa-free arrangements: first with the Group of Five, then also with Armenia and Moldova. Russia already had similar bilateral agreements with Turkmenistan (1999) and, earlier in 2000, with Uzbekistan. The Kremlin was cashing in on a new bargaining chip.

---

6. See, for example, Oleg Chekovets, "Meniu dlia sammita" [Menu for the Summit], *Sovetskaia Rossiia* (24 June 2000); On Moldova, see L. Leonov, "My tvoi deti, Rossiia" [Russia Has Two Children], *Sovetskaia Rossiia* (20 June 2000); Vadim Rechkalov, "Sodruzhestvo derzhitsia na kompromissakh" [The Commonwealth Reaches a Compromise], *Obshchaia gazeta*, No. 25 (22–28 June 2000). Earlier meetings had not been so encouraging. See, for example, Natal'ia Airapetova, "Minsodruzhestvo veleno zakryt" [Ministry of the Commonwealth Is Ordered Closed], *Sodruzhestvo NG*, No. 5 (31 May 2000).
7. "Kontseptsiia . . .," *Rossiiskaia gazeta* (11 July 2000), Pt. IV, *op. cit.*
8. See, for example, Semen Novoprudskii, "Konetz SNG, kak i bylo obeshchano" [The End of the CIS, as It Was Promised], *Izvestiia* (17 June 2000).

To facilitate closer scrutiny of border crossings, the new visa regime gave Ru
clout to hold over CIS countries whose people work in Russia and send their sala
home. Such transfer payments are especially important to Georgia, Azerbaijan,
menia and Uzbekistan. In the Caucasus, the Kremlin chose to require visas fr
Georgians and Azeris, but not of Armenians. Moreover, even though eleven of
CIS interior ministers signed an agreement on 9 September to work together agai
international terrorism, Russia insisted on setting its own rules until some work
cooperation was in place. Now it was the turn of Yevgenii Kozhokin, director of
Russian Institute for Strategic Studies, to predict that the Kremlin's attitude in 1
regard spelled the end of the CIS.[9]

Also in August, Russia's railway ministry temporarily stopped Russian trains fr
carrying goods to and from CIS countries that owed money to the ministry. Th
countries included Azerbaijan, Georgia, Moldova, Tajikistan, Turkmenistan, a
Uzbekistan, each of which had Russia as its largest trading partner. The act rep
sented a real threat to countries whose goods have to transit Russian territory
reach Europe or elsewhere. Most of them are landlocked, if one discounts
Caspian, and have very limited railway access to anywhere but former USSR te
tory. Their options are limited, especially as the goods to be shipped are usually b
(cotton, coal, grains, ores), so Russia wields important integrative authority throu
its rail system.[10] In military matters, the 1994 CIS Collective Security Pact was
newed in 1999 by only six of the member-countries (Russia, Belarus, Armenia, Ka
khstan, Kyrgyzstan, and Tajikistan). Azerbaijan, Georgia and Uzbekistan refused
follow suit. On the other hand, an Air Defense Integration agreement inclu
eleven CIS countries, leaving out only Moldova.

In the long run, it was the apparent strengthening of GUUAM that most sh
the underpinnings of the CIS. Established in 1997, GUUAM was intended mer
to facilitate the transport of goods to Europe. It was joined by Uzbekistan in 1
and increasingly took shape as a separate economic zone within the CIS. Mosc
perceived it as a creature of Washington, precisely as a means to weaken the CI
Talk of the revival of the "old silk road" as the common link in a free-trade zone
came a standby in GUUAM's informal deliberations, challenging by infere
Moscow's predominance on Central Asian trade routes.[12] By September 2000, th
was discussion of Romania joining this southern group and of its further insti

---

9. Kozhokin, "My skovany odnoi tsel'io . . ." [We Are Linked by a Single Chain] *Obshchaia gaz*
No. 36 (7–13 September 2000). The 9 September agreement was signed at a law-enforcement age
summit in Kyrgyzstan.

10. On the significance of Russia as a transportation alley for the CIS and Central Asia, connecting
and West, see Tseniia Gokoleva, "Rossii povezlo s geografiei" [Russia Is Lucky with Geography], *N
visimaia gazeta* (7 September 2000).

11. See, for example, Aleksei Guliaev, "Vashington nedovolen vlastiami Kazakhstana" [Washingto
Unhappy with the Governors of Kazakhstan], *Izvestiia* (26 May 1999), in which Kazakhstan is portra
as the front line against U.S. influence moving beyond the GUUAM.

12. On this, see Taras Kuzio, "Geopolitical Pluralism in the CIS: the Emergence of GUUAM," *E
pean Security*, 9: 2 (Summer 2000), 81–114.

tionalization. Though this did not happen in 2000, GUUAM's foreign ministers met as a group during the OSCE summit in Vienna and together held talks with U.S. Secretary of State Albright. Thus, they upgraded their association by dint of their actual deliberations.

Speaking for GUUAM, Azerbaijan's Vilayet Guliev warned against their territories being used for illegal arms deliveries or as an arena for "aggressive separatism and terrorism." Notwithstanding that such sentiments mirrored positions taken regularly by Russia, Guliev's comments were interpreted as criticisms of Russia, whose position on and involvement in Abkhazia, the Transdniester, and Nagorno-Karabakh were looked upon with great distrust by most GUUAM members. Interestingly, GUUAM representatives nominated the allegedly anti-Russian Borys Tarasyuk, who was dismissed as Ukrainian foreign minister on 30 September, for the post of OSCE commissioner for national minorities.[13]

At about the same time, Sergei Ivanov had been elected head of the CIS committee of secretaries of security councils, at a time when Moscow was looking very suspiciously on NATO maneuvers in CIS countries. These included a Tsentrazbat-2000 exercise in Kazakhstan, close to the Chinese border, two naval exercises in the Crimea (Cossack Steppe-2000), an emergency measures program (Transcarpathia-2000) in Romania and Ukraine, and a two-month PfP mine clearing training operation in Georgia fully paid for by the United States. Russia was involved in Tsentrazbat-2000, but on a minor scale compared to the USA and Turkey. Proposals from Istanbul that a NATO rapid reaction force be located in that city, with a responsibility for the Balkans, Caucasus and Central Asia, compelled Russian strategists to look harder for partners in the CIS and in Beijing.[14] Sergei and Igor Ivanov went on the offensive.[15]

A significant step in tightening up part of the CIS was taken in October when the Group of Five Customs Union recast itself as the Eurasian Economic Community (EEC). Signed by Putin and his counterparts in Astana on 10 October, the EEC accord laid foundations for the eventual economic integration of the five countries as a counterweight of sorts to the EU.[16] The next day, at Bishkek, the same five countries plus Armenia met for a CIS Collective Security Pact summit and created a common

---

13. For a detailed analysis of the GUUAM and its activities at the OSCE summit, see the *Jamestown Foundation Report*, 6: No. 23 (1 December 2000).

14. On this see, Vladimir Mukhin, "Mirotvorchestvo pod flagom NATO"[Peacekeeping under the Flag of NATO], *Nezavisimaia gazeta* (5 October 2000), and *Nezavizimoe voennoe obozrenie*, No. 37 (6–12 October 2000).

15. On the importance to the foreign ministry of the recovery of the CIS, see Igor Ivanov, *Novaia Rossiiskaia diplomatiia*, pp. 103–117.

16. On this see, for example, *Nezavisimaia gazeta* (11 October 2000), and Andrei Shafarov, "Rossiia mozhet izvlech' vygodu iz Evraziiskogo ekonomicheskogo soobshchestva" [Russia Can Extract Benefits from the Eurasian Economic Community], *Nezavisimaia gazeta* (14 October 2000). For the Eurasian Economic Community's founding statement, see ITAR-TASS (10 October 2000). For a later detailed and supportive study of the Eurasian Economic Community, see an interview with Nigmatzhan Isingarin, chairman of the integration committee, "Prezidenty reshili, chinovniki pereinachili. Poka tak budem, govorit' ob integratsii ne prikhoditsia" [The Presidents Decided, and Officials Made the Changes. If We talk this Way, Then There Will Be No Talk of Integration], *Obshchaia gazeta*, No. 45 (9–15 November 2000).

security force. The consequent agreement, "On the Status of Forces and Means
Collective Security Systems," allowed members to send troops to each other's te
tories, on request, to repel military aggression "from without," carry out joint aı
terrorist operations and conduct military exercises. Religious and political extremi
were targeted, and Afghanistan was depicted as the world's center of both "inter
tional terrorism and drug trafficking." It is clear from Russian commentary that ı
upgrading of the Collective Security Pact was seen both as a counter to NATO
pansion in the region,[17] and as a vehicle for drawing American help into the aı
terrorism campaign.[18] Suggestions that, for example, Russia and the United Stː
could work under the auspices of the UN to resolve the Afghanistan problem w
commonly heard in Moscow a full year before the events of 11 September 2(
brought Washington's full force to bear on the Taliban.

Illegal emigrants also were deemed a problem; but the most consistent the
was the notion that there existed a "conspiracy against the young independ
states" led by "Islamacists"—Chechnya and Tajikistan were offered as evidence
this assertion.[19] It did not go unnoticed that the creation of the EEC and upgr
ing of the CIS Collective Security Pact institutionalized existing splits within
CIS.[20] These developments may have been the most significant consequences
Putin's trip through Central Asia, from Astana to Bishkek, but there were other ı
portant, if less spectacular, accomplishments as well. In Kazakhstan, he ᵃ
Nazarbaev signed an agreement to cooperate fully on matters related to
Caspian Sea and they both spoke of a much strengthened partnership.[21] A feat
in the *Nezavisimaia gazeta* attributed these new tightened links to the comn
and "growing danger of Islamic extremism."[22] Separate arms sales agreements,
example, with Kyrgyzstan, were byproducts of the Collective Security Pact su
mit, and Putin himself talked enthusiastically of his ventures eastward as a natı
and historical direction for Russia.[23]

---

17. See, for example, Svetlana Babaeva, "Evraziiskoe NATO" [A Eurasian NATO], *Izvestiia* (12 O
ber 2000); Vladimir Mukhin, "Kollektivnaia oborona" [Collective Defense], *NVO*, No. 39 (20–26 O
ber 2000); Vladimir Berezovskii, "Sodruzhestvo sozdaet kollektivnye sily bezopasnosti" [The Comn
wealth Creates a Collective Security Force], *Rossiiskaia gazeta* (12 October 2000).

18. For an interview with the General Secretary of the CIS Council for Collective Security, Vɑ
Nikolaenko, see "Dogovor obrel novoe dykhanie" [The Pact Finds a New Breath], *Krasnaia zvezda*
October 2001).

19. See, for example, Yurii Kirinitsiianov, "Evraziiskii proekt: ot idei k praktike" [The Eurasian I
From Idea to Practice], *Rossiiskaia gazeta* (10 October 2000), Vladimir Berezovskii, "Sodruzhestvo soz
kollektivnyi sily bezopasnosti" [Commonwealth Creates Collective Security Forces], *Rossiiskaia gazeta*
October 2000).

20. See, for example Yekaterina Tesemnikova, Armen Khambabyan, " 'Shesterka' protiv 'piaterl
[The Six against the Five?], *Nezavisimaia gazeta* (14 October 2000).

21. See, for example, "Evraziiskii proekt: ot idei k praktike" [Eurasian Project: From Idea to Pract
Rossiiskaia gazeta (10 October 2000), and *Izvestiia* (10 October 2000).

22. See, for example, Yekaterina Tesemnikova, Armen Khanbabyan, " 'Shesterka' protiv 'piaterl
[The "Six" Against the "Five"?], *Nezavisimaia gazeta* (14 October 2000).

23. Vladimir Putin, "Rossiia: Novye vostochnye perspektivy" [Russia: New Eastern Perspectives], *N
visimaia gazeta* (14 November 2000).

By the time the final CIS heads-of-state summit for 2000 met in Minsk over 19–30 November, certain lines had been drawn. The Eurasian Economic Community and GUUAM represented a well-defined divide within the CIS, though the latter body had no formal structure as yet.[24] At the Minsk summit, Putin held bilateral conversations with Georgia's Eduard Shevardnadze, Azerbaijan's Heydar Aliev, Ukraine's Leonid Kuchma, Moldova's Petru Lucinschi, Tajikistan's Emomali Rakhmonov, and Uzbekistan's Islam Karimov. He worked especially hard to reduce tension with Georgia and Ukraine, with some success (see chapters 3, 8, 9). The summit reached a consensus on the anti-terrorist center proposed earlier, and vague plans for the expansion of inter-CIS economic relations were announced. The CIS budget was set at 237 million rubles, and Yurii Yarov's position as the Commonwealth's executive secretary was confirmed.[25]

As Putin's first year as president drew to its conclusion, the high priority allocated to the CIS in Russia's new Foreign Policy Concept still held true. Putin's first post-election visits had been to Belarus and Ukraine, followed by tours of Turkmenistan, Kazakhstan and Azerbaijan. Free-trade regulations were put in place, programs for joint use of natural resources were worked out, and tentative accords were reached on the Caspian Sea—though in this connection much still needed to be done. Combatting terrorism, especially in regards to Afghanistan, brought closer cooperation with Uzbekistan and Tajikistan.

Collaboration on specific issues had not prevented existing divisions in the CIS from effectively splitting into two groups still characterized by the degree of their bilateral relations with Russia: Belarus, Kazakhstan, Kyrgyzstan, Tajikistan and Armenia on the pro-Russian side; Georgia, Ukraine, Uzbekistan, Azerbaijan and Moldova, that is, the GUUAM states, on the other. But Moscow was by no means cut off from the GUUAM. Its relations with Kiev rapidly improved towards the end of the year, as did its associations with Uzbekistan and Azerbaijan. In short, Moscow's traditional place as the major player in Eurasia was reconfirmed, at least to a far greater extent than it had been in 1999.

CENTRAL ASIA IN 2000

During 2000, Russian observers grew increasingly edgy about American inroads into the former Soviet Central Asian republics, especially after consecutive visits to the region in March–April by CIA Director George Tenet, FBI Director Louis J. Freeh, and Madeleine Albright. In response, the notion of a common Eurasian civilization was resuscitated throughout Russia. In addition to Aleksandr Dugin's Eurasia movement, whose leadership included representatives of several nationalities and religions,

24. A GUUAM-United States consultative forum was inaugurated at the OSCE summit in Vienna, but its nature remained unclear. On the CIS summit divisions, see *Kommersant* (1 December 2000).

25. For an enthusiastic analysis of the Minsk meeting, see Vladimir Yefanov, "SNG: dolgostroi ozhivilsia" [CIS: Never-Ending Construction Project Revives], *Rossiiskaia gazeta* (5 December 2000).

ethnic Russians wrote aggressively of Eurasia as their traditional sphere of influe
on the one hand, and of Slavic solidarity on the other.[26]

Albright's mid-April tour of Kazakhstan, Kyrgyzstan and Uzbekistan was oste1
bly to follow up on discussions of the region's serious problems with border con1
and concomitant drug- and arms-running. A promise of aid in resolving these n
ters, up to $3 million, was played up in Moscow as a blatant attempt by the Uni
States to purchase a foothold in these oil-rich countries. That was why so much ฯ
made of Kazakhstan's Nazarbaev's mild rebuke of Albright for "meddling" in Kaza
stan's internal affairs.[27] More was made of Russia's need to consolidate its own p฿
tion in Central Asia, against both American inroads and the forces of "internatio
terrorism and religious extremism" emanating from Afghanistan. The villain in 1
latter threat was obvious to the FSB—Osama bin Laden.[28] In fact, Russian and C
tral Asian leaders were worried more about Bin Laden's movements than they w
about Washington.

On 21 April, a meeting in Moscow of Shanghai Five ministers of the interior
leased a communiqué calling for joint action against terrorists and separatists. M
isters of defense had issued a similar statement from Astana a week previously, ฿
Russia's MoD spokesman Leonid Ivashov called on the Shanghai Five to supp
each other in all matters, including the guarantee of Taiwan as part of China.[29] T
plainly had in mind fundamentalist Islam making Central Asia a renewed focu฿
their attention. Duma speaker, Gennadii Seleznev, in Astana as leader of a par
mentary delegation from Moscow, accused Albright of attempting to "divide ฿
conquer" the former Soviet republics (Interfax, 21 April). It has been mentioned
ready (Part I) that Nazarbaev had reproached Albright for meddling in Kazakhst฿
internal affairs, but he was restrained in comparison to a subtext common to R
sian reporting about "Islamic terrorists" and "extremists" in the region; that is,
vague suspicion that the United States might be helping the Taliban.[30] Ameri฿
sponsorship of Bin Laden during the protracted war against Soviet intervention

---

26. See, for example, Zhumagul Saadanbekov, "My neobkhodimy drug drugu" [We Need Each Ot1
Sodruzhestvo NG, No. 2 (23 February 2000), and Yurii Godin, "Slavianskaia solidarnost' i evroatlant
eskie orientiry" [Slavic Solidarity and the Euro-Atlantic Orientation], *ibid.* For the concern about A1
ican inroads, see Vladimir Skosyrev, "Pochti po Kiplingu. SShA vedut 'bol'shuiu igru' v Tsentral'noi ฿
[Almost Like Kipling. The USA Plays the "Great Game" in Central Asia], *Izvestiia* (1 April 2000); see
Vitalii Strugovets, "Neft' na dne Kaspiia" [Oil at the Bottom of the Caspian], *Krasnaia zvezda* (17 1
2000).

27. See, for example, Boris Vinogradov, "Ekzamen na demokratichnost'" [Examination on Den
racy], *Izvestiia* (18 April 2000); Vladimnir Berezovskii, "Prokhladnyi priem v teplykh kraiakh" [Cool
ception in Hot Regions], *Rossiiskaia gazeta* (20 April 2000).

28. See, for example, Oleg Falichev, Yurii Pirogov, "Novyi geopoliticheskii vyzov" [A New Geopoli
Challenge], *Krasnaia zvezda* (21 April 2000).

29. See Ivashov, "Piaterka 'Shankhaiskoi piaterke'" [The Fifth Shanghai Five" Meeting], *Kras฿
zvezda* (13 April 2000).

30. See, for example, Mekhman Gafarly, "Kto stoit za islamskimi terroristami i ekstremistami" [฿
Is behind the Islamic Terrorists and Extremists], *Nezavisimaia gazeta* (27 June 2000); Vladislav Shury
"Zachem 'Talibanu' chuzhaia zemlia?" [Why Does the Taliban Need Somebody's Land?], *Krasnaia zv฿*
(6 June 2000).

in Afghanistan had not been forgotten. All in all, however, Russia's analysts on Central Asian affairs treated, with relief, Albright's venture into the Eurasian hinterland as a failure in American policy-making.[31]

Nazarbaev remained consistently in Russia's camp, calling for greater economic integration of the CIS remnant, while still advocating close cooperation of his country with the PfP. He had been warning his population since 1999 that a domino effect of "religious extremism" was threatening their republic. In December of that year, he foresaw terrorism spreading into Kazakhstan from Tajikistan and Uzbekistan, and insisted that "partnership with Russia" was the essential condition for his country's strategic security. China and America were also singled out as crucial, if somewhat less so, to Kazakhstan's safety.[32] Nazarbaev had visited Moscow in June 2000, shortly before Albright arrived in Astana, to sign an agreement for Russia's continued use of the Baikonur space complex. Doubtless, he and Putin discussed a joint approach to the United States.

Uzbekistan's allegiances were less clear. President Karimov, another former CPSU First Secretary, openly courted NATO and friendship with Washington in 1999, and was the first state to refuse to renew the CIS collective security agreement. But he too repeated the need to remain "on friendly terms with Russia," preferring a bilateral relationship over a bloc association.[33]

Karimov had visited China in November 1999 and, having reconciled with Tajikistan, discussed the possibility of cooperation with the Shanghai Five. A Uzbekistan-China joint statement that "the forces of religious extremism and national separatism pose a serious threat" to the stability of Central Asia was a point on which Tashkent and members of the Shanghai Five clearly could agree.[34] From the Russian perspective, of course, Uzbekistan's new connection with the Shanghai Five allowed that group an insight of sorts to GUUAM.

It had taken some time for the Central Asian leaders to warm to Putin. For the most part, they had either stayed somewhat aloof, or were kept at a distance while Putin served as prime minister during the fall of 1999. It was not until well after he became president that signs of a renewed integrative and cooperative mood in the Kremlin became apparent. Political leaders in Uzbekistan and Tajikistan, and to a lesser extent Turkmenistan, had greeted Russian presidential aide Sergei Yastrzhembskii's hint in May 2000 that a preemptive Russian attack on Afghanistan's Taliban leaders was not out of the question with some trepidation. Such warnings carried mixed blessings. Central Asian presidents worried about the Taliban encouraging an Islamic revolution in their countries, but they didn't want to provoke it themselves; nor did they want Russian troops based permanently on their soil. An outbreak of

---

31. See, for example, Fedor Olegov, "SShA pytaiutsia vziat' revanch" [The USA Tries to Take Revenge], *Sodruzhestvo NG,* No. 4 (26 April 2000), and Yurii Egorov, "Tashkent ne liubit, kogda ego uchat demokratii" [Tashkent Does Not Like to be Taught Democracy], *ibid.*

32. "Nazarbaev Stresses Importance of Partnership with Russia," Interfax (15 December 1999).

33. "Karimov Discusses Foreign Policy on Television," Uzbekistan Television First Channel Network (29 April 1999), FBIS-SOV, No. 504 (5 May 1999).

34. For reports from Beijing, see ITAR-TASS (8, 9 November 1999).

violence on the borders of both Uzbekistan and Kyrgyzstan on 12 August com
cated the matter. Officials in Bishkek and Tashkent blamed the battles, in wh
dozens were killed on both sides, on "religious extremists" based in Tajikistan. 1
Tajik government denied that there were any such bases on its territory.

This situation was placed high on the agenda for the Yalta CIS summit set
18–19 August 2000. Tajikistan's Rakhmonov met with Putin at Sochi a few days
fore the summit was convoked. They agreed to coordinate their efforts against
rebels, and set the stage for what eventually became a large deployment of Russ
troops in Tajikistan.

Turkmenistan and Russia also had pulled away from each other in 1999, in part
cause of disputes over the Caspian Sea. Turkmenistan's claim to specific sectors of
Sea as its "inalienable right" was challenged by Moscow in September of that year. A
gabat's agreements with major oil companies, PSG (General Electric and Bechtel) ¿
Shell to build a gas pipeline across the floor of the Caspian to Azerbaijan, Georgia ¿
Turkey, was seen in some Russian circles as part of a giant anti-Russia conspiracy.[35]

Although President Saparmurad Niyazov, yet another former CPSU First Sec
tary (who was made president for life in December 1999 and later had him
named a "prophet"), from time to time made an effort to reassure Russians that
hoped for stronger ties with Moscow, relations remained cool. A dialogue 1
opened between Niyazov and Putin in January 2000, when natural-gas deals w
negotiated. The Turkmen president told journalists at the time that a "healthy" e
nomic partnership with Russia was clearly possible.[36] Only Tajikistan, caught up
most of the post-Soviet years in civil and religious conflict and violent disputes w
neighboring Afghanistan—and sometimes Uzbekistan—remained unwaverin
loyal to, and reliant upon, Russia. A treaty of "alliance and cooperation" signed
Yeltsin and Rakhmonov in April 1999 called for closely coordinated cooperatior
the international arena, and in "military-political matters." Tajikistan had joined
"Group of Four," making it a "Five" in 1999, and quickly agreed to renew the (
Collective Security Pact—bringing the number of signatories to six. Rakhmor
conservative pro-communist president since late 1992, made it clear that strate
economic and culture relations with Russia were his priority in foreign affairs.[37]

The continuing importance of Central Asia was such that almost immediately
ter his inauguration on 7 May 2000, Putin set out for Uzbekistan and Turkmenist
In the latter republic, he signed agreements to purchase and transport huge volu
of Turkmen gas over a long period of time. This agreement had the effect of tying

---

35. For a general report, see Interfax (22 November 1999). The "agreement" took the form of a "
laration" during the OSCE summit in Istanbul, but it had not been fully agreed-upon by year's end
cause of a dispute between Turkmenistan and Azerbaijan over export quotas.

36. See, for example, Mikhail Pereplesnin, Yegor Yashin, "Niyazov i Putin nashli obshchee" [Niy:
and Putin Come Closer], *Nezavisimaia gazeta* (20 January 2000). On the eerie and growing "Niya:
cult in Turkmenistan, see Ilan Greenberg, "When a Kleptocractic, Megalomaniacal Dictator Goes B
The New York Time Magazine (5 January 2003).

37. See Rakhmonov speech, Radio Tajikistan First Channel Network (8 September 1999), FBIS-S
No. 910 (13 September 1999).

Turkmen gas exports, and undermining the Baku to Ceyhan pipeline project.[38] The appointment, on 31 May 2000, of Vikto Kalyuzhnii, former minister for fuel and energy, to a new position as Russian deputy foreign minister with special responsibility for Caspian affairs, revealed how important the region was to Putin's new foreign and economic initiatives. Indeed, an agreement between Gazprom, Russia's monopoly gas company, and the oil conglomerates LUKoil and Yokos, to work together on Caspian exploration was another such signal.

In Uzbekistan, Putin and Karimov stressed mutual interests in opposing Islamic fundamentalism, while the RF ministry of defense made vague threats about preemptive strikes against the Taliban forces threatening both Uzbekistan and Tajikistan. Karimov and even Putin distanced themselves from the aggressive posing by the MoD. Yet no one denied that the threat was there. Certainly, at a meeting of CIS Collective Security Members in Minsk, the danger of further strife in Central Asia and the Caucasus was the main subject of conversation. "International terrorism" had merged with "aggressive separatism, religious intolerance and organized crime," they warned, while calling for closer cooperation in collective security for all of the CIS member-states (Interfax, 24 May).

In August, Uzbekistan finally requested Russian aid in combatting "religious extremists" after several months of border area conflict. Needed mostly were military and technical equipment and special services assistance (Interfax, 29 August). Russian nationalist groups had been calling for collective action against "international extremism and Islamic radicalism" for some time and the situation in Central Asia gave their claim that the dilemma was universal greater credibility.[39] Some Russian observers even made the point that continued tension in the region was to their country's advantage in that it allowed Moscow to assert its geopolitical interests.[40] It was in August as well that Kyrgyzstan withdrew its planned participation in a PfP exercise scheduled for Kazakhstan in September because fighting between extremist islamic factions on the border between its country and Tajikistan as the reason why its troops were needed at home.[41] Shortly after that Uzbekistan and Kyrgyzstan signed a military alliance specifically for the purpose of fighting "Islamic extremism."[42]

---

38. For earlier comments on this policy, see Semon Novoprudskii, "Podvig patriota. Rossiia perekupila turkmenskii gaz u Turtsii i Ukrainy" [Patriotic Deed: Russia Bought Turkmen Gas out from under Turkey and Ukraine], *Izvestiia* (21 December 1999); Arkady Dubnov, "The Big Transcaspian Pipeline Project Flops," *Moscow News* (26 January–1 February 2000). The gas deals with Turkmenistan were upgraded in September 2002.

39. On this, see for example, Vladimir Strugovits, "Vmeste protiv obshchikh ugroz. Voennoi integratsii stran Sodruzhestva—byt'!" [Together Against the General Threat. There Will Be Military Integration in the CIS!], *Krasnaia zvezda* (2 September 2000); see also *ibid.* (26 August 2000); and Semen Novoprudskii, "Sodruzhestvo zavisimykh gosudarstv" [Commonwealth of Dependent States], *Izvestiia* (2 September 2000).

40. "IDU na vy," *Kommersant vlast'* (22 August 2000); on the "domino effect" of extremism, see, for example, Maksim Yusin, "Effekt domino" [The Domino Effect], *Izvestiia* (25 August 2000).

41. On this, see Viktoriia Sokolova, "Kirgizii ne do NATO" [Kyrgyzstan Does Not Need NATO], *Izvestiia* (23 August 2000).

42. On this, see Boris Vinogradov, "S dumoi o talibakh" [With Thoughts about the Taliban], *Izvestiia* (27 September 2001).

On the military side, Moscow agreed in June to take part in the 4th Tsentraz
exercise planned for September and including troops from eleven countries:
USA, Britain and Turkey from NATO, Russia, Kazakhstan, Armenia, Uzbekist
Azerbaijan, Georgia, Ukraine and Mongolia. But Moscow limited its role strictly
was also agreed, at another CIS heads of state summit in Moscow, 21 June, that R
sia would keep a military base and troops in Tajikistan when the existing peaceke
ing force was disbanded. Kyrgyzstan's Akaev announced in July that his cour
would strongly support the CIS Collective Security Pact at its summit slated for (
tober. He was in Moscow confirming the strategic partnership between his cour
and Russia and, with Putin, signed a "Declaration of Eternal Friendship and Pi
nership between Russia and Kyrgyzstan."[43]

Kazakhstan and Russia moved still closer together after meetings between Pι
and Nazarbaev in Moscow, following the CIS summit. Both used traditional rhetι
in speaking of broadening and deepening relationships, while their prime minisι
signed a number of bilateral protocols on mutual communication and informat
technology exchanges, energy production consolidation, and joint anti-terro
undertakings. Russia remained concerned about Astana's participation in the Bal
Ceyhan oil pipeline project, especially in July after Kazakhstan announced extra
dinary new oil finds on its share of the Caspian shelf, but there appeared to be ι
son for optimism even in that sector.[44]

The meetings in Dushanbe of the Shanghai Five, called the Shanghai Forum
cause Uzbekistan sent observers, during the first week of July helped clarify the rι
tionship between Russia and the countries of former Soviet Central Asia. In addit
to a common front against Islamic fundamentalism and separatist terrorism, Ru
was the natural market for the region's products. Officials in Moscow saw the Sha
hai Forum as an ideal vehicle for the harmonization of the Central Asian grι
within the CIS in its dealings with China; and a vehicle through which Russia co
expand its interests in Central Asia.[45]

The Forum revealed a strategic potential as well: it could also counter intrusiι
by NATO. Ironically, NATO General Secretary Robertson arrived in Uzbekistan j
as the Shanghai Forum was opening. This was his third stop in a five-country C
tral Asian tour which began on 3 July. In Astana, Robertson hinted that Kazakhs

---

43. At least one writer showed little faith in Kyrgyzstan's friendship, saying that that country had
reformed and Akaev may have signed the "eternal friendship" treaty with Russia merely to ensure his ι
election. See Zurab Toduc, "U Moskvy piavilsia vechnyi drug" [Moscow Has Found an Eternal Friε
ship], *Obshchaia gazeta,* No. 31 (3–9 August 2000).

44. On this, see Armen Khanbabyan, "Moskva i Astana namereny postupatel'no razvivat' otnosheι
[Moscow and Astana Intend to Develop Relations Progressively], *Rossiiskaia gazeta* (27 June 2000). A ι
sortium of some of the world's largest oil companies, the Offshore International Operating Comr
(OKIOC) announced on 8 July that the find could contain as much as 50 billion barrels.

45. See, for example, Yurii Savenkov, "Zachem nam 'Shankhaiskaia piaterka'" [Why Do We Nee
be in the Shanghai Five], *Izvestiia* (4 July 2000); Svetlana Babaeva, "V Dushanbe za novym miropor
kom" [To Dushanbe for a New World Order], *Izvestiia* (5 July 2000); Svetlana Babaeva, "Progulk
Azii" [A Walk through Asia], *Izvestiia* (6 July 1001); Sergei Sumbaev, "Novaia vstrecha 'Shankhaisko
aterki'" [A New Meeting of the Shanghai Five], *Krasnaia zvezda* (5 July 2000).

should have a special relationship with NATO like the one "enjoyed' by Russia and Ukraine,[46] and the Alliance granted that country $450,000 to help clear up the nuclear testing damage done to Semipalatinsk. The Russian response to this tour was notably more muted than it had been to similar Solana expeditions in 1997 and 1998,—or even to Albright's venture into Central Asia in 2000—but the image of NATO as a front for the interests of Washington and international oil/gas consortia was a widely accepted one in Moscow. Kazakhstan's central place in the Shanghai Forum was one way of neutralizing NATO's inroads.

No matter how smoothly the bilateral and regional relationships were working for Moscow in Central Asia, they were subject at all times to the vicissitudes of civil war in Afghanistan. In September 2000, the Taliban claimed to have taken the town of Talikan, in northwest Afghanistan close to Tajikistan's border. The Afghan government, that is, the non-Taliban government-in-exile still recognized by the UN, Moscow and many other states, blamed Pakistan, accusing Islamabad of providing arms and mercenaries. Sergeev promised more military–technical help to the countries threatened by Afghanistan and suggested that the "6 plus 2" group offering assistance to Afghanistan (six countries bordering Afghanistan, plus Russia and the United States), become more directly involved in negotiating a settlement. As we have seen, Russian peacekeeping forces already had been posted to the Tajik-Afghan border for some time.[47] It remained to be seen how active that force would get.

Diplomacy was the first order of the day, and the Kremlin worked hard to bring Washington on board. Igor Ivanov and Madeleine Albright discussed this matter in New York during the millennium summit and agreed to "coordinate" efforts in bringing peace to the region (ITAR-TASS, 7 September). A few weeks later, presidential aide Yastrzhembskii travelled to Islamabad for talks with senior officials in that city, and was able to announce that Pakistan was prepared to host a meeting of interior ministers from Russia, Uzbekistan and Tajikistan. Yastrzhembskii and his hosts did not discuss Afghanistan directly during his two-day sojourn in Islamabad, where the more general matters of organized crime, drug trafficking, and border issues were the topics of the day, but the subtext was clear—international terrorism was becoming anathema even to countries where the religious or ideological inclinations of, in this case, radical Islamic groups might expect to find official support.[48] The perceived danger was such that Ukraine sent an observer to the CIS collective security meeting in September.

There was also a growing inclination in America to treat Central Asia as a hotbed of international terrorism. Uzbekistan's Karimov also had met with Albright during the millennium celebration in New York and she promised American help against terrorism and drug trafficking. This marked a concrete change in Washington's attitude.

46. "NATO—za osobye otnosheniia s Kazakhstanom" [NATO Wants Special Relations with Kazakhstan], *NVO*, No. 24 (7–13 July 2000).
47. See, for example, Vladimir Yermolin, "Mirotvorcheskaia missiia v Tadzhikistane okonchena" [Peacekeeping Mission in Tajikistan Ended], *Izvestiia* (22 June 2000).
48. See Yastrzhembskii, "Pakistan's Goodwill Gesture," *Moscow News* (4 October 2000).

Yet her actual commitment at that time was slight. A total of about $10 millior aid to Kazakhstan, Kyrgyzstan and Uzbekistan was small stuff, and her unwelcon wide-ranging criticisms of governments in those countries for their perceived sl(ness in moving towards economic and democratic reform had implied that United States was not much interested in major involvements the region. Parad(cally, by September Russia was encouraging American involvement in an area t the Kremlin traditionally had seen as its own sphere of influence. At that time, h(ever, it was important that Washington be brought around to Moscow's preoccu tion with international terrorism. It was hoped too that Western opinion on Che nya could be softened, and the legitimacy of Russia's self-image as Europe's bast against Islamic terrorism bolstered. Indeed, at least one Russian essayist hinted t Tajikistan was not as threatened as its government claimed. In short, a straw n may have been introduced by Tajikistan to serve the broader purpose of dragging United States into the fray.[49] Whether this tale was believed or not, it did not w at that time

Uzbekistan's Karimov also saw a straw man, but from a different source, charg on 26 September that Russia was exaggerating the peril to get agreement for milit bases on Uzbek territory. All these conspiracy theories aside, most governments the region treated the threat from Afghanistan as a real one, as the 11 October (Collective Security Pact statement would suggest. At that same time, Russia and K gyzstan signed a deal to bring planes, helicopter gun ships and armored vehicle: the latter country at "ex-works" prices.[50] A nagging fear in Moscow was the spec of conflict in Afghanistan driving refugees by the thousands into Tajikistan. Car ing arms and drugs with them, the refugees could destabilize that country furt and launch a general breakdown in Central Asia that might then serve as a vor drawing in Russia, the United States, and perhaps even China.

At any rate, there was a fine line that Moscow would not cross in attracting Wa ington to its campaign against international terrorism; that is, Russia could not ford to weaken its own integrative mechanisms in Central Asia.

Another complication was Turkey's interest in Central Asia. In October, shortly ter Putin attended the meetings in Bishkek and Astana, Turkish President Sezer's t of Uzbekistan, Turkmenistan, Kyrgyzstan and Kazakhstan startled Russian anal into sitting up and taking notice. In Uzbekistan and Kyrgyzstan, Sezer signed do ments for joint action against terrorism and on military–technical cooperati Ankara's willingness to help in the struggle against the Taliban was welcomed Moscow, but claims by the Turkish press that the tour was also an attempt to br Iran's hold on the region was looked on with some skepticism. The image of NAT

49. Aleksandr Sukhotin, "Pressa pishet, a Taliban ne idet" [The Press Writes about It, but the Tali is Not There], *Obshchaia gazeta*, No. 37 (14–20 September 2000).
50. On this, see Viktoriia Panfilova, "V otnoshenii k talibam pozitsii Moskvy i Bishkeka polnost'iu padaiut" [In Regards to the Taliban the Position of Moscow and Bishkek are Fully in Accord], *Neza maia gazeta* (10 October 2000); see also Liudmila Romanova, "Putin otstaivaet Rossiiskie interes] Kaspii" [Putin Holds Russian Interests in the Caspian], *ibid.*

with Turkey as its first agent, poised to suborn Central Asia could not be shaken even after Russian Prime Minister Kasyanov's successful diplomatic sortie to Ankara in October 2000.[51]

Be that as it may, in November 2000 Washington began actively to seek Russian endorsement of joint military action against bases in Afghanistan said to be controlled by Osama bin Laden, whom they blamed for the attack on the *USS Cole*. Moscow had been lobbying for an international effort against Bin Laden for over a year, so this was good news. Russia and the United States already were working together lobbying on the UNSC, garnering support for further sanctions against the Taliban government in Afghanistan.[52] Ironically, the idea of joint military action in Afghanistan with American troops appealed to none of the major players in Central Asia, including Russia. The Russians were at that time reluctant to facilitate a military foothold in the region for the United States, just as the Uzbeks were dubious about having Russian troops on their territory.[53] Instead, the Russian Army general staff announced that it would deploy 50,000 troops of its own to form rapid reaction forces in South and Central Asia by 2003.

On 7 December 2000, Russian and American representatives finally put together a joint resolution for the UN Security Council calling for tighter sanctions against the Taliban. They demanded that diplomatic offices and national airlines around the world be closed, and that all flights to or from Afghanistan, with the exception of humanitarian and religious missions, be prohibited.

THE CIS IN 2001–2002

In his long year-end interview published in *Nezavisimaia gazeta* on 26 December 2000, President Putin echoed the theme of his Foreign Policy Concept, that is, that "relations with CIS countries—not with the CIS as an organization, but with CIS member countries—has certainly been and will be priority Number One for us."[54] Clearly, Moscow had come to accept the divisions within the CIS structure, the only absolute consideration being the fate of the over 20 million ethnic Russians scattered throughout the CIS.

---

51. See, for example, *Nezavisimaia gazeta* (19 October 2000), *op. cit.*, Chapter 3, above. See also Muharrem Sarikaya, "Security the Issue on Sezer's Central Asia Agenda," *Hurriyet* (Turkish language daily, Ankara) (15 October 2000), translated for FBIS-SOV, No. 1018; and *Nezavisimaia gazeta* (26 October 2000).

52. See, for example, Vladimir Paklin, "Petlia szhimaetsia vokrug ben ladena" [The Noose Tightens around Bin Laden], *Rossiiskaia gazeta* (19 November 1999). For a later piece, Maksim Yusin, "Islamiskii internatsional" [The Islamic International], *Izvestiia* (30 August 1999).

53. On this, see Vladimir Mukhin, "SShA gotovy nanesti udar po gruppirovkam ben ladena iz Uzbekistana" [The USA Prepares to Launch Blows from Uzbekistan against the Bin Laden Group], *Nezavisimaia gazeta* (24 November 2000). See also *Trud* (25 November 2000), where it was warned that Russia itself did not wish to be drawn into a Central Asian war.

54. *Nezavisimaia gazeta* (26 December 2000), *op. cit.*

Even Moscow's apparent success in reintegrating parts of the CIS in 2000 was universally praised by Russian foreign policy experts. ISKRAN Director Rogov, one, insisted in a major paper published in early January 2001 that Russia had dependable allies or partners and that the "CIS is largely a burden for Russia."[5] vigorous advocate of Russia's role as the transcontinental link between Asia and] rope, Rogov was more concerned about the integrity of Russian Eurasia than he ' of the CIS *per se*. Other analysts added that the threat to Russia's security was alw present in the CIS because of foreign predominance in oil and gas exploration ¿ transit rights in both the South Caucasus and the Far East.[56]

At a Shanghai Forum meeting in mid-April 2001, informal proposals for memb ships from Uzbekistan and Pakistan were debated, but decisions in both cases w postponed. Later meetings were more constructive. Prior to the sixth summit of group set for China on 15 June, the existing five members agreed that Uzbekis should join and that the enlarged body would be called the Shanghai Cooperat Organization (ShCO).[57] Pakistan's chances were still slim because it was assumec be supporting the Taliban. New memberships had to be unanimously agreed-up Mongolia, Turkmenistan and India were considering bilateral associations with Shanghai group, making it a regional economic association of some potential. P istan applied again in July, only to be rejected once more (Interfax, 18 July).

The CIS was back in the news on 25 April when nine of its member count agreed to carry out an anti-terrorist exercise in the Osh section of Kyrgyzstan. O Armenia and Turkmenistan were absent.[58] The next day Russia's predominance CIS security matters was verified. At a meeting of CIS security council heads in Ye van, Vladimir Rushailo was elected their chairman. As he was leaving Moscow that meeting in Yerevan, Russian representative Oleg Chernov, deputy chair of RF Security Council, told reporters that there was still a real danger of "Muslim rorists" crossing into the territories of Uzbekistan and Tajikistan. It was clear fr that and similar remarks from other delegates, that the problem of the Taliban ' very high on the CIS agenda.[59]

Russia's raised profile in the once near-defunct CIS had been highlighted in F ruary 2001 after a communist victory in Moldova's parliamentary election. Pa leader Vladimir Voronin campaigned on making Russian an official language ¿

55. Rogov, "Vektory bezopasnosti 2001 goda" [Security Vectors 2001], *NVO*, No. 1 (12–18 Jani 2001).

56. See, for example, Semen Kimel'man, Vladimir Sanko, "Ugroza natsional'noi bezopasnosti real [Threat to National Security is Real], *Nezavisimaia gazeta* (18 January 2001).

57. See Vsevolod Ovchinnikov, "Shankhai: Bezopasnost' cherez sotrudnichestvo" [Shanghai: Sect through Cooperation], *Rossiiskaia gazeta* (16 June 2001).

58. See, for example, Viktoriia Panfilova, ' 'V sotrudnichestve s Moskvoi ne razocharuemsia nikog ["There Is Never Disappointment with Moscow in the Commonwealth"], *Nezavisimaia gazeta* (24 ⅄ 2001); Aleksandr Shumilin, "Pered vesennim shturmom" [Before the Spring Storm], *Izvestiia* (24 ⅄ 2001).

59. On this, see Vadim Solov'ev, "Rossiia: Iz chechenskogo ognia da v aziatskoe polymia" [Russia: F the Chechen Frying Pan into the Asiatic Fire], *NVO*, No. 15 (17 April–10 May 2001). See also Dm Gryzunov, "Afganskii uzel" [Afghan Knot], *NVO*, No. 14 (20–26 April 2001).

bringing Moldova into the Russia–Belarus Union. By year's end he was successful at least in the former ambition, when Moldova made Russian a requirement in schools (Kyrgyzstan had adopted it as a second official language). In his turn, Putin delayed the planned withdrawal of Russian troops from the self-proclaimed Transdniester Republic and, in May, Moldova recommended that Russia be invited to participate in GUUAM. The creation in May, on paper at least, of a Eurasia Transportation Corridor for the purpose of transporting goods across Eurasia from Asia to Europe also had the effect of making Central Asian countries more reliant on Russia.[60]

Yet the GUUAM kept its distance. A June meeting of its leaders, at Yalta, saw little interest shown in Russian participation and the organization adopted more institutional trappings. A charter finally was signed by member presidents and a consular convention was adhered to by each country's foreign minister. None of this enabled it to formulate a workable trade agreement, however, as existing bilateral trade arrangements and membership of two of them (Georgia and Moldova) in the WTO complicated matters.

Even though Uzbekistan remained out of the Russianist loop in the CIS, including the RRF which would incorporate troops from Russia, Kazakhstan, Kyrgyzstan and Tajikistan, its need for help against potential Taliban incursions prompted President Karimov to pay an official state visit to Moscow in early May 2001. This was the second visit of that status in three years, a somewhat unusual circumstance. Karimov was quoted as saying that Russia must provide leadership against the terrorists and the Russian press treated the visit as a major accommodation between the two CIS countries.[61] Russia's military ties with the Central Asia states were themselves institutionalized in June with the appointment of General Vladimir Yakovlev to head an army section for coordinating military relations with CIS countries. On 9 June, Putin signed two agreements for military–technical cooperation in the CIS, one with foreign countries, the other for members of the CIS Collective Security Pact. The common desire was to curb Wahhabism, that is, Islamic fundamentalism, which governments in Moscow and Central Asia tended to equate with terrorism.[62]

An informal CIS meeting of presidents held at Sochi in the first week of August was marred only by the absence of Shevardnadze and Niyazov. The leaders discussed drug trafficking, peacekeeping and the ABM, but their sessions were overshadowed by oil field disputes on the Caspian involving Azerbaijan, Turkmenistan and Iran. Putin tried to act as a broker of peaceful solutions to such disputes, and at the same

---

60. On this, see an interview with the Russian minister of transport, Sergei Frank, "Vse dorogi poidut cherez Rossiiu" [All Roads Will Go through Russia], *Rossiiskaia gazeta* (18 May 2001). The agreement was reached by CIS ministers of transport meeting in Astana, Kazakhstan.

61. See, for example, Gaiaz Alimov, "Osobyi priem" [Special Reception], *Izvestiia* (4 May 2001);Yurii Egorov, "Bezopasnost'—glavnaia tema dlia Putina i Karimova" [Security Is the Main Theme for Putin and Karimov], *Nezavisimaia gazeta* (4 May 2001).

62. On this, see, for example, Sergei Sokut, "Kreml' mostit dorogi k oboronnoi integratsii" [The Kremlin Paves the Way for Military Integration], *NVO*, No. 21 (15–21 June 2001); Aleksandr Vladimoriv, "Terror vo slavu Allakha. Ostorozhno vakhkhabizm!" [Terror for Allah's Glory. Beware of Wahhabism!], *Rossiiskaia gazeta* (6 July 2001).

time protect Russia's interests in the region. But all parties held to their positions ɛ
not much progress was achieved.[63]

After the formation of an anti-terrorist coalition with the United States in S
tember 2001, with states from both GUUAM and the EEC participating direc
the CIS was again regenerated somewhat. For the first time in several years, all mɛ
bers were present at a meeting of heads of state in Moscow at the end of Noveml
Even Shevardnadze was there in a conciliatory mood. The meeting celebrated
CIS's first decade, adopted joint anti-terrorist resolutions, and urged expanded inɪ
CIS economic relations. A communiqué claimed that the founding of the CIS,
spite of its problems, had helped ensure that the breakup of the USSR would ͪ
peaceful one, and guaranteed cooperation in infrastructure matters such as tra
portation, power and communications networks, and population transfer. Even sɪ
matters as mutual recognition of each other's academic and other specialist qual
cations had been facilitated by CIS infrastructure. The fact that the agreement
fight terrorism was pushed hard by Moscow, was evident in the communiqués'
hortation that coalition members adhere to international law and the UN Charte
Rights (presumably to forestall an American attack on Iraq), and the unanimous ·
position to any Taliban membership in the new Afghan government.[64]

The exuberant and inclusive comradeship in the CIS was short-lived, and did
survive the collapse of the Taliban for very long. By January/February, 2002, Moscc
place in Central Asia was more uncertain than it had been even a year earlier and
CIS appeared shaken yet again. Soothing comments from Moscow's officialdom t
the United States had no plans to stay permanently in Central Asia after the war w
belied both by statements from American members of Congress and the nature of
bases taken over by U.S. forces in three of the Central Asian countries.[65]

CENTRAL ASIA GEARS UP
AFTER 11 SEPTEMBER 2001—REDIVIDING THE CIS

The events of 11 September and Russia's quick entry into a worldwide anti-terro
coalition led by the United States had a special impact on circumstances in Cen

---

63. On the CIS summit, see Igor Sizov, "Bez galstukhov" [No Neckties], *Rossiiskaia gazeta* (2 Au
2001); Albert Kochetkov and Vladimir Berezovskii, "Bez Niyazova i Shevardnadze . . ." [Without N
zov and Shevardnadze . . .], *Rossiiskaia gazeta* (2 August 2001), and Aleksei Baliev, "ProSOCHIt'sia
taki nado . . ." [The Sochi Show Must Go On . . .], *Rossiiskaia gazeta* (1 August 2001).

64. See "10 let v otsutstvie liubvi i smerti" [10 Years in the Absence of Love and Death], *Nezavisin.
gazeta* (29 November 2001); Alan Kasaev, Armen Khanbabian, "Ottsu-osnovateliu SNG podyskiv
mesto v ego strukturakh" [They Seek a Place in the CIS Structure for the Founding Fathers], *Neza
maia gazeta* (30 November 2001)."Sammit SNG otkryli ministry" [The CIS Summit Opens a Minis₁
Rossiiskaia gazeta (29 November 2001); Yuyrii Yarov, "A karavan idet . . ." [A Caravan Moves Out .
Rossiiskaia gazeta (30 November 2001).

65. Serge Fedor Sukhov, "Yanki moiut sapogi v aryke. Amerikantsy ne namereny pokidat' Sredn
Aziiu" [Yankees Wash Their Boot in the Ditch. Americans Do Not Intend to Leave Central Asia],
shchaia gazeta, No. 6 (7–13 February 2002), and *Rossiiskaia gazeta* (22 January 2002).

Asia. Uzbekistan and Tajikistan were placed on high alert. The former country practically rushed into the American fold, especially after a visit by Donald Rumsfeld. An
official agreement on cooperation was signed between Tashkent and Washington,
causing Russian concern about a long-term Uzbek–American military relationship.[66]
Uzbekistan's membership in GUUAM and active participation in NATO's PfP operations had already resulted in the establishment of a NATO school for training
NCO's in Tashkent. The Russian MoD's only hope was that the association would
be short-term.[67]

On the other hand, Tajikistan announced on 9 October that American troops
would not be allowed to base on its territory. There already were 19,000 Russian
troops (8,000 regular troops from the 201st Division, and 11,000 border guards) in
Tajikistan. Rakhmonov's pronouncement came after a CIS Collective Security Pact
wound down a meeting in Bishkek. On 2 October the CIS council of directors of
security agencies issued a statement condemning terrorism, and agreed to coordinate
their efforts in the fight against the phenomenon. In short, the group chaired by
Rushailo tried to regain some initiative in central Asia's anti-terrorist campaign.

Uzbekistan, Tajikistan, and Kyrgyzstan still worried about their ability to handle
an influx of refugees. For Russia, of course, the specter of a powerful American presence in Central Asia, challenging the recently upgraded Shanghai Five, Eurasian Economic Community, and the CIS Collective Security group for influence in Eurasia
and Central Asia, was ominous. Moscow's officials rushed to tighten up Russia's links
in the region.[68] On the other hand, the same Moscow officials complained that when
the bombing campaign was finished the Americans would likely leave Russia holding the bag in the region—faced with floods of refugees, angry followers of Islam,
destabilized CIS countries, economies disrupted, and huge military debts. One analyst warned of permanent disaster and apocalypse.[69] There was some doubt as well
about the permanence of American "friendship" when the actual fighting days were
over.[70]

When, on 15 October 2001, Washington and Tashkent made official an earlier
verbal agreement guaranteeing Uzbek security in return for access to Uzbek airfields
(Khanabad), the situation darkened for Moscow. Uzbek officials did not turn up at
an extraordinary meeting in Bishkek of the ShCO even though earlier it had applied
for formal admission to the group. It appeared as well that some 2,000 American

---

66. See, for example, Vladimir Mukhin, "SShA ishchut voennye bazy v SNG" [The USA Seeks Military Bases in the CIS], *Nezavisimaia gazeta* (15 September 2001), with special emphasis on Tajikistan and
Uzbekistan.

67. Vladimir Berezovskii, "Uzbekistan vstaet v ruzh'e" [Uzbekistan Takes Up Arms], *Rossiiskaia gazeta*
(5 October 2001).

68. On this, see, for example, Sergei Sokut, Vladimir Mukhin, "Voina otkryvaet put' k peredelu mira"
[The War Opens the Way to a Changed World], *NVO*, No. 36 (28 September–4 October 2001).

69. Dmitrii Furman, "Naperegonki s apokalipsisom" [A Race against Apocalypse], *Obshchaia gazeta*,
No. 40 (4 –10 October 2001).

70. On these matters, see, for example, Edvard Batalov, "Rossiia i SShA: Druz'ia? Soperniki? Partnery?"[Russia and the U.S.: Friends? Rivals? Partners?], *Nezavisimaia* (6 October 2001); and *Izvestiia* (2
October 2001).

troops were already sited in Uzbekistan, though officials in Tashkent continued
deny it. Some Russian commentators saw this as a signal that Uzbekistan was go
to concentrate its efforts on GUUAM and move closer to NATO.[71] Because
course of events was in danger of moving quickly beyond the Kremlin's control, th
were very harrowing times for decision makers in Russia.[72] Certainly, Russia c
centrated on Tajikistan, where its troops were located and where allied meetings w
much more frequent than in Uzbekistan. Putin stopped in Dushanbe on his ret
from the Shanghai APEC conference, meeting with Rakhmonov and Northern
liance leader, Rabbani. It was to the Tajik border with Afghanistan as well t
Moscow delivered train-carloads of tents, blankets and foodstuff for refugees.

In mid-November, while Putin was in the United States, the Taliban withdi
from Kabul and the Northern Alliance walked in—against the wishes of the Uni
States. Within hours Russia had a delegation in the city, moving quickly from Ta
istan to help orchestrate the shaping of a new government. Russians met with R
bani and made it plain that they expected to play a significant role in post-Talil
Afghanistan. Instrumental in Russia's haste, one can assume, was deep-rooted ar
ety about Washington's special agreements on bases with Uzbekistan and Tajikist
Moscow did not wish to be pushed to the sidelines in Central Asia. Rumor ha
that these agreements came with grants of billions of dollars to the two host co
tries, something that Russia could never hope to match.[73]

The issue of American presence in Central Asia likely was discussed privai
when Colin Powell met with Putin and other senior Russian officials on 10 Dece
ber. Powell arrived in Moscow after a tour of Central Asia and Kazakhstan. An ag
ment allowing U.S. forces to use bases in Kyrgyzstan was reached in Bishkek, me
ing that Washington had new unilateral military ties related to the anti-terro
campaign with all members of the Shanghai Cooperative Organization, except
China. Perhaps to sooth Russia's sensibilities, Powell took the opportunity to ad
that there were terrorists in Chechnya and left a door open for eventual Russian
mission into NATO. But these minor concessions did little to assuage widespr
worry in Moscow about American presence in Central Asia.[74]

71. See, for example, Vladimir Berezovskii, "Tashkent i Vashington udarili po rukam" [Tashkent
Washington Strike a Bargain], *Rossiiskaia gazeta* (16 October 2001). In fact, by July Uzbekistan had "t
porarily" withdrawn from GUUAM.
72. For a general cautionary note about Russia (and the West's) new role in central Asia, see Yefim I
van, "Tsivilizovannyi mir dolzhen izmenit'sia—ili on proigraet" [The Civilized World Must Change-
It Will Be Lost], *Obshchaia gazeta,* No. 42 (18–24 October 2001). See also Vladimir Aleksandrov, e
"Sredniaia Aziia dzhikhada ne boitsia" [Central Asian Does Not Fear a Jihad], *ibid.,* No. 41 (11–17
tober 2001); Michael McFaul, Nikolai Zlobin, "Pogruzhenie v 'tepluiu voinu'" [Immersion in a "W
War"], *ibid.*; and Konstantin Totskii, *ibid.* No. 39.
73. On this, see Vladislav Kulikov, "Utrom den'gi, vecherom spetsnaz" [Money in the Morning, :
cial Forces in the Evening], *Rossiiskaia gazeta* (16 November 2001).
74. See, for example, Armen Khanbabyan, "Amerikanskoe prisutstvie v Tsentral'noi Azii rasshiriae
[American Presence in Central Asia Is Expanding], *Nezavisimaia gazeta* (11 December 2001); Sergei
zlov, "Vstuplenie Rossii v NATO uspokoit vsekh" [The Admission of Russia into NATO Will C
Everyone], *Nezavisimaia gazeta* (14 December 2001), accompanied by a large photo of Colin Powell sl
ing hands with Kazakhstan's Nazarbaev.

The debate over Central Asia was intensified as news of American investment in rebuilding air bases and leases circulated in Moscow. When it was calculated that over $1 billion would probably be spent in the region for infrastructure and that subsequent rents would be paid, Russian experts began to assume that Americans were there to stay.[75] Russian military and media began to warn about "encirclement" in the old Soviet style, pointing to the greatly enlarged American (and British) military presence in Central Asia, Turkey, Cyprus, Northern Europe, South Korea, and Japan—and wonder aloud if the Caucasus was next on Washington's list. The flurry of visits to Moscow by leaders of states on Russia's southern flank—Iraq, Iran, Turkmenistan, Azerbaijan—and senior Russian officials travelling to India and China, were all connected to the Kremlin's worry that its own hold on Central Asia was slipping. The sudden policy turn to the West in September 2001, became somewhat qualified in 2002 as Russia's foreign ministry reverted to its former focus on Central Asia.[76]

This did not mean that Putin gave up on his preference for the West, rather it signified that a return to the East was essential if the CIS was to be salvaged. Moreover, it demonstrated that the Russian power elite, wary of American unilateralism, still insisted on keeping Moscow's presence in Eurasia intact and strong. The resuscitated Russian diplomatic offensive in Central Asia had a public forum in March, at a ShCO meeting in Moscow, where representatives of the foreign ministries of all member countries agreed to begin drafting a formal charter for the organization. Meetings for foreign ministers were planned for Moscow in June, and the possibility of a regular meeting of the ShCO heads of state in St. Petersburg in early June was mooted as well. Clearly, Moscow was hoping to consolidate its leadership position in the Shanghai group—a point confirmed by the Russian envoy to the ShCO, Vitalii Vorobev.

The ShCO was back in the news in May 2002 when, during a meeting of its defense ministers in Moscow, it was decided that a standing mechanism and working groups be created to manage joint operations in matters of security and defense. The military leaders committed themselves to consolidated military cooperation against "terrorism, separatism, and extremism." They also supported the notion of a nuclear-free zone in Central Asia.

History might lead one to conclude that this was all talk, yet an upgrade of the CIS Collective Security Treaty bloc, creating a Collective Security Treaty Organization in part to counter NATO's expanding interest in the region, was confirmed as well. This occurred in Moscow at a conference held over 14–15 May. On 13 May, that is, a week prior to the Putin–Bush summit, a Eurasian Economic Community forum also had been opened in Moscow. The presidents of Russia, Belarus, Kazakhstan, Kyrgyzstan,

---

75. See, for example, Mikhail Khodarenok, " 'Starshego brata' sdali za milliard dollarov" [Big Brother Betrayed for $1 Billion], *Nezavisimaia gazeta* (30 January 2002).

76. On this, see for example, Andrei Ryabov, "Russia to Set Traditional Foreign Policy Priorities," *Vek*, No. 4 (2002), translated for JRL No. 191 (January 2002); Armen Khanbabyan, "Amerikanskaia morskaia pekhota v stepiakh Kazakhstana" [American Marines on the Kazakhstan Steppes], *Nezavisimaia gazeta* (29 March 2002). This latter piece was front-page, with large headlines.

and Tajikistan were in attendance, with their counterparts from Ukraine and Mold
there as observers. Admission to the WTO, continuing intrastate trade barriers ;
taxation, and a finalized charter for that organization were the main subjects on
agenda.[77] The general consensus reached on all of these matters could not hide so
of the fundamental weaknesses of this particular consortium of CIS states: Kyrgyzs
had been admitted to the WTO in 2000, making it subject to a different set of ri
than the ones applied to the CIS customs union; and widespread protective meast
still prevailed over the long-promised free trade. And the CIS itself seemed to h
reached some kind of impasse.

Among the intricate webs holding Russia's Eurasian organizations together w
the long arms of Gazprom and LUKoil. So too was the beguiling role of the Russi
language print and television media. Given the fact that the Central Asian indi
nous media is more strictly controlled by authoritarian governments than Russia's
readers and viewers turn to Russian-language papers and channels. Russian TV p
gramming, in fact, is of a far higher quality than its Central Asian counterparts, ;
it presents familiar fare. Thus, the Central Asian populations, no matter their eth
origins, are grounded in Russian interpretations of events. The importance of this
ality is hard to measure, but should not be underestimated.

Few analysts in Russia pretended that any of these integrative organizations ;
groups, or even cultural agencies in Central Asia truly rivalled the importance
Russia of NATO or the EU. But their continued existence and indeed their grov
had special significance. They provided the appearance, at least, of a Russia with
ternative cards to play in the new Great Game in international affairs. By the enc
May 2002, then, the Russian two-headed eagle saw relative stability in both dii
tions as it peered East and West.

---

77. On the significance of this forum, see Aleksei Chichkin, "Kak iz Evrazii popast' v WTO?" [F
Can One Get into the WTO from Eurasia?], *Rossiiskaia gazeta* (14 May 2002).

11

✝

Courting China and India

On 20 April 2000, Deputy Foreign Minister Aleksandr Losyukov told reporters that the importance of Russia's ties with India and China would increase in the twenty-first century. Together, he said, the three large countries were the most consistent opponents of a "monopolar world." They were also committed to "rebuffing international terrorism" as it was then defined by them, that is, various forms of religious extremism, separatism, and radical nationalism. Their governments also held opinions in common on events in Yugoslavia and Chechnya. Losyukov's perspective was representative of positions taken regularly by the RF foreign ministry since Igor Ivanov replaced Primakov as minister in September 1998.[1]

In 2000 views such as these were among the few shared across Russia's political spectrum. Along with the notion that the CIS must remain Russia's foreign affairs priority, for example, the stance taken by the CPRF both before and after the election campaign that diminished its influence in Russian politics was much the same as the government's position on China, India, and Yugoslavia, Chechnya and the question of mono- or unipolarism.[2] It remained for these connections also to be worked out by Putin.

We have already seen that Putin's eastern policy was far more complex and extensive than anything mounted by Yeltsin. By the end of 2000, in addition to the Central Asian CIS countries, he had visited every important nation of the Far East—.China, Japan, Mongolia, Vietnam, and both Koreas; and also India in Southeast Asia.

---

1. Primakov, foreign minister since January 1996, was confirmed as prime minister 11 September 1998. He too had looked to India—one of the USSR and Russia's longest-lasting strategic partners—and China as alternative "partners" after Andrei Kozyrev's westernizing approach seemed to have failed. See *Russia Faces NATO Expansion, passim.*

2. See, for example, Gennadii A. Zyuganov, "Fal'shivoe druzheliubie" [False Friendliness], *Sovetskaia Rossiia* (13 May 2000).

THE FAR EAST

Speaking to a regional forum of the Association of Southeast Asian Nati⟨
(ASEAN) countries in July 1999, Foreign Minister Ivanov used the NATO bor
ing of Yugoslavia as an example of what might happen if the concept of a multi
lar world was not soon universally adopted. Reminding his Moscow audience ⟨
speech Yeltsin had delivered to the G-8 summit in June, he warned that the Uni
States was prepared to launch an anti-missile defense program in Northeast Asia
less the ASEAN could do something to ease tension in the Koreas. Ivanov called
national reconciliation and proposed that North Korea be invited to participate
the activities of the regional forum of ASEAN members. This was one of the earl
signs that the Kremlin was worried that Washington's hostility to what came to
called "rogue" states, particularly North Korea, could greatly complicate Eurasian
fairs.[3] Moscow's policy vis-à-vis North Korea will be dealt with in this chap
mostly, rather than in the following section devoted entirely to the "rogues" beca
it cannot easily be separated from Russian relations with China.

As Ivanov set out to visit North Korea, Japan and Vietnam for the week of 9-
February 2000, Russian columnists pondered his expedition's importance. One
perienced journalist believed it to be a direct response to the "stormy polemic w
the United States and the EU" over Chechnya.[4] The "accomplishments" of each v
varied in their strategic value, naturally enough, but overall they represented a ⟨
tory in the perception of Moscow as a player in Asian affairs with renewed vigor. ⟨
fact that communists still held power in two of the states, and that Moscow's r⟨
tions with China were growing in strength, at least according to official rhetoric, p
vided Ivanov's venture an ironic historical overtone.

In Pyongyang he signed a new Treaty of Friendship, Good-Neighborly Relati⟨
and Cooperation, sparking some upset in the West. The treaty said unequivoc⟨
that it was "not aimed against a third country" and that Russia would provide no r
itary assistance to North Korea. The meetings in North Korea marked the first ti
a foreign minister (or any prominent dignitary) from Russia had travelled there si
1990. Most Russian analysts knew very well that reassociation with the unusu⟨
isolated regime in Pyongyang would provide little more than a sideshow in the
newed East–West geostrategic competition.[5] There was a faint hope that Mosc
might demonstrate by its diplomacy that direct dealing with the "rogues" could
more productive than name-calling, threats and segregation. Moreover, Moscow ⟨
Beijing recently had agreed that North Korea should not be isolated from the in⟨

---

3. The Regional Forum of the ASEAN was created in 1994. For Ivanov's statements, see ITAR-T⟨
(26 July 1999); see also Gennadii Charodeev, Maksim Yusin, "Putin letit v Pkhen'ian" [Putin Flie
Pyongyang], *Izvestiia* (10 June 2000).

4. Vsevolod Ovchinnikov, "Vostochnyi marshrut" [Eastern Route], *Rossiiskaia gazeta* (15 Febr⟨
2000).

5. See, for example, "Kak nam otkryvali Koreiu" [How We Opened Up Korea], *Obshchaia gazeta*,
30 (27 July-2 August 2000), where the optimism expressed in Moscow about its "success" in North
rea was called an "illusion."

national community, so Ivanov also was fulfilling a small role in developing the multipolar world of which Russia and China approved.

Just four months after Ivanov's talks in Pyongyang, that is, on 9 June, Putin's administration announced that the Russian president himself would visit North Korea on his way from China to Japan for the G-8 summit at Okinawa. It appeared therefore that Moscow's nurturing of a relationship with that particular maverick state had reached unexpected heights. The timing of the announcement was fortuitous: Clinton had just left Moscow, and Putin was setting out on his tour of Western Europe to discuss investment and his own nonstrategic defense system. And the presidents of North and South Korea were preparing for a historic "reconciliation" meeting to take place a mere one week later.

Following that last meeting, Foreign Minister Ivanov and some of Moscow's pundits credited their country with a mediating role, and Kremlin officials made much of the event's visible contradiction of the "evil" state image so important to American advocates of amendments to the ABM Treaty (Interfax, 29 June). Reactions at home were nonetheless mixed. Several Muscovite analysts saw the Kremlin's claims on behalf of North Korea as a "bluff" and potentially dangerous for Russia.[6] In his turn, Ivanov proclaimed that the North Korean problem could be resolved by declaring the entire Korean peninsula a nuclear-free zone. Left unsaid, at least at the official level, was the fact that no one considered Kim Jong-il to be a reliable neighbor, either for South Korea or Russia, but it was hoped that he could be persuaded to act in his and his country's best interest.

Vietnam, which with North Korea once covered the Asian flank of Moscow's socialist international camp, was quite a different matter. The country has a large population, is placed advantageously on trade routes, and has a wellspring of good feeling towards Russia. The potential for trade between the two countries was high. Vietnam actively coordinated relations between Russia and the ASEAN, providing Moscow with a real opportunity for influence in the region. Ivanov's visit was accompanied by much fanfare in Hanoi and was treated in Moscow as a big step towards countering a perceived rush to gain leverage there by American officials and energy entrepreneurs.[7]

In Japan, Ivanov was probably relieved that an expected discussion of a long-overdue peace treaty was postponed, presumably so that the issue of the Kurils would not muddy Putin's presidential campaigning. Questions about security in Southeast Asia, disarmament and UN reform were discussed in detail. Prime Minister Keizo Obuchi was handed a personal missive from Putin, who expressed a desire to maintain a "creative partnership" and cooperation within the framework of the UN and G-8. Putin, of course, was keeping the table set until more business could be done after the 26 March presidential election.

---

6. See, for example, Aleksandr Sukhotin, "Sever i Yug pozhali drug drugu ruki" [North and South Shook Hands], *Obshchaia gazeta*, No. 24 (15–21 June 2000). For Ivanov's self-congratulations, see *Novaia Rossiiskaia diplomatiia, op. cit.*, p. 159.

7. See for example, Dmitrii Kozyrev, "Igor' Ivanov pobyval v Khanoe" [Igor Ivanov Visited Hanoi], *Nezavisimaia gazeta* (15 February 2001).

His success in that election and the consequent consolidation of his polit
power base boded well for a resolution of even the Kuril issue, though in April a
tential crisis emerged when a Japanese ship was shelled and damaged by a Russ
coast guard vessel. Fortunately, neither Moscow nor Tokyo wanted to make an is
of the matter, so diplomacy prevailed. Russia apologized.

It was Putin's tour through the Russian Far East, Central Asia and Asia in June ɛ
July, culminating at the G-8 meeting in Okinawa, that brought the Asia poten
back to the forefront in Russian foreign policy deliberations. He met with Cen
Asian and Chinese leaders in Dushanbe, held further discussions with the presid
of China in Beijing and with the president of North Korea in Pyongyang, bef
conferring in Japan with the world's industrial giants. This was the proper way to
store Russia's role as a major power, or so the Russian media insisted. One longti
advocate of eastern links for Moscow, Vsevolod Ovchinnikov, raised the claim ag
that Russian and Chinese mediation could help stabilize the Korean peninsula, "
priving Washington of one of its pretexts for deploying a national anti-missile ʂ
tem."[8] Even those analysts who warned Moscow against putting too many eggs i
the Asia basket, still emphasized the tremendous importance of Asia to Russia.[9] ʈ
State Duma joined the chorus on 19 July, and approved the Treaty of Friendsh
Neighborliness and Cooperation with North Korea, 363–8 with one abstenti
Only Sergei Kovalov, of the Union of Right Wing Forces, spoke firmly against
calling North Korea a dictatorship and an unworthy friend for Russia. Koval«
warning appeared prescient in August, when Kim Jong-il told South Korean jo
nalists that his offer to suspend missile programs in return for booster rocket te
nology had been a "joke." The Kremlin's frantic denials notwithstanding, diploma
gains made by the Russian offensive in the Far East were tainted.

In the essay on potential conflicts facing Russia in the twenty-first century, p
lished in July and discussed elsewhere in this study, Andrei Kokoshin took the oʃ
mistic side when it came to the Far East (see chapter 5). Because the conflicts wo
stem, he believed, from the increased nuclear capacity of India and China, Ru
could be their natural conciliator. The potential for dispute between nuclear-arn
India and Pakistan, or Iran and an Afghanistan helped by Pakistan, and the possi
ity of China using force against Taiwan, all seemed feasible after NATO went ou
zone to bomb Yugoslavia, and Washington began to challenge the usefulness of
ABM. As an old adage would have it, one state's use of violence is another sta
excuse for violence. The onus was on Russia, Kokoshin continued, to augment
"India–China–Russia triangle" to stave off such crises.[10]

---

8. See, for example, Ovchinnikov, "Golovy Rossiiskogo orla smotriat i na Zapad, i na Vostok" [
Heads of the Russian Eagle Look Both to the West, and to the East], *Rossiiskaia gazeta* (28 June 200
9. See, for example, Dmitrii Kozyrev, "Putinu pridetsia proiti ispytanie Asiei" [Putin Will Be Put to
Test by the Asia Experience], *Dipkur'er NG*, No. 12 (13 July 2000); Sergei Merinov, "Vid s posledʜ
etazha shankhaiskogo neboskreba" [View from the Top Floor of a Shanghai Skyscraper], *Rossiiskaia ga*
(2 August 2000).
10. Kokoshin, "Kakie konflikty i soiuzy zhdut Rossiiu vo vtorom iadernom veke" [What Conflicts
Unions Await Russia in the Second Nuclear Century], *Izvestiia* (27 July 2000). At that time Kokoshin
also still a member of the CFDP.

Even as U.S. President Clinton postponed the NMD enterprise and Putin prepared for the gala UN Millennium summit in New York, Moscow–Tokyo relations
were firmed up. This does not mean that there was movement on the question of the
Kurils. There wasn't, a fact which Moscow's pundits blamed on Japanese obstinacy.[11]
The Russian president and foreign minister, with aides, paid an official state visit to
Japan on their way to New York in September. The absence of any movement either
on the Kuril Islands or a peace treaty between the two countries notwithstanding, a
number of important documents were signed by Putin and Prime Minister Toshiro
Mori. These included protocols on cooperation against organized crime, expanded
cultural ties and mutual support on matters of disarmament, the nonproliferation of
nuclear weapons, and high seas safety. Both sides acknowledged that their relationship warranted expanding, and Russia gave lip-service support to Japan's candidacy
for a permanent seat on the UN Security Council (just as it did for Germany and,
more tentatively, India).[12]

Even the peace treaty was the subject of a joint statement, both leaders agreeing
that the issue had to be resolved and promising that further negotiations were in order (Interfax, 5 September).[13] The Russian media took the visit to Japan very seriously, both as an excellent pre-UN Millennium gambit and as further evidence of
Putin's concern for Russia's eastern relationships. Most observers predicted that a
peace treaty would soon be arranged, raising the level of Russian presence in the Far
East, but not if it meant giving up the Kurils. On this they remained adamant.[14]
When the Japanese foreign minister, Yohei Kono, paid a quick call on Igor Ivanov in
Moscow on 3 November 2000 the Kuril issue again was set aside for the future.[15] In-
stead, the two foreign ministers discussed world issues in a very general way.

Nevertheless, the Asia-Pacific link continued to look very promising to some senior Russian officials. One of these was Yegor Stroev, chairman of the Federation
Council, who advocated making the development of eastern Siberia the springboard
for a major shift of Moscow's priorities eastward. China was the first country to recognize the advantages, both to Moscow and Beijing, of a new Russian surge to the
east, Stroev wrote, in a long essay for the *Nezavisimaia gazeta* in September. His interest had mainly to do with an economy that could be woven together with jointly-
owned and -built oil and gas pipelines. Yet it was no less obvious that, in his opin-

---

11. See, for example, Vasilii Golovnin, "Signal s Dal'nego Vostoka" [Signal from the Far East], *Izvestiia*
(2 August 2001), and Golovnin, "Na obeshchanii Kremlia postavlen krest" [The Kremlin Promise Is
Crossed Out], *Izvestiia* (19 August 2001).
12. On this, see, for example, Vsevolod Ovchinnikov, "Rossiia-Yaponiia: Vzgliad iz budushchego"
[Russia–Japan: View from the Future], *Rossiiskaia gazeta* (30 August 2000).
13. See Vasilii Golovnin, "Vozvrashchenie k podarku Khrushcheva" [Return to the Gift of
Khrushchev], *Izvestiia* (25 October 2000).
14. See, for example, Anatolii Koshkin, "Voina zakonchilas', no mir ne zakliuchen" [The War Is Ended,
but Peace Has Not Been Concluded], *NVO*, No. 32 (1–7 September 2000); for general praise of Putin's
action in Japan, see for example, *Rossiiskaia gazeta* (5 September 2000); *Izvestiia* (5 September 2000), and
even the communist press, for example Vasilii Safronchuk, "Rossiia i Yaponiia reshili sotrudnichat'" [Rus-
sia and Japan Decided to Cooperate], *Sovetskaia Rossiia* (5 September 2000).
15. On this, see "Moskva–Tokio: novaia glava" [Moscow–Tokyo: A New Chapter], *Nezavisimaia gazeta*
(3 November 2000).

ion, broader economic ties in the east would strengthen Russia's political positior
the world and perhaps make less urgent the current thrust for membership in the
and pleas for more investment from the West.[16] Almost simultaneously and in
other context, Dmitrii Trenin of Moscow's Carnegie Fund insisted that Russia's as
rations to be an Asian power was merely a "myth aimed at scaring Europe from ti
to time."[17] Trenin's opinion was somewhat of an anomaly at that time, for the the
of "Russia in Asia" was enjoying a burst of popularity in the Russian media and
riodical literature.[18]

Even the North Korean link had not been lost by Kim Jong-il's duplicity. Russ
communists made much of the fifty-fifth anniversary of the founding of the Work
Party of Korea. Oleg Shenin was sent to represent the CPRF at a celebratory cong
in Pyongyang, praising Kim Jong-il in the old intracommunist sycophantic mani
that is, as a "fighter against imperialism and their stooges," with "extraordinary le
ership qualities," and even as a builder of a "socialist paradise." To give the Russian
benefit of doubt, it should be pointed out that this was how the North Korean pi
reported Shenin's message. None of this maudlin silliness was reported in the Russ
communist press.[19] The Kremlin's connection with South Korea was more dire
Prime Minister Lee Han-dong was in Moscow on 9 October to meet with Kasyar
They talked about trade and the joint construction of a techno-park in South Koi
signed agreements in the fuel and energy sector, and emphasized Moscow's still-to-
played role in the inter-Korean reconciliation (Interfax, 10 October).

Madeleine Albright's trek to Pyongyang in October, marking the first meeting
tween a senior American official and a North Korean leader, may have stolen so
of Russia's thunder. But her tour certainly did not represent a change in Washi
ton's vision of what that country was all about, rather it signalled support for a No
and South Korean rapprochement. The meetings were accompanied by much ce
bration and eloquent toasts, and Albright watched and applauded a mass propagai
show featuring the heroics of North Korea's communist party, and its militaristic p
turing. Shenin was likely amused. At any rate, if anyone expected Albright's soi
what bizarre appearance with the North Korean leader to dissipate the image of
country as a "rogue" state preparing missiles against which a new American NN
could be constructed, they were in for disappointment.[20]

---

16. Stroev, "Vostochnyi vektor v Rossiiskoi strategii" [The Eastern Vector in Russian Strategy], *Ne.
isimaia gazeta* (14 September 2000); see also Ramazan Abdulatopov, "Vostochnyi vzgliad dvuglavogo (
[The Eastern Glance of the Two-Headed Eagle], *Nezavisimaia gazeta* (15 September 2000).

17. Quoted by Sophie Lambroschini, "Russia: New Study Sees NATO, EU Threat," JRL, No. 4!
#4, (20 September 2000).

18. See, for example, Vladimir Maksimenko, "Rossiia i Aziia, ili Anti-Bzhezinskii" [Russia and Asi:
Anti-Brzezinski], *Krasnaia zvezda* (28 October 2000); this was a summary of a much longer series
lining Imperial Russian and Soviet geopolitical interests in Asia, in *Vostok,* No's 1–5 (2000).

19. Translations from many Pyongyang press releases can be found on the World News Connect
FBIS-SOV.

20. See report by the head of a Russian delegation to the Russian-Korean Demarcation Commiss
Yurii Fadeev, "Rossiia iskrennie zainteresovana v vossoedinenii Korei" [Russia Sincerely Is Interested
United Korea], *Krasnaia zvezda* (28 October 2000).

On 14 November, Putin flew into Brunei from Ulan Bator, Mongolia, where he had spent a day putting pen to economic and other agreements with that country's president. These included a nonaggression pact and a confirmation that Mongolia would stay nuclear-free.[21] Some might say that neither accord mattered much in the larger international scheme of things, but they helped leave the impression that Russia was building coalitions in the East. Putin was in Brunei for the twenty-one-member Asia-Pacific Economic Cooperation (APEC) conference. There his delegation, which included Kasyanov and other Russian power officials, worked hard to bolster sagging Russian influence. In essays published in various Asian newspapers, the Russian president repeatedly put his country forward as the "integrative junction" linking Asia, Europe and North America. He offered vague commitments about expanding railroad services and roads in Eurasia for the purpose of transferring goods between Asia and Europe far quicker than by sea. In addition to the potentially important economic fallout such schemes would mean for Russia, Putin's pre-Brunei publicity campaign made it plain that the Kremlin hoped to balance its Eastern and Western affiliations. Joint projects with China, Korea, and Japan could bring infrastructure and other development to Russia's Far East that Moscow is not itself able to provide. Widespread approval of the Ulan Bator and Brunei meetings was chorused even by Russian communists, who saw them as positive steps toward reestablishing Russia as a Pacific power.[22]

The APEC gathering made it possible for Putin to hold private sessions with the American and South Korean presidents, the Japanese prime minister, and the Sultan of Brunei. At that time about 15 percent of Russia's foreign trade (roughly the same as with East and East Central Europe) was conducted with APEC, which agreed to support Russia's bid to become a member of the WTO. Russian observers saw great promise in this connection, seeing it as a potential "global center" and as an important forum in which Russia could be linked both to the ASEAN and the EU, perhaps via energy pipelines.[23]

CHINA 1999–2000

In early June 1999, a joint statement by the foreign ministers of Russia and China insisted that neither of them intended to form a "political–military alliance directed

---

21. Putin awarded Mongolian President Natsagiyn Bagabandi a Friendship Medal, and Kasyanov signed with his counterpart an agreement on inter-government cooperation.

22. On the importance of the Brunei meeting, see *Strana.Ru* (14 November 2000), and "Mirovaia biznes-elita prosit Moskvu raskryt' aziatskie karty" [The World's Business Elite Asks Russia to Disclose the Asiatic Card], *Rossiiskaia gazeta* (16 November 2000). For the more cautious communist perspective, see Vasilii Safronchuk, "Na vostochnykh shirotakh" [On the Eastern Latitude], *Sovetskaia Rossiia* (14 November 2000).

23. See, for example, *Rossiiskaia gazeta* (17 November 200), where it was predicted that APEC would become one of the "global centers"; and Vsevolod Ovchinnikov, "Bez nas i ATEC ne ATEC" [Without Us, APEC Is Not APEC], *Rossiiskaia gazeta* (14 November 2000).

APEC membership includes: Australia, Brunei, Canada, Chile, China, Hong Kong, Indonesia, Japan, Mexico, New Zealand, Papua-New Guinea, Peru, Philippines, Russia, Singapore, South Korea, Taiwan, Thailand, United States, and Vietnam. It was formed in 1989, Russia joined in 1998.

Chapter 11

against any country or group of countries" (Interfax, 2 June). This assurance did
forestall a sharp denunciation of NATO air strikes against Yugoslavia, calling thei
violation of the UN Charter. And they condemned NATO's attack on the Chin
embassy in Belgrade as a violation of both Chinese sovereignty and of internatio
law. The ministers were meeting in Beijing.

The Moscow-Beijing relationship had come a long way since 1992, when a r
Russian Foreign Policy Concept cautioned that differences in ideological and
ciopolitical systems still stood in the way of full partnership. Cooperation had b·
encouraged in that document, but it was not then a priority for a foreign mini:
headed by Andrei Kozyrev.[24] There is little doubt that NATO's "out of zone" act
ties drew Moscow and Beijing closer together. This happenstance was evident in
informal setting late in 1999 during meetings in China of the Russian–Chin
Committee of Friendship, Peace and Development for the Twenty-first Centu
Speaker after speaker, one of them China's minister of foreign affairs, reprimanc
NATO for putting the subjective concept of "human rights" above national sov
eignty and the United States for practicing "double standards" in this regard. Ch
and Russia had established a relationship of a different sort, the minister intoned
trustworthy partnership directed towards strategic cooperations for the twenty-f
century." He repeated that the partnership was aimed against no one, rather it r
resented the aspiration of both countries for a stable world. All rhetorical requ
ments aside, the mutual interest of Russia and China were very easy to see. In
analysis prepared during the first week of December, "old China hand" Vsevo
Ovchinnikov said that Russia and China had been driven closer together by
movement of NATO eastward, the broadening of U.S.–Japan relations, and Wa
ington's proposals to amend the ABM Treaty.[25] NATO's air strikes against Yugosla
merely accelerated a natural deepening of Moscow–Beijing relations and the res
rections of talk about a "great Eurasian triangle, Russia–China–India."[26]

From 10 to 11 December 1999, after three planned trips were postponed
Yeltsin for reasons of health, the Russian president finally showed up briefly in I
jing. He and Jiang Zemin issued a joint declaration on world affairs. They resta
their common views on such matters as NATO action in Yugoslavia, the U.S.
geting of the Chinese embassy in Belgrade, and Western "hysteria" against Rus:
military action in Chechnya. Russian analysts linked the declaration closely
Yeltsin's unsubtle reminder to President Clinton not to forget "for a moment t

24. For a translation of the "Kontseptsiia vneshnei politiki Rossiiskoi Federatsii," dated 25 Jani
1993, see special issue of FBIS-USR, No. 037 (25 March 1993).
25. Vsevolod Ovchinnikov, "Vmeste s Kitaem—v Tikhookeanskii vek" [Together with China into
Pacific Ocean Century], *Rossiiskaia gazeta* (8 December 1999). See also his, "Kitai: ko mne moi st
drug prikhodit" [China: My Old Friends Arrive to See Me], *Rossiiskaia gazeta* (25 November 1999);
an earlier feature by Yurii Savenkov, who wrote about China and Russia moving towards partners
"Tysiacheletnii Kitai spravliaet polveka" [A Thousand-Year-Old China Celebrates a Half-Centu
Izvestiia (2 October 1999).
26. On this, see Yurii Golotiuk, "Moscow–Pekin: Brat'ia navek-2" [Moscow–Beijing: Brothers for
Second Century], *Izvestiia* (9 June 1999).

Russia holds a full arsenal of nuclear weapons" and would not allow the United States to dictate to the entire world.[27]

The communiqué from Beijing was timely, for it demonstrated that Russia "had the support of a friendly nuclear state" exactly as EU leaders were considering the imposition of economic sanctions against Russia because of Chechnya. Participants in the EU summit then taking place in Helsinki were not troubled by the rhetoric from Beijing, but Russians were relieved to have a China card to display anyway. Analysts in Moscow saw French Foreign Minister Vedrine as their harshest tormentor, and both London and Paris as the "main instigators of the anti-Russian campaign in connection with events in Chechnya."[28]

Nothing had changed by late February 2000 when the foreign minister of China, Tang Jiaxuan, flew into Moscow and "firmly supported" Russia's policies in Chechnya (Interfax 29 February). According to Tang, the purpose of the meeting was to "deepen existing strategic and cooperative relations between the two countries."[29] This visit also was timely and important, in part because it served as preparation for another Russia–China presidential summit planned for the summer, and in part because of the mutual support Moscow and Beijing promised each other in international affairs. They both opposed U.S. attempts to amend the ABM Treaty and, in their communiqué, intervention "in the name of so-called humanitarian interference and protection of human rights" (Interfax, 2 March). On 2 March, Beijing's *People's Daily* ran articles extolling the benefits of a strategic partnership between China and Russia.[30] They spoke of creating a "just and reasonable new world order," that is, the multipolar world that both had been touting since 1992 as the antithesis to a Washington-driven unipolar world. More of the same, but perhaps comforting to those Russians who paid attention to foreign affairs.

While Tang Jiaxuan was in Moscow, Russian Deputy Prime Minister Ilya Klebanov was in Beijing discussing prospects for further sales of advanced weapons systems and energy to China. A few days afterwards a proposal to construct a pipeline to carry Russian oil through Mongolia to China was made public (Interfax, 8 March). The fact was, China needed oil from Russia (and Kazakhstan) if it was to maintain a battle-ready military. The importance of oil was given new meaning in March when a seven-year timetable for reunification of Taiwan with mainland China was announced in Beijing. If China's threats were ever to be to acted upon, oil reserves for its tanks, planes, trucks and ships were essential. The expectation in March 2000 was that, after Presidents Vladimir Putin and Jiang Zemin held their summer summit,

27. See Georgii Bovt, "Klintonu privet iz Podnebesnoi" [A Call to Clinton from the Heavenly City], *Izvestiia* (10 December 1999). For the joint declaration, "Sovmestnoe Rossiisko-Kitaiskoe zaiavlenie" [Russian–Chinese Joint Statement], *Rossiiskaia gazeta* (11 December 1999).

28. Nikolai Paklin, "Evropeiskii soiuz iavno toropitsia" [The European Union Is Clearly in a Hurry], *Rossiiskaia gazeta* (11 December 2000).

29. "Sino-Russian Strategic Alliance Slowed by Internal Issues," *Stratfor.com*. Global Intelligence Update (24 February 2000).

30. See "In Beijing. The Signs of a New Strategic Partnership," *Stratfor.com*. Global Intelligence Update (3 March 2000).

a more vigorous joint strategic agenda challenging American domination of world
fairs would follow.[31]

The issue of Russia–China relations was raised on several occasions during
Russian presidential election campaign in March. Zyuganov's communist platfc
made it explicit that China should be Russia's partner in its attempts to restore "
balance of interests in the world."[32] Chinese officials took a hand here. For exam|
when the national security adviser to Al Gore (see chapter 2), was in Moscow (
cussing START-II and the ABM Treaty, China's ambassador to Russia, Wu Tao, 1
with Deputy Foreign Minister Georgii Mamedov and voiced total support for R
sia's position on global stability and its stance on the ABM agreement (ITAR-TA
14 March). As we have seen, American proposals to amend the ABM Treaty w
consistently opposed by the Kremlin, and the China factor was often factored i
the Kremlin's calculations—at least by the Russian media. In April, ISKRAN Dii
tor Rogov mooted the possibility of Russia and China adopting joint measures in
defense field if Washington deployed a national missile defense system (Interfax,
April). He failed to mention a hidden concern for the Kremlin; that is, if the L
adopted an NMD to target missiles from, for example, North Korea, China mi
accelerate its own nuclear missile program. That outcome would be a much grea
threat to Russia than to the United States. Regardless, the China card was pla
consistently. Just as the Putin–Clinton summit got under way in June, the Russ
government announced that Putin was scheduled for a state visit to China for
July. This would be his first visit to an Asian country as president of Russia.

China's unity with Russia on the question of Yugoslavia had been demonstra
again in April by the Russian ambassador to the UN, Sergei Lavrov, and Chi
deputy ambassador, Shen Guofang. Members of an eight-person UN fact-find
mission to Kosovo who were to gather in Pristina on 26 April, the Russian and C
nese diplomats both took it upon themselves to meet first with Slobodan Milose
President of the UN Security Council, Canada's Robert Fowler, complained that
was "disappointed" with the representatives of two permanent members of
UNSC for dealing directly with "an indicted war criminal." But there was noth
else that he could do about it.

Later in the year, Li Peng, head of the Chinese parliament and former premier,
livered an address to Yugoslavia's parliament, denouncing NATO for its air campa
against that country. The UN indictment against Milosevic as a war criminal did
deter Li from meeting with the Yugoslav president either. The Chinese offi
claimed that the Serb minority in Kosovo was being subjected to genocidal practi
and called on NATO/UN forces to withdraw from Yugoslav territory. China, th
stood with Russia and, indeed, was more aggressive than Russia in its support of
ostracized Belgrade government.

---

31. For a long appraisal of potential for a true Russia–China strategic partnership, see Na
Airapetova, "Nadi li Rossii opasat'sia Kitaia?" [Should Russia Be Afraid of China?], *Nezavisimaia ga*
(3 March 2000).

32. See Zyuganov's election platform, *Rossiiskaia gazeta* (14 March 2000).

"Strategic partnership" were the buzzwords used regularly to depict the Russia–China relationship as the Shanghai Forum (see chapter 10) opened in Dushanbe on 6 July 2000. Certain Russian analysts, however, wrote that the rhetoric about "partnerships" with China had greater significance for their country than it did for Beijing. Above all, because the Dushanbe meeting preceded Putin's visit to North Korea and his participation in the G-8 summit at Okinawa, statements issued jointly with Chinese and Central Asian leaders were important as presummit position-taking. It already has been pointed out that the Shanghai Forum adopted a Declaration in which all member-states agreed to combat international terrorism, religious extremism and national separatism, thus granting Russian action in Chechnya explicit support. The Forum also called for full respect of the UN Charter and a "multipolar" world, opposed the interference of one country into the affairs of another, and granted unequivocal endorsement öf the ABM Treaty as a basis for international strategic stability (Interfax, 5 July). The degree of unanimity among Central Asian countries, Russia, and China on these matters warrants repetition. To be sure, the degree to which this like-mindedness would lead to joint political or even military stands remained untested.

At any rate, after naming China Russia's "strategic partner" in all fields, Putin set out for Okinawa with the full backing of the Shanghai Forum, plus Uzbekistan, whose President Islam Karimov had been there as an observer.[33] At the time, talk of turning the Shanghai group into a collective security system that might also include India and Iran was heard for the first time.

Two weeks after the Dushanbe meetings, Putin and Jiang again prepared a joint statement on the ABM Treaty. The statement was released in Beijing after lengthy negotiations between the two presidents over 17–18 July. It parroted exactly the Shanghai declaration and, in fact, the relevant parts of Russia's own new foreign policy concept; that is, the ABM Treaty is the "cornerstone of strategic stability."[34] The same Foreign Policy Concept had said that the "coincidence of the principal approaches of China and Russia to the key issues of world politics is one of the mainstays of regional and global stability." Putin could speak to Western and Japanese leaders with confidence that he had the backing of China.

The Kremlin's rush to highlight China's endorsement of its foreign policies was acclaimed publicly in Moscow, almost always with qualifiers showing that there were few illusions about the long-term benefits of relying on China as a partner in the international arena. In the meantime, however, the Russian delegation to Beijing was very thoroughly staffed, that is, with twenty high-level officials, only four of whom went on to Okinawa with Putin. With few exceptions, Russian analysts and officials gushed over the significance of Putin's meetings in Beijing. Stressing

---

33. Essays and editorials in the Russian media made much of these meetings, calling them breakthroughs and evidence of the correctness of the Putin approach to world affairs. See especially V. Vodolazhskii, "Piataia vstrecha 'Shankhaiskoi piaterki'" [Fifth Meeting of the "Shanghai Five"], *Rossiiskaia gazeta* (4 June 2000); see also Svetlana Babaeva, "Progulki po Azii" [A Walk through Asia], *Izvestiia* (6 July 2000).

34. "Sovmestnoe zaiavlenie" [Joint Statement], *Krasnaia zvezda* and *Rossiiskaia gazeta* (19 July 2000).

that "our positions coincide [on] strategic stability and security, [and] our appro:
to regional conflicts," the government newspaper underscored the enormous va
of the meeting's pre-G-8 timing. Less dependent papers echoed this opinion, c
gratulating Putin for "reinforcing the Asian component" of Russia's foreign pol
Even the communist media congratulated Putin for exploiting Russia's advant
with China to challenge American presumptiveness in the Far East and Cen
Asia.[35] An interview with Jiang Zemin, in which he said that Russia and China w
"good partners, good neighbors, and good friends" was printed in several Russ
papers.[36]

For all that, something as permanent as a Russian–China alliance was strikin
absent from the commentary. Among the major papers, the *Obshchaia gazeta* '
one of those to offer words of caution. Aleksandr Sukhotkin warned that, whei
the United States was a known quantity, China and Japan were unpredictable. R
sia should take care not to be drawn into any "anti-American alliance" or comn
ments to the wrong things. Sukhotkin offered similar advise about Moscow's atta
ments to India.[37]

Aleksandr Sabov tended to downplay the notion of a "strategic partnership" v
China as well, noting that Beijing had similar arrangements with the United Sta
France, Britain and Japan. He did attach great significance to the joint statem
against amendments to the ABM Treaty, which included a specific protest agai
any involvement of Taiwan in an ABM system "created by foreign states."[38] Ger
ally, however, Russian analysts treated the Asia Grand Tour taken by Putin and F
eign Minister Ivanov (who was back in Shanghai and Bangkok in August for ASE
meetings), as evidence of Russia's "new confidence" in foreign policy and an ove
strengthening of its international standing.[39]

Chinese delegations flocked to Moscow in the fall of 2000: a Chinese People's I
eration Army delegation toured Russia and Finland for two weeks, beginning on
August; a Communist Party group arrived on 23 August, meeting with Zyuganov, ‹

35. See, for example, Vasilii Safronchuk, "Dal'nevostochnyi brosok" [Far Eastern Charge], *Sovets.
Rossiia* (25 July 2000). See also, "Vostochnaia magistral'—ot Moskvy do Pekina, cherez XXI vek" [E
ern Highway, from Moscow to Pekin through the 21st Century], *Rossiiskaia gazeta* (19 July 20
Dmitrii Gornostaev, "Prezident otpravilsia v Aziiu" {The President Headed to Asia], *Nezavisimaia ga
(18, 19 July 2000).

36. See for example, "Kitai i Rossiia—khoroshie partnery, khoroshie sosedi, khoroshie druz'ia" [C]
and Russia. Good Partners, Good Neighbors, Good Friends], *Rossiiskaia gazeta* (18 July 2000).

37. Sukhotkin, "Asiatskie smotriny 'malen'kogo bratishki'" [Asian Visit of "Little Brother"],
shchaia gazeta, No. 28 (13–19 July 2000). He stressed the dangers of "swimming in the labyrint
Eastern politics."

38. *Krasnaia zvezda* (19 July 2000), *op. cit.*, and Vadim Markushin, "Za spravedlivyi miroporiac
[For a Just World Order], *Krasnaia zvezda* (21 July 2000); "Pekinskaia deklaratsiia Rossiiskoi Federai
Kitaiskoi Narodnoi Respubliki" [Pekin Declaration of the Russian Federation and the Chinese Peo
Republic], *Rossiiskaia gazeta* (20 July 2000).

39. See, for example Sergei Merinov, "Vid s poslednego etazha Shankhaiskogo neboskreba" [View f
the Last Level of the Shanghai Skyscraper], *Rossiiskaia gazeta* (2 August 2000), where it was said that I
sia's full accord with the ASEAN represented Moscow's "special confidence," and Yevgenii Belen'kii
Aziei u nas vse neplokho" [Everything Is Not Bad for Us in Asia], *Nezavisimaia gazeta* (2 August 20(

even with Zhirinovskii—who called for even closer relations between Russia and China. A few weeks later a fifty-person deputation from China's parliament, led by Li Peng, was in Moscow for a nine-day visit. This time it was the Chinese who spoke of promoting a "strategic partnership of cooperation with Russia" and of their "identical or similar" views on many issues in international affairs. Li spoke against the U.S. NMD proposal, accusing Washington of seeking to create a "mono-polar world and head it."[40] It was clear that both sides planned to maintain common cause against American and NATO intervention in sovereign countries—at least when such actions were not sanctioned fully by the UNSC. The grandiose words about strategic partnerships were mainly rhetorical insofar as this particular visit was concerned, for they were not reflected in any specific agreements related to the international situation.

Li's time in Moscow was spent primarily on energy and economic matters, and it was for those purposes that he met with Putin, Kasyanov, Gennadii Seleznev and Federation Council chairman Yegor Stroev. One consequence of these sessions was a parliamentary return visit to Beijing in October, led by Fatherland All-Russia leader Yevgenii Primakov. As a former Russian foreign and prime minister, Primakov was able also to schedule a meeting with President Jiang Zemin.

Kasyanov followed Primakov to Beijing during the first week of November, meeting mainly with Zhu Rongli, but also with Jiang Zemin and Li Peng. This marked the fifth prime ministerial meeting since the two countries established a strategic partnership in 1995. Their negotiations resulted this time in fourteen specific agreements, including a commercial arrangement covering the years 2001–005.[41] One of the accords confirmed the sale to China by Russia of an Advanced Warning and Control System (AWACS), substituting for a similar system made available to China earlier by Israel in a deal thwarted by strong pressure on Tel Aviv from Washington.

Kasyanov volunteered that he would "welcome" the formation of a Moscow–Beijing–New Delhi "axis" (Interfax, 3 November), and he confirmed Russia's absolute support of China's position on Taiwan.[42] In fact, he and Zhu signed a communiqué calling the PRC the "sole legitimate government of China and Taiwan." Zhu told reporters that the China–Russia relationship was now the firmest in their mutual history.

The requirements of diplomatic bombast aside, the consistency of Russian–Chinese public pronouncements on world affairs in 2000 was striking: they spoke as one on the need for a "multipolar world," and in opposition to NATO expansion, NATO's role in Yugoslavia, and the concept of "humanitarian intervention" by

---

40. ITAR-TASS (11 September 2000). See also reports filed from Moscow and printed in the paper *Xinhua*, FBIS-CHINA, No. 912. The China–Russia Friendship Committee for Peace and Development, founded in 1996, met in Beijing during August. For an overview of the new relationship from the Chinese perspective, see an interview with the editor of a Chinese newspaper by Vladimir Mokhin, "Ot Moskvy do Pekina gorazdo blizhe, chem my dumaem" [From Moscow to Beijing Is Much Closer than We Think], *Krasnaia zvezda* (28 September 2000).
41. All fourteen agreements are listed in a release by ITAR-TASS (3 November 2000).
42. On the revival of the "axis" concept, see *Kommersant* (4 November 2000); on the Taiwan question, see Yellena Lashkina, "Udachnye peregovory Mikhaila Kas'ianova v Pekine" [Successful negotiations of Kasyanov in Beijing], *Nezavisimaia gazeta* (4 November 2000).

NATO. They provided mutual comfort on Chechnya, Tibet, Taiwan, the NMD ¿ ABM, and in their warnings about international terrorism, separatism, and "extrε ism." Moscow and Beijing lobbied for admission to the WTO and advocated the premacy of the UN in resolving regional conflicts. In the case of the latter organi tion, they provided vocal support to India's candidacy for a permanent seat on UNSC. Ironically, it may be that Russian–Chinese unanimity in these matters { ther weakened the resolve of the United States and other NATO countries to rely the UNSC to resolve regional conflicts.

That being said, Putin greatly raised the level of Russia's profile and participat in Asian affairs during 2000. Visits to China, North and South Korea, Japan, Inι Mongolia, and Vietnam, and his participation in the APEC meeting at Brunei, stored a balance to the Kremlin's foreign policy that had been missing for some tiι

THE FAR EAST, 2001–2002

Early in 2001, the Russian foreign ministry was surprised by a bid from Pakistar join the Shanghai Five (see chapter 10). At first blush this might seem to be a ɾ jor breakthrough, for Moscow had expended considerable energy in 2000 tryin{ raise the level of its relationship with Islamabad, and persuade that country noι support the Taliban in Afghanistan. On the other hand, Moscow did not wish see its strong association with India jeopardized in any way. The situation was h dled for the time being by a Russia foreign ministry statement to the effect t there were no established "procedures" for a new membership of this sort. Interι ingly, there had been no such cover to duck under when it was rumored in 2(that Uzbekistan might join, especially after President Karimov attended a sessioɾ the Shanghai Five.

A Shanghai Five meeting of foreign ministers in April 2001 saw more arran ments reached on combatting terrorism and separatism, and more joint support the inviolability of the ABM. An agenda for the next full meeting was set for Ju when the groups would meet in Shanghai to celebrate the organization's "landma anniversary."[43]

A five-day Putin tour of South Korea and Vietnam in late February–early Ma sustained the diplomatic offensive eastward initiated in the previous year and rai Russia's star in parts of Asia where it had dimmed during the 1990s. The visit Seoul was mostly symbolic, though expanded economic cooperation was agr upon, the inviolability of the ABM Treaty was promoted, and Putin offered to h facilitate inter-Korean accommodation.[44] In Hanoi, however, a framework fo strategic partnership was deliberated along with cooperation in trade, economics ¿

---

43. See, for example *Nezavisimaia gazeta* (29, 30 April 2001), and *Izvestiia* (29 April 2001).
44. For a somewhat skeptical view of this, see Aleksandr Sukhotin, "Kreml edva ne ob'edinil dve rei" [The Kremlin Nearly United the Two Koreas], *Obshchaia gazeta*, No. 9 (1–7 March 2001).

military matters. Negotiations about Russian weapons sales to Vietnam were opened as well. In both cases, consensus was reached on energy deals and South Korea agreed to participate in the construction of a gas pipeline from Russia to the region.

Negotiations with Japan continued apace, and even a visit by the discredited Japanese premier Mori in March ended satisfactorily for Russia. He and Putin issued a communiqué promising further talks on signing a peace treaty, and to speed up talks on ownership of the Kuril Islands so as to reach "complete normalization of bilateral relations." In international affairs, they both stressed that the UN Security Council must maintain the dominant role in international conflict resolution.[45] Yet, by May, when a Russia–Japan summit was held in Irkutsk, the Russian position seemed to have hardened. Mori told reporters that an agreement to consult on the transfer of parts of the Kurils to Japan was rejected outright by Moscow. The Russian foreign ministry issued a statement denying that any such agreement had been reached and that no discussion about territory would take place until after a peace treaty had been signed. Thus, the Kurils still obstructed truly constructive diplomacy between the two countries.

That being said, data released during the Irkutsk summit showed that bilateral trade between Russia and Japan had grown by 22 percent in the previous year, reaching a total of $5.2 billion. By far the greater part of that sum was in Russian exports to Japan, so the trade balance was to the advantage of Moscow. It was assumed that this trend would continue, no matter the diplomatic difficulties related to territory.

There was progress with North Korea as well. In late April, 2001, Russia and North Korea signed a "framework agreement" on defense and military technology and cooperation. Russian Deputy Prime Minister Klebanov told reporters that the plan was to upgrade Russian equipment already in the hands of North Korea, to the tune of $777 million. Not surprisingly, this agreement angered the United States. It coincided with Bush's announcement that research on the NMD was to be upgraded. Putin made it clear that the new arrangement would not interfere with Moscow's role as facilitator of an accommodation between North and South Korea.

The return visit to Moscow by the North Korean president in August was more freakish than it was significant. The fact that Kim Jong-il and Putin signed a "Moscow Declaration" calling for the preservation of the ABM Treaty was regarded more as a tweak to the U.S. nose by Russian commentators than a matter of some international consequence. It was a public manifestation of Russia's rejection of Condoleezza Rice's offer to share missile technology if Moscow would stop providing military aid to North Korea and Iran. It was important, too, that Kim promised again to suspend ballistic missile launchings until 2003, and that Moscow could be seen as interlocutor for North Korea in the world arena. Nevertheless, with the exception of the communists, most Russian analysts saw the Stalinist Kim as an anachronism, a sense fortified by his odd and extravagant slow trip to Moscow in a

---

45. See "Statement by President of Russia and Prime Minister of Japan" (25 March 2001), *Strana.ru*. The meeting was held in Irkutsk. See also *Krasnaia zvezda* (27 March 2001).

seventeen-car luxurious train—while his people were known to be starving—and homage-paying stop at Lenin's mausoleum.[46]

Perhaps a little embarrassed about the Kim circus, Putin offered a generalist fense of Russia's relationship with North Korea in November, just as he set out his meetings with Bush in the United States. North Korea is our neighbor, he t American journalists at the Kremlin, adding that he thought it a mistake to isol any "rogue" state from the world community.[47] There were more boasts that Put policies in this regard would lay the groundwork for a "dialogue" between North ; South Korea, and the United States.[48] Months later, after George Bush inclue North Korea among his three "evil axis" states and actually delivered a speech at famous DMZ criticizing that state, Russia pushed even harder to establish long-te energy and development projects in North Korea. Improvements to rail links tween them, and an upgrade of the ice-free port facilities in Najin, were all part intensified Russian investment in North Korea.

The American tirade notwithstanding, Russia never gave up on its associat with North Korea. Indeed, shortly before Bush arrived in Moscow for his sumi meeting with Putin in May 2002, the North Korean foreign minister and a large (egation showed up in Moscow for a three-day visit. Military–technical cooperat that had gone into abeyance in 2001 was restored; more trade was planned; and Russian foreign ministry made it clear that it did not share the American belief t North Korea was preparing a missile strike against the United States in either short or long term. Igor Ivanov, in fact, delivered a welcoming speech in which stressed the importance of "good neighborly relations" with North Korea (IT/ TASS, 21 May 2002). Further embarrassments were predicted by Moscow insid(

CHINA 2001–2002

Talk of a Russia–India–China axis resurfaced in Russia in April 2001 when direc of the information and press department of the MID told an interviewer that tl common interests should be coordinated more closely.[49] Beijing almost immediai denied that any such plan was in effect but agreed that coordination on some iss of mutual importance was imperative. Trade with China was soaring by the enc

46. See, for example, Aleksandr Sukhotin, "Istoriia vozvrashchaetsia v plombirovannom vagone" [tory Returns in a Sealed Train], *Obshchaia gazeta*, No. 31 (2–8 August 2001); for the glowing commu perspective, see Vasilii Safronchuk, "Otvetnyi vizit Kim Chen Ira" [Return Visit of Kim Jong-Il], *Sc skaia Rossiia* (7 August 2001).

47. "Vladimir Putin Talks with American Journalists," *Kommersant*, No. 206 (12 November 20 RIA Novosti translation, JRL, No. 5541.

48. See, for example, Yelena Shesterina, " 'Bol'shoe puteshestvie' zavershaetsia" [The "Grand Tou Completed], *Nezavisimaia* (7 August 2001); and Andrei Vagonov, "Atomnye smotriny Kim Chen [Atomic Show for Kim Jong-Il], *ibid.*

49. Aleksandr Yakovenko, "Igor' Ivanov letit v Deli" [Igor Ivanov Flies to Delhi], *Nezavisimaia ga* (29 April 2001).

the first quarter, increasing at about the same rate but in much greater quantity than trade with Japan.

Although Russia and China have a mutual interest in a stable border and continued to speak with one voice on most international issues, a year-and-a-half of nearly uncritical praise for the newly found Moscow–Beijing fraternity from the Kremlin began to wear thin. Apprehension grew that China could be a much greater long-term source of danger to Russia than either the United States or Europe. This tendency of thought was fed by Atlanticists who insisted that Russia's long-term security depended both on Europe and Washington. According to Russian specialists, there was a coinciding growth in America of a perception that China was potentially more dangerous than the so-called rogue states and that Russia, and even India, were better bets in the face of China's arms and its threat to Taiwan.[50]

At the Kremlin level, however, friendship with China kept its high profile. A special meeting between Putin and Jiang Zemin on 14 June 2001, just prior to the Shanghai Five summit, saw a further consolidation of their positions on international affairs. With the added membership of Uzbekistan, and the transformation of the "Five" into the Shanghai Cooperation Organization (ShCO), the Russia–China connection was given a broad and institutional framework.[51] Significantly, the meeting preceded by two days the Russian president's summit with George Bush in Slovenia. Putin was banking on the Asia card again.

It was noted already that the Russo-Chinese Treaty of Neighborliness, Friendship and Cooperation provoked considerable comment when it was signed in the summer of 2001. Even though it was made clear that it was neither a real alliance, nor did it commit the two countries to help each other in case one was attacked by a third party, rumors to the contrary persisted. Doubtless it signalled close agreement in international affairs, especially against the United States' NMD, and further NATO expansion. Article 8 of the Treaty prohibits the use of either country's territory by third countries to the detriment of Chinese or Russian state sovereignty. Interestingly, in contrast to glowing official commentary, Russian media discussion of the treaty revealed a broad sense of unease in Moscow and even more so in the Russian Far East. The feeling among the fifth estate was that China needed careful watching when it came to strategic collaboration.[52]

The helpfulness of the Russian–China relationship was rethought again in August by Russian analysts in connection with ongoing negotiations between Moscow and Washington on the ABM Treaty and the NMD. Trade was still important. Russia's opportunities in Eurasia were advocated mostly by political advisers who were look-

---

50. On this, see, for example, Aleksandr Sabov, "Lysyi orel nad Aziei" [Bald Eagle over Asia], *Rossiiskaia gazeta* (29 May 2001); Vitalii Tsygichko, "S amerikoi—vmeste ili porozn'" [With America—Together or Apart], *Nezavisimaia gazeta* (9 June 2001).

51. On this, see Vsevolod Ovchinnikov, "Geopolitika: Shankhai. Bezopasnost' cherez sotrudnichestvo" [Geopolitics: Shanghai. Security through Cooperation], *Rossiiskaia gazeta* (16 June 2001).

52. On this see, for example, Aleksandr Lukin, "Rossiia-Kitai: druz'ia ili soperniki?" [Russia and China: Friends or Rivals?], *Nezavisimaia gazeta* (3 August 2001).

ing for alternatives to acquiescence to the United States and NATO in the West, ɛ
much was made of the potential of China as a source of increased arms sales. Tr.
in weaponry, of course, has an important strategic as well as economic value. In fɛ
deals signed in August by Russia's state arms dealership amounted to some $2 bill
and included the delivery of up to forty-five Russian-built fighter aircraft, to be b
at a major plant near the Amur in the Russian Far East.[53] In October, Trade Minis
reports claimed that Russia–Chinese trade was up 31 percent for the first n
months of 2001. Final ratification of the friendship treaty passed the Duma on
December (407-1-1), the same day that Gazprom opened up an office in Beijing

In the overall scheme of things, Russia–China trade was not very extensive, b
countries having greater volumes elsewhere. But for Moscow, in addition
weaponry, China remained one of the few markets for Russian-made heavy er
neering products, for example, civilian airplanes and equipment for hydro plaɪ
Even this good economic news caused discomfort to some specialists. As the fastɛ
growing economy in the world, they said, China might cast its eye on Russia's
East for resources and areas for settlement. A conflict with China is "a reali
prospect" one prominent analyst warned in late September, as he exhorted Mosc
to remain vigilant on its eastern frontiers.[54]

Russia's early participation in the worldwide anti-terrorist coalition may h
made China wonder about Putin's sudden Westward turn. When several member:
the Shanghai group signed basing agreements with Washington, their apprehens
may have been raised more. But as Russia's role faded, and the United States wi
drew from the ABM Treaty, China again became an object for Russian courtship.
it happened, consultations between high-level Chinese and Russian officials alrea
had been scheduled for Moscow on 19 December 2001. Although this regular ev
had a wide-ranging agenda, the United States decision a few days earlier to unilaɪ
ally abrogate the ABM Treaty quickly became the focus of its attention. Comn
niqués from the meetings insisted that there were no missile threats to the Uni
States and that the rationale for the American NMD, the corollary to withdraɪ
from the ABM, was so weak that Washington had now to justify its strategic dɛ
sion by reference to the events of 11 September. From the Russian and Chinese
ficial perspective, this rationale was an even weaker one than the previous assun
tion of great menace from the "rogue" states.[55]

Another major deal was signed between Moscow and Beijing in March, 20
confirming a previously discussed plan that Russia build two destroyers for China

---

53. See John Helmer, "Implications of Russia–China Deal," *The Russia Journal* (10–16 August 20
Aleksandr Sabov, "Pochemu malye shazhki luchshe bol'shikh skachkov" [Why Small Steps Are Better t
Great Leaps], *Rossiiskaia gazeta* (14 August 2001); "Rossiia—Materik, kotoryi otkryvaetsia zanovo" [I
sia Is a Continent That Is Being Discovered All over Again], *Krasnaia zvezda* (24 August 2001).

54. Aleksandr Sharavan, "Tret'ia ugroza. Voennoe stroitel'stvo Rossii vedetsia bez ucheta opasnɛ
iskhodiashchei s Vostoka," [The Third Threat. The Russian Military Structure Is Being Built Disreg
ing Danger from the East], *NVO,* No. 36 (28 September–4 October 2001).

55. See, for example, Vladimir Bogdanov, "Moskva i Pekin daleki ot isteriki" [Moscow and Beijing
Far from Hysterics], *Rossiiskaia gazeta* (20 December 2001).

few weeks later, it was announced that Russia's annual arms sales to China topped one billion U.S. dollars, that is, about one-fifth of the total trade turnover between the two countries. The PRC was then consuming 40 percent of Russia's overall arms sales. In addition to destroyers, China had been purchasing military planes of almost all types, anti-aircraft systems, multiple missile launchers, shipboard artillery systems, anti-submarine helicopters, and submarines. Part of the new negotiations included proposals for joint scientific research and development on new types of military hardware, and even joint bids for military contracts in third-world countries, above all in Africa. Obviously, Russian and Chinese ties were more binding in military–industrial matters than they were in the diplomatic sphere. Moreover, if China's fuel-dependent weaponry ever needed to be used, Russia's energy resources would become essential to Beijing's planners.

It would be a mistake to assume that the common vision of world affairs, arms and energy sales are all that hold Russia and China together. Reports printed in the summer in 2002 (Interfax, 31 July), were to show that Moscow and Beijing had completed multiple agreements in the high-tech sphere as well—thirty-five deals in 2001 and twenty-seven during the first half of 2002. Aside from energy infrastructure, these fell mainly within the transportation, metals and agricultural sectors.

INDIA, 2000–2002

The Kremlin's friendship with India has a long history, with its roots in the 1950s. So it is not surprising that in the late 1990s, New Delhi was courted by Yeltsin's senior officials. Ties between the two countries had been confirmed in July 1999 when then deputy prime minister, Viktor Khristenko, and Indian Finance Minister Yashwant Sinha initialed a wide-ranging protocol on trade, economic, scientific, technical and cultural cooperation in New Delhi. They both spoke highly of growing economic links, as diplomats do at such events, but gratuitous references to the need for continued reforms in Kosovo and the likelihood of an expanded "strategic partnership" provided observers with a glimpse of their mutual stance on world affairs.

The image of India as an ideal strategic partner was highlighted especially by Russia's communists. In Zyuganov's election platform, for example, India was granted equal billing with China as a country with which Russia could help to "restore the balance of interests in the world," that is, a multipolar world.[56] As we have seen from the opening paragraph to this section, the Kremlin also looked to India as a consistent ally in its attempts to create a multipolar international arena. Thus, when U.S. President Clinton toured South Asia in March 2000, Moscow pundits saw the event as an American attempt to lure India into its camp and away from Russia.[57]

---

56. See Zyuganov's electoral program in *Rossiiskaia gazeta* (14 March 2000).
57. See, for example, Aleksei Tamilin, "Zachem Klinton priezzhal v iuzhnuiu aziiu" [Why Clinton Travelled to South Asia], *Nezavisimaia gazeta* (28 March 2000).

The strategic relationship with India was better defined in June after an offi
visit to Moscow by New Delhi's defense minister, George Fernandes. Following a
cussions on military-technical cooperation with his Russian counterpart at so
length, and working out the details of large-volume arms purchases, including T-S
tanks,[58] Fernandes and his entourage set the stage for a state visit by Putin to In
on 2–4 October 2000. According to Fernandez, the October visit would mar
"transfer of relations between our countries to strategic partnership." In Ju
Moscow made more explicit its support for India's bid to become a permanent me
ber of the UN Security Council. Putin confirmed this position in September dur
an interview with Indian journalists.[59]

As if to confirm the upgraded relationship, an Indian military delegation sper
week (ending 26 September) in Russia and signed a purchase order for some fc
more Russian warplanes, priced at approximately $1.8 billion.[60] Shortly thereaf
between 2 and 5 October, Putin paid his long-planned state visit to India, tak
with him a large entourage from the ministry of foreign affairs, business and ene
sectors. The most spectacular result of the visit was the signing of a long-term ar
deal valued at about $3.8 billion to Russia, as India agreed to purchase a range
equipment that included more tanks, an aircraft carrier and multipurpose
planes.[61] Protocols on cooperation in matters related to military–technical affa
science, postal and legal assistance, reserve bank relations, and specific arrangeme
between Gazprom and the Gas Authority of India were also agreed upon. There
some anxiety abroad that the new level of association, praised enthusiastically in N
Delhi and Moscow, would spark an arms race between India and Pakistan. This p
sibility seemed to be of no concern to Russian officials, who stressed the importa
of a new, long-term strategic partnership—and a market for Russian arms. Mosc
and New Delhi confirmed their faith in the Russia–U.S. ABM Treaty and agreec
work together towards a "democratic" new world order.[62]

Most Russian analysts were more than enthusiastic about the accord: some e
called it an alliance, and others claimed that the trip itself was Putin's most succ
ful foreign venture. There were a few nongovernmental observers who cautioned t

---

58. On this purchase, see Viktor Litovkin, "Oruzhie dlia vcherashnei voiny" [Arms for Yesterc
Wars], *Obshchaia gazeta*, No. 29 (20–26 July 2000).

59. The journalists, representing the magazines *The Russia Journal* and *India Today* (9 October 20
quoted Putin saying that India was a prime candidate for a permanent seat in the UNSC. For a transc
of the interview, see JRL, No. 4549 (30 September 2000). For a Russian discussion of it, Aleksei Tam
"'Sravnenie ne v pol'zu Klintona'. Vmesto poslesloviia k vizitu Vladimira Putina v Indiiu" ["A Comp
son Is Not to the Advantage of Clinton." In Place of a Postscript to Vladimir Putin's Visit to India], *i*
kur'er NG, No. 15 (12 October 2000).

60. On this, see "Brakorazvodnyi protsess" [Divorce of Brothers], *Kommersant Vlast'* (26 Septen
2000); Sergei Sumbaev, "Chtob druzhba ostavalas' znachimoi i prochnoi" [For the Sake of Keeping
Friendship Important and Durable], *Krasnaia zvezda* (30 September 2000).

61. For some concern that Russia might not be able to make the military deliveries, see Aleksei Tam
"Sostoiatsia li postavki" [Will the Goods be Delivered], *Nezavisimaia gazeta* (7 October 2000).

62. See, for example, *Kommersant* (30 September 2000); *Rossiiskaia gazeta* (4 October 2000); *Kras*
zvezda (4 October 2000).

the accord might oblige Pakistan to become more aggressive in Central Asia. There was a sense as well that sometime in the future Russia might have to make a choice between "allies," that is, India or China, as they had had to do in the 1960s, but that scenario was not often raised.[63] The arrangement between Moscow and New Delhi was explicit that it was not a military alliance, while making it equally clear that they would not participate in any alliance or aggression against either of them by a third country or bloc. Practically all other types of military association were covered by their mutual declaration, however.[64]

Moscow made overtures to Pakistan as well. Presidential adviser Yastrzhembskii had a successful visit to Islamabad in late September 2000 (see chapter 3) where joint diplomatic efforts to curb the Taliban in Central Asia were agreed upon, a full year before Pakistan was dragged into the anti-terrorist coalition by Washington.[65] At the time of Yastrzhembskii's visit, it was difficult to see where the huge arms deal with India and a simultaneous courting of Pakistan's help in Central Asia could be reconciled.

As the year 2000 drew to a close, another large delegation from the Indian defense ministry toured Russia for a full week, signing in Irkutsk (28 December) a contract for the production of Su-30MKI combat planes. This was Russia's largest single sale to India since 1996 and, in fact, Russia's relations with India took another leap forward early in 2001. A $100 million contract for helicopters and more airplane construction was signed in February, and officials passed each other in the air between New Delhi and Moscow with increasing frequency. More arms sales, integrated banking systems, and lock-stepped positions on international affairs were the order of the day.

The obvious and easy quid pro quo in these deals was continued Russian support for Indian permanent membership in the UNSC. In late April 2001, for example, a representative of the Russian ministry of foreign affairs again told reporters that his country saw India "as one of the strongest and most deserving candidates for becoming a permanent member of the UN Security Council."[66] This statement preceded a three-day visit by Foreign Minister Ivanov to New Delhi where, among other things, a summit between the two countries' leaders was planned for Moscow in November.

On his arrival on 4 May, Ivanov resurrected the notion of a Russia–India–China troika working together to construct a "democratic world order." After talks with his Indian counterpart, Jaswani Singh, a communiqué was released carrying the joint opinion that the United States should not be "reckless" in regard to the ABM Treaty,

---

63. See, for example, Aleksei Tamilin, "Druz'ia i soiuzniki u nas est'" [We Have Friends and Allies], *Nezavisimaia gazeta* (4 October 2000). For strong praise of Putin's India initiative, *Izvestiia* (6 October 2000); *Kommersant* (6 October 2000). See also Aleksandr Sukhotin, "Novoi Indii Kreml' ne razgliadel" [The Kremlin Did Not Notice the New India], *Obshchaia gazeta,* No. 40 (5–11 October 2000), who said that India–Russia relations are not quite as ideal as they would seem.

64. See, for example, "Rossiia i Indiia—strategicheskie partnery" [Russia and India Are Strategic Partners], *NVO,* No. 37 (6–12 October 2000).

65. See Yastrzhembskii, "Pakistan's Goodwill Gesture," *Moscow News* (4 October 2000); *Moskovskoe novosti,* No. 39 (3–9 October 2000).

66. See, for example, Aleksandr Yakovlenko, "Igor' Ivanov letit v Deli" [Igor Ivanov Flies to Delhi], *Nezavisimaia gazeta* (29 April 2001); see also an ITAR-TASS summary, 29 April 2001. Yakovlenko was head of the MID department of information and the press.

and approving President Bush's promised nuclear arms reductions. Later, in Ju Singh flew to Moscow, where agreements were reached on joint manufacture c large transport plane and, with Israel as a third party, the construction of a rec naissance plane for India.

The "too-ing and fro-ing" continued at an astonishing pace. Further deals w signed in July during a visit to Moscow by Indian Prime Minister Atal Bihari \ payee. It was at that time as well that the visitor told reporters that a Russ India–China union was possible sometime in the future (Interfax, 25 July). Vajpa returned to Moscow in the first week of November to his name to several previou agreed protocols and to discuss mutual views on the postwar Taliban and a set ment in Afghanistan. The fact that the war in Afghanistan greatly raised the in national importance of Pakistan and its president, who suddenly became a linch for the American war effort in the region, helped draw Russia and India even cl together. The Indian position on the Taliban was the same as Russia's; that is, that member of the former ruling party be allowed in a new government. In this opin they both disagreed with Pakistan, which had proposed that "moderate" Talil members be included because they were the party of the largest single ethnic gr in Afghanistan (Pushtun), and with the United States, where the same prop briefly drew some support. Only after the Northern Alliance took the Western co tion by surprise and moved into Kabul on 13 November, did President Bush ag with Putin (who was in Washington at the time) that no Taliban member would included in a new government.

The earlier India–Russia meeting had been productive: a firm schedule was set Russian work on the Kudankulam nuclear power station, cooperation between Russian city of Astrakhan and northern regions of India was agreed upon, and t ther arms deals were signed. In the latter instance, India agreed to complete the p chase of a Russian aircraft carrier by the end of 2001.

High-level contacts between Moscow and New Delhi continued to prolifer: Deputy Prime Minister Klebanov was in Delhi in February 2002 initialing agi ments raising the military–technical cooperation between the two countries still t ther. Among the arrangements finalized were joint development of a fifth-generat fighter plane, and Russian agreement to refit and hand over to the Indian navy heavy-aircraft-carrying cruiser *Admiral Gorshkov*. To a certain extent, Moscow ; New Delhi were thrown together by Washington, whose bellicose attitude towa Iraq and Iran worried India as much as it did Moscow. The growing level of tensi between New Delhi and Islamabad over Kashmir also gave Russia and India rea: to talk and, as early as February 2002, Defense Minister Ivanov, who accompan Klebanov, announced that the Kremlin would support India "unconditionally" the case of conflict (ITAR-TASS, 7 February). This remark represented an extra dinary commitment for Moscow.

A combination of events, not the least being a general international tension, I drawn Russia and India closer than ever before. And the arms deals kept piling When George Fernandez came back to Moscow in April 2002, it was announ that the two countries were ready for the joint production of modern military equipment. At that time, India signed contracts to purchase still more Russian tanks and planes. This was big business.

Moscow did not back away from its political promises, making it unmistakable that Russia would support India as the possibility of war with Pakistan gripped the international imagination again in May. During the Putin–Bush summit in late May, the Russian president deplored Pakistan's decision to conduct tests of surface-to-surface missiles, especially while tensions in Kashmir were running so high. These missiles are capable of carrying nuclear warheads. In this instance, Bush also urged Pakistan's President Musharraf to stop the incursions of Islamic militants into Kashmir. Less than a week later, Moscow announced that leaders of India and Pakistan had both agreed to meet with him in Almaty, Kazakhstan, at a security summit of sixteen regional leaders. It appeared, therefore, that Russia had an opportunity to act as mediator in a very important international conflict. Putin was doomed to disappointment, as the Indian and Pakistani presidents did little more than cast aspersions on each other.

As the "merry month of May," 2002, drew to a close, Moscow's presentation of itself as a mediator in Southeast Asia seemed to have gone the way of Moscow as mediator in the Middle East; that is, into the dustbin of history.

CONCLUSION

In concluding this chapter, it is worth remembering that in two-and-a-half years, Putin's ministry of foreign affairs had met with considerable success in Far East, Central Asia, and Southeast Asia. Already-healthy relations with China and India were raised to partnership levels, grounded mostly on guns and energy, but also on their similar perspective in world affairs.

Putin had been taken seriously by leaders of the G-8 in Okinawa, the APEC in Brunei, and at the UN Millennium in New York in 2000. So he was off to a good start. More importantly, Russia then restaked its claims in Eurasia more firmly than at any time during the 1990s. Its prominent place in the Shanghai Cooperative Organization, which includes China, the Eurasian Economic Community, and the CIS Collective Security Treaty Organization, combined to provide Moscow with its first usefully integrative mechanisms in post-Soviet Eurasia, Central Asia, and the Far East.

China and India remained cornerstones of the Kremlin's Eastward policy. One might wonder, therefore, why the relationship with China had not been raised even further, to an alliance level. The reason for this can be put down to expediency: an alliance would serve neither side any more than the current strategic partnership. It would commit both sides, above all Russia, to policies on which they could quickly have second thoughts. There was a second factor for Russians, that is, a deeply rooted foreboding that the huge Chinese population lusts after Russia's vast and relatively uninhabited spaces. For that reason, a strict visa regime remained in force on Russia–China border, and multiple obstacles against freer trade at the ground lc were kept in place—encouraging tens of thousands of Chinese to busy themselves stead in the Russian shadow economy. This issue will remain difficult to resolve e· as the state-to-state relationship thrives.

In the spring of 2002, it remained to be seen how these Eurasian starting poi would play out as Moscow became more entrenched, by dint of treaties with United States and NATO, in the Western scheme of things.

12

✠

Dealing with
"Rogue" States

In August 2000, observers of Russian foreign policy began to discern a new pattern in Moscow's international behavior, that is, a determination to renew relationships with countries named as "rogue" or "maverick" by Madeleine Albright in the 1990s. In addition to North Korea, about which much has been said already, the rogues included Iraq, Iran and Libya—countries against which sanctions of various kinds had been imposed either by the UN Security Council or the U.S. Congress. It was claimed and perhaps believed in Washington that the governments of these particular countries represented real threats to the territory of the United States. After 11 September 2001, the presentation by President Bush of some of these states as part of a dangerous "axis" of evil gained greater credence. Cuba fit America's outsider category as well, though by the 1990s Fidel Castro was considered more of an irritant than a threat, and even the Russian bureaucracy had lost interest in him.[1] The fact that, from the mid- to late-1990s, Moscow looked to these same countries as potential markets and diplomatic partnerships, and for voices to add to the clamor against American and NATO global policy, greatly complicated the Russia–U.S. relationship.

Other long-standing thorns in Washington's side found audiences in Moscow. A two-day working visit to Moscow by Palestinian leader Yasser Arafat in August 2000, shortly after the Camp David peace talks chaired by President Clinton failed, demonstrated that the PLO leader hoped to bring Moscow in on his side. According to the Palestinian envoy in Moscow, Arafat wanted a specific Russian proposal for Middle East peace talks and support for his plan to declare a Palestinian state on 13 September (ITAR-TASS, 7 August). Putin took the opportunity to telephone both

---

1. See especially a long interview with Fidel Castro published in the communist *Sovetskaia Rossiia* (29 July 2000).

Egyptian President Hosni Mubarek and Israeli Prime Minister Ehud Barak, to form them of the content of his conversations with Arafat and try to work out so sort of compromise (Interfax, 15 August). On 11 August, Foreign Minister Ivaı told journalists that there were no reasons why Russia should not support Araf declaration of an independent Palestinian state, no matter when it was issued.

So the door was opened for Russia to resuscitate its influence in Middle East   ˙ fairs. Foreign Minister Ivanov made telephone calls on the peace process to his coı terparts in the United States, Syria, Spain, Israel, the Vatican, Italy and France (terfax, 17 August). Two days later he followed up by sending Vasilii Sredin, dep foreign minister and presidential envoy for the Middle East settlement, of wh Moscow is co-sponsor, on a tour of Israel, Palestine and Egypt (19–23 August).

Most Russian analysts cheered on this trend, yet little of substance was to comє it.[2] Moscow had little political clout to bring to bear on the situation, and even feˑ economic weapons. And there was too much ambiguity in its approach to the laı Middle East scene. Even at that time, there were voices in the wilderness urg Moscow to take care when it came to talks with Iraq and Libya. These were "odi states," a writer for *Obshchaia gazeta* warned, and open friendship with them could ː peril Russia's chances of full accession to the G-8 and other beneficial collectives.[3] the time, however, the Kremlin felt that it needed association with the "rogue" state a way to demonstrate Russia's independent posture in international affairs. More spe ically, renewed or upgraded relations with Iraq, Libya, Angola, and others signallєc the Russian people that the Russian government had fully shaken off the "euphoria' expectation of help from the United States that had been so blatant in the early 199ı

Putin himself told Russian TV and press journalists on 25 December that Ruˌ would continue to cultivate relations with the "problem regimes," referring to Cu North Korea, Iraq, and Iran. In the case of Cuba, which still owed Russia up to ʃ billion, Moscow stood to gain very little other than a sense of going Russia's o way. The MID recognized that Canadian, Spanish and French companies had lє since overtaken Russia's place in business there, and would be virtually impossiblє replace. Iraq and Iran posed other kinds of problems. As a member of the UNSC ₂ the G-8, Russia had to take international security concerns into account when dє ing with these states, yet they too provided business opportunities that Mosc could not afford to ignore.

At the end of 2000, Putin told Russian journalists that Iran and Iraq were imp tant to Russia's national interests, and that he had no reason to be embarrassed

---

2. See, for example, Vladimir Lapskii, "Shory politikam ne k litsu" [Blinkers Do Not Suit Politiciₐ *Rossiiskaia gazeta* (3 August 2000); and Marianna Belen'kaia, "Putin poedet i k Kaddafi" [Putin Goє Qaddafi As Well], *Nezavisimaia gazeta* (2 August 2000), the subtitle of which was "West Dislikes In sification of Russia's Foreign Policy." The radical communist paper, *Zavtra* (No.31, August 2000) praised this trend, but accused Putin of still being dependent on the West and "America's regional ₐ because of his economic policies.

3. Boris Yunanov, "Vneshniaia politika—ne povod dlia samoutverzhdeniia" [Foreign Policy Not Cː for Self-Determination], *Obshchaia gazeta*, No. 31 (3–9 August 2000).

4. On this, see for example, *Komsomol'skaia pravda* (7 December 2000).

dealing with such countries. In fact, he pointed out, Germany had also raised its involvement with Iran, and France was active in Iraq.[5] The Iraq question was a little more complex, though Putin argued that favorable changes were under way in that country. For a while after 11 September 2001 the "rogue" notion itself began to fade as the United States suddenly needed help, or at least some form of neutrality, from countries that it had regularly been accusing of harboring or otherwise abetting terrorists (e.g., Iran), and explosively Muslim Pakistan became a key partner in the antiterrorist campaign.

The respite was brief. As soon as the situation in Afghanistan appeared controllable, the "rogues" were thrust back into the limelight. In November 2001, speaking in Geneva to a United Nations review of the 1972 Biological Weapons Convention, U.S. Undersecretary of State for Arms Control and International Security John Bolton accused Iraq of building up its offensive biological weapons stockpile during the three years of no UN inspections. He went on to name that country the greatest threat to launch a germ-war campaign against the United States. North Korea, Syria, Libya and Iran also were labelled biological weapons threats, and Russia's association with those countries, especially Iraq and Iran, was again under unspecified suspicion.

Iraq

A familiar face resurfaced on the Russian presidential election scene on 6 March 2000. Vladimir Zhirinovskii, a longtime advocate of strengthening Russian ties with Iraq, India, and Iran, had been declared ineligible for the election campaign (his third) by the Central Electoral Committee (CEC), but was reinstated by the Russian Supreme Court. His first campaign statement included a promise that India and Iraq would become Moscow's "strategic partners" if he was elected. The United States, China and Turkey would be declared "enemies of the Fatherland" (Interfax, 9 March). Zhirinovskii's formal presidential platform, published on 18 March, was a little more temperate. It called for a "new foreign policy" which would include cooperation with the West ("our rival"), but Russia's closest geopolitical partners were still to be "Iraq, Libya, Iran, Serbia, Armenia and Belarus."[6] Some six weeks earlier, Zhirinovskii had informed reporters that he had reached a personal agreement with Saddam Hussein on siting Russian warships at naval bases in Iraq. It is quite unlikely that this was done with the support, or even the knowledge, of the Russian government, but Iraq remained one of the "rogue" states to which Moscow took a vastly different approach than the NATO countries. For his troubles, Zhirinovskii came in at a distant fifth in the election.

The Russian media had, in fact, been generally supportive of Iraq and Saddam Hussein for a long time, sharply criticizing the West for demonizing him to the

5. Putin, *Nezavisimaia gazeta* (26 December 200), *op. cit.*
6. Zhirinovskii, "Pochenu Ya—kandidat v Prezidenty Rossii" [Why I Am a Candidate for the Presidency of Russia], *Rossiiskaia gazeta* (18 March 2000). Zhirinovskii made these points about Iraq and Iran as well at a conference on "Russia-2000" in London, 5 March 2000.

detriment of the Iraqi people.[7] By the spring of 2000, there were rumors afloat t
Russia was facilitating a military link between Belgrade and Baghdad, driven mo:
by a visit to Moscow in April by the Iraqi defense minister, Col. Gen. Sul
Hashimn Ahmad, who had been in Yugoslavia shortly before his arrival in Mosc
In June, Russia twice supported Baghdad's official protests to the UN against Am
ican and British air strikes in the "no-fly" zones. The Russian position was that
air attacks against Iraq must stop (Interfax, 1 June 2000). Sredin confirmed t
stance on 21 June while meeting with an adviser to Hussein, H. Hammadi,
Moscow (Interfax, 21 June). A month later, Foreign Minister Ivanov confirn
Moscow's desire that sanctions against Iraq be lifted during talks with Iraqi amb
sador to Moscow, Hasan Juma (Interfax, 21 July), and criticized air strikes agai
Iraq again on 24 July, two days before Iraq's Deputy Prime Minister Tariq Aziz '
scheduled to meet with Putin in Moscow. Washington's State Department pro
against this high-level meeting with an envoy from a UN-sanctioned coun
prompted outbursts from Zhirinovskii, who called for all Russian air links with I
to be restored, and Zyuganov, who urged his government to extend full diplom;
relations to Baghdad. The Russian mainstream media fully supported Putin's sta
on Iraq, calling the U.S. State Department's objections "jealousy" driven by the
ject failure of its own policies towards that country. Russia's diplomacy is proving
be a viable "alternative to the forceful U.S. methods," one columnist wrote, typ
ing the mood in Moscow.[8]

Another writer accused Washington (and London) of behaving towards the Ir
people as it had towards the Serbs: "Hoping to finish off a regime, they destro
country and make life miserable for the common people." U.S. policies towards I
and Libya were lumped into this category as well, whereas the Kremlin's attitude '
termed without prejudice. It was concluded that the "political baggage of 'sanctio
'blockades,' and 'embargoes' should be consigned to the dustbin of history."[9]

The communist media differed from the Russian government in its level of sh
ness when it came to Iraq, but supported the government in its "more active" M
dle East policy. After Tariq Aziz met with Zyuganov and other CPRF leaders on
July, *Sovetskaia Rossiia* rejoiced that the visit signalled that the "euphoria with
West had died down" in government circles—naming Andrei Kozyrev as the per:
most guilty of establishing that early trend. The communists lauded Putin for 1
ommending that UN sanctions against Iraq be lifted, and ridiculed the U.S. St
Department and the American media for their objections.[10]

---

7. See, for example, Vladimir Dunaev, "Fotografiia na pamiat'. Saddam Khusein izuchaet mir iz l
mosa po rossiiskiim snimkam" [Photographs for Keepsake. Saddam Hussein Studies the World from
Cosmos by Russian Pictures], *Izvestiia* (20 October 1999).

8. Vladimir Dunaev, "Saddam pishet Putinu" [Saddam Writes to Putin], *Izvestiia* (27 July 2000);
also *Komsomol'skaia pravda* (28 July 2000).

9. Lapskii, *Rossiiskaia gazeta* (3 August 2000), *op. cit.*

10. See, for example, Yu. Zinin, G. Muslaelian, "Vizit Tarika Aziza v Moskvu. Kak razmorozit' ais!
sanktsii" [Visit of Tariq Aziz to Moscow. How to Melt the Iceberg of Sanctions], *Sovetskaia Rossiia* (29
2000).

On 15 August, following more British and American bombings (of the southern city of Samawa), Moscow's foreign ministry issued an angry statement demanding that all such attacks cease. The Russian statement claimed that the raids destroyed food supplies and would affect only civilians, several of whom had been killed in the attacks. Zhirinovskii echoed these demands in his capacity as vice chairman of the Duma, insisting again that the UN sanctions be lifted. The allied command's assurances that the strikes hit only air defense sites from which anti-aircraft artillery had fired on planes patrolling the "no-fly" zone met with widespread disbelief in Russia. Although air strikes against Iraq did not generate the same degree of public fury in Moscow as NATO's bombing of Yugoslavia had done, the two events increasingly were coupled in Russian official pronouncements, media features, and political rhetoric as characteristic of the West's (usually meaning Washington) ruthless urge to world hegemony.

Russia's delegate to the United Nations raised the matter in the Security Council on 18 August, calling the American and British behavior "gross violations of international law."[11] The very next day, a delegation led by Emergencies Minister Sergei Shoigu flew to Baghdad for a two-day discussion of both emergency measures, and the implementation of humanitarian programs. In the case of Iraq, indeed, Moscow's consistency struck an increasingly sympathetic chord worldwide. The president of Venezuela paid a state visit to Baghdad a few days prior to Shoigu's arrival; the president of Indonesia was scheduled to come later in the year; and a large group of French celebrities announced plans to participate in a "sanction-busting" flight to Iraq. Interest groups throughout the Western world spoke out on behalf of the Iraqi people. Iraqi relations with Syria and other Arab countries were much improved—leaving only Kuwait and Saudi Arabia still actively opposing the Saddam Hussein regime by the end of the summer, 2000.

Russia began taking the question of sanctions against Iraq to a broader forum than the UNSC in September. Foreign Minister Ivanov, for example, strongly recommended that the sanctions be lifted during separate conference meetings with both the G-8 foreign ministers and the permanent members of the UNSC. A Russian aircraft with permission to carry humanitarian aid to Baghdad took along unsanctioned oil-industry officials on 17 September, including the president of Stroitransgaz. And at about the same time, Aeroflot announced that it planned to open an office in Baghdad and resume regular air communications sometime in October.

Another Russian plane, from Vnukovo Airlines, carrying a soccer team, musicians, medical supplies and business executives, arrived in Baghdad a week later. The Russian flight was preceded by two days by a plane from France, causing both the United States and Britain to protest, and illustrating an erosion of sorts in the UNSC regime of sanctions against Iraq. Moscow began cautiously to claim victory in this matter. Ironically, there were mixed feelings among Russian economists on the Iraq question.

---

11. On Moscow's attempt to ameliorate UN sanctions against Iraq, see Vladimir Dunaev, "Mir bez kontributsii" [Peace without Contributions], *Izvestiia* (25 August 2000).

Several of them warned that if sanctions were lifted, then a new influx of Iraqi
could bring world prices down, robbing Russia of an opportunity to benefit fr
high world prices and OPEC's refusal to raise production levels. Other econom
hoped that the end of sanctions would allow Iraq to pay Russia the some $8 bill
owed Moscow from the Soviet era.[12]

In the long run, caution appeared to have carried the day. By late Septeml
Moscow had backed off somewhat from opening regular flights to Iraq, and e·
asked Baghdad to be more flexible about the UN inspections. Permission had b·
granted for the two flights mentioned above, post-facto, by Hans Blix, chair of
inspections committee. The Russian press reported Madeleine Albright's vigor·
objections to the flight, and noted that the matter had become part of the U.S. p·
idential election campaign.[13] Moscow's hesitation proved fruitful when Vedrine s
in Moscow that his country fully supported Moscow's position on Iraq. More Frei
flights were on their way to Baghdad as well. On 30 September, with much less f
fare, another Russian plane carrying oil executives landed in Baghdad.

A political crisis between the United States and Turkey brought Russia another
tential ally in the struggle to have sanctions eased against Iraq. After the U.S. House
ternational Relations Committee insisted on putting forward a bill calling the Turk·
army slaughter of Armenians in 1916 "genocide," an irked government in Ank
decided to improve its relations with Iraq. Opening border gates for railway serv·
between the two countries and constructing a natural-gas pipeline between them w
two of Turkey's considerations. Iraq's international position was helped as well by
newed crisis in the Middle East as the peace talks between the Israeli government ·
Palestinian authorities dissipated into uncontrolled violence in October. Angry
what they perceived as Washington's application of double standards when it cam·
Israel's treatment of Palestinians, Arab leaders began to follow the lead set by tl
populations and fly into Baghdad. The prime minister of Jordan, Ali Abu al-Ragh
for one, led a delegation of Jordanian journalists and politicians to the newly ope·
Baghdad airport during the first week of November. The Russians reported this ev
with unbridled glee.[14] Nongovernment Arab groups from Egypt and elsewhere, of
including doctors and celebrities, chartered planes and flocked to Iraq with food, s·
plies and much moral support—just as Russia's Zhirinovskii already had done.

In October, Turkey upgraded its diplomatic relations with Iraq to the ambassa·
rial level, and Syria agreed that its cross-border pipeline with Iraq should be
opened. All this was to the benefit of Russian policy. Indeed, the Russian positior
Iraq itself was abetted in November when Slavneft, the Russia–Belarus oil compa
signed a preliminary agreement with the government in Baghdad to participate

12. See, for example, Vladislav Kuzmichev, Sergei Pravosudov, "Neft'"—eto politika" [Oil Spells l
tics], *Nezavisimaia gazeta* (21 September 2000).

13. See, for example, Yevgenii Artemov, "Rossii razreshili letat' v Irak" [Russia Allowed to Fly into I·
Obshchaia gazeta, No. 38 (21–27 September 2000).

14. See, for example, Marianna Belen'kaia, "V Bagdad priletel pervyi arabskii samolet" [The First ·
Plane Has Arrived at Baghdad], *Nezavisimaia gazeta* (28 September 2000).

the development of Iraq's Subba oil field (Interfax, 8 November). Less than a week later, Foreign Minister Ivanov opened a seven-day grand tour (13–19 November) of the Middle East with a visit to Iraq. He went on to Egypt, Jordan, Kuwait, Saudia Arabia, Palestine and Israel, hoping to augment Russia's role in the region and also to get local support, or at least acquiescence, for lifting the sanctions against Iraq.[15] Aziz was back in Moscow shortly after Ivanov returned, urging Russia to broker a deal to have UN sanctions lifted in return for one final inspection of Iraqi arms sites. The large debt owed Russia by Iraq was, of course, still a strong incentive for Moscow to assist Baghdad in this. Russian commentators agreed that Iraq must fulfill the UN's resolution on arms inspections, but believed that this had been for the most part accomplished and that the sanctions must be lifted. In an old-style approach, several analysts in Moscow described the continuing sanctions as a means for the American government to protect its large corporations.[16]

Thus, by the end of 2000 Russia's position on Iraq could be said to have been consistent, firm and independent—and also neither very productive, nor particularly disruptive for Moscow's relationships with Western countries. Since that time Moscow's dealings with Baghdad were to became more problematic.

As Washington slowly formulated its post-Clinton foreign policy, certain trends became clear. In the first instance, in early February 2001, Secretary of State Colin Powell revealed that the Persian Gulf and Iraq were now the American priorities in the Middle East. In the same breath, he distanced his office from the Palestinian–Israeli crisis, saying that a broader perspective would be brought to U.S. interests in the region. This marked a major change from the direct involvement in the Middle East peace process urged by President Clinton and Madeleine Albright. At the same time, CIA Director George Tenet claimed that the "rogue" states were still dangerous and specifically accused Russia of providing far more ballistic missile technology to Iran than it admitted.[17] American and British air strikes against radar stations outside the "no fly" zone in mid-February revealed plainly the differences between Moscow and Washington on the Iraq question. Powell and Bush called these attacks "routine" and said they would continue. The Russian government objected to them vociferously. For a change, the communists represented the Russian consensus when they termed the raids "renewed Bushism" aimed against Iraq and the Iraqi people.[18]

---

15. On this trip, which Russian analysts saw as a great opportunity for Russian role-playing, see Mari-anna Belen'kaia, "Igor' Ivanov zavershaet turne" [Igor Ivanov Completes Tour], *Nezavisimaia gazeta* (18 November 2000).

16. On this see, for example, Marianna Belen'kaia, Sergei Pravosudov, "SShA vydavlivaiut Rossiiu iz Iraka" [The USA Squeezes Russia out of Iraq], *Nezavisimaia gazeta* (29 November 2000); Vladimir Lapskii, "Kogda v Bagdade budet spoikoino? [When Will There Be Calm in Baghdad?], *Rossiiskaia gazeta* (1 Dec 2000).

17. Tenet was making his annual report on global threats to the United States to the U.S. Senate Intelligence Committee, 7 February 2001. The greater threat, he said, was international terrorism.

18. For an interesting analysis of the Bush administration's likely take on the Iraq situation, see Nicholas Lemann, "The Iraq Factor," *The New Yorker* (22 January 2001), 34–38. Vasilii Safronchuk, "Yanki vnov' BUSHuiut" [Yankees Renew Bushism], *Sovetskaia Rossiia* (20 February 2001). On the raids, see Sergei Sokut, "V pritzelakh—Bagdad" [In the Target—Baghdad], *NVO*, No. 7 (23–29 February 2001), who also saw the event as a renewal of George Bush senior's policies.

Media rhetoric on this issue far outdid the calmer approach taken by both R sian and Western leaders. In Washington on 25 February, George Bush and Brita Tony Blair maintained the correctness of their attacks on Iraq, while acknowledg that something needed to be done about the harsh toll the sanctions were taking the Iraqi people. On the same day in Cairo, Ivanov and Powell agreed to take a c structive approach to the Iraq question, and concurred that Iraq should not be lowed to acquire weapons of mass destruction.

The Iraq question remained problematic even for Russia. Not only did it serv a real obstacle against a modus vivendi with the United States, friendship with Ba dad made the expansion of relationships with moderate Arab States difficult. M to the point, the government was still reminded that lifting economic sancti against Iraq, for which Moscow lobbied so aggressively, would release that count oil supplies onto the world market, costing Russia much of its energy-related r enue. Nevertheless, the foreign ministry promised on 3 April that a formula for c last UN monitoring exercise in Iraq would soon be ready, and predicted that a se of agreements would be in place allowing Iraq reentry to the concert of sta Among Moscow's recommendations was a Persian Gulf zone free of weapons of m destruction (ITAR-TASS, 3 April).

A visit to Moscow by Iraqi Prime Minister Taha Yasin Ramadan two weeks l; was greeted enthusiastically by Russian political leaders, the foreign ministry, and mament industry, but with less anticipation on the part of Moscow's other busir and financial circles. Ramadan, the highest-ranked Iraqi official to come to Russi; fifteen years, met with Putin, to whom he conveyed a message from Saddam H sein and the power ministers. The meetings were widely-covered by Russia's me yet not much was revealed about what Ramadan accomplished in Moscow ot than photo-ops and rhetoric about sanctions and historical friendships. Sho thereafter, however, it was made plain that trade-offs had been made related to lo term oil and gas development, and marketing had been negotiated.

Later in the spring the Russian permanent ambassador to the United Natic Sergei Lavrov, took exception to a British proposal that sanctions against Iraq modified, but not abolished. While the suggestion was being discussed in New Yc American and British planes again bombed parts of Iraq, angering Moscow e more—especially in light of the action's timing. Russia now finally came up wit proposal of its own, calling for the sanctions to be lifted and a permanent system monitoring disarmament to be deployed in Iraq. Russia's trade turnover with Irac 2000 had been about $2.4 billion. This amount notwithstanding, Russia was los billions due to the sanctions. In addition to the some $7 billion already owed R sia, which Iraq could not pay until its oil was again on the open market, that cou try was lost to Russia as a major arms customer.[19]

This dilemma was eased somewhat in July when Iraq accepted a new UNSC i olution, after Britain and the United States dropped their original proposal and

---

19. On this, see Nadezhda Spiridonova, "Sanctions against Iraq Lose Russia Billions," *Moscow Ti* No. 24 (13–19 June 2001).

stead supported a simple extension of the oil-for-food program (Interfax, 27 June). The compromise was largely a consequence of Russia's threat to veto the original sanction-based British resolution. Iraq, which had halted limited oil exports on 4 June in protest of the British–U.S. proposal, resumed exports (about 5 percent of the world's supply) within a few days of accepting the new terms. And Moscow was credited with a "victory" in this particular diplomatic exercise.

A few weeks later, Putin referred directly to Iraq during a long and much-publicized press conference with some 500 Russian and foreign journalists. In response to a query about the G-8, he called sanctions against Iraq "unproductive" and repeated the Russian alternative proposal for lifting the restrictions against that country.[20] By August, Russia's longtime support of Iraq finally produced some real bilateral dividends, as the Iraqi government agreed that it would grant priority to Russia in signing oil contracts (ITAR-TASS, 2 August 2001). Within a month, contracts were signed calling for Russian assistance in developing oil deposits and providing equipment authorized by the UN. The value of these agreements was judged to be some $2.5 billion, making Iraq Russia's leading trade partner in the Arab East (ITAR-TASS, 16 August).

All was going well, therefore, until the anti-terrorism coalition's bombing assault on Afghanistan drew Iraq back into the American gun-sight. Rumors to the effect that Iraq could be subjected to similar attacks spread through Washington. Saddam Hussein was accused by Western officials of supplying biological weapons to terrorists, though no evidence in support of such charges was made public. Russian policy in the region was undermined again. The Kremlin did not want separatists in Chechnya and elsewhere gaining access to such weapons if they were made available to them, yet Russian officials also made it clear that they would be greatly angered by any attack on Iraq without irrefutable evidence of wrongdoing. This was a bit of a catch-22 situation. Indeed, in November, stories that Putin planned to visit Iraq caused consternation in London and Washington. Putin's staff denied these stories shortly after they appeared, but a message had been sent. It was assumed that the status of Iraq would be one of the questions discussed by Putin and Bush during their meetings over 13–15 November 2001. In fact, immediately prior to his session with President Bush, Putin told American journalists in Moscow that Iraqi leaders should allow international observers to check weapons sites, and at the same time the "anti-Iraqi sanctions should be lifted."[21]

It was a few days afterwards that Bolton told UN delegates that Iraq was a potential threat as a bio-weapon distributor, lending credence in some circles to the view that the United States was preparing to invade that country. Ironically, a rather strange Russian delegation was in New York at the time, appealing directly to the UN that it lift sanctions from Iraq. The Russian Centre for Cooperation with Iraq,

---

20. "Vladimir Putin's Press Conference with Russian and Foreign Journalist," *strana.ru* (18 July 2001). A complete translated transcript is available via the BBC Monitoring Service (Russian TV, Moscow, 18 July 2002).

21. "Vladimir Putin Talks with American Journalists," *Kommersant*, No. 206 (12 November 2001), RIA Novosti translation; JRL, No. 5541.

made up of academics, politicians and businessmen, has no official status in Rus
It was led by Adam Shegunts, head of the Russian Academy of Sciences Institute
International Relations, and had a hearing with a number of UN delegates. Am
can policy was untouched by the appeal. At any rate, a compromise was reached
the last day of November and the possibility of "Gulf War 2" was postponed. Ru
and the United States agreed that the UNSC could extend the oil-for-food progr
to Iraq for six months while negotiations on revising economic sanctions against t
country would continue.

President Bush changed the situation almost overnight when, in his State of
Nation message, he depicted Iraq as one member of an "axis of evil" and set the st
for a pre-emptive American strike against Baghdad. Russia was very unlikely to p
ticipate in any such operation and Kremlin officials regularly appealed to the Eu
pean countries and the UN to help them mute the American approach. It was cl
that the still tightly-knit anti-terrorist coalition could not easily be transformed i
an anti-Iraq coalition. A visit to Moscow by Canada's Prime Minister Jean Chrét
resulted in statements that could be—and were—interpreted as a common Russi
Canadian stance on the Iraq file. Condoleeza Rice quickly demanded clarificat
from the Canadian foreign minister, John Manley, who hedged but still insisted t
Iraq was a matter for the UN. Manley said that Canada would continue to part
pate in the war against terrorism in Afghanistan and elsewhere but needed conc
reasons before it could agree to the invasion of a sovereign state. On the Russian si
it was recognized by both official and private analysts that the Kremlin was fa
with a complex problem; that is, as one expert put it, how to maintain a "pro-W
orientation" and at the same time "defend Iraq from invasion by the USA."[22]

As the American plan to bring down the Hussein regime became more open in
winter of 2002, and was probably the incentive behind President Bush's turnarou
April intervention in the Middle East crisis, Russian officialdom became still m
concerned about its diplomatic investment in Iraq. Yevgenii Primakov took up
challenge and regularly spoke of the alleged U.S. campaign against Baghdad a
"historic" mistake—which is what he had said often about NATO expansion wl
serving as foreign and prime minister (Interfax, 23 March). At the ministerial le
relations between Moscow and Baghdad officials were busy—even hectic. 1
Russia–Iraq Intergovernmental Commission on trade, economic and science-a
technology cooperation met in Moscow on 18 March and discussed large proje
including a construction contract won by Russia to build an irrigation system in E
Al-Jazirah, valued at some $70 million. By this time, as well, Russia was handl
close to half of Iraq's controlled oil exports, so economic links between the two co
tries were being consolidated.

A few weeks later, during festivities in Baghdad marking the thirtieth annivers
of a treaty of friendship with the USSR, more projects and trade agreements w

22. Aleksandr Kuranov, "Pod pritselom—Irak" [Under the Gun—Iraq], *Nezavisimaia* (27 Decen
2001); see also Aleksei Pushkin, "Rossiia i SShA: predely sblizheniia" [Russia and the USA: Limit
Closeness], *Nezavisimaia* (27 December 2001).

itemized and signed, projected to be valued up to $40 billion. It is little wonder that Moscow continued to lobby actively on Iraq's behalf in the UN and to issue joint criticisms of both the proposed "smart" sanctions and American "threats" against Hussein. The notion that the United States was planning to attack Iraq was taken very seriously in Russia and it became a point of departure for a number of analytical commentaries on the choices Moscow was soon going to have to make in international affairs. Several pundits warned, for example, that in such an event the Kremlin would have to again rely on China for support and, one writer shuddered, perhaps eventually become a colony of China.[23]

For most Russian analysts and even more so the Russian public, Washington's war talk was a by-product of a "cowboy" approach to world affairs taken by a trigger-happy administration, whose first choice was to use its great military advantage to crush any regime it disliked. The fact that none of this had happened yet made few inroads against the assumption that it would. The image of little boys in the Pentagon gleefully playing with guns permeated Russian accounts: who will be next?—was the common journalistic query. This image was strikingly different from the old, ideologically driven stereotypes of back-room imperialists driving the political machine for the good of big business, and was more harmful to discourse precisely because of its spontaneous and deep-rooted nature.

It was also pointed out often that the Arab world would not support an attack on Iraq this time and that Russia must take that fact into consideration when it came time to decide on a role for itself. None of this meant that people in Moscow supported Saddam Hussein, they didn't; nor did they favor an American invasion.[24]

During the month of April, in fact, it was the Russian delegate's turn to chair the UNSC and he took the opportunity to mediate the Iraqi cause whenever he could. During that period a compromise was worked out that eased the process of trade with Iraq, though the sanction regime was not altered. Hans Blix, UN chief of the commission for monitoring and inspecting Iraq, was in Moscow on the last day of the month talking to Igor Ivanov about a suggestion from Moscow that Iraq was ready to allow a resumption of UN monitoring. The relevant UNSC Resolution 1409 was not adopted until mid-May (Interfax, 15 May), but Russia's hand was evident in it. As it happened, Iraq's foreign minister, Naji Sabri, was in Moscow at the same time, though he and Blix did not meet.

Russia and Iraq signed some sixty economic contracts in early May, well before the Putin–Bush summit. These included more oil and gas projects scheduled over a ten-year

---

23. See, for example, Aleksandr Khramichikhin, "V ob'iatiia kitaiskoi kolonizatsii. Voina SShA s Irakom privedet Rossiiu k ekspansii Kitaia na Dal'nem Vostoke" [In the Embrace of Chinese Colonization. A USA War with Iraq Will Subject Russia to the Expansion of China in the Far East], *NVO*, No. 13 (19–15 March 2002).

24. On this, see for example, Dmitrii Nikolaev, "SShA gotovy nanesti udar po Iraku" [The USA Prepares an Attack on Iraq], *NVO*, No. 10 (29 March–4 April 2002). See also Stanislav Kondrashov, "Saddam in Place of Osama?" *Moscow News*, No. 13 (3–9 April 2002), and Yevgenii Bai, "Poslednii argument Saddama" [Saddam's Final Argument], *Izvestiia* (25 April 2002), on the inevitability of Hussein using nuclear weapons if he is attacked again.

period (ITAR-TASS, 6 May). Towards the end of the month, Moscow and Bagh‹ must have been delighted with the story out of Washington that the U.S. Joint Ch of Staff had strongly advised their president to postpone any direct military confror tion with Iraq. Nevertheless, talk in the American capital of forced "regime change' Baghdad rose in volume and intensity, generating still more misgivings in Mosc where the "moral authority" of the United States now was regularly questioned.

At the same time, insiders in Moscow let it be known that their government ˈ not planning to take its support for Iraq much further as long as new governmen Baghdad adhered to the recently signed economic deals and agreed to pay off country's debt to Russia. Dmitrii Rogozin, chair of the Duma's international rʻ tions committee, represented a common perspective among Russia's foreign poˈ elite when he wrote that it was in Moscow's best interest that Iraq "have a stable ˂ predictable regime, friendly to Russia. But of course we do not want to see weapʻ of mass destruction manufactured there." The United States, however, must "corı its intolerable urge to fight," and allow a political solution to be reached.[25] At t time the chance of the latter scenario prevailing seemed very slim.

Clearly Russia would not participate in a U.S.-led invasion of Iraq, but nor wo they attempt to prevent the Pentagon from doing so.[26] In the long run, of course, most any regime change would mark an improvement over Hussein's and, if deals ready made were to be honored, then any change but one induced by war would to Russia's advantage.

Iran

Among the states identified in the United States as "rogue," it was actually Iran— Iraq—that had been most catered to by Moscow. A common interest in defusing (somewhat different reasons) America's hegemony in international affairs and, m specifically, ensuring their own mutual predominance on the Caspian Sea, contin﹐ to spearhead their bilateral relationship.[27] Oil and gas considerations were to glue th together, at least for a while. Moscow continued to supply Teheran with arms and a﹐ clear reactor, and they cooperated in opposing Islamic fundamentalism in Central A at least in the form espoused by the Taliban government in Afghanistan.[28]

To a certain extent, increased Russian involvement with Iran was a by-producı American policy. The U.S. Congress's Iran–Iraq Arms Non-Proliferation Act of 1ˢ had warned that Washington would impose sanctions against any country foı

25. Rogozin, "V Irake net svoego Severnogo al'iansa" [Iraq Does Not Have Its Northern Alliar *Izvestiia* (30 April 2002).

26. On this, see Georgii Mirskii, "Rossiia ne stanet meshat' amerikantsam" [Russia Will Not Hiı the Americans], *Izvestiia* (30 April 2002).

27. On this, see a long analytical essay on Iran's ambitions for regional leadership by Radzhab Safː "Sredstvo izmeneniia geopolitiki" [Remedy for Changing Geopolitics], *NVO*, No. 24 (25 June–1 1999).

28. On this generally, see Robert O Freedman, "Russian–Iranian Relations in the 1990s," *Meria J* nal, 4:2 (June 2000), 1–15. Website.

dealing in weaponry with either of those two countries. It was made explicit too that aid to Russia would be cut off if Moscow did not comply in this matter. The accession of Primakov, advocate of an independent Russian foreign policy, to the office of foreign minister in January 1996, brought with it an inclination to deal with both Iran and Iraq. These were his areas of expertise, both as a troubleshooting diplomat for Gorbachev and as director of the Foreign Intelligence Service.[29] Embargoes were, in fact, imposed against Russian companies and this remained a sore spot in Russia–U.S. Relations. Further congressional legislation against Iran, for example, the Iran Non-Proliferation Act which became law in March 2000, complicated matters for Russia. Nationalist urges aside, Teheran had been important to Moscow in the 1990s by providing diplomatic support in both the Nagorno-Karabakh dispute and in resolving Tajikistan's civil war. So there was more to the issue than the natural inclination of both countries to thwart perceived American desires for the region they shared.

Existing links between Moscow and Teheran were confirmed in late November, 1999, when Igor Ivanov visited the latter city to meet with his counterpart, Kamal Kharrazi. Ivanov, of course, had been Primakov's "No. 2" in the foreign ministry. In their post-meeting joint communiqué, Ivanov and Kharrazi said that "Iran and Russia can and should enter the 21st century as good neighbors and close partners" (ITAR-TASS, 28 November). Their close association was especially timely, Ivanov insisted, because of U.S. attempts to impose a new "world order" on the international community without taking the UN into account. The Russian foreign minister's comments in this regard repeated the basic themes of his own address to the UN General Assembly two months earlier. Clearly instrumental in the new Russia–Iran dialogue was the fact that, at the OSCE meeting in Istanbul (18 November), a "go-ahead" had been given on the Baku–Ceyhan pipeline, which would bypass Iran and Russia. Moreover, a gas pipeline from Turkmenistan, across the Caspian seabed, to Baku and then Turkey, reached the "declaration of intent" stage at the same meetings.

In connection with these developments, head of the Iranian security council, Hassan Rouhani, visited Moscow from 11 to 14 January 2000, to hold conversations with his counterpart Sergei Ivanov. Their joint communiqué announced closer strategic and economic ties between their two countries. Rouhani's call on Ivanov marked a further strengthening of the Russian–Iranian relationship on the Caspian Sea and made a point in the face of alleged Western, mainly American, insistence that the two be isolated from new oil pipeline construction.

Their closeness was confirmed in February by Teheran's ambassador to Moscow, Mehdi Safari, who told reporters that the two countries shared a "strategic partnership . . . immune to the influence of third parties" (Interfax, 11 February). He denied reports in the Western media that Russia was supplying Iran with missile tech-

29. On this, see Mikhail Shchipanov, "Takov Evgenii Primakov, *Rossiiskaia gazeta* (12 January 1996); Primakov, "Vneshniaia politika Rossii dolzhna byt' mnogovektornoi" [Russian Foreign Policy Must Be Multi-Vectored], *Krasnaia zvezda* (2 April 1996); Anatolii Repin, "Rol' vedomogo—ne dlia nas. Yevgenii Primakov o printsipial'nykh napravleniiakh vneshnei politiki Rossii" [The Role of Follower Is Not for Us. Yevgenii Primakov on the Principle Directions of Russian Foreign Policy], *Trud* (25 June 1996).

nology, accusing the United States and Israel of willfully spreading false stories. D
ing a later trip to Moscow, the Iranian Deputy Foreign Minister Sayed Kharrazi p
claimed that Teheran firmly supported Russian policy in Chechnya, calling it enti
an "internal affair."[30] Officials in Moscow and Teheran both expressed anger ¿
concern over incidents in which American ships seized Russian oil tankers in the I
sian Gulf, many commentators charging NATO and the United States with "pro
cation."[31] Times had changed, however, for at least one mainstream paper regret
that the Russian foreign ministry and media had rushed into denial so quickly—
cause the oil was contraband. "We lied," a writer for *Izvestiia* groaned, "[and so
hurt] our image unnecessarily."[32]

There was scattered concern in Moscow as well that Iran might try to assert it
as a player equal to Moscow in both the Caspian Sea and in Central Asia. Moreo
the new Iranian president, reformer Mohammad Khatami, seemed inclined to co
to terms with the West—a policy to which Moscow could not openly object, but ¢
that had the potential of undermining the source of Russia's influence in Iran in
long run. However, their joint action in undermining the Baku–Ceyhan pipeline
mained a symbol of their combined strength.

Iran had been among the main buyers of Russian weaponry since the mid-19
when it was at war with Iraq's Saddam Hussein, who at that time was being func
in part by the United States.[33] Sanctions imposed by the UN in 1995 against sell
weapons to Iran had not prevented Russia from shipping arms on the basis, Mosc
said, of contracts signed prior to the UN decision. Whereas it had agreed not to 1
dertake any new arms deals with Iran, Russia still refused in February 2000 to c
tail construction of a nuclear energy plant at Bushehr, nor would it give up o
planned airplane manufacturing plant. Both these projects, Moscow's officials c
tended, were civilian in nature and not subject to sanctions imposed by the UN (
terfax, 15 March 2000).[34]

The possibility of a three-way compromise loomed large in the summer as Pt
prepared to participate in the UN Millennium summit. The Iranian governme
now led by Khatami, and Putin were ready to make a case to American officials
lifting embargoes.[35] Their prospects of success were diminished, however, when

---

30. See Dmitrii Gornostaev, "Iranskoe posol'stvo otmetilo godovshchinu revoliutsii" [Iranian Emb
Celebrates Anniversary of the Revolution] *Dipkur'er NG,* No. 3 (17 February 2000).
31. See, for example, Andrei Volokhin, Aleksei Chichkin, "A byla li neft'" [But Was There Any C
Rossiiskaia gazeta (5 February 2000); Vsevolod Ovchinnikov, "Skol'zkii otkos k konfrontatsii" [Slip|
Slope to Confrontation], *Rossiiskaia gazeta* (8 February 2000).
32. Maksim Yusin, "Po ushi v mazute" [Up to Our Ears in Fuel Oil], *Izvestiia* (8 February 2000).
33. In March Iran even purchased Soviet-trained marine animals (dolphins, Belugas, sea lions)—
mals purported to be trained to kill enemy divers and blow up ships. The purchase was made in Ukra
however, from Crimean officials in Sevastopol who claimed they were no longer able to feed and m
tain the animals. Story in the *Ottawa Citizen* (10 March 2000), citing from *Komsomol'skaia pravda.*
34. For an interesting interview with Yurii P. Savel'ev, rector of Baltic State Technical University, ir
Petersburg, and a longtime advocate of teaching rocket technology to Iranians, see Patrick E. Tyler, "1
sia's Links to Iran Offer a Case Study in Arms Leaks," *New York Times* (10 May 2000). For the refus:
suspend work at Bushehr, see Interfax (10 February 2000).

issue of Russian arms sales to Teheran was resurrected again in October. In the heat of presidential election campaigning, the U.S. House International Affairs Committee claimed that Russia had broken a 1995 Gore–Chernomyrdin agreement not to sell arms to Iran after December 1999. The Clinton Administration rejected the sanctions then proposed by the House Committee, saying that Moscow had made no new arms sales, rather it was continuing delivery of arms covered under the 1995 agreement. But damage had been done to the credibility of proposals from Russia on Iran, at least in the United States.

As usual, Moscow rejected these charges as politically motivated, and continued to build up relations with Teheran. Talks between transportation ministries in October, 2000, led to plans for the re-opening of Iran–Russia railway communications as part of a North–South transport corridor. Significantly, at precisely the time that the Middle East peace process was disintegrating, Moscow was upgrading its courtship of Iran. Sergei Ivanov was in Teheran on 18 October while Iran's oil minister was in Moscow discussing energy cooperation with members of Russia's government. According to Russian pundits, Washington was angered by this cooperation—especially as it coincided with the publication in the United States of the previously secret Chernomyrdin–Gore correspondence about Russia–Iranian arms deals.[36] The importance of Iran to Moscow's ambitions for the Caspian Sea was such that Russian journalists insisted that in terms of such relations "there must be no compromise with Washington."[37]

A noteworthy turning point came on 3 November 2000, when Igor Ivanov informed Madeleine Albright that Russia would no longer observe the 1995 promise not to sell tanks and battlefield weapons to Iran. Claiming that the Chernomyrdin–Gore secret agreement was invalidated as soon as it was made public in the United States, Ivanov said that such sales would become legitimate in Russia once again by 1 December 2000. Subsequent U.S. warnings that sanctions could still be imposed against Russian firms dealing with Iran had little effect on Moscow, and Russian analysts treated the matter as one of preserving their country's "dignity and national interests"—and very large contracts.[38] Tempers cooled after a long meeting between Sergeev and William Cohen at NATO headquarters in Brussels, on 6 December. Sergeev agreed that only defensive weapons would be sold to Iran, along with service and maintenance of old Soviet equipment in that country. The announcement of this conclusion to journalists coincided with an unusual joint U.S.–Russia resolution

---

35. On this see, for example, Georgii Bovt, "Tsepnaia reaktsiia v 'miagkom podbriush'e'" [A Chain Reaction in the "Underbelly"], *Izvestiia* (7 September 2000).

36. A letter from Chernomyrdin, then prime minister of Russia, to Gore in 1995 promised that Russia would stop sending arms to Iran and conducting joint research in that country's nuclear sector, if the United States would agree not to impose sanctions against Russian firms. Gore agreed, but allowed Russia to continue to fill signed long-term contracts—which they were still doing in 2000.

37. See, for example, Nikolai Kamenskii, "Dlia Ameriki vrag, dlia Rossii—partner. Moskva ukrepliaet sviazi s Tegeranom" [For America an Enemy—for Russia a Partner. Moscow Strengthens Connections with Teheran], *Vremia* (19 October 2000).

38. See, for example, Aleksei Podymov, Aleksei Vladimirov, "Sekretnyi paragraf sdelki veka" [Secret Paragraph of the Deal of the Century], *Rossiiskaia gazeta* (9 December 2000); Andrei Stepanov, "It Smells of Cold War in the USA", *Trud* (25 November 2000), translated in JRL, No. 4655.

against the Taliban at the UN Security Council and Sergeev's strong endorsemen
a reconstituted Russian relationship with NATO.

Still, Sergeev later spent three days in Iran, that is, from 26 to 28 December 20
boosting weapons sales and joint military cooperation. Continued Russian conv
tional arms sales to Iran and assistance to that country's nuclear-energy program c
tinued to handicap the advent of smooth Russian–American relations. Sergeev's
journ in Teheran was followed up when President Khatami arrived in Moscow w
his defense minister for a two-day state visit, 13–14 March. The meeting was p
ceded by Russian press commentary on the importance of close military and e
nomic ties with Iran.[39] Putin served notice that Russia had the full right to proc
with conventional arms sales to Iran and complete the construction of a nucl
power plant there (Interfax, 13 March).

Russia's press and officials spoke of Iran as an important "direction" in Russian f
eign policy-making, and accused the United States of "counter-productive" reacti
to their joint initiatives.[40] Moscow took care, however, to avoid calling Iran a "str
gic partner," even though that was the term used in Teheran. Russian analysts to
note of this, and reminded their several types of audiences that Russia and Iran w
still potential competitors in the Caucasus, Central Asia and on the Caspian,
though they reached a tentative accord on the latter region as well—to Kazakhst
open discomfort.

A joint communiqué stressed that the two countries would continue to cooper
in "peaceful uses of atomic energy" and step up trade and economic cooperati
Specific agreements were signed on constructing a thermal-power station at Ta
and carry out joint development of the Iranian coalfield in Mazino. Prelimin
technology agreements were worked out as well, including the manufacture a
launch of a geostationary telecommunication satellite (Interfax, 16 March). All in
these were pretty extensive undertakings. The fact that Sergei Ivanov was in Wa
ington holding discussion with Powell and Rice while the Iranian president wa
Moscow was likely coincidence, but it certainly highlighted the two countries' (
ferences of opinion on that issue.[41] Interestingly, the Russian media began regul
to refer to Khatami as Iran's "Gorbachev."[42]

39. See, for example, Igor Korotchenko, "Rossiia i Iran vozobnovili sotrudnichestvo" [Russia and Resurrected Cooperation], *NVO*, No. 1 (12–18 January 2001).

40. The communist press took delight in America's assumed "great dissatisfaction" over Khatami's v see Vasilii Safronchuk, "Diadia Sem serditsia, a Sergei Ivanov opravdyvaetsia" [Uncle Sam Is Angry, Sergei Ivanov Justifies Himself], *Sovetskaia Rossiia* (20 March 2001).

41. See Andranik Migranyan, "Vneshniaia politika Rossii: Ispytanie Iranom" [The Foreign Policy of I sia: Test with Iran], *Nezavisimaia gazeta* (15 March 2001). See also Yelena Shesternina, "Moskva ob'iasnil Vashingtonom" [Washington Has a Talk with Washington] (on Iran), *Nezavisimaia gazeta* (16 March 20

42. See, for example, Marianna Belen'kaia, " 'Iranskii Gorbachev' v Moskve" [The "Iranian Gorbacl in Moscow], *Nezavisimaia gazeta* (13 March 2001), where it was noted that Iran was an important tential partner, but still a "rival" in many areas; Vladimir Mukhin, "Zachem Iranskii prezident pried Rossiiu" [Why the Iranian President Will Come to Moscow], *Nezavisimaia gazeta* (12 March 2001); *Izvestiia* (13 March 2001), where Russia's failure to call Iran a "strategic partner" was called realistic; k stantin Kapitobov, "Prezident Khatami—Iranskii Gorbachev" [President Khatami is the Iranian (bachev], *Nezavisimaia gazeta* (Figury i litsa, No. 6), (29 March 2001).

There were Russian analysts who cautioned that Russian–Iranian relations should be pursued for pragmatic, mutual-interest reasons, and that anti-American rhetoric clouded the issue and was counter-unproductive. The fact that the strongly Islamic Iranian government did not support Chechen rebels and opposed the Taliban in Afghanistan was very important to Russia; so too were their common interests in the Caspian; except that angering the United States could undermine Russia's case against the NMD and NATO enlargement. For these reasons, A. Bovin recommended strengthening ties with Iran and at the same time advised that the anti-American rhetoric be toned down.[43] The fact that in July 2001 an agreement that Teheran would buy Russian transport helicopters was finalized with little backlash from Washington lent credence to Bovin's approach (ITAR-TASS, 9 July).

Although arms deals with Iran were generally condoned in Moscow both because of their financial significance and as a symbol of independence from the West, there was some suspicion that the Kremlin might inadvertently be supporting an Islamic revolutionary movement. This was an obvious dilemma after followers of Islam were so obviously responsible for the airplane-highjacking attacks on New York and Washington in September. Moreover, the arms deals with Iran put Russia in a position of having to choose between Iran and Azerbaijan as partners on the Caspian Sea.[44] As it happened, the extremist attacks on the United States cast the Russia–Iran relationship in an unexpected new light. Moscow and Teheran issued a joint anti-terrorist statement, and moved together to join with the United States in combatting what both Russia and NATO called the "scourge" of the world. Suddenly, the U.S.-Iran accommodation advocated by Zbigniew Brzezinski in 1997 edged closer to reality. Perhaps this development made Russia a little nervous, but unequivocal choices had to be made in both Washington and Moscow.[45]

In late September, early October 2001, an Iranian defense delegation spent four days in Moscow hammering out military–technical agreements, without evoking the usual loud protest from the United States. Terrorism and drug trafficking were recognized as the main problem in international affairs, and a new conventional arms deal was signed. Russia sold border protection equipment to Iran and guaranteed to deliver the long-awaited nuclear reactor in November.[46] All in all, the new arms deal was valued at about $7 billion over several years. Although Condoleeza Rice told the U.S.–Russia Business Council on 4 October that Washington still had "concerns" about Russian arms sales to Iran, and charged that Russian companies were helping

43. Aleksandr Bovin, "Partnerstvo bez epitetov" [Partnership without Epithets], *Obshchaia gazeta,* No. 13 (29 March–4 April 2001).

44. On this, see Aleksandr Sukhotin, "Tanki dlia islamskoi revoliutsii" [Tanks for the Islamic Revolution], *Obshchaia gazeta,* No. 35 (30 August–5 September 2001).

45. See, for example, Yurii Sumbatian, "Voiny 'Mirovoi islamskoi revoliutsii'" [Wars of the "World Islamic Revolution"], *NVO,* No. 31 (24–30 August 2001). The author predicted that the aim in Iran was to build an army of 20 million. See also Brzezinski, "A Geostrategy for Eurasia," *Foreign Affairs,* 76: 5 (September/October 1997).

46. See, for example, Aleksei Bolotnikov, "Iran uzhe opredelilsia" [Iran Has Already Decided], *Nezavisimaia gazeta* (20 September 2001).

Iran develop nuclear, biological and chemical weapons, official American objecti·
to the most recent arms deal was decidedly less aggressive than earlier ones. Rus:
promise to make between $30–45 million worth of arms (including tanks) availa
to the Northern Alliance in Afghanistan, and Iran's agreement to serve as the conc
for those arms, may have been responsible for this relative disinterest.

The respite was a short one. American anxiety about Russia's alleged sales of n
sile and nuclear technology to Iran was reintroduced to the RF–U.S. discourse c
arms reduction by President Bush on the very eve of the summit in Moscow. Spe
ing in Berlin on 23 May, the day before he flew to Moscow, Bush warned that
Iran with weapons of mass destruction posed a threat to everyone, including Rus
Putin rejected this indirect admonition directly, pointing out that several other ɪ
jor European countries had as much dealing with Iran as Russia did, and that inɪ
national corporations, many based in the United States, were less likely than g
ernments to heed warnings when profits were to be made in Iran.

All was not friendly in the Russian–Iran relationship either, for issues of owr
ship and access on and under the Caspian Sea remained a source of tension. Th
issues were confronted openly at a forum of Caspian heads of state in April 20
and a general consensus that their resolution was necessary was reached.[47] The qɪ
tion of access to Caspian Sea oil deposits (i.e., the sea bottom) remained a poinɪ
contention. After Russia reached accords with Kazakhstan and Azerbaijan in M
Iran still refused to budge on its claim that its share of the seabed should be gre;
expanded, a claim that had helped cause the collapse of the Caspian states' sumɪ
held in Ashgabat in April. Iran and Russia had then ordered displays of their m
tary presence on the Sea in early May, and the governments in Moscow and Tehe
issued angry statements about the other's intransigence on the matter. The comn
nist press came to the defense of Iran, charging Putin with a "brutish and unmɪ
vated threat." Non-communists worried that Iran might be lost as an important aɪ
customer, or even as a useful foil to the United States.[48]

But geo-strategic issues remained significant to Moscow. At least one writer
a mainstream, normally moderate Russian paper, accused the United States of
ing international terrorism as an excuse to attack Iran as part of a much larɪ
scheme likened to Hitler's "Drang nach Osten" (Drive to the East), that is, agaɪ
China, and cautioned Russia not to be caught between them.[49] In the spring
2002, however, the Kremlin's interests in Iran were more immediate. A cooperaɪ
framework was in place on paper, but was obviously subject to major adjustm
if the United States achieved its ambitions in Iraq, the relative peace in Afghanis
deteriorated dramatically, or the Caspian Sea disputes proved impossible to resoɪ

---

47. See, for example, Aleksei Chichkin, "Granitsu ne nashli" [Borders Not Found], and Vladɪ
Vorob'ev, "Proryva ne poluchilos" [Failure of the Breakthrough], *Rossiiskaia gazeta* (25 April 2002).

48. On this see Andrei Piontkovsky, director of the Centre of Strategic Research in Moscow, "The ɪ
Russian Patriot: Not Exactly Rallying around the Flag," *Ottawa Citizen* (11 June 2002).

49. Viktor Novikov, "Iran v Amerikanskoi 'vilke'" [Iran in the American "Bracket"], *NVO*, No
(7–13 June 2002).

At that juncture there was little telling as to what adjustment the Russian foreign ministry foresaw.

Libya

An upgraded Libyan connection in the second half of 2000 was somewhat more startling and unexpected than the expanded ties with Iraq and Iran. Moscow had for a long time been courting Libya mildly, but mostly to chide the United States for demonizing Colonel Moammar Qaddafi.[50] In early August, Libyan Foreign Minister Abdel Rahman Mohammed Shalgham paid a state visit to Moscow, where he met Putin and the senior power officials. Among other things, he handed Putin an invitation from Qaddafi inviting him to pay a state visit to Tripoli. Putin agreed to do so, sparking an uproar in the West and a round of congratulations from Russians on the "realism" of their president's policy. It is better to deal directly with "rogue" leaders than to adopt sanctions, was the common theme—though *Krasnaia zvezda* added a little realism of its own by acknowledging that such relations would be good for the arms business.[51]

The military commentators got it right. Tripoli already owed Russia nearly $4 billion, but UN sanctions against Libya rendered payment difficult. During the August meeting, Moscow agreed to repair and upgrade Libyan military hardware (anti-aircraft systems and armored vehicles), help increase the capacity of its thermal nuclear plant, and build new electric power lines (Interfax, 1 August).[52] Most of these systems had been set up by the USSR in the first place. A joint statement released in Moscow called for "a fair, multi-polar world free from double standards and Cold War era stereotypes," and the lifting of UN sanctions against Libya; these themes were echoed in much of the Russian press.

The connection with Libya was re-confirmed in New York during the 55th session of the UN General Assembly, and after the millennium summit. On 17 September 2000, Foreign Minister Ivanov and Shalgham met again and declared that they were ready to raise the level of bilateral relations in trade and other sectors. Dates were set for the 4th session of the Russian–Libyan Inter-government Commission on trade, economic, scientific and technical cooperation—in Tripoli in October; and the usual rhetorical pronouncement about their "unity of opinion" on a "just world order with a multi-polar structure" was featured by the Russian media (ITAR-TASS, 17 September).

---

50. See, for example, Vladimir Dunaev, "Mechta liviiskogo polkovnika" [Dreams of the Libyan Colonel], *Izvestiia* (3 September 2000).

51. See Vadim Karkushin, "Oboiudnyi interes" [Mutual Interest], *Krasnaia zvezda* (2 August 2000). See also Vladimir Lapskii, "Priglashenie polkovnika Kaddafi priniato" [Invitation of General Qaddafi Accepted], *Rossiiskaia gazeta* (2 August 2000); Belen'kaia in *Rossiiskaia gazeta* (2 August 2000), *op. cit.*, and *Komsomol'skaia pravda* (2 August 2000).

52. "Putin poedet k Kaddafi" [Putin Will Go to Qaddafi], *Nezavisimaia gazeta* (2 August 2000).

In fact, Libya's image in the United States as a "rogue" had been muted for so time. Even Qaddafi was not regarded as so great a risk as he once had been in Wa ington. Nor was the North African state a priority for the government in Mosc Nevertheless, it was an object for renewed Russian global diplomacy in 2001. I Ivanov, the first Russian foreign minister to visit that country, arrived in Tripoli 6 May carrying a message to Qaddafi from Putin. Ivanov had just come from In so the tour was part of Putin's program for resurrecting old Russian ties.[53]

While Putin was in Washington and Crawford in mid-November, the Libyan f eign minister returned to Moscow, talking mostly with middle-level officials si Igor Ivanov was also in the United States, attending meetings at the UN. But n of this concerned the United States as much as Russia's accelerated dealings with I and Iran.

Cuba

The Cuban–Russian relationship had a long and well-known history before it star to break down in the late 1980s, when Gorbachev began both to cater to the Uni States and also to call in the huge financial debt Havana owed Moscow. Relati were never broken, of course, and remained an important if greatly played do Russian link to Latin America. The reasonably regular meetings between mid level officials and trade-debt negotiators took an upswing in 1999–2000, though that time Russian analysts had become quite open in their distaste for the lack of tain freedoms in Cuba.[54] Hoping to repair the damage, Cuba's Foreign Minister lipe Perez Roque paid a working visit to Moscow on 25–27 January 2000, and vited Putin to Havana. The Russian press gave widespread coverage to the eve sometimes emphasizing with open eagerness that it was an affront to Washingtoi

Cuba was back in the news in May, when the Russian foreign ministry issued angry response to a U.S. House International Relations Committee vote to rest financial assistance to Russia. The Committee based their decision on the fact t the large Russian radar station was still deployed at Lourdes. Ivanov claimed that vote violated international law and, rightly as it turned out, assumed that the L administration would not approve the resolution ((Interfax, 6 May). It was obvic however, that Cuba remained a sore spot between Moscow and Washington e though, as we have seen, the Lourdes base was later closed.

There was talk in August, in fact, that Russian would consider helping compl the construction of a nuclear power plant started by the Soviet Union as long ag

53. On this, see for example, Marianna Belen'kaia, "Stremitel'nyi brosok v Tripoli" [A Quick Dash Tripoli], *Nezavisimaia gazeta* (8 May 2001).
54. See, for example, Yekaterina Korotaeva, "Ostrov Svobody protiv svobody slova" [The Island of F dom is against Freedom of the Word], *Izvestiia* (31 August 1999).
55. See, for example, Andrei Dmitriev, "Rossiia-Kuba: Vzgliad na perspektivu" [Russia–Cuba. V on Prospects], *Rossiiskaia gazeta* (27 January 2000).

1976. The project had been slowed in 1986, when the USSR curtailed funding, but the construction site was preserved and awaited a restart. But it was the UN Millennium summit that first put Cuba back on the Russian viewing screen when Putin met with the Cuban delegation in New York. Subsequent Russian, mainly communist, attention to Cuba and Fidel Castro was consistent and sympathetic, and Castro's speeches and presentations began reappearing in the Russian print media.

Putin paid the promised visit to Cuba in mid-December 2000, the first by a head of government in Russia since Gorbachev flew there in 1989 as president of the USSR. Pre-trip hype was extensive and, because he scheduled a visit to Ottawa after Havana, often made much of the fact that Russia's president planned to visit America's neighbors without stopping off in Washington.[56] No one suggested that some kind of a Cuba–Canada resistance to American domination would be raised, but it was quite obvious that Russia was démonstrating its renewed global aspirations. Discussion in Cuba focussed on trade and the likelihood of Russia restarting the nuclear power station project, at Juragua, on which it had stopped work altogether in 1992. The Cuban debt to Russia, approximately $20 billion, also needed to be negotiated, as did the expansion of trade—to that date mostly oil for sugar. Putin took advantage of the Havana forum to urge the USA to adhere to the ABM Treaty and proclaimed that the cooling of Russia–Cuba relations had been a mistake. Castro was invited to Russia, but no date was set. Most Russian analysts agreed that rebuilding ties with Cuba was a good thing, but advised that the debt be dealt with first.[57]

On the face of it, Putin's trip to Havana accomplished very little. But it helped raise Castro's flagging profile, perhaps even at home where he had had so few "accomplishments" lately that the Elián González case had to be touted as a great victory. So Putin was helping Castro and at the same time triggering nostalgia at home and setting up yet another point of contention between Russia and the incoming George W. Bush. Russian communists underscored excerpts from Castro's speeches ("Our task is to preserve the revolution, independence, and achieve social gains"), and even skeptics in Russia admired Castro's consistency in his convictions.[58] *Sovetskaia Rossiia*, the CPRF's main newspaper, chose Castro as the only foreign recipient of its newly instituted "Words to the People" prize for inspiring writing in the year 2000.[59]

In the long run, nostalgia generated by Putin's visit to that Caribbean island was not enough to sustain an interest in Cuba among members of Russia's political elite and the media. In fact, with the exception of a brief outburst of pro-Cuban excitement over the

---

56. See, for example, Dmitrii Gornostaev, "A pri chem zdes' SShA?" [And What Has the USA to Do with This?], *Dipkur'er NG*, No. 19 (7 December 2000).

57. See, for example, Oleg Falichev, "Vremena meniaiutsia, druzhba ostaetsia" [Times Are Changing, Friends Remain], *Rossiiskaia gazeta* (16 December 2000); *Izvestiia* (16 December 2000).

58. See, for example, Boris Yunanov, "Neutrachennye illiuzii" [Recovered Illusions], *Obshchaia gazeta*, No. 50 (14–20 December 2000); "Rossiia—Kuba: shagi k sblizheniiu" [Russia and Cuba: Steps Closer], *Sovetskaia Rossiia* (16 December 2000); "Fidel' Kastro: 'Nasha zadacha—sokhranit' revoliutsiiu, nezavisimost' i dostignutye sotsial'nye zavoevaniia'" [Fidel Castro: "Our Task Is to Preserve the Revolution, Independence, and Achieve Social Gains], *Sovetskaia Rossiia* (19 December 2000); Yurii Rost, "Vypivanie s Fidelem" [Drinking with Fidel], *Obshchaia gazeta*, No. 51 (21–27 October 2000).

59. "'Slovo k narodu'" [Word to the People], *Sovetskaia Rossiia* (30 December 2000).

González story, Russian writers for the most part expressed little sympathy for C
tro. To cite but one example: a Cuban writer living in Miami, author of a book
the Cuban leader, was interviewed by *Obshchaia gazeta* in February 2001, and m;
unsavory details on Castro's family life were featured.[60] To be sure, Russia's comn
nists continued to tout the significance of a renewed level of relations with Cuba, ;
Castro's major speeches continued to appear in full or summarized in the p;
press.[61] The fact that the communist party continued to do well in public opin
ratings, that is, regularly between 25–35 percent of popular support, made
CPRF's position in such matters worthy of attention. For the most part, thou
they were preaching to the converted.

The Russian government was unequivocal in its support for the Cuban peo]
however, and continued lobbying for the long-standing American embargo agai
Cuba to be lifted. In May 2001, for example, Foreign Minister Igor Ivanov called
embargo "unacceptable" and an "obvious anachronism." Contacts between Mosc
and Havana at the ministerial level increased during 2001, and trade relations g
steadily. Yet the dilemma of Cuba's debt to Russia, the distance between the t
countries, Castro's unbending ideological perspective, and Moscow preference
tidy relations with Washington all mitigated against a return to the old closeness

The exclusion of Cuba from the Summit of the Americas held in June, in Cana
was ridiculed in Russia. The only state in the Western hemisphere not invited, Cu
was said by both left-wing and mainstream analysts in Russia to be less abusive
human rights than governments of several countries who were asked to particip;
Castro's long rebuttal of the explanation offered by Canada's Prime Minister Ch
tien was published in full in the CPRF daily newspaper.[63]

Putin had choices to make. The renewed honeymoon between the Russian g
ernment and Havana was jolted abruptly in mid-October 2001 when Putin deci
to close the Lourdes surveillance base, since 1964 the site of Soviet electronic s
veillance on the United States. This was both a cost-saving decision, and a seri
nod to Russia's new relationships with America. Russian communists and some r
itary politicoes parroted Cuba's fury, but Putin, expecting some kind of quid pro ;
from Washington, ignored their protest.[64] As we have seen, officials in Mosc

60. "Pochemu Fidel' ne p'et 'a granel'" " [Why Fidel Does Not Drink Rum], *Obshchaia gazeta* , N
(22–28 February 2001).

61. See, for example, V. I. Vorotnikov, "Gavana-Moskva" [Havana–Moscow], *Sovetskaia Rossiia* (20 J;
ary 2001), extracts from a memoir; "Fidel' Kastro na Otkrytoi tribune. Ne otrechemsia! . ." [Fidel Castr
the Open Tribune. We Don't Renounce! . .], *Sovetskaia Rossiia* (12 April 2001); Fidel' Kastro (Castro), "
myslima Kuba bez sotsializma" [Cuba without Socialism Is Unthinkable], *Sovetskaia Rossiia* (12 May 20

62. See Igor Ivanov, "Russia and Latin America: Forward Looking Relations," *Latin America* (A
2001), full translation released by the Embassy of the Russian Federation in Canada (10 May 2001).

63. Fidel' Kastro [Castro], "Istoriia rassudit" [History Will Judge], *Sovetskaia Rossiia* (7 June 2001)
also Fidel Kastro, "My znaem, kak dolzhny zashchishchat'sia" [We Know How We Must Defend (
selves], *Sovetskaia Rossiia* (24 July 2001).

64. See, for example, Gennadii Zyuganov, "Putin prodolzhaet politiku Gorbacheva-Yeltsina" [P
Continues the Policies of Gorbachev and Yeltsin], *Sovetskaia Rossiia* (20 October 2001). This paper
ried a Russian translation of the official note of protest from the Cuban government.

looked forward to the upcoming APEC meetings in Shanghai, where they hoped to hear what they had gained by closing the base in which there had been some 1,000 personnel housed. Confusion on this issue was common in Moscow, where misguided rumors circulated that it was not to be fully closed down.[65] Certainly the Russian communist press kept pressure on the Kremlin and the public to maintain links with Cuba and, above all, to prevent the U.S. from fitting Cuban for a terrorist jacket, making it subject to attack by the coalition.[66] The left wing's stance was rounded up at year's end by Sergei Tetekin, who prepared a long feature on "Cuba, Which We Have Lost." The withdrawal from Lourdes on strictly financial grounds was "absurd", he said, adding that it weakened Russia severely in world strategic balance, and helped drive Russia into a position of greater subservience to Washington. In addition, the insult to Castro was at the same time a blow against Russia's heritage of greatness in world affairs.[67] That too remained to be seen.

CONCLUSION

Moscow's attachment to "rogue" states and Cuba was not universally popular in Russia, and was detested in Washington. Yet, because Putin himself remained very popular at home and such policies caused few ripples in Europe, they could be called a success by the Kremlin. In fact, there is little doubt that in spite of some unease, the Kremlin's dealings with the "rogues" was accepted as logical and practical in the Russian mainstream. Satisfaction from tweaking America's nose was but one of the reasons for that, and likely a minor one exploited by the media's liking for melodrama.

When it comes down to economic progress, which all members of the power elite acknowledge as vital to their country's survival, Russia has been handicapped by the fact that the West is interested primarily in its natural resources and market potential. Russia's manufactured goods cannot now find markets in Europe or North America; tariff walls have been set up against many of its products; and the long-promised entry into the WTO seems further away than it was even a year ago. Where else but to the "rogues" can it go to sell its weapons, factories, and power plants? Diplomatic drawbacks aside, building railroads in North Korea, modernizing Iran's nuclear power sector, and signing huge oil deals with Iraq, all made eminent sense in Moscow. So did weapons sales to Iran, and also to China and India.

And one cannot disregard out of hand as some governments do, the Russian notion that it is less dangerous in the long run to deal with the "rogues" than it is to isolate them.

---

65. See, for example, Oleg Vladykin, "Da ne oslepnet oko razvedki. Lurdes ob'iavili zakrytym, chtoby sokhranit'?" [But the Eye of Intelligence Won't Be Blinded. Lourdes Is Proclaimed Closed, in Order to Preserve It?"], *Obshchaia gazeta*, No. 43 (25–31 October 2001).

66. See, for example, a reprint of a long Castro speech delivered on Cuban TV, "Fidel' Kastro: Vystuplenie po kubinskomu televideniiu," *Sovetskaia Rossiia* (15 November 2001).

67. Tetekin, "Kuba, kotoruiu my teriaem," *Sovetskaia Rossiia* (27 December 2001).

Conclusion:
Where We Were in May 2002

When Yeltsin handpicked Putin to succeed him, it was assumed by most observers and presumably by Yeltsin that the younger man would follow the leads set by his patrons. It was clear also that Putin was much preferred by the Yeltsin team over either Yevgenii Primakov or Yurii Luzhkov, the two most prominent candidates for the presidency at that time.

At the outset, it appeared that the cynics were right. Putin granted Yeltsin and his immediate family immunity from legal charges and kept all the major power holders in office. Yet within a very short time, it appeared that Putin had an agenda of his own and "saving Russia," both from itself and from terrorism and separatism, was part of it. In the former case, saving Russia came to mean strengthening the state apparatus, challenging the "oligarchs" for control, combatting organized crime, and getting the economy in order. Recentralization was one means to those ends, as was accommodation with international economic agencies: the G-7 (G-8), the IMF, World Bank, the EBRD, and so on. Saving Russia also meant, on the one hand, pursuing the war in Chechnya at all costs and, on the other, coming to terms with, but not falling subservient to, the most important international political and security agencies, above all the EU and NATO. In the tradition of Gorbachev, Putin and his power ministers were among the leading advocates of the preservation of the UN Security Council, on which Russia has a privileged position, as the sole initial source of authority in the resolution of regional conflicts in the international arena. Redefining and upgrading Moscow's bilateral relationships with the major Western industrial powers and Japan were crucial to his chances of success in all of these potentially contradictory ambitions.

Putin also had to eliminate all vestiges of what the opposition in Russia still called "Yeltsinism," that is, reactive, erratic and ambiguous policy-making with no apparent goal in sight. He was helped here by the results of elections to the Duma in late

345

1999, and the subsequent slide of opposition parties into near irrelevance. Put consistent popularity, even in the wake of such tragedies as the *Kursk* affair, was greatest asset in quickly defusing real and potential opponents. In two-and-a-l years, the influence of the CPRF, though it retained many seats in the Duma, minished rapidly. Yabloko almost disappeared as an organized mouthpiece of "liberal" perspective in Russia; and the nationalists had many of their goals co-op by Putin. Power wielded by provincial governors in the Federation Council was f tially legislated away, the Federation Council was weakened, and Putin's represer tives in seven large districts provided the presidential office with a direct oversight Russia's federalism. The media remained alone as an oppositional voice, althoug] too was semi-muzzled by the government. Interestingly, as the state strengthened self, Putin and his policies grew in popularity and his foreign policy was more ¿ more trusted by the media and general public.

This is not to say that nothing had been accomplished during the Yeltsin ye Russia had successfully and reasonably smoothly acquired status as the only nucl power on former Soviet territory. Relations with NATO had been institutionali in 1997 and, in spite of a year of frozen activity and an upsurge of Russian popu hostility because of events in Yugoslavia, their joint agencies had not disappeared the long run, NATO expanded twice without major upheaval in Moscow.

It was with Europe that the greatest heights of cooperation were reached. After l ting an all-time low in its general relations with Europe and PACE, in 1999–20 by mid-2002 a combination of Putin's personal diplomacy and rising world oil pri had brought Russia to an enthusiastic rapprochement with the major countrie: Western Europe, and particularly with the EU. Only the problem of Kaliningrad l gered on as a source of friction, and that situation was on its way to resoluti Pipeline diplomacy helped glue Russia and the EU to a format of mutual dep dency. The most spectacular accomplishment, however, was the formation in Ma) 2002 of what amounts to an alliance with NATO. Cynics have pointed out the m iad weak spots in these new arrangements with Europe, from the Russian persp tive; but few would deny their potential for integrating Russia into the concert of l ropean states. It can be said fairly that Putin had carried on and improved up M. S. Gorbachev's "Common European Home" campaign of the late 1980s. O time will tell if there is to be a permanence to this development.

Within the Russian neighborhood, the CIS still existed after a decade of prec tions of its demise, and this was an accomplishment of sorts. There were twenty-t CIS summits during the decade of the nineties and they had declined in frequei in the last few years of the 1990s. The Commonwealth tended to split according the degree to which member countries remained reliant on Moscow. The continu existence of GUUAM aside, during the first year-and-a-half of Putin's leadershi trend towards reestablishing Russia's predominance in the CIS and Eurasia acce ated greatly. The most striking and positive change came with the striking imprc ment in the Russia–Ukraine relationship. The CIS, in fact, celebrated its tenth niversary on an upswing.

The marked improvement in Russia's economic performance was a major reason for Moscow's improved standing within the CIS and Eurasian framework. Even the events of 11 September 2001 introduced quite new ingredients to Russia–Eurasia relations, including an American military presence in Georgia and Central Asia, but after initial disruptions, did not radically alter the mix.

Russia also had come to terms with the Caspian Sea littoral states (with the sometime exception of Iran), was a leading force with China in the greatly upgraded Shanghai Cooperation Organization (ShCO), and had become a player in APEC. In fact, the institutionalization of the ShCO, the CIS Collective Security Treaty Organization, and the Eurasian Economic Community were more important to Moscow than the fate of the larger CIS itself. Visits by Putin to China and India already scheduled for December of 2002 were expected to help strengthen Russia's integrative process to the East.

After the terrorist attacks on New York and Washington, Russia for a while was an important participant in the U.S.-led anti-terrorist coalition. Although Moscow's place in that undertaking began to fade after several months and the U.S. presence in Central and Southeast Asia grew exponentially, it remained obvious that the West needed Russian cooperation if the war against terrorism was to be won. That being said, Moscow's relationship with Washington survived many bumps to reach a degree of cooperation that had not been seen since 1992–1993. The fact is, the Russian and American presidents had worked out an unusual relationship well before the terrorist assault on the United States. Putin adopted a vastly different approach than Yeltsin would have done to such matters as the abrogation of the ABM Treaty, American troop deployment to both Georgia and Central Asia, and even to the further expansion of NATO: he shrugged them off. Russian analysts were split in their interpretation of what these muted responses meant: were they a pragmatic, matured approach to international affairs; or a fearful, indecisive inability to protect Russia's national interests? The great majority leaned towards the former assessment of what Putin was all about in the global arena.

By the end of our period of study, Russia's level of understanding with both NATO and the EU had surpassed all previous heights; so too had partnership and economic agreements with China and India. Even with the Kuril Islands issue left unresolved, relations with Japan had been normalized. Moscow played a role in the slow-moving reconciliation of the two Koreas and expanded already-extensive dealings with Vietnam. Long-standing associations with Iran and Iraq had been given real substance in the form of substantial trade, development and diplomatic arrangements.

Obviously, some of these bold and controversial accommodations, above all those with Baghdad and Teheran, had the potential of seriously setting back Putin's accomplishments in other areas of foreign policy. Indeed, as our story ends, two specters loomed with the capacity of completely undoing Putin's previous achievements in international relations: an American-led war on Iraq; and a Russian war against Georgia. The rhetoric of preemptive strike on both sides of the Atlantic began to sound remarkably alike in the summer of 2002, that is, post-May; as did the

rhetoric of opposition to each other's stated grounds for war. Fortunately, the lik
hood of Russia going to war against Georgia diminished quickly.

There was a lot of business left unfinished by the end of May 2002. NATO '
poised for its second wave of expansion and Russia's foreign and defense minist
were still proclaiming that Russia would "rethink" its military strategy if the Ba
States became members. This time, however, few people even in Russia took si
threats seriously and Putin, who may well have approved them privately, igno
them in his discourse with Washington. With the ABM Treaty about to expire o
cially on 13 June, the long-term implications of the still unratified arms reduct
treaty signed by Putin and Bush in Moscow on 24 May 2002 remained to be se
The war in Chechnya was no closer to resolution in May 2002 than it had beer
January 2000.

Residual friction-causing phenomena between Russia and the United States, si
as the Jackson–Vanik amendment and the NMD, and with Western Europe, sucl
the status of Kaliningrad and PACE's irritating jabs, did not alter Putin's comn
ment to integration with the West. Russia had recently been designated a full me
ber of the G-8 and confirmed as a country with a market economy by both
United States and the EU, so the long-promised membership in the WTO seen
closer to reality in mid-2002. The Eurasianism touted by Primakov and others '
still important, but always secondary to the Kremlin's longing for acceptance
Western Europe and North America.

As Vladimir Putin's first half-term as President of the Russian Federation wou
down, the multipolarism pushed by Moscow in the 1990s may have faded as an ov
arching policy, but Russia's presence in both Eurasian and European integrative
sociations had surpassed expectations. To a certain extent, in fact, the competing
sions put forward in the nineties by Eurasianists and Atlanticists had been fus
answering for now the perennial Russian question. Moscow's two-headed eagle '
committed to looking westward for signs of welcome, yet still kept all its option:
the East wide open. To a very large extent, the ball was left in the West's court.

Appendix: Changing "Dividing Lines" in Europe and Eurasia as of May 2002

EUROPE

NATO

- 16 + 3 (1997): Poland, Czech Republic, Hungary
- "Second Wave" decision(s) scheduled for November 2002
- Five to seven new members, including Baltic States

European Union

- 15 + 12 (no schedule): including ten former USSR Republics and Warsaw Pact countries
- Northern Dimension Initiative (1997)
- Rapid Reaction Force of 60,000 debated

RUSSIAN FEDERATION

Commonwealth of Independent States

- 1992–2002 fluctuating membership of eleven to twelve former Soviet republics, dominated by Russia

Collective Security Pact (1994, 1999)

Russia, Armenia, Belarus, Kazakhstan, Kyrgyzstan, Tajikistan (Azerbaijan, Uzbekistan and Georgia did not renew in 1999).

- Common security force established (11 October 2001, Bishkek)
- Collective Security Treaty Organization (15 May 2002)

Russia–Belarus Union (December 1999)
Customs Union

Russia, Belarus, Kazakhstan (1995), Kyrgyzstan (1996), Tajikistan (1999).

Eurasian Economic Community (Astana, 10 October 2000)

- All ratified May 2001; membership as above, new members pending (e Moldova)

Shanghai Five

- Russia, Kazakhstan, Tajikistan, Kyrgyzstan, China (1996)
- Shanghai Forum after Uzbekistan associated with it in July 2000
- Shanghai Cooperation Organization (ShCO) (June 2001)
- Military cooperation upgrade (May 2002). Charter pending, making ShCO o| to new members (e.g., India)

BY-PRODUCTS

- GUAM (1997): Georgia, Ukraine, Azerbaijan, Moldova; joined by Uzbekistar 1998
- (GUUAM) [Uzbekistan withdrew "temporarily" in 2002]
- Moscow–Beijing–New Delhi Axis: an idea voiced by Primakov (December 19ς Kasyanov (November 2000), and Igor Ivanov (September 2002)

EUROPE, EURASIA, AND CENTRAL ASIA ARE ALSO DIVIDE BY MEMBERSHIPS IN THE FOLLOWING:

- World Trade Organization (WTO)
- Regional economic integrative organizations (APEC, ASEAN, Caspian Gro OPEC, and so on)
- Permanent and nonpermanent membership of the UNSC

Bibliography

Alekseeva, Tat'iana A. *Nuzhna li filosofiia politike?: Sbornik.* Moscow: Editorial URSS, 2000.

Alison, Roy, and Christoph Bluth, eds. *Security Dilemmas in Russia and Eurasia.* Washington, D.C.: Brookings Institute, 1998.

Arbatov, Alexei G. "Russia's Foreign Policy Alternatives." *International Security* 18: 2 (1993).

Aron, Leon, et al. *The Emergence of Russian Foreign Policy.* Washington, D.C.: National Institute of Peace, 1994.

Asmus, Ronald D. *Opening NATO's Door.* New York: Columbia University Press, 2002.

Avakov, R. M., and A. G. Lisov, eds. *Rossiia i Zakavkaz'e: Realii nezavisimosti i novoe partnerstvo.* Moscow: ZAO Finstatinform, 2000.

Baranovsky, Vladimir, et al. *Russia and Europe: The Emerging Security Agenda.* Oxford University Press, 1997.

Bebler, Anton. *The Challenge of NATO Enlargement.* Westport, Conn.: Praeger, 1999.

Bjelakovic, Nebojsa. "The Foreign Policy Debate in Russia of the 1990s: An Analysis of Russian Security Discourse." Ph.D. Dissertation. Political Science. Carleton University, 2000.

Black, J. L. *Russia Faces NATO Expansion. Bearing Gifts or Bearing Arms?* Lanham, Md.: Rowman & Littlefield, 2000.

Black, J. L. *Vladimir Putin and the New World Order. Debating Security and Defence in Year One.* CRCR Occasional Paper No. 9 (March 2001).

Blacker, Coit D. *Hostage to Revolution: Gorbachev and Soviet Security Policy, 1985–1991.* Washington, D.C.: Council on Foreign Relations, 1993.

Blackwill, R. D., and Sergei Karaganov, et al., eds. *Damage Limitation or Crisis? Russia and the Outside World.* Cambridge: Brassey's, 1994.

Bowker, Mike. *Russian Foreign Policy and the End of the Cold War.* Vermont: Dartmouth Publishing, 1997.

Brzezinski, Zbigniew. "A Geostrategy for Eurasia." *Foreign Affairs,* 76: 5 (Sept/Oct 1997).

Brzezinski, Zbigniew, and Paige Sullivan, eds. *Russia and the Commonwealth of Independent States. Documents, Data, and Analysis.* Cambridge: Harvard University Press, 1997.

Carnegie Endowment for International Peace. *An Agenda for Renewal. U.S.–Russian Relati* New York: (December 2000).

Charles-Philippe, David, and Jacques Levésque, eds. *The Future of NATO: Enlargement, 1 sia and European Security.* Montreal-Kingston: McGill-Queen's, 1999.

Clem, James, and Nancy Popson, eds. *Ukraine and Its Western Neighbors.* Washington, D Woodrow Wilson Center and Harvard Ukrainian Research Center, 2000.

Cohen, Stephen F. *Failed Crusade: America and the Tragedy of Post-Communist Russia.* N York: M. E. Sharpe, 2000.

Cooper, Leo. *Russia and the World. New State-of-Play on the International Stage.* Lond Macmillan, 1999.

Crow, Suzanne. "Russia Debates Its National Interests." *RFE/RL Research Report,* 1: 28 (19!

Crow, Suzanne. "Competing Blueprints for Russian Foreign Policy." *RFE/RL Research Rep* l: 50 (1992).

Crow, Suzanne. "Why Has Russian Foreign Policy Changed?" *RFE/RL Research Report,* 3: (1994).

Daniels, Robert V. "Putin's Patient Strategy." *The New Leader* (July/Aug 2002).

Dashichev, V. I. *Natsional'naia bezopasnost' Rossii i ekspansiia NATO.* Moscow: IMERI R/ 1996.

Dawisha, Karen, et al. *The International Dimension of Post-Communist Transitions in Ru and the New States of Eurasia.* New York: M. E. Sharpe, 1997.

Dwan, R., and O. Pavliuk, eds. *Building Security in the New States of Eurasia: Subregional operation in the Former Soviet Space.* New York: M. E. Sharpe, 2000.

Feldhusen, Anka. "The 'Russia Factor' in Ukrainian Foreign Policy." *Fletcher Forum on In national Relations,* 23: 2 (Fall 2000).

Gardner, Hall. *NATO, Russia, and Eastern European Security. Beyond the Interwar Anat* London: Macmillan, 1998.

Gardner, Hall. "NATO and the EU: The Risks of the 'Double Enlargement.'" *Geostrate* (10 Jan 2001).

Goldgeier, James, and Michael McFaul. "George W. Bush and Russia." *Current History* (' tober 2002).

Gorbachev, M. S. *Perestroika. New Thinking for Our Country and the World.* New York: Hai & Row, 1987.

Government of Canada. *Canada, Russia and Ukraine: Building a New Relationship.* Repor the Standing Senate Committee on Foreign Affairs (June 2002).

Hopf, Ted, ed. *Understandings of Russian Foreign Policy.* Pittsburgh: Pennsylvania State l versity Press, 1999.

Hunns, Derek. *Russia and NATO.* New York: Columbia University Press, 1998.

Ito, Takayuki, and Hayashy Tadayuki, eds. *Russian Foreign Policy in the Post-Cold War* Tokyo: Yuushindo, 1999.

Ivanov, Igor. "The Missile-Defense Mistake: Undermining Strategic Stability and the A Treaty." *Foreign Affairs* (Sept/Oct, 2000).

Ivanov, Igor. "New Priorities in Russian Foreign Policy." *Internationale Politik,* 1: 3 (2000

Ivanov, Igor. *Novaia Rossiiskaia diplomatiia. Desiat' let vneshnei politiki strany.* Moscow: Ol Press, 2002.

Jonson, Lena. *Russia and Central Asia: A New Web of Relations.* London: RIIA, 1998.

Ivanov, Igor Sergeevich, *Novaia rossiiskaia diplomatiia: desiat' let vneshnei politiki str.* Moscow: Olma-Press, 2001.

Ivanov, V., and K. Smith, eds. *Japan and Russia in Northeast Asia.* London: Praeger, 1999.

Kanet, Roger E., and A.V. Kozhemiakin, eds. *The Foreign Policy of the Russian Federation.* London: Macmillan, 1997.

Karaganov, Sergei, et al., eds. *Damage Limitation of Crisis? Russia and the Outside World.* CSIA Studies in International Security, No. 5. London: Brassey's, 1994.

Karaganov, Sergei. "A New Foreign Policy. What Is Russia To Do? What Is to Be Done with Russia?" *Moscow News,* No. 9 (8–14 March 2000).

Kozyrev, Andrei. "An Interview with Russian Foreign Minister Andrei Kozyrev." *RFE/RL Research Report,* 3: 28 (1994).

Kremenyuk, Victor A. *Conflicts in and around Russia: Nation-Building in Difficult Times.* London: Greenwood, 1994.

Kubicek, Paul. "End of the Line for the Commonwealth of Independent States." *Problems of Post-Communism,* 46: 2 (March/April 1999).

Kullberg, Judith S. *The End of New Thinking? Elite Ideologies and the Future of Russian Foreign Policy.* Mershon Center. Ohio State University (July 1993).

Kuzio, Taras. "Geopolitical Pluralism in the CIS: The Emergence of GUUAM." *European Security,* 9: 2 (Summer 2000).

Lebed, Aleksandr. *Za derzhavu obidno . . .* Moscow: Moskovskaia pravda, 1995.

Lisichkin, G.S. *O nashikh reformatorakh, ikh reformakh i natsional'noi idee.* Moscow: Epikon-IMEPI RAN, 1999.

Livermore, Gordon, ed. *Russian Foreign Policy Today.* 5th edition. Columbus, Ohio: Current Digest Foreign Policy Series, 1992.

Lo, Bobo, *Russian Foreign Policy in the Post-Soviet Era: Reality, Illusion, and Myth-making.* New York: Macmillan, 2002.

Makarenko, Vadim. *Kto soiuzniki Rossii? Mental'nosti geopolitika: paradoksy politiki bezopasnosti Rossii.* Moscow: Stradiz, 2000.

Malcolm, Neil, et al., eds. *Internal Factors in Russian Foreign Policy.* New York: Oxford University Press, 1996.

Mandelbaum, Michael, ed. *The New Russian Foreign Policy.* New York: Council of Foreign Relations, 1998.

Mihalka, Michael. "European–Russian Security and NATO's Partnership for Peace." *RFE/RL Research Report,* 3: 33 (1994).

Mlechen, Leonid. *Yevgenii Primakov: istoriia odnoi kar'ery.* Moscow: Tsentrpoligraf, 1999.

Molchanov, Mikhail A. *Political Culture and National Identity in Russian–Ukrainian Relations.* College Station, TX: Texas A & M University Press, 2002.

Naray, Peter. *Russia and the World Trade Organization.* London: Antony Rowe, 2001.

Olcott, Martha Brill, Anders Aslund, and Sherman W. Garnett. *Getting It Wrong: Regional Cooperation and the Commonwealth of Independent States.* Washington, D.C.: Carnegie Endowment for International Peace, 1999.

Parrish, Scott. "Chaos in [Russian] Foreign-Policy Decision-Making." *Transition,* 2: 10 (1996).

Pellerin, Alain. *NATO Enlargement—Where We Came From and Where It Leaves Us.* Ottawa: CCIPS (Aurora papers, 29), May 1997.

Petro, Nicolai N., Alvin Z. Rubinstein. *Russian Foreign Policy; from Empire to Nation-State.* New York: Longman, 1997.

Primakov, Yevgenii. *Gody v bol'shoi politike.* Moscow: Sovershenno sekretno, 1999.

Prizel, Ilya. *National Identity and Foreign Policy: Nationalism and Leadership in Poland, Ru and Ukraine.* Cambridge University Press, 1998.

Ra'anan, Uri, and Kate Martin, eds. *Russia: A Return to Imperialism?* New York: St. Mart 1995.

Rossiia-SShA-NATO. Dinamika sovremennykh vzaimootnoshenii i vozmozhnosti preodole; krizisa doveriia. Moscow: Nizhnii Novgorod, 2000.

Rossiia–Ukraina, 1990–2000. Dokumenty i materialy. 2 Vols. Moscow: Mezhdunarodnye nosheniia, 2001.

"Russia and Its Southern Neighbours." *Pro et Contra,* Vol. 5, No. 3 (Summer 2000). Spe issue [pubs.carnegie.ru]

Sakwa, Richard, Mark Webber. "The Commonwealth of Independent States: Stagnation Survival, 1992–1999." *Europe–Asia Studies,* 51: 3 (1999), 379–415.

Sestanovich, Stephen, ed. *Rethinking Russia's National Interests.* Washington, D.C.: Centre Strategic and International Studies, 1994.

Skak, Mette. *From Empire to Anarchy: Post-Communist Foreign Policy and International Affi* New York: St. Martin's, 1996.

Solchanyk, Roman, *Ukraine and Russia: The Post-Soviet Transition.* Lanham, Md.: Rowmaı Littlefield, 2000.

Spillmann, Kurt R., Andreas Wenger, eds. *Russia's Place in Europe. A Security Debate.* Bern: ter Lang AG, 1999.

Trenin, Dmitrii. "Vladimir Putin's Autumn Marathon: Toward the Birth of a Russian Forc Policy Strategy." Carnegie Central (Moscow), *Briefing Paper* 3:11 (November 2001).

Valasek, Tomas, Theresa Hitchens, eds. *Growing Pains. The Debate on the Next Rounc NATO Enlargement.* Washington, D.C.: Center for Defense Information, 2002.

Vneshniaia politike Rossiiskoi Federatsii. 1991–1999: Uchebnoe posobie. Moscow: ROSSPl 2000. (Textbook prepared at the Russian State Institute of International Affairs).

Vozzenikov, Anatolii V. *Natsional'naia bezopasnost': teoriia, politika, strategiia.* Moscow: N Modul, 2000.

Wallander, Celeste, A., et al. *The Sources of Russian Foreign Policy after the Cold War.* Boul Colo.: Westview, 1996.

Wallander, Celeste A. "Russia's New Security Policy and the Ballistic Missile Defense Deba *Current History* (October 2000).

Webber, Mark, ed. *Russia and Europe: Conflict or Cooperation.* New York: Gower & St. N tin's, 2000.

Zolotarev, Vladimir Antonovich, *Voennaoa bezopasnost' Gosudarstva Rossiiskogo.* Mosc Kuchkovo Pole, 2001.

Zyuganov, G. A. *Voennaia reforma: Otsenka ugroz natsional'noi bezopasnosti Rossii.* Mosc Narodno-patrioticheskii Soiuz Rossii, 1997.

Name Index

Subject Index

Belarus, 24, 42, 50, 95, 166, 263, 266–73;
  and NATO, 266, 270, 275
Black Sea Fleet, 16, 251, 253, 260, 264
Black Sea Region, 223f
Brezhnev Doctrine, 26
Brunei, 303
Bulgaria, 10, 28, 29, 54
"Bush doctrine," 174, 327

Cam Ranh naval base, 149, 163, 215
Canada, 25, 51, 75, 102n142, 117, 130,
  152, 153, 165, 306, 322, 341
Caspian Sea region, 162, 223f, 229f,
  237–38, 281, 286, 291, 323ff, 337ff, 347
Caucasus, 109, 162, 175
central Asia, 84, 91ff, 105, 142–43, 145f,
  147, 162, 215–16, 238, 281–89
Central Asian Economic Community, 276
CFDP. *See* Council for Foreign and Defense
  Policy
CFE. *See* Conventional Armed Forces in
  Europe
Chechens, 77, 112, 166
Chechnya, 24–25, 31, 42ff, 56, 69, 79,
  86f, 91, 92, 99, 106, 109–10, 117, 142,
  144, 152, 155, 160, 172, 185, 202,
  204–5, 208f, 254, 280, 288, 305, 309,
  334
China, 25, 57, 65, 74, 81, 84, 89, 105,
  116, 132, 135, 136, 138–39, 142–43,
  195, 209, 273, 303, 312–15, 323
Christianity. *See* religion
Cold War, 14, 95, 100, 198
Commonwealth of Independent States
  (CIS), 20, 71, 93, 121, 146, 173f, 227,
  229, 243–44, 247, 257, 275, 281,
  289–96, 346–71; air defense, 278; antiterrorist center, 276
Collective Security Pact (Treaty), 54, 91,
  173, 176–77, 192, 215, 227, 231, 247,
  273, 278, 279–80, 288, 291, 293, 295,
  319, 347; Council of Heads of State, 77,
  255, 263; Customs Union, 20–21, 276;
  Eurasian Economic Community, 173,
  227, 235, 257, 279–80, 281, 293, 295f,
  319, 347; Inter-Parliamentary Assembly,
  249

Communist Party of the Russian Federat
  (CPRF), 18f, 20, 23, 45, 55, 76, 89, 1
  180–81, 188ff, 302, 324, 342
Communist Party of Ukraine, 248f, 252
Comprehensive Test Ban Treaty (CTBT),
  17, 46, 58, 62, 111, 219
Concept of National Security. *See* nation:
  security concept
Constitution, Russian Federation, 23; Ar
  cle VI, 23
Conventional Armed Forces in Europe
  (CFE), 14, 201, 218, 224
Council of Europe, 68, 69, 88, 225. *See ι*
  PACE
Council for Foreign and Defense Policy
  (CFDP), 13, 30f, 150
Crimea, 263
CTBT. *See* Comprehensive Test Ban Trea
Cuba, 53, 159, 176, 322, 340–43
Cyprus, 162, 227
Czech Republic, 87, 112

Dagestan, 234
Davos. *See* world economic forum
debt: of Russia, 67n26, 108f; to Russia,
  253, 322, 326, 339, 341–42; Ukrainia
  253, 254, 256–57, 263
Denmark, 112
drug trafficking, 92, 279, 337
Dukhovnoe nasledie, 108

EBRD. *See* European Bank for Reconstrι
  tion and Development
economy, Russian, 106, 112, 115, 120,
  167f
education, Russian, 105, 185–86
Egypt, 93, 256, 322
elections, Russian, 323, 346. *See also*
  Ukraine
espionage, 117ff
Estonia. *See* Baltic States
Eurasia, 124, 125, 281
Eurasian Transportation Corridor, 291
Eurasian Economic Community. *See* CIS
Eurocorps, 85. *See also* rapid reaction for
Europe, 108ff, 113
European Investment Bank, 95

Subject Index

Tajikistan, 91, 333
Taliban, 25, 91, 112, 146, 147, 149, 156,
  160, 165, 215, 236, 280, 283, 285, 287,
  290, 291, 294, 310, 318, 332, 335
Technical Assistance to CIS (TACIS),
  44–45
terrorism, 8, 12f, 16, 92f, 99, 117; international, 35, 56, 64, 91–92, 98, 99, 112,
  115, 128, 141–43, 146–47, 151, 152,
  155, 156, 164, 166, 169, 202, 214, 216,
  224, 228, 235, 245, 276, 279, 285, 295,
  329, 337; domestic, 18–19, 77, 80–82,
  112, 117, 166, 172f, 204–5, 242, 290
Tibet, 310
Transdniester, 276, 277, 279, 290
Transdneft, 234
Tsentrazbat, 229, 279, 286
Turkey, 162, 226, 227, 229, 242, 288–89,
  323, 326
Turkmenistan, 226, 227, 258

Ukraine, 29, 42, 50, 85, 95, 127, 166, 227,
  232, 247–66, 275, 276; anti-Russianism,
  252, 254–55, 259–60, 261, 263, 274;
  and NATO, 50, 249, 250ff, 253, 266;
  elections, 248–49, 253
"Ukraine Year in Russia," 264f
unilateralism. *See* United States
Union of Right-Wing Forces, 19–20, 45
Union of Serb Communities, 37
United Nations, 7, 71, 72, 80, 127, 161,
  174, 205, 244–45, 330; General Assembly,
  9, 83; Human Rights Commission, 225;
  millennium, 287, 301, 319, 339; Security
  Council, 18, 71, 72, 83, 121, 170, 289,
  316, 317, 325, 327–29, 331, 336, 345;

Resolution 1244, 26, 30, 35, 38, 50, 5[
  69, 90, 133, 157, 192, 251
United States, 5–6, 8, 58–59, 69, 71, 78.
  86, 96f, 101, 105, 116, 123, 135, 160
  190, 224f, 229, 248f, 256, 287ff, 292,
  293, 298, 305, 309, 323, 327, 332ff,
  337ff; Trade Wars (with Russian Feder
  tion), 167f; unilateralism, 51, 126, 16
  164, 174, 331
Unity Party, 19–20, 45, 48
USS Cole, 92
Uzbekistan, 132, 147, 226

Vatican, 262
Venezuela, 325
Vietnam, 23, 149, 176, 298, 299f, 310–[

wahhabitism, 146
War Crimes Tribunal, 25, 52–53, 54, 64,
  136, 166–67
Warsaw Treaty Organization, 3
Westernizers, 76
World Bank, 69, 261
World Economic Forum (Davos), 112, 1
World Trade Organization (WTO), 4, 2(
  42, 94, 102, 120, 138, 148, 163, 182,
  296, 303, 310, 343, 348
World War II, 16, 33, 36–37, 51, 154

Yabloko, 19, 33, 45
Yavoriv training grounds, 250, 251
Yemen, 167
Yugoslavia, 26f, 30, 36f, 68, 83, 88–90,
  133, 136, 188–89, 225, 249–50, 275,
  298, 304, 306, 309, 325. *See also*
  Balkans

About the Author

J. L. (Larry) Black was born in Sackville, New Brunswick, Canada, and educated at Mount Allison University (Sackville), Boston University, and McGill University (Montreal). Black has been a professor of history at Carleton University in Ottawa since 1976. He was director of the Institute of Soviet and East European Studies from 1982 to 1990 and has been the director of the Centre for Research on Canadian–Russian Relations (CRCR) at Carleton since 1990.

The recipient of seven university and provincial research honors and two teaching awards, he was also a NATO research fellow for two years (1997–1999). Black has written or edited more than thirty books on Soviet and Russian history, foreign policy, and education, including *Russia Faces NATO Expansion: Bearing Gifts or Bearing Arms?* (2000) and *The Peasant Kingdom: Canada in the 19th–Century Russian Imagination* (2002).